Microsoft® SQL Server™ 2000 Programming

BY EXAMPLE

800 East 96th Street
Indianapolis, Indiana 46240

Fernando G. Guerrero
Carlos Eduardo Rojas

Microsoft® SQL Server™ 2000 Programming by Example

Copyright © 2001 by Que® Corporation

International Standard Book Number: 0-7897-2449-9

Library of Congress Catalog Card Number: 00-111702

Printed in the United States of America

First Printing: April, 2001
Reprinted with corrections: May 2003

05   04   03   8 7 6 5 4

Trademarks

Warning and Disclaimer

Acquisitions Editor
Michelle Newcomb

Development Editor
Sean Dixon

Managing Editor
Thomas Hayes

Project Editor
Tonya Simpson

Copy Editor
Kay Hoskin

Indexer
Kelly Castell

Proofreader
Maribeth Echard

Technical Editor
Vincent Mayfield

Team Coordinator
Cindy Teeters

Media Developer
Michael Hunter

Interior Designer
Karen Ruggles

Cover Designer
Duane Rader

Page Layout
Brad Lenser
Liz Patterson

Contents at a Glance

Table of Contents

About the Authors

Carlos Eduardo Rojas is a program manager with Planeta Networks, an Internet company headquartered in Coral Gables, Florida that provides broadband applications to Internet service providers in Ibero-America. He specializes in the design of n-tier applications, database implementation, and administration of SQL Server databases. Prior to this role, he was a consultant and trainer with Manapro in Caracas, Venezuela, where he is originally from. Also, he has participated as a speaker in various TechNet conferences in Venezuela.

Carlos earned a B.S. degree in Computer Science from University Simón Bolívar, Caracas, Venezuela. He is a Microsoft Certified Systems Engineer + Internet (MCSE+I), Microsoft Certified Database Administrator (MCDBA), Microsoft Certified Sales Specialist (MCSS), and has been awarded with the MVP (Most Valuable Professional) status on SQL Server. He is also a voting member and volunteer of PASS, the professional association for SQL Server.

Carlos can be reached at `carlos@sqlserverbyexample.com`.

Fernando G. Guerrero is a principal technologist and SQL Server product consultant in QA, United Kingdom. His main role involves IT training, course development, and internal mentoring.

He writes for *SQL Server Magazine* (`www.sqlmag.com`), presented a session on SQL Server 2000 at TechEd 2000 Europe, and has accepted to speak at PASS2001, TechEd Europe 2001, VBUG 2001, VBITS 2001, VSLive, and SQL2THEMAX conferences during the year 2001.

He is a Civil and Hydrologic Engineer with almost 20 years' experience in software development and design, in many cases applied to engineering environments.

He holds seven Microsoft Professional Certifications, including MCSE+Internet, MCSD, MCDBA, MCT, and has been awarded with the MVP (Most Valuable Professional) status on SQL Server. He is also a voting member and volunteer of PASS, the professional association for SQL Server.

His professional experience covers six years (1981–1987) as a lecturer in the Valencia's Polytechnic University (Spain, `www.upv.es`), where he was lecturing on surveying, photogrammetry, technical drawing, and applied numerical methods in the Civil Engineering School and the Agricultural Engineering School.

He built his own software company in Spain, TOU S.A., focused on desktop publishing and graphical tools for the professional market, and was technical director in that company for four years (1987–1991).

Before joining QA (Nov. 1998), he spent eight years (1991–1998) as an international consultant for a prestigious Spanish engineering firm (www.inypsa.es), living in different countries, designing, developing, and implementing information systems for projects financed by the World Bank, the European Union, and the European Investment Bank.

Fernando can be reached at fernan@sqlserverbyexample.com.

Dedication

This book is dedicated to Carlos and Yumaira, who taught me the key elements for success in life: discipline and persistence.

—Carlos Eduardo Rojas

To Manuela, for being my wife, my confidant, my shelter, my partner, warmth for my winters, and refreshing breeze for my summers.

—Fernando Guerrero

Acknowledgments

First of all, I want to thank all my family, friends, and co-workers, all of whom made this book possible. I wish I could name each and every one of you who contributed directly or indirectly to this book.

To my family, Carlos, Yumaira, Jesús Eduardo, and María Angélica. You were a great source of motivation for this book. Also, a special gratitude to my uncle and aunt, José and María; the CD you gave me helped me relax during those endless nights writing the book.

To all my teachers, professors, and classmates from high school and university—I'll never forget those wonderful years of my life and all the moments we shared. Special thanks to Juan Carlos Guzmán, who, since then, has been a great source of support.

Thanks to all the teachers at the English Language Institute (ELI), University of Pittsburgh, for helping me improve my writing skills, especially Stephanie Maietta-Pircio, Dorolyn Smith, Holly Stark, and Lois Wilson. Also, thanks to Professor Janusz Szczypula from Carnegie Mellon University for all his help and support during my time in Pittsburgh.

During my work experience, I've met a lot of exciting people who, in one way or the other, have helped me grow in my professional career. Thanks to all of you in Database ACCESS, NetPeople, Manapro, and Planeta Networks. Special thanks to José Alberto Nuñez, Carlos Guanchez, and María Dolores Nardi. Also, thanks to the extraordinary Planeta Networks team, especially Rodolfo Tancredi, who always has been willing to guide me since I began to work for Planeta Networks.

I want to express special gratitude to the group of SQL Server MVPs for honoring me as a new member. This has been one of the most important awards in my professional career. In particular, thanks to Fernando Guerrero, a great friend and very talented professional, for taking the time to review all the chapters of the book.

Thanks to Holly Allender for making my dream of writing a book a reality. The editorial team at Que Publishing also deserves my gratitude, in particular Michelle Newcomb for her patience and understanding throughout the whole process of writing the book, and for her dedication and persistence to meet the deadlines. Thanks to all the editorial team: Sean Dixon, Vincent Mayfield, Tonya Simpson, and Kay Hoskin.

Last, but not least, my most sincere thanks to those who believed in me, and to those who, by reading this book, will inspire me for future publications.

Carlos Eduardo Rojas

January 2001

My life has had plenty of amazing opportunities and challenges, and I was very fortunate to meet amazing people along the way. Each one of them has contributed to what I am now, and what I will be in the future. I would like to pay tribute to them, as an honest gratitude gesture, for all the help that they generously gave me. In chronological order:

To my father, Fernando, the intelligent, honest, and caring person, who gave me his love, dedication, and help and taught me the importance of quality at work. To my mother, Maruja, who gave me her love, optimism, and unbreakable happiness. They both are responsible for most of the good values that guide my life. They built a great family, and I only hope to live long enough to enjoy their company. To my brothers and sisters: Ana, Inmaculada, Carlos, Rocío, and José Ignacio, I hope you know how important you are to me. I wish I could spend more time with all of you.

To Professor Manuel Chueca, excellent professor and amazing human being, who gave me the opportunity to teach on his team and helped me beyond any reasonable limit. To Dr. José Herráez, who generously gave me his full support and friendship. To Dr. Luis Angel Alonso, who always helped me move forward. It was for me an honor learning from all of you the joy of teaching. I miss you and the years we spent together.

To Tom Peters, whose books have inspired me for almost 15 years.

To Bernardo Cebolla and Vicente Cebolla, excellent friends and partners. We lived together an unforgettable business and human experience, during the first years of the personal computing market. Our friendship will remain forever.

Inypsa, one of the best Spanish engineering firms, gave me the opportunity to work on important international projects around the world for almost eight years. I'd like to thank specially Juan Hernández, Casimiro del Pozo, and José Luis Muñoz, for their trust, professionalism, and friendship. I wish you all the best.

During those years in Inypsa, I had the privilege of meeting excellent professionals and friends along the way. To Reynaldo Barboza, who continuously encouraged me and wisely advised me to join Inypsa; to Javier Gras, excellent engineer and friend; to José María Pastor, my brother-in-law, dear friend, and excellent engineer; to the amazing professionals and friends who worked with me during those years: Esther Pineda, Poernomo Widrobo, Alvaro Chucatiny, Ludwing Céspedes, David Plaza, José Luis Sacristán, Samuel Sánchez, Oscar Rocha, Víctor Hugo Durán, and Anil Pillai.

I want to thank Patrick Beasley, Jonathan Finch, Mike Shammas, and Barbara Savage for giving me the opportunity to work in the best learning environment in the world: QA. I wish to thank Bill Walker for his continuous support. To Patrick Beasley and Aaron Johal, you both offered me your hand from the very first day, when I needed it most. Working for QA represents for me the possibility to learn from the greatest training team you can ever imagine.

As a SQL Server MCT, I spend some time with other SQL Server MCTs in an amazing private newsgroup where we share our experiences, fears, challenges, and achievements. Among these great MCTs, I would want to express my gratitude to Dejan Sarka, one of the best SQL Server trainers of this galaxy and an excellent and generous friend. I will always remember the excitement I felt when I finally met Itzik Ben-Gan. Itzik is one of the most recognized SQL Server experts, an excellent friend, and the one who makes me work at warp speed many Fridays with his puzzles. One sunny day at San Diego, Dejan and Itzik, by surprise, introduced me to Kalen Delaney, and I felt like a novice actor meeting John Ford. I cannot forget other great SQL Server MCTs, such as Ted Malone, Chris Randall, Robert Vieira, Tibor Karaszi, Victor Isakov, Aaron Johal, and many others.

Last year I was honored with the SQL Server MVP award. My most sincere gratitude to Juan T. Llibre (ASP and IIS MVP), Carlos Sánchez (Microsoft Spain), and Alberto Borbolla (VB MVP) for generously proposing me as an MVP, and to the other SQL Server MVPs for accepting me on their team. I still cannot believe that I am part of the amazing SQL Server MVP group. It is easy to feel small being surrounded by Bob Pfeiff, B.P. Margolin, Brian Moran, Carlos Eduardo Rojas, Darren Green, Dejan Sarka, Gianluca Hotz, Itzik Ben-Gan, Kalen Delaney, Michael Hotek, Neil Pike, Olivier Matrat, Ron Talmage, Roy Harvey,

Russell Fields, Sharon Dooley, Tibor Karaszi, Tony Rogerson, Trevor Dwyer, Umachandar Jayachandran, and Wayne Snyder. Together we try to help the SQL Server community in different ways, mainly providing free user support in the SQL Server newsgroups. We share ideas, wishes, and experiences in the most challenging newsgroup you could imagine, together with a selected group of Microsoft support engineers and members of the SQL Server developer team.

From the SQL Server group at Microsoft, I wish to thank Gert Drapers, Euan Garden, Lubor Kollar, Jim Gray, Tom Barclay, Hal Berenson, Don Vilen, Adam Shapiro, Margo Crandall, Karl Dehmer, LeRoy Tutle, Rick Byham, Shawn Aebi, Steve Dibbing, and Peter Kalbach. Their SQL Server courses, presentations, white papers, classes, messages, and continuous support helped me understand this technology a little bit more every day. And especially to Richard Waymire, the most knowledgeable SQL Server professional I ever met—attending any of your speeches was a tremendous learning experience for me.

I wish to express my gratitude to the great professionals who made the Spanish SQL Server newsgroup one of the best public SQL Server newsgroups. Among them: Antonio Soto, Carlos Paz, Carlos Sacristán, Claudio Alabarce, Deman Thierry, Eladio Rincón, Emilio Boucau, Jesús López, Jorge López, Julián Valencia, Mariano Melgar, Miguel Ángel Sanjuán, Miguel Egea, Norman Armas, Rodrigo Estrada, and Salvador Ramos.

I wish to thank Michelle Crocket, Kathy Blomstrom, Carol Martin, and the amazing technical edit team at *SQL Server Magazine* for their continuous support. Writing for *SQL Server Magazine* is nothing but a pleasure when you're surrounded by these great professionals.

To Carlos Rojas, the generous friend who gave me the opportunity to co-write this book, I will always thank you for this great opportunity. Your continuous support to the SQL Server users' community, and especially to the Spanish SQL Server newsgroup, proves your tremendous generosity and incredible knowledge level.

Writing a book like this would be impossible without the continuous help and support from the Que Publishing editorial team: Vincent Mayfield, Sean Dixon, Kay Hoskin, Tonya Simpson, and especially Michelle Newcomb. I am really impressed by their review process. However, if you still find any mistakes, or something you don't like, in this book, you can blame only the authors.

Thanks to Ian Dolan, who helped me correct the style on my first chapters of this book.

Finally, I want to thank my wife, Manuela, and my daughters, Rocío, Marta, and Marina. They were extremely supportive during these months that I've been working full time, day and night, writing this book. They came to my room from time to time to give me a big smile, a kiss, a hug, and to tell me how much they love me, despite the fact that I could not spend much time with them. Thank you for helping me fulfill this dream. Now you can have your revenge— I promise to spend more quality time with you from today.

Fernando G. Guerrero

January 2001

We Want to Hear from You!

As the reader of this book, *you* are our most important critic and commentator. We value your opinion and want to know what we're doing right, what we could do better, what areas you'd like to see us publish in, and any other words of wisdom you're willing to pass our way.

As an associate publisher I welcome your comments. You can email or write me directly to let me know what you did or didn't like about this book—as well as what we can do to make our books better.

Please note that I cannot help you with technical problems related to the topic of this book. We do have a User Services group, however, where I will forward specific technical questions related to the book.

When you write, please be sure to include this book's title and author as well as your name, email address, and phone number. I will carefully review your comments and share them with the author and editors who worked on the book.

Email: Greg Wiegand
Associate Publisher
Que Publishing
800 East 96th Street
Indianapolis, IN 46240 USA

For more information about this book or another Que title, visit our Web site at www.quepublishing.com. Type the ISBN (excluding hyphens) or the title of a book in the Search field to find the page you're looking for.

Introduction

The *by Example* Series

How does the *by Example* series make you a better programmer? The *by Example* series teaches programming using the best method possible. After a concept is introduced, you'll see one or more examples of that concept in use. The text acts as a mentor by figuratively looking over your shoulder and showing you new ways to use the concepts you just learned. The examples are numerous. While the material is still fresh, you see example after example demonstrating the way you use the material you just learned.

The philosophy of the *by Example* series is simple: The best way to teach computer programming is by using multiple examples. Command descriptions, format syntax, and language references are not enough to teach a newcomer a programming language. Only by looking at many examples in which new commands are immediately used and by running sample programs can programming students get more than just a feel for the language.

Who Should Use This Book?

Microsoft SQL Server 2000 Programming by Example is targeted toward people with previous experience in any programming language.

As a database programming book, we expect you to have some background knowledge about logical database design. Understanding how to define entities, attributes, and relationships between entities is essential in producing any good database system. We will provide you with some comments about this subject when required, but we will not go into deeper detail. If you feel uncomfortable about this subject, we suggest that you read a general database design book first.

No prior experience in Transact-SQL is necessary; however, if you have experience working with the SQL language, from any other database system, this book can be used as a reference in which you will find a lot of useful examples that you can use to program applications in SQL Server.

If you do have experience with any previous version of SQL Server, you will find many examples that you can use to practice the extended functionality of SQL Server 2000. However, this is not an upgrading book for users of previous versions, so we do not assume any prior knowledge of previous versions.

If you are a Web developer, this book can teach you how to use SQL Server's new XML functionality to access data from the Internet. If you are a SQL Server developer and you want to introduce yourself to the new XML world, you can find in this book some useful examples on how to use this exciting new functionality.

Learning a new programming language is a mixture of theory and practice. We try to provide as many examples as possible about every topic. We advise you to apply these new concepts as soon as possible in a real scenario, because this is the best way to reinforce your learning effort. If you are not working in a database design right now, create your own personal database to manage appointments, books, pictures, or your personal music library.

This Book's Organization

This book provides you with the skills needed to develop and maintain SQL Server applications. Also, it contains the enhancements introduced in SQL Server 2000.

We highly recommend that you go over all the examples in this book. They were designed to help you understand each concept and feature of Transact-SQL. You can use Query Analyzer, which is explained in Appendix B, "Using SQL Query Analyzer," to execute all examples presented in this book.

Commonly, there are some tasks that can be performed using Enterprise Manager instead of Transact-SQL. Be aware that every task that you perform in Enterprise Manager translates to a set of instructions in Transact-SQL executed behind the scenes. Because the purpose of this book is to teach you the Transact-SQL language, examples are based in Transact-SQL and, in some specific cases, the way to perform the task in Enterprise Manager is also explained.

Appendix A, "Using SQL Server Instances," shows you how to use one of the new features of SQL Server 2000, multi-instance support. This appendix is useful to practice the distributed queries examples that appear in Chapter 15, "Working with Heterogeneous Environments: Setting Up Linked Servers."

Chapter 6, "Optimizing Access to Data: Indexes," is an advanced chapter that teaches you how to optimize access to databases using indexes efficiently. The information contained in this chapter, although very important, is not essential to understand the next chapters. You can read this chapter when you feel confident enough using SQL Server 2000 and you want to optimize your database.

As a programming book, we deliberately do not cover administration subjects. However, we do include information about two important administrative subjects:

- Security—Understanding how SQL Server 2000 manages security is crucial to create a secure database. In Chapter 1, "Relational Database Management Systems and SQL Server," we explain this subject in detail from a programmer's point of view.

- Importing and exporting data—Because almost every programmer must import and export data from time to time, we cover this subject in Chapter 14, "Transferring Data to and from SQL Server."

Chapter 16, "Working with XML Data in SQL Server 2000," is not included in this book's printed material. Due to the late availability of the latest version of the SQL Server 2000 Web Release, we had to provide this chapter in an online format only. You can download Chapter 16 from the www.mcp.com site (http://www.mcp.com/que/byexample_que.cfm).

Unfortunately, some exciting new features are not covered in this book, such as

- SQL Server 2000 Administration
- Data Transformation Services Development—however, we cover basic creation of DTS packages
- English Query
- Full-Text Search
- Analysis Services

SQL Server 2000 is a vast product, and we decided to focus on what we consider to be the basic set of features that every database developer should know about SQL Server 2000.

An evaluation version of SQL Server 2000 Enterprise Edition is included in this book. If you don't have SQL Server installed on your machine, this evaluation version can be used to practice with all examples shown throughout the book.

This book prepares you for one of the core exams of the Microsoft Certified Database Administrator (MCDBA) certification: Exam 70-229 Designing and Implementing Databases with Microsoft SQL Server 2000 Enterprise Edition. This exam is also an elective of the Microsoft Certified Systems Engineer (MCSE) certification. For details on this exam, you can visit Microsoft's Web site at http://www.microsoft.com/trainingandservices/exams/examsearch.asp?PageID=70-229.

Conventions Used in This Book

Examples are identified by the icon shown at the left of this sentence.

Listing, code, Transact-SQL keywords, and object names appear in monospace font, such as

EXAMPLE

EXEC sp_help

Many examples contain output, either as warning and error messages, and result sets. In those cases, you can identify the output by the icon shown at the left of this sentence.

OUTPUT

We do not show the output for some examples if the output is obvious, irrelevant, or does not offer any benefit to the reader. In general, we prefer to show the output, so you can check whether you executed the example properly.

NOTE

Special notes augment the material you read in each chapter. These notes clarify concepts and procedures.

TIP

You'll find numerous tips offering shortcuts, tested tricks, and solutions to common problems.

CAUTION

The cautions warn you about common problems and misconceptions when writing Transact-SQL code. Reading the caution sections will save you time and trouble.

What's Next?

Microsoft SQL Server 2000 is a powerful tool, capable of managing big-scale databases fast and efficiently. However, not even the most powerful hardware and the best relational database management system can improve a poorly designed database application.

Learning the Transact-SQL language will help you create an efficient, versatile, and feature-rich database application.

Please visit the *by Example* Web site for code examples or additional material associated with this book:

`http://www.mcp.com/que/byexample_que.cfm`

You can find comments, error logs, and additional code about this book on its own Web site:

`http://www.sqlserverbyexample.com`

You can contact the authors by email at

Carlos Eduardo Rojas: `carlos@sqlserverbyexample.com`

Fernando G. Guerrero: `fernan@sqlserverbyexample.com`

The public Microsoft newsgroups represent an amazing learning opportunity as well. You can find free support from other SQL Server colleagues, SQL Server MVPs, and members of the Microsoft SQL Server group:

```
news://msnews.microsoft.com/microsoft.public.sqlserver.programming
news://msnews.microsoft.com/microsoft.public.sqlserver.ce
news://msnews.microsoft.com/microsoft.public.sqlserver.clients
news://msnews.microsoft.com/microsoft.public.sqlserver.clustering
news://msnews.microsoft.com/microsoft.public.sqlserver.connect
news://msnews.microsoft.com/microsoft.public.sqlserver.datamining
news://msnews.microsoft.com/microsoft.public.sqlserver.datawarehouse
news://msnews.microsoft.com/microsoft.public.sqlserver.dts
news://msnews.microsoft.com/microsoft.public.sqlserver.fulltext
```

```
news://msnews.microsoft.com/microsoft.public.sqlserver.mseq
news://msnews.microsoft.com/microsoft.public.sqlserver.odnc
news://msnews.microsoft.com/microsoft.public.sqlserver.olap
news://msnews.microsoft.com/microsoft.public.sqlserver.replication
news://msnews.microsoft.com/microsoft.public.sqlserver.security
news://msnews.microsoft.com/microsoft.public.sqlserver.server
news://msnews.microsoft.com/microsoft.public.sqlserver.setup
news://msnews.microsoft.com/microsoft.public.sqlserver.tools
news://msnews.microsoft.com/microsoft.public.sqlserver.xml
news://msnews.microsoft.com/microsoft.public.es.sqlserver
news://msnews.microsoft.com/microsoft.public.espanol.sqlserver.administracion
news://msnews.microsoft.com/microsoft.public.espanol.sqlserver.olap
news://msnews.microsoft.com/microsoft.public.fr.sqlserver
news://msnews.microsoft.com/microsoft.public.ae.arabic.sqlserver
news://msnews.microsoft.com/microsoft.public.arabic.sqlserver
news://msnews.microsoft.com/microsoft.public.de.sqlserver
news://msnews.microsoft.com/microsoft.public.il.hebrew.sqlserver
news://msnews.microsoft.com/microsoft.public.jp.sqlserver.server
```

Microsoft provides many white papers on SQL Server at the following address:

```
http://www.microsoft.com/sql/Index.htm
```

Go to Chapter 1 and start learning *Microsoft SQL Server 2000 Programming by Example* today!

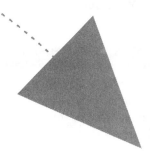

Relational Database Management Systems and SQL Server

From the beginning of human history, knowledge has meant power. The success or failure of individuals, companies, and countries depends on the amount and quality of knowledge they have about their environment.

Knowledge is based on facts. In some cases, facts are made of abstract data, difficult to represent in precise mathematical terms. However, the economic life of every company relies on precise data obtained from external and internal sources.

Knowledge management is based on the ability to use this absolute data to interpret reality and arrive at conclusions about how their environment reacts to specific conditions.

Data has value if it is accurate and comprehensive enough to serve business needs. However, the way the data is stored and the mechanisms available to retrieve it are important factors to consider. Database management systems provide reliable data storage systems and flexible data retrieval tools.

In this book, you learn how to develop database applications, using one of the latest and more powerful database management systems: Microsoft SQL Server 2000.

This chapter teaches you the main concepts of Microsoft SQL Server 2000:

- Basic concepts about relational database systems

- SQL Server architecture and server components

- SQL Server client tools

- How to protect your data in SQL Server

- Basic principles about client/server application design and how SQL Server fits in this model

Database Models

To provide the required durability, data is stored in physical storage devices. These files are stored in different logical formats depending on the database model selected by every particular database management system. You can find many database models in the database market:

- Flat files
- Hierarchical
- Networked
- Relational
- Object
- Object-relational
- Document

Flat files, hierarchical, and networked models are mainly used in mainframes, whereas the other models have been ported to client/server environments, based on personal computers. Discussing these database models is out of the scope of this book. SQL Server 2000 implements the relational model, and the following section teaches you the basic theory behind this popular database model.

The Relational Model

In the *relational* model, data is arranged in tables in which the physical location of every value is not permanently predefined and is transparent to the data retrieval strategy. Every table is defined with a fixed set of columns that map the entity attributes.

Data from different tables is related by logical links that are dynamically defined by the database application or by the end user who sends a data request. Figure 1.1 shows a typical example of a relational database.

Users access data using an industry standard query language, called SQL. This means that the database design focuses mainly on the data to store, producing a flexible database that can be used by many different applications. This flexibility contrasts with the databases stored in a hierarchical or networked model, in which the database structure was designed to solve a specific business problem.

As you can imagine, this flexibility represents more complexity for the database engine. This is the reason you can expect better performance for the same hardware platform, using hierarchical or networked databases rather than relational databases. However, the continuous improvements on relational database management systems (RDBMS) is switching the database market to this technology, even at mainframe level, where a big percentage of available data is still in hierarchical and networked format.

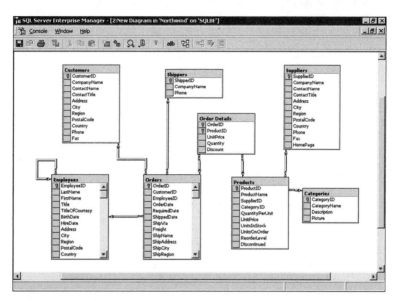

Figure 1.1: *The relational model arranges data in tables with logical dynamically defined links.*

The relational model is based on the relational theory, in which modifications to the data are based on relational algebra and relational calculus.

Dr. E. F. Codd, an IBM mathematician, published *A Relational Model of Data for Large Shared Data Banks* (Communications of the ACM, Vol. 3, No. 6, June 1970). This document establishes the rules of the relational databases. Many database vendors started to implement his theories soon after this publication. IBM DB2, Oracle, Sybase, and Microsoft SQL Server are typical RDBMS products.

The language used to request information from RDBMS, SQL, is part of the ANSI standard since the ANSI SQL 86 version. Many products are based on the ANSI SQL 89 and ANSI SQL 92 standards, but every product offers different extensions. A new standard is available now, ANSI SQL 99, which expands the traditional relational model nearer to the object-oriented model.

Microsoft SQL Server 2000 is based in a special SQL dialect, called Transact-SQL, which is an expanded version of the ANSI SQL 92 standard.

A Brief History of SQL Server

Figure 1.2 shows the SQL Server timeline in which you can see the evolution of SQL Server compared with the evolution of the Windows operating systems, the Intel and AMD processors, and the typical CPU speed available at that time.

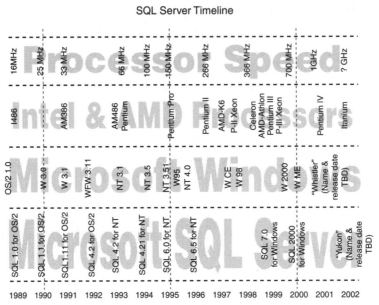

Figure 1.2: The SQL Server timeline.

Microsoft SQL Server was born as a joint commercial venture between Sybase and Microsoft and signed on March 27, 1987. It was developed for the 16-bit OS/2 platform, an operating system jointly developed between IBM and Microsoft. SQL Server started its commercial life with the commercial support of Ashton-Tate, whose mainstream database product, dBase, was the market leader at that time. Ashton-Tate/Microsoft SQL Server 1.0 arrived on the market in May 1989.

If you do not remember those remote years, personal computers were equipped with Intel I286 and I386 processors, and the I486 processor was just a newcomer. Personal computers had processors running at 12MHz and 16MHz and had a typical 20MB–40MB hard disk. Perhaps you do not remember those years where RAM was measured in kilobytes.

During those first years, Sybase developed Microsoft SQL Server for OS/2 and Microsoft commercialized and supported the product on this platform. Ashton-Tate abandoned the project soon after the first version.

Starting in 1992, Microsoft SQL Server 4.2 for OS/2 was released. In this case, it was a joint development between Sybase and Microsoft, with active development collaboration from Microsoft. It was still a 16-bit database product, running on a 16-bit operating system (OS/2 1.3). In that personal computer market, ruled by 32-bit processors (Intel I386, I486, and AMD AM386) at more than 33MHz and running Windows 3.1, working with a 16-bit backend database was not a good selling point.

About a year later, Microsoft SQL Server 4.2 for Windows NT was released. This product was the final point in the joint development agreement between Sybase and Microsoft, although Sybase code remained in SQL Server code for several more versions to come—up to version 6.5.

For Microsoft this was a no-way-back decision, and SQL Server has since been a Windows-only product. This was the first 32-bit release and for many customers was, perhaps, just an excuse for buying the new Windows NT 3.1 operating system.

Remember, 1995 was the year of Windows 95, the Pentium processor, and amazing 150MHz CPU speeds on personal computers equipped with hard disks as big as 400MB or 600MB and with 4MB–8MB of RAM. That year was the release of the new SQL Server 6.0 for Windows NT. It didn't have the new Windows 95 interface, but it included new features, which made this product an important contender in the database market.

SQL Server 6.5 was the final version of the Sybase-based era. This version included client tools based on the widely accepted Windows 95 interface, which runs on Windows NT 4.0.

Starting in 1999, a brand-new version came to the market: Microsoft SQL Server 7.0. It was a completely new product, with exciting new tools, an enhanced database engine, and graphical user interface inherited from the popular DaVinci Tools (or Visual Database Tools) already available in the Enterprise Edition of Microsoft Visual Studio. New services, such as Full-Text Search, English Query, Data Transformation Services (DTS), and OnLine Analytical Processing (OLAP), as well as a faster database engine, made this product a big market success.

This was a Microsoft-only database engine, in a nearly Microsoft-only personal computing market, where processors ran at 200MHz–300MHz, hard disk sizes were already measured in gigabytes, and RAM available in personal computers was more than 32MB.

The end of the second millennium was the birth of the newest SQL Server version which, to be in sync with all the new Microsoft products of that year, was named Microsoft SQL Server 2000.

Changes have occurred since 1989. Corporations look at the PC market searching for powerful servers equipped with Intel or AMD processors, running Windows 2000 and Windows 2000-compatible server applications and services. The highest database transaction benchmarks are based on PC-like servers—running Windows 2000—and the database market has changed forever.

The Microsoft SQL Server developer team does not stop here. They are already writing new versions that will appear on the market soon, improving Internet support, providing support for new 64-bit Windows versions and 64-bit processors, the new Windows XP operating system, new file systems, scaling up, out, and down, and adding more functionality to this database management system.

Basics of SQL Server Architecture

SQL Server is a client/server relational database management system. Figure 1.3 shows the process that every query must follow, from its origin as a SQL query in the client application running in the client computer, to the final result set received by the client application.

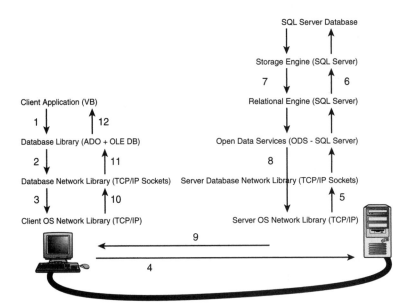

Figure 1.3: *Client access to a SQL Server database.*

These steps are defined as follows:

1. The user selects an option in a client application. This option calls a function in the client application that generates a query that is sent to SQL Server. The application uses a database access library to send the query in a way SQL Server can understand.

2. The database library transforms the original request into a sequence of one or more Transact-SQL statements to be sent to SQL Server. These statements are encapsulated in one or more Tabular Data Stream (TDS) packets and passed to the database network library to be transferred to the server computer.

3. The database network library uses the network library available in the client computer to repackage the TDS packets as network protocol packets.

4. The network protocol packets are sent to the server computer network library across the network, where they are unwrapped from their network protocol.

5. The extracted TDS packets are sent to Open Data Services (ODS), where the original query is extracted.

6. ODS sends the query to the relational engine, where the query is optimized and executed in collaboration with the storage engine.

7. The relational engine creates a result set with the final data and sends it to ODS.

8. ODS builds one or more TDS packets to be sent to the client application, and sends them to the server database network library.

9. The server database network library repackages the TDS packets as network protocol packets and sends them across the network to the client computer.

10. The client computer receives the network protocol packets and forwards them to the network libraries where the TDS packets are extracted.

11. The network library sends the TDS packets to the database access library, where these packets are reassembled and exposed as a client result set to the client application.

12. The client application displays information contained in the result sets to the user.

These are some important points to consider about this process:

- The client application sends only a database request to the server computer.

- SQL Server sends only the final result set to the client application, saving network bandwidth.

- SQL Server receives the SQL request and sends result sets in return. SQL Server does not spend server resources on user interaction.

- SQL Server is not responsible for the final output format; it is the responsibility of the client application. The client application does not use client resources to solve low-level query solving and data access processes.

- The client application can be designed independently of the database system used in the back end. Data access operations are based in a high-level data access library, which can be easily changed to connect to other types of database systems.

- The client application is not aware of the network protocol used to connect to the server, and this protocol can be changed at any time, provided that the server and client share a common protocol.

When you install SQL Server 2000, you install two different sets of components:

- Server components are back-end services, responsible for data storage, data integrity, security, concurrency, and so on.

- Client components are front-end applications, used by administrators, developers, and even end users, to administer, develop, test, and use a SQL Server 2000 database system.

Server Components

What we call SQL Server 2000 is actually a collection of several Windows services:

- Microsoft SQL Server service (MSSQLServer)—The main service, responsible for data storage, data integrity, consistency, concurrency, security, query processing, optimization, and execution.

- Microsoft SQL Server Agent (SQLServerAgent)—Responsible for scheduling jobs, managing alerts, and Notifying operators. SQL Server Agent is an important service in SQL Server Administration because so many administrative operations depend on it to be executed automatically at fixed intervals—for example, backups, data consistency checks, rebuilding indexes, importing and exporting data, replication, and so on.

- Microsoft Search—Provides full-text search capabilities to SQL Server, as well as to Microsoft Exchange and Index Server.

- Microsoft SQL Server OLAP Service—Provides back-end support for Analysis Services.

- Microsoft Distributed Transaction Coordinator (MS-DTC)—Provides transaction support in multiserver and heterogeneous environments.

- Server Network libraries—SQL Server can listen to several network libraries at the same time, waiting for queries to answer, and use any of these libraries to send results to the client. The selected database network library must have a compatible server network library to work with. SQL Server 2000 currently supports the following network libraries: TCP/IP Sockets, Named Pipes, Multiprotocol, NWLink IPX/SPX, VIA ServerNET II SAN, VIA GigaNet SAN, Banyan VINES, and AppleTalk ADSP.

CAUTION

Make sure that both client and server use the same network library or they will not be able to communicate.

TIP

You do not need all these services to work with SQL Server 2000. Select only the services you really need and you will save server resources.

Microsoft SQL Server Service contains different components that collaborate to provide back-end data services. The three main components are

- Open Data Services—This component receives client requests from the network library and passes them on to SQL Server. When SQL Server terminates the query process, it sends the result set to ODS to be transferred through the network to the client application.

- Relational Engine—This component is responsible for parsing, optimizing, executing queries, and enforcing security.

- Storage Engine—This component manages physical storage operations, such as data storage, allocation and deallocation of data pages, transaction logging and recovery, database backups and restoring, locking, and so on.

NOTE

Developers can extend the functionality of SQL Server by writing their own libraries based on ODS. This is the basis of the extended stored procedures you see in Chapter 8, "Implementing Business Logic: Programming Stored Procedures."

Client Tools

The preceding section discussed the different server components. In the client side, we can identify the following components:

- The client application—This application, developed using any programming language, provides user interaction, prepares requests to the database server, and shows query results to the user in a user-friendly way.

- Database library—This library is responsible for translating application requests into specific statements that the database server can understand.

- Client network libraries—This is the component that talks to the server network library to send and receive TDS packets through the network.

Figure 1.4 shows the different database libraries you can use to connect a client application to SQL Server 2000:

- Direct HTTP access from an HTML page or an Active Server Page (ASP)—In this case, you use the SQL ISAPI extension through a virtual directory in Internet Information Server, supporting direct XPath queries through HTTP and XML input/output.

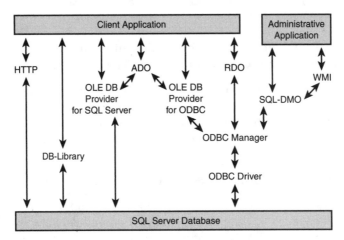

Figure 1.4: *Data access options to connect to SQL Server from a client application.*

- Native SQL Server. DB-Library access—This is not the recommended solution because most of the new SQL Server 2000 functionality is not exposed through DB-Library.

- Access to the ODBC API—Using any programming language, although C or C++ is recommended.

- Indirect access to the ODBC library through Remote Data Objects (RDO)—This solution provides an object-oriented library that encapsulates database access objects. RDO is maintained for backward compatibility with existing applications, but Microsoft recommends ActiveX Data Objects instead.

- Direct access to the OLE DB Provider library, in which case using C++ is recommended—This solution provides full access to SQL Server 2000 through a comprehensive data-access object model with specific properties available in the native SQL Server OLE DB provider.

- Indirect access to the OLE DB provider for SQL Server through ActiveX Data Objects (ADO) or ADO.Net—ADO exposes an object model, as OLE DB does, easier to implement than direct access to the OLE DB provider, and is suitable to any programming and scripting language, including any version of Visual Basic and ASP.Net.

- Indirect access to the SQL Server ODBC driver through the OLE DB provider with or without the ADO library—This solution is not recommended because of the extra steps involved in the data access, unless specific ODBC functionality is required.

- Access to database metadata through ADOX and OLE DB—This is an alternative way to connect to SQL Server, to send Data Definition Language (DML) statements, and metadata discovery. This connectivity solution is not represented in the diagram because it is not a very common solution.

- Administrative access to SQL Server through SQL-DMO (Distributed Management Objects)—This is the object model library that SQL Server Enterprise Manager uses to connect to SQL Server. Developers can use all this functionality to build small administration applications, as subsets of what Enterprise Manager can do.

- Windows Management Instrumentation (WMI)—WMI is a scalable Windows 2000 component, common to other server applications, which exposes an object model to control and administer SQL Server, as well as other server services and devices.

NOTE

WMI install is not part of the SQL Server setup. You can install WMI support for SQL Server 2000 from the folder x86\OTHER\wmi on the SQL Server 2000 compact disc.

Currently, WMI access to SQL Server is based on SQL-DMO, but future releases might implement it in a different way.

TIP

If you want to create a new application to connect to SQL Server 2000, write your application using ADO and the native OLE DB provider for SQL Server. This will help the compatibility with the new Microsoft.net development framework.

You can search for extra information on ADONET (ADO+) at the .NET Microsoft site: http://www.microsoft.net

SQL Server 2000 includes some client applications you can use to administer and develop databases:

- Enterprise Manager
- Query Analyzer
- Profiler
- Upgrade Wizard
- Service Manager
- Command-line utilities

CAUTION

If you install SQL Server 2000 in the same computer as SQL Server 7.0, the version 7.0 client utilities will be replaced with the new ones. This will give you extra benefits, but you might be surprised at first by the different user interface.

ENTERPRISE MANAGER

You can use Enterprise Manager to manage any SQL Server 2000 instance, including the default SQL Server 2000 instance, running locally or remotely. You also can use Enterprise Manager to manage any local or remote SQL Server 7.0 installation. However, this version of Enterprise Manager is not compatible with SQL Server 6.5.

Figure 1.5 shows the Enterprise Manager environment, similar to the well-known Windows Explorer interface, in which you can identify different sections for every server:

- The SQL Server Administration Tree—This panel uses the TreeView control to display the structure of every registered server. It displays different icons for every database object and shows context menus for every object, according to the methods that can be applied to each specific object.

- The menu bar—In this menu bar, you can find the Action menu, which is equivalent to the object context menu available from the tree; the View menu to specify how to display information about the selected object in the tree; and the Tools menu to show general commands you can use in Enterprise Manager to administer SQL Server.

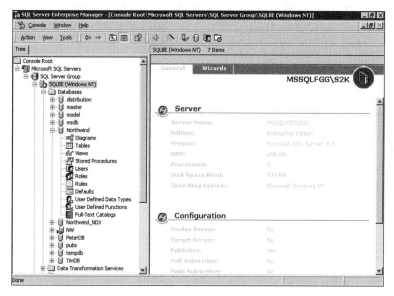

Figure 1.5: *SQL Server Enterprise Manager.*

- The taskbar—This is a dynamic list of icons that represents processes you can run in the current context, as well as navigation keys through the tree.

- The information panel—This panel shows information in different formats, depending on the selected object. Figure 1.5 shows the Taskpad, which, in this case, is an HTML page with information about the Northwind database.

For every server, the Enterprise Manager tree shows the following sections (folders):

- Databases—This section includes the list of available databases in the connected server.

- Data Transformation Services—This section gives you access to the DTS Designer and the Import/Export Wizard.

- Management—Enter this section to see the current activity of the connected server; to access SQL Server Agent objects, alerts, jobs, and operators; to manage backups and database maintenance plans; and to look at the SQL Server event log.

- Replication—This is where you can administer publications and sub-scriptions, if this server publishes or subscribes to any database.

- Replication Monitor—This section is available only if Replication is installed on this server. In that case, you can use this section to monitor and administer replication agents.

- Security—This section gives you access to the administration of SQL Server logins, server roles, linked servers, and remote servers. Later in this chapter, in the "Security Model" section, you will learn about SQL Server security and Chapter 15, "Working with Heterogeneous Environments: Setting Up Linked Servers," covers linked and remote servers.

- Support Services—Access this section to administer other services, such as Distributed Transaction Coordinator, Full-Text Search, and SQL Mail.

- Meta Data Services—This section gives you access to the Microsoft Repository.

CAUTION

Do not confuse SQL Mail with SQLServerAgent Mail.

SQL Mail is a service that allows SQL Server users to use the mail-extended stored procedures, to send and receive messages from Transact-SQL scripts, stored procedures, and triggers. SQL Mail uses the MAPI profile defined for the MSSQLServer service account.

SQLServerAgent Mail is the feature that allows SQLServerAgent to send messages to operators by email to notify job success, failure, or completion, and alerts notifications. SQLServerAgent Mail uses the MAPI profile defined for the SQLServerAgent service account.

In many servers, both services use the same service account, so they use the same MAPI profile. However, they are different services and they use email for different purposes and in different circumstances.

SQL Server Enterprise Manager provides wizards to perform most of the standard administrative activities. These wizards are available from the Tools menu and from the Taskpad, at server and database level. Figure 1.6 shows the Wizards list from the Taskpad. To access the Taskpad, select a server in the Enterprise Manager tree, and in the View menu, select Taskpad. To show the wizards, click on the Wizard tab in the Taskpad.

From SQL Server Enterprise Manager, you can design a database in a similar way to Visual Database Tools (from Visual Studio Enterprise Edition). Figure 1.7 shows the Northwind database diagram. You can create this diagram by opening the list of databases and opening the subtree for the

Northwind database. There you can right-click on Diagrams and select New Database Diagram. This menu will open the Create Database Diagram Wizard that will lead you step-by-step through the creation of this diagram.

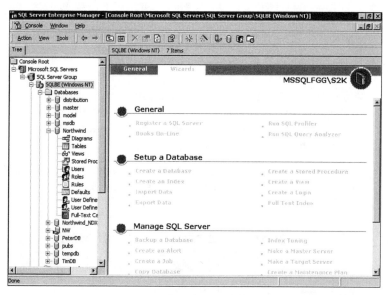

Figure 1.6: *Access to the Wizards list from the Taskpad.*

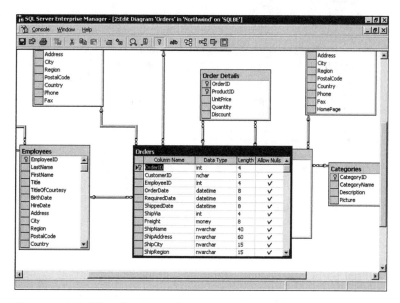

Figure 1.7: *The database diagram tool from Enterprise Manager.*

TIP

If you run SQL Server in a network, you can install the SQL Server client tools, including Enterprise Manager, in any workstation, without any server component. Then, you can register the servers you have to administer in Enterprise Manager. This provides centralized administration, without producing any overhead in the server, because the client administration tools runs in the client computer, not in the server.

QUERY ANALYZER

Query Analyzer is a client tool designed to send queries to SQL Server and to display results. This is not an end-user application; instead, it is a developer tool used to manage databases and create database applications through the use of Transact-SQL scripts.

Query Analyzer is the tool you will use throughout this book to practice the examples. Figure 1.8 shows Query Analyzer after retrieving a query result set from SQL Server.

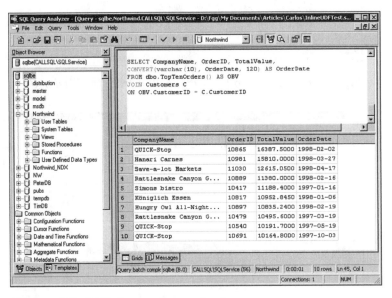

Figure 1.8: SQL Server Query Analyzer.

Appendix B gives you a comprehensive coverage of Query Analyzer.

PROFILER

SQL Server Profiler is a client tool that captures SQL Server activity and sends this activity to a file, database table, or the screen, giving you a powerful analysis tool. For every trace you can

- Select which events to trace.

- Select which information to show for every event.

- Select how to group the events.

- Apply filters to include or exclude specific values, such as applications, logins, databases, hosts, and so on.

- Save the trace in a trace file or a database table.

Using Profiler, you can

- Monitor real-time activity in SQL Server.

- Detect long-running queries.

- Trace locks and deadlocks.

- Summarize activity per database, user, host, and so on.

- Select which database objects are more heavily used to prioritize optimization decisions.

- Detect actual SQL Server activity from applications in which the source code is not available. You can create a trace to look at what Enterprise Manager does when you administer SQL Server using graphical user interface commands.

- Monitor database autogrowth or autoshrink.

- Perform security audits.

To start a trace, follow these instructions:

1. Open Profiler from the Microsoft SQL Server program group.

2. Choose File, New, Trace.

3. Select the server to monitor, and connect to the server.

4. The Trace properties form appears. There you can give a name to the trace and select the SQLProfilerTSQL_Replay template from the drop-down list.

5. Click Save to File and select a location for the trace file (using the standard .trc extension).

6. Leave the default values for the other fields and click Run.

7. Profiler will show you an empty window with several columns and only one row.

8. In the Tools menu, click Query Analyzer to open Query Analyzer.

9. In Query Analyzer, connect to the same server as in step 3.

10. In the query window type SELECT @@VERSION and press F5 to execute the query.

11. Go back to Profiler, and you will see many rows where before it was a single row trace. Scroll down through the trace to the last row and you should see something similar to Figure 1.9.

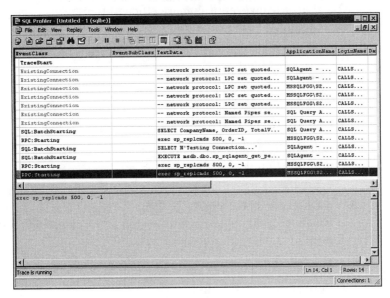

Figure 1.9: *SQL Server Profiler.*

12. Stop the trace by choosing File, Stop Trace menu.

13. The instructions traced on Profiler include all the events selected by the trace template. Choose File, Properties, and then click the Events tab to see the selected events.

14. Look at the Data Columns and Filters tabs in the Trace Properties window to see how this trace template is defined.

15. Exit Profiler.

THE UPGRADE WIZARD

The SQL Server Upgrade Wizard converts SQL Server 6.5 databases to the SQL Server 2000 format. You can upgrade the entire server or selected databases. The upgrade process will transfer and convert the database catalog, most of the server and database settings, and user data.

NOTE

After the wizard completes the upgrade, SQL Server 6.5 is still available. If you want to remove SQL Server 6.5, you must uninstall it.

Using the SQL Server Upgrade Wizard, you can upgrade a SQL Server 6.5 database to the default SQL Server 2000 instance running in the same computer. In this case, you can use a tape device to avoid space problems in the hard disk. However, it is more efficient to upgrade from one computer to another in the same network.

CAUTION

To run the Upgrade Wizard, you must have already installed a default instance of SQL Server 2000 in your import server. If the default instance in the target computer is SQL Server 7.0, the Upgrade Wizard available will be the one installed with SQL Server 7.0.

You can find the SQL Server Upgrade Wizard in the Microsoft SQL Server—Switch programs group. Figure 1.10 shows the main form of this wizard, right after the Wizard Welcome form.

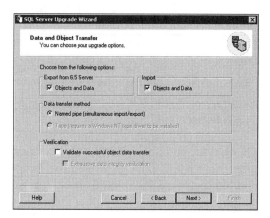

Figure 1.10: *The SQL Server Upgrade Wizard.*

NOTE

The Tape option will be available only if you have a tape physically attached to the computer that is running SQL Server.

SERVICE MANAGER

Using Service Manager, you can start, pause, and stop SQL Server services on any available SQL Server in your network. Figure 1.11 shows the SQL Server Service Manager. There you can specify to autostart a service whenever the operating system starts.

Figure 1.11: *SQL Server Service Manager.*

When you stop, the SQL Server Service, SQL Server

1. Disables new logins, excluding system administrators.

2. Performs a CHECKPOINT in every database to shorten recovery time the next time SQL Server starts. Checkpoint is an internal process in SQL Server that ensures that every data modified in memory is sent to disk.

3. Waits for all active statements and stored procedures to finish their work.

4. Shuts down.

CAUTION

Note that batches can be interrupted when you stop SQL Server, and if the batch was inside a transaction, the transaction is automatically rolled back.

Chapter 13, "Maintaining Data Consistency: Transactions and Locks," teaches you how to use transactions in SQL Server.

When you pause SQL Server, you only prevent new connections, but existing users can continue their work. This gives you the opportunity to send a message to the connected users, so they can finish their work before stopping SQL Server.

COMMAND-LINE UTILITIES

SQL Server 2000 setup installs several utilities that can be started from the command prompt. To use them, you must open a command prompt window and type any of the following commands:

- bcp—Bulk Copy Program. Use this utility to import or export data to and from SQL Server 2000. Chapter 14, "Transferring Data to and from SQL Server," contains information on how to use bcp.

- console—Displays backup and restore messages when the operation uses a tape device.

- dtsrun—This utility runs Data Transformation Packages from the command prompt.

- dtswiz—Use this utility to start the DTS Import/Export Wizard.

- isql—This is a query tool that uses DB-Library to connect to SQL Server. Use this tool to execute scripts in SQL Server 2000 that do not require user interaction, such as administrative scripts. You can send the output to a file.

- isqlw—Use this command to run SQL Query Analyzer.

- osql—This is a similar tool to isql, but it uses ODBC to connect to SQL Server.

- itwiz—Runs the Index Tuning Wizard, which will advise you about the best strategy to tune your database. Chapter 6, "Optimizing Access to Data: Indexes," teaches you how to use the Index Tuning Wizard.

- makepipe—This utility creates a pipe that helps you test the Named Pipes protocol with the readpipe utility.

- readpipe—This utility reads from a pipe created using the makepipe utility.

- odbccmpt—Enables or disables the compatibility flag for ODBC applications, which solves some compatibility problems related to the ODBC 3.7 drivers.

- odbcping—Tests connectivity to an ODBC data source.

- rebuildm—Rebuild Master utility. This utility rebuilds all the system databases.

- distrib—Configures and runs the Replication Distribution Agent.

- logread—Configures and runs the Replication Log Reader Agent.

- replmerg—Configures and runs the Replication Merge Agent.

- queueread—Configures and runs the Replication Queue Reader Agent.

- snapshot—Configures and runs the Replication Snapshot Agent.

- scm—Service Control Manager. This utility is the command-line version of the SQL Server Service Manager, with extra functionality.

- sqlagent—Starts the SQLServerAgent service.

- sqldiag—Produces a full diagnostics report about SQL Server current environment and activity.

- sqlftwiz—Starts the Full-text Indexing Wizard.

- `sqlmaint`—Runs specific database maintenance tasks.

- `sqlservr`—Starts, stops, or pauses any instance of SQL Server 2000.

- `vswitch`—Switches the default instance of SQL Server between SQL Server 6.5 and either SQL Server 7.0 or the default instance of SQL Server 2000.

CAUTION

Setup does not install the `makepipe`, `readpipe`, or `odbcping` utilities. You can find them in the x86\Binn directory from the distribution CD.

Database Components (Objects)

A SQL Server 2000 database contains different types of objects. Some objects contain user data, whereas other objects are just definitions of objects, business rules declarations, and programs.

Data is arranged in tables and every field, identified by its name and data type, represents a different attribute. Tables are the main database objects because you store your data in tables. You will learn how to create tables in Chapter 3, "Working with Tables and Views."

Every individual value uses a specific data type. SQL Server provides a collection of data types, compatible with the ANSI SQL 92 standard, but you can create your own user-defined data types, based on existing system supplied data types. Chapter 2, "Elements of Transact-SQL," teaches you how to use data types and how to define and apply user-defined data types.

To guarantee data integrity and consistency, you can define constraints in the following manner:

- Primary key and unique constraints provide entity integrity, maintaining uniqueness in one or more columns.

- Check and default constraints maintain domain integrity, checking for specific business rules to apply to the inserted data.

- Foreign keys maintain referential integrity, maintaining links between related information in different tables.

Chapter 7, "Enforcing Data Integrity," covers constraints in detail, as well as Rule and Default objects.

Complex queries can be defined as views, which can be reused in other queries, providing better readability and easier maintenance. You learn about views in Chapter 3, "Working with Tables and Views."

To speed up access to data, you can create indexes on tables and views. Indexes store subsets of the available information in an ordered way, as keys and pointers to the actual data, to provide fast access to the data. Chapter 6, "Optimizing Access to Data: Indexes," discusses indexes in detail.

You can expand the SQL Server capabilities creating user-defined functions. These functions can be as simple as a scalar function or as complex as a multistatement table-valued user-defined function. To know more about user-defined functions, read Chapter 10, "Enhancing Business Logic: User-Defined Functions (UDF)."

Complex processes can be defined as stored procedures. In this way, SQL Server can optimize the stored procedure's execution plan on the first execution, and reuse this optimized execution plan for every further call. Chapter 8, "Implementing Business Logic: Programming Stored Procedures," teaches you how to create and use stored procedures.

You can define special stored procedures, called triggers, which, linked to a table, execute automatically whenever you attempt any data modification to the table.

Security Model

SQL Server stores important data for your company, and you want to guarantee that every user can access only the data she needs and with the appropriate access rights.

Ensuring a proper security policy in a SQL Server database is a task that starts in your IT environment. To plan this security policy, you should find answers to the following questions:

- Who can access your company premises?
- Who can physically access your corporate servers?
- Who, and from where, can connect to your corporate network?
- Do you apply proper password policies in your network?
- Do you isolate sensitive servers in restricted networks?
- Do you follow adequate security auditing policies?

Your network is secure if you can identify and ensure

- What resources need shared access by nonadministrators
- Who can access shared resources
- Which users have access to a resource, from which places users can access this resource, and during what period of time

- A password policy that prevents misuse of logins and passwords

- A proper audit policy to trace unauthorized access attempts to any resource, by tracing information about failed access

In other words: To control access to important resources in your company, you need to identify the users who access these resources, the date and time of each access, and the location from where each access is made.

SQL Server enforces security at different levels. Any data access, such as reading the unit price of a given product, forces SQL Server to check data access security, following predefined steps, according to the SQL Server security model. Figure 1.12 shows how SQL Server checks for data access security, which is in summary:

1. A user needs a valid login to gain access to SQL Server.

2. After a user has entered SQL Server, access to specific databases is controlled by the existence of a valid user on the target database.

3. Users need specific permissions to execute specific statements at the database level.

4. Users need permissions per object and action.

5. Incomplete permissions to execute a given statement prevent the entire statement from being executed.

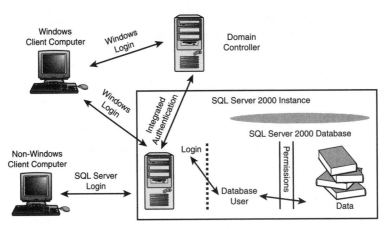

Figure 1.12: *The SQL Server security model.*

According to the preceding comments, a login gives you access to SQL Server, and a user gives you access to a specific database. You learn in more detail this important process in the following sections.

N O T E

Security management is an administrative task, usually out of the scope of database developers. However, many common problems in database applications are related to security. As a database developer, you will benefit from understanding the implications of database security. Having security in mind helps you design a better database system that is more adequate to the business requirements.

AUTHENTICATION MODES

SQL Server 2000 is integrated with Windows, and it can use the authentication mode defined in your Windows network. SQL Server 2000 can collaborate with Windows NT or Windows 2000 to authenticate this user. In other cases, some users will access SQL Server from other networks, not members of any Windows domain, yet you still need to provide them secure access to SQL Server. In these cases, SQL Server is the only service responsible for user authentication.

SQL Server supports two authentication modes:

- Windows Authentication only, when only valid Windows users will have access to SQL Server.

- Mixed mode, when SQL Server accepts either Windows authentication or SQL Server authentication.

To specify the authentication mode for your server, use Enterprise Manager, open the SQL Server properties form, and select the required authentication mode in the Security tab, as you can see in Figure 1.13. After you change the authentication mode, you must stop and restart SQL Server.

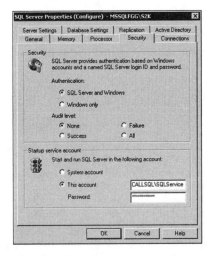

Figure 1.13: SQL Server authentication mode.

WINDOWS INTEGRATED AUTHENTICATION   Usually, you have your SQL Server 2000 installed in a member server of a Windows domain. In this case, every user needs a valid domain login and password to start a session on any computer member of this domain.

Every domain user can be a member of any number of domain groups, and every domain group can belong to one or more local groups on every specific server. In other words, one specific domain user can be authenticated in a specific server by his or her direct or indirect membership in one or more local or domain groups.

The permissions that any user has when trying to access any server resource, printer, shared folder or file, or network application, is the combination of permissions applied to every group where this particular user has membership; the only exception is no access, which cancels any possible permissions that this user has.

When a user tries to connect to SQL Server using Windows Integrated Authentication, it is not necessary to supply the login name and password again. Windows has already checked this data and SQL Server does not need to check it again. Windows informs SQL Server about the identity of this user and the windows groups' membership.

SQL Server must check whether the user has a valid login defined on SQL Server for his or her own Windows login, or for any windows group where this user has membership. If this search is successful, SQL Server checks whether any of these valid SQL Server logins has denied access to SQL Server, in which case the user connection is rejected. If none of the valid logins for this Windows user has denied access to SQL Server, the connection is established.

Windows authentication has an important advantage: You use Windows to control who can access your network and how, why not use Windows to control who can access SQL Server and how? SQL is a networked Windows application, after all.

Using this type of authentication, SQL Server doesn't store password information for Windows logins.

CAUTION

If you try to provide a login name and password to connect to SQL Server 2000 and this particular server accepts only Windows Authentication, the connection will be rejected, even if the attempted login was sa with the valid sa password.

MIXED (SQL AND WINDOWS) AUTHENTICATION   In some environments, you can have users who are authenticated by Windows and users without Windows credentials, or in other words, they don't have a Windows account. If this is the case, you should use Mixed Authentication Mode. In this case, any user can connect to SQL Server either by Windows Authentication or by SQL Server Authentication.

Perhaps you want to have an extra security layer to access your databases and, even if Windows has authenticated the user, you want to force the user to provide a valid login and password to connect to SQL Server. In other cases, users access SQL Server from remote networks, perhaps from the Internet, and Windows cannot authenticate them.

CAUTION

It is the user's responsibility to decide which credentials to use when trying to connect to SQL Server. If the user selects Windows Authentication, the connection will be successful only if SQL Server accepts his Windows credentials.

If the user selects SQL Server Authentication, the supplied login name and password must correspond to a valid login name and password in SQL Server; otherwise, the connection will be refused and SQL Server will not try to connect with the user's Windows credentials.

CONNECTING TO SQL SERVER: LOGINS

To allow users access to SQL Server, you must create a login for them. When you install a new instance of SQL Server, you have only the following logins:

- BUILTIN\Administrators—This is the login associated with the local Administrator group in the local server where SQL Server is installed. Members of this group are considered SQL Server administrators by default. You can remove this login.

- sa—This is the SQL Server system administrator login account used for SQL Server authentication. This login cannot be removed, even if you select Windows Integrated Authentication only.

- YourDomain\SQLService—This is the login account for the SQL Server service account, if you selected, as recommended, to use a domain account as a SQL Server service account (SQLService, in this case).

NOTE

The service account should be a member of the local Administrators account, and in that case it already has a valid login as a member of the BUILTIN\Administrators group. However, it is recommended that you maintain a separate login for this account, because it should not depend on the existence of other logins.

You can add more logins using Enterprise Manager or using the sp_addlogin or sp_grantlogin system-stored procedures, as in Listing 1.1.

To create new logins in SQL Server you have the following choices:

- Execute `sp_addlogin` to create a new login using SQL Server Authentication. In this case, you can specify the password, default language, and default database for this login.

- Execute `sp_grantlogin` to grant access to SQL Server to an existing local user in the server that is running SQL Server. In this case, the name of the login should have the format `'BUILTIN\User'`.

- Execute `sp_grantlogin` to grant access to SQL Server to an existing local group in the server that is running SQL Server. In this case, the name of the login should have the format `'BUILTIN\LocalGroup'`. A typical example of this is the default `'BUILTIN\Administrators'` login created during setup.

- Execute `sp_grantlogin` to grant access to SQL Server to an existing domain user in a domain trusted by the domain in which SQL Server is running. In this case, the name of the login should have the format `'DomainName\User'`. This is the case used by the service account login `'YourDomain\SQLService'`.

- Execute `sp_grantlogin` to grant access to SQL Server to an existing domain global group in a domain trusted by the domain where SQL Server is running. In this case, the name of the login should have the format `'DomainName\GlobalGroup'`.

CAUTION

Local users and groups are valid only in the computer in which they are created, so they cannot be used to grant access to SQL Server in a different computer.

NOTE

To execute Listing 1.1, and the other examples in this chapter, you must log in to SQL Server 2000 from Query Analyzer using an administrator account.

EXAMPLE

Listing 1.1: Create Logins Using the `sp_addlogin` and `sp_grantlogin` System Stored Procedures

```
-- Create a SQL Server login
-- using English as a default language
-- with Northwind as a default database

EXEC sp_addlogin
@loginame = 'Tim'
, @passwd = 'TimPassword'
, @defdb = 'Northwind'
, @deflanguage = 'English'

-- Create a SQL Server login
```

Listing 1.1: continued

```
-- using Spanish as a default language
-- without password, and without default database

EXEC sp_addlogin
@loginame = 'Pedro'
, @deflanguage = 'Spanish'

-- Create a SQL Server login
-- for the local Guest Windows account

EXEC sp_grantlogin 'BUILTIN\Guest'

-- Create a SQL Server login
-- for the domain Guest account

EXEC sp_grantlogin 'YourDomain\Guest'

-- Create a SQL Server login
-- for the local group Users Windows account

EXEC sp_grantlogin 'BUILTIN\Users'

-- Create a SQL Server login
-- for the domain group Domain Users account

EXEC sp_grantlogin 'YourDomain\Domain Users'
```

OUTPUT

```
New login created.
New login created.
Granted login access to 'BUILTIN\Guest'.
Granted login access to 'YourDomain\Guest'.
Granted login access to 'BUILTIN\Users'.
Granted login access to 'YourDomain\Domain Users'.
```

CAUTION

If the server where SQL Server is installed is a domain controller, it does not have local users. Therefore, the third example from Listing 1.1 will fail.

As you see in Listing 1.1, when you add a new SQL Server login, you can specify a password, a default database, and default language for this particular login. When you add a Windows login using sp_grantlogin, you cannot specify these options. However,

- The password cannot be specified because Windows will check the password when the user tries to connect to Windows. SQL Server does not need to know this password.

- You can use the sp_defaultlanguage system stored procedure to modify the default language that this particular login will use to communicate with SQL Server. This setting affects custom error messages and date output formats. This procedure is valid for SQL Server and Windows logins.

- You can execute the sp_defaultdb system stored procedure to modify the default database for this login. This procedure is valid for SQL Server and Windows logins.

CAUTION

Having a default database does not guarantee access to this database. To have access to a database, you must be mapped to a valid user in that database.

The next section teaches you how to create database users.

To deny access to SQL Server to a particular login, you can use the following:

- EXECUTE sp_denylogin 'Domain\User' denies access to SQL Server to a domain user. The login still exists, but nobody can connect to SQL Server using this login. If the login is a Windows group, none of the members of this group will be able to connect to SQL Server—regardless of the existence of other logins they might have access to.

- EXECUTE sp_revokelogin 'Domain\User' permanently removes this Windows login from SQL Server. This does not guarantee that the users or members of this Windows group will not have access to SQL Server, because they can still belong to one or more Windows groups with valid logins in SQL Server.

- EXECUTE sp_droplogin 'SQLUser' denies access to SQL Server to a SQL Server login. In this case, this login will be deleted from SQL Server permanently.

NOTE

You can change the password for an existing SQL Server login using the sp_password system stored procedure.

USING DATABASES: USERS

After the user connects to SQL Server using a valid login, the connection is established, but there is not much to do. To access real data, the user needs access to a database. This is achieved by creating a user on that database.

When you set up SQL Server, the systems databases contain the following users:

- dbo—This is the database owner with full permissions, by default, on the entire database. This user cannot be removed.

- guest—This is the default user for logins that don't have a specific user in a database. Because every system database, Northwind, and Pubs databases have a guest user, any valid login can use these databases directly. This user can be removed to guarantee authenticated access to a database only.

CAUTION

SQL Server uses the Model database as a template to create new databases. The Model database does not have a Guest account; therefore, new databases will not have a guest user unless you create it explicitly.

To create a user in the current database, you can use the sp_grantdbaccess stored procedure, as in Listing 1.2. Each login can be mapped to a single user per database. Even if the login were related to a Windows group, the mapped user in the database is considered a logically individual user.

EXAMPLE

Listing 1.2: Use sp_grantdbaccess to Grant Logins Access to a Database

```
USE Northwind
GO

-- Create a Tim user in the Northwind database

EXEC sp_grantdbaccess
@loginame = 'Tim'

-- Create a User in Northwind
-- for the local Guest login

EXEC sp_grantdbaccess
@loginame = 'BUILTIN\Guest'
, @name_in_db = 'LocalGuest'

-- Create a user in Northwind
-- for the domain Guest account

EXEC sp_grantdbaccess
@loginame = 'YourDomain\Guest'
, @name_in_db = 'GlobalGuest'

-- Create a user in Northwind
-- for the local group Users Windows account

EXEC sp_grantdbaccess
@loginame = 'BUILTIN\Users'
```

Listing 1.2: continued

```
, @name_in_db = 'LocalUsers'

-- Create a user in Northwind
-- for the domain group Domain Users account

EXEC sp_grantdbaccess
@loginame = 'YourDomain\Domain Users'
, @name_in_db = 'GlobalUsers'
```

OUTPUT

```
Granted database access to 'Tim'.
Granted database access to 'BUILTIN\Guest'.
Granted database access to 'CallSQL\Guest'.
Granted database access to 'BUILTIN\Users'.
Granted database access to 'CallSQL\Domain Users'.
```

As you saw in Listing 1.2, users in a database do not have to have exactly the same names as the corresponding logins in SQL Server. However, it is recommended that users and logins have the same names to avoid maintenance problems.

SERVER AND DATABASE ROLES

After a login has been granted access to a database, because it has a user defined on that database, it does not have access to specific data yet. The user needs specific permissions to access data from database objects.

Applying and managing to individual users can be very complex. SQL Server 2000 provides roles, at server and database levels, to simplify permissions management:

- Fixed server roles—Group logins by general server permissions to simplify general logins administration. These fixed server roles cannot be modified or dropped, not even their permissions. You can only change their membership.

- Fixed database roles—Group users in a database by functionality, reducing permissions maintenance overhead. Fixed database roles cannot be modified or dropped, not even their permissions. You can only change their membership.

- User-defined database roles—Extend the functionality of fixed database roles, providing extra flexibility on grouping users at the database level to apply specific permissions.

The most important fixed server role is sysadmin (System Administrators). Login members of the sysadmin server role are not affected by SQL Server security at all.

If you want to differentiate between users with only specific administrative privileges, you can use other fixed server roles:

- Members of the serveradmin role can configure and stop or restart SQL server.

- Members of the setupadmin role can manage linked servers and specify which stored procedures will automatically run when SQL Server starts.

- Members of the securityadmin role can manage logins, including changing passwords, and assign permissions to create databases.

- Members of the processadmin role can stop processes running in SQL Server.

- Members of the dbcreator role can manage databases.

- Members of the diskadmin role can manage disk files and backup devices.

- Members of the bulkadmin role can execute BULK INSERT statements.

You can use system stored procedures to retrieve information about server roles and to manage server roles membership, as in Listing 1.3.

EXAMPLE

Listing 1.3: Stored Procedures to Manage Server Roles

```
-- Get a list of the server roles

EXEC sp_helpsrvrole

-- get a list of permissions of a specific server role

EXEC sp_srvrolepermission setupadmin

-- Make Tim member of the sysadmin role

EXEC sp_addsrvrolemember
@loginame = 'Tim'
```

Listing 1.3: continued

```
, @rolename = 'sysadmin'

-- Get a list of sysadmin role members

EXEC sp_helpsrvrolemember sysadmin

-- Remove Tim from the sysadmin role

EXEC sp_dropsrvrolemember
@loginame = 'Tim'
, @rolename = 'sysadmin'
```

OUTPUT

```
ServerRole                          Description
---------------------------------   ---------------------------------
sysadmin                            System Administrators
securityadmin                       Security Administrators
serveradmin                         Server Administrators
setupadmin                          Setup Administrators
processadmin                        Process Administrators
diskadmin                           Disk Administrators
dbcreator                           Database Creators
bulkadmin                           Bulk Insert Administrators

(8 row(s) affected)


ServerRole                          Permission
---------------------------------   ---------------------------------
setupadmin                          Add member to setupadmin
setupadmin                          Add/drop/configure linked servers
setupadmin                          Mark a stored procedure as startup

(3 row(s) affected)

'Tim' added to role 'sysadmin'.


ServerRole   MemberName             MemberSID
----------   ------------------     -----------------------------------
sysadmin     BUILTIN\Administrators  0x010200000000000520000000020200000
sysadmin     YourDomain\SQLService   0x0105000000000000515000000003FAD1462
➥FD43461E1525AF47EF030000
sysadmin     distributor_admin       0xBAC6B1014B4F23408F6B0CEF54A0AB5E
sysadmin     sa                      0x01
sysadmin     Tim                     0x6E00C5CC4408ED47A33C5B210029109F

'Tim' dropped from role 'sysadmin'.
```

At database level, you can group users in database roles. Every database contains a fixed set of fixed database roles:

- `db_owner`—Database owners or users who have, by default, granted permissions to perform any action on every database object.

- `db_accessadmin`—Database access administrators manage users in the database.

- `db_securityadmin`—Database security administrators manage permissions.

- `db_ddladmin`—Database DDL administrators can execute any Data Definition Language statement.

- `db_backupoperator`—Database backup operators.

- `db_datareader`—Database users with permissions to read data from any table in the database.

- `db_datawriter`—Database users with permissions to modify data on any table in the database.

- `db_denydatareader`—Database users with denied permissions to read data from this database.

- `db_denydatawriter`—Database users with denied permissions to modify data from this database.

You can use system-stored procedures to retrieve information about fixed database roles, as in Listing 1.4.

EXAMPLE

Listing 1.4: Stored Procedures to Manage Fixed Database Roles

```
USE Northwind
GO

-- Get a list of the database roles

EXEC sp_helpdbfixedrole

-- Get a list of permissions of a specific database role
```

Listing 1.4: continued

```
EXEC sp_dbfixedrolepermission db_ddladmin

-- Make Tim member of the db_owner role

EXEC sp_addrolemember
@rolename = 'db_owner'
, @membername = 'Tim'

-- Get a list of db_owner database role members

EXEC sp_helprolemember 'db_owner'

-- Remove Tim from the db_owner role

EXEC sp_droprolemember
@rolename = 'db_owner'
, @membername = 'Tim'
```

OUTPUT

```
DbFixedRole            Description
-------------------    ----------------------------------
db_accessadmin         DB Access Administrators
db_backupoperator      DB Backup Operator
db_datareader          DB Data Reader
db_datawriter          DB Data Writer
db_ddladmin            DB DDL Administrators
db_denydatareader      DB Deny Data Reader
db_denydatawriter      DB Deny Data Writer
db_owner               DB Owners
db_securityadmin       DB Security Administrators

(9 row(s) affected)

DbFixedRole            Permission
-------------------    ----------------------------------
db_ddladmin            All DDL but GRANT, REVOKE, DENY
db_ddladmin            dbcc cleantable
db_ddladmin            dbcc show_statistics
db_ddladmin            dbcc showcontig
db_ddladmin            REFERENCES permission on any table
db_ddladmin            sp_changeobjectowner
db_ddladmin            sp_fulltext_column
db_ddladmin            sp_fulltext_table
db_ddladmin            sp_recompile
db_ddladmin            sp_rename
db_ddladmin            sp_tableoption
db_ddladmin            TRUNCATE TABLE
```

Listing 1.4: continued

```
(12 row(s) affected)

'Tim' added to role 'db_owner'.

DbRole          MemberName   MemberSID
-------------   -----------  ----------------------------------
db_owner        dbo          0x01
db_owner        Tim          0x6E00C5CC4408ED47A33C5B210029109F

(2 row(s) affected)

'Tim' dropped from role 'db_owner'.
```

You can create your own database roles. This is useful in some specific circumstances:

- If you cannot create Windows groups to group your SQL Server users, you can create database roles to group users according to the different set of permissions they must have.

- If you have Windows users and non-Windows users, you will have Windows logins and SQL Server logins, and you want to apply permissions to them as a group, regardless of their login origin.

TIP

Try to use Windows groups instead of user-defined database roles whenever possible. Windows users are grouped by functionality, and they share common permissions to access different resources at Windows level, printers, directories, and so on. It usually makes sense to maintain them as a group in SQL Server, creating a single login for all of them and a single user on the database they need. In this case, there is no need for a database role.

You can manage database roles with several stored procedures similar to the ones used in Listings 1.3 and 1.4. Listing 1.5 shows how to create a database role, how to manage membership of the role, and how to remove the database role when it is no longer necessary.

EXAMPLE

Listing 1.5: Stored Procedures to Manage User-Defined Database Roles

```
USE Northwind
GO

-- Add a new role

EXEC sp_addrole 'SalesAdmin'

-- Get a list of the database roles
```

Listing 1.5: continued

```
EXEC sp_helprole

-- Make the SqlesAdmin role member of the
-- db_datareader database role

EXEC sp_addrolemember
@rolename = 'db_datareader'
, @membername = 'SalesAdmin'

-- Make Tim member of the SalesAdmin role

EXEC sp_addrolemember
@rolename = 'SalesAdmin'
, @membername = 'Tim'

-- Get a list of SalesAdmin database role members

EXEC sp_helprolemember 'SalesAdmin'

-- Remove Tim from the SalesAdmin role

EXEC sp_droprolemember
@rolename = 'SalesAdmin'
, @membername = 'Tim'

-- Drop the SalesAdmin role

EXEC sp_droprole 'SalesAdmin'
```

OUTPUT

```
New role added.

RoleName             RoleId IsAppRole
-------------------- ------ -----------
public               0      0
db_owner             16384  0
db_accessadmin       16385  0
db_securityadmin     16386  0
db_ddladmin          16387  0
db_backupoperator    16389  0
db_datareader        16390  0
db_datawriter        16391  0
db_denydatareader    16392  0
db_denydatawriter    16393  0
SalesAdmin           16400  0

(11 row(s) affected)
```

Listing 1.5: continued

```
'SalesAdmin' added to role 'db_datareader'.

'Tim' added to role 'SalesAdmin'.

DbRole          MemberName   MemberSID
-------------   -----------  -----------------------------------
db_owner        Tim          0x6E00C5CC4408ED47A33C5B210029109F

 (1 row(s) affected)

'Tim' dropped from role 'SalesAdmin'.

Role dropped.
```

There is a special group on every SQL Server database; its name is public and every user and role in that database belongs to public. The public role is very useful to define the default permissions that every user has in the database.

PERMISSIONS

Now that you have users in a database and you grouped them by database roles, you can apply permissions to them. These permissions can be

- Statement permissions—Permissions to execute specific Transact-SQL statements, to create database objects, and to execute backups.

- Data access permissions—Permissions to read, delete, insert, update, or reference data, or permissions to execute stored procedures and user-defined functions.

Regardless of the type of permission to apply, the user permission to perform any action on a specific database object or statement can have any of these three states:

- Neutral—No permissions. In this case, the user will have permissions to perform the required action, depending on permissions applied to other roles or Windows groups the user might belong to.

- Denied—The user cannot perform the required action. It does not matter whether the user belongs to other roles or groups with permissions to perform this action. Deny overrides everything else.

- Granted—In principle, the user has permissions to proceed with this action. However, the final permissions depend on other existing permissions on the same action applied to other groups or roles this particular user belongs to.

To decide which permissions a particular user has, SQL Server must combine permissions from the user with permissions from the different roles and groups in which this user has membership. The only exception to this is if any permission is denied to the user or any of the user's roles or groups, the final permission will be denied.

NOTE

Remember, members of the sysadmin role are not affected by permissions.

STATEMENT PERMISSIONS   You can define permissions for the following statements:

- BACKUP DATABASE—To execute full or differential database backups

- BACKUP LOG—To perform transaction log backups

- CREATE DATABASE—To create databases

- CREATE DEFAULT—To create independent DEFAULT objects

- CREATE FUNCTION—To create user-defined functions

- CREATE PROCEDURE—To create stored procedures

- CREATE RULE—To create independent RULE objects

- CREATE TABLE—To create tables

- CREATE VIEW—To create views

To grant statement permissions, you use the GRANT statement with the following syntax:

```
GRANT Statement TO Security_account
```

or

```
GRANT ALL TO Security_account
```

Security_account can be a database user or a user-defined database role.

To deny statement permissions, use the DENY statement with the following syntax:

```
DENY Statement TO Security_account
```

or

```
DENY ALL TO Security_account
```

To revoke previously granted or denied statement permission, use the REVOKE statement with the following syntax:

```
REVOKE Statement FROM Security_account
```

or

```
REVOKE ALL FROM Security_account
```

You can manage statement permissions in Enterprise Manager as well, in the Permissions tab available in the Database Properties form, as shown in Figure 1.14.

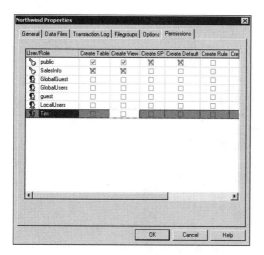

Figure 1.14: *Manage statement permissions from Enterprise Manager.*

CAUTION

By default, when a user creates an object, the user becomes the owner of that object. However, the dbo, or any member of the db_owner role, can take ownership of any existing object in the database they own.

TIP

It is not recommended to grant statement permissions to any user other than dbo. In this way, the same user, dbo, will own every object and permissions management will be much easier.

It is not necessary to grant statement permissions to dbo because it has all these permissions by default.

NOTE

DROP and ALTER statement permissions are granted only to the object owner and members of the db_owner role.

RESTORE DATABASE and RESTORE LOG permissions are granted to members of the sysadmin and dbcreator server roles. Note that members of the db_owner role do not have permissions to restore the database they own.

DATA ACCESS PERMISSIONS   You can protect access to the data using the GRANT, DENY, and REVOKE statements you saw already in the preceding section.

Depending on the object, you can manage permissions for different actions. Figure 1.15 shows the permissions that can be applied to every different object.

	SELECT	INSERT	UPDATE	DELETE	EXECUTE	REFERENCES
TABLES	●	●	●	●		●
COLUMNS	●		●			
VIEWS	●	●	●	●		●
STORED PROCEDURES					●	
INLINE UDFs	●	●	●	●		●
SCALAR UDFs					●	●
TABLE-VALUED UDFs	●					●

Data Access Permissions per Database Object

Figure 1.15: *Data access permissions available per database object.*

You can access object permissions in Enterprise Manager in three ways:

- Through the Object Permissions form, you can see the permissions applied to every user and role for a particular object. Figure 1.16 shows you the Object Permissions form.

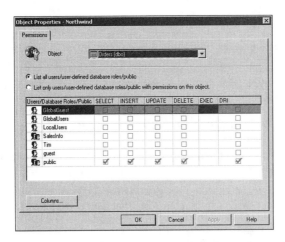

Figure 1.16: *Data access permissions through the Object Permissions form.*

- Through the Database User Permissions form, where for every user you can see the permissions applied on every object in the database. Figure 1.17 shows the User Permissions form.

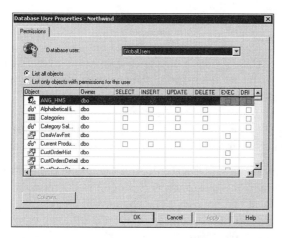

Figure 1.17: *Data access permissions through the Database User Permissions form.*

- Through the Database Role Permissions form, where for every role you can see the permissions applied on every object in the database, as in Figure 1.18.

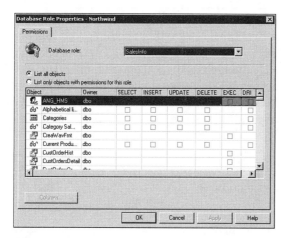

Figure 1.18: *Data access permissions through the Database Role Permissions Form.*

Some users have special data access permissions:

- Members of the sysadmin server role have full permissions on all objects and all databases available in the server they manage. Even if you specifically deny permissions to these users, they can still perform any action because SQL Server security does not affect SQL Server administrators.

- Members of the db_owner database role have, by default, full permissions on all objects from the database they own. However, it is possible to deny permissions on specific actions and objects to members of the db_owner role. In that case, DENY affects them, as with any other database user. However, members of the db_owner role can revoke previously denied permissions and take ownership of any object if necessary.

- Object owners have, by default, full permissions on the objects they own. However, the object owner, members of the sysadmin server role, or members of the db_owner database role can deny permissions on specific actions to the object owner. In that case, DENY affects the object owner, as with any other database user. However, object owners can revoke previously denied permissions as long as they are still owners of the target object.

NOTE

An object owner is not necessarily the database owner, and vice versa. However, it is recommended that all objects in a database be owned by the user dbo.

APPLICATION SECURITY   In the preceding sections, you learned how to manage permissions to execute specific Data Manipulation Language (DML) or Data Definition Language (DDL) statements, affecting database users and roles. Managing permissions in this way can be complex as soon as the number of database objects and users increases. Using SQL Server 2000, you can simplify permissions management using Application Security in different ways:

- Creating stored procedures to retrieve and modify data—You can give users access to the data through these stored procedures only, denying permissions to access directly the underlying tables. Chapter 8 covers in detail how to implement applications security using stored procedures.

- Provide indirect access to the data through views—You can design your views to provide access to particular columns only and to particular sets of rows, hiding the actual tables to the users. Chapter 3, "Working with Tables and Views," covers how to implement applications security using views in detail.

- Provide indirect access to the data through inline user-defined functions—Inline user-defined functions are similar to views, but they expose parameters that give your users extra flexibility. You learn in Chapter 10, "Enhancing Business Logic: User-Defined Functions (UDF)," how to implement applications security using inline user-defined functions.

- Provide indirect read-only access to the data through multistatement table-valued user-defined functions—These functions work similar to stored procedures, but they do not modify actual data. Users can work with these user-defined functions as if they were tables. You can find examples of table-valued functions in Chapter 10.

When a user invokes a stored procedure, view, or user-defined function, SQL Server checks first whether every required object belongs to the same owner. In this case, SQL server will check permissions only in the invoked object, and it does not check permissions on the underlying objects at all. However, if the ownership chain is broken on any of the referenced objects, SQL Server must check permissions on every individual object.

Chapters 3, 8, and 10 contain information and examples about implications of ownership chains on application security.

Imagine now a different situation:

Your company has a sales application, called SalesInfo, to manage sales orders. Customers call your company to place orders and you have a dedicated team of sales specialists who take orders on the phone and enter them into your database using the SalesInfo application.

You have a call center with 100 computers and you have in total about 200 sales specialists who use these computers in different shifts. Sales specialists sit every day at a different computer, and you give them an individual domain account to log in to your network. Other employees can use the SalesInfo application from their desktops or mobile computers.

Different employees might have different permissions in SQL Server, through different Windows groups and database roles. However, the SalesInfo application must execute specific actions in the database, regardless of the employee who is using the application. You want to make sure that if an employee has access to this application, he or she will be able to use it at full functionality, regardless of the individual database permissions the user might have.

To solve this problem, you could create a database role and assign permissions to this new role. However, permissions on this database role will be merged with other permissions the user might have, resulting in different actual permissions per employee.

SQL Server 2000 provides a solution to this problem through application roles. An *application role* is a special type of database role that has no members and whose permissions are not combined with any user's permissions.

You can create an application role using the `sp_addapprole` system stored procedure, providing a name for the new application role and a password for its activation. To change the application role password, you can execute the `sp_setapprolepassword` system stored procedure.

Applications can activate an application role using the `sp_setapprole` system stored procedure. User permissions are disregarded when an application role is active.

CAUTION

As we mentioned earlier in this chapter, every user and role belongs to the public role, including application roles. After activating an application role, the only active permissions are the permissions applied to the application role and to any group to which the application role belongs.

To drop an application role, you can use the `sp_dropapprole` system stored procedure. Listing 1.6 contains an example of how to create an application role, change its password, and activate the application role. It also shows an example of how to drop the application role.

EXAMPLE

Listing 1.6: Application Role Management

```
USE Northwind
GO

-- Create an Application Role

EXEC sp_addapprole
@rolename = 'SalesInfo'
,@password = 'SIPassword'
GO

-- Change the Application Role password

EXEC sp_approlepassword
@rolename = 'SalesInfo'
, @newpwd = 'NewSIPassword'
GO

-- Drop the Application Role
-- Note: execute this code alone
-- to drop the SalesInfo application role

/*
```

Listing 1.6: continued

```
EXEC sp_dropapprole 'SalesInfo'

*/

-- Activate the Appliction role
-- with encryption

EXEC sp_setapprole
@rolename = 'SalesInfo'
, @password = {Encrypt N 'NewSIPassword'}
, @encrypt = 'ODBC'

-- Activate the Appliction role
-- without encryption
-- Note: execute this conde instead of
-- the preceding statement
-- if you do not want to use encryption

/*

EXEC sp_setapprole
@rolename = 'SalesInfo'
, @password = 'NewSIPassword'

*/
```

```
New application role added.

(1 row(s) affected)
```

OUTPUT

```
The password for application role 'SalesInfo' has been changed.
The application role 'SalesInfo' is now active.
```

Applications can activate an application role at any time, providing the application role name and the specific application role password. The general security process for the SalesInfo application could be as follows:

1. Every employee uses a personal windows login to connect to the network.

2. Create a Windows group called SalesInfoGroup to group all users of the SalesInfo application.

3. Create a login in SQL Server for the SalesInfoGroup Windows group. Provide the Northwind database (or your particular target database) as a default database for this login.

4. Create the SalesInfoGroup user in the target database.

5. Create the SalesInfo application role in the target database as described in Listing 1.6.

6. The SalesInfo application can be designed to connect to SQL Server using Windows Integrated Authentication, using in this way the Windows login of the user who executes the application.

7. Every time the SalesInfo application connects to SQL Server, the application must call the stored procedure sp_setapprole to activate the application role.

8. When the application role is active, user permissions are disregarded.

CAUTION

Application roles are defined in a single database and they can access this database only. If an application role tries to access another database, it will use permissions available to the Guest account, if the Guest account exists in the target database.

TIP

If you use application roles and you want to know which Windows user is actually connected, use the SYSTEM_USER function. Even after an application role is active, SYSTEM_USER returns the actual login.

Client/Server Applications Design

You can design client/server applications to connect to SQL Server in many different ways. If you think about the basic activities every application does, you can group these activities in three conceptual layers:

- Data—This layer deals with the actual data your application uses. Some data can be stored in a relational database; some other data can be stored somewhere else, on any other format.

- Presentation—This layer is responsible for user interaction, accepting input from the user and presenting results to the user.

- Business—This layer interacts with the data layer to access data, and with the presentation layer to receive user requests and send results. This layer enforces business rules and executes business processes.

You can design your application as a monolithic standalone client-side application, including these three layers. This was the way many programs were created some years ago. If you deploy your application to several users, every user works with a private set of data. If you need to apply any change to the programming logic, you must rebuild and redeploy the application.

Trying to share data from different users forces you to separate the data layer from the other two and store the data in a separate database server. You can still design your application to manage presentation and business layers. In this case, changes on the business rules will force you to rebuild and redeploy the application to every user.

You can use constraints, views, stored procedures, user-defined functions, and triggers to translate part of the business layer to SQL Server. In this way, the database can be somehow a self-contained application with data, and business rules and processes. This approach can give you great flexibility, because changes on any business rules can be made in a central location: the SQL Server database.

In the previous examples, changes to the presentation layer force you to rebuild and redistribute your application. However, you can base your presentation layer in Active Server Pages (ASP), running in Internet Information Server (IIS). In this case, the only thing that the users need is an Internet browser. Changes to the presentation layer can be done easily in IIS, without any manual redistribution to the final users.

Using COM+ in Windows 2000 or Microsoft Transaction Server (MTS) in Windows NT 4.0, you can create components that encapsulate some functionality from the business and data layers. The presentation layer can use business components from COM+, and these business components can either use data components in COM+ or use database objects directly in SQL Server.

Designing your application in this way, you can change your database system to a different database structure or to a different database management system, if you need to, and the only changes to apply will be in your COM+ components. The presentation layer will be unaware of the changes in the database system.

Figure 1.19 shows a typical schema of a multilayer, or multitier, application.

In Figure 1.19, you can identify the following components:

  A. Data is stored in a SQL Server 2000 database and Exchange 2000 Server folders.

  B. Data components running in COM+ encapsulate data access to other components and applications.

  C. Business components expose complex data and business operations to other components.

  D. Network applications provide user interaction to local users, based on business components from COM+.

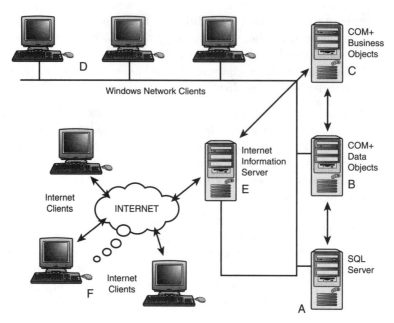

Figure 1.19: *A multitier system.*

E. Active Server Pages, running on Internet Information Server, provide user interaction to local and remote users, based on functionality provided by business components from COM+.

F. Local and remote users connect to IIS with an Internet browser to display the results of the Active Server Pages.

What's Next?

This book is about Microsoft SQL Server 2000. In some cases, you will see some comments about previous versions, but we wrote this book with SQL Server 2000 and for SQL Server 2000 database developers. This book provides comprehensive information about the new features available in SQL Server 2000:

- In Appendix A, you can learn how to install multiple instances of SQL Server 2000, and Chapter 15 teaches you how to write distributed queries, spanning multiple servers and instances.

- Appendix B covers the increased functionality of the new Query Analyzer.

- You will find information about new datatypes and built-in functions in Chapters 2 and 3.

- Chapter 6 is about optimizing data access using indexes. It covers new features, such as indexed views and indexes on computed columns.

- Cascade Declarative Referential Integrity is covered in Chapter 7.

- In Chapter 8, you will learn how to use the new Transact-SQL Debugger to test the execution of stored procedures.

- Information on and examples of new trigger functionality, such as index order and INSTEAD OF triggers, are available in Chapter 9.

- Chapter 10 provides comprehensive coverage of user-defined functions, which is one of the most exciting features of this new SQL Server version.

- Chapter 14 teaches you how to use the new Copy Database Wizard and how to create your own DTS packages.

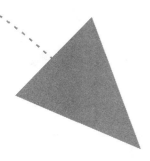

Elements of Transact-SQL

SQL, or Structured Query Language, is the language used to access and interact with a relational database. It was created by IBM in the 1970s and first standardized by the *American National Standards Institute (ANSI)* in 1989. ANSI released a new version of the standard in 1992, known as SQL-92 or SQL2.

Although all relational management systems, including SQL Server, are ANSI compliant at different levels, they provide extensions to the SQL language that extend the language's functionality. However, be aware that the code becomes less portable by using these extensions. Therefore, it's up to the programmer to comply or not comply with the ANSI standard.

Transact-SQL is the SQL Server implementation of the ANSI SQL-92 standard. In addition to the ANSI SQL-92 basic elements, Transact-SQL has extensions or enhancements that improve the capabilities of the language. For example, Transact-SQL adds procedural control-of-flow elements, such as IF .. ELSE, WHILE, BREAK, and CONTINUE.

Unlike procedural languages, Transact-SQL is a set-oriented database language (set-oriented means that it processes groups of data at once). As such, it was designed to work efficiently with set operations, instead of row-by-row operations. Thus, using Transact-SQL, you specify what you want to do with the whole set of data, instead of indicating what to do with each piece of data, or in database terminology, each row.

This chapter teaches you the following elements of Transact-SQL:

- The Data Definition Language (DDL)
- The Data Manipulation Language (DML)
- The Data Control Language (DCL)
- Extensions of Transact-SQL, such as variables, operators, functions, control of flow statements, and comments

Data Definition Language (DDL)

The Data Definition Language is used to create and manage databases and database objects, such as tables, stored procedures, user-defined functions, triggers, views, defaults, indexes, rules, and statistics. Transact-SQL provides a CREATE and a DROP statement for all these elements. Listing 2.1 shows the creation and removal of a table in the Northwind database.

EXAMPLE

Listing 2.1: Creating a Table Using the CREATE TABLE Statement

```
USE Northwind

CREATE TABLE Employeedependents
(
dependentid INT IDENTITY(1,1),
lastname VARCHAR(20),
firstname VARCHAR(20),
)
GO
```

OUTPUT

```
The command(s) completed successfully.
```

In addition to CREATE and DROP statements, an ALTER statement is provided to modify the properties of some of these objects (databases, tables, stored procedures, user-defined functions, triggers, and views). Listing 2.2 demonstrates how to add a new column to a table, using the ALTER TABLE statement.

EXAMPLE

Listing 2.2: Adding a New Column to the Employeedependent Table Using the ALTER TABLE Statement

```
USE Northwind

ALTER TABLE Employeedependents ADD birthdate DATETIME
GO
```

OUTPUT

```
The command(s) completed successfully.
```

In SQL Server, objects must be unique within users. This allows two users to own an object with the same name. For example, consider two users in a certain database. Each one of these two users could own a table with the same name. Therefore, in this case, there would be two tables with the same name in the database. In the following example, users user1 and user2 successfully create a table with the same name (Table×) in the Northwind database.

1. Using Query Analyzer, connect to SQL Server with the sa login and execute the following code, which creates both logins (login1 and login2 with blank password), adds users (user1 and user2) to the Northwind database for these logins, and grants CREATE DATABASE permissions to these two users:

```
USE Northwind

EXEC sp_addlogin 'login1'
EXEC sp_addlogin 'login2'
EXEC sp_adduser 'login1','user1'
EXEC sp_adduser 'login2','user2'
GRANT CREATE TABLE TO user1
GRANT CREATE TABLE TO user2
GO
```

2. Using Query Analyzer, open another connection to SQL Server, but use the newly created login1 login with blank password, and execute the following code:

```
USE Northwind

CREATE TABLE Tablex
(col1 INT)
GO
```

3. Using Query Analyzer, open a third connection to SQL Server using the newly created login2 login with blank password, and execute the following code:

```
USE Northwind

CREATE TABLE Tablex
(col1 INT)
GO
```

4. Finally, to check that both tables were successfully created, execute the following code from the first connection (the one with the sa login):

```
USE Northwind

PRINT 'user1'
SELECT * FROM user1.Tablex
PRINT 'user2'
SELECT * FROM user2.Tablex
GO
```

OUTPUT

```
user1
col1
-----------
(0 row(s) affected)

user2
col1
-----------
(0 row(s) affected)
```

Notice that in the last piece of code, the name of the tables had to be qualified with the owner's name.

A fully qualified name has four parts:

`Servername.databasename.owner.objectname`

The first three parts can be omitted. Thus, if you specify only the object name, SQL Server uses the current user, current database, and local server. The first part, the server name, must be specified when working with distributed queries (queries that span servers). The second part, the database name, must be specified when executing queries across databases. For example, Listing 2.3 shows a SELECT statement that is executed from the Northwind database that queries a table in the Pubs database.

EXAMPLE

Listing 2.3: Using the Database Name to Fully Qualify Names

```
USE Northwind

SELECT * FROM Pubs.dbo.Jobs
GO
```

OUTPUT

```
job_id job_desc                                                  min_lvl max_lvl
------ -------------------------------------------------------- ------- -------
1      New Hire - Job not specified                              10      10
2      Chief Executive Officer                                   200     250
3      Business Operations Manager                               175     225
4      Chief Financial Officer                                   175     250
5      Publisher                                                 150     250
6      Managing Editor                                           140     225
7      Marketing Manager                                         120     200
8      Public Relations Manager                                  100     175
9      Acquisitions Manager                                      75      175
10     Productions Manager                                       75      165
11     Operations Manager                                        75      150
12     Editor                                                    25      100
13     Sales Representative                                      25      100
14     Designer                                                  25      100

(14 row(s) affected)
```

Finally, the third part or owner specifies the object owner. This is useful in cases when two or more users own an object with the same name, like the previous example, in which both user1 and user2 own a table called Table1.

Rules for Identifiers

When creating databases or database objects, the name (object identifier) can have up to 128 characters and 116 characters for temporary objects (because SQL Server adds a suffix to the object's name).

A regular identifier is the one that complies with the following rules:

- The first character is either a letter, the at sign (@), the number sign (#), or the underscore character (_).

- The identifier doesn't contain any spaces.

- The identifier is not a Transact-SQL reserved keyword.

Any identifier that doesn't comply with any of these rules is not considered a regular identifier and must be enclosed in brackets. For example, Listing 2.4 shows the use of brackets when creating an object whose name contains spaces (a delimited identifier).

Listing 2.4: Using Delimited Identifiers

```
USE Northwind

CREATE TABLE [Name contains spaces]
(
cola INT,
colb VARCHAR(20)
)
GO
```

EXAMPLE

The command(s) completed successfully.

There are some special considerations regarding identifiers:

OUTPUT

- If the first character is #, it represents a local temporary object (either a local temporary table or a local temporary stored procedure). Listing 2.5 shows the creation of a local temporary table called #EmployeeBasicInfo.

Listing 2.5: Creating a Local Temporary Table

```
USE Northwind

CREATE TABLE #EmployeeBasicInfo
(
employeeid INT,
lastname VARCHAR(20),
firstname VARCHAR(20)
)
GO
```

EXAMPLE

The command(s) completed successfully.

- If the first character is ##, it represents a global temporary object (either a global temporary table or a global temporary stored procedure). Listing 2.6 shows the creation of a global temporary table called ##ProductBasicInfo.

OUTPUT

EXAMPLE

Listing 2.6: Creating a Global Temporary Table

```
USE Northwind

CREATE TABLE ##ProductBasicInfo
(
productid INT,
productname VARCHAR(40)
)
GO
```

OUTPUT

The command(s) completed successfully.

- If the first character is @, it represents a local variable. Because of this, you can't use the @ sign as the first character of the name of any database object. The statement used to define a local variable is the DECLARE statement. Listing 2.7 shows how to define a local variable (notice that the first character of the variable's name is @).

EXAMPLE

Listing 2.7: Creating a Local Variable

```
USE Northwind

DECLARE @age INT
SET @age = 25
GO
```

OUTPUT

The command(s) completed successfully.

Transact-SQL Programming Conventions

As a good programming practice, these are some conventions you can follow:

- Use uppercase characters for all reserved keywords.

- Capitalize all table names. In general, you should capitalize all objects that are collections.

- Use lowercase characters for all scalars, such as column names and variables.

- Keep names unique. In other words, try not to use the same name for more than one object.

- Regarding object ownership, the *database owner (dbo)* should be the owner of all objects in the database because this makes database administration easier and prevents a broken ownership chain. If, by any chance, the owner of a certain object must be changed, use the sp_changeobjectowner system stored procedure. Moreover, if you want to change the database owner, use the sp_changedbowner system stored procedure.

Data Manipulation Language (DML)

The Data Manipulation Language (DML) is the most commonly used component of Transact-SQL by database developers. Basically, it is used to retrieve, insert, modify, and delete information from databases. These four operations are performed through the commands that compose the DML, respectively:

- SELECT
- INSERT
- UPDATE
- DELETE

Therefore, any application or client who wants to interact with SQL Server to retrieve, insert, modify, or delete information has to do it through one of these four elements of the Transact-SQL DML.

Listing 2.8 shows a basic example of each one of the four statements that comprise the Data manipulation language (DML).

EXAMPLE

Listing 2.8: Using the DML to Interact with the Database

```
USE Northwind

INSERT INTO Customers (customerid, companyname, contactname, contacttitle)
VALUES ('ACME1','ACME Publishing','Fernando','DBA')
GO

UPDATE Customers
SET contactname = 'Fernando Guerrero'
WHERE customerid = 'ACME1'
GO

SELECT customerid,companyname
FROM Customers
WHERE customerid = 'ACME1'
GO

DELETE Customers
WHERE customerid = 'ACME1'
GO
```

OUTPUT

```
(1 row(s) affected)

(1 row(s) affected)

customerid companyname
---------- -------------------------------------
```

Listing 2.8: continued

```
ACME1      ACME Publishing

(1 row(s) affected)

(1 row(s) affected)
```

Data Control Language (DCL)

The Data Control Language is the subset of Transact-SQL used to manage security in databases. Specifically, it is used to set permissions on database objects and statements. In general, after you create the database and database objects (through DDL), you are ready to set up permissions using the statements provided by the Data Control Language. The three statements that comprise the Data Control Language are

- GRANT—Used to grant access on an object or a statement to a user.

- DENY—Used to explicitly deny any permission on any object or statement. This always takes precedence over any other permission inherited by role or group membership.

- REVOKE—Removes any entry in the permissions table (syspermissions) that either granted or denied access on an object or a statement to a user. Hence, REVOKE is used to revert a previous GRANT or DENY.

The syntax used for these statements varies depending on the kind of permissions you want to set—either on an object or statement. The syntax used to set permissions on objects is

```
GRANT permission ON object TO user
DENY permission ON object TO user
REVOKE permission ON object TO user
```

Listing 2.9 shows how you can use the GRANT statement to allow user1 to see the contents of the Categories table.

EXAMPLE

Listing 2.9: Using the GRANT Statement to Set Object Permissions

```
USE Northwind

GRANT SELECT ON Categories TO user1
GO
```

The command(s) completed successfully.

OUTPUT

On the other hand, the syntax used to set permissions on statements is

```
GRANT statement TO user
DENY statement TO user
REVOKE statement TO user
```

Listing 2.10 shows an example of the GRANT statement, which gives user1 permission to create tables in the Northwind database.

Listing 2.10: Using the GRANT Statement to Set Statement Permissions

```
USE Northwind

GRANT CREATE TABLE TO user1
GO
```

EXAMPLE

The command(s) completed successfully.

OUTPUT

Permissions can be set on either objects or statements. A database object can be a table, view, user-defined function, stored procedure, or extended stored procedure. Thus, different permissions can be applied for each kind of object. Table 2.1 lists permissions that apply for each database object. Notice that the three kinds of user-defined functions have different sets of permissions that can be set.

Table 2.1: Permissions on Database Objects

Objects	Permissions
Table, view, inline table valued function	SELECT, INSERT, UPDATE, DELETE, REFERENCES
Scalar valued function	EXECUTE, REFERENCES
Multistatement table valued function	SELECT, REFERENCES
Stored procedure, extended stored procedure	EXECUTE

All these kinds of permissions are very straightforward; they allow users to do what they say—SELECT, INSERT, UPDATE, DELETE, and EXECUTE. Regarding the REFERENCES permission, to be able to create a foreign key to a certain table, you need to have REFERENCES permissions on that table.

The second kind of permissions is statement permissions. Statements basically allow users to create objects in the database and back up the database and the transaction log. These statements are BACKUP DATABASE, BACKUP LOG, CREATE DEFAULT, CREATE FUNCTION, CREATE PROCEDURE, CREATE RULE, CREATE TABLE, and CREATE VIEW. One statement in which permissions can be granted only in the MASTER database is the CREATE DATABASE statement. Listing 2.11 demonstrates this fact; first, it creates a new login (login3), then it adds a user (user3) in master for this new login, and then the CREATE DATABASE permission is granted to user3. Notice that this permission is granted in the MASTER database.

EXAMPLE

Listing 2.11: Using the GRANT Statement to Set the CREATE DATABASE Statement Permission

```
USE Master

EXEC sp_addlogin 'login3'
EXEC sp_adduser 'login3','user3'
GRANT CREATE DATABASE TO user3
GO
```

OUTPUT

```
New login created.
Granted database access to 'login3'.
```

Permissions are managed in the local database. In other words, you can set permissions on objects or statements to users or roles only in the current database. If you want to set permissions on objects or statements in some other database, you need to change the database context.

TIP

There is a way to set permissions (either on objects or statements) to all users in a database. Because the PUBLIC database role contains all users and roles in a database, if you set permissions to public, all users will inherit these permissions.

In Listing 2.12, the public database role in Northwind is allowed to create tables in the local database. As a result, any user in Northwind will now be able to create tables.

EXAMPLE

Listing 2.12: Using the GRANT Statement to Set Permissions to Public

```
USE Northwind

GRANT CREATE TABLE TO public
GO
```

OUTPUT

```
The command(s) completed successfully.
```

Security information is stored in the Syspermissions system table. The sp_helprotect system stored procedure displays user permissions information on an object or statement and gets this information from Syspermissions. sp_helprotect can receive the name of an object or a statement as a parameter and return the security information associated with this object or statement. When used with no parameters, it returns permissions information for all objects and statements in the current database. Listing 2.13 shows the security information of the CREATE TABLE statement in the Northwind database.

EXAMPLE

Listing 2.13: Listing Security Information Through the sp_helprotect System Stored Procedure

```
USE Northwind

EXEC sp_helprotect 'CREATE TABLE'
GO
```

Listing 2.13: continued

OUTPUT

```
Owner Object Grantee     Grantor ProtectType Action       Column
..... ...... ..........  ....... ........... ............ ......
.     .      public      dbo     Grant       Create Table .
.     .      user1       dbo     Grant       Create Table .
.     .      user2       dbo     Grant       Create Table .
```

Data Types

Transact-SQL provides 27 different data types, which basically control the data that you can store in columns, variables, parameters, and expressions.

SQL Server 2000 introduced three new data types: BIGINT, TABLE, and SQL_VARIANT. BIGINT uses 8 bytes to store integers, which is 4 bytes more than the INT data type, which uses only 4 bytes of storage size. The TABLE data type behaves like a table, storing sets of rows. Be aware that the TABLE data type cannot be used by columns in tables. And finally, the SQL_VARIANT data type allows you to store almost any value (integer, character, numeric, and so on), except TEXT, NTEXT, IMAGE, TIMESTAMP, and SQL_VARIANT values. The SQL_VARIANT data type is similar to the variant data type in Visual Basic.

The data types supplied by Transact-SQL are divided in these main categories: limited character, unlimited character, binary, binary large objects, integers, approximate numeric, exact numeric, date and time, currency, and other. Table 2.2 lists all these categories with their respective data types and a brief description of each data type.

Table 2.2: Transact-SQL Data Types

Category	Data Type	Description
Limited character	CHAR	Fixed-length character data (up to 8,000 characters)
	VARCHAR	Variable-length character data (up to 8,000 characters)
	NCHAR	Fixed-length Unicode character data (up to 4,000 characters)
	NVARCHAR	Variable-length Unicode character data (up to 4,000 characters)
Unlimited character	TEXT	Variable-length character data (up to 2,147,483,647 characters)
	NTEXT	Variable-length Unicode character data (up to 1,073,741,823 characters)
Binary	BINARY	Fixed-length binary data (up to 8,000 bytes)
	VARBINARY	Variable-length binary data (up to 8,000 bytes)

Table 2.2: continued

Category	Data Type	Description
Binary large objects	IMAGE	Variable-length binary data (up to 2,147,483,647 bytes)
Integers	BIGINT	Integer from -2^63 to 2^63 - 1
	INT	Integer from -2,147,483,648 to 2,147,483,647
	SMALLINT	Integer from -32,768 to 32,767
	TINYINT	Integer from 0 to 255
	BIT	Binary integer with only two possible values (0 or 1)
Approximate numeric	REAL	Approximate numbers with a precision between 1 and 7 (4 bytes of storage)
	FLOAT	Approximate numbers with a precision between 8 and 15 (8 bytes of storage)
Exact numeric	DECIMAL	Exact numbers that can use up to 17 bytes to store data
	NUMERIC	Synonym of DECIMAL
Date and time	DATETIME	Date and time data from January 1, 1753 to December 31, 9999. Time is accurate to the 1/300 of a second
	SMALLDATETIME	Date and time data from January 1, 1900 to June 6, 2079. Time is accurate to the minute
Currency	MONEY	Currency data from -922,337,203,685,477.5808 to 922,337,203,685,477.5807
	SMALLMONEY	Currency data from -214,748.3648 to 214,748.3647
Other	UNIQUEIDENTIFIER	16-byte GUID
	TABLE	Similar to a table database object, and used just for temporary storage
	SQL_VARIANT	Can store any Transact-SQL data type, but TEXT, NTEXT, IMAGE, TIMESTAMP, and itself
	TIMESTAMP or ROWVERSION	8-byte binary number that changes every time a column is inserted or updated
	CURSOR	Used only for variables and stored procedures output parameters

Note that Unicode data types (NCHAR, NVARCHAR, and NTEXT) use two bytes per character. This is why they can store only half the space of the same non-Unicode data types (CHAR, VARCHAR, and TEXT). However, because Unicode data uses two bytes per character, it can store data in any language. To specify Unicode data, use the N prefix, as shown in Listing 2.14.

EXAMPLE

Listing 2.14: Specifying Unicode Data

```
USE Northwind

DECLARE @unicode_data NCHAR(20)
SET @unicode_data = N'This is unicode data'
GO
```

OUTPUT

The command(s) completed successfully.

The UNIQUEIDENTIFIER data type has an associated system function, NEWID, that generates new values for these data types. Therefore, if you use the UNIQUEIDENTIFIER data type in a table, you can use the NEWID system function as the column's default value, as Listing 2.15 shows.

EXAMPLE

Listing 2.15: Using the NEWID System Function

```
USE Northwind

CREATE TABLE Bigidentifiers
(
col1 UNIQUEIDENTIFIER DEFAULT NEWID()
)
GO
```

OUTPUT

The command(s) completed successfully.

The new SQL_VARIANT data type can store up to 8,016 bytes of almost any base data type. Listing 2.16 shows how to use the SQL_VARIANT with character and integer data.

EXAMPLE

Listing 2.16: Using the SQL_VARIANT Data Type

```
USE Northwind

DECLARE @integer_data SQL_VARIANT, @char_data SQL_VARIANT
SET @integer_data = 845
SET @char_data = 'This is character data'
GO
```

OUTPUT

The command(s) completed successfully.

The TIMESTAMP data type is not related at all to DATETIME or SMALLDATETIME. Moreover, you cannot directly update a TIMESTAMP column because it updates itself when you insert or update a row that contains a TIMESTAMP. Also, there can be only one TIMESTAMP column per table.

Creating Customized Data Types: User-Defined Data Types

Users can create their own data types using the data types provided by Transact-SQL as the base types. To create user-defined data types, or

UDDT, use the sp_addtype system stored procedure, and to drop them, use sp_droptype. The basic syntax of the sp_addtype system stored procedure is

`sp_addtype uddt_name, uddt_base_type, nullability`

For example, suppose that you want to create a UDDT to store phone numbers that could be null. You can define this user-defined data type using the CHAR data type as the base type with a length of 12, as shown in Listing 2.17.

Listing 2.17: Creating User-Defined Data Types (UDDTs)

```
USE Northwind

EXEC sp_addtype phone_number,'CHAR(12)',NULL
GO
```

EXAMPLE

```
(1 row(s) affected)

Type added.
```

OUTPUT

Information about user-defined data types is stored in the systypes system table, which is located in all databases. When created, the properties of user-defined data types can be displayed using the sp_help system stored procedure, which receives an object name as a parameter, which, in this case, would be the name of the user-defined data type, as shown in Listing 2.18.

Listing 2.18: Using sp_help to Display UDDT's Properties

```
USE Northwind

EXEC sp_help phone_number
GO
```

EXAMPLE

Type_name	Storage_type	Length	Prec	Scale	Nullable	Default_name	Rule_name
phone_number	char	12	12	NULL	yes	none	none

OUTPUT

> **TIP**
>
> UDDTs are stored in the database where they are created. However, if you want all your user databases to have a set of predefined, user-defined data types when they're created, create these UDDT in the model database. This is because every new database that is created in SQL Server is a copy of the model database.

Listing 2.19 creates a UDDT called ssn in Model. This UDDT will be automatically transferred to every user database that is created afterward.

Listing 2.19: Creating UDDTs in Model

```
USE Model

EXEC sp_addtype ssn,'CHAR(11)','NOT NULL'
GO
```

```
(1 row(s) affected)
```

Type added.

UDDTs can be created also in Enterprise Manager. To accomplish this, right-click User Defined Data Types (which is located inside the database folder) and then choose New User-Defined Data Type, which opens the window shown in Figure 2.1.

Figure 2.1: *Creating UDDTs in Enterprise Manager.*

Data Type Selection Criteria

You should be very careful when choosing data types. Always make sure that the data type you're choosing is the correct one and the length is appropriate, because it is very common to choose data types that are oversized. For example, let's say that you choose CHAR(100) as the data type and length for a ZIP code column. Although CHAR(100) is able to store this kind of data, you will waste a lot of space because ZIP codes have only five characters. In a small table, this isn't a problem, but in big tables this can lead to performance problems.

The same rule applies for integer data. Take a look at the maximum and minimum value of each integer data type when choosing among them. This way, you avoid using a big data type when you could have used a smaller one. For example, a very efficient way to store IP addresses in a table is to use four TINYINT columns, because this data type can store integers from 0 to 255.

If the length is not specified when declaring character (CHAR, NCHAR, VARCHAR, and NVARCHAR) or binary (BINARY and VARBINARY) data, SQL Server uses 1 as the length by default. Listing 2.20 shows the declaration of a variable in which you will be able to store just one character because the length was not specified. Notice that although you don't get an error if you assign more than one character to the variable, SQL Server stores only the first character.

EXAMPLE

Listing 2.20: Using the Default Length with Character Data

```
USE Northwind

DECLARE @onecharacter VARCHAR
SET @onecharacter = 'String'
SELECT @onecharacter
GO
```

```
----
S
```

OUTPUT

```
(1 row(s) affected)
```

Be aware that fixed-length data types always use the length you defined. On the other hand, variable-length data types use only the actual space that is being used by the value. For example, look at the table shown in Listing 2.21. If you insert a row and the length of the lastname is 5, SQL Server will use just 5 bytes for the storage of this value because the data type is VARCHAR. On the other hand, if the length of the firstname is 5, SQL Server has to use 20 bytes to store this value because the data type is CHAR. Therefore, when using the CHAR data type, even if the length of the value is less than the length of the column, SQL Server uses the length of the whole column to store this value.

EXAMPLE

Listing 2.21: Using Variable- and Fixed-Length Character Data

```
USE Northwind

CREATE TABLE Authors
(
lastname VARCHAR(20),
firstname CHAR(20)
)
GO
```

```
The command(s) completed successfully.
```

OUTPUT

If you want to store data that can hold more than 8,000 bytes, use the TEXT, NTEXT, or IMAGE data types, which can store up to 2GB. However, make sure that you really need to store more than 8,000 bytes, because these data types use another set of statements (WRITETEXT, READTEXT, and UPDATETEXT).

TIP

You can use standard DML commands with TEXT, NTEXT, and IMAGE data, but only a portion of the data can be accessed (using the SUBSTRING function, for example).

Be careful when you use approximate numeric data because, by definition, these data types (FLOAT and REAL) store an approximation of the number. Therefore, they should not be used to perform exact comparisons in WHERE clauses.

The TABLE data type cannot be used as a column data type when creating tables; thus, it is not possible to have tables inside tables. Whenever possible, use the TABLE data type instead of temporary tables because the first one is stored in memory, improving performance considerably. Usually, the TABLE data type is used to store temporary result sets, as shown in Listing 2.22, in which a variable is created using the TABLE data type and then two rows are inserted.

Listing 2.22: Using the TABLE Data Type

```
USE Northwind

DECLARE @Authors TABLE(lastname VARCHAR(20), firstname VARCHAR(20))
INSERT @Authors VALUES ('Guerrero','Fernando')
INSERT @Authors VALUES ('Rojas','Carlos')
SELECT * FROM @Authors
GO
```

EXAMPLE

OUTPUT

```
(1 row(s) affected)

(1 row(s) affected)

lastlame             firstname
-------------------- --------------------
Guerrero             Fernando
Rojas                Carlos

(2 row(s) affected)
```

Although TIMESTAMP and ROWVERSION are synonyms, you should use ROWVERSION instead of TIMESTAMP, because Microsoft could change the functionality of TIMESTAMP in the future to be compliant with the ANSI SQL-92 standard, which states that the TIMESTAMP data type stores date and time data.

Additional Elements

In addition to DDL, DML, DCL, and data types, Transact-SQL has some additional elements or extensions that make life easier for programmers and administrators, and also make Transact-SQL a more powerful language. Be aware that these extensions are not ANSI-SQL standard; therefore, they are not portable. If you are concerned about portability, you should avoid using any of these extensions.

SQL Server is not the only relational database management system that adds new elements to the standard language; this is done by the majority of the commercial database systems today. If you want to check that your code is compliant with the ANSI standard, use the SET FIPS_FLAGGER statement provided by SQL Server, which receives as a parameter the level of compliance that you want to check: ENTRY, INTERMEDIATE, or FULL. Listing 2.23 shows how this statement is used to check the compliance of a query that contains the TOP clause, which is a Transact-SQL extension.

Listing 2.23: Using the SET FIPS_FLAGGER Statement to Check for ANSI Compliance

```
USE Northwind

SET FIPS_FLAGGER 'FULL'

SELECT TOP 3 lastname
FROM Employees
ORDER BY hiredate

GO
```

EXAMPLE

OUTPUT

```
FIPS Warning: Line 1 has the non-ANSI statement 'USE'.
FIPS Warning: Line 3 has the non-ANSI statement 'SET'.
FIPS Warning: Line 5 has the non-ANSI clause 'TOP'.
lastname
------------------

Leverling
Davolio
Fuller
```

To deactivate the checking of the ANSI compliance (because it remains activated for the session), use the same statement (SET FIPS_FLAGGER) with the OFF parameter; that is, SET FIPS_FLAGGER OFF.

Variables

In Transact-SQL, local variables are used in stored procedures, user-defined functions, triggers, and user scripts. Variables are valid in the session that created them; for example, if a stored procedure creates a variable, it is valid only during the execution of the stored procedure.

Variables are first declared, using the DECLARE statement and specifying the variables' name (which has to begin with @) and data type. The syntax is

```
DECLARE @variable_name datatype
```

Then, a value is set to the variable using either SET or SELECT. When a variable is declared, its value is initialized to NULL until a value is assigned. Listing 2.24 shows the creation of the @firstname variable, which uses the VARCHAR data type with a length of 20. Next, its value is set using the SET statement, and finally, its value is shown using the SELECT statement.

EXAMPLE

Listing 2.24: Using Variables in Transact-SQL

```
DECLARE @firstname VARCHAR(20)
SET @firstname = 'Maria'
SELECT @firstname
GO
```

OUTPUT

```
. . . . . . . . . . . . . . . . . . . .
Maria
```

You can also assign values to variables in a query. Using this approach, make sure that the query returns only one row because, otherwise, you will get just one value in the variable. For example, Listing 2.25 demonstrates how to assign variables (@ln and @fn) in a query to the Employees table. This query stores the value of the first and last name of the employee whose ID equals 1 in the @fn and @ln variables. Then, it shows the value that was assigned to each one of these variables.

EXAMPLE

Listing 2.25: Assigning Values to Variables in Queries

```
USE Northwind

DECLARE @ln VARCHAR(20), @fn VARCHAR(20)

SELECT @ln = lastname, @fn = firstname
FROM Employees
WHERE employeeid = 1

SELECT @fn, @ln
GO
```

OUTPUT

```
. . . . . . . . . . . . . . . . . . . .    . . . . . . . . . . . . . . . . . . . .
Nancy                Davolio
```

System functions that begin with @@ used to be called global variables. In fact, they are system functions that don't have any parameters, and they are not global variables because you cannot declare and assign a value to them; they are managed by SQL Server instead. Table 2.3 lists some of these system functions and the value they return.

Table 2.3: System Functions That Begin with @@

System Function	Return Value
@@CONNECTIONS	Number of connections to SQL Server since the service was started.
@@ERROR	Error code of the last statement executed (if it succeeded, it returns 0).
@@IDENTITY	Last identity value inserted in the current session.
@@MAX_CONNECTIONS	Maximum number of connections allowed.
@@OPTIONS	Information about set options in the current session.
@@ROWCOUNT	Number of rows affected by the last statement executed.
@@SERVERNAME	Name of the server where SQL Server is installed.
@@SPID	ID of the current process.
@@VERSION	Current version of SQL Server.

For example, Listing 2.26 shows how to use these system functions, specifically @@servername (the name of this server is SQLBYEXAMPLE).

Listing 2.26: Using System Functions

```
SELECT @@servername
GO
```

EXAMPLE

OUTPUT

- -

SQLBYEXAMPLE

CAUTION

There are no global variables in SQL Server. The @@ prefix is used just by SQL Server's system functions. Although you can declare variables using the @@ prefix, they won't behave as global variables; they will behave just as local ones.

Operators

Operators are used in Transact-SQL to deal with variables, scalars, and, in general, expressions. There are different kinds of operators, and each kind is used to manipulate different kinds of data types.

The assignment operator is the equal sign (=). It is used to set values to variables, as shown in the preceding section (see Listings 2.24 and 2.25).

The arithmetic operators are + (addition), − (subtraction), * (multiplication), / (division), and % (modulo or remainder of division). These operators are used to work with integers, approximate numeric, and exact numeric. The + and - operators also behave as unary operators (positive and negative), which deal with only one expression. In Listing 2.27, you can see an example of the use of the division and modulo operators and the negative unary operator.

EXAMPLE

Listing 2.27: Using Arithmetic Operators

```
SELECT 8/4
SELECT 9%4
SELECT -7
GO
```

OUTPUT

```
-----------
2

-----------
1

-----------
-7
```

The comparison operators are = (equal to), <> (not equal to), < (less than), > (greater than), <= (less than or equal to), and >= (greater than or equal to). Comparison operators are used to deal with any kind of data types but TEXT, NTEXT, and IMAGE. Listing 2.28 shows an example that uses the less than or equal to (<=) operator.

EXAMPLE

Listing 2.28: Using the Less Than or Equal to Operator

```
USE Northwind

SELECT employeeid, lastname, firstname
FROM Employees
WHERE employeeid <= 8
GO
```

OUTPUT

```
employeeid  lastname              firstname
-----------  --------------------  ----------
1            Davolio               Nancy
2            Fuller                Andrew
3            Leverling             Janet
4            Peacock               Margaret
5            Buchanan              Steven
6            Suyama                Michael
7            King                  Robert
8            Callahan              Laura

(8 row(s) affected)
```

The logical operators are AND, OR, NOT, BETWEEN, IN, and LIKE. These operators check a condition and evaluate to true or false. AND evaluates to true if all expressions are true. OR evaluates to true if any of the expressions are true. NOT evaluates to false if the expression is true, and true if the expression is false. Listing 2.29 shows how to use the AND logical operator in the WHERE clause of a SELECT statement.

Listing 2.29: Using the AND Logical Operator

```
USE Northwind

SELECT employeeid, lastname, firstname, city
FROM Employees
WHERE firstname='anne' AND city='london'
GO
```

```
employeeid  lastname              firstname  city
----------- --------------------- ---------- ---------------
9           Dodsworth             Anne       London
```

OUTPUT

```
(1 row(s) affected)
```

BETWEEN is used to check for an inclusive range (in an inclusive range the limits are included), and its syntax is

```
1st_expression BETWEEN 2nd_expression AND 3rd_expression.
```

The first expression, usually a column, is checked to see whether it falls within the range of the second expression and the third expression (both included in the range). The syntax of BETWEEN is equivalent to (using >= and <=):

```
(1st_expression >= 2nd expression) AND (1st_expression <= 3rd_expression)
```

Listing 2.30 shows an example of BETWEEN, which gets all the rows in the Employees table whose ID is between 2 and 5 (including 2 and 5).

Listing 2.30: Checking for Ranges Using the BETWEEN Operator

```
USE Northwind

SELECT employeeid, firstname, lastname
FROM Employees
WHERE employeeid BETWEEN 2 AND 5
GO
```

```
employeeid  firstname  lastname
----------- ---------- --------------------
2           Andrew     Fuller
3           Janet      Leverling
4           Margaret   Peacock
```

OUTPUT

Listing 2.30: continued

```
5           Steven      Buchanan

(4 row(s) affected)
```

The IN operator is, at some level, similar to BETWEEN. Instead of a range, it checks whether the first expression is contained in a list of expressions. The syntax is the following:

```
expression IN (expression_1, expression_2, ..., expression_n)
```

Listing 2.31 shows an example of IN, which gets all the rows from the Employees table whose ID is 2, 6, or 9.

EXAMPLE

Listing 2.31: Using the IN Logical Operator

```
USE Northwind


SELECT employeeid, firstname, lastname
FROM Employees
WHERE employeeid IN (2,6,9)
GO
```

OUTPUT

```
employeeid  firstname  lastname
----------- ---------- --------------------
2           Andrew     Fuller
6           Michael    Suyama
9           Anne       Dodsworth

(3 row(s) affected)
```

The LIKE operator is used to find patterns in strings (pattern matching). Typically, you will want to look for a specific pattern in the values of the rows in a given table. The syntax of LIKE is (the expression is usually a column)

```
expression LIKE pattern_to_find
```

You specify the pattern you are looking for by using wildcards. Transact-SQL provides four types of wildcards you can use with the LIKE operator. The first wildcard, and the most commonly used, is the percentage character (%), which is used to specify any string of any length (0 or more). For those of you who have previously worked with DOS or Access, the percentage character (%) is similar to * in these environments. Listing 2.32 shows three queries that use %: The first one gets all employees whose first name begins with *a*, the second one gets all employees whose first name ends with *e*, and the last one gets all employees whose last name contains the character sequence *ae*, no matter the position.

EXAMPLE

Listing 2.32: Using the Percentage (%) Wildcard with LIKE

```
USE Northwind

SELECT firstname, lastname
FROM Employees
WHERE firstname LIKE 'a%'

SELECT firstname, lastname
FROM Employees
WHERE firstname LIKE '%e'

SELECT firstname, lastname
FROM Employees
WHERE firstname LIKE '%ae%'
GO
```

OUTPUT

```
firstname   lastname
---------   -------------------
Andrew      Fuller
Anne        Dodsworth

firstname   lastname
---------   -------------------
Anne        Dodsworth

firstname   lastname
---------   -------------------
Michael     Suyama
```

The second wildcard is the underscore character (_), which denotes any single character. The third wildcard is used to search for a character within a range or a set, which is delimited by brackets. For example, [a-z] denotes a range that contains all characters between *a* and *z*, and [abc] denotes a set that contains three characters: *a*, *b*, and *c*. The last wildcard is a variation of the third one, in which you want to search for a character not within a range or set. Listing 2.33 shows an example of each of these wildcards. The first query gathers all the employees whose first name begins with any character, and the last four characters are *anet*. The second one returns all employees whose first name begins with either *j* or *s*. The third query gets all employees whose first name does not begin with the character *a*, *m*, *j*, *s*, *l*, or *r*.

Listing 2.33: Using Wildcards with LIKE

```
USE Northwind

SELECT firstname, lastname
FROM Employees
```

EXAMPLE

Listing 2.33: continued

```
WHERE firstname LIKE '_anet'

SELECT firstname, lastname
FROM Employees
WHERE firstname LIKE '[js]%'

SELECT firstname, lastname
FROM Employees
WHERE firstname LIKE '[^amjslr]%'
GO
```

OUTPUT

```
firstname  lastname
---------- -------------------
Janet      Leverling


firstname  lastname
---------- -------------------
Janet      Leverling
Steven     Buchanan


firstname  lastname
---------- -------------------
Nancy      Davolio
```

The last operator is the plus sign (+), which is used to concatenate strings, as shown in Listing 2.34.

EXAMPLE

Listing 2.34: Using the String-Concatenation Operator

```
DECLARE @first VARCHAR(10), @second VARCHAR(10)
SET @first = 'SQL '
SET @second = 'Server'
SELECT @first + @second
GO
```

OUTPUT

```
-------------------
SQL Server
```

Generally, + is used to concatenate columns when querying tables, as Listing 2.35 shows.

EXAMPLE

Listing 2.35: Using the String-Concatenation Operator to Concatenate Columns

```
USE Northwind

SELECT firstname + ' ' +lastname
FROM Employees
```

Listing 2.35: continued

```
WHERE employeeId = 1
GO
```

Nancy Davolio

OUTPUT

Control of Flow Statements

Transact-SQL provides statements that you can use to control the flow of the code in your scripts. The most common statements are IF .. ELSE and WHILE, which are very common among modern programming languages.

NOTE

Transact-SQL does not provide a FOR statement, like many other programming languages. Instead, it provides a WHILE statement, which can expose basically the same functionality of the FOR statement.

IF .. ELSE

The IF statement contains a condition that is evaluated by SQL Server; if it is true, the code right after IF is executed, and if it is not true, the code right after ELSE is executed. Notice that the ELSE statement is optional.

If there is more than one statement to execute in IF or ELSE, these have to be delimited by the BEGIN and END statements. For example, Listing 2.36 demonstrates the use of IF .. ELSE with multiple statements. This example uses EXISTS, which evaluates to true if there is at least one row in the query (in this case, the query is SELECT * FROM Shippers), or false if there are no rows in the query. Also, this example returns a message to the client using the PRINT statement, which takes a string as a parameter (this is why the integer must be converted to character).

Listing 2.36: Using IF .. ELSE Control of Flow Statements

EXAMPLE

```
USE Northwind

IF EXISTS (SELECT * FROM Shippers)
BEGIN
    DECLARE @number_rows INT
    SELECT @number_rows = count(*) FROM Shippers
    PRINT 'There are ' + CAST(@number_rows AS VARCHAR(10))
        + ' rows in the Shippers table'
END
ELSE
    PRINT 'This table does not contain any rows'

GO
```

Listing 2.36: continued

```
There are 3 rows in the Shippers table
```

RETURN

OUTPUT

RETURN is used to exit unconditionally from a script or stored procedure. When used in stored procedures, RETURN receives a parameter, the return code. As a standard coding convention, a return code of 0 means success, and any other number than 0 indicates than an error occurred.

Listing 2.37 shows an example of RETURN. Observe that the statement that is right after RETURN is not executed.

Listing 2.37: Aborting Script Execution Using RETURN

EXAMPLE

```
PRINT 'First step'
RETURN 2
PRINT 'Second step (this is not executed)'
GO
```

OUTPUT

```
First step
```

WAITFOR

WAITFOR can be used in one of two ways. Using the first one, it instructs SQL Server to wait until a specific time, and the syntax is

```
WAITFOR TIME 'time'
```

Using the second way, WAITFOR indicates SQL Server to wait a specific amount of time.

```
WAITFOR DELAY 'time'
```

Listing 2.38 shows an example of each of these two approaches. The first WAITFOR statement waits until 8:00 a.m., and the second one waits for 1 minute before following the execution.

Listing 2.38: Using WAITFOR

EXAMPLE

```
WAITFOR TIME '08:00:00'
PRINT getdate()
WAITFOR DELAY '00:01:00'
PRINT getdate()
GO
```

OUTPUT

```
Jan 9 2001  8:00AM
Jan 9 2001  8:01AM
```

WHILE

WHILE iterates (executing some statements) until a certain condition is true. If there is more than one statement to execute until the condition is true, enclose them between BEGIN and END.

Listing 2.39 shows an implementation of multiplication that uses WHILE to loop as many times as the second number indicates.

EXAMPLE

Listing 2.39: Looping with WHILE Statements

```
DECLARE @a INT, @b INT, @result INT
SET @a = 3
SET @b = 4
SET @result = 0
WHILE @b > 0
BEGIN
    SET @result = @result + @a
    SET @b = @b - 1
END
SELECT @result
GO
```

OUTPUT

```
- - - - - - - - - - -
12

(1 row(s) affected)
```

BREAK

BREAK is used inside a WHILE statement to exit unconditionally from the WHILE loop. When SQL Server finds a BREAK inside a WHILE, it continues the execution with the instruction right after the END of the WHILE.

CONTINUE

CONTINUE is used inside a WHILE statement to transfer the execution to the beginning of the WHILE statement, restarting the loop. Listing 2.40 demonstrates how CONTINUE and BREAK are used inside a WHILE loop.

EXAMPLE

Listing 2.40: Using CONTINUE and BREAK

```
DECLARE @count INT
SET @count = 0
WHILE @count < 10
BEGIN
    IF @count = 3
        BREAK
    SET @count = @count + 1
    PRINT 'This line is executed'
    CONTINUE
    PRINT 'This line is never executed'
END
GO
```

OUTPUT

Listing 2.40: continued

```
This line is executed
This line is executed
This line is executed
```

GOTO

GOTO directs SQL Server to continue the execution in the place where a label is defined. It is very useful for error handling because you can define a generic error handler and then use GOTO to execute this error handler in the code. Listing 2.41 shows how to alter the execution of a script using GOTO.

EXAMPLE

Listing 2.41: Altering the Execution Using GOTO

```
IF NOT EXISTS (SELECT * FROM Suppliers)
    GOTO no_rows

IF NOT EXISTS (SELECT * FROM Employees)
    GOTO no_rows

GOTO finished
no_rows:
PRINT 'An error occurred'

finished:
PRINT 'The program has finished its execution'
```

OUTPUT

```
The program has finished its execution
```

Comments

Transact-SQL provides two ways to include comments inside code. Using the first way, you can include one-line comments, which are specified using "--" (two dashes). In this case, anything that follows "--" in a specific line is considered a comment and is not evaluated by SQL Server.

The other type of comments are multiline comments, which are delimited by "/*" and "*/". Anything between these two delimiters is considered as a comment.

Listing 2.42 shows an example of both kinds of comments that can be used in Transact-SQL.

EXAMPLE

Listing 2.42: Inserting Comments in the Code

```
/*
This is an example of the use
of comments in Transact-SQL
*/
```

Listing 2.42: continued

```
SELECT @@version -- this query shows the current version of SQL Server
GO
```

OUTPUT

```
-------------------------------------------------------------
Microsoft SQL Server  2000 - 8.00.194 (Intel X86)
    Aug  6 2000 00:57:48
    Copyright (c) 1988-2000 Microsoft Corporation
    Enterprise Edition on Windows NT 5.0 (Build 2195: )


(1 row(s) affected)
```

Programming Scripts and Batches

The main characteristic of a batch is that it is processed by SQL Server as a unit, similar to stored procedures. A batch might contain one or more Transact-SQL instructions, and the last statement in a batch is the GO statement. However, some restrictions apply to batches. The statements CREATE DEFAULT, CREATE PROCEDURE, CREATE RULE, CREATE TRIGGER, and CREATE VIEW cannot appear more than once in a batch. If any of these statements appears in a batch, it must be the only statement. Hence, if you want to have more than one of these statements in the code, add a GO statement right after each one of them (thus creating multiple batches).

A script comprises one or more batches—each of them separated by a GO statement. Using scripts, you can store the schema of your database (DDL that creates all database objects) in a file. Scripts can be generated using the Generate scripts utility in the Enterprise Manager. To use this utility, go to the databases folder in the Enterprise Manager, then right-click the database name, and choose All Tasks, Generate SQL Script. This window appears in Figure 2.2.

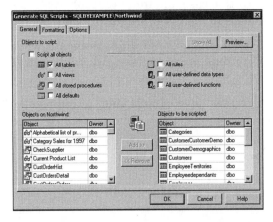

Figure 2.2: *Generating scripts in Enterprise Manager.*

The GO Statement

The GO statement is used to separate batches. Even though it is not a Transact-SQL element; it is used just by the SQL Server utilities. Actually, it can be changed in the Query Analyzer to any other word, if you go to the Options menu and then to the Connections tab. This tab appears in Figure 2.3.

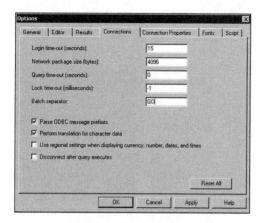

Figure 2.3: *Changing the batch separator in the Query Analyzer.*

What's Next?

You already know the basics of the Data Definition Language (DDL) and the data types that can be used in Transact-SQL. In the next chapter, we will use these two elements to create tables and views. In the case of tables, we will show you how to create different types of tables and to alter the definition of tables. Regarding views, you will learn how to create, maintain, and manipulate data through views.

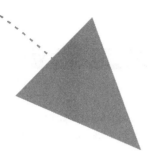

Working with Tables and Views

A table is the basic unit of storage in a relational database. Tables and relationships (elements that link tables) are the most important elements of the relational model, which was designed by E. F. Codd in 1970. A table is composed of columns and a set of rows. First, a *column* represents an attribute of the entity described by the table. For example, an employee table might have these columns: Social Security number (SSN), first name, and last name. Second, a *row*, or a *tuple*, contains the actual data that is stored in a table. In the employee's example, if there are 10 employees in the company, this table will contain 10 rows.

A database object similar to tables in the way it is queried is a view. A *view*, also called a *virtual table*, is basically a predefined query stored in a database; every time the view is queried, SQL Server reads its definition and uses this definition to access the underlying table. Views add a layer between applications and tables because, through views, applications don't have to query tables directly.

In previous versions of SQL Server, a view never stored data. Now, using a new feature of SQL Server 2000 called indexed views, you can create indexes on views (with some restrictions), and this translates into permanent storage of the result set produced by the view.

This chapter teaches you the following:

- How to create and modify tables

- The types of tables available in SQL Server

- The advantages and usage of views

- How to use extended properties to store *metadata* (information that describes objects) in a database

Creating and Altering Tables

The first step in the database design process is creating the entity relationship model, which is a conceptual representation of the database. The entity relationship model is comprised of entities, attributes, and relationships. An *entity* represents a real-world object, such as cars, employees, orders, students, courses, and teachers. Each entity has characteristics, which are called *attributes*. For example, the entity called employee has these attributes: Social Security number (SSN), last name, and first name. The last piece is the *relationship*, which is a link between two or more tables. There are three types of relationships: one-to-one (1:1), one-to-many (1:M), and many-to-many (M:N). For example, there's a one-to-many relationship between employees and orders because one employee can place many orders, and an order can be placed by just one employee.

The study of entity-relationship models is out of the scope of this book. However, it's important that you understand that entity-relationship modeling is the core of database design, and that good applications cannot be developed without a good database design.

After the entity-relationship model is finished, the next step is to convert it into the database structure. Specifically, a new table is created to represent each entity, and the table will have as many columns as attributes in the entity. Also, a table is created to represent each many-to-many relationship. The columns of this table will be the primary keys of the tables involved in the many-to-many relationship.

Some CASE (computer-aided software engineering) tools out there transform an entity-relationship model into a script that you can run against a database server to create the database schema.

CAUTION

Be careful when using the terms "relation" and "relationship," because they can lead to confusion. A *relationship* links two or more tables in a database, whereas *relation* is a synonym of table in the relational theory.

CAUTION

By definition, a set has no ordering. Thus, in a table, rows have no specific order because a table contains a set of rows. For this reason, there is no concept of first or last row in a table.

In SQL Server, the smallest unit of storage is the page. A page is 8KB in size and can store one or more rows; however, a row cannot span pages. For this reason, a single row can store up to 8,060 bytes, unless you use TEXT, NTEXT, or IMAGE data types, which are stored separately in their own pages.

Each group of eight pages forms an *extent*, which is the unit of storage of tables and indexes. There are two types of extents: uniform and mixed. A uniform extent stores data for only a single object, whereas a mixed extent stores multiple objects' data. In other words, a uniform extent is a set of eight pages (64KB) that stores a single object's (table or index) data (see Figure 3.1). Refer to Chapter 6, "Optimizing Access to Data: Indexes," for more information on data storage.

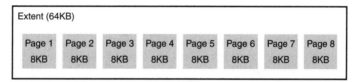

Figure 3.1: *Data storage in SQL Server: pages and extents.*

Types of Tables

In versions of SQL Server prior to SQL Server 2000, there were only two types of tables: permanent and temporary. The TABLE data type is a new feature of SQL Server 2000 that we can add to our set of tools.

NOTE

Generally, for simplicity, *permanent tables* are just called *tables*. In contrast, when refer-ring to temporary tables, the whole term is used (*temporary table*).

PERMANENT TABLES

Permanent tables store the actual data in a database. These are the tables you create as a result of the conversion of the entity relationship model to a database structure.

Permanent tables are stored in the database where they are created. There are system tables (sysobjects, syscolumns, and sysconstraints) that keep track of the configuration information of tables such as owner, creation date, name and type of each column, and constraints defined on the table, among others.

System tables are permanent tables that are created automatically by SQL Server at installation time. Their name begins with sys—for example, sysobjects. The purpose of system tables is to store metadata of databases, such as objects in the database (tables, views, stored procedures, extended stored procedures, and user-defined functions), users, roles, permissions, data and log files, and so on. By default, users cannot insert or modify the data in system tables. If you want to modify the data in system tables—

which is not recommended—use the `sp_configure` system stored procedure to enable the `'allow updates'` configuration option. Listing 3.1 shows how to enable this option.

Listing 3.1: Using `sp_configure` to Allow Modifications to System Tables

```
sp_configure 'allow updates', 1
GO
RECONFIGURE WITH OVERRIDE
GO
```

One of the most important system tables in every database is `sysobjects`, which stores information of every object in a database. The object type is stored in the `type` column of `sysobjects`. Table 3.1 lists the possible values of the `type` column of the `sysobjects` system table.

Table 3.1: Types of Objects in SQL Server

Value in the Type Column	Type of Object
C	Check constraint
D	Default constraint
F	Foreign key constraint
FN	Scalar function
IF	Inline table function
K	Primary key or Unique constraint
P	Stored procedure
R	Rule
S	System table
TF	Multistatement table function
TR	Trigger
U	User table
V	View
X	Extended stored procedure

For example, if you want to list all system tables in the Northwind database, you can query `sysobjects` and filter by the `'S'` type, as shown in Listing 3.2.

Listing 3.2: Listing System Tables in the Northwind Database

```
USE Northwind

SELECT name,crdate
FROM sysobjects
WHERE type = 'S'
```

OUTPUT

Listing 3.2: continued

```
name                     crdate
.....................    ............................
sysobjects               2000-04-18 01:51:58.910
sysindexes               2000-04-18 01:51:58.910
syscolumns               2000-04-18 01:51:58.910
systypes                 2000-04-18 01:51:58.910
syscomments              2000-04-18 01:51:58.910
sysfiles1                2000-04-18 01:51:58.910
syspermissions           2000-04-18 01:51:58.910
sysusers                 2000-04-18 01:51:58.910
sysproperties            2000-04-18 01:51:58.910
sysdepends               2000-04-18 01:51:58.910
sysreferences            2000-04-18 01:51:58.910
sysfulltextcatalogs      2000-04-18 01:51:58.910
sysindexkeys             2000-04-18 01:51:58.910
sysforeignkeys           2000-04-18 01:51:58.910
sysmembers               2000-04-18 01:51:58.910
sysprotects              2000-04-18 01:51:58.910
sysfulltextnotify        2000-04-18 01:51:58.910
sysfiles                 2000-04-18 01:51:58.910
sysfilegroups            2000-04-18 01:51:58.910

(19 row(s) affected)
```

TEMPORARY TABLES

Temporary tables, like any other temporary object in SQL Server, are stored in `tempdb` and dropped automatically by SQL Server if they are not dropped explicitly. This type of table is used as a temporary working area for many purposes, such as multistep calculations and, also, to split up large queries.

There are two types of temporary tables: local and global. The name of local temporary tables begins with #, whereas the name of global temporary tables begins with ##. Local temporary tables are available only in the connection that created them, and when the connection is finished, the table is automatically dropped by SQL Server, unless it is dropped explicitly using `DROP TABLE`. This type of table is very useful for applications that run more than one instance of a process simultaneously, because each connection can have its own copy of the temporary table, without interfering with the other connections executing the same code. For example, if you create a stored procedure that uses temporary tables, every user or application running the stored procedure will have its own copy of these temporary tables.

On the other hand, global temporary tables are available to all connections in SQL Server. Therefore, when a connection creates a global temporary table, and other connections reference the table, they will be accessing the same table. Global temporary tables last until the connection that created them finishes its execution.

TABLE VARIABLES

In previous versions of SQL Server, temporary tables were the only way to store temporary data or result sets. In SQL Server 2000, the TABLE data type can be used for this purpose. This new data type is more efficient than temporary tables because it is stored in memory, whereas a temporary table is stored in tempdb.

Regarding scope, the TABLE data type is similar to local temporary tables, which have only local scope. As a result, any variable that uses the TABLE data type is available only in the session where the variable is used, and if this session calls a stored procedure, for example, table variables are not visible inside the stored procedure, whereas temporary tables are visible.

To define a variable whose data type is TABLE, use the DECLARE statement specifying TABLE as the data type followed by the table structure. After declared, it is treated like any other table in SQL Server. Listing 3.3 shows how to declare a variable that uses the TABLE data type. This example also inserts a row in the table, and then gets all rows on it.

EXAMPLE

Listing 3.3: Using the TABLE Data Type

```
DECLARE @employees TABLE (ssn INT, firstname VARCHAR(20), lastname VARCHAR(30))

INSERT @employees (ssn, firstname, lastname)
VALUES ('555555555','Rojas','Yumaira')

SELECT *
FROM @employees
(1 row(s) affected)
```

OUTPUT

```
ssn           firstname              lastname
----------    -------------------    -----------------------------
555555555     Rojas                  Yumaira

(1 row(s) affected)
```

Table variables can also be used as the return value of user-defined functions. This will be covered in Chapter 10, "Enhancing Business Logic: User-Defined Functions (UDF)."

Creating Tables

To create a table, you must specify the table's name, the columns that make up the table, and the data types of the columns. You can create tables using a graphical interface in Enterprise Manager or using Transact-SQL in Query Analyzer. The Transact-SQL statement used is CREATE TABLE, and the syntax is

```
CREATE TABLE Table_name (
column_1 data_type,
column_2 data_type,
.

.

column_n data_type
)
```

Listing 3.4 shows an example that creates the Drivers table, which contains three columns: license, firstname, and make.

Listing 3.4: Creating Tables Using Transact-SQL

```
USE Northwind

CREATE TABLE Drivers (
license VARCHAR(15),
firstname VARCHAR(30),
lastname VARCHAR(30)
)
```

In SQL Server, a table can have up to 1,024 columns and a database can contain up to 2,147,483,647 objects, including tables. As you already know, the maximum size of a row in a table is 8,060 bytes. Nonetheless, you can still create tables that have columns of variable data types (VARCHAR, NVARCHAR, and VARBINARY) whose row size exceeds 8,060 bytes. In these cases, SQL Server creates the table, but it gives you a warning. Be careful when creating these tables because you won't have all this space available. For example, suppose you create a table that has two columns which use the VARCHAR data type, and the length is 5,000 bytes on each column. You won't have 10,000 bytes available for each row—you will have only 8,060; therefore, if you try to insert a row with more than 8,060 bytes, you will get an error. Listing 3.5 shows this example and the warning message.

Listing 3.5: Creating Tables with a Row Size That Exceeds 8,060 Bytes

```
USE Northwind

CREATE TABLE Bigtable(
firstcolumn VARCHAR(5000),
```

Listing 3.5: continued

```
secondcolumn VARCHAR(5000)
)
GO
```

```
Warning: The table 'Bigtable' has been created but its maximum row size
(10025) exceeds the maximum number of bytes per row (8060). INSERT or
UPDATE of a row in this table will fail if the resulting row length
exceeds 8060 bytes.
```

When a table is created, SQL Server automatically adds a new row to sysobjects (in the local database) with the information about the newly created table. Also, a new row is added to syscolumns for each column in the table. Be aware that dealing directly with system tables is not recommended, because their functionality might change in future versions of SQL Server. The alternative is to use the INFORMATION_SCHEMA views (INFORMATION_SCHEMA.COLUMNS and INFORMATION_SCHEMA.TABLES in this case), which, by the way, are ANSI standard. Moreover, you can use the system stored procedure sp_help to show information of any object in SQL Server, including tables.

Listing 3.6 demonstrates the use of sp_help to get a table's information. Notice that, for reasons of space, two columns were removed from the output of sp_help (TrimTrailingBlanks and FixedLenNullInSource).

Listing 3.6: Displaying a Table's Information

```
USE Northwind
GO
sp_help 'Drivers'
```

Name	Owner	Type	Created_datetime
Drivers	dbo	user table	2000-11-16 02:10:31.320

Column_name	Type	Computed	Length	Prec	Scale	Nullable
license	varchar	no	15			yes
firstname	varchar	no	30			yes
lastname	varchar	no	30			yes

Identity	Seed	Increment	Not For Replication
No identity column defined.	NULL	NULL	NULL

RowGuidCol
No rowguidcol column defined.

Listing 3.6: continued

```
Data_located_on_filegroup
-----------------------------------------
PRIMARY


The object does not have any indexes.

No constraints have been defined for this object. .

No foreign keys reference this table.
No views with schema binding reference this table.
```

As already stated, another option to get an object's metadata is using
INFORMATION_SCHEMA views. Basically, metadata is information about the
object and its components. The advantages of using these views is that,
first, they're ANSI compatible (SQL-92 Standard), and second, they are
independent of system tables, in the way that if the functionality or schema
of system tables changes in future versions, these views will still be supported. Listing 3.7 shows how to get a table's metadata (the Drivers table)
using two INFORMATION_SCHEMA views: TABLES and COLUMNS.

EXAMPLE

Listing 3.7: Using INFORMATION_SCHEMA Views to Get Metadata

```
USE Northwind

SELECT *
FROM INFORMATION_SCHEMA.TABLES
WHERE table_name = 'Drivers'

SELECT *.
FROM INFORMATION_SCHEMA.COLUMNS
WHERE table_name = 'Drivers'

GO
```

OUTPUT

TABLE_CATALOG	TABLE_SCHEMA	TABLE_NAME	TABLE_TYPE
Northwind	dbo	Drivers	BASE TABLE

(1 row(s) affected)

TABLE_CATALOG	TABLE_SCHEMA	TABLE_NAME	COLUMN_NAME	ORDINAL_POSITION	DEFAULT
Northwind	dbo	Drivers	license	1	NULL
Northwind	dbo	Drivers	firstname	2	NULL
Northwind	dbo	Drivers	lastname	3	NULL

(3 row(s) affected)

After a table is created, it must be populated. If you want to know how much space a table is using, use the sp_spaceused system stored procedure. It takes the table's name as the parameter and displays the number of rows and the used space. Listing 3.8 shows space information of the Employees table in the Northwind database.

EXAMPLE

OUTPUT

Listing 3.8: Displaying Space Information of Tables

```
USE Northwind
.
EXEC sp_spaceused 'Employees'
GO
name           rows    reserved    data        index_size    unused
-------------  ------  ----------  ----------  ------------  ----------------
Employees      9       320 KB      232 KB      48 KB         40 KB
```

Any object created by users, including tables, can be renamed using the sp_rename system stored procedure, which has three arguments (the last one is optional). The first parameter is the old name of the object, the second is the new name, and the third is the type of object to rename: column, database, index, and userdatatype. When renaming tables the third parameter is not necessary, but it is required to rename columns. When renaming columns, in the first parameter the name of the table that contains the column must be specified, using the following syntax:
'table_name.column_name'.

User databases can be renamed if you specify database as the third parameter. Another system-stored procedure, sp_renamedb, is used only to. rename user databases.

Listing 3.9 renames the Drivers table to Safedrivers, and then renames the column license to licensenumber.

EXAMPLE

OUTPUT

Listing 3.9: Renaming User Objects Using sp_rename

```
USE Northwind

EXEC sp_rename 'Drivers','Safedrivers'
GO

EXEC sp_rename 'Safedrivers.license','licensenumber','column'
GO
Caution: Changing any part of an object name could break
scripts and stored procedures.
The object was renamed to 'Safedrivers'.
Caution: Changing any part of an object name could break
scripts and stored procedures.
The column was renamed to 'licensenumber'.
```

In tables, columns can allow null values, which represent unknown values. A null doesn't mean that the value is either 0 for numbers or a zero-length string for characters, it just means unknown or undefined. The nullability of a column is specified when the table is created and can be modified by altering the properties of the column.

By default, Query Analyzer assumes that columns allow nulls if the nullability status is not specified when tables are created using Transact-SQL. This is due to the fact that Query Analyzer automatically activates ANSI settings every time a connection is made to SQL Server (the statement used for this setting is SET ANSI_NULL_DFLT_ON).

In particular, when you create tables using the CREATE TABLE statement, the nullability status is specified after the column data type. If the column allows null values, use the NULL keyword; otherwise, use NOT NULL. For example, if you take a look at Listing 3.4, which creates the Drivers table, it doesn't specify the nullability status for any of the columns, and this is why all of them allow null values (this can be seen in the output of Listing 3.6).

Listing 3.10 illustrates how to explicitly specify the nullability status of columns when creating a table. It also executes sp_help on this table to show whether each column is nullable.

Listing 3.10: Specifying Nullability Status When Creating Tables

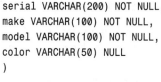

EXAMPLE

```
USE Northwind

CREATE TABLE Cars (
serial VARCHAR(200) NOT NULL,
make VARCHAR(100) NOT NULL,
model VARCHAR(100) NOT NULL,
color VARCHAR(50) NULL
)

EXEC sp_help 'Cars'
GO
```

OUTPUT

Name	Owner	Type	Created_datetime
Cars	dbo	user table	2000-11-19 16:06:09.947

Column_name	Type	Computed	Length	Prec	Scale	Nullable
serial	varchar	no	200			no
make	varchar	no	100			no
model	varchar	no	100			no

Listing 3.10: continued

```
color          varchar      no          50                          yes


Identity                         Seed      Increment   Not For Replication
------------------------------   --------  ----------- -------------------
No identity column defined.      NULL      NULL        NULL


RowGuidCol
-------------------------------
No rowguidcol column defined.


Data_located_on_filegroup
-------------------------------
PRIMARY


The object does not have any indexes.

No constraints have been defined for this object.

No foreign keys reference this table.
No views with schema binding reference this table.
```

A table should always have a primary key, which is a column or set of columns that uniquely identifies each row in a table. For example, the Social Security number can be the primary key in the Employees table because there aren't two employees with the same Social Security number. Primary keys are part of the integrity of tables (entity integrity), and this will be covered in Chapter 7, "Enforcing Data Integrity."

In case a table doesn't have an inherent primary key, the IDENTITY property can be used, which is basically a number that auto-increments by itself and cannot be NULL. The IDENTITY property is similar to the AUTONUMBER data type in Access. A seed and an increment can be specified with the IDENTITY column when creating a table. If they're not specified, the default value is 1 for each of them.

Listing 3.11 creates the Dealers table, which contains an IDENTITY column, dealerid, with a seed of 10 and increment of 1.

EXAMPLE

Listing 3.11: Using the IDENTITY Property

```
USE Northwind

CREATE TABLE Dealers(
dealerid INT IDENTITY(10,1) NOT NULL,
dealername VARCHAR(100) NOT NULL,
```

Listing 3.11: continued

```
address VARCHAR(200) NULL,
city VARCHAR(100) NULL,
state CHAR(2) NULL,
zipcode VARCHAR(10) NULL
)
GO
```

C A U T I O N

The IDENTITY property used in tables is different from the IDENTITY function, which is used to add an identity column to a table created by a SELECT INTO statement (the IDENTITY function is covered in Chapter 4, "Querying and Modifying Data").

In SQL Server, only one IDENTITY column is allowed per table, and it cannot be updated. Also, because the value of an IDENTITY column is automatically incremented every time a new row is inserted, you don't need to specify this column when inserting data in the table. However, if you want to insert a specific value in an IDENTITY column, use the SET IDENTITY_INSERT statement. The syntax of this statement is the following:

```
SET IDENTITY_INSERT Name_of_the_table {ON|OFF}
```

Every time you activate IDENTITY_INSERT in a table, don't forget to deactivate it (using the OFF keyword in the SET IDENTITY_INSERT statement) after values are explicitly inserted in the IDENTITY column. Listing 3.12 shows how to insert data in the IDENTITY column of the Dealers table. In the first INSERT statement the dealerid column is not specified, therefore, the next identity value is used (1 in this case). In the second INSERT statement, a value of 8 is explicitly inserted in the dealerid column (notice the use of SET IDENTITY_INSERT).

EXAMPLE

Listing 3.12: Inserting Data in IDENTITY Columns

```
USE Northwind

INSERT Dealers (dealername) VALUES ('Acme BMW')
GO

SET IDENTITY_INSERT Dealers ON
INSERT Dealers (dealerid,dealername) VALUES (18,'USA Toyota')
SET IDENTITY_INSERT Dealers OFF
GO

SELECT * FROM Dealers
GO
```

OUTPUT

Listing 3.12: continued

```
(1 row(s) affected)

(1 row(s) affected)

dealerid    dealername       address          city             state zipcode
----------  ---------------  ---------------  ---------------  ----- ----------
10          Acme BMW         NULL             NULL             NULL  NULL
18          USA Toyota       NULL             NULL             NULL  NULL

(2 row(s) affected)
```

There are some system functions related to IDENTITY columns, including IDENT_SEED, IDENT_INCR, IDENT_CURRENT, SCOPE_IDENTITY, and @@IDENTITY. The first two functions, IDENT_SEED and IDENT_INCR, return information about the increment and seed of an IDENTITY column in a specified table, which is passed as the argument. Listing 3.13 demonstrates how these two functions are used.

EXAMPLE

Listing 3.13: Using IDENTITY System Functions (IDENT_SEED and IDENT_INCR)

```
USE Northwind

SELECT IDENT_SEED('Dealers'), IDENT_INCR('Dealers')
GO
```

OUTPUT

```
----- -----
10    1

(1 row(s) affected)
```

The last three functions, IDENT_CURRENT, SCOPE_IDENTITY, and @@IDENTITY, return last-generated identity values. IDENT_CURRENT takes the name of a table as a parameter and returns the last identity value inserted in this table. SCOPE_IDENTITY returns the last identity generated in the current scope, which can be a stored procedure, trigger, user-defined function, or batch. Similarly, @@IDENTITY returns the last identity value generated in the current session. The difference between these two functions is that @@IDENTITY is not limited to the current scope; instead, it is limited to the current session, whereas SCOPE_IDENTITY is limited to the current scope. A session might have one or more than one scope. Listing 3.14 shows how to call these functions.

EXAMPLE

Listing 3.14: Using IDENT_CURRENT, SCOPE_IDENTITY, and @@IDENTITY

```
USE Northwind

SELECT IDENT_CURRENT('Dealers'), SCOPE_IDENTITY(), @@IDENTITY
GO
```

Listing 3.14: continued

OUTPUT

```
----- ----- -----
18     18     18

(1 row(s) affected)
```

CAUTION

@@IDENTITY behaves differently from any other system function that begins with @@. These functions usually have serverwide scope. In contrast, @@IDENTITY is always associated with the current session. To illustrate, if two users are connected to SQL Server (two different connections) and these users insert a row in a table with an identity column, each one of them will get the value they just inserted if they use @@IDENTITY.

TIP

Sometimes the IDENTITY property is not an option, because you might need to guarantee uniqueness across tables, databases, or servers. For these cases, use the UNIQUEIDENTIFIER (globally unique identifier, or GUID) data type, which is a 16-byte (128 bits) binary value.

After tables are created, you might want to change their owners. The sp_changeobjectowner system stored procedure is used to change the owner of any object in SQL Server. This system-stored procedure is very useful when you want to delete a user from a database and want to transfer all objects owned by this user to another user in the database.

The statement used to drop user tables (system tables cannot be dropped) is DROP TABLE followed by the name of the table. Be aware that if you create views or user-defined functions with the SCHEMABINDING option and they reference tables, these objects (views or user-defined functions) have to be dropped first before dropping the tables they reference.

Listing 3.15 illustrates how to drop a user table.

EXAMPLE

Listing 3.15: Using the DROP TABLE Statement

```
USE Northwind

DROP TABLE Dealers
GO
```

Notice that when you delete all rows from a table and it becomes an empty table, it still exists in the database; therefore, it isn't dropped when it has no rows. want

Altering a Table's Definition

After tables are created, their structure can be modified using the ALTER TABLE statement. This statement can be used to add columns, drop columns, change column properties (including data types), add constraints, drop constraints, disable constraints and triggers, and re-enable constraints and triggers.

CAUTION

ALTER TABLE cannot be used if the compatibility level of the database is set to 65 (compatible with SQL Server 6.5). To change this setting, use the sp_dbcmptlevel system stored procedure.

If you want to add a column or columns to a table, use the following syntax:

```
ALTER TABLE Table_name ADD column_name data_type [NULL|NOT NULL]
```

Listing 3.16 adds a new column, mileage, to the Cars table.

Listing 3.16: Adding a New Column to a Table

```
USE Northwind

ALTER TABLE Cars ADD mileage INT NULL
GO
```

EXAMPLE

To drop a column or columns, the following syntax is used:

```
ALTER TABLE Table_name DROP COLUMN column_name
```

For example, Listing 3.17 drops the mileage and color columns of the Cars table.

Listing 3.17: Dropping Columns from a Table

```
USE Northwind

ALTER TABLE Cars DROP COLUMN mileage,color
GO
```

EXAMPLE

If you want to change the properties of a specific column, use this syntax:

```
ALTER TABLE Table_name ALTER COLUMN column_name new_data_type [NULL|NOT NULL]
```

Listing 3.18 changes the properties of three columns in the Safedrivers table. The first statement sets the length of the licensenumber column to 30 and sets this column to not allow nulls. The second and the third statements leave intact the data type and length of the firstname and lastname columns, but change the nullability status of these columns to NOT NULL.

Listing 3.18: Changing the Data Types and Nullability Status of Columns

```
USE Northwind

ALTER TABLE Safedrivers ALTER COLUMN licensenumber VARCHAR(30) NOT NULL
GO

ALTER TABLE Safedrivers ALTER COLUMN firstname VARCHAR(30) NOT NULL
GO
```

EXAMPLE

Listing 3.18: continued

```
ALTER TABLE Safedrivers ALTER COLUMN lastname VARCHAR(30) NOT NULL
GO
```

Be aware that when adding a new column that doesn't allow NULL values, you must specify a default value for all the rows in the table (using a DEFAULT constraint). The statement needed to add a new column with a default constraint appears in Listing 3.19, which adds the state column (this column doesn't allow NULL values) to the Safedrivers table, with a default value of FL.

Listing 3.19: Adding New Columns with a Constraint

```
USE Northwind

ALTER TABLE Safedrivers ADD state CHAR(2) NOT NULL
CONSTRAINT addstate DEFAULT 'FL'
GO
```

EXAMPLE

To drop a constraint:

```
ALTER TABLE Table_name DROP constraint_name
```

To disable a constraint (allowing data that normally would be rejected by the constraint):

```
ALTER TABLE Table_name NOCHECK CONSTRAINT constraint_name
```

Then, to re-enable the constraint:

```
ALTER TABLE Table_name CHECK CONSTRAINT constraint_name
```

To disable a trigger of a table (preventing the trigger from being executed):

```
ALTER TABLE Table_name DISABLE TRIGGER trigger_name
```

Then, to re-enable the trigger:

```
ALTER TABLE Table_name ENABLE TRIGGER trigger_name
```

Refer to Chapter 7, "Enforcing Data Integrity," for more information on constraints, and to Chapter 9, "Implementing Complex Processing Logic: Programming Triggers," for more information on triggers.

Creating and Altering Views

A *view* is basically a predefined query (a SELECT statement) that is stored in the database for later use. Therefore, whenever you want to execute this predefined query again, you just have to query the view. The tables that are referenced by the view are called *base tables*.

For example, suppose there is a complex query that involves many joins, and it is executed frequently by an application. You can create a view that contains this query, and change the application to query this view instead of executing the whole query.

CAUTION

Views are often called *virtual tables*. Be careful when using this terminology because some special system tables in SQL Server are kept in memory; these are called virtual tables.

Benefits of Views

Many benefits are associated with the use of views. Here's a summary of these benefits:

- Using views, users don't query the tables directly; therefore, you are creating a security layer between users (or applications) and base tables. This, in turn, has another benefit: If the underlying database schema changes, you don't have to change the application, just the views that access the tables.

- Views can be used to vertically partition the data in a table. For example, suppose there is a table with three columns, but some users are allowed to see only two of these three columns. You can create a view that queries just the two columns they can see. Using this approach, these users will be able to issue a SELECT * query against the view, which is not possible with the table.

- Information schema views can be used as an alternative way to deal directly with system tables. They were introduced in SQL Server 7.0 as a method to provide information (metadata) about objects in SQL Server. The benefit of using these views is that the functionality of system tables might change in future releases of SQL Server, whereas these views' functionality will remain intact because they are ANSI standard.

- Indexes can be created on views. This is a new feature of SQL Server 2000, which basically stores the result set of a view in the database, or in other words, materializes the view. In general, the advantage of indexed views is that this makes queries run faster, because SQL Server can take advantage of the indexed view even if the view is not referenced in the query. When you create indexes on views, SQL Server automatically updates the data of the index. Therefore, whenever the data changes in the underlying tables, SQL Server updates the index.

- Another feature of SQL Server 2000 is the federated databases technology or distributed partitioned views that are updatable. This is Microsoft's answer to the scale-out technology, in which the database is spread across many servers, each server containing a subset of the whole data. This technique is useful when you reach the point where scale-up (adding RAM, CPUs, and disks to the database server) is not enough, and the database server cannot scale any more for whatever reason. The trick is to create a view with the same name, in all the federated servers, that basically merges the data in all these servers using UNION ALL statements. Then, when users access data, SQL Server automatically takes the piece you need from the servers where it resides, making transparent to users the fact that data is split in more than one server. The benefit of this new feature is that these views are updatable, which allows applications to issue SELECT, INSERT, DELETE, and UPDATE statements against these views, and SQL Server does the rest (queries or modifies the data in the server where it resides).

- The last feature of SQL Server 2000 related to views is the introduction of *instead-of triggers*. In previous versions of SQL Server, triggers could not be defined on views. Now, this new type of trigger can be defined on views, which enhances tremendously the power of views in SQL Server. An instead-of trigger, as its name indicates, executes the code of the trigger instead of the triggering action (INSERT, UPDATE, or DELETE). This is covered in Chapter 9.

Creating and Dropping Views

Views are created using the CREATE VIEW statement. When you create a view, SQL Server checks that all objects that the view references exist in the current database. Then, the code of the view is stored in the syscomments system table, general information about the view is stored in sysobjects, and the columns of the view are stored in syscolumns. A view can reference up to 1,024 columns.

The following is the basic syntax of CREATE VIEW:

```
CREATE VIEW View_name
AS
select_statement
```

Next, a SELECT statement is used to query the view. For example:

```
SELECT * FROM View_name
```

Listing 3.20 creates a view on the Customers table that gets all customers from Spain. Then, it contains a SELECT statement to query this view.

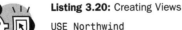

EXAMPLE

Listing 3.20: Creating Views

```
USE Northwind
GO

CREATE VIEW Spaincustomers
AS
SELECT *
FROM Customers
```

Listing 3.20: continued

```
WHERE country = 'Spain'
GO

SELECT * FROM Spaincustomers
GO

-- Partial results shown
```

OUTPUT

```
CustomerID CompanyName                                  ContactName
---------- -------------------------------------------- ----------------
BOLID      Bólido Comidas preparadas                    Martín Sommer
FISSA      FISSA Fabrica Inter. Salchichas S.A.         Diego Roel
GALED      Galería del gastrónomo                        Eduardo Saavedra
GODOS      Godos Cocina Típica                          José Pedro Freyre
ROMEY      Romero y tomillo                             Alejandra Camino

(5 row(s) affected)
```

Views can be nested 32 levels deep. In other words, a view can reference another view, and so on, up to 32 levels of nesting.

The system stored procedures that return a view's metadata are sp_help, which returns general information about views; sp_helptext, which returns the definition of the view (if it's not encrypted); and sp_depends, which displays object dependencies information, or, in other words, objects referenced by the view. Listing 3.21 shows how to use the first of these stored procedures, sp_help.

EXAMPLE

Listing 3.21: Displaying Views' Information

```
USE Northwind

EXEC sp_help 'Spaincustomers'
GO
```

OUTPUT

```
Name                Owner      Type       Created_datetime
------------------- ---------- ---------- ----------------------------
Spaincustomers      dbo        view       2000-11-21 00:50:00.263

Column_name    Type      Computed  Length  Nullable
-------------- --------- --------- ------- --------
CustomerID     nchar     no        10      no
CompanyName    nvarchar  no        80      no
ContactName    nvarchar  no        60      yes
ContactTitle   nvarchar  no        60      yes
Address        nvarchar  no        120     yes
City           nvarchar  no        30      yes
Region         nvarchar  no        30      yes
PostalCode     nvarchar  no        20      yes
```

Listing 3.21: continued

```
Country        nvarchar  no       30      yes
Phone          nvarchar  no       48      yes
Fax            nvarchar  no       48      yes

Identity                         Seed    Increment    Not For Replication
------------------------------   ------- ------------ -------------------
No identity column defined.      NULL    NULL         NULL

RowGuidCol
----------------------------------------------
No rowguidcol column defined.

No constraints have been defined for this object.
No foreign keys reference this table.
The object does not have any indexes.
```

Listing 3.22 shows an example of the sp_helptext system stored procedure that shows the definition of the Spaincustomers view.

Listing 3.22: Displaying the View's Definition with sp_helptext

EXAMPLE

```
USE Northwind

EXEC sp_helptext 'Spaincustomers'
GO
```

OUTPUT

```
Text
-----------------------------------------
CREATE VIEW Spaincustomers
AS
SELECT *
FROM Customers
WHERE country = 'Spain'
```

Listing 3.23 demonstrates how to use sp_depends with views.

Listing 3.23: Displaying Objects Referenced by the View

EXAMPLE

```
USE Northwind

EXEC sp_depends 'Spaincustomers'
GO
```

OUTPUT

```
In the current database, the specified object references the following:
name                          type            updated selected column
----------------------------  --------------- ------- -------- ------------
dbo.Customers                 user table      no      yes      Phone
dbo.Customers                 user table      no      yes      Fax
dbo.Customers                 user table      no      yes      Region
dbo.Customers                 user table      no      yes      PostalCode
```

Listing 3.23: continued

```
dbo.Customers                    user table      no      yes      Country
dbo.Customers                    user table      no      yes      ContactTitle
dbo.Customers                    user table      no      yes      Address
dbo.Customers                    user table      no      yes      City
dbo.Customers                    user table      no      yes      CustomerID
dbo.Customers                    user table      no      yes      CompanyName
dbo.Customers                    user table      no      yes      ContactName
```

Another way to get metadata information of views is using these INFORMATION_SCHEMA views: INFORMATION_SCHEMA.TABLES and INFORMATION_SCHEMA.VIEWS. For example, Listing 3.24 uses these two views to show information of the Spaincustomers view.

EXAMPLE

Listing 3.24: Using INFORMATION_SCHEMA Views to Show Views' Metadata

```
USE Northwind

SELECT *
FROM INFORMATION_SCHEMA.TABLES
WHERE table_name = 'Spaincustomers'

SELECT *
FROM INFORMATION_SCHEMA.VIEWS
WHERE table_name = 'Spaincustomers'
GO
```

OUTPUT

```
TABLE_CATALOG   TABLE_SCHEMA   TABLE_NAME       TABLE_TYPE
-------------   ------------   ---------------  ----------
Northwind       dbo            Spaincustomers   VIEW

(1 row(s) affected)

TABLE_CATALOG   TABLE_SCHEMA   TABLE_NAME       VIEW_DEFINITION
-------------   ------------   ---------------  --------------------------
Northwind       dbo            Spaincustomers   CREATE VIEW Spaincustomers
                                                AS
                                                SELECT *
                                                FROM Customers
                                                WHERE country = 'Spain'

(1 row(s) affected)
```

Notice that when a view is created, if its definition contains a SELECT *, the query is expanded to get all the columns referenced by the query to be able to store this information in syscolumns. In other words, SQL Server translates the * into the actual list of columns. Sometimes, this can cause problems, because if you create a view that queries all columns of a table (using a SELECT * query), and then add a new column to the base table, this new column won't be included in the view. If you come across this problem, use the sp_refreshview system-stored procedure to update the definition of the view in the system tables. This stored procedure takes the name of the view as the parameter.

Listing 3.25 adds a new column to the Customers table, and then executes sp_depends to show that this new column is not part of the view (because the SELECT * of this view was expanded when it was created). Therefore, the output of sp_depends is exactly the same as the one of the preceding example (it doesn't show the new column as part of the view).

EXAMPLE

Listing 3.25: Adding Columns to the Views' Base Tables

```
USE Northwind

ALTER TABLE Customers ADD Mobile VARCHAR(12) NULL
GO

sp_depends 'Spaincustomers'
GO
```

OUTPUT

```
In the current database, the specified object references the following:
name                           type              updated selected column
------------------------------ ----------------- ------- -------- ------------
dbo.Customers                  user table        no      yes      Phone
dbo.Customers                  user table        no      yes      Fax
dbo.Customers                  user table        no      yes      Region
dbo.Customers                  user table        no      yes      PostalCode
dbo.Customers                  user table        no      yes      Country
dbo.Customers                  user table        no      yes      ContactTitle
dbo.Customers                  user table        no      yes      Address
dbo.Customers                  user table        no      yes      City
dbo.Customers                  user table        no      yes      CustomerID
dbo.Customers                  user table        no      yes      CompanyName
dbo.Customers                  user table        no      yes      ContactName
```

The next step uses sp_refreshview to update the view definition. This is shown in Listing 3.26. Notice that the new column (mobile) now appears in the output of sp_depends.

EXAMPLE

Listing 3.26: Using sp_refreshview

```
USE Northwind

EXEC sp_refreshview 'Spaincustomers'

EXEC sp_depends 'Spaincustomers'
GO
```

Listing 3.26: continued

OUTPUT

```
In the current database, the specified object references the following:
name                          type              updated selected column
----------------------------- ----------------- ------- -------- -------------
   dbo.Customers              user table        no      yes      Phone
   dbo.Customers              user table        no      yes      Fax
-> dbo.Customers              user table        no      yes      Mobile
   dbo.Customers              user table        no      yes      Region
   dbo.Customers              user table        no      yes      PostalCode
   dbo.Customers              user table        no      yes      Country
   dbo.Customers              user table        no      yes      ContactTitle
   dbo.Customers              user table        no      yes      Address
   dbo.Customers              user table        no      yes      City
   dbo.Customers              user table        no      yes      CustomerID
   dbo.Customers              user table        no      yes      CompanyName
   dbo.Customers              user table        no      yes      ContactName
```

The definition of a view can be encrypted in the syscomments system table using the WITH ENCRYPTION option when creating the view. Using this option, the definition of the view cannot be seen by any user after the view is created. If anybody tries to see the definition of the view, using sp_helptext for example, SQL Server will display this message: "The object comments have been encrypted." Listing 3.27 creates a view using the WITH ENCRYPTION option, and then tries to display its definition using sp_helptext.

EXAMPLE

Listing 3.27: Preventing Users from Reading the Code of Views

```
USE Northwind
GO

CREATE VIEW Mexicancustomers
WITH ENCRYPTION
AS
SELECT *
FROM Customers
WHERE country = 'Mexico'
GO

sp_helptext 'Mexicancustomers'
GO
```

OUTPUT

```
The object comments have been encrypted.
```

Another feature of views is that you can create a virtual association between a view and the objects it references. The advantage of this feature is that, when you activate it, any object that is referenced by the view cannot be dropped. To create this virtual association, use the WITH SCHEMABINDING option when creating the view.

The SCHEMABINDING option has two restrictions:

- The objects referenced by the view must also specify the owner—for example, 'dbo.Table_name'.

- The column list must be explicitly specified in the view; therefore, you cannot use SELECT *.

For example, Listing 3.28 creates a view (Toyotacars) that is schemabound to the Cars table. Note that the SELECT statement contains the column list, and the name of the table specifies the object owner. Then, SQL Server throws an error when trying to drop the base table (Cars).

Listing 3.28: Using the SCHEMABINDING Option

```
USE Northwind
GO

CREATE VIEW Toyotacars
WITH SCHEMABINDING
AS
SELECT serial, make, model
FROM dbo.Cars
WHERE make = 'Toyota'
GO

DROP TABLE Cars
GO
```

```
Server: Msg 3729, Level 16, State 1, Line 2
Cannot DROP TABLE 'Cars' because it is being referenced by object 'Toyotacars'.
```

Normally, if you don't use SCHEMABINDING, objects referenced by views can be dropped, creating inconsistencies in the database.

In general, a view cannot contain an ORDER BY clause. However, if you use the TOP 100 PERCENT clause (which is covered in Chapter 4, "Querying and Modifying Data") in the view, it is possible to add the ORDER BY clause. For example, Listing 3.29 shows the creation of a view that contains an ORDER BY clause.

Listing 3.29: Using the ORDER BY Clause in Views

```
USE Northwind
GO

CREATE VIEW Customersbyname
AS
SELECT TOP 100 PERCENT *
FROM Customers
ORDER BY contactname
GO
```

In general, you can modify data through views in the same way that you modify data in tables. However, some restrictions need to be taken into consideration when modifying data through views. Specifically, just one table at a time can be updated when working through views. Thus, if a view references more than one table, you cannot update data in all tables at once through the view. Also, data that is not modified through the view must have a default value or accept nulls.

Regarding delete operations, if you want to delete data from a certain table through a view, the view must reference only one table (the table from which you want to delete data).

Listing 3.30 shows how to modify data stored in the `Customers` table through the `Spaincustomers` view.

EXAMPLE

Listing 3.30: Modifying Data Through Views

```
USE Northwind

UPDATE Spaincustomers
SET contactname = 'Maria Angelica Rojas',
    contacttitle = 'Owner'
WHERE customerid = 'ROMEY'
GO
```

Sometimes, you want to make sure that when views are used for data modification, the new values of the modified rows still belong to the result set of the view. To solve this problem, specify WITH CHECK OPTION when creating the view. For example, if there's a view that lists all Brazilian customers and WITH CHECK OPTION is specified, SQL Server throws an error when you try to change the country of any row through this view, because the new value would not allow this row to be part of the view's result set. This example appears in Listing 3.31.

EXAMPLE

Listing 3.31: Using WITH CHECK OPTION

```
USE Northwind
GO

CREATE VIEW Braziliancustomers
AS
SELECT *
FROM Customers
WHERE country = 'Brazil'
WITH CHECK OPTION
GO

UPDATE Braziliancustomers
SET country = 'USA'
WHERE customerid = 'WELLI'
```

Listing 3.31: continued

OUTPUT

```
GO

Server: Msg 550, Level 16, State 1, Line 1
The attempted insert or update failed because the target view either
specifies WITH CHECK OPTION or spans a view that specifies
WITH CHECK OPTION and one or more rows resulting from the operation
did not qualify under the CHECK OPTION constraint.
The statement has been terminated.
```

Similar to stored procedures, views can be used to enforce security in the database. Specifically, views can be used to allow users to see only subsets of data. In some cases, views are better than assigning column permissions in tables because, through a view, a user would be able to issue a SELECT * statement, whereas with column permissions, the user wouldn't be allowed to issue a SELECT * against the table.

DROP VIEW is the statement used to drop the definition and permissions associated with a view. It can be used to remove one or more views from the database, as shown in Listing 3.32.

EXAMPLE

Listing 3.32: Removing Views from the Database

```
USE Northwind

DROP VIEW Customersbyname,Toyotacars
GO
```

Altering a View's Definition

The ALTER VIEW statement is used to change the definition or the options of views, keeping permissions intact. If you drop the view, and then re-create it, permissions are lost.

You must specify the view's definition and options when using ALTER VIEW, because SQL Server overwrites the old definition and options with the new ones specified in ALTER VIEW. Therefore, if you want to retain functionality provided by options of the view, you must specify these options when altering the view.

For example, suppose that you want to alter the Mexicancustomers view to add the SCHEMABINDING option. In this case, the ENCRYPTION option must be specified again if you want the view's definition to be encrypted. Listing 3.33 shows this example.

EXAMPLE

Listing 3.33: Using ALTER VIEW

```
USE Northwind
GO

ALTER VIEW Mexicancustomers
```

Listing 3.33: continued

```
WITH ENCRYPTION, SCHEMABINDING
AS
SELECT customerid, companyname, contactname
FROM dbo.Customers
WHERE country = 'Mexico'
GO
```

TIP

Be sure to store the definition of views in a safe place when you create views using the WITH ENCRYPTION option, because after it is created, there is no way to show the definition. Therefore, if you want to alter a view that is encrypted, you will need the source code.

What's Next?

You can create tables and views using the CREATE TABLE and the CREATE VIEW statements, respectively. Furthermore, you can change their definition and properties by using the ALTER TABLE and ALTER VIEW statements. After they're created, you can insert, modify, delete, and extract data in tables using the Data Manipulation Language. This subset of the Transact-SQL language is covered in depth in the next chapter, "Querying and Modifying Data."

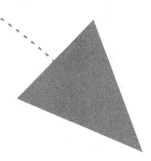

4

Querying and Modifying Data

In Chapter 2, "Elements of Transact-SQL," you learned the basics of all the statements that make up the Data Manipulation Language (DML), which are used to interact with the information stored in the database. Moreover, these four elements of the DML (SELECT, INSERT, UPDATE, and DELETE) are the core of database programming.

This chapter teaches you the following:

- The components and syntax of the SELECT statement
- How to insert data in the database using the INSERT statement
- How to create a table and populate it on-the-fly from result sets
- How to modify data through the UPDATE statement
- How the data is removed using the DELETE statement

Querying Data

One of the main purposes of a database is to have a repository or a data storage system where information can be extracted quickly. The SQL statement used to extract information from tables in a database is the SELECT statement.

The SELECT Statement

The SELECT statement is used to extract information from the database or, in other words, to ask questions (or queries) to the database.

The clauses or elements of the SELECT statement are FROM, WHERE, ORDER BY, GROUP BY, HAVING, TOP, and INTO. The only element that is always required for queries is the FROM clause, which is used to specify the table or view from which to extract information.

The basic syntax of SELECT is

```
SELECT column_list
FROM Table_name
```

When you issue a SELECT statement using this syntax, all rows are returned to the client because there are no restrictions (the query doesn't have a WHERE clause).

The output of the SELECT statement is a result set that is composed of rows that come from one or more tables or views (working with multiple tables at the same time using JOIN is covered in Chapter 5, "Querying Multiple Tables: JOINs"). If you want to get all columns of a table in a SELECT statement, use the * wildcard instead of specifying the whole column list. However, if you want only certain columns to appear in the output, these specific columns must be specified in the column list.

Listing 4.1 shows how to query a table using the * wildcard and using a column list. Notice that in both cases the query returns all rows on the table without restrictions, but the second one shows only certain columns.

EXAMPLE

Listing 4.1: Using a Basic SELECT Statement

```
USE Northwind

SELECT *
FROM Shippers

SELECT ShipperID,CompanyName
FROM Shippers
GO
```

Listing 4.1: continued

OUTPUT

```
ShipperID   CompanyName                               Phone
----------- ----------------------------------------  ----------------------
1           Speedy Express                            (503) 555-9831
2           United Package                            (503) 555-3199
3           Federal Shipping                          (503) 555-9931

(3 row(s) affected)

ShipperID   CompanyName
----------- ----------------------------------------
1           Speedy Express
2           United Package
3           Federal Shipping

(3 row(s) affected)
```

Notice that the SELECT statement can be used by itself when printing constants or values of variables. Also, SELECT is used to assign values to variables; similar to SET, which is used for the same purpose, but you can assign only one variable for each SET statement. On the other hand, you can assign values to more than one variable using one SELECT statement. In these cases (variable assignment and output), SELECT doesn't need a FROM clause. Listing 4.2 demonstrates how to use SELECT and SET to assign values to variables, and then it uses SELECT to show these values.

EXAMPLE

Listing 4.2: Using SELECT and SET to Assign Values to Variables and to Show These Values

```
DECLARE @firstname VARCHAR(10), @middlename VARCHAR(10), @lastname VARCHAR(10)
SET @firstname = 'Maria'
SELECT @middlename = 'Angelica', @lastname = 'Rojas'

SELECT @firstname, @middlename, @lastname
GO
```

OUTPUT

```
---------- ---------- ----------
Maria      Angelica   Rojas
```

In the column list of a SELECT statement, you also can include constants (or literals), which appear as new columns in the result set. Furthermore, columns can be concatenated (using the + string concatenation operator) to form a new column. These two techniques can be useful when populating tables using SELECT .. INTO, to calculate values, and to build scripts dynamically.

Listing 4.3 contains two queries. The first one has a constant ('The name of the table is: ') and a column (the name of the table that is extracted from the INFORMATION_SCHEMA.TABLES view). Notice that in the output of the first query, the constant appears as the first column. The second query uses

+ to concatenate two strings (a constant and a column) and generates one string (or a column resulting from the concatenation). This query generates a script as output that can be used later.

Listing 4.3: Using Constants and Concatenating Strings in the Column List of SELECT

```
USE Northwind

SELECT 'The name of the table is: ', table_name
FROM INFORMATION_SCHEMA.TABLES
WHERE table_type = 'base table'

SELECT 'DROP TABLE ' + table_name
FROM INFORMATION_SCHEMA.TABLES
WHERE table_type = 'base table'
GO
```

OUTPUT

```
-- partial results are shown

                                  table_name
.........................  ...........................
The name of the table is:  Cars
The name of the table is:  Categories
The name of the table is:  CategoriesBudget

(20 row(s) affected)


.........................................
DROP TABLE Cars
DROP TABLE Categories
DROP TABLE CategoriesBudget

(20 row(s) affected)
```

When concatenating columns, make sure that the data type of the column is character. Otherwise, use CONVERT or CAST to change it to character data to be able to use the concatenation operator. Listing 4.4 illustrates how to use CAST with a column whose data type is MONEY to change it to VARCHAR to be able to concatenate it with other columns and constants.

Listing 4.4: Using String Concatenation and CAST in SELECT Statements

```
USE Northwind

SELECT 'The cost per unit of ' + productname + ' is ' +
        CAST(unitprice as VARCHAR(10))
FROM Products
GO
```

Listing 4.4: continued

OUTPUT

```
-- partial results are shown

.............................................................
The cost per unit of Chai is 18.00
The cost per unit of Chang is 19.00
The cost per unit of Aniseed Syrup is 10.00
The cost per unit of Chef Anton's Cajun Seasoning is 22.00
The cost per unit of Chef Anton's Gumbo Mix is 21.35
```

The DISTINCT clause is used to eliminate duplicates in a result set. For example, the Employees table has more than one person with the same title. If you want to display all possible values of this column, you will get repeated data, but if DISTINCT is used in the SELECT clause, only unique values will be listed. Listing 4.5 shows the difference between a query without DISTINCT and another one with it.

EXAMPLE

Listing 4.5: Using DISTINCT to Remove Duplicate Rows from a Result Set

```
USE Northwind

SELECT title
FROM Employees

SELECT DISTINCT title
FROM Employees
GO
```

OUTPUT

```
title
----------------------------
Sales Representative
Vice President, Sales
Sales Representative
Sales Representative
Sales Manager
Sales Representative
Sales Representative
Inside Sales Coordinator
Sales Representative

(9 row(s) affected)

title
----------------------------
Inside Sales Coordinator
Sales Manager
Sales Representative
Vice President, Sales

(4 row(s) affected)
```

In SELECT statements, the IDENTITYCOL keyword can be used instead of the name of an IDENTITY column. For example, the Shippers table has a column with the IDENTITY property, shipperid. Therefore, when referencing this column in a SELECT statement, you can use either its name or the IDENTITYCOL keyword, which appears in Listing 4.6.

Listing 4.6: Using IDENTITYCOL Instead of the IDENTITY Column Name

```
USE Northwind

SELECT shipperid
FROM Shippers

SELECT IDENTITYCOL
FROM Shippers
GO
```

```
shipperid
-----------
1
2
3

(3 row(s) affected)

ShipperID
-----------
1
2
3.

(3 row(s) affected)
```

COLUMN ALIASES

You can use aliases to change default column names. Sometimes, assigning labels or aliases to the columns in a SELECT statement can be beneficial because

- There is more than one column with the same name—This usually happens when you're working with more than one table (using JOINs) and they have a column with the same name. In this case, it is beneficial to use column aliases to differentiate between these columns.

- The column is the result of a calculation, becoming an expression—In these cases, SQL Server doesn't assign a column name to these kinds of columns.

A column alias is specified using the following syntax:

```
column_name AS alias_name
```

The AS keyword is optional; therefore, the column name can be followed by the alias name. Also, the alias name can contain up to 128 characters.

CAUTION

The alias name must be enclosed in single quotation marks or brackets if it contains spaces.

Listing 4.7 shows how to use column aliases.

EXAMPLE

Listing 4.7: Using Column Aliases

```
USE Northwind


SELECT productname + ' (' + quantityperunit + ')' as product_quantities,
       unitsinstock + unitsonorder units
FROM Products
GO
```

OUTPUT

```
partial results shown

product_quantities                                              units
-------------------------------------------------------------   -------
Chai (10 boxes x 20 bags)                                       39
Chang (24 - 12 oz bottles)                                      57
Aniseed Syrup (12 - 550 ml bottles)                             83
Chef Anton's Cajun Seasoning (48 - 6 oz jars)                   53
Chef Anton's Gumbo Mix (36 boxes)                               0
Grandma's Boysenberry Spread (12 - 8 oz jars)                   120
Uncle Bob's Organic Dried Pears (12 - 1 lb pkgs.)               15
Northwoods Cranberry Sauce (12 - 12 oz jars)                    6
```

The FROM Clause

You use the FROM clause to specify the tables or views involved in a query. In the case of multiple tables, the type of JOIN and the JOIN condition are also specified in the FROM clause. Listing 4.8 shows a SELECT statement that retrieves information from two tables, Territories and Region (Chapter 5 goes over queries that involve multiple tables using JOINs).

EXAMPLE

Listing 4.8: Using the FROM Clause to Specify the Tables from Which Data Will Be Retrieved

```
USE Northwind

SELECT Territories.territorydescription, Region.regiondescription
FROM Territories JOIN Region
ON Territories.regionid = Region.regionid
GO
```

Listing 4.8: continued

OUTPUT

```
partial results shown

territorydescription      regiondescription
------------------------  -----------------
Westboro                  Eastern
Bedford                   Eastern
Georgetown                 Eastern
Boston                    Eastern
Cambridge                 Eastern
Braintree                 Eastern
```

Tables in other databases can be referenced in the FROM clause if you qualify them with the database name and the owner (the last is optional). Furthermore, if you're working with linked servers (which are covered in Chapter 15, "Working with Heterogeneous Environments: Setting Up Linked Servers"), you can access tables in those servers, but in this case you must qualify the table with the name of the server, and then the database name (or catalog) and owner (or schema). Listing 4.9 illustrates this situation, retrieving data stored in the Authors table in Pubs, from the Northwind database.

EXAMPLE

Listing 4.9: Using the FROM Clause to Specify Tables in Other Databases

```
USE Northwind

SELECT au_fname + ' ' + au_lname AS name
FROM Pubs..Authors
GO
```

OUTPUT

```
name
---------------------------------
Abraham Bennet
Reginald Blotchet-Halls
Cheryl Carson
Michel DeFrance
Innes del Castillo
Ann Dull
Marjorie Green
Morningstar Greene
Burt Gringlesby
Sheryl Hunter
Livia Karsen
Charlene Locksley
Stearns MacFeather
Heather McBadden
Michael O'Leary
Sylvia Panteley
Albert Ringer
Anne Ringer
```

Listing 4.9: continued

```
Meander Smith
Dean Straight
Dirk Stringer
Johnson White
Akiko Yokomoto

(23 row(s) affected)
```

A maximum of 256 tables can be referenced in a SELECT statement. If you have a query that requires extracting information from more than 256 tables, use temporary tables or derived tables to store partial results.

TABLE ALIASES

You can use table aliases to make queries more readable, adding a label to a table (usually an identifier that is shorter than the name of the table), and using this label to reference the table in the rest of the query. Generally, table aliases are useful when you are writing queries that involve multiple tables (joining tables).

A table alias is specified using the following syntax (similar to column aliases):

```
Table_name AS alias_name
```

Notice that the AS keyword can be omitted. Therefore, specifying the table name followed by the alias name is also valid. Listing 4.10 shows a query similar to the one shown in Listing 4.8, but this one uses table aliases, which are used to qualify the columns in the column list and in the JOIN condition.

EXAMPLE

Listing 4.10: Using Table Aliases

```
USE Northwind

SELECT T.territorydescription, R.regiondescription
FROM Territories T JOIN Region R
ON T.regionid = R.regionid
GO
```

OUTPUT

```
partial results shown

territorydescription        regiondescription
------------------------    -----------------
Westboro                    Eastern
Bedford                     Eastern
Georgetown                  Eastern
Boston                      Eastern
Cambridge                   Eastern
Braintree                   Eastern
```

CAUTION

If an alias is specified for a table, it must be used in the rest of the query—the name of the table cannot be used.

The WHERE Clause

You have learned how to query a table (retrieving all rows) using the SELECT statement and the FROM clause. Generally, you must restrict the number of rows that a query returns; therefore, only rows that meet certain criteria or conditions will be part of the result set of the query. The WHERE clause restricts the result set of a query based on a search condition. As a result, just the rows that meet the search condition will be returned by the query. The syntax of a query that contains a WHERE clause is

```
SELECT column_list
FROM Table_name
WHERE conditions
```

Listing 4.11 shows a SELECT statement that retrieves the lastname, firstname, and hiredate of the employees who live in Seattle.

Listing 4.11: Using the WHERE Clause to Restrict the Output of a Query

```
USE Northwind

SELECT lastname, firstname, hiredate
FROM Employees
WHERE city = 'seattle'
GO
```

EXAMPLE

```
lastname              firstname   hiredate
------------------    ----------  --------------------------
Davolio               Nancy       1992-05-01 00:00:00.000
Callahan              Laura       1994-03-05 00:00:00.000
```

OUTPUT

```
(2 row(s) affected)
```

In Transact-SQL, operators are used to work with expressions. Because a WHERE clause contains one or more expressions to restrict the output of a query, all operators covered in Chapter 2 can be used in WHERE clauses. These are LIKE, NOT LIKE, IN, NOT IN, BETWEEN, NOT BETWEEN, and comparison operators (=, <>, <, >, <=, and >=). Listing 4.12 demonstrates how these operators are used in queries.

Listing 4.12: Using Operators in WHERE Clauses

```
USE Northwind

-- Returns all employees whose last name begins with 'b'
SELECT lastname, firstname
```

EXAMPLE

Listing 4.12: continued

```
FROM Employees
WHERE lastname LIKE 'b%'

-- Returns all employees who don't live in Seattle, Redmond or Tacoma
SELECT lastname, firstname, city
FROM Employees
WHERE city NOT IN ('seattle','redmond','tacoma')

-- Returns all employees that were hired between 1/1/1993 and 12/31/1993
SELECT lastname, firstname, hiredate
FROM Employees
WHERE hiredate BETWEEN '1993.1.1' AND '1993.12.31'

-- Returns all employees that live in any other city than London
SELECT lastname, firstname, city
FROM Employees
WHERE city <> 'london'.
GO
```

OUTPUT

```
lastname              firstname
--------------------  ----------
Buchanan              Steven

(1 row(s) affected)

lastname              firstname  city
--------------------  ----------  --------------
Leverling             Janet       Kirkland
Buchanan              Steven      London
NewFamily             Michael     London
King                  Robert      London
Dodsworth             Anne        London

(5 row(s) affected)

lastname              firstname  hiredate
--------------------  ----------  ----------------------------
Peacock               Margaret    1993-05-03 00:00:00.000
Buchanan              Steven      1993-10-17 00:00:00.000
NewFamily             Michael     1993-10-17 00:00:00.000

(3 row(s) affected)

lastname              firstname  city
--------------------  ----------  --------------
Davolio               Nancy       Seattle
Fuller                Andrew      Tacoma
```

Listing 4.12: continued

```
Leverling        Janet      Kirkland
Peacock          Margaret   Redmond
Callahan         Laura      Seattle.
```

```
(5 row(s) affected)
```

In a WHERE clause, many expressions can be combined using the AND and OR logical operators. Therefore:

- If AND is used, the rows returned by the query will be the ones that meet all the search conditions.

- On the other hand, if OR is used, the result set will contain the rows that meet any of the search conditions.

An example of how these logical operators (AND and OR) are used in the WHERE clause that appears in Listing 4.13.

EXAMPLE

Listing 4.13: Combining Expressions in the WHERE Clause Using AND and OR

```
USE Northwind

-- Returns all employees whose last name begins with 'b'
-- and don't live in Seattle, Redmond or Tacoma
SELECT lastname, firstname, city
FROM Employees
WHERE lastname LIKE 'b%'
AND city NOT IN ('seattle','redmond','tacoma')

-- Returns all employees that either:
-- were hired between 1/1/1993 and 12/31/1993
-- or live in any other city than London
SELECT lastname, firstname, city, hiredate
FROM Employees
WHERE hiredate BETWEEN '1993.1.1' AND '1993.12.31'.
OR city <> 'london'
GO
```

OUTPUT

```
lastname             firstname   city
-------------------- ----------- ----------------
Buchanan             Steven      London
```

```
(1 row(s) affected)
```

```
lastname             firstname   city             hiredate
-------------------- ----------- ---------------- ----------------------------
Davolio              Nancy       Seattle          1992-05-01 00:00:00.000
Fuller               Andrew      Tacoma           1992-08-14 00:00:00.000
Leverling            Janet       Kirkland         1992-04-01 00:00:00.000
```

Listing 4.13: continued

```
Peacock            Margaret   Redmond      1993-05-03 00:00:00.000
Buchanan           Steven     London       1993-10-17 00:00:00.000
NewFamily          Michael    London       1993-10-17 00:00:00.000
Callahan           Laura      Seattle      1994-03-05 00:00:00.000
```

(7 row(s) affected)

When comparing DATETIME values in WHERE clauses, be aware that this data type stores both date and time. Hence, if you want to compare just the date portion of the whole value, use the CONVERT function to get just the portion you want. For example, if you need to retrieve all orders posted on 7/4/1996 no matter the time they were posted, you can use the query shown in Listing 4.14.

EXAMPLE

Listing 4.14: Comparing DATETIME Values in WHERE Clauses

```
USE Northwind

SELECT orderid, customerid, employeeid, orderdate
FROM Orders
WHERE CONVERT(VARCHAR(20),orderdate,102) = '1996.07.04'
GO
```

OUTPUT

```
orderid      customerid employeeid  orderdate
-----------  ---------- ----------- ---------------------------
10248        VINET      5           1996-07-04 00:00:00.000
```

(1 row(s) affected)

CAUTION

NULL values should be handled with care when comparing them in WHERE clauses. Specifically, use IS NULL or IS NOT NULL, according to each case, to check for NULL values, and avoid using comparison operators with NULL values—for example, 'column_name = NULL'—because their behavior depends on the SET ANSI_NULLS setting.

Listing 4.15 shows an example of how IS NULL and IS NOT NULL are used within expressions in a WHERE clause to search for NULL values.

EXAMPLE

Listing 4.15: Using IS NULL and IS NOT NULL to Make Comparisons with NULL Values

```
USE Northwind

-- Retrieves all suppliers whose region doesn't have a NULL value
SELECT companyname, contactname, region
FROM Suppliers
WHERE region IS NOT NULL

-- Retrieves all suppliers whose region is NULL (or unknown)
SELECT companyname, contactname, region
```

Listing 4.15: continued

```
FROM Suppliers
WHERE region IS NULL
GO
```

-- the output has been simplified

OUTPUT

companyname	contactname	region
New Orleans Cajun Delights	Shelley Burke	LA
Grandma Kelly's Homestead	Regina Murphy	MI
Cooperativa de Quesos 'Las Cabras'	Antonio del Valle Saavedra	Asturia

(9 row(s) affected)

.

companyname	contactname	region
Exotic Liquids	Charlotte Cooper	NULL
Tokyo Traders	Yoshi Nagase	NULL
Mayumi's	Mayumi Ohno	NULL.

(21 row(s) affected)

Multiple expressions and the ISNULL function can be used in a WHERE clause as an elegant solution for queries that contain optional search fields. For example, suppose you want to search for employees based on city, title, or both. Two variables can be created to store the value of the city or title to search for (@city and @title). If a variable equals NULL—for example, @city—this means that you are searching for a specific title (which is stored in the @title variable). If both variables are NULL, you want to retrieve all rows in the table.

Usually, to solve this problem, you can validate each variable and create a query accordingly. These are the possible cases:

- If just the city is used (@title equals NULL), build a query that just searches for employees who live in this city.

- If just the title is used (@city equals NULL), build a query that just searches for employees whose title is the one stored in the @title variable.

- If both values are used (city and title), build a query with two expressions in the WHERE clause, and connect these two expressions with an AND operator.

Listing 4.16 shows how to code these three queries (each of them is based on the value of the @title and @city variables). In this example, the @title variable is set to NULL and @city is set to London to retrieve all employees who live in London.

EXAMPLE

Listing 4.16: Using Optional Search Fields with Different Queries

```
USE Northwind

DECLARE @title VARCHAR(60), @city VARCHAR(30)

-- Setting @title to NULL and searching for all employees
-- who live in London

SET @title = NULL
SET @city = 'London'

IF @title IS NOT NULL AND @city IS NULL

  SELECT lastname, firstname, title, city
  FROM Employees
  WHERE title = @title

IF @title IS NULL AND @city IS NOT NULL

  SELECT lastname, firstname, title, city
  FROM Employees
  WHERE city = @city

IF @title IS NOT NULL AND @city IS NOT NULL

  SELECT lastname, firstname, title, city
  FROM Employees
  WHERE city = @city
  AND title = @title..

GO
```

OUTPUT

```
lastname            firstname  title                           city
------------------- ---------- ------------------------------- ----------------
Buchanan            Steven     Sales Manager                   London
NewFamily           Michael    Sales Representative            London
King                Robert     Sales Representative            London
Dodsworth           Anne       Sales Representative            London

(4 row(s) affected)
```

However, as stated before, you can build just one query using the ISNULL function to validate each variable, and one expression per variable; thus, solving the problem of the optional search fields with just a query and not using any IF statements. This query appears in Listing 4.17 (notice that it has the same output as the preceding example).

EXAMPLE

Listing 4.17: Using Optional Search Fields Using One Query

```
USE Northwind
DECLARE @title VARCHAR(60), @city VARCHAR(30)

-- Setting @title to NULL and serarching for all employees
-- who live in London

SET @title = NULL
SET @city = 'London'

SELECT lastname, firstname, title, city
FROM Employees
WHERE city = ISNULL(@city,city)
AND title = ISNULL(@title,title) .
GO
```

OUTPUT

```
lastname              firstname   title                                city
-------------------   ---------   ---------------------------------    ---------------
Buchanan              Steven      Sales Manager                        London
NewFamily             Michael     Sales Representative                 London
King                  Robert      Sales Representative                 London
Dodsworth             Anne        Sales Representative                 London.

(4 row(s) affected)
```

CAUTION

Be aware that IS NULL is different from the ISNULL function. The IS NULL clause is used to make comparisons with NULL values, whereas ISNULL is a function that takes two arguments. If the first one is NULL, it returns the second one; otherwise, the first argument is returned.

Data Aggregation and the GROUP BY Clause

One of the benefits of the SQL language is that it enables you to generate summaries of the data stored in a database. Sometimes, data as a whole might not make sense, but when summarized, it can be used for many purposes.

Transact-SQL provides aggregate functions, which are used to generate summary values. Basically, they return a single value based on a calculation on a set of values. Table 4.1 shows the most common aggregate functions used in Transact-SQL.

Table 4.1: Transact-SQL's Aggregate Functions

Aggregate Function	Description
AVG	Returns the average or arithmetic mean.

Table 4.1: continued

Aggregate Function	Description
COUNT	Returns the number of values (an INT data type). COUNT(*) can be used to return the number of rows in a group (the group can be the whole table, obtaining the number of rows in the table).
COUNT_BIG	Similar to COUNT in that it returns the number of values, but it returns a BIGINT data type. COUNT_BIG(*) can be used to return the number of rows in a group (the group can be the whole table, obtaining the number of rows in the table).
MAX	Returns the maximum value.
MIN	Returns the minimum value.
SUM	Returns the sum of the values. Takes only numbers as arguments.

Listing 4.18 indicates how these aggregate functions are used to return summary values based on the values on the whole table.

EXAMPLE

Listing 4.18: Using Aggregate Functions

```
USE Northwind


-- Returns the average of unitsinstock
SELECT AVG(unitsinstock)
FROM Products

-- Returns the number of rows in the Employees table
SELECT COUNT(*)
FROM Employees

-- Returns the price of the most expensive product
SELECT MAX(unitprice)
FROM Products

-- Returns the birthdate of the oldest employee
SELECT MIN(birthdate)
FROM Employees

-- Returns the number of products in stock
SELECT SUM(unitsinstock)
FROM Products
GO
```

```
- - - - - - - - - - -
40
```

OUTPUT

Listing 4.18: continued

```
. . . . . . . . . . .
9


. . . . . . . . . . . . . . . . . . .
263.5000


. . . . . . . . . . . . . . . . . . . . . . . . . . . . . . .
1937-09-19 00:00:00.000:


. . . . . . . . . . .
3119
```

The DISTINCT keyword can be used in any aggregate function to consider repeating values just once. For example, to retrieve how many different titles the Employees table has, you can use the COUNT aggregate function with the DISTINCT keyword, as shown in Listing 4.19. In this case, the DISTINCT keyword is needed because more than one employee has the same title, and you want to count each title once to see how many different titles are in this table.

Listing 4.19: Using DISTINCT in Aggregate Functions

```
USE Northwind

SELECT COUNT(DISTINCT title)
FROM Employees
GO
```

EXAMPLE

```
. . . . . . . . . . .
4
```

OUTPUT

You use the GROUP BY clause to group rows in a result set, generating a summary row for each group of data. All columns specified in SELECT must also be specified in GROUP BY. However, columns specified in the GROUP BY clause don't have to be in the SELECT column list.

To illustrate, Listing 4.20 shows an example that retrieves the number of employees per title. SQL Server generates a row per each title (this is the column specified in the GROUP BY clause) and counts the number of rows per title.

Listing 4.20: Using the GROUP BY Clause

```
USE Northwind

SELECT title, COUNT(*)
FROM Employees
GROUP BY title
GO
```

EXAMPLE

Listing 4.20: continued

```
title
............................ ..........
Inside Sales Coordinator     1
Sales Manager                1
Sales Representative         6
Vice President, Sales        1

(4 row(s) affected)
```

It might be necessary to generate a summary row for a table (just one row and not a row for each group). In this case, because it is just one group (the whole table), use aggregate functions without the GROUP BY clause, as previously shown in Listing 4.18. Moreover, you can use more than one aggregate function in the same query. For example, to get the most recent date in which an order was placed, and the minimum orderid in the Orders table, use the query shown in Listing 4.21.

Listing 4.21: Summarizing Data

```
USE Northwind

SELECT MAX(orderdate), MIN(orderid)
FROM orders
GO
```

```
............................ ..........
1998-05-06 00:00:00.000      10248

(1 row(s) affected)
```

If there's a WHERE clause in the query, it must be specified before the GROUP BY clause. SQL Server evaluates the WHERE clause first, and then it generates the groups based on the columns specified in GROUP BY. For example, to retrieve the number of customers in Spain and Venezuela, use the query shown in Listing 4.22.

Listing 4.22: Restricting the Groups Generated by GROUP BY

```
USE Northwind

SELECT country, COUNT(*)
FROM Customers
WHERE country IN ('Spain','Venezuela')
GROUP BY country
GO
```

Listing 4.22: continued

OUTPUT

```
country
--------------- -----------
Spain            5
Venezuela        4
```

(2 row(s) affected)

TIP

As a new feature of SQL Server 2000, BIT columns can be used in a GROUP BY clause. This was a limitation of GROUP BY in previous versions.

The use of column aliases is recommended when working with aggregate functions, because when any function is applied to a column, the result set doesn't show the original name of the column. Listing 4.23 shows an example of column aliases when using aggregate functions.

EXAMPLE

Listing 4.23: Using Column Aliases and Aggregate Functions

```
USE Northwind

SELECT country, COUNT(*) AS [number of customers]
FROM Customers
WHERE country IN ('Spain','Venezuela')
GROUP BY country
GO
```

OUTPUT

```
country          number of customers
--------------- --------------------
Spain            5
Venezuela        4
```

(2 row(s) affected)

THE HAVING CLAUSE

When using GROUP BY in a query to generate groups, you might want to set restrictions on these groups. Specifically, the HAVING clause sets restrictions on the groups generated by GROUP BY. HAVING is similar to WHERE in the sense that it restricts the output of the query, but HAVING is evaluated by SQL Server after the groups are generated.

It's important to know that WHERE is evaluated first, then groups are generated (as a result of GROUP BY), and finally, the HAVING clause is evaluated. Therefore, aggregate functions cannot be referenced in the WHERE clause; they can be referenced only in the HAVING clause.

Listing 4.24 retrieves the number of customers of the countries that have more than five customers. This is done by setting a restriction after the groups are generated (using a HAVING clause); hence, showing only the countries that have more than five customers.

Listing 4.24: Setting Restrictions on the Groups Generated by GROUP BY Using HAVING

```
USE Northwind

SELECT country, COUNT(*) AS [number of customers]
FROM Customers
GROUP BY country
HAVING COUNT(*) > 5
GO
```

```
country          number of customers
---------------  -------------------
Brazil           9
France           11
Germany          11
UK               7
USA              16
```

OUTPUT

```
(5 row(s) affected)
```

Similar to WHERE, multiple conditions can be specified in the HAVING clause, combining them with a logical operator (OR or AND). Listing 4.25 shows how conditions can be combined in a HAVING clause.

Listing 4.25: Combining Conditions in a HAVING Clause

```
USE Northwind

SELECT country, COUNT(*) AS [number of customers]
FROM Customers
GROUP BY country
HAVING COUNT(*) > 5
AND COUNT(*) < 10
GO
```

```
country          number of customers
---------------  -------------------
Brazil           9
UK               7
```

OUTPUT

```
(2 row(s) affected)
```

The ORDER BY Clause

A table comprises a set of rows, and a set, by definition, is unordered. Therefore, when retrieving data from tables, SQL Server doesn't guarantee the order of the rows in the result set. This is because SQL Server might optimize the query in a different way each time it is executed, depending on the data; resulting in a different order of the rows each time the same query is executed. To guarantee a specific order in a result set, use the ORDER BY clause. Listing 4.26 retrieves information from the Shippers table ordered by company name in ascending order (this is the default in SQL Server).

EXAMPLE

Listing 4.26: Using ORDER BY to Guarantee the Order of Rows

```
USE Northwind

SELECT companyname, phone
FROM Shippers
ORDER BY companyname
GO
```

OUTPUT

```
companyname                                phone
-----------------------------------------  --------------------------
Federal Shipping                           (503) 555-9931
Speedy Express                             (503) 555-9831
United Package                             (503) 555-3199
```

(3 row(s) affected)

You can include more than one column in the ORDER BY clause, and you also can specify how these values will be sorted, either ascending (using the ASC keyword), which is the default, or descending (using the DESC keyword). If more than one column is specified in the ORDER BY clause, SQL Server sorts the result set in the order in which these columns appear (first, the first column, then the second column, and so on). Listing 4.27 shows how to specify multiple columns and how to order them (either ascending or descending) in the ORDER BY clause.

Listing 4.27: Using Multiple Expressions in the ORDER BY Clause

```
USE Northwind

SELECT lastname, firstname
FROM Employees
ORDER BY lastname ASC, firstname DESC
GO
```

EXAMPLE

OUTPUT

```
lastname            firstname
------------------  ----------
Buchanan            Steven
Callahan            Laura
Davolio             Nancy
Dodsworth           Anne
Fuller              Andrew
King                Robert
Leverling           Janet
NewFamily           Michael
```

Listing 4.27: continued

```
Peacock              Margaret

(9 row(s) affected)
```

TIP

As discussed in previous chapters, use TOP if you want to specify the ORDER BY clause when creating a view.

The TOP N Clause

TOP is used to limit the results of a query. It can be used in two ways: to retrieve the first N rows or to retrieve the first N percent of the rows in the result set. The TOP clause must be used along with ORDER BY; otherwise, SQL Server doesn't guarantee a specific ordering, and the TOP clause will be meaningless.

TOP returns the least significant values if they are sorted in ascending order. On the other hand, TOP retrieves the most significant values if they are sorted in descending order. For example, to retrieve the most expensive products, use a TOP clause and an ORDER BY clause sorting the unitprice column in descending order, as shown in Listing 4.28.

EXAMPLE

Listing 4.28: Limiting the Output of a Query Using the TOP Clause

```
USE Northwind

SELECT TOP 10 productid, productname, unitprice
FROM Products
ORDER BY unitprice DESC

SELECT TOP 1 PERCENT productid, productname, unitprice
FROM Products
ORDER BY unitprice DESC
GO
```

OUTPUT

productid	productname	unitprice
38	Côte de Blaye	263.5000
29	Thüringer Rostbratwurst	123.7900
9	Mishi Kobe Niku	97.0000
20	Sir Rodney's Marmalade	81.0000
18	Carnarvon Tigers	62.5000
59	Raclette Courdavault	55.0000
51	Manjimup Dried Apples	53.0000
62	Tarte au sucre	49.3000
43	Ipoh Coffee	46.0000
28	Rössle Sauerkraut	45.6000

Listing 4.28: continued

```
(10 row(s) affected)

productid   productname                                     unitprice
----------- ----------------------------------------------  ----------
38          Côte de Blaye                                   263.5000

(1 row(s) affected)
```

CAUTION

If you're concerned about portability, be careful when using TOP because it is not ANSI standard. Instead, it is a feature of Transact-SQL.

The argument of TOP is a positive integer in either case (percent or fixed number of rows).

CAUTION

The argument of the TOP clause must be an integer; it cannot be a variable. If you want to use a variable, use dynamic queries (EXEC or sp_executesql).

In previous versions of SQL Server (6.5 and earlier), the only way to limit the result set of a query was by using SET ROWCOUNT, which stops the processing of the query when it reaches the number of rows specified by SET ROWCOUNT.

Be aware that TOP is more efficient than SET ROWCOUNT because TOP is evaluated at parse time, not at execution time like SET ROWCOUNT. Another disadvantage of using SET ROWCOUNT is that it remains set until you execute SET ROWCOUNT 0 to reset it to its original behavior (all rows are returned when executing a query). When SET ROWCOUNT is enabled, it also affects modification operations (INSERT, UPDATE, and DELETE). Listing 4.29 demonstrates the usage of SET ROWCOUNT (notice that the result set is equivalent to the one shown in Listing 4.28).

EXAMPLE

Listing 4.29: Using SET ROWCOUNT

```
USE Northwind

-- Use SET ROWCOUNT 10 to limit the output of all queries to 10 rows
SET ROWCOUNT 10

SELECT productid, productname, unitprice
FROM Products
ORDER BY unitprice DESC

-- Use SET ROWCOUNT 0 to reset it to its original state (all rows are returned)
SET ROWCOUNT 0
GO
```

Listing 4.29: continued

OUTPUT

productid	productname	unitprice
38	Côte de Blaye	263.5000
29	Thüringer Rostbratwurst	123.7900
9	Mishi Kobe Niku	97.0000
20	Sir Rodney's Marmalade	81.0000
18	Carnarvon Tigers	62.5000
59	Raclette Courdavault	55.0000
51	Manjimup Dried Apples	53.0000
62	Tarte au sucre	49.3000
43	Ipoh Coffee	46.0000
28	Rössle Sauerkraut	45.6000

(10 row(s) affected)

CAUTION

If you use SET ROWCOUNT, don't forget to execute SET ROWCOUNT 0 to turn this setting off; otherwise, it remains set during the connection, affecting all subsequent queries.

Use the WITH TIES keyword of the TOP clause when you want to include ties in the result set. If WITH TIES is specified, the result set may contain more rows than the number of rows specified in the TOP clause because all ties would be included. For example, Listing 4.30 shows a query that retrieves the top six units in stock. Notice that seven rows are returned because there's a tie in the sixth position, and the query returns all ties (two in this case).

EXAMPLE

Listing 4.30: Using WITH TIES in TOP Clauses

```
USE Northwind

SELECT TOP 6 WITH TIES productid, productname, unitsinstock
FROM Products
ORDER BY unitsinstock DESC
GO
```

OUTPUT

productid	productname	unitsinstock
75	Rhönbräu Klosterbier	125
40	Boston Crab Meat	123
6	Grandma's Boysenberry Spread	120
55	Pâté chinois	115
61	Sirop d'érable	113
33	Geitost	112
36	Inlagd Sill	112

(7 row(s) affected)

Using Dynamic Queries

In some situations, you might want to parameterize queries using variables to specify, for example, the table to query. However, some elements cannot be specified dynamically in queries, such as the table name and column names. In these specific cases, dynamic queries might be beneficial. Specifically, there are two ways to execute dynamic queries: using EXEC (or EXECUTE), and using the sp_executesql system stored procedure. These two ways are listed in Listing 4.31.

CAUTION

The string (a dynamic query) that is passed as an argument to sp_executesql must be a Unicode string (to specify Unicode strings, use the N prefix when building the string).

EXAMPLE

Listing 4.31: Dynamically Generating and Executing Queries Using EXEC and sp_executesql

```
USE Northwind

DECLARE @tablename VARCHAR(20), @query NVARCHAR(100)
SET @tablename = 'Shippers'
SET @query = N'SELECT * FROM ' + @tablename

-- Executing the dynamic query using EXEC
EXEC (@query)

-- Executing the dynamic query using sp_executesql
EXEC sp_executesql @query
GO
```

OUTPUT

```
ShipperID   CompanyName                           Phone
----------  ------------------------------------  ------------------------
1           Speedy Express                        (503) 555-9831
2           United Package                        (503) 555-3199
3           Federal Shipping                      (503) 555-9931

ShipperID   CompanyName                           Phone
----------  ------------------------------------  ------------------------
1           Speedy Express                        (503) 555-9831
2           United Package                        (503) 555-3199
3           Federal Shipping                      (503) 555-9931

(3 row(s) affected)
```

The following are the disadvantages of using dynamic queries:

- The statements inside EXEC or sp_executesql are executed inside its own batch; therefore, these statements cannot access variables declared in the outside batch.

- If the query to be executed by EXEC is not similar enough to a previously executed query due to different format, values, or data types, SQL Server cannot reuse a previously executed query plan. However, sp_executesql overcomes this limitation, allowing SQL Server to reuse the execution plan of the query (because it can be cached in memory).

TIP

Use sp_executesql whenever possible when executing dynamic queries, because the plan has a better chance of being reused.

Sometimes the dynamic query is very long and it becomes illegible. In these cases, you can use a variable to store the entire string and then use this variable as the argument of EXEC or sp_executesql, as shown in Listing 4.31. Also, you might want to insert carriage returns (using CHAR(13)) in the query to make it more legible (in case you want to display it). Listing 4.32 indicates how to insert carriage returns in a dynamic query.

EXAMPLE

Listing 4.32: Inserting Carriage Returns When Building Dynamic Queries

```
USE Northwind

DECLARE @query NVARCHAR(100)
SET @query = N'SELECT * ' + CHAR(13)+ 'FROM Shippers'

-- To display the query (which has a carriage return)
SELECT @query

-- Executing the dynamic query
EXEC sp_executesql @query
GO
```

OUTPUT

```
---------------------------
SELECT * FROM Shippers

(1 row(s) affected)

ShipperID   CompanyName                         Phone
----------  ----------------------------------  ----------------------
1           Speedy Express                      (503) 555-9831
2           United Package                      (503) 555-3199
3           Federal Shipping                    (503) 555-9931

(3 row(s) affected)
```

CAUTION

In SQL Server, EXECUTE can be used for three different purposes: to execute dynamic queries, to execute stored procedures, and to assign execute permissions to users on stored procedures (using GRANT, DENY, or REVOKE). The difference between executing a stored procedure and a dynamic statement using EXECUTE is that the first one doesn't need to be enclosed in parentheses, whereas the dynamic statement does.

There are some security issues when dynamic statements are executed inside a stored procedure. Usually, to be able to execute a stored procedure, a user just needs to have EXECUTE permissions on the stored procedure. However, if a dynamic query is used, the user also needs permissions on every object referenced by the dynamic query. This is because the dynamic query is not parsed until the stored procedure is executed, and SQL Server must check permissions on every object referenced by the dynamic query.

Modifying Data

As you already know, SELECT is the element of the Data Manipulation Language (DML) that is used to extract information from tables. The other elements of the DML are used to add, modify, and remove data from tables. These elements are INSERT, UPDATE, and DELETE.

The INSERT Statement

INSERT is used to add new rows in a table. The following is the basic syntax to insert a row in a table:

```
INSERT INTO Table_name (column_1,column_2,..,column_n)
VALUES (value_1,value_2,..,value_n)
```

The order of the values to be inserted must be the same order of the columns specified in the column list. Also, the INTO keyword can be omitted when using the INSERT statement, as shown in Listing 4.33.

EXAMPLE

Listing 4.33: Adding a New Row Using the INSERT Statement

```
USE Northwind

INSERT Territories (territoryid,territorydescription,regionid)
VALUES ('77777','Fort Lauderdale',4)
GO
```

OUTPUT

```
(1 row(s) affected)
```

If you want to insert data in all columns of a table, the column list can be omitted, but keep in mind that the values must be ordered in the same way that their respective columns appear in the table's definition (you can see the order of the columns using the sp_help system stored procedure).

For example, Listing 4.34 inserts a row in the `Territories` table, omitting the column list.

Listing 4.34: Omitting the Column List When Inserting Data in All Columns of the Table

```
USE Northwind

INSERT Territories VALUES ('88888','Miami',4)
GO
```

```
(1 row(s) affected)
```

SQL Server automatically handles `IDENTITY` columns by default. Therefore, when a row is inserted in a table that has an `IDENTITY` column, you don't have to specify the `IDENTITY` column in the `INSERT` statement because SQL Server provides a value automatically, as shown in Listing 4.35.

Listing 4.35: Inserting a Row in a Table with an `IDENTITY` Column

```
USE Northwind

INSERT Shippers (companyname, phone)
VALUES ('Super Fast Shipping','(503) 555-6493')
GO
```

```
(1 row(s) affected)
```

However, if you want to explicitly insert a value in an `IDENTITY` column, use `SET IDENTITY_INSERT` with the table's name as an argument. This is demonstrated in Listing 4.36.

Listing 4.36: Inserting a Value in an `IDENTITY` Column

```
USE Northwind

SET IDENTITY_INSERT Shippers ON
INSERT Shippers (shipperid,companyname, phone)
VALUES (20,'ACME Shipping','(503) 555-8888')
SET IDENTITY_INSERT Shippers OFF
GO
```

```
(1 row(s) affected)
```

There are two ways to insert `NULL` values in nullable columns: either explicitly (using the `NULL` keyword when inserting data) or implicitly (the column is not referenced in the `INSERT` statement).

Similarly, there are two ways to use default values in `INSERT` statements: either explicitly (using the `DEFAULT` keyword) or implicitly (if the column is not specified in the `INSERT` statement).

As a result, when columns are omitted in the column list of `INSERT`, SQL Server automatically provides a default value (if one is defined on the column) or, if a default value is not defined and the column is nullable, a `NULL` is used. On the other hand, if a column doesn't have a default value and it doesn't accept NULLs, a value must be specified in the INSERT statement; otherwise, the INSERT operation will fail.

Listing 4.37 shows two equivalent INSERT statements. The first one uses the NULL and DEFAULT keywords, whereas the second one omits these columns, producing the same result.

EXAMPLE

Listing 4.37: Omitting Specific Columns and Using the NULL and DEFAULT Keywords

```
USE Northwind

INSERT Products (productname,supplierid,categoryid,quantityperunit,
reorderlevel,discontinued)
VALUES ('Donut',NULL,NULL,'6 pieces',DEFAULT,DEFAULT)

-- INSERT Products (productname,quantityperunit)
-- VALUES ('Donut','6 pieces')
GO
```

OUTPUT

```
(1 row(s) affected)
```

CAUTION

Keywords, such as NULL or DEFAULT, don't need to be enclosed in single quotation marks like strings.

Furthermore, if you want to insert default values in all columns and NULL values in the nullable ones without a default, use the following syntax (which also takes care of IDENTITY values):

```
INSERT Table_name DEFAULT VALUES
```

Be aware that to be able to use this syntax, all columns must meet at least one of these conditions:

- It must be an IDENTITY column.
- The column must have a default value defined on it.
- The column must be nullable.

Listing 4.38 shows an example of this syntax.

EXAMPLE

Listing 4.38: Inserting Default Values in All Columns

```
USE Northwind

INSERT Orders DEFAULT VALUES
GO
```

OUTPUT

```
(1 row(s) affected)
```

INSERT may also be used to insert multiple rows in a table. This can be done through two approaches:

- Using a SELECT statement along with INSERT. In this case, the output of the SELECT statement is inserted into the table. Listing 4.39 indicates how to insert multiple rows in a table using this approach.

EXAMPLE

Listing 4.39: Inserting a SELECT Statement's Output into a Table

```
USE Northwind

CREATE TABLE #employees_in_wa (
lastname NVARCHAR(40),
firstname NVARCHAR(20)
)

-- Inserting into the temporary table the last name
-- and first name of all employees from WA

INSERT #employees_in_wa
SELECT lastname,firstname
FROM Employees
WHERE region = 'WA'

SELECT * FROM #employees_in_wa
GO
```

OUTPUT

```
(5 row(s) affected)

lastname                                 firstname
---------------------------------------- --------------------
Davolio                                  Nancy
Fuller                                   Andrew
Leverling                                Janet
Peacock                                  Margaret
Callahan                                 Laura

(5 row(s) affected)
```

- Executing a stored procedure that has a SELECT statement on it, and inserting this output into a table. Notice that this approach is similar to the first one; the only difference is that the SELECT statement is wrapped into a stored procedure. Listing 4.40 shows how the output of a stored procedure is inserted into a table.

EXAMPLE

Listing 4.40: Inserting the Output of a Stored Procedure into a Table

```
USE Northwind
GO

CREATE PROC get_uk_employees
```

Listing 4.40: continued

```
AS
SELECT lastname,firstname
FROM Employees
WHERE country = 'UK'
GO

CREATE TABLE #employees_in_uk (
lastname NVARCHAR(40),
firstname NVARCHAR(20)
)

-- Inserting into the temporary table the last name
-- and first name of all employees from UK

INSERT #employees_in_uk
EXEC get_uk_employees

SELECT * FROM #employees_in_uk
GO
```

OUTPUT

```
(4 row(s) affected)

lastname                                    firstname
------------------------------------------  --------------------
Buchanan                                    Steven
NewFamily                                   Michael
King                                        Robert
Dodsworth                                   Anne

(4 row(s) affected)
```

The DELETE Statement

You use DELETE to remove one or more rows permanently from a table. A DELETE statement may contain a WHERE clause to restrict the rows to be deleted. The basic syntax of DELETE is

```
DELETE Table_name WHERE condition
```

If WHERE is not used in the DELETE statement, all rows are removed from the table. Listing 4.41 shows how to delete specific rows from a table (using a WHERE clause).

EXAMPLE

Listing 4.41: Deleting Rows from a Table

```
USE Northwind

DELETE Orders
WHERE customerid IS NULL
GO
```

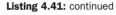

Listing 4.41: continued

OUTPUT

(1 row(s) affected)

The TRUNCATE statement is also used to remove permanently all rows from a table. However, it has some restrictions:

- The table cannot have foreign keys defined.

- TRUNCATE cannot contain a WHERE clause. Therefore, all rows in the table are removed.

- TRUNCATE reseeds the IDENTITY value of the table (if there is one).

TIP

TRUNCATE is faster than DELETE because SQL Server only logs the deallocation of pages, not the removal of each row (like it does when dealing with DELETE statements).

Listing 4.42 illustrates the use of the TRUNCATE statement to remove all rows from a table.

EXAMPLE

Listing 4.42: Using the TRUNCATE Statement to Delete All Rows from a Table

```
USE Northwind
GO

CREATE TABLE #shippers (
companyname NVARCHAR(20),
phone NVARCHAR(20)
)

INSERT #shippers
SELECT companyname,phone FROM Shippers

-- Using TRUNCATE to remove all rows from the #shippers table
TRUNCATE TABLE #shippers

SELECT * FROM #shippers
GO
```

OUTPUT

(5 row(s) affected)

```
companyname          phone
------------------   -------------------
```

(0 row(s) affected)

The UPDATE Statement

The UPDATE statement sets new values in existing rows of a specific table. UPDATE modifies information in just one table. Therefore, if you want to change data in some other table, use another UPDATE statement. The basic syntax of UPDATE is

```
UPDATE Table_name
SET column_1 = new_value,
column_2 = new value,
  .

  .

column_n = new_value
WHERE condition
```

The new value of a column can be either a constant or an expression that may or may not contain the previous value of the column.

A WHERE clause can be used to restrict the rows to be modified by the UPDATE statement.

Listing 4.43 shows an UPDATE statement that restricts the column to be modified with a WHERE clause. Also, the new value of one of the columns, companyname, is based in the old value (concatenating the word 'Express' to the old value).

EXAMPLE

Listing 4.43: Using the UPDATE Statement

```
USE Northwind

UPDATE Shippers
SET companyname = companyname + ' Express',
phone = '(305) 555 8888'
WHERE shipperid = 20
GO
```

OUTPUT

```
(1 row(s) affected)
```

Using an UPDATE statement, the new values of columns can be stored in local variables when updating a single row. This method is useful because you don't have to update the row first, and then use a SELECT statement to get the new values. The following is the basic syntax:

```
UPDATE table
SET @variable = column = value
```

Listing 4.44 indicates how to store the new value of a column in a local variable.

EXAMPLE

Listing 4.44: Storing in Variables the New Values of Columns When Updating a Single Row

```
USE Northwind

DECLARE @availableunits SMALLINT

UPDATE Products
SET @availableunits = unitsinstock = unitsinstock + 20
```

Listing 4.44: continued

```
WHERE productname = 'Chai'

SELECT @availableunits
GO
```

OUTPUT

```
(1 row(s) affected)


. . . . . . .
59

(1 row(s) affected)
```

The SELECT INTO Statement

SELECT INTO enables you to create a table on-the-fly and populate it using just one instruction. The new table is populated with the output of the SELECT statement. SELECT INTO can be used to create either permanent or temporary tables. Listing 4.45 shows the syntax of SELECT INTO.

EXAMPLE

Listing 4.45: Using SELECT INTO to Create and Populate Tables

```
USE Northwind

SELECT lastname, firstname
INTO #salesrep_employees
FROM employees
WHERE title = 'sales representative'

SELECT * FROM #salesrep_employees
GO
```

OUTPUT

```
(6 row(s) affected)

lastname               firstname
-------------------    ----------
Davolio                Nancy
Leverling              Janet
Peacock                Margaret
NewFamily              Michael
King                   Robert
Dodsworth              Anne

(6 row(s) affected)
```

Column aliases must be used for calculated columns. These aliases are the column names that SQL Server will use when creating the new table specified in SELECT INTO. For example, Listing 4.46 uses an alias for the first column, which is the result of the concatenation of two columns (firstname and lastname).

Listing 4.46: Using Column Aliases with SELECT INTO

USE Northwind

EXAMPLE

```
SELECT firstname + ' ' + lastname AS fullname, country
INTO #employeescountry
FROM Employees
ORDER BY fullname

SELECT * FROM #employeescountry
GO
```

OUTPUT

```
(9 row(s) affected)

fullname                         country
-------------------------------  ---------------
Andrew Fuller                    USA
Anne Dodsworth                   UK
Janet Leverling                  USA
Laura Callahan                   USA
Margaret Peacock                 USA
Michael Suyama                   UK
Nancy Davolio                    USA
Robert King                      UK
Steven Buchanan                  UK

(9 row(s) affected)
```

The IDENTITY function is used to generate a column with consecutive numbers when using SELECT INTO. Similar to the IDENTITY property, the IDENTITY function accepts three parameters: the data type, the seed (or first number), and the increment (the last two are the arguments of the IDENTITY property). Listing 4.47 demonstrates how the IDENTITY function is used in SELECT INTO statements.

Listing 4.47: Using the IDENTITY Function

USE Northwind

EXAMPLE

```
SELECT IDENTITY(INT,1,1) as companyid, companyname
INTO #italiancompanies
FROM Customers
WHERE country = 'Italy'

SELECT * FROM #italiancompanies
GO
```

Listing 4.47: continued

OUTPUT

```
(3 row(s) affected)

companyid    companyname
...........  ......................................
1            Franchi S.p.A.
2            Magazzini Alimentari Riuniti
3            Reggiani Caseifici

(3 row(s) affected)
```

In previous versions of SQL Server (7.0 and earlier), the SELECT INTO/ BULKCOPY database option had to be set to TRUE if you wanted to use SELECT INTO to create permanent tables. In SQL Server 2000, the SELECT INTO/ BULKCOPY and the TRUNC. LOG ON CHKPT. database options are no longer used. Now, SQL Server provides three recovery models (SIMPLE, BULK LOGGED, and FULL), and basically, SELECT INTO can be used with any of these models. For more information on recovery models, refer to Books Online.

What's Next?

You already know how to interact with single tables and extract data from them. In the next chapter, you will learn how to extract data from multiple tables through JOINs, the different type of JOINs, and how to combine the results of more than one query using the UNION operator.

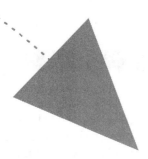

5

Querying Multiple Tables: JOINs

In previous chapters, you have been dealing with queries that involve just one table. Sometimes the data you need to manipulate is spread across more than one table and, in this case, these tables must be combined or joined to be able to retrieve all this data. Basically, a JOIN operation merges two or more tables into one result set.

The capability to link or join tables and generate one result set from the data stored in many tables is one of the most important characteristics of a relational database. Usually, tables are linked using foreign keys, and these foreign key columns are used in JOIN operations to combine tables and generate one result set. Notice that tables don't necessarily need to have a foreign key defined to be able to join them.

Additionally, not only can JOIN be used in SELECT statements, but also in modification operations, as UPDATE and DELETE. A DELETE operation can be based on information from more than one table if they are joined in the FROM clause. The same rule applies for UPDATE operations.

This chapter teaches you the following:

- How to use the ANSI SQL-92 JOIN syntax

- How the different types of joins (inner joins, outer joins, cross joins, and self joins) work, and the differences among them

- How to combine result sets from more than one query using the UNION operator

ANSI SQL-92 Syntax

In earlier versions of the SQL language (ANSI SQL-89), a JOIN operation was specified in the FROM clause and the WHERE clause. Specifically, the tables involved in the JOIN operation were specified in the FROM clause, and the JOIN conditions in the WHERE clause. For example, Listing 5.1 indicates how this old syntax is used to specify an inner join. (This type of join will be explained in the next section.) As you can see in this example, the two tables involved are listed in the FROM clause separated by a comma, and the columns that link these two tables are specified in the WHERE clause (the JOIN condition).

EXAMPLE

Listing 5.1: Using the ANSI SQL-89 Syntax in Inner Joins

```
USE Northwind

SELECT *
FROM Products, Categories
WHERE Products.categoryid = Categories.categoryid
GO
```

In regard to outer joins, the *= and =* operators were used in the WHERE clause to specify LEFT OUTER JOIN and RIGHT OUTER JOIN, respectively. This syntax appears in Listing 5.2, which performs a LEFT OUTER JOIN between Territories and Region.

EXAMPLE

Listing 5.2: Using the ANSI SQL-89 Syntax in Outer Joins

```
USE Northwind

SELECT *
FROM Territories, Region
WHERE territories.regionid *= region.regionid
GO
```

Listing 5.3 shows a slight variation of the query shown previously in Listing 5.2. Notice that the WHERE clause contains both the JOIN condition and an additional condition that forces SQL Server to show only rows in which regionid equals 1.

EXAMPLE

Listing 5.3: Using the ANSI SQL-89 OUTER JOIN Syntax Along with Conditions

```
USE Northwind

SELECT *
FROM Territories, Region
WHERE territories.regionid *= region.regionid
AND region.regionid = 1
GO
```

As you might have noticed, using the old ANSI SQL-89's JOIN syntax, SQL Server may interpret a query in an unexpected way, getting a totally different result set. This is because of the fact that SQL Server must evaluate JOIN conditions and restrictions of the query together, because both elements are specified in the WHERE clause. This issue was solved by the ANSI committee in the SQL-92 standard, which states that all elements of a JOIN operation (tables involved in the JOIN and conditions of the JOIN) are specified in the FROM clause, thus eliminating any ambiguity.

The ANSI SQL-92 standard introduced, among other things, five JOIN keywords: INNER JOIN, LEFT OUTER JOIN, RIGHT OUTER JOIN, FULL OUTER JOIN, and CROSS JOIN. These keywords are used to specify the type of join between two tables.

Listing 5.4 illustrates this new syntax for inner joins. Notice that this query is similar to the one shown in Listing 5.1, but this uses the new JOIN syntax.

EXAMPLE

Listing 5.4: Using the ANSI SQL-92 JOIN Syntax

```
USE Northwind

SELECT *
FROM Products INNER JOIN Categories
ON Products.categoryid = Categories.categoryid
GO
```

Through this new approach, SQL Server evaluates JOIN conditions first (which are specified in the FROM clause), and then restrictions of the query (specified in the WHERE clause). In particular, the order of processing of conditions in a join using the SQL ANSI-92 syntax is first, the conditions in the FROM clause are evaluated, then the WHERE clause, and finally, the HAVING clause, if there is one. This process is used by SQL Server to parse joins. However, SQL Server does not necessarily execute the FROM clause before the WHERE clause.

Listing 5.5 shows a JOIN operation using the SQL ANSI-92 syntax, along with a restriction in the WHERE clause.

EXAMPLE

Listing 5.5: Using Restrictions Along with a JOIN Operation Using the New Syntax

```
USE Northwind

SELECT *
FROM Territories LEFT OUTER JOIN Region
ON territories.regionid = region.regionid
WHERE region.regionid = 1
GO
```

The new JOIN syntax has a very powerful feature, which basically allows you to specify a condition of the query in the FROM clause along with the JOIN condition. This is useful in cases in which we want this condition to be evaluated before the JOIN operation, taking advantage of the order of processing of the query. Listing 5.6 shows a query similar to the one illustrated in Listing 5.5, but different in that because a condition is specified in the FROM clause, it is evaluated before the JOIN operation.

EXAMPLE

Listing 5.6: Using Restrictions in the FROM Clause

```
USE Northwind

SELECT *
FROM Territories LEFT OUTER JOIN Region
ON territories.regionid = region.regionid
AND region.regionid = 1
GO
```

Queries are easier to read using the new JOIN syntax because all components of the JOIN operation are specified in the FROM clause. Also, the conditions of the query are specified in the WHERE clause, unless you want the condition to be evaluated before the JOIN operation. In that case, the condition must be specified in the FROM clause, as shown in the previous listing.

Although SQL Server 2000 supports both JOIN syntaxes (ANSI SQL-89 and ANSI SQL-92), you should change all queries to the new ANSI SQL-92 syntax because, in future releases, the SQL Server development team might decide not to support the old syntax. Therefore, all applications you develop should use the new ANSI SQL-92 JOIN syntax to avoid incompatibility problems in future versions of SQL Server.

INNER JOIN

In general, a JOIN operation combines two or more tables, generating one result set from the information stored in such tables. These tables should have similar columns, commonly foreign keys, which are the ones used in JOIN operations to link tables. Also, as you might have noticed in previous examples, the columns involved in a JOIN condition don't need to have the same name.

An INNER JOIN operation between two tables returns all common rows in these two tables. Specifically, INNER JOIN evaluates the JOIN condition for each row in both tables and if this condition is met, the row is included in the result set. For example, if you want to retrieve information about products and the name of the supplier of each product, the Products table and the Suppliers table must be joined (through an INNER JOIN), thus generating a result set with all the information needed (products and suppliers). Listing 5.7 shows the query that retrieves each product and its supplier.

EXAMPLE

Listing 5.7: Using INNER JOIN to Retrieve Information from Two Tables

```
USE Northwind

SELECT productid, productname, companyname
FROM Products INNER JOIN Suppliers
ON Products.supplierid = Suppliers.supplierid
GO

-- Partial result
```

OUTPUT

```
productid productname                          companyname
--------- ----------------------------------- -----------------------------------
1         Chai                                Exotic Liquids
2         Chang                               Exotic Liquids
3         Aniseed Syrup                       Exotic Liquids
4         Chef Anton's Cajun Seasoning        New Orleans Cajun Delights
5         Chef Anton's Gumbo Mix              New Orleans Cajun Delights
6         Grandma's Boysenberry Spread        Grandma Kelly's Homestead
7         Uncle Bob's Organic Dried Pears     Grandma Kelly's Homestead
8.        Northwoods Cranberry Sauce          Grandma Kelly's Homestead
9         Mishi Kobe Niku                     Tokyo Traders
10        Ikura                               Tokyo Traders
11        Queso Cabrales                      Cooperativa de Quesos 'Las Cabras'
12        Queso Manchego La Pastora           Cooperativa de Quesos 'Las Cabras'
13        Konbu                               Mayumi's
14        Tofu                                Mayumi's
15        Genen Shouyu                        Mayumi's
```

Figure 5.1 shows a graphical representation of the INNER JOIN performed in Listing 5.7. In this figure, you can see how an INNER JOIN is processed: For every row in the first table, SQL Server goes through the second table trying to find a corresponding row based on the join column (supplierid in this case), and if a row matches, it is returned in the result set.

CAUTION

Be aware that columns with NULL values don't match any values, because NULL is not equal to anything. In particular, NULL is not equal to NULL.

TIP

To specify an INNER JOIN operation, you can use either JOIN or INNER JOIN (they're equivalent).

The columns specified in a JOIN condition don't necessarily need to have the same data type but, at least, they have to be compatible. Basically, compatible means one of the following two things:

- Both columns have the same data type.

- If the columns have different data types, the data type of one column can be implicitly converted to the data type of the other column.

```
SELECT productid, productname, companyname
FROM Products INNER JOIN Suppliers
ON Products.supplierid = Suppliers.supplierid
```

Products table

productid	productname	supplierid
4	Chef Anton's Cajun Seasoning	2
5	Chef Anton's Gumbo Mix	2
65	Louisiana Fiery Hot Pepper Sauce	2
66	Louisiana Hot Spice Okra	2
6	Grandma's Boysenberry Spread	3
7	Uncle Bob's Organic Dried Pears	3
8	Northwoods Cranberry Sauce	3
34	Sasquach Ale	16
35	Steeleye Stout	16
67	Laughing Lumberjack Lager	16
40	Boston Crab Meat	19
41	Jack's New England Clam Chowder	19

Suppliers table

supplierid	companyname
2	New Orleans Cajun Delights
3	Grandma Kelly's homestead
16	Bigfoot Breweries
19	New England Seafood Cannery

Result set

productid	productname	company name
4	Chef Anton's Cajun Seasoning	New Orleans Cajun Delights
5	Chef Anton's Gumbo Mix	New Orleans Cajun Delights
65	Louisiana Fiery Hot Pepper Sauce	New Orleans Cajun Delights
66	Louisiana Hot Spice Okra	New Orleans Cajun Delights
6	Grandma's Boysenberry Spread	Grandma Kelly's Homestead
7	Uncle Bob's Organic Dried Pears	Grandma Kelly's Homestead
8	Northwoods Cranberry Sauce	Grandma Kelly's Homestead
34	Sasquach Ale	Bigfoot Breweries
35	Steeleye Stout	Bigfoot Breweries
67	Laughing Lumberjack Lager	Bigfoot Breweries
40	Boston Crab Meat	New England Seafood Cannery
41	Jack's New England Clam Chowder	New England Seafood Cannery

Figure 5.1: *Processing INNER JOIN operations.*

For example, when two tables are joined and the JOIN condition has two columns with different data types, SQL Server tries to perform an implicit conversion; otherwise, CAST or CONVERT must be used to perform an explicit conversion. An example of this implicit conversion appears in Listing 5.8. Notice that the data types of the columns in the JOIN condition are different (VARCHAR and INT), thus SQL Server performs an implicit conversion to process the JOIN.

EXAMPLE

Listing 5.8: Performing an INNER JOIN with Columns of Different Data Types in the JOIN Condition

```
USE Northwind

CREATE TABLE Parents (
parentid INT IDENTITY(1,1) PRIMARY KEY,
fullname VARCHAR(50),
relationship VARCHAR(50),
employeeid VARCHAR(10))
GO
```

Listing 5.8: continued

```
SET SHOWPLAN_TEXT ON
GO

SELECT lastname, firstname, fullname
FROM employees JOIN Parents
ON employees.employeeid = parents.employeeid
GO

SET SHOWPLAN_TEXT OFF
GO

DROP TABLE Parents
GO
```

OUTPUT

```
-- Notice that a convert operation is performed in the last line of the
-- execution plan

StmtText
-----------------------------------------------

SELECT lastname, firstname, fullname
FROM employees JOIN Parents
ON employees.employeeid = parents.employeeid

(1 row(s) affected)

StmtText
-------------------------------------------------------------------
|--Nested Loops(Inner Join, OUTER REFERENCES:([Parents].[employeeid]))
  |--Clustered Index Scan(OBJECT:([Northwind].[dbo].[Parents].
        [PK__Parents__1F98B2C1]))
   |--Clustered Index Seek(OBJECT:([Northwind].[dbo].[Employees].
        [PK_Employees]),
        SEEK:([Employees].[EmployeeID]=Convert([Parents].[employeeid]))
        ORDERED FORWARD)

(3 row(s) affected)
```

The column list of a query that joins tables can reference any of the columns in any of these tables. There are many different ways to show columns in the result set of a JOIN operation. Be aware that when more than one table has a column with the same name, you must qualify the name of the column with the table's name—for example, `tablename.columnname`. If a column name doesn't have a duplicate in any of the other joined tables, it doesn't have to be qualified with the table name or alias. Listing 5.9 demonstrates how columns with the same name are included in the result set of a JOIN.

Listing 5.9: Qualifying the Name of Columns in the Column List

```
USE Northwind

-- Notice that both tables that are being joined contain the regionid column
-- (this is the only column that has to be fully qualified in the query)

SELECT Region.regionid, territorydescription, regiondescription
FROM Territories JOIN Region
ON Territories.regionid = Region.regionid
ORDER BY Region.regionid
GO

-- Partial result
```

```
regionid     territorydescription      regiondescription
----------   -----------------------   ------------------------
1            Westboro                  Eastern
1            Bedford                   Eastern
1            Georgetown                Eastern
1            Boston                    Eastern
1            Cambridge                 Eastern
1            Braintree                 Eastern
1            Providence                Eastern
1            Wilton                    Eastern
1            Morristown                Eastern
1            Edison                    Eastern
1            New York                  Eastern
1            New York                  Eastern
1            Mellvile                  Eastern
1            Fairport                  Eastern
```

If you want to reference all the columns in a table, this syntax can be used: tablename.*. If you specify only * in the column list, all columns from all tables involved in the query will be returned. These two approaches are shown in Listing 5.10.

Listing 5.10: Specifying All Columns from a Table in a Column List Using the * Keyword

```
USE Northwind

SELECT Territories.*
FROM Territories JOIN Region
ON Territories.regionid = Region.regionid

SELECT *
FROM Territories JOIN Region
ON Territories.regionid = Region.regionid
GO
```

OUTPUT

-- Partial results

territoryid	territorydescription	regionid
01581	Westboro	1
01730	Bedford	1
01833	Georgetown	1
02116	Boston	1
02139	Cambridge	1
02184	Braintree	1
02903	Providence	1
03049	Hollis	3
03801	Portsmouth	3
06897	Wilton	1
07960	Morristown	1
08837	Edison	1

TerritoryID	TerritoryDescription	RegionID	RegionID	RegionDescription
01581	Westboro	1	1	Eastern
01730	Bedford	1	1	Eastern
01833	Georgetown	1	1	Eastern
02116	Boston	1	1	Eastern
02139	Cambridge	1	1	Eastern
02184	Braintree	1	1	Eastern
02903	Providence	1	1	Eastern
03049	Hollis	3	3	Northern
03801	Portsmouth	3	3	Northern
06897	Wilton	1	1	Eastern
07960	Morristown	1	1	Eastern
08837	Edison	1	1	Eastern

Table aliases can be used when referencing tables in JOIN operations to make queries easier to read. However, make sure that if an alias is specified, every reference to the table uses the alias; otherwise (if the name of the table is used and an alias was specified), you will get a syntax error. Listing 5.11 illustrates the use of table aliases in JOIN operations.

EXAMPLE

Listing 5.11: Using Table Aliases in JOIN Operations

USE Northwind

-- Notice that the aliases of the tables are used
-- in the column list and in the JOIN condition

Listing 5.11: continued

```
SELECT P.productname, C.categoryname
FROM Products P JOIN Categories C
ON P.categoryid = C.categoryid
GO

-- Partial result
```

OUTPUT

```
productname                              categoryname
---------------------------------------- --------------
Chai                                     Beverages
Chang                                    Beverages
Aniseed Syrup                            Condiments
Chef Anton's Cajun Seasoning             Condiments
Chef Anton's Gumbo Mix                   Condiments
Grandma's Boysenberry Spread             Condiments
Uncle Bob's Organic Dried Pears          Produce
Northwoods Cranberry Sauce               Condiments
Mishi Kobe Niku                          Meat/Poultry
Ikura                                    Seafood
Queso Cabrales                           Dairy Products
Queso Manchego La Pastora                Dairy Products
```

TIP

In general, the performance of a JOIN operation can be improved if the columns involved in the JOIN condition are indexed.

A query can involve more than one JOIN operation; therefore, more than two tables can be joined in a query to generate one result set. In particular, to join more than two tables, specify two tables first, and then specify the remaining tables one by one along with the JOIN condition. As stated earlier, not all columns from all tables have to be specified in the column list; you just have to specify the ones you need.

For example, if you want to know all regions associated with employees in the Northwind database, you must retrieve the territory for each employee first, and then retrieve the region of each territory. This is accomplished by joining the Employees, Employeeterritories, Territories, and Region tables, as shown in Listing 5.12.

EXAMPLE

Listing 5.12: Joining More Than Two Tables

```
USE Northwind

SELECT firstname, lastname, territorydescription, regiondescription
FROM Employees E JOIN Employeeterritories ET
ON E.employeeid = ET.employeeid
JOIN Territories T
```

Listing 5.12: continued

```
ON ET.territoryid = T.territoryid
JOIN Region R
ON T.regionid = R.regionid
GO

-- Partial result
```

OUTPUT

firstname	lastname	territorydescription	regiondescription
Nancy	Davolio	Wilton	Eastern
Nancy	Davolio	Neward	Eastern
Andrew	Fuller	Westboro	Eastern
Andrew	Fuller	Bedford	Eastern
Andrew	Fuller	Georgetown	Eastern
Andrew	Fuller	Boston	Eastern
Andrew	Fuller	Cambridge	Eastern
Andrew	Fuller	Braintree	Eastern
Andrew	Fuller	Louisville	Eastern
Janet	Leverling	Atlanta	Southern
Janet	Leverling	Savannah	Southern
Janet	Leverling	Orlando	Southern
Janet	Leverling	Tampa	Southern
Margaret	Peacock	Rockville	Eastern
Margaret	Peacock	Greensboro	Eastern
Margaret	Peacock	Cary	Eastern
Steven	Buchanan	Providence	Eastern
Steven	Buchanan	Morristown	Eastern
Steven	Buchanan	Edison	Eastern
Steven	Buchanan	New York	Eastern
Steven	Buchanan	New York	Eastern
Steven	Buchanan	Mellvile	Eastern
Steven	Buchanan	Fairport	Eastern

Internally, a JOIN that involves more than three tables works this way:

1. A result set is generated joining the first two tables.

2. This result set is joined with the third table and so on.

3. The columns specified in the result set are the ones shown in the
   result set of the JOIN operation.

A JOIN operation can also be used in UPDATE and DELETE statements.
Basically, this allows us to update or delete rows based on information
stored in many tables. For example, suppose that you have to increase the
price of all products of a certain supplier. In this case, you have to update
the Products table and join it with the Suppliers table because the name of

the supplier is stored in the Suppliers table and not in the Products table. Listing 5.13 increases by 5 dollars the unitprice of all products of the 'Exotic Liquids' supplier.

EXAMPLE

Listing 5.13: Using JOIN in UPDATE Statements

```
USE Northwind

SELECT productid, unitprice, companyname
FROM Products P JOIN Suppliers S
ON P.supplierid = S.supplierid
WHERE companyname = 'Exotic Liquids'

UPDATE Products
SET unitprice = unitprice + 5
FROM Products P JOIN Suppliers S
ON P.supplierid = S.supplierid
WHERE companyname = 'Exotic Liquids'

SELECT productid, unitprice, companyname
FROM Products P JOIN Suppliers S
ON P.supplierid = S.supplierid
WHERE companyname = 'Exotic Liquids'
GO
```

OUTPUT

```
productid   unitprice            companyname
---------   ------------------   ----------------------------------------
1             18.0000            Exotic Liquids
2             19.0000            Exotic Liquids
3             10.0000            Exotic Liquids

(3 row(s) affected)


(3 row(s) affected)

productid   unitprice            companyname
---------   ------------------   ----------------------------------------
1             23.0000            Exotic Liquids
2             24.0000            Exotic Liquids
3             15.0000            Exotic Liquids

(3 row(s) affected)
```

A JOIN operation can also be used in a DELETE statement in the same way as it is used in an UPDATE statement.

OUTER JOINs

An OUTER JOIN operation returns all rows that match the JOIN condition, and it may also return some of the rows that don't match, depending on the type of OUTER JOIN used. There are three types of OUTER JOIN: RIGHT OUTER JOIN, LEFT OUTER JOIN, and FULL OUTER JOIN.

In INNER JOIN, the order of the tables in the query doesn't matter, whereas in OUTER JOIN, the order of the tables in the query is important.

TIP

A LEFT OUTER JOIN can be translated into a RIGHT OUTER JOIN, and vice versa if you change the order of the tables in the join.

An OUTER JOIN can be seen as the result of the union of an INNER JOIN and all unmatched rows in

- The left table in the case of LEFT OUTER JOIN

- The right table in the case of RIGHT OUTER JOIN

- Or both in the case of FULL OUTER JOIN

RIGHT OUTER JOIN

A RIGHT OUTER JOIN operation returns all matching rows in both tables, and also rows in the right table that don't have a corresponding row in the left table. In the result set of a RIGHT OUTER JOIN operation, the rows that don't have a corresponding row in the left table contain a NULL value in all columns of the left table.

For example, imagine that you want to retrieve all regions with their respective territories and also the regions that don't have a corresponding territory. To solve this problem, a RIGHT OUTER JOIN can be performed between Territories and Region, thus preserving all rows in the Region table that don't have a corresponding row in the Territories table. This query is shown in Listing 5.14, which also shows a query that gets regions that don't have territories.

Notice that the last three rows of the result set are rows from the Region table that don't have a corresponding row in the Territories table. This is the reason they have a NULL value in the first two columns (which belong to the Territories table).

EXAMPLE

Listing 5.14: Using RIGHT OUTER JOIN

USE Northwind

INSERT Region VALUES (5, 'Europe')

Listing 5.14: continued

```
INSERT Region VALUES (6,'Latin America')
INSERT Region VALUES (7,'Asia')

-- Get regions with their respective territories
SELECT territoryid, territorydescription, R.regionid, regiondescription
FROM Territories T RIGHT OUTER JOIN Region R
ON T.regionid = R.regionid

-- Get regions that don't have territories
SELECT territoryid, territorydescription, R.regionid, regiondescription
FROM Territories T RIGHT OUTER JOIN Region R
ON T.regionid = R.regionid
WHERE territoryid IS NULL
GO
```

OUTPUT

territoryid	territorydescription	regionid	regiondescription
01581	Westboro	1	Eastern
01730	Bedford	1	Eastern
01833	Georgetown	1	Eastern
02116	Boston	1	Eastern
02139	Cambridge	1	Eastern
02184	Braintree	1	Eastern
02903	Providence	1	Eastern
06897	Wilton	1	Eastern
07960	Morristown	1	Eastern
08837	Edison	1	Eastern
10019	New York	1	Eastern
10038	New York	1	Eastern
11747	Mellvile	1	Eastern
14450	Fairport	1	Eastern
19713	Neward	1	Eastern
20852	Rockville	1	Eastern
27403	Greensboro	1	Eastern
27511	Cary	1	Eastern
40222	Louisville	1	Eastern
60179	Hoffman Estates	2	Western
60601	Chicago	2	Western
80202	Denver	2	Western
80909	Colorado Springs	2	Western
85014	Phoenix	2	Western
85251	Scottsdale	2	Western
90405	Santa Monica	2	Western
94025	Menlo Park	2	Western
94105	San Francisco	2	Western
95008	Campbell	2	Western
95054	Santa Clara	2	Western

Listing 5.14: continued

```
95060              Santa Cruz          2    Western
98004              Bellevue            2    Western
98052              Redmond             2    Western
98104              Seattle             2    Western
03049              Hollis              3    Northern
03801              Portsmouth          3    Northern
19428              Philadelphia        3    Northern
44122              Beachwood           3    Northern
45839              Findlay             3    Northern
48075              Southfield          3    Northern
48084              Troy                3    Northern
48304              Bloomfield Hills    3    Northern
53404              Racine              3    Northern
55113              Roseville           3    Northern
55439              Minneapolis         3    Northern
29202              Columbia            4    Southern
30346              Atlanta             4    Southern
31406              Savannah            4    Southern
32859              Orlando             4    Southern
33607              Tampa               4    Southern
72716              Bentonville         4    Southern
75234              Dallas              4    Southern
78759              Austin              4    Southern
NULL               NULL                5    Europe
NULL               NULL                6    Latin America
NULL               NULL                7    Asia
```

```
(56 row(s) affected)
```

```
territoryid   territorydescription   regionid   regiondescription
------------  ---------------------  ---------  -----------------
NULL          NULL                   5          Europe
NULL          NULL                   6          Latin America
NULL          NULL                   7          Asia
```

```
(3 row(s) affected)
```

Figure 5.2 shows a graphical representation of the RIGHT OUTER JOIN performed in Listing 5.14 (this figure doesn't contain all data stored in the original tables). In this figure, you can see the rows of the right table (Region) that don't have a corresponding row in the left table (Territories).

TIP

RIGHT OUTER JOIN is equivalent to RIGHT JOIN, so either one of them can be used to specify a RIGHT OUTER JOIN operation.

```
SELECT  territoryid, territorydescription, R.regionid, regiondescription
FROM Territories T RIGHT OUTER JOIN Region R
ON T.regionid = R.regionid
```

Territories table

TerritoryID	TerritoryDescription	RegionID
29202	Columbia	4
30346	Atlanta	4
31406	Savannah	4
32859	Orlando	4
33607	Tampa	4
72718	Bentonville	4
75234	Dallas	4
78759	Austin	4

Region table

RegionID	RegionDescription
4	Southern
5	Europe
6	Latin America
7	Asia

4

Result set

territoryid	territorydescription	regionid	regiondescription
29202	Columbia	4	Southern
30346	Altanta	4	Southern
31406	Savannah	4	Southern
32859	Orlando	4	Southern
33607	Tampa	4	Southern
72716	Bentonville	4	Southern
75234	Dallas	4	Southern
78759	Autsin	4	Southern
NULL	NULL	5	Europe
NULL	NULL	6	Latin America
NULL	NULL	7	Asia

Figure 5.2: *Processing RIGHT OUTER JOIN operations.*

Listing 5.15 shows a query that uses RIGHT JOIN instead of RIGHT OUTER JOIN. Notice that this query is equivalent to the one shown in Listing 5.14.

EXAMPLE

Listing 5.15: Using RIGHT JOIN to Perform a RIGHT OUTER JOIN Operation

```
USE Northwind

SELECT territoryid, territorydescription, R.regionid, regiondescription
FROM Territories T RIGHT JOIN Region R
ON T.regionid = R.regionid
GO
```

LEFT OUTER JOIN

In addition to the rows that match the JOIN condition, a LEFT OUTER JOIN returns the rows from the left table that don't have a corresponding row in the right table.

In a LEFT OUTER JOIN operation, the unmatched rows of the result set have NULL values in the columns of the right table.

Basically, a LEFT OUTER JOIN can be translated into a RIGHT OUTER JOIN if the order of the tables is changed (the right table becomes the left and vice versa). This is why the order of the tables in an OUTER JOIN operation is important.

Listing 5.16 shows a LEFT OUTER JOIN operation between Region and Territories. This query is similar to the one shown in Listing 5.14, but the order of the tables was changed and also the type of JOIN, thus generating the same result set seen earlier in Listing 5.14.

Listing 5.16: Using LEFT OUTER JOIN

EXAMPLE

```
USE Northwind

SELECT territoryid, territorydescription, R.regionid, regiondescription
FROM Region R LEFT OUTER JOIN Territories T
ON R.regionid = T.regionid
GO
```

OUTPUT

territoryid	territorydescription	regionid	regiondescription
01581	Westboro	1	Eastern
01730	Bedford	1	Eastern
01833	Georgetown	1	Eastern
02116	Boston	1	Eastern
02139	Cambridge	1	Eastern
02184	Braintree	1	Eastern
02903	Providence	1	Eastern
06897	Wilton	1	Eastern
07960	Morristown	1	Eastern
08837	Edison	1	Eastern
10019	New York	1	Eastern
10038	New York	1	Eastern
11747	Mellvile	1	Eastern
14450	Fairport	1	Eastern
19713	Neward	1	Eastern
20852	Rockville	1	Eastern
27403	Greensboro	1	Eastern
27511	Cary	1	Eastern
40222	Louisville	1	Eastern
60179	Hoffman Estates	2	Western
60601	Chicago	2	Western
80202	Denver	2	Western
80909	Colorado Springs	2	Western
85014	Phoenix	2	Western
85251	Scottsdale	2	Western
90405	Santa Monica	2	Western
94025	Menlo Park	2	Western
94105	San Francisco	2	Western
95008	Campbell	2	Western
95054	Santa Clara	2	Western
95060	Santa Cruz	2	Western
98004	Bellevue	2	Western
98052	Redmond	2	Western

Listing 5.16: continued

98104	Seattle	2	Western
03049	Hollis	3	Northern
03801	Portsmouth	3	Northern
19428	Philadelphia	3	Northern
44122	Beachwood	3	Northern
45839	Findlay	3	Northern
48075	Southfield	3	Northern
48084	Troy	3	Northern
48304	Bloomfield Hills	3	Northern
53404	Racine	3	Northern
55113	Roseville	3	Northern
55439	Minneapolis	3	Northern
29202	Columbia	4	Southern
30346	Atlanta	4	Southern
31406	Savannah	4	Southern
32859	Orlando	4	Southern
33607	Tampa	4	Southern
72716	Bentonville	4	Southern
75234	Dallas	4	Southern
78759	Austin	4	Southern
NULL	NULL	5	Europe
NULL	NULL	6	Latin America
NULL	NULL	7	Asia

(56 row(s) affected)

TIP

LEFT OUTER JOIN and LEFT JOIN are interchangeable, so either one of them can be used to specify a LEFT OUTER JOIN operation.

FULL OUTER JOIN

A FULL OUTER JOIN operation returns

- All rows that match the JOIN condition.

- Rows from the left table that don't have a corresponding row in the right table. These rows have NULL values in the columns of the right table.

- Rows from the right table that don't have a corresponding row in the left table. These rows have NULL values in the columns of the left table.

Therefore, the result set of a FULL OUTER JOIN operation is like the intersection of the result sets generated by LEFT OUTER JOIN and RIGHT OUTER JOIN.

For example, imagine that you want to know which suppliers are located in a country where a customer is located. This is solved by performing an INNER JOIN between Suppliers and Customers on their country column. If you also want to know the suppliers that are located in a country where there are no customers, and vice versa (customers that are located in countries where there are no suppliers), you would have to perform a FULL OUTER JOIN between Suppliers and Customers on their country column. Listing 5.17 shows this FULL OUTER JOIN operation. Notice that NULL values in the result set indicate that either there is no corresponding customer for a certain supplier in a country or, on the contrary, there is no corresponding supplier for a specific customer in a country.

EXAMPLE

Listing 5.17: Using FULL OUTER JOIN

```
USE Northwind

SELECT S.companyname as suppliername, S.country as supcountry,
       C.companyname as customername, C.country as cuscountry
FROM Suppliers S FULL OUTER JOIN Customers C
ON S.country = C.country
GO

-- Partial results
```

OUTPUT

suppliername	supcountry	customername	cuscountry
Heli Süßwaren GmbH & Co. KG	Germany	Alfreds Futterkiste	Germany
NULL	NULL	Antonio Moreno Taquería	Mexico
Exotic Liquids	UK	Around the Horn	UK
Specialty Biscuits, Ltd.	UK	Around the Horn	UK
PB Knäckebröd AB	Sweden	Berglunds snabbköp	Sweden
Svensk Sjöföda AB	Sweden	Berglunds snabbköp	Sweden
NULL	NULL	Cactus Comidas para llevar	Argentina
NULL	NULL	Centro comercial Moctezuma	Mexico
NULL	NULL	Chop-suey Chinese	Switzerland
NULL	NULL	Tortuga Restaurante	Mexico
Refrescos Americanas LTDA	Brazil	Wellington Importadora	Brazil
New England Seafood Cannery	USA	White Clover Markets	USA
New Orleans Cajun Delights	USA	White Clover Markets	USA
Grandma Kelly's Homestead	USA	White Clover Markets	USA
Bigfoot Breweries	USA	White Clover Markets	USA
Karkki Oy	Finland	Wilman Kala	Finland
NULL	NULL	Wolski Zajazd	Poland
Zaanse Snoepfabriek	Netherlands	NULL	NULL
Leka Trading	Singapore	NULL	NULL
Pavlova, Ltd.	Australia	NULL	NULL
G'day, Mate	Australia	NULL	NULL
Tokyo Traders	Japan	NULL	NULL
Mayumi's	Japan	NULL	NULL

TIP

FULL JOIN is equivalent to FULL OUTER JOIN; they can be used interchangeably.

CROSS JOINs

A CROSS JOIN generates a Cartesian product of the tables specified in the JOIN operation. In other words, the result set of a CROSS JOIN operation contains every possible combination of rows of the tables involved in the query. In particular, if there are n rows in the first table and m rows in the second table, the result set will have n*m rows.

These are the two possible ways to specify a CROSS JOIN operation:

```
SELECT * FROM Table1, Table2
SELECT * FROM Table1 CROSS JOIN Table2
```

Listing 5.18 shows an example that generates a Cartesian product using CROSS JOIN. The tables involved in the CROSS JOIN have 7 and 8 rows, respectively, and the result set has 56 rows (7*8).

EXAMPLE

Listing 5.18: Using CROSS JOIN to Generate a Cartesian Product

```
USE Northwind

SELECT *
FROM Region

SELECT categoryid, categoryname
FROM Categories

SELECT regionid, regiondescription, categoryid, categoryname
FROM region CROSS JOIN categories
GO
```

OUTPUT

```
RegionID    RegionDescription
----------- --------------------------------------------------------
1           Eastern
2           Western
3           Northern
4           Southern
5           Europe
6           Latin America
7           Asia

(7 row(s) affected)

categoryid  categoryname
```

Listing 5.18: continued

```
---------- ---------------
1          Beverages
2          Condiments
3          Confections
4          Dairy Products
5          Grains/Cereals
6          Meat/Poultry
7          Produce
8          Seafood
```

(8 row(s) affected)

regionid	regiondescription	categoryid	categoryname
1	Eastern	1	Beverages
1	Eastern	2	Condiments
1	Eastern	3	Confections
1	Eastern	4	Dairy Products
1	Eastern	5	Grains/Cereals
1	Eastern	6	Meat/Poultry
1	Eastern	7	Produce
1	Eastern	8	Seafood
2	Western	1	Beverages
2	Western	2	Condiments
2	Western	3	Confections
2	Western	4	Dairy Products
2	Western	5	Grains/Cereals
2	Western	6	Meat/Poultry
2	Western	7	Produce
2	Western	8	Seafood
3	Northern	1	Beverages
3	Northern	2	Condiments
3	Northern	3	Confections
3	Northern	4	Dairy Products
3	Northern	5	Grains/Cereals
3	Northern	6	Meat/Poultry
3	Northern	7	Produce
3	Northern	8	Seafood
4	Southern	1	Beverages
4	Southern	2	Condiments
4	Southern	3	Confections
4	Southern	4	Dairy Products
4	Southern	5	Grains/Cereals
4	Southern	6	Meat/Poultry
4	Southern	7	Produce
4	Southern	8	Seafood
5	Europe	1	Beverages

Listing 5.18: continued

5	Europe	2	Condiments
5	Europe	3	Confections
5	Europe	4	Dairy Products
5	Europe	5	Grains/Cereals
5	Europe	6	Meat/Poultry
5	Europe	7	Produce
5	Europe	8	Seafood
6	Latin America	1	Beverages
6	Latin America	2	Condiments
6	Latin America	3	Confections
6	Latin America	4	Dairy Products
6	Latin America	5	Grains/Cereals
6	Latin America	6	Meat/Poultry
6	Latin America	7	Produce
6	Latin America	8	Seafood
7	Asia	1	Beverages
7	Asia	2	Condiments
7	Asia	3	Confections
7	Asia	4	Dairy Products
7	Asia	5	Grains/Cereals
7	Asia	6	Meat/Poultry
7	Asia	7	Produce
7	Asia	8	Seafood

(56 row(s) affected)

A JOIN condition is not needed when using CROSS JOIN. However, a JOIN condition may be specified in the WHERE clause, and in this case, the CROSS JOIN operation behaves like an INNER JOIN.

Listing 5.19 shows two equivalent queries. The first one performs a CROSS JOIN and has a join condition, and the second one is an INNER JOIN operation. Both queries produce the same result set.

EXAMPLE

Listing 5.19: Using CROSS JOIN with a JOIN Condition

```
USE Northwind

SELECT territoryid, territorydescription, R.regionid, regiondescription
FROM Territories T CROSS JOIN Region R
WHERE T.regionid = R.regionid
AND R.regiondescription = 'Southern'

SELECT territoryid, territorydescription, R.regionid, regiondescription
FROM Territories T INNER JOIN Region R
ON T.regionid = R.regionid
AND R.regiondescription = 'Southern'
GO
```

Listing 5.19: continued

OUTPUT

territoryid	territorydescription	regionid	regiondescription
29202	Columbia	4	Southern
30346	Atlanta	4	Southern
31406	Savannah	4	Southern
32859	Orlando	4	Southern
33607	Tampa	4	Southern
72716	Bentonville	4	Southern
75234	Dallas	4	Southern
78759	Austin	4	Southern

(8 row(s) affected)

territoryid	territorydescription	regionid	regiondescription
29202	Columbia	4	Southern
30346	Atlanta	4	Southern
31406	Savannah	4	Southern
32859	Orlando	4	Southern
33607	Tampa	4	Southern
72716	Bentonville	4	Southern
75234	Dallas	4	Southern
78759	Austin	4	Southern

(8 row(s) affected)

Usually, the purpose of a CROSS JOIN operation is to generate data for testing purposes because you can generate a big result set from small tables. Furthermore, similar to the other JOIN operations, a CROSS JOIN can involve more than two tables. In particular, the syntax used to perform a CROSS JOIN that involves three tables is

```
SELECT *
FROM Table1 CROSS JOIN Table2
CROSS JOIN Table3
```

CAUTION

Be aware that a FULL OUTER JOIN operation is different from a CROSS JOIN operation. Usually, a CROSS JOIN returns more rows because it returns every combination of rows in both tables.

Self Joins

A self join is a special type of join, in which a certain table is joined to itself. Basically, in a self join, two virtual copies of the same table are merged, generating a result set based on information stored in this table.

Generally, self joins are used to represent hierarchies in a table. For example, the Employees table has a column called reportsto, which has a foreign key pointing to the employeeid column in this table. Therefore, if you want to retrieve the manager of any employee, the Employees table must be joined to itself.

Listing 5.20 demonstrates how to extract information from this hierarchy represented in the Employees table, using a self join. Specifically, the query performs a self join to retrieve the name of Anne Dodsworth's manager (her manager is also an employee).

EXAMPLE

Listing 5.20: Using a Self Join to Retrieve Hierarchy Information

```
USE Northwind

SELECT E1.employeeid, E1.firstname, E1.lastname,
       E2.firstname as managerfirstname, E2.lastname as managerlastname
FROM Employees E1 JOIN Employees E2
ON E1.reportsto = E2.employeeid
WHERE E1.lastname = 'Dodsworth'
AND E1.firstname = 'Anne'
GO
```

OUTPUT

employeeid	firstname	lastname	managerfirstname	managerlastname
9	Anne	Dodsworth	Steven	Buchanan

(1 row(s) affected)

CAUTION

Notice that table aliases must be used when working with self joins to differentiate between the two copies of the table.

The UNION Operator

UNION is an operator used to combine two or more SELECT statements and generate one result set. These SELECT statements must meet some conditions, such as the following:

- They must have the same number of columns. You can work around this restriction if you use constants in the SELECT statement with fewer columns, as shown in Listing 5.21.

EXAMPLE

Listing 5.21: Using a UNION Operator with Constants in the SELECT Statements

```
-- A constant has to be used in the second SELECT statement
-- because Shippers doesn't have a contactname column

USE Northwind
```

Listing 5.21: continued

```
SELECT companyname, contactname FROM Suppliers WHERE country = 'USA'
UNION
SELECT companyname, 'N/A' FROM Shippers
GO
```

```
companyname                              contactname
---------------------------------------- ----------------------------
New Orleans Cajun Delights               Shelley Burke
Grandma Kelly's Homestead                Regina Murphy
Bigfoot Breweries                        Cheryl Saylor
New England Seafood Cannery              Robb Merchant
Speedy Express                           N/A
United Package                           N/A
Federal Shipping                         N/A
```

(7 row(s) affected)

- The column's data types must be compatible. In other words, the data types must be equivalent, can be converted implicitly, or must be explicitly converted using either CAST or CONVERT. In the previous example (Listing 5.21), the companyname column of both tables has the same data type (NVARCHAR), and the other column (contactname) is compatible with the 'N/A' constant.

The column names of the result set in a UNION operation are taken from the column names of the first SELECT statement of UNION. By default, UNION removes all duplicates from the result set. However, if you want to keep duplicates in the result set, use the ALL keyword when performing a UNION operation. Listing 5.22 shows the difference between using UNION and UNION ALL.

Listing 5.22: Using the ALL Option in UNION Operators

```
USE Northwind

SELECT city, country FROM Customers WHERE country = 'UK'
UNION
SELECT city, country FROM Suppliers WHERE country = 'UK'

SELECT city, country FROM Customers WHERE country = 'UK'
UNION ALL
SELECT city, country FROM Suppliers WHERE country = 'UK'
GO
```

```
city            country
--------------- ---------------
Cowes           UK
London          UK
Manchester      UK
```

Listing 5.22: continued

```
(3 row(s) affected)

city            country
--------------- ---------------
London          UK
London          UK
London          UK
London          UK
Cowes           UK
London          UK
London          UK
London          UK
Manchester      UK

(9 row(s) affected)
```

The result set of a UNION operation can be ordered, but be aware that only one ORDER BY clause can be specified when using UNION, and it must be specified in the last SELECT statement. Listing 5.23 demonstrates how to use ORDER BY in a UNION operation.

EXAMPLE

Listing 5.23: Using an ORDER BY in a UNION Operation

```
USE Northwind

SELECT city, country FROM Customers WHERE country = 'UK'
UNION ALL
SELECT city, country FROM Suppliers WHERE country = 'UK'
ORDER BY city
GO
```

OUTPUT

```
city            country
--------------- ---------------
Cowes           UK
London          UK
London          UK
London          UK
London          UK
London          UK
London          UK
London          UK
Manchester      UK

(9 row(s) affected)
```

When using UNION, only the first SELECT statement can have an INTO keyword, which allows you to create a table on-the-fly with the result set of the UNION operation. Listing 5.24 creates a temporary table that stores the full name of employees and suppliers.

EXAMPLE

Listing 5.24: Creating a Table On-the-Fly with the Result of a UNION

```
USE Northwind

SELECT firstname + ' ' + lastname as fullname
       INTO #employeesandsuppliers
FROM Employees
UNION
SELECT contactname FROM Suppliers WHERE country = 'usa'
ORDER BY fullname

SELECT * FROM #employeesandsuppliers
GO
(13 row(s) affected)
```

OUTPUT

```
fullname
-------------------------------
Andrew Fuller
Anne Dodsworth
Cheryl Saylor
Janet Leverling
Laura Callahan
Margaret Peacock
Michael Suyama
Nancy Davolio
Regina Murphy
Robb Merchant
Robert King
Shelley Burke
Steven Buchanan

(13 row(s) affected)
```

What's Next?

You have been studying different ways to access data in databases. Until now, performance hasn't been an issue. However, as you might have experienced, databases are constantly growing, and sometimes this can hurt the performance of queries and applications that access the database. This performance degradation can turn out to be a very serious problem, because we want to be able to issue queries against the database and get the result set right away.

In general, indexes can be used to improve the performance of queries. The main characteristic of indexes is that they speed up data retrieval, even when working with big tables. In the next chapter, you go through all the steps and guidelines needed to create useful indexes that can improve the performance of queries and applications.

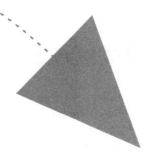

Optimizing Access to Data: Indexes

Perhaps the main reason to install a database system is to be able to search efficiently for data. Commercial systems use vast amounts of data, and users have come to expect a reasonably short response time when searching for information irrespective of how the search is carried out or the criteria used in the search.

Many other programming books and technical papers have already covered searching and sorting algorithms, so it is not the purpose of this book to introduce any new theories on this subject.

To produce results in the quickest and most efficient way, SQL Server must have fast access to the data. It does this by allowing every operation to have optimized access to any resource that it might need to use.

This chapter teaches you

- How to use indexes in everyday operations
- How SQL Server 2000 implements indexes
- How SQL Server 2000 accesses data from tables
- The differences between clustered and nonclustered indexes
- How to create, modify, and delete indexes
- How SQL Server 2000 accesses data stored as a clustered index
- How SQL Server 2000 accesses data stored as a heap
- How to create an index to cover a query
- What index fragmentation is and how to manage it
- How to use the Index Tuning Wizard

Introduction to Indexes

You are used to working with indexes in daily life. Many books have a *table of contents*. This table of contents shows the book's outline, and in this outline, you can see on which page every topic starts. You can read just the table of contents and search for a subject that interests you. After you find an interesting topic, you can quickly go straight to the correct page number.

In this example, the book is organized according to the table of contents. The table of contents is not ordered alphabetically but it is ordered by its outline. If you want to search for a specific topic, you have to search the table of contents sequentially from the beginning to the end.

Every entry in the table of contents can be considered a key to the index, whereas the page number is no more than a pointer to the physical page where the topic starts.

Most books have an *index* at the end. The index is just a collection of keywords that are organized alphabetically. These keywords represent different topics: For every keyword the index shows the page or pages where this topic is covered. Because these keywords are alphabetically ordered, it is easy to search for a specific topic without having to read the index sequentially.

An index key in SQL Server is like a keyword in the index of a book, and the page number of the index in the book is the pointer to the physical page where the topic is covered.

Perhaps it is difficult to visualize a book as a table in a database, but a book is information that is stored in a sequence of physical pages, which is not very different from the way SQL Server 2000 stores data, as you will see later in this chapter.

Let's consider another familiar example. Every telephone company maintains a database of customers. This database has, at least, the family name, first name, address, and telephone number of every customer.

Applications for new telephone lines are stored in order, but the telephone directory shows entries in alphabetical order. If you know the customer's family name, you can easily search for their telephone number by browsing the telephone directory. To help us carry out this search, every page in the telephone directory is labeled with either the first or the last entry on the page, so you can read the labels and search for the entry you want to find.

To search for a specific entry in the directory, you follow a process that could be called a binary search. SQL Server uses binary search when it scans an index searching for specific information.

Having the data ordered by more than one attribute—that is, surname, first name, and address as in this case—is what you do when you use a composite index. In this case, the combination of surname, first name, and address is the index key. Telephone directory data is physically written in this order, and this is what you call a clustered index in SQL Server. You will look at clustered indexes later in this chapter.

Because you often need to search for businesses offering a specific kind of service, some companies offer special yellow pages books to help people search for specific businesses. The yellow pages order telephone entries by activity. Entries are ordered alphabetically for every activity.

The yellow pages show a typical example of a nonclustered index in SQL Server.

Searching for customers living in a specific street or area will mean having to sequentially read the standard telephone book and extract, one by one, every entry that matches the searching criteria. Just as in the preceding case, when SQL Server doesn't have a suitable index to execute a query, the only choice available is to read the entire table first and then filter out every entry that matches the searching criteria.

Benefits of Indexes

SQL Server queries can benefit from the existence of suitable indexes in the following cases:

- Exact-match queries—When searching for rows with specific key values. These are queries with a WHERE clause to restrict the query to specific values for every key column.

- Range queries—When solving queries that search for a range of values in a column.

- Filtering for values in the foreign key to solve a join operation—When using a JOIN predicate to search for rows in a table based on keys from a second table.

- Hash and merge join operations—In some cases, having an index can speed up the execution of a JOIN algorithm, because the data is exactly in the order that the JOIN algorithm uses.

- Covering a query—To avoid a full-table scan, when a narrow index contains all the required data.

- Avoiding duplicates—To check for the existence of suitable indexes in an INSERT or UPDATE operation in an attempt to avoid duplicates.

- Sorting data—To produce an ordered output when using the ORDER BY clause.

In the following sections, you will see one example of each of these cases.

For every example, you can see the estimated execution plan before the query is executed. We do not provide the result of the queries because we want you to pay attention to the execution plan, not to the final result of the query.

If a query plan shows that it accesses a table with a table scan, SQL Server must read the entire table to execute the query. This is not very efficient on big tables because SQL Server must read every data page.

If the query plan shows Index Scan as a table access method, SQL Server must read the entire index to solve the query. If the index is a clustered index, this is equivalent to a table scan. If the index is a nonclustered index, this strategy is usually more efficient than a table scan because the clustered index key usually is shorter than the row in the table. Therefore, the number of index pages to read is smaller than the number of data pages. We will discuss clustered and nonclustered indexes later in this chapter, in the "Clustered Indexes" and the "Nonclustered Indexes" sections.

If you see in the query plan the words Index Seek, this usually represents good news for you, because SQL Server can traverse the index searching for the required rows, following a binary search strategy, without entirely reading the index.

NOTE

To show the estimated execution plan without running the query, you can use the menu Query-Display Estimated Execution Time, the Ctrl+L keyboard shortcut, or click the Display Estimated Execution Time icon in the toolbar.

Using Indexes on Point Queries

If you execute a query that searches for an exact match between fields and specific values, call this query a Point Query. SQL Server might find it efficient to use an index to search for these values. Listing 6.1 shows an example of this type of query, where you search for the product identified by ProductID = 10.

Figure 6.1 shows the query plan that SQL Server uses to execute the query of Listing 6.1. The query plan shows Clustered Index Seek, which means that SQL Server uses the index to seek for the requested value, without reading the entire table or the entire index.

Listing 6.1: SQL Server Uses an Index to Solve a Point Query

```
USE Northwind
GO
```

EXAMPLE

Listing 6.1: continued
```
SELECT *
FROM Northwind.dbo.Products
WHERE ProductID = 10
```

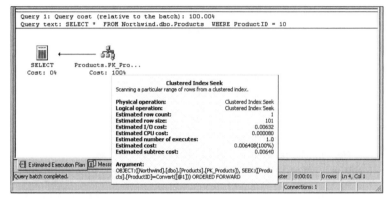

Figure 6.1: *SQL Server can use an index to solve point queries, as in Listing 6.1.*

NOTE

Readers can visit the book's Web site (www.sqlserverbyexample.com) to download a more complex and bigger database to practice with more complex scripts that can show differences on timing when they use indexes.

Using Indexes in Range Queries

A range query searches for data using a condition that specifies minimum and maximum values, such as products with a stock level lower than the minimum essential level (UnitsInStock BETWEEN 0 AND 25). Another example of a range query is a query that uses the LIKE operator, such as searching for customers living in a specific urban area (Telephone LIKE '321%'). The filtering condition uses a range of possible values (Telephone >= '321' AND Telephone < '322').

Listing 6.2 shows different cases of range queries using comparison operators, the BETWEEN operator, and the LIKE operator. Figure 6.2 shows the execution plan for a range query using the BETWEEN operator. You can identify that SQL Server uses an index on the PostalCode column because the query plan shows the Index Seek icon.

Execute each query from Listing 6.2 individually to study the estimated query execution plan for every query.

NOTE

You can select which part of a script to execute by marking the required block of statements in SQL Query Analyzer with the mouse or the keyboard—in the same way you mark a block using any text editor.

EXAMPLE

Listing 6.2: SQL Server Can Use Indexes When the Query Is Defined for a Range of Values

```
USE Northwind
GO

-- Combining > or >= with < or <=

SELECT *
FROM Northwind.dbo.Products
WHERE UnitPrice > 10
AND UnitPrice <= 20

-- Using the BETWEEN operator

SELECT *
FROM Northwind.dbo.Customers
WHERE PostalCode BETWEEN 'WX1' AND 'WXZZZZZ'

-- Which is equivalent to:

SELECT *
FROM Northwind.dbo.Customers
WHERE PostalCode >= 'WX1'
AND PostalCode <= 'WXZZZZZ'

-- Using the LIKE Operator with trailing wildcards

SELECT *
FROM Northwind.dbo.Customers
WHERE CompanyName LIKE 'Hungry%'

-- Which is equivalent to:

SELECT *
FROM Northwind.dbo.Customers
WHERE CompanyName >= 'Hungry'
AND CompanyName < 'HungrZ'
```

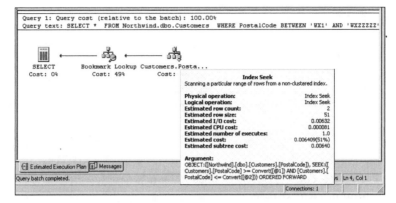

```
Query 1: Query cost (relative to the batch): 100.00%
Query text: SELECT * FROM Northwind.dbo.Customers  WHERE PostalCode BETWEEN 'WX1' AND 'WXZZZZZ'
```

SELECT   Bookmark Lookup Customers.Posta...
Cost: 0%   Cost: 49%   Cost:

Index Seek
Scanning a particular range of rows from a non-clustered index.

Physical operation:	Index Seek
Logical operation:	Index Seek
Estimated row count:	2
Estimated row size:	51
Estimated I/O cost:	0.00632
Estimated CPU cost:	0.000081
Estimated number of executes:	1.0
Estimated cost:	0.006409(51%)
Estimated subtree cost:	0.00640

Argument:
OBJECT:([Northwind].[dbo].[Customers].[PostalCode]), SEEK:([
Customers].[PostalCode] >= Convert([@1]) AND [Customers].[
PostalCode] <= Convert([@2])) ORDERED FORWARD

Figure 6.2: *SQL Server can use an index to solve queries restricted to a range of values, as in Listing 6.2.*

Using Indexes to Search for Foreign Key Values to Solve Join Operations

An example of this case is when SQL Server has to execute a join to retrieve data from two tables, such as searching for orders containing products from a specific category.

NOTE

You can learn more about join algorithms in Chapter 5.

Listing 6.3 shows the query to solve this example where, to produce the required information, the query must join the Products and Order Details tables. You can see in Figure 6.3 that SQL Server uses an index seek on the Products table to solve this join.

EXAMPLE

Listing 6.3: SQL Server Uses an Index to Execute This Query That Joins Two Tables

```
USE Northwind
GO

SELECT Products.ProductID,
[Order Details].UnitPrice,
[Order details].Quantity
FROM Products
JOIN [Order Details]
ON Products.ProductID = [Order Details].ProductID
WHERE Products.CategoryID = 1
```

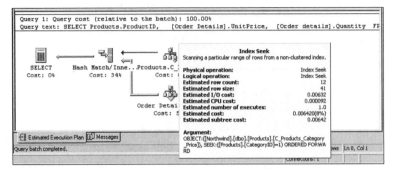

Figure 6.3: *SQL Server uses an index to solve queries with a* JOIN *predicate and a* WHERE *clause.*

Using Indexes to Speed Up the Execution of Hash and Merge JOIN Operations

If the columns used to join two tables have an index on every table that participates in the JOIN operation, SQL Server can use the merge join algorithm. For example, if you join the Categories table and the Products table by the CategoryID column, and there is an index on the CategoryID column in the Categories table and another index on the CategoryID column in the Products table, SQL Server can very efficiently use a merge join to connect both tables.

To execute the hash join algorithm, you do not need to have an index on the joining columns, but having an index on the joining columns can speed up the process as well.

NOTE

You can learn more about join algorithms in Chapter 5.

Listing 6.4 shows a query where you join the Products table and the Order Details table by using the ProductID column. The ProductID column has an index defined in the Products table and the Order Details table; this is why SQL Server solves the query with an index scan on every table plus a hash join operation. Figure 6.4 shows the estimated execution plan for this query.

Listing 6.4: SQL Server Can Use Indexes to Join Tables

EXAMPLE

```
USE Northwind
GO

SELECT Products.ProductID,
[Order Details].UnitPrice,
[Order details].Quantity
```

Listing 6.4: continued
```
FROM Products
JOIN [Order Details]
ON Products.ProductID = [Order Details].ProductID
```

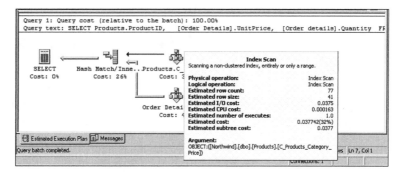

Figure 6.4: SQL Server uses indexes to help in the hash-match/Inner join operation.

Using Indexes That Cover a Query

In some cases, you can find that an index contains all the information required to execute a query. For example, if you want to produce a list of customers by name and you had an index on name, just reading the index SQL Server provides is enough information to produce the required results.

In these cases, the index covers the query, and reading the index is more efficient than reading the table because, usually, an index key is shorter than a table row.

NOTE

Later in this chapter, in the "Covered Queries and Index Intersection" section, covered indexes are discussed in detail.

Listing 6.5 shows a query that can be executed using just an index defined on the CategoryID column of the Products table. Figure 6.5 shows that SQL Server uses an index scan on the CategoryID index to solve this query.

EXAMPLE

Listing 6.5: SQL Server Can Use an Index to Avoid Access to Data Pages
```
USE Northwind
GO

SELECT DISTINCT CategoryID
FROM Products
```

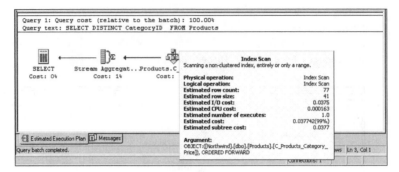

Figure 6.5: SQL Server uses an index to solve a query with no access required to data pages.

Using an Index to Enforce Uniqueness

Every time you try to insert a new value in a column with a PRIMARY KEY or UNIQUE CONSTRAINT, SQL Server must check to see whether the new value already exists. To speed up this process, SQL Server uses the index created during the CONSTRAINT creation.

NOTE

Constraints are covered in Chapter 7.

Listing 6.6 inserts a new row in the Categories table. This table has a unique index on the CategoryID column because this column has a FOREIGN KEY CONSTRAINT defined. Figure 6.6 shows that SQL Server uses the index on the CategoryID column to solve the clustered index insert operation.

EXAMPLE

Listing 6.6: SQL Server Uses Unique Indexes to Check for Duplicate Values in INSERT and UPDATE Operations

```
USE Northwind
GO

-- Execute this instruction first

SET IDENTITY_INSERT Categories ON
GO

-- Retrieve the Estimated Execution Plan of the following query

INSERT Categories (CategoryID, CategoryName, Description)
VALUES (9, 'Liquors', 'Whiskies, Brandies and other Spirits')
GO
```

Listing 6.6: continued

```
-- Execute this instruction at the end

SET IDENTITY_INSERT Categories OFF
GO
```

Query 1: Query cost (relative to the batch): 100.00%
Query text: INSERT Categories (CategoryID, CategoryName, Description) VALUES (9, 'Liquors', 'Whi

| | Clustered Index Insert/Insert | |
| | Insert rows in a clustered index. | |

INSERT	Clustered In	Physical operation:	Clustered Index Insert
Cost: 0%	Cost: 10	Logical operation:	Insert
		Estimated row count:	1
		Estimated row size:	4
		Estimated I/O cost:	0.0108
		Estimated CPU cost:	0.000001
		Estimated number of executes:	1.0
		Estimated cost:	0.010847(100%)
		Estimated subtree cost:	0.0108

Argument:
OBJECT:([Northwind].[dbo].[Categories].[PK_Categories]), SET:([Cate
gories].[CategoryID]=RaiseIfNull(setidentity([@1], 2041058307, 6, N
ULL)), [Categories].[CategoryName]=RaiseIfNull([Expr1001]), [Catego
ries].[Description]=[Expr1002], [Categories].[Picture]=NULL), DEFINE:
([Expr1005]=setideInsert

Estimated Execution Plan   Messages

Query batch completed.   0:00:00   0 rows   Ln 3, Col 1

Connections: 1

Figure 6.6: *SQL Server uses an index to guarantee uniqueness in* INSERT *and* UPDATE *operations.*

Using Indexes to Help Produce Ordered Output

This is the more obvious use of indexes. If SQL Server can retrieve the data in order, it will not need to reorder the data before it can display it.

Using the query from Listing 6.7 you can retrieve the ProductName and UnitPrice for the entire products table, ordering the result by the ProductName column. SQL Server uses an index on ProductName to solve the query, as you can see in Figure 6.7, because in this way it can retrieve the data already in ProductName order.

Listing 6.7: SQL Server Can Use Indexes to Produce an Ordered Output

```
USE Northwind
GO


SELECT ProductName, UnitPrice
FROM Products
ORDER BY ProductName ASC
```

EXAMPLE

If none of the indexes available matches the ordering criteria, SQL Server must execute a SORT process to order the final result set.

Listing 6.8 shows a similar example as in Listing 6.7, but in this case we order by UnitPrice. Because the UnitPrice column is not indexed, SQL Server must execute the SORT process, as shown in Figure 6.8.

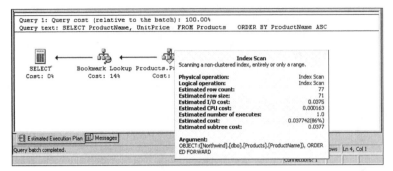

```
Query 1: Query cost (relative to the batch): 100.00%
Query text: SELECT ProductName, UnitPrice  FROM Products    ORDER BY ProductName ASC
```

```
    SELECT        Bookmark Lookup  Products.P    Index Scan
                                                 Scanning a non-clustered index, entirely or only a range.
    Cost: 0%        Cost: 14%       Cost:
                                                 Physical operation:                      Index Scan
                                                 Logical operation:                       Index Scan
                                                 Estimated row count:                             77
                                                 Estimated row size:                              71
                                                 Estimated I/O cost:                          0.0375
                                                 Estimated CPU cost:                       0.000163
                                                 Estimated number of executes:                  1.0
                                                 Estimated cost:                       0.037742(86%)
                                                 Estimated subtree cost:                      0.0377

 Estimated Execution Plan   Messages
Query batch completed.                           Argument:
                                                 OBJECT:([Northwind].[dbo].[Products].[ProductName]), ORDER
                                                 ED FORWARD                                    ws  Ln 4, Col 1
```

Figure 6.7: *SQL Server can use indexes when sorting data is required.*

EXAMPLE

Listing 6.8: SQL Server Must Execute a SORT Process If None of the Indexes Available Matches the Ordering Criteria

```
USE Northwind
GO

SELECT ProductName, UnitPrice
FROM Products
ORDER BY UnitPrice ASC
```

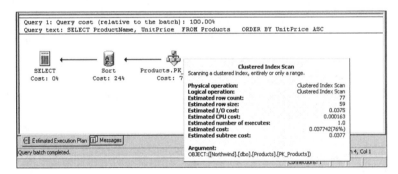

```
Query 1: Query cost (relative to the batch): 100.00%
Query text: SELECT ProductName, UnitPrice  FROM Products    ORDER BY UnitPrice ASC
```

```
    SELECT          Sort        Products.PK_    Clustered Index Scan
                                                Scanning a clustered index, entirely or only a range.
    Cost: 0%      Cost: 24%      Cost: 7
                                                Physical operation:              Clustered Index Scan
                                                Logical operation:               Clustered Index Scan
                                                Estimated row count:                             77
                                                Estimated row size:                              59
                                                Estimated I/O cost:                          0.0375
                                                Estimated CPU cost:                       0.000163
                                                Estimated number of executes:                  1.0
                                                Estimated cost:                       0.037742(76%)
                                                Estimated subtree cost:                      0.0377

 Estimated Execution Plan   Messages
Query batch completed.                          Argument:
                                                OBJECT:([Northwind].[dbo].[Products].[PK_Products])    n 4, Col 1
```

Figure 6.8: *SQL uses a SORT step to order data when no suitable index exists.*

How to Create Indexes

To create an index on a table, you have to select on which columns to build the index, and then use the CREATE INDEX statement. As an example, to create the index called ndx_Customers_City on the City field of the Customers table, you must execute the statement of Listing 6.9.

EXAMPLE

Listing 6.9: Creating an Index Is Easy Using the CREATE INDEX Statement

```
USE Northwind
GO

CREATE INDEX ndx_Customers_City
ON Customers(City)
```

You can use Enterprise Manager to create indexes on tables using the Manage Indexes form. To open the Manage Indexes form, you must display the list of tables in a database, select the table in which you want to create the index, right-click with the mouse on the table name, or choose Action, All Tasks, Manage Indexes. Figure 6.9 shows the Manage Indexes form.

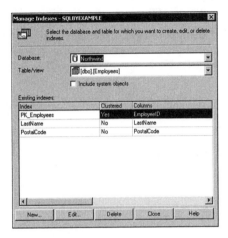

Figure 6.9: *Getting information on indexes available for every table or view is easy using the Manage Indexes form.*

You can select the database and the table in which to create the index by using the Database and Table/view drop-down list boxes.

To create an index, you can click the New command button, and the Create New Index form will appear. Figure 6.10 shows the Create New Index form.

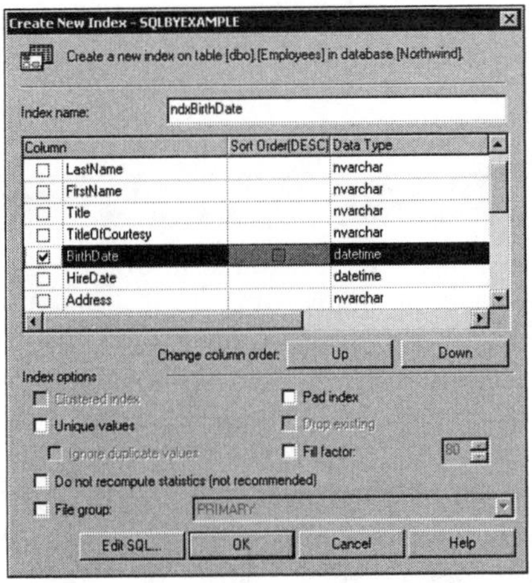

Figure 6.10: *Creating indexes is easy using the Create New Index form.*

Every index must have a name, and the name must be unique for the table or view where the index is defined.

Below the index name, you can see the list of columns you can make part of the index. Clicking the check boxes on the left of the column name, you can specify which columns to include in the index. You also can select whether the column must be included in ascending or descending order.

You can change the order of the columns in the index by using the Up and Down buttons.

CAUTION

The order of columns in an index is important: An index created on the (CompanyName, Phone) columns, as in Listing 6.10, can be useful to search for telephone numbers of a certain company; however, an index on (Phone, CompanyName) could be useful to search for the company where a specific telephone number is installed.

EXAMPLE

Listing 6.10: You Can Create an Index on More Than One Column Using the CREATE INDEX Statement

```
USE Northwind
GO

CREATE INDEX ndx_Customers_Company_Phone
ON Customers(CompanyName, Phone)

CREATE INDEX ndx_Customers_Phone_Company
ON Customers(Phone, CompanyName)
```

After the index is created, nothing special happens. Our data still looks the same. However, having indexes gives SQL Query Optimizer more ways to optimize a query—and it will use them as necessary.

Later in this chapter, in the "Types of Indexes" and "Index Maintenance" sections, you will learn about more options that you can use to create different type of indexes.

How SQL Server 2000 Stores Data

SQL Server stores the data of every database in one or more data files. These files are stored directly on the hard disk and are treated like other operating system files; however, SQL Server locks them as soon as it opens a database.

It is inside the data files that SQL Server stores tables and indexes, as well as a definition of every object in the database. Properties of objects are stored in the database, too. Every database is almost self contained, so it can be easily moved to another server if required.

Accessing the hard disk every time a user wants to retrieve some information, such as a product's price, is inefficient. To read information from disk, the hard disk heads must physically move to access specific information stored in a specific sector and track of the hard disk. The movement of heads on a hard disk can be a slow process and can be carried out just a few times per second; however, after the hard disk heads are in position, they can read the disk and access data very quickly.

Hard disks are designed to move blocks of data efficiently, not short sequences of bytes. SQL Server 2000 reads data in 8KB-page blocks, providing faster access to the data than reading individual fields or rows.

Every data page belongs to an individual table or index. Every table or index has a collection of pages that it uses to store rows of data. Every row in a table must be contained in a single page, and because the page contains some information required for internal SQL Server management, the maximum row size is 8,060 bytes.

If a table contains BLOB fields (Binary Large Objects such as image, text, or ntext), these fields are stored in a separate collection of pages. That's why the limit of 8,060 bytes/row doesn't affect the BLOB fields.

Figure 6.11 shows the data page structure with the following sections:

- Page Header, where SQL Server stores information to help the management of this page. This section has 96 bytes.

- Data block, where rows are stored. This section is limited to 8,060 bytes.

- Row offset, where SQL Server stores 2 bytes per row slot, as a pointer to the position where the row starts inside the page.

Data pages, index pages, and text/image pages have the same general structure. The page header identifies the type of data stored in the page and the data block structure is different for every type of page but, as a rule, the general structure is the same.

SQL Server has other types of pages, which can be used in general allocation pages. They are used to keep track of space used by every object and to keep control of unused space in every file. Because these general allocation pages are defined as bitmaps, they provide very fast access to the information they hold. The study of these pages is outside the scope of this book, but you can read about them in Books Online.

Because reading page by page is not very efficient, SQL Server arranges pages in groups of eight contiguous pages. This group of eight contiguous pages is called an *extent*, and SQL Server tries to read and write data extent by extent if possible. The allocation pages mentioned in the preceding paragraph track extents as a unit of allocation.

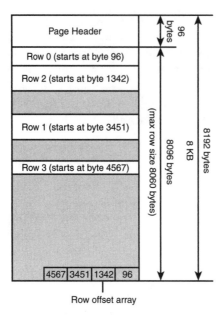

Figure 6.11: *This is the structure of a data page.*

SQL Server tries to access the hard disk one extent at a time, if possible, reading 64KB per extent. In addition, because reading sequentially from a hard disk is always faster than reading randomly, SQL Server tries whenever possible to optimize hard-disk access by reading several extents in sequence.

A mixed extent can contain data pages from different objects, but a uniform extent contains data from only one object. The first eight pages of any object can be held in mixed extents, but as soon as the object needs more than eight pages, SQL Server allocates uniform extents for it.

The preceding paragraph has explained how SQL Server stores and retrieves data. However, if you want to retrieve only a few bytes of data, why does SQL Server read 8KB or 64KB of data?

SQL Server keeps data pages in a reserved space in RAM as a buffer, or data cache. Access to RAM is much faster than access to a hard disk; so, keeping information in RAM provides a boost to performance to any database application. Every time a process needs to access any data, it searches RAM to see whether the data pages are already being held in cache. If the pages are not already in RAM, the process must request the copy of the data pages from disk to RAM before trying to do any operation with them. If the data page is modified by the process, the page will be marked as a *dirty page* because it does not contain the same information as the copy available in the disk, and it will be copied to the disk by a separate process.

How SQL Server 2000 Modifies Data

To guarantee consistency and recoverability of the information, SQL Server considers every data modification as part of a transaction. It will record transaction information, and every modification made as part of every transaction, in a transaction log. In other words, SQL Server first records how the data will be modified, and then it modifies the data. The logical process could be explained as follows:

1. A data modification is requested.

2. SQL Server creates a query plan to execute the data modification request.

3. SQL Server starts a transaction and records it in the transaction log.

4. SQL Server writes every operation to apply to the data in the transaction log before modifying the data.

5. After the operations are registered in the transaction log, the affected data is modified in cache, and the pages are marked as dirty. These changes are provisional. They will be permanent only if the transaction completes successfully.

6. SQL Server applies steps 4 and 5 for every individual operation in the transaction.

7. If every operation was successful, SQL Server records a transaction commit in the transaction log, and the changes are considered permanent.

8. If any operation in this transaction failed, SQL Server requests a rollback and will register in the transaction log the operations required to roll back all the changes applied to the modified data pages. The transaction is marked as rolled back in the transaction log.

We will cover transactions in Chapter 13, "Maintaining Data Consistency: Transactions and Locks," but as demonstrated in the preceding points, a transaction is a unit of work that must be completely committed or completely rolled back.

Index Enhancements in SQL Server 2000

SQL Server 2000 provides some important index enhancements over previous versions:

- It is possible to create indexes in views. This feature can speed up the process of repetitive queries using aggregate functions or multiple joins. This topic is covered in the section "Indexed Views," later in this chapter.

- It is possible to create indexes on computed columns, providing faster retrieval and sorting for data calculated dynamically. This topic is covered in the "Indexes on Computed Columns" section, later in this chapter.

- You can define the index on ascending or descending order. If you have a composite index, every field can be ordered in ascending or descending order independently. Composite indexes are covered in the "Clustered Indexes" and "Nonclustered Indexes" sections, later in this chapter.

- It is possible to use the Tempdb database for index creation, providing better performance if Tempdb is stored in a different physical disk subsystem.

- The index creation process can be executed in parallel, providing a faster execution than previous versions.

Accessing Data Without Indexes: Table Scan

As explained before, table data is stored in pages, and pages are grouped in extents. Special pages called *IAM (Index Allocation Map)* keep information about which extents are used by a particular table.

Information related to table definition is stored in different system tables:

- The name of the table, as well as the owner, creation date, and other general information, is stored in the sysobjects system table. The sysobjects table has a field called ID, which provides a unique object identification number for every object stored in a database. The ID field is used to relate this object to extra information in other systems' tables. It is possible to retrieve the table ID calling the OBJECT_ID system function.

- Column definitions are stored in the syscolumns system table.

- UNIQUE, PRIMARY KEY, and FOREIGN KEY constraints are treated as objects, which is why there is an entry in the sysobjects system table to identify them.

- Other constraints, such as CHECK and DEFAULT constraints, are identified in sysobjects, too, but their definition is stored in the syscomments table.

- The sysindexes table stores information about indexes' definitions. Every index is identified in the sysindexes table by its name, its table ID, and a special value unique to every index on the same table, called indid, with values from 0 to 255.

The sysindexes system table stores important information about how to start reading actual data or index keys. Every table has at least one entry in the sysindexes table.

If a table doesn't have a clustered index, it is stored as a heap, because the rows are not in any specific order. In this case, the table itself is defined in the sysindexes table as a row with indid = 0. The allocation map of a table or index is stored in special pages, called the Index Allocation Map (IAM), and sysindexes stores the address of the first IAM page of a specific table or index in the FirstIAM field.

IAM pages are special SQL Server pages that contain a sequence of bits, which is why they are called bitmaps. Every bit indicates whether the correspondent extent in the file uses the page.

If SQL Server needs to retrieve data from a table that doesn't have any clustered index defined, it uses the IAM pages to select which pages belong to the table and reads the pages in sequence to retrieve the information.

Because the IAM pages reflect the physical order of the data pages, the reading process can be quite efficient. However, using indexes can usually provide better performance than table scans.

Types of Indexes

SQL Server can create two general types of indexes:

- Regular SQL Server indexes, which are created by Transact-SQL commands and maintained automatically by SQL Server. Query Optimizer uses these indexes to speed the execution of queries.

- Full-text indexes, which are created by system-stored procedures, managed by the Microsoft Search Service, and accessed by specific Transact-SQL extended commands. Query Optimizer doesn't use full-text indexes automatically to optimize the execution of queries.

Full-text indexes are used by specific Transact-SQL functions. This type of index is out of the scope of this book, but you can get information about them in Books Online.

This chapter covers in detail the regular SQL Server indexes because of their importance in query optimization.

The information of the index is stored in pages in a similar way as the data pages. Index pages are organized in a binary tree to speed up searching operations. These trees have three main sections:

- Root node—The root node is the page at the top of the tree, the beginning of any search operation. This page contains one entry per every page in the next level of the index.

Figure 6.12 shows the root node and its relationship with pages in the next level. Every entry in the root node contains the first key of one page of the next level and the physical address of that page. This physical address is a combination of the data file number and the page number.

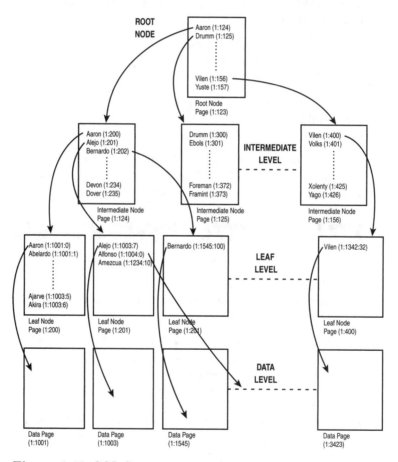

Figure 6.12: *SQL Server stores indexes in pages organized in a binary tree structure.*

Every index has a root node. If the table is so small that it is possible to store all the index entries in a single page, the index will have only one page—the root node.

- Leaf level—The base of an index is a collection of pages that contain one entry per every row in the table. The actual composition of this level depends on the type of index, as you will see later. The entries in the leaf level are in order.

  Every index has a leaf level.

- Nonleaf level—If the root node doesn't have enough space to store one entry per every page in the leaf level, it is necessary to create more pages, arranged in intermediate levels to maintain the link between the root node and the leaf level. These intermediate pages form the nonleaf level of the index.

  Not every index has a nonleaf level.

SQL Server tables can be organized in two ways:

- As a heap, where data is stored without any specific order.

- As a clustered index, where data is stored in order according to the order of specific key fields.

In a clustered index, the actual data pages are the leaf level of the index, because the data is already in order.

Clustered Indexes

As explained before with the telephone directory example, SQL Server can create clustered indexes, ordering the actual data using the selected key columns as ordering criteria.

Figure 6.13 shows the schema of a clustered index. You can see in the schema that the leaf level of the index is the actual data. Because the data is physically in order, there is no need for an extra layer with ordered key values plus pointers to the physical rows.

Because a clustered index physically orders the actual data, it is not possible to create more than one clustered index per table.

When you create a clustered index, perhaps the keys of the index are not unique in the table. If you created a clustered nonunique index, SQL Server creates an extra hidden-integer field to uniquely identify every physical row.

CAUTION

As you will see in Chapter 7, when you create a PRIMARY KEY, SQL Server creates a CLUSTERED INDEX by default, unless you specify NONCLUSTERED in the PRIMARY KEY definition. Thus, creating a PRIMARY KEY with the default settings prevents you from creating a new clustered index.

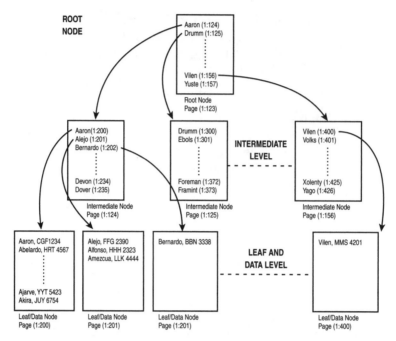

Figure 6.13: *A clustered index has a leaf level and a root node, plus more nonleaf levels if required.*

CREATING AND DROPPING CLUSTERED INDEXES

As Listing 6.11 shows, to create a clustered index you must specify CLUSTERED in the CREATE INDEX statement.

EXAMPLE

Listing 6.11: You Must Specify the CLUSTERED Keyword to Create a Clustered Index

```
USE Northwind
GO

IF OBJECT_ID('OrderDetails') IS NOT NULL
DROP TABLE OrderDetails
GO

-- Create a new table with the same structure and data
-- as the Order Details table

SELECT *
INTO OrderDetails
FROM [Order Details]

-- Create a Clustered index on the new table

CREATE CLUSTERED INDEX C_ORDER_DETAILS_ORDER_PRODUCT
ON OrderDetails (OrderID, ProductID)
```

To drop a CLUSTERED INDEX, you have to execute a DROP INDEX statement, as in Listing 6.12. Note that you must qualify the index name with the table name, because index names are not unique in the database.

EXAMPLE

Listing 6.12: You Must Execute the DROP INDEX Statement to Remove an Index from a Table

```
USE Northwind
GO

DROP INDEX OrderDetails.C_ORDER_DETAILS_ORDER_PRODUCT
```

> ### NOTE
>
> If you did not execute the code from Listing 6.11 and you try to execute the code from Listing 6.12, you will get an error message because the OrderDetails table does not exist.

When you drop a clustered index, the leaf level is not removed; otherwise, the data itself would be removed. Only the root node and the nonleaf levels will be deallocated.

> ### CAUTION
>
> You cannot specify the CLUSTERED keyword in the DROP INDEX statement.

Specify the UNIQUE keyword to declare a CLUSTERED INDEX as unique, as you can see in Listing 6.13.

EXAMPLE

Listing 6.13: You Must Specify the UNIQUE Keyword to Create a Unique Clustered Index

```
USE Northwind
GO

CREATE UNIQUE CLUSTERED INDEX UC_ORDER_DETAILS_ORDER_PRODUCT
ON OrderDetails (OrderID, ProductID)
```

> ### NOTE
>
> If you did not execute the code from Listing 6.11 and you try to execute the code from Listing 6.13, you will get an error message, because the OrderDetails table does not exist.

In SQL Server 2000, every column of the key in an index can be sorted using ascending or descending order. Listing 6.14 shows an example of this new feature.

EXAMPLE

Listing 6.14: You Can Specify Descending or Ascending Order for Every Column in the Index Key

```
USE Northwind
GO

CREATE INDEX C_Products_Category_Price
ON Products (CategoryID ASC, UnitPrice DESC)
```

ACCESSING DATA THROUGH CLUSTERED INDEXES

If a table is stored as a clustered index and the Query Optimizer decides to use the clustered index to return the result, SQL Server can access data in that table in different ways:

- As a Clustered Index Scan if the query doesn't restrict the data to be returned.

- As a Clustered Index Seek when the query is restricted to a certain number of rows.

ACCESSING DATA THROUGH A CLUSTERED INDEX SCAN   When a Clustered Index Scan is required, it is not guaranteed that the data will be returned in order, because SQL Server could use the information stored in the IAM pages to access the data more efficiently than navigating the index. If you need results in order, you must specify an ORDER BY clause in the query. This is the case of the example of Figure 6.14.

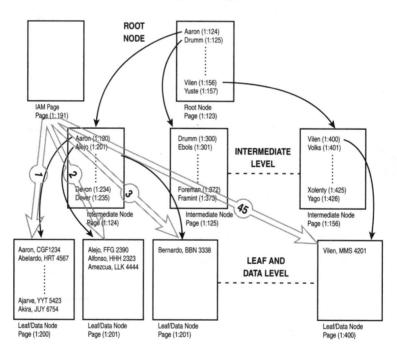

Figure 6.14: *SQL Server uses a Clustered Index Scan to execute unrestricted queries.*

USING A CLUSTERED INDEX SEEK TO EXECUTE POINT QUERIES   SQL Server can use a Clustered Index Seek to retrieve individual rows. Figure 6.15 shows an example.

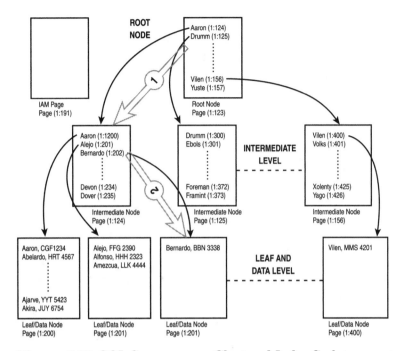

Figure 6.15: *SQL Server uses a Clustered Index Seek to execute restricted queries.*

In this example, SQL Server navigates the index from the root node to the leaf level, applying a binary search until reaching the required data.

USING A CLUSTERED INDEX SEEK TO EXECUTE QUERIES WITH A RANGE SEARCH   Perhaps a more interesting use of a clustered index is to execute queries restricted to a range of values. Figure 6.16 shows an example of a range search.

In this example, SQL Server navigates the index from the root node to the leaf level, searching for the lower limit of the range, and then continues reading from the leaf level until it reaches the upper limit of the range.

Nonclustered Indexes

The leaf level of a nonclustered index contains one entry for every row in the table. Each entry in the index contains the key columns and a pointer to identify the row in the table where this index entry points.

As explained earlier in this chapter, if the table doesn't have a clustered index, the pointer included on every entry of the nonclustered index is a binary value. This binary value is a combination of the file number, page number, and row slot number where the original row is stored. In this way, every entry in the index is connected to the physical location of the row. If a row changes its physical location, the index pointer must be modified. This process can produce some overhead on SQL Server.

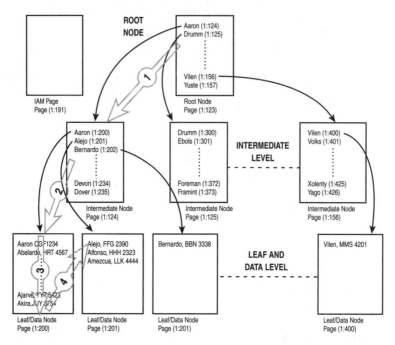

Figure 6.16: *SQL Server uses a Clustered Index Seek to execute queries that contain a range search.*

If the table has a clustered index, the index entries don't point to the physical location of the rows. In this case, the pointer is the clustered key of the corresponding row. You will see later in this chapter how to access data using a nonclustered index when the data is stored as a clustered index.

CREATING AND DROPPING NONCLUSTERED INDEXES

You can specify the keyword NONCLUSTERED to create a nonclustered index using the CREATE INDEX statement. This is the default option. Listing 6.15 shows how to create a NONCLUSTERED index.

Listing 6.15: You Can Specify the NONCLUSTERED Keyword to Create a Nonclustered Index

```
USE Northwind
GO

CREATE NONCLUSTERED INDEX C_ORDER_DETAILS_PRODUCT
ON [Order Details] (ProductID)
```

EXAMPLE

To drop a NONCLUSTERED INDEX, you have to execute a DROP INDEX statement, as in Listing 6.16.

EXAMPLE

Listing 6.16: You Must Execute the DROP INDEX Statement to Remove an Index from a Table

```
USE Northwind
GO

DROP INDEX [Order Details].C_ORDER_DETAILS_PRODUCT
```

When you drop a nonclustered index, the complete index is removed, including the leaf level, the root node, and the nonleaf levels.

CAUTION

You cannot specify the NONCLUSTERED keyword in the DROP INDEX statement.

Specify the UNIQUE keyword to declare a NONCLUSTERED INDEX as unique, as you can see in Listing 6.17.

EXAMPLE

Listing 6.17: You Must Specify the UNIQUE Keyword to Create a Unique Nonclustered Index

```
USE Northwind
GO

IF OBJECT_ID('NewOrders') IS NOT NULL
DROP TABLE NewOrders
GO

SELECT *
INTO NewOrders
FROM Orders
GO

CREATE UNIQUE NONCLUSTERED INDEX UNC_ORDERS_ORDERID
ON NewOrders (OrderID)
```

ACCESSING DATA THROUGH NONCLUSTERED INDEXES

The way SQL Server retrieves data through nonclustered indexes depends on the existence of a clustered index on the table. As explained earlier in this chapter, the reason for this difference in behavior is to optimize index maintenance, trying to avoid the continuous physical pointer modifications when data rows must be moved because of reordering the clustered index.

DATA STORED AS A HEAP   If table data is stored as a heap, the nonclustered index is a binary structure built on top of the actual data. Figure 6.17 shows an example of index navigation.

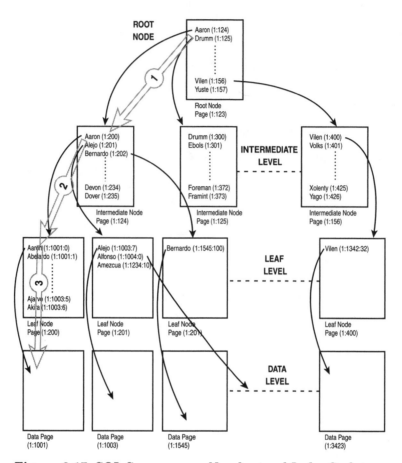

Figure 6.17: *SQL Server uses a Nonclustered Index Seek to search for rows within a search condition.*

SQL Server searches for entries in the nonclustered index, starting from the root node and going down to the leaf level of the index.

Every entry in the leaf level has a pointer to a physical row. SQL Server uses this pointer to access the page where the row is located and reads it.

DATA STORED AS A CLUSTERED INDEX If table data is stored as a clustered index, it is stored in the order specified by the clustered index definition. The index is a binary structure built on top of the actual data, which in this case is the leaf level of the clustered index.

Nonclustered indexes don't have a pointer to the physical position of the rows. They have as a pointer the value of the clustered index key.

Figure 6.18 shows an example of nonclustered index navigation on top of a clustered index.

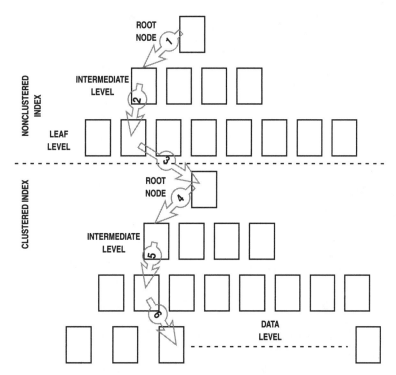

Figure 6.18: SQL Server uses a Nonclustered Index Seek to search for rows within a search condition, and it must navigate the clustered index as well.

If SQL Server decides to use a Nonclustered Index Seek to execute a query, it must follow a process similar to the one described in the preceding section, with an important difference: It also must navigate the clustered index to arrive at the physical rows.

You have to consider the extra work when you use a nonclustered index on top of a clustered index. However, if you consider the number of pages to read, you will consider this solution quite efficient.

The customers table could have 20,000 pages, so to execute a table scan, SQL Server will have to read 20,000 pages. For this reason, in most cases we should use a different strategy reducing the number of pages to read. As an example of a better strategy you should consider that the number of pages to read when searching for a particular row, traversing the index tree structure, depends on the number of levels on the index tree (usually very small) instead of the number of data pages used on this table.

Indexes don't have many levels, often less than four. The right index image should be a pyramid with a base of thousands of pages and only three or four pages high. Even if you have two pyramids to navigate, the number of pages to read is still much smaller than reading through a full table scan.

Covered Queries and Index Intersection

Mentioned earlier in this chapter were different ways to access data, depending on the available indexes. Let's consider the example of Listing 6.18. If you had an index on (`City`, `CompanyName`, `ContactName`), this index has every field required to execute the query. In this case, it is not required to access the data pages, resulting in a more efficient access method. Figures 6.19 and 6.20 show the query plan with and without this index.

EXAMPLE

Listing 6.18: This Query Can Be Covered by an Index on the Columns (`City`, `CompanyName`, `ContactName`)

```
USE Northwind
GO

SELECT CompanyName, ContactName
FROM Customers
WHERE City = 'Madrid'
```

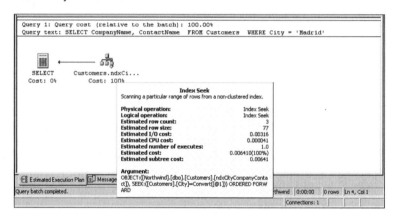

Figure 6.19: *SQL Server uses the index on (`City`, `CompanyName`, `ContactName`) to cover the query.*

In these situations, you can say that the selected index covers the query.

If you consider the example in Listing 6.19, you can see in the query execution shown in Figure 6.21 that the index in (`City`, `CompanyName`, `ContactName`) still covers the query, even if you added a new field called `CustomerID`.

EXAMPLE

Listing 6.19: This Query Can Be Covered by an Index on the Columns (`City`, `CompanyName`, `ContactName`)

```
USE Northwind
GO
```

```
SELECT CustomerID, CompanyName, ContactName
FROM Customers
WHERE City = 'Madrid'
```

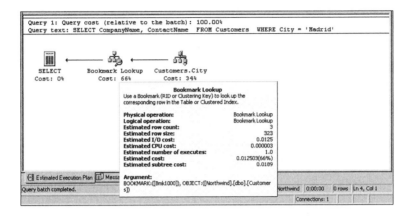

Figure 6.20: *SQL Server needs access to the data pages to execute the query if an index on* (`City, CompanyName, ContactName`) *doesn't exist.*

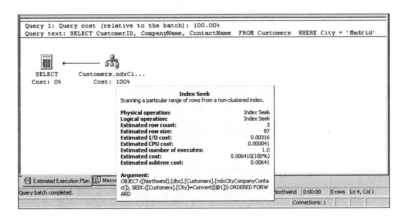

Figure 6.21: *SQL Server uses the index on* (`City, CompanyName, ContactName`) *to cover the query even when you add the field* `CustomerID`.

The Customers table has a clustered index on the field `CustomerID`, and this field is used as a pointer for every nonclustered index, such as the one you created on (`City, CompanyName, ContactName`). In other words, every key entry in the index actually contains four fields: City, CompanyName, ContactName, and CustomerID. That's why this index covers this query, too.

Trying to cover every query is almost impossible and requires too much space and maintenance cost. SQL Server 2000 can combine indexes, if required, to execute a query, and this technique is called index intersection. Listing 6.20 shows a query that selects three fields from the [Order

Details] table and applies two conditions to two of the selected fields. In this case, you could be tempted to create a composite index on these three fields to cover the query, but if you had already an index on UnitPrice and another index on OrderID, SQL Server can combine these two indexes to solve the query. Figure 6.22 shows the query plan of this query.

EXAMPLE

Listing 6.20: This Query Can Be Solved by an Index on OrderID and Another Index on UnitPrice

```
USE Northwind
GO

SELECT OrderID, UnitPrice
FROM [Order details]
WHERE UnitPrice > 15
AND OrderID > 11000
```

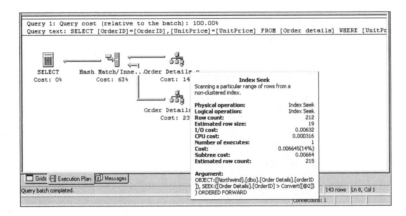

Figure 6.22: *SQL Server combines two indexes to solve the query.*

Index Maintenance

SQL Server automatically maintains indexes on tables. Every INSERT, UPDATE, or DELETE operation forces SQL Server to update the index information to keep it up to date. This maintenance produces some overhead on these operations.

Any time you insert a new row and you had a clustered index, SQL Server must search for the correct page to insert this new row. If the page is full, SQL Server decides the best way to insert this row, depending on the following conditions:

- If the row has to be inserted at the end of the table and the last page doesn't have any free space, SQL Server must allocate a new page for this new row.

- If the row has to be inserted into an existing page and there is enough free space in the page to allocate this new row, the row will be inserted in any free space in the page, and the row-offset will be reordered to reflect the new row order.

- If the row has to be inserted into an existing page and the page is full, SQL Server must split this page into two. This is done by allocating a new page and transferring 50% of the existing rows to the new page. After this process, SQL Server will evaluate on which one of these two pages the new row must be inserted. The row-offset list must be reordered according to new row order.

Figure 6.23 shows the split-page process. This Page Split process produces some overhead for SQL Server as well.

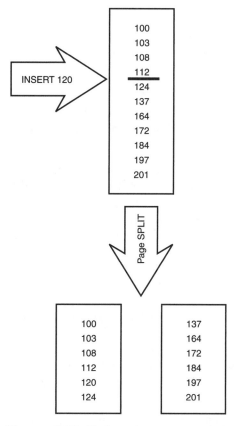

Figure 6.23: *To insert a new row into a full page, SQL Server must split the page.*

The same process must be done to accommodate a new key into a leaf-level page of a nonclustered index.

Rebuilding Indexes

If you would like to change the index definition, you can use the CREATE INDEX statement with the DROP_EXISTING option. Listing 6.21 shows an example where you want to convert a nonclustered index on (OrderID, ProductID) on the [Order Details] table into a clustered index on the same fields.

EXAMPLE

Listing 6.21: You Can Modify Existing Indexes with the CREATE INDEX Statement and the DROP_EXISTING Option

```
USE Northwind
GO

CREATE UNIQUE CLUSTERED INDEX UC_ORDER_DETAILS_ORDER_PRODUCT
ON OrderDetails (OrderID, ProductID)
WITH DROP EXISTING
```

> **NOTE**
>
> If you did not execute the code from Listing 6.11 and you try to execute the code from Listing 6.21, you will get an error message because the OrderDetails table does not exist.

In this case, other nonclustered indexes must be rebuilt because they must point to the clustered keys, and not to the physical row locations.

If you had a table with a clustered index and several nonclustered indexes and you wanted to modify the clustered index definition, you could drop the index and create it again. In this case, the nonclustered indexes must be rebuilt after the clustered index is dropped, and they must be rebuilt again after the clustered index is re-created. However, using the DROP_EXISTING option to rebuild the clustered index will save time, because the nonclustered indexes will be rebuilt automatically just once, instead of twice, and only if you select different key columns for the clustered index.

> **TIP**
>
> Create the clustered index before the nonclustered indexes. In this way, you can avoid rebuilding the nonclustered indexes because of the creation of the clustered index.

When an index is rebuilt, the data is rearranged, so external fragmentation is eliminated and internal fragmentation will be adjusted, as you'll see later in this chapter.

Another alternative to CREATE INDEX... WITH DROP EXISTING is to use the DBCC DBREINDEX. This statement can rebuild all the indexes of a given table with a single command. This is the preferred way to rebuild indexes if they are part of a constraint definition. Listing 6.22 shows the statement to rebuild all the indexes of the [Order Details] table. In this case, indexes are rebuilt with the same definition they were created.

Listing 6.22: Use DBCC DBREINDEX to Rebuild All the Indexes of a Table

```
USE Northwind
GO
```

EXAMPLE

```
DBCC DBREINDEX ('[Order details]')
```

Index Fragmentation

Every time a page is split, the index suffers some fragmentation. If fragmentation were important, it would be necessary to read more pages than normal to retrieve the same information. For read-only tables, fragmentation must be as minimal as possible. However, for read/write tables it is better to have some fragmentation to accommodate new rows without splitting too many pages.

You can adjust the fragmentation of an index using the FILLFACTOR option. FILLFACTOR expects a value between 1 and 100, which specifies the percentage of the page that should be full at the time the index is created. The actual percentage will be less than or equal to the specified fill factor.

Applying a FILLFACTOR will pack or expand the leaf-level pages to accommodate this new filling factor. For nonleaf-level pages, there will be one free entry per page. Listings 6.23 and 6.24 show two examples of rebuilding an index with a new FILLFACTOR. Listing 6.23 uses CREATE INDEX, and Listing 6.24 uses DBCC DBREINDEX.

Listing 6.23: You Can Specify a New FILLFACTOR for an Existing Index with the CREATE INDEX Statement and the FILLFACTOR Option

```
USE Northwind
GO
```

EXAMPLE

```
CREATE NONCLUSTERED INDEX OrderID
ON [Order Details] (OrderID)
WITH DROP_EXISTING, FILLFACTOR = 80
```

Listing 6.24: Use DBCC DBREINDEX to Rebuild All the Indexes of a Table with a Different FILLFACTOR

```
USE Northwind
GO
```

EXAMPLE

```
DBCC DBREINDEX ('[Order details]', '', 70)
```

Considering that fragmentation on nonleaf-level pages will be produced only when allocating and deallocating new pages at leaf level, having a free entry per page should be considered normal. If you expected many new rows and many new pages in the leaf level, you could be interceding to specify the PAD_INDEX option, which will apply the FILLFACTOR value to nonleaf-level pages as well. Listing 6.25 shows how to apply this option to one of the indexes of the [Order Details] table.

EXAMPLE

Listing 6.25: You Can Specify a New FILLFACTOR for an Existing Index with the CREATE INDEX Statement and the FILLFACTOR Option, and Apply This FILLFACTOR to the Nonleaf-Level Pages with the PAD_INDEX Option

```
USE Northwind
GO

CREATE NONCLUSTERED INDEX OrderID
ON [Order Details] (OrderID)
WITH DROP_EXISTING, FILLFACTOR = 80, PAD_INDEX
```

If you want to avoid fragmentation on data pages, you can build a clustered index and specify a FILLFACTOR option with a value of 100. If there is already a clustered index on the table, you can rebuild the index and specify a value of 100 for FILLFACTOR. Listing 6.26 shows how to pack the data pages on the Products table by rebuilding the index PK_Products with a FILLFACTOR of 100.

EXAMPLE

Listing 6.26: Use DBCC DBREINDEX to Pack the Data Pages by Rebuilding the Clustered Index with a FILLFACTOR of 100

```
USE Northwind
GO

DBCC DBREINDEX ('Products', PK_Products, 100)
```

If the clustered index is not required to provide a normal use of the table, and you want to pack data pages, you can create a clustered index with FILLFACTOR 100 and drop the clustered index when it's created.

Index Statistics

SQL Query Optimizer selects the best strategy based on indexes available for every table to be used in the query and for specific information about every index. For every index, Query Optimizer gets general information from the sysindexes table about

- The number of data pages in the index (the field dpages)
- The approximate number of rows (the field rowcnt)
- Density of the index (information included in the statblob field)
- Average length of the key (information included in the statblob field)

However, this information is not enough to predict whether the index is useful in a particular query.

Consider the Customers table. To filter customers who live in a specific city, having an index on the City column can be useful. However, if 95% of your customers live in Toronto, the index on City will be useless when searching for customers living in Toronto. In this case, a table scan will produce better results.

SQL Server maintains distribution statistics about every index. Statistic information is stored in the statblob field of the sysindexes table.

SQL Server samples the data to select information organized in ranges of data. For every range, SQL Server stores

- The number of rows where the key is in the specific range, excluding the maximum value of the range

- The maximum value of the range

- The number of rows where the value of the key is equal to the maximum value of the range

- The number of distinct key values in the range, excluding the maximum value of the range

SQL Server calculates the average density of every range as well, dividing number of rows by number of distinct key values on every range.

Listing 6.27 shows how to use the DBCC SHOW_STATISTICS statement to get statistics information about the (Products.SupplierID) index.

EXAMPLE

OUTPUT

Listing 6.27: Use DBCC SHOW_STATISTICS to Get Information About Index Statistics

```
USE Northwind
GO

DBCC SHOW_STATISTICS (Products, SupplierID)
```

```
Statistics for INDEX 'SupplierID'.
Updated              Rows  Rows Sampled  Steps  Density      Average key length
------------------   ----- ------------- ------ ---------    ----------------------
Oct 23 2000  5:16PM  77    77            20     3.3189032E-2  8.0
(1 row(s) affected)
```

```
All density              Average Length           Columns
---------------------    ----------------------   -----------------------------
3.4482758E-2             4.0                      SupplierID
1.2987013E-2             8.0                      SupplierID, ProductID

(2 row(s) affected)
```

RANGE_HI_KEY	RANGE_ROWS	EQ_ROWS	DISTINCT_RANGE_ROWS	AVG_RANGE_ROWS
1	0.0	3.0	0	0.0
2	0.0	4.0	0	0.0
4	3.0	3.0	1	3.0
5	0.0	2.0	0	0.0
6	0.0	3.0	0	0.0
7	0.0	5.0	0	0.0

Listing 6.27: continued

```
8               0.0         4.0         0               0.0
9               0.0         2.0         0               0.0
10              0.0         1.0         0               0.0
11              0.0         3.0         0               0.0
12              0.0         5.0         0               0.0
13              0.0         1.0         0               0.0
17              9.0         3.0         3               3.0
19              2.0         2.0         1               2.0
20              0.0         3.0         0               0.0
22              2.0         2.0         1               2.0
24              3.0         3.0         1               3.0
26              2.0         2.0         1               2.0
27              0.0         1.0         0               0.0
29              2.0         2.0         1               2.0

(20 row(s) affected)

DBCC execution completed. If DBCC printed error messages,
contact your system administrator.
```

SQL Server by default automatically creates statistics when you create an index and automatically maintains these statistics as you add rows to the base table. It is possible, but not advisable, to avoid automatic statistics maintenance by setting an option at database level, as shown in Listing 6.28.

EXAMPLE

Listing 6.28: By Using sp_dboption, It Is Possible to Avoid Automatic Statistics Creation and Maintenance for the Entire Database

```
USE Northwind
GO

-- Change the database setting to avoid
-- statistics creation and maintenance

EXEC sp_dboption 'Northwind', 'auto create statistics', 'false'

EXEC sp_dboption 'Northwind', 'auto update statistics', 'false'

-- To test the present settings

PRINT 'After changing to manual statistics maintenance'

EXEC sp_dboption 'Northwind', 'auto create statistics'

EXEC sp_dboption 'Northwind', 'auto update statistics'
```

Listing 6.28: continued

OUTPUT

```
After changing to manual statistics maintenance
OptionName                             CurrentSetting
------------------------------------  --------------
auto create statistics                 off


OptionName                             CurrentSetting
------------------------------------  --------------
auto update statistics                 off
```

It is possible to create statistics on individual columns, or groups of columns, without creating an index. These statistics can be helpful for Query Optimizer to select efficient query execution strategies. Listing 6.29 shows different ways to create statistics.

EXAMPLE

Listing 6.29: It Is Possible to Create Statistics on Nonindexed Columns

```
USE Northwind
GO

-- To create statistics in an individual column

CREATE STATISTICS stProductsStock
ON Products(UnitsInStock)

-- To create statistics in a group of columns

CREATE STATISTICS stProductsStockOrder
ON Products(UnitsInStock, UnitsOnOrder)

-- To create single column statistics for all eligible  columns
-- on all user tables in the current database

EXEC sp_createstats
```

To retrieve information about available statistics in a table, you can use the sp_helpstats system stored procedure. Listing 6.30 shows an example of sp_helpstats execution.

EXAMPLE

Listing 6.30: Use the sp_helpstats System Stored Procedure to Get Information About Statistics

```
USE Northwind
GO

EXEC sp_helpstats Products
```

OUTPUT

```
statistics_name                   statistics_keys
-------------------------------   ----------------------------
_WA_Sys_UnitPrice_07020F21        UnitPrice
QuantityPerUnit                   QuantityPerUnit
ReorderLevel                      ReorderLevel
```

Listing 6.30: continued

```
stProductsStock            UnitsInStock
stProductsStockOrder       UnitsInStock, UnitsOnOrder
UnitsOnOrder               UnitsOnOrder
```

Getting Information About Indexes

You can use the sp_help system stored procedure to retrieve general information about a table, including the list of available indexes. Using the sp_helpindex system stored procedure you can get only the list of indexes available for a specific table, as in the example included in Listing 6.31.

EXAMPLE

Listing 6.31: Use the sp_helpindex System Stored Procedure to Retrieve Information About Indexes in a Table

```
USE Northwind
GO

EXEC sp_helpindex customers
```

OUTPUT

```
index_name    index_description                                         index_keys
------------  --------------------------------------------------------  ------------
City          nonclustered located on PRIMARY                           City
CompanyName   nonclustered located on PRIMARY                           CompanyName
Contact       nonclustered located on PRIMARY                           ContactName
PK_Customers  clustered, unique, primary key located on PRIMARY CustomerID
PostalCode    nonclustered located on PRIMARY                           PostalCode
Region        nonclustered located on PRIMARY                           Region
```

To get specific information about individual index properties, you can use the INDEXPROPERTY system function as demonstrated in Listing 6.32.

EXAMPLE

Listing 6.32: Use the INDEXPROPERTY Function to Retrieve Information About Any Index

```
USE Northwind
GO

-- To retrieve number of index levels

SELECT INDEXPROPERTY(OBJECT_ID('Products'), 'PK_Products', 'IndexDepth')
AS 'Index Levels'
-- To determine if the index is clustered

SELECT CASE
INDEXPROPERTY(OBJECT_ID('Products'), 'PK_Products', 'IsClustered')
WHEN 0 THEN 'No'
ELSE 'Yes' END as 'Is Clustered'

-- To determine if it is not a real index
-- So it cannot be used for data access
-- because it contains only statistics
```

Listing 6.32: continued
```
SELECT CASE
INDEXPROPERTY(OBJECT_ID('Products'), 'PK_Products', 'IsStatistics')
WHEN 0 THEN 'No'
ELSE 'Yes' END as 'Is Statistics only'

-- To know if the index is unique

SELECT CASE
INDEXPROPERTY(OBJECT_ID('Products'), 'PK_Products', 'IsUnique')
WHEN 0 THEN 'No'
ELSE 'Yes' END as 'Is Unique'
```

OUTPUT

```
Index Levels
-----------
1


Is Clustered
-----------
Yes


Is Statistics only
------------------
No


Is Unique
---------
Yes
```

Indexes on Computed Columns

In SQL Server 2000, you can create computed columns in a table. These columns don't use storage space, and SQL Server maintains them automatically whenever the underlying data changes.

You can create a computed column SalePrice in the [Order Details] table to get the total sale value of every row, considering the unit price and quantity. To speed up the process of searching, or sorting, for this SalePrice column, you can create an index on this computed column, and Query Optimizer might use it, if necessary. Listing 6.33 shows the complete process.

Listing 6.33: It Is Possible to Create Indexes on Computed Columns
```
USE Northwind
GO
```

EXAMPLE

```
-- Create the computed column SalePrice
```

Listing 6.33: continued

```
ALTER TABLE [order details]
ADD SalePrice AS (UnitPrice * Quantity)

-- Create an index on SalePrice

CREATE INDEX ndxSale ON [order details] (SalePrice)
```

To create an index on a computed column, you have to check the following requirements:

- The expression defining the computed column must be *deterministic*. An expression is deterministic if it always produces the same results for the same arguments. Every function referenced in the expression must be deterministic, too.

  An example of a nondeterministic expression is (Month(GetDate()) because it uses a nondeterministic function, GetDate, which changes every time you call it.

- The expression must be precise. To be precise, the expression cannot use the float or real data types, or any combination of them, even if the final result uses a precise data type.

  If you define the SalePrice computed column as (UnitPrice * Quantity * (1 - Discount)), the expression is not precise because it uses an imprecise field: Discount. In this case, you cannot create an index on this computed column.

- Because connection settings can affect results, the connection that creates the index in the computed column, and every connection that modifies data affecting this index, must have settings according to the following list:

  ```
  SET ANSI_NULLS ON
  SET ANSI_PADDING ON
  SET ANSI_WARNINGS ON
  SET ARITHABORT ON
  SET CONCAT_NULS_YIELDS_NULL ON
  SET QUOTED_IDENTIFIER ON
  SET NUMERIC_ROUNDABORT OFF
  ```

Indexed Views

SQL Server 2000 can create indexes on views. This functionality is implemented by extensions in the CREATE VIEW and CREATE INDEX statements. If a view is not indexed, it doesn't use any storage space. Whenever you use the view in a Transact-SQL statement, SQL Server merges the view definition with the statement to produce a single execution plan and it directly accesses the underlying tables on which the view is defined.

After a view is indexed, its index needs storage space, as any standard index.

The process of creating an indexed view is as follows:

1. Create the view with SCHEMABINDING, which prevents modifications on the definition of referenced objects.

2. Create a clustered index on the view to physically save the view results in a clustered index structure where the leaf level will be the complete resultset of the view. The index key should be as short as possible to provide good performance.

3. Create nonclustered indexes, if required.

After the creation of the clustered index, the view is stored like a clustered index for a table, but this information is maintained automatically whenever data changes in the underlying tables.

If you reference the view, Query Optimizer will use the indexed view directly, and it will be unnecessary to access the underlying tables.

SQL Server 2000 Enterprise Edition can use indexed views to optimize the execution of queries that don't reference the indexed views explicitly, improving execution performance.

Listing 6.34 shows how to create an index on a view. Figure 6.24 shows how SQL Server uses the view definition to access the base tables directly. Figure 6.25 shows that by having an indexed view, SQL Server can avoid accessing the base tables, reducing the amount of IO required to execute the query.

EXAMPLE

Listing 6.34: In SQL Server 2000, You Can Create Indexes on Views

```
USE Northwind
GO

-- Create the view

CREATE VIEW Customers_UK
WITH SCHEMABINDING
AS
```

Listing 6.34: continued

```
SELECT CustomerID, CompanyName, ContactName, Phone
FROM dbo.Customers
WHERE Country = 'UK'

-- Test how a normal query uses the view

SELECT CustomerID, CompanyName, ContactName, Phone
FROM Customers
WHERE Country = 'UK'
AND CompanyName like 'C%'

-- Create a clustered index on the view

CREATE UNIQUE CLUSTERED INDEX CustUK ON Customers_UK (CustomerID)

-- Create a nonclustered index on the CompanyName field on the view

CREATE NONCLUSTERED INDEX CustUKCompany ON Customers_UK (CompanyName)

-- Test how a normal query uses the view after indexing the view

SELECT CustomerID, CompanyName, ContactName, Phone
FROM Customers
WHERE Country = 'UK'
AND CompanyName like 'C%'
```

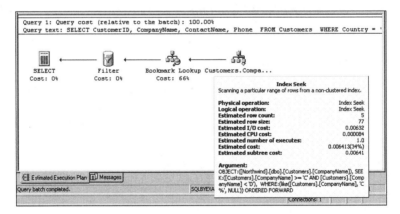

Figure 6.24: *When using nonindexed views, SQL Server accesses data directly from tables.*

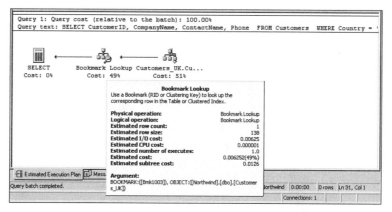

Figure 6.25: *When using indexed views, SQL Server doesn't require access to the tables.*

Not every view can be indexed because some requirements must be met. Some requirements affect the definition of the view, and others the creation of the index. To create a view that can be indexed, it is necessary to meet the following requirements:

- The ANSI_NULLS option must be set to ON to create the base tables and the view.

- The QUOTED_IDENTIFIER must be set to ON to create the view.

- The view must reference only base tables, from the same database and owner.

- The view must be created with the SCHEMABINDING option set to prevent changes on the underlying objects. If the view uses a user-defined function, this must be created as well with SCHEMABINDING.

- To avoid ambiguity, objects must be referenced with two part names, owner, and object name. Three- or four-part names are not allowed because the view cannot reference objects from other databases or servers.

- All the expressions used in the view definition must be deterministic, and the expressions used in key columns must be precise, as explained earlier, for indexes on computed columns.

- The view must specifically name all columns, because SELECT * is not allowed.

- You cannot use a column more than once in the SELECT clause, unless every time the column was used as a part of a complex expression.

- It is not allowed to use subqueries, and that includes derived tables in the FROM clause.

- You cannot use Rowset functions, such as OPENROWSET, OPENQUERY, CONTAINSTABLE, or FREETEXTTABLE.

- It cannot contain the UNION operator.

- It cannot contain outer or self-joins.

- It cannot contain the ORDER BY clause, and that includes the use of the TOP clause.

- You cannot use the DISTINCT keyword.

- The only aggregate functions allowed are COUNT_BIG and SUM. To use the SUM function, you must select COUNT_BIG as well, and you must specify a GROUP BY clause.

- SUM cannot be used on a nullable column or expression.

- It cannot use full-text functions.

- COMPUTE or COMPUTE BY clauses are not allowed.

- The view cannot contain BLOB columns, as text, ntext, and image.

To create an index in a view, some more requirements must be met:

- Only the owner of the view can create indexes on the view.

- The connection settings must be the same as the settings for indexes on computed columns.

- If the view has a GROUP BY clause, only the columns specified in the GROUP BY clause can participate in the index key.

CAUTION

To modify data that is used in an indexed view, you must set the seven connection settings in the same way as for the index creation, or the operation will fail.

NOTE

Using the SCHEMABINDING option means you cannot alter or drop the base objects, and to do so, you must drop the view to break the schema binding.

Index Tuning Wizard

Deciding which indexing strategy to apply is not an easy task. Different queries can be optimized in different ways using different indexes. To decide which is the best indexing strategy, it would be necessary to consider statistically which strategy produces the best global performance.

The Index Tuning Wizard does just that. It uses a trace from SQL Profiler to analyze, propose, and apply, if required, the best indexing strategy for the actual database workload.

With the integration of the Index Tuning Wizard in SQL Query Analyzer, it is possible to optimize a single query or batch in Query Analyzer, without creating a trace with SQL Profiler. This can be considered as a provisional solution, to speed up the process of one specific query. However, the best approach is still to use a trace that is representative of the actual database workload.

The process of using the Index Tuning Wizard is almost the same in both cases; that's why you will learn how to optimize a single query from Query Analyzer in this chapter. The query to optimize is represented in Listing 6.35.

EXAMPLE

Listing 6.35: You Can See How to Optimize the Following Query Using Index Tuning Wizard

```
USE Northwind
GO

SELECT OD.OrderID, O.OrderDate,
C.CompanyName, P.ProductName,
OD.UnitPrice, OD.Quantity, OD.Discount
FROM [Order Details] AS OD
JOIN [Orders] AS O
ON O.OrderID = OD.OrderID
JOIN [Products] AS P
ON P.ProductID = OD.ProductID
JOIN [Customers] AS C
ON C.CustomerID = O.CustomerID
WHERE Country = 'UK'
```

Write the query in Query Analyzer and select the complete query with the mouse.

Open the menu Query—Index Tuning Wizard, or press Ctrl+I. The Index Tuning Wizard will start and it will show the Welcome form. Click Next in this form and you will see the form shown in Figure 6.26.

In this form, you can decide whether you want to keep existing indexes; for the example, uncheck the check box so you don't consider any index as fixed.

You can select whether the wizard can consider the creation of indexed view. Leave the check box checked.

Select Thorough Tuning Mode to get better results. Click Next.

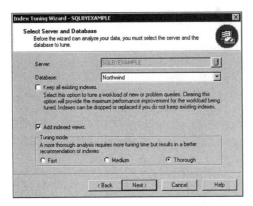

Figure 6.26: The Index Tuning Wizard has different analysis modes.

To Specify Workload, leave the SQL Query Analyzer Selection option set and click Next. If you followed the preceding instructions, the Index Tuning Wizard will be as shown in Figure 6.27.

Select the Orders, Products, Customers, and Order Details tables to tune, and then click Next.

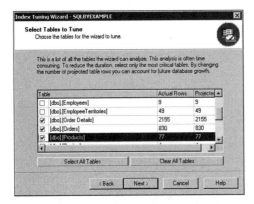

Figure 6.27: The Index Tuning Wizard can analyze individual tables or a group of tables.

The Index Tuning Wizard starts analyzing and, after a few minutes, shows index recommendations. You can review and select which recommendations are valid for you, according to your experience and the knowledge of the actual data. Note that the Index Tuning Wizard estimates the relative performance improvement when applying the new index strategy.

Click Next. Now either you can apply the changes directly or scheduled to a certain time, or you can script these changes for further analysis. Select to save the script and provide a filename. You should receive a script similar to that in Listing 6.36.

Click Finish to end the wizard.

Listing 6.36: These Are the Recommendations of the Index Tuning Wizard to Optimize the Query of Listing 6.35

```
/* Created by: Index Tuning Wizard    */
/* Date: 25/10/2000          */
/* Time: 23:36:33          */
/* Server Name: BYEXAMPLE          */
/* Database Name: Northwind          */
USE [Northwind]
go

SET QUOTED_IDENTIFIER ON
SET ARITHABORT ON
SET CONCAT_NULL_YIELDS_NULL ON
SET ANSI_NULLS ON
SET ANSI_PADDING ON
SET ANSI_WARNINGS ON
SET NUMERIC_ROUNDABORT OFF
go

DECLARE @bErrors as bit

BEGIN TRANSACTION
SET @bErrors = 0

DROP INDEX [dbo].[Orders].[ShipPostalCode]
DROP INDEX [dbo].[Orders].[ShippedDate]
DROP INDEX [dbo].[Orders].[CustomersOrders]
DROP INDEX [dbo].[Orders].[OrderDate]
DROP INDEX [dbo].[Orders].[CustomerID]
DROP INDEX [dbo].[Orders].[ShippersOrders]
DROP INDEX [dbo].[Orders].[EmployeesOrders]
DROP INDEX [dbo].[Orders].[EmployeeID]
CREATE NONCLUSTERED INDEX [Orders7]
ON [dbo].[Orders] ([OrderID] ASC, [CustomerID] ASC, [OrderDate] ASC )

IF( @@error <> 0 ) SET @bErrors = 1

IF( @bErrors = 0 )
COMMIT TRANSACTION
ELSE
ROLLBACK TRANSACTION

BEGIN TRANSACTION
SET @bErrors = 0

DROP INDEX [dbo].[Order Details].[ProductID]
```

Listing 6.36: continued

```
DROP INDEX [dbo].[Order Details].[orderID]
DROP INDEX [dbo].[Order Details].[price]
DROP INDEX [dbo].[Order Details].[OrdersOrder_Details]
DROP INDEX [dbo].[Order Details].[ProductsOrder_Details]
DROP INDEX [dbo].[Order Details].[ndxSale]

IF( @bErrors = 0 )
COMMIT TRANSACTION
ELSE
ROLLBACK TRANSACTION

BEGIN TRANSACTION
SET @bErrors = 0

DROP INDEX [dbo].[Customers].[Region]
DROP INDEX [dbo].[Customers].[CompanyName]
DROP INDEX [dbo].[Customers].[Contact]
DROP INDEX [dbo].[Customers].[ndx_Customers_City]
DROP INDEX [dbo].[Customers].[PostalCode]
DROP INDEX [dbo].[Customers].[City]

IF( @bErrors = 0 )
COMMIT TRANSACTION
ELSE
ROLLBACK TRANSACTION

BEGIN TRANSACTION
SET @bErrors = 0

DROP INDEX [dbo].[Products].[C_Products_Category_Price]
DROP INDEX [dbo].[Products].[CategoriesProducts]
DROP INDEX [dbo].[Products].[SuppliersProducts]
DROP INDEX [dbo].[Products].[CategoryID]
DROP INDEX [dbo].[Products].[ProductName]
DROP INDEX [dbo].[Products].[SupplierID]

IF( @bErrors = 0 )
COMMIT TRANSACTION
ELSE
ROLLBACK TRANSACTION


/* Statistics to support recommendations */

CREATE STATISTICS [hind_325576198_1A_2A_3A_4A_5A]
ON [dbo].[order details] ([OrderID], [ProductID], [UnitPice],
[Quantity], [Discount])
```

Now you can modify this script to meet other requirements and execute against the server to apply the changes.

Summary

Understanding the way SQL Server 2000 stores, modifies, and retrieves data helps you to design databases for optimal performance.

Which index strategy to apply has a big impact on the overall performance of the database. Different uses require different indexing strategies.

Decision Support Systems (DSSs) are based on reading operations, which read many rows to produce a report, usually with data aggregation. *Online Transaction Processing Systems (OLTP)* are based in fast access to a small number of rows, producing modifications on the data, forcing index maintenance.

Many systems are a mixture of DSS and OLTP operations. SQL Profiler can help us to determine the actual workload, and the Index Tuning Wizard can suggest an efficient strategy to apply.

New SQL Server 2000 features, such as indexes on computed columns and indexed views, could speed up the execution of complex queries in many scenarios.

What's Next?

Indexes play an important role in some types of data integrity, and Chapter 7, "Enforcing Data Integrity," shows how SQL Server uses indexes to enforce primary key and unique constraints.

Having an adequate index strategy provides the basis for an efficient database system. The way SQL Server produces query plans to execute stored procedures and triggers depends on the available indexes. Stored procedures and triggers are covered in Chapter 8, "Implementing Business Logic: Programming Stored Procedures," and Chapter 9, "Implementing Complex Processing Logic: Programming Triggers."

User-defined functions benefit from indexes as well, because their query plan depends on the existence of suitable indexes. In Chapter 10, "Enhancing Business Logic: User-Defined Functions (UDF)," you learn how to define user-defined functions to solve business problems as a flexible alternative to using views or stored procedures.

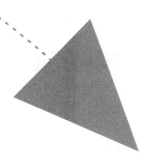

Enforcing Data Integrity

Databases are as useful as the quality of the data they contain. The quality of the data is determined by many different factors, and every phase in the life cycle of a database contributes to the ultimate quality of the data. The logical database design, the physical implementation, the client applications, and the final user entering the data in the database all have key roles in the final quality of the data.

Data integrity is an important factor that contributes to the overall quality of the data, and SQL Server 2000, as a relational database management system, provides different ways to enforce data integrity. This chapter teaches you

- Types of data integrity and how SQL Server helps you enforce them

- How to uniquely identify rows in a table using PRIMARY KEY and UNIQUE constraints

- How to validate values in new rows using CHECK constraints and RULE objects

- How to provide default values for columns using DEFAULT constraints and DEFAULT objects

- How to enforce referential integrity between tables using FOREIGN KEY constraints and how to use cascade referential integrity

- Which constraint is appropriate in each case

Types of Data Integrity

Consider a commercial database in which you store information about products, customers, sales, and so on. You can measure the integrity of the data contained in that database in different ways:

- Is the information related to one specific product stored in a consistent way, and is it easy to retrieve?

- Do you have different products with the same name or code?

- Can you identify your customers in a unique manner, even if they have the same name?

- Are there any sales that are not related to a specific customer?

- Do you have any sales of nonexistent products?

- Do you have a consistent price structure for your products?

To guarantee the integrity of the data contained in a database, you should ensure

- That every individual value conforms to specific business rules (domain integrity)

- That every object can be uniquely and unequivocally identified (entity integrity)

- That related data is properly connected (relational integrity)

Domain Integrity

Applying business rules to validate the data stored in the database enforces domain integrity. Your database application has different ways to validate the data entered in a database, such as the following:

- The column data type restricts the values you can enter in this column. This prevents you from entering textual descriptions in data columns or dates in price columns.

- The column length enforces the length of the data you can enter in a specific column.

- You can enforce the minimum and maximum length for any given value. For example, you can determine that product codes should be at least five characters long and fewer than ten.

- You can restrict data that conforms to a specific format. This can be useful to validate ZIP or postal codes or telephone numbers.

- It might be useful to restrict the valid range of values. You can limit the value to enter, as a date of birth of a new bank customer, to dates between 1880-01-01 and today's date, to avoid possible mistakes.

- The business meaning of a column might need to enforce that the values entered into the column must be one of the possible values in a fixed list. Your sales application, for example, might classify customers as individual customers, public institutions, or businesses.

Entity Integrity

Every real object should be easily identified in a database. It is difficult to refer to a customer as "the customer who lives in Seattle, has four children and 300 employees, is 40 years old, his first name is Peter, and his telephone number ends with 345." For humans this data could be enough for searching our memory and identifying a customer. However, for a computer program, such as SQL Server 2000, this way of customer identification will force SQL Server to apply different conditions in sequence, one condition per attribute. Perhaps it would be easy to identify every customer by a single unique value, such as 25634, stored in a identification column, such as CustomerID. In this way, to search for a customer, SQL Server will have to apply a simple condition: CustomerID = 25634.

This is especially important if you want to relate information from other entities, because every relationship should be based on the simplest possible link.

Referential Integrity

Relational databases are called "relational" because the data units stored in them are linked to each other through relationships:

- Customers have sales representatives who take care of them

- Customers place orders

- Orders have order details

- Every item in an order references a single product

- Products are organized by categories

- Products are stored in warehouses

- The products come from suppliers

You must make sure that all these links are well established, and that our data does not contain any orphan data that is impossible to relate to the rest of the data.

User-Defined Integrity

In some situations, you are required to enforce complex integrity rules that are impossible to enforce by using standard relational structures. In these situations, you can create stored procedures, triggers, user-defined functions, or external components to achieve the extra functionality you require.

Enforcing Integrity: Constraints (Declarative Data Integrity)

SQL Server uses Transact-SQL structures to enforce data integrity. You can create these structures during table creation or by altering the table definition after the creation of the table and even after data has been inserted into the table.

To enforce entity integrity, SQL Server uses PRIMARY KEY and UNIQUE constraints, UNIQUE indexes, and the IDENTITY property. UNIQUE indexes are covered in Chapter 6, "Optimizing Access to Data: Indexes."

NOTE

The IDENTITY function is used to create an IDENTITY field in a table created by using the SELECT INTO statement.

For domain integrity, SQL Server provides system-supplied and user-defined data types, CHECK constraints, DEFAULT definitions, FOREIGN KEY constraints, NULL and NOT NULL definitions, and RULE and DEFAULT objects. Data types were covered in Chapter 2, "Elements of Transact-SQL."

NOTE

DEFAULT definitions are called DEFAULT constraints as well. Because DEFAULT constraints don't restrict the values to enter in a column but rather provide values for empty columns in INSERT operations, SQL Server 2000 calls them properties, instead of constraints, reflecting their purpose more accurately.

To enforce referential integrity, you can use FOREIGN KEY and CHECK constraints. Using complex structures, such as stored procedures, triggers, and user-defined functions as part of constraint definitions, it is possible to enforce complex business integrity rules.

Primary Keys

To enforce entity integrity in a given table, select the fields or combination of fields that uniquely identifies every row.

Tables usually represent an entity, such as Products, and the primary key can be as simple as one single field, which contains the unique identifiers for objects of that entity. You could consider the name of a product as the unique identifier, but usually names are not unique in a table. That's why to uniquely identify every product, you introduce a unique value in the field `ProductID`. This avoids ambiguity when referring to one specific product.

Following a pure relational database design, you should identify which set of natural attributes uniquely identifies every object of that entity. In some cases, this set will be a single attribute although, in most cases, this set will be a collection of different attributes. In a pure relational design, you should define the `PRIMARY KEY` on this set of attributes. However, you can create an artificial attribute, called a *surrogate key*, that uniquely identifies every row, working as a simplification of the natural `PRIMARY KEY`.

NOTE

Whether to use a natural `PRIMARY KEY` or a surrogate artificial key as a `PRIMARY KEY` depends on the implementation of the particular database product you use.

The recommendations in this chapter refer to SQL Server 2000. If you need to implement your database on different database systems, we recommend you follow a more standard relational approach.

Providing a new artificial integer column to be used as a primary key has some advantages. It is a short value—only 4 bytes—and SQL Server uses this value very efficiently on searching operations and joining tables through this field.

You can define the primary key constraint at column level, after the column definition, or at table level, as part of the table definition. Another possibility is to create the table first and add the primary key constraint later, using the `ALTER TABLE` statement.

TIP

Providing a user-friendly name to the primary key constraints will help when referring to the constraint in other statements and to identify the constraint after receiving a message from SQL Server.

Because there is only a `PRIMARY KEY` constraint per table, a recommended naming standard for a `PRIMARY KEY` can be PK_TableName.

You can use the code in Listing 7.1 to create a `PRIMARY KEY` in a single column of a table, using the `CREATE TABLE` statement.

EXAMPLE

Listing 7.1: Define a `PRIMARY KEY` in a Single Column

```
-- Define a PRIMARY KEY in a single column
-- using the DEFAULT constraint name

CREATE TABLE NewRegions (
RegionID int NOT NULL
PRIMARY KEY NONCLUSTERED,
```

Listing 7.1: continued

```
RegionDescription nchar (50) NOT NULL ,
)
GO


DROP TABLE NewRegions
GO


-- Define a PRIMARY KEY in a single column
-- specifying the constraint name

CREATE TABLE NewRegions (
RegionID int NOT NULL
CONSTRAINT PK_NewRegions
PRIMARY KEY NONCLUSTERED,
RegionDescription nchar (50) NOT NULL ,
)
GO


DROP TABLE NewRegions
GO


-- Define a PRIMARY KEY in a single column
-- specifying the constraint name
-- and defining the constraint at table level

CREATE TABLE NewRegions (
RegionID int NOT NULL,
RegionDescription nchar (50) NOT NULL ,
CONSTRAINT PK_NewRegions
PRIMARY KEY NONCLUSTERED (RegionID),
)
GO


DROP TABLE NewRegions
GO


-- Define a PRIMARY KEY in a single column
-- specifying the constraint name
-- and defining the constraint at table level
-- using the ALTER TABLE statement

CREATE TABLE NewRegions (
RegionID int NOT NULL,
RegionDescription nchar (50) NOT NULL)
GO
```

Listing 7.1: continued

```
ALTER TABLE NewRegions
ADD CONSTRAINT PK_NewRegions
PRIMARY KEY NONCLUSTERED (RegionID)
GO

DROP TABLE NewRegions
GO
```

To define a primary key in a column, the column cannot accept nulls.

Because primary key values must be unique, SQL Server creates a UNIQUE index to help check whether new values already exist in the column. Without an index, as explained in Chapter 6, SQL Server would have to read every single row to determine the uniqueness of each new value. This index takes the same name as the primary key constraint, and it cannot be removed without removing the constraint.

You can provide properties for the index, such as CLUSTERED, NONCLUSTERED, or FILLFACTOR, in the constraint definition. Listing 7.2 shows how to declare the index of a PRIMARY KEY as NONCLUSTERED and with a FILLFACTOR of 70%. Index properties were detailed in Chapter 6.

EXAMPLE

Listing 7.2: Define a PRIMARY KEY and Select Properties for Its UNIQUE INDEX

```
-- Define a PRIMARY KEY in a single column
-- and create the index a nonclustered
-- and 70% FillFactor

CREATE TABLE NewRegions (
RegionID int NOT NULL
PRIMARY KEY NONCLUSTERED WITH FILLFACTOR = 70,
RegionDescription nchar (50) NOT NULL ,
)
GO

DROP TABLE NewRegions
GO
```

CAUTION

It is important to understand that a constraint is a definition that enforces data validation, whereas an index is a storage structure that speeds up the searching processes. A primary key is not an index, but it uses an index for performance reasons.

It is possible to create a primary key in a group of columns. In this case, none of the columns in the primary key can accept nulls.

CAUTION

You can use up to 16 columns in a PRIMARY KEY definition, as long as the total key size is less than 900 bytes. It is advisable to keep the key size as short as possible.

Listing 7.3 shows how to create a PRIMARY KEY constraint on the combination of the ProductID and the SaleID columns using two different versions: The first version creates the PRIMARY KEY directly in the CREATE TABLE statement; the second version creates the PRIMARY KEY using the ALTER TABLE statement, after the creation of the table.

EXAMPLE

Listing 7.3: Defining a Multicolumn PRIMARY KEY

```
-- Define a composite PRIMARY KEY in two columns
-- specifying the constraint name


CREATE TABLE ProductSales (
ProductID int NOT NULL,
SaleID int NOT NULL,
Quantity int NOT NULL,
Price money NOT NULL,
Description varchar(200) NULL,
CONSTRAINT PK_ProductSales
PRIMARY KEY NONCLUSTERED (ProductID, SaleID)
)
GO


DROP TABLE ProductSales
GO


-- Define a composite PRIMARY KEY in two columns
-- using the ALTER TABLE statement


CREATE TABLE ProductSales (
ProductID int NOT NULL,
SaleID int NOT NULL,
Quantity int NOT NULL,
Price money NOT NULL,
Description varchar(200) NULL)

ALTER TABLE ProductSales
ADD CONSTRAINT PK_ProductSales
PRIMARY KEY NONCLUSTERED (ProductID, SaleID)
GO


DROP TABLE ProductSales
GO
```

SQL Server can automatically provide values for a primary key defined in a single column in the following ways:

- By using the IDENTITY property for the column to specify the seed and increment values.

- By using the uniqueidentifier data type combined with the NEWID function as a DEFAULT definition to supply automatic GUID (Global Unique Identifier) values.

- By declaring a user-defined function as a DEFAULT definition, to provide unique values to the column.

- By declaring the column using a data type timestamp or rowversion. Although this is a technically correct option, it is not a recommended solution because these values change whenever the row is modified. Having a PRIMARY KEY defined in a timestamp column will make this constraint unsuitable as a reference for FOREIGN KEY constraints defined on related tables.

CAUTION

For many relational database systems, following the ANSI SQL-92 standard, a time-stamp column holds the data and time of the latest modification of a row. SQL Server 2000 implements timestamp values in a different way, and it is not a date and time value. This is the reason for the new term: rowversion.

You should use the rowversion data type, instead of the timestamp, because future versions of SQL Server could implement the timestamp data type in a different way, perhaps in the way suggested in the ANSI SQL-92 standard.

CAUTION

If you use a rowversion or timestamp data type for a primary key column and you don't specify NONCLUSTERED, the row will physically move every time the row changes because SQL Server will change the value of the column automatically.

You can use Enterprise Manager to define a PRIMARY KEY in a table. To do it, right-click the table and select Design Table to display the Design Table form.

Figure 7.1 shows the Design Table form in which you can see the key icon on the PRIMARY KEY field. To delete the PRIMARY KEY, click the Set Primary Key icon on the toolbar.

To specify more properties about the PRIMARY KEY, you can open the Properties form by clicking the Table and Index Properties icon on the tool-bar. In the Indexes/Keys tab, you can modify or delete the PRIMARY KEY definition, but you cannot create a PRIMARY KEY using this form.

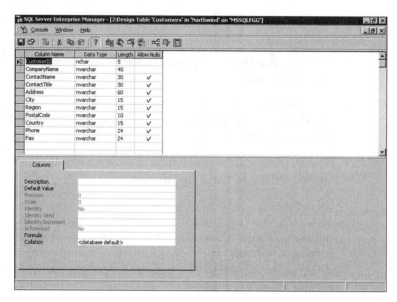

Figure 7.1: *Use the Design Table form to edit the* PRIMARY KEY.

Figure 7.2 shows the Properties form in which you can see how to change the FILLFACTOR or the CLUSTERED property of the index associated to the PRIMARY KEY.

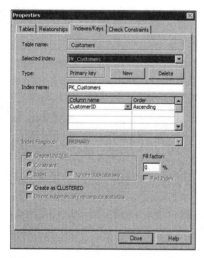

Figure 7.2: *Use the index Properties form to change properties of a* PRIMARY KEY *index.*

UNIQUE Constraints

You can create a PRIMARY KEY to enforce uniqueness in a field or group of fields, but you can have only one PRIMARY KEY per table.

If you require enforcing uniqueness in other columns, you can create a UNIQUE constraint. For example, you can have a PRIMARY KEY defined in the EmployeeID surrogate key in the Employees table, but you want to enforce uniqueness on

- Social security number if all your employees have one
- National identification number in countries where this is the standard identification
- Passport number on overseas projects
- Driver's license number for your Drivers table.

Full Name is not usually a good candidate for a UNIQUE constraint, because you can have many employees with the same name.

ProductName can be a good candidate, unless you have multiple products with the same name and different size, color, or any other attribute. In this case, you either provide a name with the full description, including all these attributes, or consider the combination of name and attributes as unique in your table.

A UNIQUE constraint is similar to a PRIMARY KEY, but you can have more than one UNIQUE constraint per table. When you declare a UNIQUE constraint, SQL Server creates a UNIQUE index to speed up the process of searching for duplicates. In this case, the index defaults to NONCLUSTERED, because you can have more than one UNIQUE constraint but only one clustered index.

NOTE

The number of UNIQUE constraints in a table is limited by the maximum number of indexes per table, which is 249 nonclustered indexes plus one possible clustered index, as mentioned in Chapter 6.

Contrary to PRIMARY KEY constraints, UNIQUE constraints can accept NULL values, but just one. If the constraint is defined in a combination of fields, every field can accept NULL and have some NULL values on them, as long as the combination of values is unique.

Suppose you declared a UNIQUE constraint in the combination of the fields (HouseNumber, HouseName, Apartment, Address, City). In this case, you can have many rows where any of these fields are NULL, but only one row can have all these fields NULL. In this example, the table can have different combinations of NULL entries:

- Only one row with NULL in all these fields.

- Many rows with NULL value in HouseNumber, HouseName, Apartment, Address or City, as long as the other fields are not NULL at the same time.

- Many rows with NOT NULL values in these fields.

If you want to enforce uniqueness in a column that accepts many NULL values, a UNIQUE constraint cannot help you. In this case, you should use a trigger or a CHECK constraint with a user-defined function. You can see examples of both strategies in Chapters 9 and 10.

Trying to create a UNIQUE constraint in a row or combination of rows with nonunique values will give you an error message.

You can specify options for the UNIQUE index, in the same way as in the PRIMARY KEY definition. For more index options, you can create a UNIQUE index instead of a UNIQUE constraint.

You can use the code of Listing 7.4 to create a UNIQUE constraint in a single column of a table, using the CREATE TABLE and the ALTER TABLE statements, using different syntax options.

EXAMPLE

Listing 7.4: Create UNIQUE Constraints

```
-- Define a UNIQUE constraint in a single column
-- using the default constraint name

CREATE TABLE NewRegions (
RegionID int NOT NULL
UNIQUE NONCLUSTERED,
RegionDescription nchar (50) NOT NULL ,
)
GO


DROP TABLE NewRegions
GO


-- Define a UNIQUE constraint in a single column
-- specifying the constraint name

CREATE TABLE NewRegions (
RegionID int NOT NULL
CONSTRAINT UC_NewRegions
UNIQUE NONCLUSTERED,
RegionDescription nchar (50) NOT NULL ,
)
GO
```

Listing 7.4: continued

```
DROP TABLE NewRegions
GO

-- Define a UNIQUE constraint in a single column
-- specifying the constraint name
-- and defining the constraint at table level

CREATE TABLE NewRegions (
RegionID int NOT NULL,
RegionDescription nchar (50) NOT NULL ,
CONSTRAINT UC_NewRegions
UNIQUE NONCLUSTERED (RegionID),
)
GO

DROP TABLE NewRegions
GO

-- Define a UNIQUE constraint in a single column
-- specifying the constraint name
-- and defining the constraint at table level
-- using the ALTER TABLE statement

CREATE TABLE NewRegions (
RegionID int NOT NULL,
RegionDescription nchar (50) NOT NULL)

ALTER TABLE NewRegions
ADD CONSTRAINT UC_NewRegions
UNIQUE NONCLUSTERED (RegionID)
GO

DROP TABLE NewRegions
GO
```

As detailed earlier in this chapter for PRIMARY KEYs, you can provide properties for the index, such as CLUSTERED, NONCLUSTERED, or FILLFACTOR, in the constraint definition. Listing 7.5 shows how to declare the index of a UNIQUE constraint as nonclustered and with a FILLFACTOR of 70%. Index properties were detailed in Chapter 6.

Listing 7.5: Create a UNIQUE Constraint and Define Properties of Its UNIQUE INDEX

```
-- Define a UNIQUE constraint in a single column
-- and create the index a nonclustered
-- and 70% FillFactor
```

EXAMPLE

Listing 7.5: continued

```
CREATE TABLE NewRegions (
RegionID int NOT NULL
UNIQUE NONCLUSTERED WITH FILLFACTOR = 70,
RegionDescription nchar (50) NOT NULL ,
)
GO


DROP TABLE NewRegions
GO
```

Listing 7.6 shows how to create a multicolumn UNIQUE constraint. A composite UNIQUE constraint is limited to 16 columns and 900 bytes for the key size.

EXAMPLE

Listing 7.6: Create a Multicolumn UNIQUE Constraint

```
-- Define a composite UNIQUE in two columns
-- specifying the constraint name


CREATE TABLE ProductSales (
ProductID int NOT NULL,
SaleID int NOT NULL,
Quantity int NOT NULL,
Price money NOT NULL,
Description varchar(200) NULL,
CONSTRAINT UC_ProductSales
UNIQUE NONCLUSTERED (ProductID, SaleID)
)
GO


DROP TABLE ProductSales
GO


-- Define a composite UNIQUE constraint in two columns
-- using the ALTER TABLE statement


CREATE TABLE ProductSales (
ProductID int NOT NULL,
SaleID int NOT NULL,
Quantity int NOT NULL,
Price money NOT NULL,
Description varchar(200) NULL)
```

Listing 7.6: continued

```
ALTER TABLE ProductSales
ADD CONSTRAINT UC_ProductSales
UNIQUE NONCLUSTERED (ProductID, SaleID)
GO

DROP TABLE ProductSales
GO
```

You can provide default values for a UNIQUE field in the same way as for the PRIMARY KEY:

- Using the IDENTITY property for the column, specifying the seed and increment values.

- Using the uniqueidentifier data type combined with the NEWID function as a DEFAULT constraint to supply automatic GUID (Global Unique Identifier) values.

- Declare a user-defined function as a DEFAULT constraint, to provide unique values to the column.

- Declare the column using a data type timestamp or rowversion. However, this option is useless because timestamp values are unique, regardless of the existence of a UNIQUE constraint, and they change whenever the row changes.

CAUTION

An IDENTITY property does not guarantee uniqueness on its column. SQL Server does not guarantee uniqueness on IDENTITY columns unless you define a PRIMARY KEY constraint, a UNIQUE constraint, or a UNIQUE index on that column.

You can use Enterprise Manager to define a UNIQUE constraint in a table. To do it, right-click the table and select Design Table to display the Design Table form, and then click the Table and Index Properties icon on the toolbar. In the Indexes/Keys tab, you can create, modify, or delete UNIQUE constraints.

In the Properties form, you have the choice to create a UNIQUE constraint or a UNIQUE index. Use UNIQUE index if you want to provide extra functionality as Ignore Duplicate Key or Do Not Automatically Recompute Statistics.

Figure 7.3 shows the Properties form in which you can see how to define Properties for a UNIQUE constraint. Figure 7.4 shows a similar form to specify properties for the UNIQUE index associated to the UNIQUE constraint.

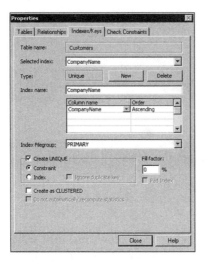

Figure 7.3: *Using the Properties form, you can define properties for a*
UNIQUE constraint.

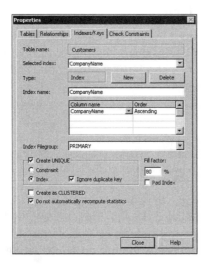

Figure 7.4: *Using the Properties form, you can define properties for a*
UNIQUE index.

CHECK Constraints

A CHECK constraint defines a condition for one or more columns in a table on
INSERT and UPDATE operations. This condition can be defined by any expression that returns TRUE or FALSE. If the condition returns TRUE, the operation
continues, but if the condition returns FALSE, the operation is automatically
rolled back.

It is possible to have many CHECK constraints per table, in which case they will be checked in creation order. If one CHECK constraint fails, the operation is rolled back and no more CHECK constraints are tested. In these situations, the client receives a single error message with information about the CHECK constraint that failed.

To define a CHECK constraint, you can use any expression as long as it references only columns in the same table. A CHECK constraint cannot reference other rows in the same table or other tables, but it is valid to use a user-defined function as part of the CHECK definition, and the user-defined function can use data from other tables, databases, or servers. In Chapter 10, we'll discuss how to use user-defined functions in CHECK constraints.

You can use a CHECK constraint to verify

- That the value has a valid format. For example, the Postcode should be a five-digit number.

- That the value is in a specific range of valid data. For example, the UnitPrice should be between 1 and 1,000, or greater than 0.

- That the value is not equal to any specific reserved value. For example, the name of a new product shouldn't be an empty string (").

- The result of a function applied to this value. For example, PaymentDue should be not later than 90 days from the SaleDate.

You can define single column CHECK constraints during the creation of a table. Listing 7.7 shows how to create a CHECK constraint on the NewEmployees table to ensure that the PostCode column accepts only strings with five digits. The second example in Listing 7.7 creates a CHECK constraint that enforces positive values for the UnitPrice column in the Products table.

EXAMPLE

Listing 7.7: Create a CHECK Constraint with the CREATE TABLE Statement

```
-- Define a CHECK constraint in a single column
-- using the default constraint name

CREATE TABLE NewEmployees (
EmployeeID int NOT NULL,
EmployeeName varchar(50) NOT NULL,
PostCode char(5) NOT NULL
CHECK (PostCode LIKE '[0-9][0-9][0-9][0-9][0-9]')
)
GO


DROP TABLE NewEmployees
GO
```

Listing 7.7: continued

```
-- Define a CHECK constraint in a single column
-- specifying the constraint name

CREATE TABLE NewProducts (
ProductID int NOT NULL,
ProductName varchar(50) NOT NULL,
UnitPrice money NOT NULL
CONSTRAINT CC_Prod_UnitPrice
CHECK (UnitPrice > 0)
)
GO

DROP TABLE NewProducts
GO
```

You can create a CHECK constraint at table level in the CREATE TABLE statement. This is the only way to define it if the CHECK constraint references more than one column. The expression can contain any number of subexpressions using logical operators as long as the total expression evaluates to TRUE or FALSE.

Listing 7.8 contains three examples of CHECK constraints:

- The CC_Prod_Name CHECK constraint forces the ProductName column to accept only nonempty strings.

- The CC_Order_DueDate CHECK constraint checks that the time between DueDate and SaleDate is less than or equal to 90 days.

- The third example creates the CC_Order_DueDate CHECK constraint to check three conditions simultaneously:

  - The DueDate should be on or prior to 90 days after the SaleDate.

  - The SaleDate cannot be a future date.

  - The ShipmentMethod can have only three possible values: air ('A'), land ('L'), or sea ('S').

Listing 7.8: Create Multicolumn CHECK Constraints with the CREATE TABLE Statement

```
-- Define a CHECK constraint in a single column
-- specifying the constraint name
-- and defining the constraint at table level

CREATE TABLE NewProducts (
ProductID int NOT NULL,
ProductName varchar(50) NOT NULL,
UnitPrice money NOT NULL ,
```

Listing 7.8: continued

```
CONSTRAINT CC_Prod_Name
CHECK (ProductName <> '')
)
GO

DROP TABLE NewProducts
GO

-- Define a CHECK constraint in a single column
-- specifying the constraint name
-- and defining the constraint at table level
-- as an expression

CREATE TABLE NewOrders (
OrderID int NOT NULL,
CustomerID int NOT NULL,
SaleDate smalldatetime NOT NULL ,
DueDate smalldatetime NOT NULL,
CONSTRAINT CC_Order_DueDate
CHECK (DATEDIFF(day, SaleDate, DueDate) <= 90)
)
GO

DROP TABLE NewOrders
GO

-- Define a CHECK constraint in a single column
-- specifying the constraint name
-- and defining the constraint at table level
-- as a multiple expressions linked by
-- logical operators

CREATE TABLE NewOrders (
OrderID int NOT NULL,
CustomerID int NOT NULL,
SaleDate smalldatetime NOT NULL ,
DueDate smalldatetime NOT NULL,
ShipmentMethod char(1) NOT NULL,
CONSTRAINT CC_Order_DueDate
CHECK
((DATEDIFF(day, SaleDate, DueDate) <= 90)
AND
(DATEDIFF(day, CURRENT_TIMESTAMP, SaleDate) <= 0)
AND (ShipmentMethod IN ('A', 'L', 'S'))
)
)
```

Listing 7.8: continued

```
GO

DROP TABLE NewOrders
GO
```

It is possible to create CHECK constraints for existing tables using the ALTER TABLE statement, as in Listing 7.9. In this case, you can specify whether it is necessary to check existing data.

The first example in Listing 7.9 creates three CHECK constraints on the NewOrders table: one CHECK constraint for every condition used in the last example from Listing 7.8.

The second example in Listing 7.9 creates the same CHECK constraints as in the first example, but in this case it specifies not to check existing data for the first and third CHECK constraints.

TIP

If you create a CHECK constraint as a sequence of multiple conditions, linked with the AND operator only, break it into several single-condition CHECK constraints. The maintenance of these CHECK constraints will be easier, and you will have more flexibility for enabling and disabling individual conditions, if required.

Listing 7.9: Create CHECK Constraints with the ALTER TABLE Statement

```
-- Define multiple CHECK constraint
-- in existing tables specifying
-- the constraint name and defining
-- the constraint at table level
-- using the ALTER TABLE statement
-- checking existing data

CREATE TABLE NewOrders (
OrderID int NOT NULL,
CustomerID int NOT NULL,
SaleDate smalldatetime NOT NULL ,
DueDate smalldatetime NOT NULL,
ShipmentMethod char(1) NOT NULL)

ALTER TABLE NewOrders
ADD CONSTRAINT CC_Order_DueDate
CHECK (DATEDIFF(day, SaleDate, DueDate) <= 90)

ALTER TABLE NewOrders
ADD CONSTRAINT CC_Order_SaleDate
CHECK (DATEDIFF(day, CURRENT_TIMESTAMP, SaleDate) <= 0)
```

Listing 7.9: continued

```
ALTER TABLE NewOrders
ADD CONSTRAINT CC_Order_Shipment
CHECK (ShipmentMethod IN ('A', 'L', 'S'))

GO

DROP TABLE NewOrders
GO

-- Define multiple CHECK constraint
-- in existing tables specifying
-- the constraint name and defining
-- the constraint at table level
-- using the ALTER TABLE statement
-- checking existing data
-- only for one of the constraints

CREATE TABLE NewOrders (
OrderID int NOT NULL,
CustomerID int NOT NULL,
SaleDate smalldatetime NOT NULL ,
DueDate smalldatetime NOT NULL,
ShipmentMethod char(1) NOT NULL)

ALTER TABLE NewOrders
WITH NOCHECK
ADD CONSTRAINT CC_Order_DueDate
CHECK (DATEDIFF(day, SaleDate, DueDate) <= 90)

ALTER TABLE NewOrders
ADD CONSTRAINT CC_Order_SaleDate
CHECK (DATEDIFF(day, CURRENT_TIMESTAMP, SaleDate) <= 0)

ALTER TABLE NewOrders
WITH NOCHECK
ADD CONSTRAINT CC_Order_Shipment
CHECK (ShipmentMethod IN ('A', 'L', 'S'))

GO

DROP TABLE NewOrders
GO
```

To modify a CHECK constraint, you must drop the constraint and re-create it or use Enterprise Manager to do it. To modify a CHECK constraint using Enterprise Manager, right-click the table and select Design Table to display the Design Table form. Click the Table and Index Properties icon on the toolbar to display the Properties form, and select the Check Constraints tab. Figure 7.5 shows the Check Constraints tab of the Properties form. Using this form, you can

- Change the name of the CHECK constraint.

- Change the expression of the constraint.

- Specify whether you want to check existing data.

- Select whether you want to enforce this constraint when receiving data from replication (on by default).

- Enable the constraint for INSERT and UPDATE statements (on by default).

CAUTION

When you modify a CHECK constraint using Enterprise Manager, Check Existing Data is off by default. However, when you create a new constraint using Transact-SQL, this option is on by default.

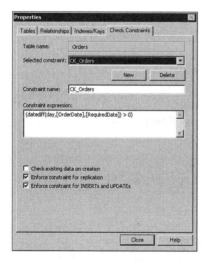

Figure 7.5: *Use Enterprise Manager to modify a CHECK constraint.*

NOTE

If you use Enterprise Manager to modify a CHECK constraint, Enterprise Manager will drop and re-create the constraint for you, using the new settings.

CAUTION

Check constraints are evaluated when you insert data and when you try to update a column referenced by a check constraint. However, if you update a column in a preexisting row, only this column will be checked against CHECK constraints; the other columns will remain unchecked.

Checking constraints produces some overhead. You can disable a CHECK constraint for INSERT and UPDATE operations if the data to insert is checked already with the same conditions. To disable a constraint for INSERT and UPDATE operations, you can use the ALTER TABLE statement.

Listing 7.10 shows how to disable and reenable a CHECK constraint.

EXAMPLE

Listing 7.10: Use the ALTER TABLE Statement to Disable and Reenable Constraints

```
-- Create a CHECK constraint
-- in existing tables specifying
-- the constraint name and defining
-- the constraint at table level
-- using the ALTER TABLE statement
-- checking existing data


-- Create table

CREATE TABLE NewOrders (
OrderID int NOT NULL,
CustomerID int NOT NULL,
SaleDate smalldatetime NOT NULL ,
DueDate smalldatetime NOT NULL,
ShipmentMethod char(1) NOT NULL)

-- Create constraint

ALTER TABLE NewOrders
ADD CONSTRAINT CC_Order_DueDate
CHECK (DATEDIFF(day, SaleDate, DueDate) <= 90)

-- Disable constraint

ALTER TABLE NewOrders
NOCHECK CONSTRAINT CC_Order_DueDate

-- Reenable constraint
```

Listing 7.10: continued

```
ALTER TABLE NewOrders
CHECK CONSTRAINT CC_Order_DueDate
GO

DROP TABLE NewOrders
GO
```

TIP

Disable constraints before importing the data to speed up the importing process, and reenable them after the data has been imported.

Replicated data has been checked already in the Publisher. Checking the same data again in the subscriber is usually unnecessary. You can create a CHECK constraint that is disabled for replicated data specifying NOT FOR REPLICATION after the CHECK keyword.

Listing 7.11 shows how to use the NOT FOR REPLICATION option in the CREATE TABLE and ALTER TABLE statements.

EXAMPLE

Listing 7.11: Using the NOT FOR REPLICATION Option to Avoid Checking Replicated Data

```
-- Define a CHECK constraint in a single column
-- using the default constraint name
-- specifying NOT FOR REPLICATION

CREATE TABLE NewEmployees (
EmployeeID int NOT NULL,
EmployeeName varchar(50) NOT NULL,
PostCode char(5) NOT NULL
CHECK NOT FOR REPLICATION (PostCode LIKE '[0-9][0-9][0-9][0-9][0-9]')
)
GO

DROP TABLE NewEmployees
GO

-- Define multiple CHECK constraint
-- in existing tables specifying
-- the constraint name and defining
-- the constraint at table level
-- using the ALTER TABLE statement
-- checking existing data
-- specifying NOT FOR REPLICATION

CREATE TABLE NewOrders (
OrderID int NOT NULL,
CustomerID int NOT NULL,
```

Listing 7.11: continued

```
SaleDate smalldatetime NOT NULL ,
DueDate smalldatetime NOT NULL,
ShipmentMethod char(1) NOT NULL)

ALTER TABLE NewOrders
ADD CONSTRAINT CC_Order_DueDate
CHECK NOT FOR REPLICATION
(DATEDIFF(day, SaleDate, DueDate) <= 90)

ALTER TABLE NewOrders
ADD CONSTRAINT CC_Order_SaleDate
CHECK NOT FOR REPLICATION
(DATEDIFF(day, CURRENT_TIMESTAMP, SaleDate) <= 0)

ALTER TABLE NewOrders
ADD CONSTRAINT CC_Order_Shipment
CHECK NOT FOR REPLICATION
(ShipmentMethod IN ('A', 'L', 'S'))

GO

DROP TABLE NewOrders
GO
```

CAUTION

If you disable a CHECK constraint to import data, test the data to see whether the check condition can still be valid before reenabling the constraint.

You can remove a CHECK constraint by using the ALTER TABLE statement. Removing a table removes constraints associated with the table.

Use the example in Listing 7.12 to create the NewProducts table, including the CC_Prod_UnitPrice CHECK constraint, and drop the constraint using the ALTER TABLE statement.

Listing 7.12: Use the ALTER TABLE Statement to Remove CHECK Constraints

```
-- Define a CHECK constraint in a single column
-- specifying the constraint name

CREATE TABLE NewProducts (
ProductID int NOT NULL,
ProductName varchar(50) NOT NULL,
UnitPrice money NOT NULL
CONSTRAINT CC_Prod_UnitPrice
CHECK (UnitPrice > 0)
)
```

Listing 7.12: continued

```
GO

-- Drop the constraint
-- Specifying its name

ALTER TABLE NewProducts
DROP CONSTRAINT CC_Prod_UnitPrice
GO

DROP TABLE NewProducts
GO
```

TIP

Providing names to constraints makes it easier to drop, disable, and reenable them. Otherwise, you must use the sp_helpconstraint system stored procedure to retrieve information about existing constraints in a table.

DEFAULT Definitions

You can define a DEFAULT definition for columns to avoid repetitive data entry. If a column has a DEFAULT definition, this value will be supplied if you don't provide a specific value for the column in the INSERT statement. DEFAULT definitions are applied only in INSERT operations.

You can provide as a DEFAULT definition any expression that evaluates to a single scalar value with a data type compatible with the data type of the column in which the DEFAULT definition is defined. This expression can be

- A constant value

- Any system scalar function

- The result of a scalar user-defined function

- Any scalar expression made from any combination of the previous points, including mathematical expressions

You can create a DEFAULT definition for a new column using the CREATE TABLE or ALTER TABLE statements, defining the DEFAULT constraint at column level. To force the use of the default value, you can omit the column, provide the DEFAULT keyword, or use the DEFAULT VALUES for the INSERT statement, as detailed in Listing 7.13.

CAUTION

If you explicitly insert a NULL value into a column that accepts NULL, and the column has a DEFAULT definition, the DEFAULT definition won't be applied.

CAUTION

You can have only one DEFAULT definition per column; otherwise, SQL Server will not know which value to use. If you try to create more than one DEFAULT definition for a column, you will receive an error message.

EXAMPLE

Listing 7.13: Create DEFAULT Definitions Using the CREATE TABLE Statement

```
-- Create the table NewCustomers
-- providing the value 'London'
-- as a column DEFAULT definition
-- for the City column,
-- a named DEFAULT constraint
-- for the CustomerName column,
-- The current date and time
-- for the CreaDate column
-- and the login name
-- for the CreaUser column


CREATE TABLE NewCustomers(
CustomerID int NOT NULL
IDENTITY(1,1)
PRIMARY KEY,
CustomerName varchar(30) NOT NULL
CONSTRAINT Def_CustName
DEFAULT 'To be entered',
City varchar(30)
DEFAULT 'London',
CreaDate smalldatetime
DEFAULT Getdate(),
CreaUser nvarchar(128)
DEFAULT System_User)
GO

-- Insert data into the NewCustomers table
-- Providing values for CustomerName
-- and City fields

INSERT NewCustomers (CustomerName, City)
VALUES ('MyComp corp.', 'New York')

-- Insert data into the NewCustomers table
-- Omitting to enter the City field

INSERT NewCustomers (CustomerName)
VALUES ('ACME Inc.')
```

Listing 7.13: continued

```
SELECT *
FROM NewCustomers

-- Insert data into the NewCustomers table
-- Providing the default value
-- for the City field

INSERT NewCustomers (CustomerName, City)
VALUES ('NewDotCompany Ltd.', DEFAULT)

SELECT *
FROM NewCustomers

-- Insert data into the NewCustomers table
-- Providing the default value
-- for every nonnull field

INSERT NewCustomers
DEFAULT VALUES

SELECT *
FROM NewCustomers

-- Drop the test table

DROP TABLE NewCustomers
```

OUTPUT

```
CustomerID  CustomerName          City       CreaDate                  CreaUser
----------- --------------------- ---------- ------------------------- --------
1           MyComp corp.          New York   2000-11-11 17:35:00       sa
2           ACME Inc.             London     2000-11-11 17:35:00       sa

CustomerID  CustomerName          City       CreaDate                  CreaUser
----------- --------------------- ---------- ------------------------- --------
1           MyComp corp.          New York   2000-11-11 17:35:00       sa
2           ACME Inc.             London     2000-11-11 17:35:00       sa
3           NewDotCompany Ltd.    London     2000-11-11 17:35:00       sa

CustomerID  CustomerName          City       CreaDate                  CreaUser
----------- --------------------- ---------- ------------------------- --------
1           MyComp corp.          New York   2000-11-11 17:35:00       sa
2           ACME Inc.             London     2000-11-11 17:35:00       sa
3           NewDotCompany Ltd.    London     2000-11-11 17:35:00       sa
4           To be entered         London     2000-11-11 17:35:00       sa
```

NOTE

You can refer to the DEFAULT definitions as DEFAULT constraints or DEFAULT properties as well. SQL Server 2000 Books Online refers to them as DEFAULT definitions, but earlier versions called them DEFAULT constraints, and using SQL-DMO refer to them as DEFAULT properties.

You can add a DEFAULT definition to an existing column using the ALTER TABLE statement, as in Listing 7.14.

EXAMPLE

Listing 7.14: Create new DEFAULT Properties for New and Existing Columns with the ALTER TABLE Statement

```
-- Create the table NewCustomers
-- providing the value 'London'
-- as a column DEFAULT definition
-- for the City column,
-- and a named DEFAULT constraint
-- for the CustomerName column


CREATE TABLE NewCustomers(
CustomerID int NOT NULL
IDENTITY(1,1)
PRIMARY KEY,
CustomerName varchar(30) NOT NULL
CONSTRAINT Def_CustName
DEFAULT 'To be entered',
City varchar(30)
DEFAULT 'London',
CreaDate smalldatetime)
GO

-- Use ALTER TABLE
-- to add a new column
-- with a DEFAULT definition

ALTER TABLE NewCustomers
ADD CreaUser nvarchar(128)
DEFAULT SYSTEM_USER

-- Use ALTER TABLE
-- to add a DEFAULT definition
-- to an existing column

ALTER TABLE NewCustomers
ADD CONSTRAINT Def_Cust_CreaDate
DEFAULT CURRENT_TIMESTAMP
FOR CreaDate
```

Listing 7.14: continued

```
GO

-- Drop the test table

DROP TABLE NewCustomers
```

> **NOTE**
> You can use the system function CURRENT_TIMESTAMP as a synonym of GetDate(), and
> the system function SYSTEM_USER as a synonym of SUSER_SNAME().

When you add a new column with a DEFAULT definition, the column gets the
DEFAULT value automatically for existing rows if

- The column does not accept NULL

- The column accepts NULL but you specify WITH VALUES after the DEFAULT
  definition

Listing 7.15 shows how to add a column with a DEFAULT definition to a table
with existing data, specifying the WITH VALUES option.

EXAMPLE

Listing 7.15: Use the WITH VALUES Option to Provide a Default Value to a New Column on
Existing Rows

```
-- Create the table NewCustomers
-- providing the value 'London'
-- as a column DEFAULT definition
-- for the City column,
-- and a named DEFAULT constraint
-- for the CustomerName column

CREATE TABLE NewCustomers(
CustomerID int NOT NULL
IDENTITY(1,1)
PRIMARY KEY,
CustomerName varchar(30) NOT NULL
CONSTRAINT Def_CustName
DEFAULT 'To be entered',
City varchar(30)
DEFAULT 'London',
CreaDate smalldatetime
DEFAULT CURRENT_TIMESTAMP)
GO

-- Insert some data

INSERT NewCustomers (CustomerName, City)
VALUES ('MyComp corp.', 'New York')
```

Listing 7.15: continued

```
INSERT NewCustomers (CustomerName)
VALUES ('ACME Inc.')

INSERT NewCustomers (CustomerName, City)
VALUES ('NewDotCompany Ltd.', DEFAULT)

INSERT NewCustomers
DEFAULT VALUES

SELECT *
FROM NewCustomers
GO

-- Use ALTER TABLE
-- to add a new column
-- with a DEFAULT definition
-- filling this new column
-- in existing rows

ALTER TABLE NewCustomers
ADD CreditLimit money
DEFAULT 1000.0
WITH VALUES

SELECT *
FROM NewCustomers

GO

-- Drop the test table
DROP TABLE NewCustomers
```

OUTPUT

CustomerID	CustomerName	City	CreaDate
1	MyComp corp.	New York	2000-11-11 17:35:00
2	ACME Inc.	London	2000-11-11 17:35:00
3	NewDotCompany Ltd.	London	2000-11-11 17:35:00
4	To be entered	London	2000-11-11 17:35:00

CustomerID	CustomerName	City	CreaDate	CreditLimit
1	MyComp corp.	New York	2000-11-11 17:58:00	1000.0000
2	ACME Inc.	London	2000-11-11 17:58:00	1000.0000
3	NewDotCompany Ltd.	London	2000-11-11 17:58:00	1000.0000
4	To be entered	London	2000-11-11 17:58:00	1000.0000

Foreign Keys

If you have two related tables—such as TableA and TableB—their relationship can be any of these three types:

- One to one—Figure 7.6 shows the relationship between the Customers table and the PublicCustomers table (this table does not exist in the Northwind database). Every row in the PublicCustomers is related to a single row in the Customers table, but not every row in the Customers table has a related row in the PublicCustomers table. As in this example, you can use one-to-one relationships to expand a table creating a subtable to store information related only to some specific rows.

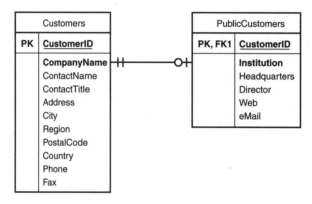

Figure 7.6: *A one-to-one relationship.*

- One to many—Figure 7.7 shows the relationship between the Products and [Order Details] tables. For every product, you can have none, one, or many related rows in the [Order Details] table. And every row in the [Order Details] table is related to only one row in the Products table.

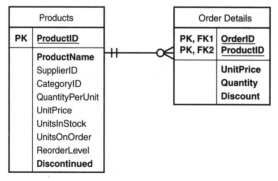

Figure 7.7: *A one-to-many relationship.*

- Many to many—Every employee can work in different territories, and in every territory you can have many employees. Figure 7.8 shows the relationships between the Employees and the Territories tables. As you can see in the diagram, the problem is solved by an intersection table, EmployeesTerritories, that contains the keys to connect to both tables.

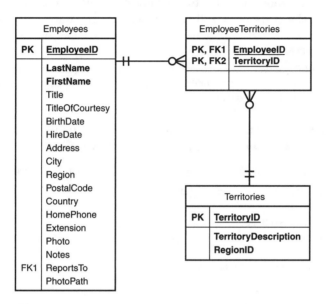

Figure 7.8: *A many-to-many relationship.*

To establish a relationship from one table, which can be called the "children" table, to another table, which can be called the "parent" table, you must create in the children table a FOREIGN KEY constraint.

When you define a FOREIGN KEY in the children table, this constraint enforces some rules in both parent and children tables:

- In the parent table, you cannot modify the related field on any row that has any related rows in the children table. For example, you cannot change the product code, or sales in this product will be invalid.

- You cannot delete a row in the parent table that has related rows in the children table. For example, you cannot delete a product with sales, or the sales about this product will be orphans.

- You cannot insert new rows in the children table where the related field contains nonexisting values in the related field on the parent table. For example, you cannot create a sale for a nonexisting product.

- You cannot modify the related field in the children table to a new value that does not exist in the parent table. For example, you cannot change the product code in a sale for a nonexisting product code.

After the FOREIGN KEY is created, SQL Server will check every statement involving the related tables to prevent any violation of the relationship. In that case, the statement will be rejected and the data will not be modified.

CAUTION

Because SQL Server checks constraints before modifying the data, if any constraint fails, the data will never be modified. Therefore, this cancelled action will not fire any trigger you might have defined.

You can declare a FOREIGN KEY constraint either using the CREATE TABLE or the ALTER TABLE statements. Listing 7.16 shows a complete example.

EXAMPLE

Listing 7.16: Create FOREIGN KEY Constraints with the CREATE TABLE or ALTER TABLE Statement

```
-- Create Customers and Orders tables

CREATE TABLE Customers(
CustomerID int
PRIMARY KEY,
CustomerName varchar(20) NOT NULL)

CREATE TABLE Orders(
OrderID int
IDENTITY(1,1)
PRIMARY KEY,
CustomerID int NOT NULL,
OrderDate smalldatetime NOT NULL
DEFAULT CURRENT_TIMESTAMP)
GO


-- Create the FOREIGN KEY constraint

ALTER TABLE Orders
ADD CONSTRAINT FK_Orders
FOREIGN KEY (CustomerID)
REFERENCES Customers (CustomerID)
GO

/*

-- Or you could define the Orders
-- table with References
-- without using the ALTER TABLE
-- statement to define the FOREIGN KEY
```

Listing 7.16: continued

```
CREATE TABLE Orders(
OrderID int
IDENTITY(1,1)
PRIMARY KEY,
CustomerID int NOT NULL
REFERENCES Customers(CustomerID),
OrderDate smalldatetime NOT NULL
DEFAULT CURRENT_TIMESTAMP)
--GO

*/


-- Insert some Customers

INSERT Customers
VALUES (1, 'MyComp corp.')

INSERT Customers
VALUES (2, 'ACME Inc.')

INSERT Customers
VALUES (3, 'NewDotCompany Ltd.')

-- Insert some Orders
-- with the default Date

INSERT Orders (CustomerID)
VALUES (1)

INSERT Orders (CustomerID)
VALUES (2)

INSERT Orders (CustomerID)
VALUES (3)

INSERT Orders (CustomerID)
VALUES (3)

-- Try to update customer 3 PRIMARY KEY
-- to a different value

PRINT CHAR(10) + 'Trying to update a customer PK' + CHAR(10)

UPDATE Customers
SET CustomerID = 30
```

Listing 7.16: continued

```
WHERE CustomerID = 3

-- Try to insert a new order for a
-- nonexisting customer

PRINT CHAR(10) + 'Trying to insert an orphan Order' + CHAR(10)

INSERT Orders (CustomerID)
VALUES (10)

GO

DROP TABLE Orders

DROP TABLE Customers
```

OUTPUT

```
Trying to update a customer PK

Server: Msg 547, Level 16, State 1, Line 1
UPDATE statement conflicted with COLUMN REFERENCE constraint 'FK_Orders'.
➥The conflict occurred in database 'ByExample',
➥table 'Orders', column 'CustomerID'.
The statement has been terminated.

Trying to insert an orphan Order

Server: Msg 547, Level 16, State 1, Line 1
INSERT statement conflicted with COLUMN FOREIGN KEY constraint 'FK_Orders'.
➥The conflict occurred in database 'ByExample',
➥table 'Customers', column 'CustomerID'.
The statement has been terminated.
```

CAUTION

Having a FOREIGN KEY defined in a column does not prevent this column from being NULL. Therefore, it is possible to have orphan rows not related to any row in the parent table. To solve this situation, you should declare the related columns as NOT NULL.

NOTE

It is required that the related field or group fields in the parent table must have defined a UNIQUE index. Therefore, it is recommended to use the primary key as the related field.

You can use Enterprise Manager to create FOREIGN KEY constraints. The easiest way is by using the Diagram tool. Figure 7.9 shows a diagram for the Northwind database, including the relationships between tables.

To create a FOREIGN KEY in the Diagram tool, you can just drag a column from the children table and drop it on the parent table.

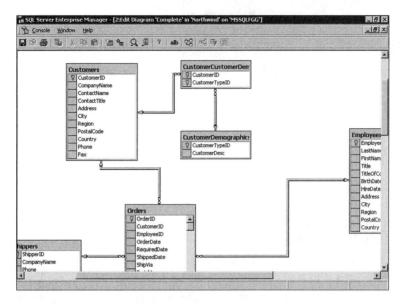

Figure 7.9: *To view and edit relationships between tables, you can use the Diagram tool in Enterprise Manager.*

TIP

In complex databases, create one diagram for every main table, showing only one or two levels of relationship. In this way, it will be easier to manage. However, you can have a complete diagram as well to get the full picture, if required.

Figure 7.10 shows how to create and modify FOREIGN KEY constraints using the Properties form of the children table.

You can prevent checking existing data when you create the FOREIGN KEY constraint by using the WITH NOCHECK option.

To modify a FOREIGN KEY constraint, you must drop the constraint and re-create it.

NOTE

Remember that you can use ALTER TABLE... NOCHECK CONSTRAINT to disable constraint checking and ALTER TABLE... CHECK CONSTRAINT to reenable the constraint.

To prevent the FOREIGN KEY constraint from checking replicated data, use the NOT FOR REPLICATION predicate.

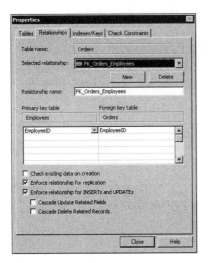

Figure 7.10: *Using the Properties form, you can define relationships with related tables.*

CAUTION

To create a FOREIGN KEY constraint that references a multicolumn UNIQUE index, PRIMARY KEY or UNIQUE constraint, in the parent table, you must create the FOREIGN KEY in the group of related fields.

FOREIGN KEY constraints are dropped automatically when the table is dropped. However, to drop a constraint you can use the ALTER TABLE... DROP CONSTRAINT statement, specifying the name of the constraint to drop.

NOTE

When you create a FOREIGN KEY constraint, SQL Server does not create any index on the selected columns. However, the columns included in a FOREIGN KEY constraint are good candidates for an index.

Cascading Operations: Cascaded Declarative Referential Integrity

The ANSI standard establishes four modes to solve changes that could break referential integrity definitions:

- RESTRICT or NO ACTION—Trying to delete or modify a row that is linked to some rows in a children table produces an error message and the operation is rolled back. This is the default for SQL Server 2000.

- CASCADE—Modifications to a UNIQUE field are cascaded to every FOREIGN KEY that references the field. Deleting a row forces a deletion of every related row where the FOREIGN KEY references the deleted row. This mode is optional in SQL Server 2000.

- SET NULL—When the referential integrity is broken for some FOREIGN KEY values, because of an update or delete operation in the parent table, those values are set to NULL. This mode is not implemented in SQL Server 2000.

- SET DEFAULT—If the referential integrity is broken for some FOREIGN KEY values due to an update or delete operation in the parent table, the FOREIGN KEY values are set to a default value. This mode is not implemented in SQL Server 2000.

The standard mode of FOREIGN KEY constraints has been covered in a previous section. In the following sections, you are going to see how to implement cascade operations in SQL Server 2000.

Nested cascade operations interact with nested triggers in the following way:

1. INSTEAD OF triggers, in the original table, execute first, usually with the execution of modifications on individual tables, which you will consider the first level of update.

2. All cascade operations, from tables of the first level of update, execute without a predefined order. The cascade operations continue through the related tables, eventually forcing further cascade operations to be executed affecting other tables, until there are no more tables to apply cascade operations.

3. AFTER triggers on the deepest level of the cascade operation fire first. On this level, the triggers of the affected tables fire without predefined order. The execution of triggers moves one level up at a time, firing every required trigger from affected tables. In this way, for a given table, SQL Server tries to fire every AFTER trigger only once. The AFTER triggers on these levels fire only if the trigger is fired due to the modification of one or more rows.

4. AFTER triggers on the first level of update fire regardless of the number of affected rows.

CAUTION

Because the interaction between constraints and triggers can be very complex, always document your design and keep it simple.

NOTE

You can use the Transact-SQL Debugger to debug triggers (INSTEAD OF and AFTER triggers). You must create a stored procedure to do the first modification, and debug this procedure. The debugger will jump from trigger to trigger if required.

CASCADING DELETES

To define a FOREIGN KEY constraint as a cascaded DELETE action, you must use the ON DELETE CASCADE in the REFERENCES clause of the FOREIGN KEY definition on the CREATE TABLE or ALTER TABLE statements.

In Listing 7.17, you create the Customers table and the Orders table. You define a FOREIGN KEY constraint between these two tables with the ON DELETE CASCADE option. Customer 2 has three related rows in the Orders table. The operation that deleted customer 2 from the Customers table forces the deletion of the three related rows in the Orders table.

CAUTION

Cascade operations can be nested from table to table producing potentially undesired results.

EXAMPLE

Listing 7.17: Cascade Deletion of Rows in Related Tables with FOREIGN KEY Constraints Defined As ON DELETE CASCADE

```
-- Create Customers and Orders tables

CREATE TABLE Customers(
CustomerID int
PRIMARY KEY,
CustomerName varchar(20) NOT NULL)

CREATE TABLE Orders(
OrderID int
IDENTITY(1,1)
PRIMARY KEY,
CustomerID int NOT NULL,
OrderDate smalldatetime NOT NULL
DEFAULT CURRENT_TIMESTAMP)
GO

-- Create the FOREIGN KEY constraint
-- with CASCADE

ALTER TABLE Orders
ADD CONSTRAINT FK_Orders
FOREIGN KEY (CustomerID)
REFERENCES Customers (CustomerID)
ON DELETE CASCADE

GO

-- Insert some Customers
```

Listing 7.17: continued

```
INSERT Customers
VALUES (1, 'MyComp corp.')

INSERT Customers
VALUES (2, 'ACME Inc.')

INSERT Customers
VALUES (3, 'NewDotCompany Ltd.')

-- Insert some Orders
-- with the default Date

INSERT Orders (CustomerID)
VALUES (1)

INSERT Orders (CustomerID)
VALUES (1)

INSERT Orders (CustomerID)
VALUES (2)

INSERT Orders (CustomerID)
VALUES (2)

INSERT Orders (CustomerID)
VALUES (2)

INSERT Orders (CustomerID)
VALUES (3)

INSERT Orders (CustomerID)
VALUES (3)

-- Show the data

PRINT CHAR(10) + 'Original Customers table' + CHAR(10)

SELECT *
FROM Customers

PRINT CHAR(10) + 'Original Orders table' + CHAR(10)

SELECT *
FROM Orders

GO
```

Listing 7.17: continued

```
-- Delete Customer 2

DELETE Customers
WHERE CustomerID = 2

PRINT CHAR(10) + 'Customers table after delete Customer 2' + CHAR(10)

SELECT *
FROM Customers

PRINT CHAR(10) + 'Orders table after delete Customer 2' + CHAR(10)

SELECT *
FROM Orders

GO

DROP TABLE Orders

DROP TABLE Customers
```

OUTPUT

```
Original Customers table

CustomerID  CustomerName
----------- --------------------
1           MyComp corp.
2           ACME Inc.
3           NewDotCompany Ltd.


Original Orders table

OrderID     CustomerID  OrderDate
----------- ----------- ------------------------------
1           1           2000-11-12 23:55:00
2           1           2000-11-12 23:55:00
3           2           2000-11-12 23:55:00
4           2           2000-11-12 23:55:00
5           2           2000-11-12 23:55:00
6           3           2000-11-12 23:55:00
7           3           2000-11-12 23:55:00


Customers table after delete Customer 2

CustomerID  CustomerName
----------- --------------------
```

Listing 7.17: continued

```
1          MyComp corp.
3          NewDotCompany Ltd.


Orders table after delete Customer 2

OrderID    CustomerID  OrderDate
---------- ----------- ----------------------------
1          1           2000-11-12 23:55:00
2          1           2000-11-12 23:55:00
6          3           2000-11-12 23:55:00
7          3           2000-11-12 23:55:00
```

CASCADING UPDATES

To define a FOREIGN KEY constraint as a cascaded UPDATE action, you must use the ON UPDATE CASCADE in the REFERENCES clause of the FOREIGN KEY definition on the CREATE TABLE or ALTER TABLE statements.

Listing 7.18 is based in the same example as in Listing 7.17. You create the Customers table and the Orders table. You define a FOREIGN KEY constraint between these two tables with the ON UPDATE CASCADE option. You want to change the ID of customer 3 to 30. Customer 3 has two related rows in the Orders table. The UPDATE operation changes the CustomerID from 3 to 30 in both tables automatically.

CAUTION

It is not recommended to change PRIMARY KEY values. This can produce identity integrity problems in your applications.

EXAMPLE

Listing 7.18: Cascade Changes on Primary Keys to Related Foreign Keys with FOREIGN KEY Constraints Defined As ON UPDATE CASCADE

```
-- Create Customers and Orders tables

CREATE TABLE Customers(
CustomerID int
PRIMARY KEY,
CustomerName varchar(20) NOT NULL)

CREATE TABLE Orders(
OrderID int
IDENTITY(1,1)
PRIMARY KEY,
CustomerID int NOT NULL,
OrderDate smalldatetime NOT NULL
DEFAULT CURRENT_TIMESTAMP)
GO
```

Listing 7.18: continued

```
-- Create the FOREIGN KEY constraint
-- with CASCADE

ALTER TABLE Orders
ADD CONSTRAINT FK_Orders
FOREIGN KEY (CustomerID)
REFERENCES Customers (CustomerID)
ON DELETE CASCADE -- This is optional
ON UPDATE CASCADE
GO

-- Insert some Customers

INSERT Customers
VALUES (1, 'MyComp corp.')

INSERT Customers
VALUES (2, 'ACME Inc.')

INSERT Customers
VALUES (3, 'NewDotCompany Ltd.')

-- Insert some Orders
-- with the default Date

INSERT Orders (CustomerID)
VALUES (1)

INSERT Orders (CustomerID)
VALUES (1)

INSERT Orders (CustomerID)
VALUES (2)

INSERT Orders (CustomerID)
VALUES (2)

INSERT Orders (CustomerID)
VALUES (2)

INSERT Orders (CustomerID)
VALUES (3)

INSERT Orders (CustomerID)
VALUES (3)
```

Listing 7.18: continued

```
-- Show the data

PRINT CHAR(10) + 'Original Customers table' + CHAR(10)

SELECT *
FROM Customers

PRINT CHAR(10) + 'Original Orders table' + CHAR(10)

SELECT *
FROM Orders

GO


-- Update Customer 3
-- Change CustomerID from 3 for 30

UPDATE Customers
SET CustomerID = 30
WHERE CustomerID = 3

PRINT CHAR(10) + 'Customers table after update Customer 3' + CHAR(10)

SELECT *
FROM Customers

PRINT CHAR(10) + 'Orders table after update Customer 3' + CHAR(10)

SELECT *
FROM Orders

GO

DROP TABLE Orders

DROP TABLE Customers
```

OUTPUT

```
Original Customers table

CustomerID  CustomerName
----------- --------------------
1           MyComp corp.
2           ACME Inc.
3           NewDotCompany Ltd.


Original Orders table
```

Listing 7.18: continued

```
OrderID      CustomerID  OrderDate
...........  ..........  .................................
1            1           2000-11-12 23:59:00
2            1           2000-11-12 23:59:00
3            2           2000-11-12 23:59:00
4            2           2000-11-12 23:59:00
5            2           2000-11-12 23:59:00
6            3           2000-11-12 23:59:00
7            3           2000-11-12 23:59:00


Customers table after update Customer 3

CustomerID   CustomerName
...........  ...................
1            MyComp corp.
2            ACME Inc.
30           NewDotCompany Ltd.


Orders table after update Customer 3

OrderID      CustomerID  OrderDate
...........  ..........  .................................
1            1           2000-11-12 23:59:00
2            1           2000-11-12 23:59:00
3            2           2000-11-12 23:59:00
4            2           2000-11-12 23:59:00
5            2           2000-11-12 23:59:00
6            30          2000-11-12 23:59:00
7            30          2000-11-12 23:59:00
```

Transact-SQL–Specific Integrity Structures

Transact-SQL language provides an alternative to the CHECK and DEFAULT constraints with the RULE and DEFAULT objects. RULE and DEFAULT objects are not ANSI standard, so it is advisable to use constraints as a general way to provide the same functionality.

One of the reasons to use these Transact-SQL objects is to create self-contained user-defined data types, including not only the data type, but also the DEFAULT value and the RULE to check for domain integrity. If a column uses one of these self-contained user-defined data types as a data type, this column will inherit the DEFAULT definition and the RULE definition as well.

User-defined data types were covered in Chapter 2.

Using DEFAULT and RULE objects can help during the development process, if the same condition must be applied to multiple columns. However, remember that they are not ANSI compliant.

DEFAULT OBJECTS

DEFAULT objects are similar to the DEFAULT definition of a column, but you can create a DEFAULT object independently of any column and bind it to specific columns or user-defined data types later.

To create a DEFAULT object, you use the CREATE DEFAULT statement, providing a unique name for the DEFAULT object and defining the object as a constant, built-in function or any valid scalar expression.

To delete a DEFAULT object, you must use the DROP DEFAULT statement. You cannot drop a DEFAULT object if it is used anywhere in your database.

CAUTION

The only way to modify a DEFAULT or RULE object definition is by dropping and re-creating the object. Before dropping the object, you must unbind the object from any field and user-defined data type.

To bind a DEFAULT object to a field or user-defined data type, you must use the sp_bindefault system stored procedure, and the sp_unbindefault disconnects a bound DEFAULT object from a field or user-defined data type. Only one DEFAULT definition or DEFAULT object can be defined per column; binding a new DEFAULT object to a column overrides the existing one.

NOTE

DEFAULT and RULE objects are local to a database. Therefore, DEFAULT and RULE objects created in the Master database can be used only in the Master database.

You can see a complete example of how to use DEFAULT objects in Listing 7.19.

EXAMPLE

Listing 7.19: Create Independent DEFAULT Objects and Bind Them Later to Any Field or User-Defined Data Type

```
-- Create a DEFAULT object using a constant

CREATE DEFAULT NoSales
AS 0
GO


-- Create DEFAULT objects using expressions
-- based on built-in functions

CREATE DEFAULT ThisMonth
AS Month(CURRENT_TIMESTAMP)
GO
```

Listing 7.19: continued

```
CREATE DEFAULT UserDB
AS SYSTEM_USER
+ ' - ' + DB_NAME(DB_ID())
GO


-- Create two User-Defined Data Types

EXEC sp_addtype 'UDDTLoginDB', 'nvarchar(256)', 'NULL'

EXEC sp_addtype 'UDDTSales', 'money', 'NULL'
GO


-- Create a table to test the DEFAULT objects
-- and the User-Defined Data Types

CREATE TABLE TestDefaults(
ID int NOT NULL
IDENTITY(1,1)
PRIMARY KEY,
TotalSales money NULL,
SalesMonth tinyint NULL,
WhoWhere UDDTLoginDB)
GO


-- Insert a new empty row in the table

INSERT TestDefaults
DEFAULT VALUES

PRINT char(10) + 'No defaults defined' + CHAR(10)

SELECT *
FROM TestDefaults
GO


-- Bind the NoSales DEFAULT object
-- to the TotalSales field in the TestDefaults table

EXEC sp_bindefault 'NoSales', 'TestDefaults.TotalSales'
GO


-- Insert a new empty row in the table

INSERT TestDefaults
DEFAULT VALUES
```

Listing 7.19: continued

```
PRINT  CHAR(10) + 'Only DEFAULT on TotalSales defined' + CHAR(10)

SELECT *
FROM TestDefaults
GO

-- Bind the ThisMonth DEFAULT object
-- to the SalesMonth field in the TestDefaults table

EXEC sp_bindefault 'ThisMonth', 'TestDefaults.SalesMonth'

GO

-- Insert a new empty row in the table

INSERT TestDefaults
DEFAULT VALUES

PRINT  CHAR(10) + 'DEFAULT defined on TotalSales and SalesMonth' + CHAR(10)

SELECT *
FROM TestDefaults
GO

-- Bind the UserDB DEFAULT object
-- to the UDDTLoginDB User-Defined Data Type

EXEC sp_bindefault 'UserDB', 'UDDTLoginDB'

GO

-- Insert a new empty row in the table

INSERT TestDefaults
DEFAULT VALUES

PRINT  CHAR(10) + 'DEFAULT defined on TotalSales, SalesMonth'
PRINT 'and the UDDTLoginDB User-Defined Data Type' + CHAR(10)

SELECT *
FROM TestDefaults
GO

-- Add a new column to the TestDefaults table
-- Using the UDDTSales data type
```

Listing 7.19: continued

```
ALTER TABLE TestDefaults
ADD ProjectedSales UDDTSales
GO

PRINT CHAR(10) + 'Add an empty field using the UDDTSales data type' + CHAR(10)

SELECT *
FROM TestDefaults
GO

-- Bind the NoSales DEFAULT object
-- to the UDDTSales User-Defined Data Type
-- for future columns only

EXEC sp_bindefault 'NoSales', 'UDDTSales', 'futureonly'
GO

-- Insert a new empty row in the table

INSERT TestDefaults
DEFAULT VALUES

PRINT CHAR(10) + 'DEFAULT defined on UDDTSales data type as futureonly'
PRINT 'does not affect the existing fields using this UDDT' + CHAR(10)

SELECT *
FROM TestDefaults
GO

-- Drop everything in order
-- Table first
-- UDDT next
-- DEFAULT last

DROP TABLE TestDefaults

EXEC sp_droptype 'UDDTSales'

EXEC sp_droptype 'UDDTLoginDB'

DROP DEFAULT NoSales

DROP DEFAULT ThisMonth

DROP DEFAULT UserDB
```

Listing 7.19: continued

OUTPUT

```
Type added.
Type added.

No defaults defined

ID     TotalSales       SalesMonth WhoWhere
------ ---------------- ---------- --------------
1      NULL             NULL       NULL


Default bound to column.

Only DEFAULT on TotalSales defined

ID     TotalSales       SalesMonth WhoWhere
------ ---------------- ---------- --------------
1      NULL             NULL       NULL
2      .0000            NULL       NULL

Default bound to column.

DEFAULT defined on TotalSales and SalesMonth

ID     TotalSales       SalesMonth WhoWhere
------ ---------------- ---------- --------------
1      NULL             NULL       NULL
2      .0000            NULL       NULL
3      .0000            11         NULL

Default bound to data type.
The new default has been bound to columns(s) of the specified user data type.

DEFAULT defined on TotalSales, SalesMonth
and the UDDTLoginDB User-Defined Data Type

ID     TotalSales       SalesMonth WhoWhere
------ ---------------- ---------- --------------
1      NULL             NULL       NULL
2      .0000            NULL       NULL
3      .0000            11         NULL
4      .0000            11         sa - ByExample


Add an empty field using the UDDTSales data type
```

Listing 7.19: continued

ID	TotalSales	SalesMonth	WhoWhere	ProjectedSales
1	NULL	NULL	NULL	NULL
2	.0000	NULL	NULL	NULL
3	.0000	11	NULL	NULL
4	.0000	11	sa - ByExample	NULL

Default bound to data type.

DEFAULT defined on UDDTSales data type as future only
does not affect the existing fields using this UDDT

ID	TotalSales	SalesMonth	WhoWhere	ProjectedSales
1	NULL	NULL	NULL	NULL
2	.0000	NULL	NULL	NULL
3	.0000	11	NULL	NULL
4	.0000	11	sa - ByExample	NULL
5	.0000	11	sa - ByExample	NULL

Type has been dropped.
Type has been dropped.

RULE OBJECTS

RULE objects are similar to CHECK constraints. However, you can create a
RULE object independently of any column and bind it later to specific
columns or user-defined data types.

To create a RULE object, you use the CREATE RULE statement, providing a
unique name for the RULE object and defining the object as any expression
that returns TRUE or FALSE.

CAUTION
You can't use user-defined functions as part of a DEFAULT or RULE object definition.

To delete a RULE object, you must use the DROP RULE statement. You cannot
drop a RULE object if it is used anywhere in your database.

To bind a RULE object to a field or user-defined data type, you must use the
sp_bindrule system stored procedure, and the sp_unbindrule disconnects a
bound RULE object from a field or user-defined data type.

You can bind only one rule to a user-defined data type or a table field.
However, a rule can coexist with one or more CHECK constraints in a field; in
this case, all the conditions will be checked. If you bind a new rule to a field
or user-defined data type, the old rule will be unbound automatically.

You can see an example of how to use RULE objects in Listing 7.20.

EXAMPLE

Listing 7.20: Create Independent RULE Objects and Bind Them Later to Any Field or User-Defined Data Type

```
-- Define a Table to test RULE Creation

CREATE TABLE NewEmployees (
EmployeeID int NOT NULL,
EmployeeName varchar(50) NOT NULL,
PostCode char(5) NOT NULL )
GO


-- Create the RULE object

CREATE RULE RUPostCode
AS
(@PCode LIKE '[0-9][0-9][0-9][0-9][0-9]')
GO


-- Bind the RULE to the PostCode column

EXEC sp_bindrule 'RUPostCode', 'NewEmployees.PostCode'
GO


-- Insert data in the table to test the RULE

INSERT NewEmployees
VALUES (1, 'Paul', 'GL513')

INSERT NewEmployees
VALUES (2, 'Eladio', '01380')

SELECT *
FROM NewEmployees

GO


DROP TABLE NewEmployees
GO

DROP RULE RUPostCode
GO
```

OUTPUT

```
Rule bound to table column.
Server: Msg 513, Level 16, State 1, Line 1
A column insert or update conflicts with a rule imposed by
➥a previous CREATE RULE statement. The statement was terminated.
➥The conflict occurred in database 'ByExample',
```

Listing 7.20: continued

```
➡table 'NewEmployees', column 'PostCode'.
The statement has been terminated.
EmployeeID  EmployeeName                    PostCode
----------  ----------------------------    --------
2           Eladio                          01380
```

NOTE

The definition of the RULE object contains a variable. The name of this variable is not relevant; it just represents the column to where the RULE object will be bound.

NOTE

Remember to keep it simple. Overengineering a database will produce execution overhead and a difficult maintenance.

What's Next?

This chapter covered the creation and use of structures to enforce data integrity.

Chapter 8 covers the creation of stored procedures, where you can test the integrity of the data before attempting any modification, having extra data control and access to more complex condition checking.

Chapter 9 covers triggers, which is another way to enforce data integrity. In that chapter, you will see how to create triggers to enforce domain integrity and referential integrity.

User-defined functions are covered in Chapter 10. It is possible to use UDF as part of constraint definitions. This new feature gives you tremendous flexibility in the definition of DEFAULT and CHECK constraints.

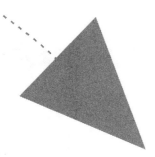

Implementing Business Logic: Programming Stored Procedures

A stored procedure is a database object that comprises one or more Transact-SQL statements. The main difference between a stored procedure and a set of statements is that a stored procedure can be reused just by calling its name. Therefore, if you want to rerun the code, you don't have to execute the whole set of statements that compose the stored procedure one by one.

As a database developer, you will spend most of your time coding, fixing, and optimizing stored procedures because they can be used for thousands of purposes. Not only can they be used to encapsulate business logic for your applications, they also can be used for administrative purposes inside SQL Server.

This chapter teaches you the following:

- The benefits of using stored procedures
- The types of stored procedures in SQL Server
- The types of stored procedure parameters
- How to create, alter, and execute stored procedures
- How to handle errors in stored procedures
- Security considerations when working with stored procedures

Benefits of Using Stored Procedures

Usually, stored procedures are used to encapsulate or enforce business rules in your databases. For example, if you have to do some calculations before inserting data in a table, you can embed this logic in a stored procedure and then insert the data using this stored procedure. Similarly, if you don't want users to directly access tables and any other objects, you can create stored procedures to access these objects and have users use them, instead of manipulating objects directly. For example, Microsoft discourages users from making direct modifications to system tables; however, SQL Server comes with system stored procedures to manipulate system tables.

CAUTION

If you develop applications that modify system tables, you should stop doing this. Be advised that in future releases of SQL Server, Microsoft won't allow users to modify system tables directly.

The following are the benefits and advantages of stored procedures:

- They are precompiled statements—An execution plan (or access plan) is created and stored in memory the first time the stored procedure is run, and it is subsequently used each time you execute the stored procedure, thus minimizing the time it takes to run. This is more efficient than executing each statement separately, one by one, because SQL Server would have to generate an access plan for each statement every time it is run.

- They optimize network traffic—You might say that stored procedures aren't related to network traffic at all. However, when you execute a stored procedure that contains many statements, you just have to call the stored procedure once, not each statement separately. In other words, the entire block of code (the whole set of statements) doesn't need to be sent from the client to the server. For example, if you create a stored procedure with 10 statements and execute it, you need to send only one instruction to SQL Server instead of 10 separate instructions. This translates into fewer round trips to SQL server, thus optimizing network traffic.

- They can be used as a security mechanism—In particular, if the owner of an object doesn't want to give direct permissions to users on database objects, he can create stored procedures that manipulate these objects, and then give execute permissions on these stored procedures to users. This way, users will be allowed only to execute these stored procedures, and they won't be able to directly manipulate the objects that stored procedures reference. System stored procedures are an example of this approach. SQL Server provides system stored procedures to prevent users from dealing directly with system tables.

- They allow modular programming—You can encapsulate your business logic inside stored procedures, and then just call them from applications. Therefore, all statements that make up a stored procedure are executed as a whole in the server. Furthermore, you can embed conditional logic in a stored procedure using any of the control of flow statements (IF...ELSE, WHILE) available in Transact-SQL.

- They can be set to execute automatically when SQL Server starts— Any routine task that must be executed whenever the SQL Server service starts can be programmed as a stored procedure and then configured to run automatically using the sp_procoption system stored procedure.

- They can use parameters—This is one of the ways that stored procedures have to receive data from and return it to the calling application. Parameters can be either input, which are similar to variables passed by value, or output, which behave as variables passed by reference.

Types of Stored Procedures

In SQL Server, there are four types of stored procedures: *system stored procedures*, *user-defined stored procedures*, *temporary stored procedures*, and *extended stored procedures*. System and extended stored procedures are created automatically at installation time. The other types (user-defined, temporary) are the ones users create explicitly.

System Stored Procedures

System stored procedures are created automatically in system databases when you install SQL Server. They are basically a way to interact with system tables. Moreover, there is a system stored procedure for almost any administrative task you perform in SQL server. Also, because Microsoft doesn't recommend dealing directly with system tables, this is the preferred way to deal with them.

Every global system stored procedure's name has the sp_ prefix, and for this reason they can be executed from any database. Listing 8.1 demonstrates this feature, calling the sp_helpdb system stored procedure (which gives general information about databases) from the Northwind database.

EXAMPLE

Listing 8.1: Executing a System Stored Procedure (Which Is Stored in Master) from the Northwind Database

```
USE Northwind
GO

sp_helpdb
```

Listing 8.1: continued

OUTPUT

`--The output has been simplified`

name	db_size	owner	dbid	created	compatibility_level
master	12.19 MB	sa	1	Aug 6 2000	80
model	1.13 MB	sa	3	Aug 6 2000	80
msdb	13.50 MB	sa	4	Aug 6 2000	80
Northwind	3.94 MB	sa	6	Aug 6 2000	80
pubs	2.13 MB	sa	5	Aug 6 2000	80
tempdb	8.50 MB	sa	2	Jan 22 2001	80

Transact-SQL provides a system function, OBJECTPROPERTY, that is used to check for a variety of object properties. Specifically, the property 'IsMSShipped' checks whether an object is a system object. Thus, it can be used to identify whether a stored procedure is a system stored procedure. This system function, like many others in SQL Server, receives the object's ID as a parameter, which can be obtained using the OBJECT_ID system function. The OBJECTPROPERTY function returns 0 if the property is true, or 1 if not. Listing 8.2 shows the use of this property.

EXAMPLE

Listing 8.2: Using the OBJECTPROPERTY System Function to Check Whether an Object Was Created During SQL Server Installation

```
USE Master
SELECT OBJECTPROPERTY(OBJECT_ID('sp_help'),'IsMSShipped')
GO
```

OUTPUT

```
-----------
1
(1 row(s) affected)
```

CAUTION

Books Online states that 'IsMSShipped' returns 1 (true) for any object created in the SQL Server installation process. This is not completely true, because 'IsMSShipped' returns 0 (false) for any user object created when SQL Server was installed—for example, Northwind.dbo.Shippers. Therefore, 'IsMSShipped' returns 1 for any system object created at installation time. Notice that although Pubs and Northwind are created during the installation process, they are not considered system databases.

User-Defined Stored Procedures

You create user-defined stored procedures in SQL Server to implement business logic. Any task, no matter how simple or complex, that comprises multiple statements and conditions can be programmed as a stored procedure, and then the calling application just needs to execute the stored procedure, instead of executing the whole set of statements separately.

User-defined stored procedures are created using the CREATE PROCEDURE statement, and then SQL Server stores them in the current database.

Stored procedures' names, like any other object's name, must be unique within the database and unique to the user who creates them (the owner). Hence, in a certain database, it is possible that two stored procedures exist with the same name but with different owners.

Any stored procedure that is created in the master database with the sp_ prefix—for example, sp_myprocedure—can be accessed from any other database. In general, when a stored procedure is executed and its name has the sp_ prefix, SQL Server looks for it, first in the current database, and then, if it's not found in the current database, SQL Server looks for it in the master database.

CAUTION

If you create a user-defined stored procedure in any database other than master, with the sp_ prefix on its name, and there is a stored procedure in master with the same name, the user-defined stored procedure that resides in the user's database will be executed only when called from the user database. This is because when SQL Server executes any stored procedure that contains the sp_ prefix, SQL Server looks for it first in the current database, and then in master if it doesn't find it in the current database. Be aware that Books Online incorrectly states that SQL Server looks for it first in master and then in the current database.

For example, you can create a user-defined stored procedure in master, as Listing 8.3 shows, and call it from other databases.

EXAMPLE

Listing 8.3: Creation of a Stored Procedure, with the sp_ Prefix, in Master, and Execution in Pubs

```
USE Northwind
GO
CREATE PROCEDURE sp_showdatabasename
AS
SELECT 'Northwind'
GO

USE Master
GO
CREATE PROCEDURE sp_showdatabasename
AS
SELECT 'Master'
GO

-- When executed from Northwind, SQL Server executes
-- the one stored in Northwind
USE Northwind
EXEC sp_showdatabasename
GO

-- When executed from Pubs, SQL Server executes
```

Listing 8.3: continued

```
-- the one stored in Master, because there isn't
-- a stored procedure called sp_showdatabasename
-- in the Pubs database
USE Pubs
EXEC sp_showdatabasename
GO

----------
Northwind

(1 row(s) affected)
```

OUTPUT

```
------
Master

(1 row(s) affected)
```

Temporary Stored Procedures

These are stored procedures created by users and stored in the `tempdb` database. They are called temporary because they are dropped automatically by SQL Server, unless you explicitly issue a `DROP PROCEDURE` statement. Like any other temporary object in SQL Server, when creating temporary stored procedures, use the # prefix for local and the ## prefix for global temporary stored procedures. Listing 8.4 shows the creation of a temporary stored procedure. After executing the code shown in Listing 8.4 in Query Analyzer, expand the Stored Procedures folder of `tempdb` in the Object Browser, and you will see the stored procedure `#getdatabasename` listed. Then, close the current connection to SQL Server (close the window if you're working in Query Analyzer), and refresh the Stored Procedures folder of `tempdb`; the table will be gone.

Listing 8.4: Creation of a Temporary Stored Procedure

```
CREATE PROC #getdatabasename
AS
SELECT db_name() AS database_name
GO
```

EXAMPLE

Basically, temporary stored procedures have the same functionality as user-defined stored procedures, with one exception; they are dropped when the connection that creates them is finished.

TIP

A temporary stored procedure, once created (and stored in `tempdb` automatically by SQL Server), can be called from any database.

Extended Stored Procedures

Extended stored procedures are DLL programs written in C++ that extend the capabilities of SQL Server. The links to these external libraries are defined in the master database and exposed as extended stored procedures inside SQL Server.

SQL Server has its own set of extended stored procedures whose name begins with xp_, which are used mainly for administrative purposes. However, there are some extended stored procedures that start with sp_ just to consider them as global—for example, sp_OACreate.

You can create your own extended stored procedure, coding a DLL using C++ and then adding it to SQL Server as an extended stored procedure, using the sp_addextendedproc system stored procedure. Be very careful when coding extended stored procedures (trap any kind of errors, deallocate memory, and so on) because they run in the same memory space as SQL Server; thus, any error in an extended stored procedure can crash SQL Server.

Creating and Dropping Stored Procedures

Stored procedures are created using the CREATE PROCEDURE statement or the equivalent statement CREATE PROC. When a stored procedure is created, its properties are stored in the sysobjects system table, and its definition (all the statements it contains) in the syscomments system table. A stored procedure is stored in the current database; therefore, if you want to create a stored procedure in other databases, you have to make the other database the current one before creating it (using the USE statement).

After a stored procedure is created, you can view its parameters and definition using the sp_helptext system stored procedure. You can view its properties using sp_help.

In Listing 8.5, you can see an example of the syntax used to create a stored procedure. Followed by the creation, it shows the retrieval of the stored procedure's properties, using sp_help, and then its code, using sp_helptext.

EXAMPLE

Listing 8.5: Creating a Stored Procedure and Retrieving Its Properties and Code

```
USE Northwind
GO

CREATE PROC dbo.getcurrenttime
AS
SELECT CURRENT_TIMESTAMP
GO
```

Listing 8.5: continued

```
EXEC sp_help 'getcurrenttime'
EXEC sp_helptext 'getcurrenttime'
GO
```

OUTPUT

```
Name                Owner   Type                Created_datetime
----------------    ------  ----------------    ------------------------
getcurrenttime      dbo     stored procedure    2000-09-18 01:35:06.257
```

```
Text
----------------------------------
CREATE PROC getcurrenttime
AS
SELECT CURRENT_TIMESTAMP
```

There are three steps that SQL Server performs with stored procedures: *parsing*, *name resolution*, and *optimization*.

SQL Server parses a stored procedure when it is created to check for correct syntax. Then, the stored procedure's information is stored in sysobjects and syscomments.

The first time the stored procedure is executed, SQL Server checks that all the objects it references exist. This is a feature of SQL Server called *deferred name resolution*, which allows you to create stored procedures that reference objects that haven't been created yet. This is why this step is performed the first time the stored procedure is executed, not when it is created.

In the last step, SQL Server finds an optimized execution plan, looking for the best way to execute each statement inside the stored procedure. Then, an optimized execution plan is generated and stored in the procedure cache, which is part of the memory that SQL Server allocates for its use (the other part of the memory, the data cache, is used to store the data pages that SQL Server manipulates).

Figure 8.1 shows this three-step process (parse, name resolution, and optimization).

The execution plan of a stored procedure will remain in memory until SQL Server is stopped or when SQL Server needs the memory allocated for the plan. Therefore, if SQL Server doesn't have any more memory available for new execution plans, it needs to drop from memory some of these existing plans, or some data pages, to make room for new ones.

After the execution plan is created and stored in the procedure cache (memory), any time you execute the stored procedure, SQL Server just needs to reuse the plan to manipulate the data. SQL Server shows this cache information if you query the syscacheobjects system table. Be aware that syscacheobjects is a virtual table, not a real one. The only purpose of this virtual table is to provide support for internal procedures and DBCC commands, and the table is filled automatically with data when you use it. Specifically, you can retrieve information about the procedure cache by querying this virtual table (master.dbo.syscacheobjects).

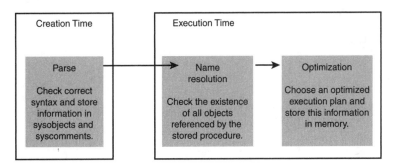

Figure 8.1: *Creation and execution of stored procedures in SQL Server.*

The process of generating a good access plan involves evaluating many factors, such as indexes and data in tables. This is one of the reasons you should have good indexes on tables and views referenced by stored procedures, and also keep statistics up to date, which is a database option that is set by default when you create a database.

TIP

In a stored procedure, it's better to create the objects first (DDL), and then manipulate them (DML), because this prevents the query processor from recompiling the stored procedure while it is executed.

In SQL Server 6.5 and earlier, the only way to create an access plan was by using stored procedures. In version 7.0 and later, the query processor can store execution plans in the procedure cache for all Transact-SQL statements (including ad hoc queries). When reexecuting a Transact-SQL statement, if the query processor detects that it can reuse the plan, it takes it from the procedure cache, optimizing the execution time of the whole statement.

A feature of stored procedures, as mentioned earlier, is that they can be set to execute automatically when the SQL Server service is started. Because they won't have any interaction with any application, they can't have any input parameters. The stored procedure must be created by the system administrator in the master database, and then the system stored procedure sp_procoption must be used to set it to execute when the SQL Server service is started.

For example, suppose that you want to be able to know every time the SQL Server service was started. To accomplish this, you can create a table in master to store the date and time when the SQL Server service has been started, and then create a stored procedure that inserts a row in this table with the current date. Finally, set this stored procedure to execute automatically whenever SQL Server is started. Listing 8.6 shows the code needed to achieve these steps.

EXAMPLE

Listing 8.6: Using the sp_procoption System Stored Procedure

```
USE Master
GO

CREATE TABLE dbo.Sqlstatus (
lasttime DATETIME
)
GO

CREATE PROC dbo.insertsqlstatus
AS
INSERT Sqlstatus (lasttime)
VALUES (CURRENT_TIMESTAMP)
GO

EXEC sp_procoption 'insertsqlstatus','startup','true'
```

To test this example, follow the next steps:

1. Using Query Analyzer, connect to SQL Server as sa, or if using integrated authentication, with a member of the System Administrators server role.

2. Run the code shown in Listing 8.6, which will create the Sqlstatus table and the insertsqlstatus stored procedure, and then set this stored procedure to run automatically whenever SQL Server is started.

3. Close any applications that might be using SQL Server (Query Analyzer, Enterprise Manager, and so on).

4. Stop and restart SQL Server.

5. Connect to SQL Server using Query Analyzer, and issue a SELECT query against the Sqlstatus table.

To verify that a stored procedure that was configured to execute automatically was successfully executed, you can check the SQL Server error log. The error log will show the following message to indicate that the stored procedure was executed successfully:

```
Launched startup procedure 'name_of_the_stored_procedure'
```

TIP

Another way to find the last time when SQL Server was started is by using the crdate column in the sysdatabases system table in master. This column stores the creation date of the database, and because tempdb is re-created every time the SQL Server service starts, you can get the last time that SQL Server was started.

Some statements can't be included in a stored procedure's code. These statements are CREATE DEFAULT, CREATE PROCEDURE, CREATE RULE, CREATE TRIGGER, and CREATE VIEW.

Stored procedures can be created using the WITH ENCRYPTION option, which encrypts the definition in the syscomments system table; therefore, nobody can read the definition. If you try to see the code of a stored procedure (using sp_helptext or any other method) and it has been encrypted, you will get this error:

```
The object comments have been encrypted
```

Be cautious when you encrypt a stored procedure's definition, because you won't be able to display it again unless you keep the original source code. Therefore, if you need to modify the definition of a stored procedure that was created using the WITH ENCRYPTION option, you must use the original source code. It is always a good idea to keep a copy of the original scripts that you used to generate the database schema.

Listing 8.7 creates the getcurrentuser stored procedure using the WITH ENCRYPTION option, and then tries to show the code of the stored procedure using sp_helptext, without success.

EXAMPLE

Listing 8.7: Creation of a Stored Procedure Using the WITH ENCRYPTION Option

```
USE Northwind
GO

CREATE PROC dbo.getcurrentuser
WITH ENCRYPTION
AS
SELECT USER
GO

sp_helptext 'getcurrentuser'
The object comments have been encrypted.
```

OUTPUT

Using Parameters

Like any function or procedure in any other programming language, stored procedures communicate with applications or clients through parameters. The maximum number of parameters in a stored procedure is 2,100 (this was significantly increased from SQL Server 7, which had a maximum of 1,024 parameters per stored procedure).

CAUTION

Be aware that Books Online incorrectly states in the "Maximum Capacity Specifications" section that the maximum number of parameters in a stored procedure is 1,024.

When you develop stored procedures, to be able to access the value of a parameter inside the stored procedure's body, you just have to specify the parameter's name (including the @ character).

Once created, information about stored procedures' parameters is stored in the syscolumns system table (you already know that sysobjects stores general information and syscomments stores the code of the stored procedure).

Parameters are defined right after the stored procedure's name when creating the stored procedure. The parameter's name must have the @ character as the first character (like any variable in Transact-SQL). After the name of the parameter, the data type must be specified, and then a default value, if there's one (the default value is optional).

Listing 8.8 shows an example of the creation of a stored procedure (getemployeesbylastname) that contains a parameter (@emplastname). This stored procedure gets the employees whose last name contains the string indicated by the @emplastname parameter. Notice that, when creating stored procedures, parameters are declared between the stored procedure's name and the AS keyword.

EXAMPLE

Listing 8.8: Creation of a Stored Procedure Using Parameters

```
USE Northwind
GO

CREATE PROC dbo.getemployeesbylastname
@emplastname VARCHAR(40)
AS
SELECT *
FROM Employees
WHERE lastname LIKE '%' + @emplastname + '%'
GO
```

The default value of a parameter can be set to NULL. If a parameter doesn't have a default value, a value must be supplied by the calling application when executing the stored procedure. On the other hand, if a parameter has a default value, the calling application doesn't have to supply a value for this parameter if it wants to use the default.

Listing 8.9 creates a stored procedure (`getemployeesbylastname_default`, a slight variation of the stored procedure shown in Listing 8.8), which contains a parameter (`@emplastname`) with a default value. Notice that the default value is specified just after the parameter's data type.

Listing 8.9: Creation of a Stored Procedure Using Default Parameters

```
USE Northwind
GO

CREATE PROC dbo.getemployeesbylastname_default
@emplastname VARCHAR(40) = 'a'
AS
SELECT *
FROM Employees
WHERE lastname LIKE '%' + @emplastname + '%'
GO
```

EXAMPLE

There are two types of parameters, *input* and *output*:

- An input parameter is similar to a variable passed by value. Therefore, the stored procedure gets a copy of the data and this doesn't affect the data outside the stored procedure. In other words, if you pass a variable as a parameter of a stored procedure, and the value of this variable is modified inside the stored procedure, this doesn't change the value of the variable outside the stored procedure.

- An output parameter is like a variable passed by reference. Hence, because the stored procedure gets a pointer to a variable, any changes made to it are reflected outside the scope of the stored procedure. Using this type of parameter, a stored procedure can send values back to the calling application. To take advantage of output parameters, and to distinguish them from input parameters, the OUTPUT keyword must be specified when creating the stored procedure, and also when it is executed.

Listing 8.10 shows the creation of a stored procedure (`getemployeeaddress`) that contains an input parameter (`@employeeid`) and an output parameter (`@employeeaddress`). This stored procedure stores the complete address of a given employee in the `@employeeaddress` output parameter. Notice that the OUTPUT keyword must be specified when declaring output parameters.

Listing 8.10: Using Input and Output Parameters

```
USE Northwind
GO

CREATE PROC dbo.getemployeeaddress
@employeeid INT,
```

EXAMPLE

Listing 8.10: continued

```
@employeeaddress NVARCHAR(120) OUTPUT
AS

SELECT @employeeaddress = address + '. ' + city + '. ' + region + '. ' +
       postalcode + '. ' + country
FROM Employees
WHERE employeeid = @employeeid
GO
```

An advantage of using stored procedures is that they can return result sets, using SELECT statements in the body of the stored procedure. However, one of the limitations of using parameters is that you can't use a parameter to pass the name of a database object (table, column, or stored procedure) to the stored procedure. For this purpose, you must build the query at runtime, generating a dynamic query (using EXEC or sp_executesql). Notice that this is not a restriction of parameters; it is a restriction of the Data Definition Language (DML).

To illustrate this idea, imagine that you want to create a stored procedure with one parameter, and this parameter is the table you want to query. Listing 8.11 shows the code necessary to create this stored procedure, using the EXEC statement.

EXAMPLE

Listing 8.11: Using Objects As Parameters and Building Queries at Runtime

```
USE Northwind
GO

CREATE PROC dbo.issuequery
@tablename NVARCHAR(256)
AS
DECLARE @query NVARCHAR(1000)
SET @query = 'SELECT * FROM ' + @tablename
EXEC (@query)
GO
```

Altering Stored Procedure Definitions

The code of a stored procedure can be modified using the ALTER PROCEDURE statement, or its equivalent ALTER PROC. In SQL Server 6.5 and earlier, the only way to change a stored procedure's definition was to drop and re-create it, but this approach has one drawback: Permissions and properties set on the stored procedure are lost. Therefore, after re-creating the stored procedure, the database administrator had to set permissions again.

Listing 8.12 modifies the definition of the stored procedure created in Listing 8.11. The new stored procedure, in addition to the table's name, receives a column's name as a parameter.

EXAMPLE

Listing 8.12: Using ALTER TABLE to Modify the Code of a Stored Procedure

```
USE Northwind
GO

ALTER PROC dbo.issuequery
@tablename NVARCHAR(256),
@columname NVARCHAR(256)
AS
DECLARE @query NVARCHAR(1000)
SET @query = 'SELECT ' + @columname + ' FROM ' + @tablename
EXEC (@query)
GO
```

When you alter a stored procedure's definition (using the ALTER PROC statement):

- SQL Server keeps permissions intact on the stored procedure. As a result, any permissions set on the stored procedure are kept after changing the stored procedure's code using ALTER TABLE.

- This doesn't affect any dependent objects (tables, triggers, or stored procedures). For example, if you alter a stored procedure's definition and it references a table, the table isn't affected.

- This doesn't affect the property to run automatically when SQL Server starts, if this was previously set using the sp_procoption system stored procedure. For example, if you alter the code of the stored procedure created in Listing 8.6 (insertsqlstatus, which was set to run automatically whenever SQL Server is started), SQL Server keeps this property intact.

In other words, if you either want to change the procedure's code without affecting permissions and properties, or want to change the options of the stored procedure (WITH ENCRYPTION or WITH RECOMPILE), you can use the ALTER PROCEDURE statement. However, notice that if you just need to change an option, you still must specify the entire code of the stored procedure. Similarly, if you just have to change the code and preserve the options, you also must specify the options.

For example, if you want to encrypt the code shown in Listing 8.12, you would have to add the WITH ENCRYPTION option to the definition of the stored procedure. Listing 8.13 shows you how to accomplish this, and also shows that the code is in fact encrypted after executing this script.

EXAMPLE

Listing 8.13: Using ALTER TABLE to Modify the Code of a Stored Procedure

```
USE Northwind
GO

ALTER PROC dbo.issuequery
@tablename NVARCHAR(256),
@columname NVARCHAR(256)
WITH ENCRYPTION
AS
DECLARE @query NVARCHAR(1000)
SET @query = 'SELECT ' + @columname + ' FROM ' + @tablename
EXEC (@query)
GO

sp_helptext issuequery
GO
```

OUTPUT

```
The object comments have been encrypted.
```

Notice that if you only want to add an option to the stored procedure's code (WITH ENCRYPTION, in the previous example), you still have to specify the entire code.

The RETURN Statement

The RETURN statement is used to exit unconditionally from a stored procedure. In other words, if SQL Server reaches a RETURN statement when executing a stored procedure, it stops processing and returns the control to the calling application.

The RETURN statement has one parameter, the *return value*, which is an integer that can be used to communicate with the calling application. When creating a stored procedure, if you use a data type other than integer for the return value, SQL Server allows you to create the stored procedure, but you will get an error when it is executed.

The return value is 0 by default; therefore, if a stored procedure contains a RETURN statement without this parameter, the return value will be 0. Therefore, it is equivalent to say RETURN 0 or RETURN. Similarly, if a stored procedure doesn't have any return statement at all, the return value is 0.

In general, a return value of 0 indicates a successful completion of the stored procedure. Any return value other than 0 usually indicates that there was an error in the execution of the stored procedure. The general convention used in system stored procedures is 0 means success, and any other value indicates that an error occurred.

Usually, the RETURN statement is very useful in the error-checking phase of the stored procedure; thus, if there's any error that you want to trap in the calling application, the RETURN statement can be used to return an error code.

Because you can use numbers other than 0 to return error codes to the calling application, if you want to have customized error codes in your application, you can choose a number for each type of error, and then when the application receives one of these error codes, it knows how to interpret them.

Listing 8.14 shows an example of a stored procedure (getemployee) that uses return values to indicate whether a certain employeeid exists in the Employees table. Getemployee returns –1 if the employeeid doesn't exist in the Employees table, and returns 0 if it does exist. Notice that the second RETURN statement doesn't have the return value, so it's 0 (the default).

EXAMPLE

Listing 8.14: Using the RETURN Statement in Stored Procedures

```
USE Northwind
GO

CREATE PROC dbo.getemployee
@employeeid INT
AS
IF NOT EXISTS (SELECT * FROM Employees WHERE employeeid = @employeeid)
    RETURN -1
ELSE
    SELECT * FROM Employees WHERE employeeid = @employeeid

RETURN
GO
```

CAUTION

The return value is not a stored procedure's output parameter; these are different things. Database developers sometimes confuse the return value with an output parameter. Keep in mind that a stored procedure can have more than one output parameter but just one return value.

Executing Stored Procedures

There are a variety of ways to execute stored procedures. All depend on the calling application, language used, and the programming interface (OLE-DB, ODBC, ADO, and so on). In Transact-SQL, the basic syntax to execute a stored procedure is the following:

```
EXECUTE @return_value = procedure_name parameter_1,..,parameter_n
```

The EXECUTE statement must be used if there's more than one instruction in the batch. Otherwise, if you want to execute just the stored procedure and there are no more instructions in the batch, you can omit the EXECUTE statement.

TIP

If there's more than one instruction in the batch and the stored procedure is called in the first line of the batch, you can omit the EXECUTE statement.

There are two ways to specify input parameters when executing a stored procedure:

- Use the name of the variables used in the parameter declaration of the stored procedure and their value—With this approach, you can omit variables if you want to use their default values. Also, the order of the parameters is not important. For example, Listing 8.15 creates a stored procedure that inserts a row in the Customers table, and then executes it. Notice that all the parameters that don't have a default value have to be specified.

Listing 8.15: Executing a Stored Procedure with Parameters

```
USE Northwind
GO

CREATE PROC dbo.InsertCustomer
@customerid NCHAR(10),
@companyname NVARCHAR(80),
@contactname NVARCHAR(60),
@contacttitle NVARCHAR(60) = 'Owner',
@address NVARCHAR(120) = NULL,
@city NVARCHAR(30) = 'Miami',
@region NVARCHAR(30) = 'FL',
@postalcode NVARCHAR(20) = '33178',
@country NVARCHAR(30) = 'USA',
@phone NVARCHAR(48) = NULL,
@fax NVARCHAR(48) = NULL
AS

INSERT INTO Customers (customerid,companyname,contactname,contacttitle,address,
            city,region,postalcode,country,phone,fax)
VALUES (@customerid,@companyname,@contactname,@contacttitle,@address,@city,
        @region,@postalcode,@country,@phone,@fax)
GO

InsertCustomer @customerid='MACMI',@contactname='Carlos Eduardo Rojas',
        @companyname = 'Macmillan'
GO
```

- Use just the actual values that you want to pass to the stored procedure—With this method, the order of the values is important. For this reason, values must be specified in the same order in which variables appear in the parameter declaration section of the stored procedure. Also, default values can be used, but they must be the last ones in the parameter declaration; otherwise, you would break the sequence. Listing 8.16 shows the execution of the stored procedure created in Listing 8.15, using this approach.

EXAMPLE

Listing 8.16: Another Way to Pass Parameters When Calling a Stored Procedure

```
USE Northwind
GO

InsertCustomer 'QUEPU','QUE Publishing','Jesus Rojas'
GO
```

The values can also be passed as local variables used in the same batch in which the stored procedure is being called. Listing 8.17 illustrates this variation.

EXAMPLE

Listing 8.17: Using Local Variables As Parameters When Calling a Stored Procedure

```
USE Northwind
GO

DECLARE @custid NCHAR(10),
@contname VARCHAR(60),
@compname VARCHAR(80)

SELECT @custid = 'SAMSP',
@contname = 'Maria Rojas',
@compname = 'Sams Publishing'

EXEC InsertCustomer @custid,@contname,@compname
GO
```

When output parameters are used in a stored procedure, the OUTPUT keyword must be specified again when the stored procedure is executed. In addition to the OUTPUT keyword, a variable must be used to store the value of the parameter after the stored procedure's execution. Listing 8.18 shows how to use output parameters. It creates a stored procedure that gets customer information given its ID. Note that the code that executes the stored procedure contains the OUTPUT keyword.

EXAMPLE

Listing 8.18: Using Output Parameters

```
USE Northwind
GO
```

Listing 8.18: continued

```
CREATE PROC dbo.getCustomerInfo
@customerid NCHAR(10),
@contact NVARCHAR(60) OUTPUT,
@company NVARCHAR(80) OUTPUT
AS
SELECT    @contact = contactname,
      @company = companyname
FROM    Customers
WHERE    customerid = @customerid
GO



DECLARE @customer_id NCHAR(10),@customer_name NVARCHAR(60),
      @customer_company NVARCHAR(80)
SET @customer_id = 'SAMSP'

EXEC getCustomerInfo @customer_id, @customer_name OUTPUT,
    @customer_company OUTPUT
SELECT @customer_name + ' - ' + @customer_company
GO
```

OUTPUT

```
Maria Rojas - Sams Publishing

(1 row(s) affected)
```

CAUTION

If the OUTPUT keyword is omitted when the stored procedure is executed, the parameter behaves as an input parameter.

Listing 8.19 contains the execution of the same stored procedure executed in Listing 8.18, but 8.19 omits the OUTPUT keyword in both variables. Notice that these values are lost after the stored procedure's execution.

EXAMPLE

Listing 8.19: Using Output Parameters Without the OUTPUT Keyword

```
USE Northwind
GO

DECLARE @customer_id NCHAR(10),@customer_name NVARCHAR(60),
      @customer_company NVARCHAR(80)
SET @customer_id = 'SAMSP'
EXEC getCustomerInfo @customer_id, @customer_name, @customer_company
SELECT @customer_name + ' - ' + @customer_company
GO
```

Listing 8.19: continued

OUTPUT

```
- - - - - - - - - - - - - - - - - - - - - - - - - - - - - - - - - - - - - - - - - - - - - - - - - - - - -
NULL

(1 row(s) affected)
```

If you want to process the return value of a stored procedure, you must store it in a variable when executing the stored procedure. Listing 8.20 executes the stored procedure created in Listing 8.14 (getemployee), and demonstrates how to store the return value in a local variable for further processing.

EXAMPLE

Listing 8.20: Storing the Return Value of a Stored Procedure in a Variable

```
USE Northwind
GO

DECLARE @employeeexists INT
EXEC @employeeexists = getemployee 88
SELECT @employeeexists
GO
```

OUTPUT

```
- - - - - - - - - - -
-1
```

The result set returned by executing a stored procedure (if it contains a SELECT statement) can be inserted into a table using the INSERT statement followed by the execution of the stored procedure. The data types of the result set must be compatible with the ones of the table. Compatible means that the data types must be either the same or they can be implicitly converted by SQL Server. Also, the number of columns of the stored procedure's result set must match the table's definition. For example, if the stored procedure produces a result set with three columns, you can't insert it in a table with two columns. In Listing 8.21, a stored procedure is created to get all the employees of a given country, and then a temporary table is created to store the result set returned by the execution of the stored procedure.

EXAMPLE

Listing 8.21: Inserting in a Table a Result Set Returned by a Stored Procedure

```
USE Northwind
GO

CREATE PROC dbo.GetEmployeesCountry
@country NVARCHAR(30)
AS
SELECT    employeeid,lastname,firstname
FROM      Employees
WHERE     country = @country
GO
```

Listing 8.21: continued

```
CREATE TABLE #Employees_in_usa (
emp_id INT NOT NULL,
emp_lname NVARCHAR (20) NOT NULL,
emp_fname NVARCHAR (10) NOT NULL
)
GO

INSERT INTO #Employees_in_usa
EXEC GetEmployeesCountry 'USA'

SELECT * FROM #Employees_in_usa
GO
```

OUTPUT

```
emp_id        emp_lname               emp_fname
-----------   --------------------    ----------
1             Davolio                 Nancy
2             Fuller                  Andrew
3             Leverling               Janet
4             Peacock                 Margaret
8             Callahan                Laura
```

(5 row(s) affected)

A stored procedure can be called from any database using fully qualified names. Notice that when calling a stored procedure from any other database than the one where it resides (where it was created), you must fully qualify the name of the stored procedure. This way, SQL Server knows where to look for the stored procedure. If you call a stored procedure from the database where it resides, you just have to call it by its name. For example, if you want to execute an extended stored procedure from any other database than master, you must indicate that this stored procedure resides in master. Specifically, Listing 8.22 shows the execution of xp_fixeddrives, which lists all the drives and space available, from the Northwind database. Notice that the output you get can vary according to the number of drives available in your computer and the space available on each one of them.

EXAMPLE

Listing 8.22: Using Fully Qualified Names to Call Stored Procedures

```
USE Northwind
GO

EXEC master..xp_fixeddrives
drive MB free
----- -----------
C     8315
```

OUTPUT

Listing 8.22: continued

```
D      8487
E      8316

(3 row(s) affected)
```

Using Query Analyzer's Object Browser to Execute Stored Procedures

In SQL 2000, the new object browser (one of the best additions to the Query Analyzer) allows us to execute stored procedures using a graphical interface. Using this method, you just have to enter the value of each parameter using the GUI, and then Query Analyzer automatically generates the code necessary to execute the stored procedure.

To execute a stored procedure using the object browser, follow these steps:

1. Open the Query Analyzer.

2. Connect to the server and choose the database.

3. Make sure that the object browser is open. If it is not open, choose Tools, Object Browser, or press F8.

4. In the object browser, expand a database, and then the stored procedures folder.

5. Right-click the stored procedure, and then click the Open option.

6. Query Analyzer opens the Execute Procedure window, in which you can enter the value of each parameter.

7. Click the Execute button.

CAUTION

When entering any kind of string in the Execute Procedure window in the Query Analyzer, don't use quotes to enclose the string.

If you follow these steps to execute the stored procedure created in Listing 8.21 (GetEmployeesCountry), you'll see the Execute Procedure window shown in Figure 8.2. Notice that the data type of the parameter is NVARCHAR, and when typing the value of this parameter, you don't have to use quotes to enclose it.

Figure 8.3 shows the results of the execution of the GetEmployeesCountry stored procedure. Query Analyzer generated all the code needed to execute the stored procedure using the parameters you provided in the window.

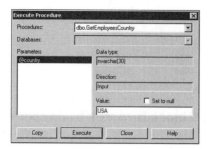

Figure 8.2: *Executing stored procedures using the Execute Procedure option in Query Analyzer.*

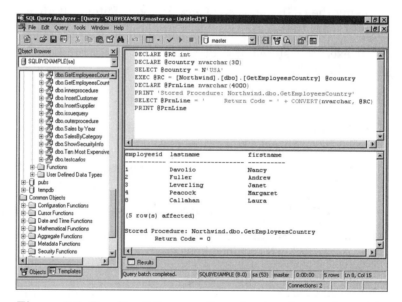

Figure 8.3: *Results of the execution of a stored procedure using the Execute Procedure option.*

Stored Procedure Recompilation

As you already know, SQL Server creates an optimized execution plan, which is stored in memory, the first time a stored procedure is executed. In general, you want SQL Server to reuse this execution plan for subsequent executions of stored procedures. However, for diverse reasons, sometimes you might want to force SQL Server to modify an execution plan. The reason might fall among one of these: The value of parameters changed significantly, the objects referenced by the stored procedure changed in some way, the data changed significantly or, last but not less important, indexes changed.

There are three ways to explicitly force SQL Server to generate another execution plan:

- Use the WITH RECOMPILE option when creating the stored procedure (CREATE PROC .. WITH RECOMPILE)—With this approach, SQL Server doesn't cache the stored procedure's execution plan. Instead, SQL Server compiles the stored procedure every time it is executed, generating a new execution plan. Listing 8.23 illustrates a stored procedure created using the WITH RECOMPILE option.

EXAMPLE

Listing 8.23: Creating a Stored procedure Using the WITH RECOMPILE Option

```
USE Northwind
GO

CREATE PROC dbo.GetEmployeesCountry2
@country NVARCHAR(30)
WITH RECOMPILE
AS
SELECT    employeeid,lastname,firstname
FROM      Employees
WHERE     country = @country
GO
```

- At execution time, use the WITH RECOMPILE option (EXECUTE .. WITH RECOMPILE)—If this method is used, SQL Server generates a new execution plan that is used in subsequent executions of the stored procedure. Listing 8.24 shows the execution of a stored procedure, using the WITH RECOMPILE option, forcing SQL Server to generate a new execution plan.

EXAMPLE

Listing 8.24: Using the WITH RECOMPILE Option in the Stored Procedure's Execution

```
USE Northwind
GO

EXEC GetEmployeesCountry 'USA' WITH RECOMPILE
GO
```

- Use the sp_recompile system stored procedure—This is a slightly different way to recompile a stored procedure. sp_recompile receives the name of an object as a parameter; the object can be a stored procedure, table, view, or trigger. If a stored procedure's name or a trigger's name is used as a parameter, this object (trigger or stored procedure) is recompiled the next time it is executed. On the other hand, if the parameter specified is the name of a table or a view, any stored procedure that references this table or view will be recompiled the next time it is executed. This is the preferred way to request recompilation of all stored procedures (that reference a specific table or view) with just one instruction. Listing 8.25 shows the use of the sp_recompile system stored procedure, forcing SQL Server to recompile any stored procedure that references the Employees table in the Northwind database.

Listing 8.25: Using sp_recompile to Force SQL Server to Generate a New Execution Plan for Every Stored Procedure That References the Authors Table

EXAMPLE

```
USE Northwind
GO

sp_recompile 'Employees'
GO

Object 'Employees' was successfully marked for recompilation.
```

OUTPUT

Handling Errors

An important element of any program you write is the error-checking section. During software development, it is a good programming technique to check for errors in your code, and abort the execution of the program or trap the error when it is found. If the program crashes, there's a high probability that it crashed because you neglected to check or trap an error.

Transact-SQL provides two elements that allow us to check and throw errors programmatically. These elements are the @@ERROR parameterless (or niladic) system function and the RAISERROR statement.

The @@ERROR system function returns the error code (an integer different from 0) of the last statement executed, if there was an error. On the other hand, if the last statement was executed successfully, @@ERROR returns 0. Be aware that this value changes from one statement to the next one; hence, you must check this value right after the statement is executed.

RAISERROR is used to explicitly throw an error. You can either use an ad hoc message or a message stored in the Sysmessages system table (all SQL Server error messages are stored in Sysmessages). You can add your own messages to this system table through the sp_addmessage system stored procedure, and to delete messages, through sp_dropmessage. Notice that when creating a user-defined message with sp_addmessage, you must specify a message ID greater than 50,001 (message IDs less than 50,000 are reserved by SQL Server).

This is the syntax of RAISERROR:

```
RAISERROR (msg_id | msg_text, severity, state) WITH option
```

The first parameter is the message ID or the message text. If you specify a message ID, you need to have previously created a user-defined message with sp_addmessage. If you want to use an ad hoc message, the message text can have up to 400 characters. The second parameter is the severity level of the error, which is a number between 0 and 25 (severity levels

greater than 20 must be used by system administrators for critical errors).
If the severity level falls in the range of 0 through 10, it's considered an
informational message. Then, severity levels from 10 to 19 are used for
trappable errors, and from 20 to 25 for critical errors (which close the connection after the client receives the error message).

The third parameter, the state of the error, is an integer between 0 and 127
which, by the documentation, isn't significant to SQL Server. Finally, there
are two options (either can be used) in the last parameter, which are optional:

- LOG—Stores the error information in the SQL Server error log and in
  the NT Application log. This option must be specified when using
  severity levels higher than 19.

- NOWAIT—This option sends the error message immediately to the client
  application.

After executing RAISERROR, @@ERROR returns the value of the message ID
of the error or, if you use an ad hoc message, it will return 50,000.

Listing 8.26 demonstrates the use of sp_addmessage, @@ERROR, and
RAISERROR.

EXAMPLE

Listing 8.26: Using @@ERROR and RAISERROR

```
USE Northwind
GO


sp_addmessage 50001,11,'An error occurred'
GO



CREATE PROC generateerror
AS
RAISERROR (50001,11,1) WITH LOG
SELECT @@ERROR
GO


generateerror
(1 row(s) affected)
```

OUTPUT

```
Server: Msg 50001, Level 11, State 1, Procedure generateerror, Line 4

An error occurred


-----------
50001


(1 row(s) affected)
```

Nesting Stored Procedures

Stored procedures can be nested up to 32 levels. *Nested* means that one stored procedure calls another, and so on. If the nesting level exceeds 32, the execution of the whole group of stored procedures fails. SQL Server provides a way to check the nesting level using the @@nestlevel system function.

When a stored procedure calls another stored procedure, the nesting level is incremented by one, and then when the inner stored procedure finishes its execution, the nesting level decreases by one.

Listing 8.27 shows the creation of two stored procedures. The first one, CheckSupplier, returns −1 if a given supplier name already exists in the Suppliers table, and 0 if it doesn't. The second one, InsertSupplier, calls the CheckSupplier stored procedure to check whether the data is already stored in the database, and if it's not, it's inserted. Observe in the output of Listing 8.27 that the nesting level is incremented by one each time a stored procedure is called from another one.

EXAMPLE

Listing 8.27: Using the @@nestlevel System Function

```
USE Northwind
GO

CREATE PROC dbo.CheckSupplier
@supplier_name VARCHAR(40)
AS

PRINT '3) The nesting level is ' + CAST(@@nestlevel AS VARCHAR(5))

IF EXISTS (SELECT * FROM Suppliers WHERE companyname = @supplier_name)
    RETURN -1
ELSE
    RETURN 0
GO

CREATE PROC dbo.InsertSupplier
@suppliername NVARCHAR(40),
@contactname NVARCHAR(30),
@contacttitle NVARCHAR(30)
AS
DECLARE @supplier_exists INT
PRINT '2) The nesting level is ' + CAST(@@nestlevel AS VARCHAR(5))
EXEC @supplier_exists = CheckSupplier @suppliername
PRINT '4) The nesting level is ' + CAST(@@nestlevel AS VARCHAR(5))
IF @supplier_exists = 0
    INSERT INTO dbo.Suppliers (companyname,contactname,contacttitle)
    VALUES (@suppliername,@contactname,@contacttitle)
ELSE
```

Listing 8.27: continued

```
    PRINT 'This supplier already exists in the database'
GO


PRINT '1) The nesting level is ' + CAST(@@nestlevel AS VARCHAR(5))
EXEC InsertSupplier 'ACME','Fernando Guerrero','Owner'
PRINT '5) The nesting level is ' + CAST(@@nestlevel AS VARCHAR(5))
GO
```

OUTPUT

```
1) The nesting level is 0
2) The nesting level is 1
3) The nesting level is 2
4) The nesting level is 1

(1 row(s) affected)

5) The nesting level is 0
```

When a main stored procedure calls other stored procedures, it must call them one after the other, and, as you might already know, this is not considered nesting. Thus, because this is not considered nesting, you can call more than 32 stored procedures from the main one. Listing 8.28 illustrates this situation. Pay close attention to the nesting level in the output; the maximum value it reaches is 1 (because there's no nesting).

EXAMPLE

Listing 8.28: Using the @@nestlevel System Function

```
USE Northwind
GO

CREATE PROC dbo.ShowSecurityInfo
AS
EXEC sp_helpgroup
PRINT '2) The nesting level is ' + CAST(@@nestlevel AS VARCHAR(5))
EXEC sp_helpuser
PRINT '3) The nesting level is ' + CAST(@@nestlevel AS VARCHAR(5))
GO


PRINT '1) The nesting level is ' + CAST(@@nestlevel AS VARCHAR(5))
EXEC ShowSecurityInfo
PRINT '4) The nesting level is ' + CAST(@@nestlevel AS VARCHAR(5))
GO
```

OUTPUT

```
1) The nesting level is 0
Group_name                        Group_id
-------------------------------   --------
db_accessadmin                    16385
db_backupoperator                 16389
db_datareader                     16390
db_datawriter                     16391
```

Listing 8.28: continued

```
db_ddladmin              16387
db_denydatareader        16392
db_denydatawriter        16393
db_owner                 16384
db_securityadmin         16386
public                   0

2) The nesting level is 1
UserName   GroupName        LoginName DefDBName    UserID SID
..........  ...............  .........  ...........  ......  ........

dbo        db_owner         sa         master       1       0x01
guest      public           NULL       NULL         2       0x00

3) The nesting level is 1
4) The nesting level is 0
```

An advantage of nesting is that when a stored procedure is called from another stored procedure, the inner one can access all objects created by the outer stored procedure. For example, Listing 8.29 shows the creation of two stored procedures, outerprocedure and innerprocedure, and as you can see, innerprocedure can access the temporary table created by outerprocedure.

EXAMPLE

Listing 8.29: Accessing Objects Created by an Outer Stored Procedure, in an Inner Stored Procedure

```
USE Northwind
GO

CREATE PROC outerprocedure
AS
SELECT orderid, orderdate
INTO #Spain_orders
FROM Orders
WHERE Shipcountry = 'Spain'
AND Shipcity = 'Barcelona'
EXEC innerprocedure
GO

CREATE PROC innerprocedure
AS
SELECT *
FROM #Spain_orders
GO

EXEC outerprocedure
```

Listing 8.29: continued

OUTPUT

```
orderid      orderdate
----------   ------------------------------------------------
10366        1996-11-28 00:00:00.000
10426        1997-01-27 00:00:00.000
10568        1997-06-13 00:00:00.000
10887        1998-02-13 00:00:00.000
10928        1998-03-05 00:00:00.000

(5 row(s) affected)
```

Application Security Using Stored Procedures

One of the advantages of stored procedures is that they can be used as a security mechanism to prevent users from dealing directly with tables. The process is very straightforward: First, create the stored procedure, and then assign execute permissions to the users on the stored procedure. Therefore, users don't need to have permissions on every object referenced by the stored procedure. For example, if you create a stored procedure that retrieves data from a certain table (using a SELECT query), you just have to grant execute permissions on the stored procedure to the users, and then they will be able to run the stored procedure (without having direct permissions on the table referenced by the stored procedure).

The first step SQL Server performs when a user executes a stored procedure is to check permissions on it. In general, the user who is executing the stored procedure just has to have EXECUTE permissions on it. However, there are two exceptions to this rule:

- If there's a dynamic query in the stored procedure (it contains either the EXECUTE statement or the sp_executesql system stored procedure), the user executing it must have permissions on the objects referenced by the dynamic query. In other words, SQL Server checks permissions on every object referenced by the dynamic query. This is because if the stored procedure contains a dynamic query at creation time, SQL Server doesn't know which objects are referenced by the dynamic query until it is executed. To illustrate, if you create a stored procedure that accesses the Orders table through a dynamic query, any user who executes the stored procedure, besides execute permissions, has to have appropriate permissions in the Orders table.

- If the ownership chain is broken, SQL server checks permissions on each object with a different owner, and only statements with sufficient permissions will be executed. This is why it's highly recommended that the owner of a stored procedure owns all objects referenced by it, to avoid a broken ownership chain.

For example, suppose there are three users in a database, Fernando, Carlos, and Michelle. Fernando owns a table called Countries, and Carlos owns a table called Cities. This scenario appears in Figure 8.4.

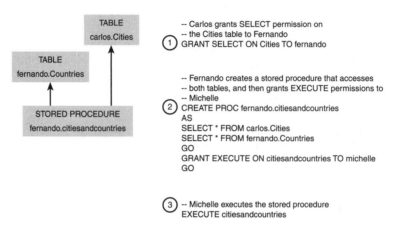

Figure 8.4: *Using ownership chains.*

Carlos grants SELECT permissions on the Cities table to Fernando. Then, Fernando creates a stored procedure called citiesandcountries that accesses these two tables (Cities and Countries). After creating the stored procedure, Fernando grants EXECUTE permissions to Michelle on the stored procedure, and when Michelle executes it, she only gets the result set of the second query in the stored procedure. This is because Michelle is accessing indirectly Carlos' table, and Carlos hasn't granted permissions on his table to Michelle.

In this case, the ownership chain is broken because a stored procedure is accessing a table that has a different owner than the stored procedure. In particular, SQL Server must check permissions on the Cities table because this table's owner is not the same owner of the citiesandcountries stored procedure.

To solve this problem, Carlos would have to grant SELECT permissions to Michelle on his table. Notice that Fernando doesn't have to grant SELECT permissions on his table to Michelle, because he's also the owner of the stored procedure, which he already granted EXECUTE permissions to Michelle on, thus implicitly allowing Michelle to access any object in the stored procedure owned by Fernando.

To summarize, if all objects referenced by a stored procedure belong to the stored procedure's owner, and there aren't dynamic queries inside the stored procedure's definition, any user with just execute permissions can successfully execute the stored procedure.

What's Next?

In this chapter, you learned the concepts that enable you to create and maintain stored procedures as efficient and safe ways to access data. In the next chapter, we will go over a special kind of stored procedures, triggers, which are executed automatically by SQL Server when modification operations take place.

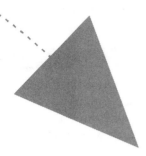

Implementing Complex Processing Logic: Programming Triggers

You can include programmatic capabilities into your database using stored procedures, as described in Chapter 8, "Implementing Business Logic: Programming Stored Procedures." However, tables are considered as passive objects that accept modifications, and you must rely on your programs to build complex business requirements.

You can incorporate complex business logic directly into your tables, defining special procedures that react to specific actions automatically. These special procedures are called *triggers*. In this way, a table can be a self-contained object with attributes (columns and properties), business rules (constraints), and application logic (triggers).

This chapter teaches you the following:

- How to create triggers and how to specify whether they execute before or after the base object is modified

- How to define a trigger to accomplish complex data modifications through views

- How to compare the before and after state of the object during the trigger execution, and detect which columns have been modified

- How to write a trigger that detects whether the action affected only one row or multiple rows, and reacts accordingly

- How to control nested and recursive execution of triggers

- How and when you can disable trigger execution

- How to select between triggers and constraints to enforce business rules

Benefits of Triggers

In Chapter 7, "Enforcing Data Integrity," you learned how to enforce business rules by defining constraints. In some real case scenarios, you can find problems that cannot be solved by using constraints. However, using the programmatic capabilities of triggers, you can create complex rules with endless possibilities.

A *trigger* is a stored procedure that is called automatically whenever you execute the action to which the trigger is defined. You cannot call a trigger directly, but you can execute the action that fires the trigger.

A trigger does not accept parameters and cannot call the RETURN statement to return a value, but it can return results, as any other stored procedure, although it is not recommended. A trigger executes in the background and it shouldn't return anything other than error messages, if required.

You can define several triggers for every INSERT, UPDATE, or DELETE action, or any combination of them.

To define a trigger to fire automatically whenever you insert or update data in the Products table, you can use the simplified syntax from Listing 9.1. Later in this chapter, you will study the CREATE TRIGGER syntax in detail.

EXAMPLE

Listing 9.1: Use the CREATE TRIGGER Statement to Define Triggers

```
CREATE TRIGGER TriggerName ON Products
AFTER INSERT, UPDATE
AS
-- Here you write your program logic
```

CAUTION

You cannot define a trigger on a SELECT action because this action does not modify data.

When you have a trigger defined in a table, it does not matter how you modify the table. The trigger is always fired whether you write DML statements directly, execute stored procedures, or use a database library from a client application.

TIP

A trigger is defined in a table or view inside a database, but the code inside the trigger can refer to objects in other databases, providing a unique way to implement referential integrity between objects in different databases.

Using Triggers to Enforce Complex Domain Integrity

Think about an Employees table where you register employees' data. The field DriverNo stores the driver license number, and because not every employee drives, this field must accept NULL. However, you want to enforce uniqueness in this field because two employees cannot have the same driver license number. Let's consider different ways to enforce this rule:

- You cannot create a UNIQUE constraint because you can have more than one employee without a driver's license and, as you remember, UNIQUE constraints can accept only one NULL value.

- You cannot create a CHECK constraint to see whether you already have the same value in other rows in the same table, because a CHECK constraint cannot access other rows in the same table.

- You cannot create a RULE object because these objects check for values in the selected field and affected row only.

- You can create a stored procedure to insert data into the table, and inside the procedure you can check for uniqueness of this value. In this case, you need two stored procedures, one to insert data and another one to modify data. Because this business rule is enforced only through these two stored procedures, you must make sure that your client applications insert and update employees' data only through these stored procedures. System administrators can modify the base tables directly and break this business rule.

- The solution could be a trigger that checks for uniqueness of the newly inserted value and either accepts or rejects the modification. This trigger could be implemented as detailed in Listing 9.2.

EXAMPLE

Listing 9.2: You Can Create a Trigger to Enforce Complex Uniqueness

```
USE Northwind
GO

-- Add the DriverNo fields to the Employees table

ALTER TABLE Employees
ADD DriverNo varchar(15) NULL
GO

-- Create the trigger to check
-- for uniqueness of the DriverNo field

CREATE TRIGGER isrEmployees
ON Employees
FOR INSERT, UPDATE
AS

IF UPDATE (DriverNo)
```

Listing 9.2: continued

```
IF EXISTS (

SELECT DriverNo, COUNT(*)
FROM Employees
WHERE DriverNo IS NOT NULL
AND DriverNo IN
(SELECT DISTINCT DriverNo
FROM Inserted)
GROUP BY DriverNo
HAVING COUNT(*) > 1)

BEGIN

RAISERROR ('Driver license number not unique, INSERT aborted', 16, 1)
ROLLBACK TRAN

END

-- This statement succeeds

UPDATE Employees
SET DriverNo = '74914173'
WHERE EmployeeID = 5

-- This statement fails
-- the driverno is not unique

UPDATE Employees
SET DriverNo = '74914173'
WHERE EmployeeID = 6

-- This statement fails
-- Trying to insert multiple repeated
-- DriverNo values

UPDATE Employees
SET DriverNo = '74914175'
WHERE EmployeeID BETWEEN 6 AND 10

-- reset to NULL succeeds because
-- NULL values are not considered
-- in this trigger

UPDATE Employees
SET DriverNo = NULL
```

Listing 9.2: continued

OUTPUT

```
Server: Msg 50000, Level 16, State 1, Procedure isrEmployees, Line 16
Driver license number not unique, INSERT aborted
```

Triggers do not represent much overhead for SQL Server because their execution time depends mostly on data access to other tables. However, it is not advisable to create complex logic inside triggers.

Triggers always run inside the transaction context of the action that fires them.

CAUTION

Be careful when using ROLLBACK TRAN inside a trigger, because it cancels the execution of the batch that fired the trigger. The complete transaction is rolled back, including any other actions performed during the transaction scope

---

Using Triggers to Maintain Denormalized Data

Let's consider a different example. You want to know the total sales for product categories. You want to know this total for any given category at any time, and the results must reflect the actual data. You have several different ways to do this.

USE AGGREGRATE FUNCTIONS

Execute the query from Listing 9.3 every time you want to obtain this information, modifying the value for CategoryName. This is not very efficient, because you must remember the complete syntax or save the query in a script or template. Every time you execute this query, SQL Server must parse, compile, and execute the query with the overhead associated to aggregate functions. If you rarely need to call this script, this could be an acceptable solution.

EXAMPLE

Listing 9.3: Use Aggregate Functions to Get Summary Information

```
USE Northwind
GO

SELECT P.CategoryID, C.CategoryName,
SUM(OD.UnitPrice * Quantity * (1 - Discount)) as Total
FROM [Order Details] OD
JOIN Products P
ON P.ProductID = OD.ProductID
JOIN Categories C
ON C.CategoryID = P.CategoryID
WHERE CategoryName = 'Confections'
GROUP BY P.CategoryID, C.categoryName
```

OUTPUT

Listing 9.3: continued

```
CategoryID  CategoryName     Total
..........  ...............  .............................
3           Confections      167357.22483158112
```

CREATE A VIEW

Create the `TotalSalesByCategory` view, as in Listing 9.4, to produce this result and select from this view filtering to the required `CategoryName`. This solution is flexible and provides good security control, but it does not provide any improvements in speed because the view definition must be merged with the outer query, and the final resulting query plan will be executed every time you use this view, with the overhead inherent to the use of aggregate functions. This could be an adequate solution if the view is not going to be executed frequently.

EXAMPLE

Listing 9.4: Create a View to Retrieve Summary Information

```
USE Northwind
GO

-- Create the view

CREATE VIEW TotalSalesByCategory
AS
SELECT P.CategoryID, C.CategoryName,
SUM(OD.UnitPrice * Quantity * (1 - Discount)) as Total
FROM [Order Details] OD
JOIN Products P
ON P.ProductID = OD.ProductID
JOIN Categories C
ON C.CategoryID = P.CategoryID
GROUP BY P.CategoryID, C.categoryName
GO

-- Use the view to search
-- for 'Confections' totals

SELECT *
FROM TotalSalesByCategory
WHERE CategoryName = 'Confections'
```

CREATE A STORED PROCEDURE

Create the stored procedure `GetSalesByCategory`, as in Listing 9.5, to produce the required results for a given category. This solution can be efficient and faster than the previous ones, due to the reuse of the query plan. If this procedure is not frequently used, compared to the insert and update operations on the underlying tables, this solution is sufficiently efficient.

Listing 9.5: Create a Stored Procedure to Retrieve Summary Information

```
-- Create the procedure

CREATE PROCEDURE GetSalesByCategory
@CatName nvarchar(15)
AS
SELECT P.CategoryID, C.CategoryName,
SUM(OD.UnitPrice * Quantity * (1 - Discount)) as Total
FROM [Order Details] OD
JOIN Products P
ON P.ProductID = OD.ProductID
JOIN Categories C
ON C.CategoryID = P.CategoryID
WHERE CategoryName = @CatName
GROUP BY P.CategoryID, C.categoryName
GO


-- Use the procedure to search
-- for 'Confections' totals

EXEC GetSalesByCategory 'Confections'
```

NOTE

The query plan of the last three examples is exactly the same, so it is the execution performance. The latest method, using a stored procedure, is more efficient for repeated execution because it avoids the need for parsing, optimizing, and compiling the query. The query plan can be reused more easily than direct queries, and it produces lower network traffic.

USE TRIGGERS

The fastest way to retrieve this information is to have the precomputed total in a new table `TotalCategoriesSales`, and create triggers, as in Listing 9.6, to maintain this information automatically, whenever you change data in the Order Details table. If your more frequent query is to get these totals, you should provide this information as fast as possible. In this case, retrieving these values is highly efficient, but modifying data is less efficient because triggers must run after every data modification.

Listing 9.6: Use Triggers to Maintain Summary Data

```
USE Northwind
GO

-- Create denormalized table

CREATE TABLE TotalCategoriesSales
```

Listing 9.6: continued

```
(CategoryID int NOT NULL PRIMARY KEY,
CategoryName nvarchar(15) NOT NULL,
TotalSales money DEFAULT 0)

-- Synchronization Procedure
-- Including initial data population

CREATE PROCEDURE SyncTotalCategoriesSales
AS
TRUNCATE TABLE TotalcategoriesSales

INSERT TotalCategoriesSales
SELECT CategoryID, CategoryName, 0
FROM Categories

UPDATE TC
SET TotalSales =
(SELECT SUM(OD.UnitPrice * Quantity * (1 - Discount))
FROM [Order Details] OD
JOIN Products P
ON P.ProductID = OD.ProductID
WHERE P.CategoryID = TC.categoryID)
FROM TotalCategoriesSales TC
GO

-- Synchronize totals
-- We can run this procedure if necessary

EXEC SyncTotalcategoriesSales

GO


CREATE TRIGGER modOrderDetails
ON [Order Details]
AFTER INSERT, UPDATE, DELETE
AS

UPDATE TC
SET TotalSales = TotalSales
- D.UnitPrice * Quantity * (1 - Discount)
FROM TotalCategoriesSales TC
JOIN Products P
ON P.CategoryID = TC.CategoryID
JOIN Deleted D
ON D.ProductID = P.productID
```

Listing 9.6: continued

```
UPDATE TC
SET TotalSales = TotalSales
+ I.UnitPrice * Quantity * (1 - Discount)
FROM TotalCategoriesSales TC
JOIN Products P
ON P.CategoryID = TC.CategoryID
JOIN Inserted I
ON I.ProductID = P.productID
GO

-- Select initial values

PRINT CHAR(10) + 'Initial summary values' + CHAR(10)

SELECT *
FROM TotalCategoriesSales

-- Insert a new Order

INSERT Orders (CustomerID)
SELECT 'ALFKI'

DECLARE @id int

SET @id = @@IDENTITY

-- Show the @@identity for later reference

SELECT @id AS OrderID

-- Sell 10 units of Ikura (cat 8) at $30.00 and 10% discount

PRINT CHAR(10) + 'Insert Ikura (cat 8) Order' + CHAR(10)

INSERT [Order Details]
(orderID, ProductID, UnitPrice, Quantity, Discount)
VALUES (@id, 10, 30, 10, 0.1)

-- Sell 20 units of Tofu (cat 7) at $20.00 and 20% discount

PRINT CHAR(10) + 'Insert Tofu (cat 7) Order' + CHAR(10)

INSERT [Order Details]
(orderID, ProductID, UnitPrice, Quantity, Discount)
VALUES (@id, 14, 20, 100, 0.2)
```

Listing 9.6: continued

```
-- Sell 5 units of Queso Cabrales (cat 4) at $20.00 and no discount

PRINT CHAR(10) + 'Insert Queso Cabrales (cat 4) Order' + CHAR(10)

INSERT [Order Details]
(orderID, ProductID, UnitPrice, Quantity, Discount)
VALUES (@id, 11, 20, 5, 0.0)

-- Test the new totals

SELECT *
FROM TotalCategoriesSales

-- Update quantity of the Queso Cabrales to 100

PRINT CHAR(10) + 'Increase Queso Cabrales (cat 4) to 100' + CHAR(10)

UPDATE [Order Details]
SET Quantity = 100
WHERE OrderID = @id
AND ProductID = 11

-- Test the new totals

SELECT *
FROM TotalCategoriesSales

-- Remove Tofu from this order

PRINT CHAR(10) + 'Remove Tofu (cat 7) Order' + CHAR(10)

DELETE [Order Details]
WHERE OrderID = @id
AND ProductID = 14

-- Test the new totals

SELECT *
FROM TotalCategoriesSales

-- remove the order completely

PRINT CHAR(10) + 'Remove Ikura (cat 8) Order' + CHAR(10)

DELETE [Order Details]
WHERE OrderID = @id
AND ProductID = 10
```

Listing 9.6: continued

```
PRINT CHAR(10) + 'Remove Queso Cabrales (cat 4) Order' + CHAR(10)

DELETE [Order Details]
WHERE OrderID = @id
AND ProductID = 11

DELETE Orders
WHERE OrderID = @id

-- Test the new totals

SELECT *
FROM TotalCategoriesSales
Initial summary values
```

OUTPUT

```
CategoryID  CategoryName     TotalSales
----------  --------------   --------------------
1           Beverages        267868.1805
2           Condiments       106047.0850
3           Confections      167357.2248
4           Dairy Products   234507.2813
5           Grains/Cereals   95744.5875
6           Meat/Poultry     163022.3591
7           Produce          99984.5781
8           Seafood          131261.7344


OrderID
----------
11083



Insert Ikura (cat 8) Order


Insert Tofu (cat 7) Order


Insert Queso Cabrales (cat 4) Order

CategoryID  CategoryName     TotalSales
----------  --------------   --------------------
1           Beverages        267868.1805
2           Condiments       106047.0850
3           Confections      167357.2248
4           Dairy Products   234607.2813
5           Grains/Cereals   95744.5875
```

Listing 9.6: continued

```
6          Meat/Poultry    163022.3591
7          Produce         101584.5781
8          Seafood         131531.7344


Increase Queso Cabrales (cat 4) to 100

CategoryID  CategoryName    TotalSales
----------- --------------- --------------------
1          Beverages       267868.1805
2          Condiments      106047.0850
3          Confections     167357.2248
4          Dairy Products  236507.2813
5          Grains/Cereals  95744.5875
6          Meat/Poultry    163022.3591
7          Produce         101584.5781
8          Seafood         131531.7344


Remove Tofu (cat 7) Order

CategoryID  CategoryName    TotalSales
----------- --------------- --------------------
1          Beverages       267868.1805
2          Condiments      106047.0850
3          Confections     167357.2248
4          Dairy Products  236507.2813
5          Grains/Cereals  95744.5875
6          Meat/Poultry    163022.3591
7          Produce         99984.5781
8          Seafood         131531.7344


Remove Ikura (cat 8) Order


Remove Queso Cabrales (cat 4) Order

CategoryID  CategoryName    TotalSales
----------- --------------- --------------------
1          Beverages       267868.1805
2          Condiments      106047.0850
3          Confections     167357.2248
4          Dairy Products  234507.2813
5          Grains/Cereals  95744.5875
6          Meat/Poultry    163022.3591
7          Produce         99984.5781
8          Seafood         131261.7344
```

CAUTION

The example from Listing 9.6 only works with single-row operations. Later in this chapter you will see how to deal with multirow operation using the same example.

NOTE

To complete the example, you should create triggers in the Products and Categories tables as well, because a product could be moved to a new category, and a category can change its name.

You could drop the CategoryName field from the TotalCategoriesSales table, but in that case you have to join to the Categories table to filter the category by name. After you denormalized your database to maintain summary values, why not denormalize one step further? In this way, you need to access only one table to produce the required results.

USE INDEXED VIEWS

A different possibility would be to create an index on the SalesByCategory view, as in Listing 9.7. In this case, no triggers are necessary to maintain this information, and the Query Optimizer can decide to use this view to solve queries requesting data compatible with the data generated by this view, even if the queries do not reference the view. This is the optimal solution for summary data retrieval, but it is not as efficient as the solution based on triggers—if you expect many data updates.

EXAMPLE

Listing 9.7: Use Indexed Views to Retrieve Precomputed Summary Information

```
-- Drop the existing view

IF OBJECT_ID('TotalSalesByCategory') IS NOT NULL
DROP VIEW TotalSalesByCategory
GO


-- Setting required to create an indexed view

SET ANSI_NULLS ON
SET ANSI_PADDING ON
SET ANSI_WARNINGS ON
SET ARITHABORT ON
SET CONCAT_NULL_YIELDS_NULL ON
SET QUOTED_IDENTIFIER ON
SET NUMERIC_ROUNDABORT OFF
GO


-- Create the view
-- With Schemabinding
-- and use two part names for objects
```

Listing 9.7: continued

```
CREATE VIEW TotalSalesByCategory
WITH SCHEMABINDING
AS
SELECT P.CategoryID, C.CategoryName,
SUM(OD.UnitPrice * Quantity * (1 - Discount)) as Total,
COUNT_BIG(*) as CB
FROM dbo.[Order Details] OD
JOIN dbo.Products P
ON P.ProductID = OD.ProductID
JOIN dbo.Categories C
ON C.CategoryID = P.CategoryID
GROUP BY P.CategoryID, C.categoryName
GO

-- Create the index on the view

CREATE UNIQUE CLUSTERED INDEX ndx_CatTotals
ON TotalSalesByCategory (CategoryName)

-- Use the view to search
-- for 'Confections' totals
-- set SHOWPLAN_TEXT
-- to show that the view is used
-- instead of the base tables

SET SHOWPLAN_TEXT ON

SELECT CategoryID, CategoryName, Total
FROM TotalSalesByCategory (NOEXPAND)
WHERE CategoryName = 'Confections'
```

StmtText

OUTPUT

```
----------
  |--Clustered Index Scan(
  ➥OBJECT:([Northwind].[dbo].[TotalSalesByCategory].[ndx_CatTotals]),
  ➥ WHERE:([TotalSalesByCategory].[CategoryName]='Confections'))
```

NOTE

Using indexed views in similar situations to the example from Listing 9.7 has been improved dramatically since SQL Server 2000 Service Pack 1. To avoid performance problems related to indexed views maintenance, for views defined on aggregations, we recommend that you install the latest Service Pack available for SQL Server 2000.

Trigger Enhancements in SQL Server 2000

SQL Server 2000 includes exciting new features for triggers. Some of these features are discussed later in this chapter, but here we want to mention them briefly.

In previous versions, you were forced to use triggers to implement cascading operations. SQL Server 2000 provides cascade declarative referential integrity by FOREIGN KEY constraints with the ON DELETE CASCADE and ON UPDATE CASCADE options, as explained in Chapter 7. This is the recommended way to implement cascade operations.

SQL Server 2000 provides a new type of trigger: the INSTEAD OF trigger. These triggers are executed instead of the firing actions, providing a mechanism to check for data changes before the data is actually modified. Later in this chapter you will learn about the applications of these new triggers.

It is possible to create an INSTEAD OF trigger on a view, providing new ways to deal with data modifications through views. Later in this chapter you will find some examples of this exciting feature.

As in version 7.0, you can create multiple triggers per action, but now you can specify which trigger will be the first one to fire, providing some kind of initialization process for other triggers. You also can specify the last trigger to execute, providing a cleansing mechanism to finish the triggering action.

The list of restricted statements to be executed inside triggers has been reduced from previous versions. A very useful new possibility is the capability to create tables inside the triggers—mainly temporary tables—using DDL statements.

NOTE

In SQL Server 7.0, you could create a table inside a trigger only by using the SELECT INTO statement.

Inside INSTEAD OF triggers, you can inspect the previous and after state of BLOB columns, because they appear in the Inserted and Deleted tables.

Checking for changes in specific columns is now easier using the new COLUMNS_UPDATED function.

Inserted and Deleted Tables

Inside the trigger, you can check the previous and after column values for the affected rows by reading two virtual tables: Inserted and Deleted. The Inserted and Deleted tables are read-only in-memory virtual tables with the same columns as the base table.

The Inserted table contains the new inserted rows in a trigger defined for an INSERT statement or the new values for modified rows in a trigger defined for an UPDATE statement. In a trigger defined for a DELETE statement, the Inserted table exists, but it is empty.

The Deleted table contains the deleted rows in a trigger defined for a DELETE statement or the old values for modified rows in a trigger defined for an UPDATE statement. In a trigger defined for an INSERT statement, the Deleted table exists, but it is empty.

If the original action modified several rows at once, the trigger is fired just once and the Inserted and Deleted tables are multirow tables containing the modified rows.

Inside a trigger, it is possible to modify the base table again. In this case, it is possible to join the base table to the Inserted table to remodify only affected rows. Listing 9.8 shows an example of this possibility.

EXAMPLE

Listing 9.8: Inside a Trigger, You Can Remodify the Affected Rows

```
-- Create a new table

CREATE TABLE NewCategories (
CategoryID int NOT NULL
IDENTITY(1,1) PRIMARY KEY,
CategoryName nvarchar(15) NOT NULL ,
Modified smalldatetime
DEFAULT CURRENT_TIMESTAMP,
Modifier nchar(128)
DEFAULT SYSTEM_USER)
GO


-- Populate the table with data

INSERT NewCategories
(CategoryName)
SELECT CategoryName
FROM Categories
GO


-- Create an AFTER UPDATE trigger

CREATE TRIGGER udt_NewCategories
ON NewCategories
AFTER UPDATE
AS
UPDATE NewCategories
SET Modified = CURRENT_TIMESTAMP,
Modifier = SYSTEM_USER
FROM NewCategories
```

Listing 9.8: continued

```
JOIN Inserted
ON Inserted.CategoryID = NewCategories.CategoryID
GO

-- Show actual values

SELECT *
FROM NewCategories
WHERE CategoryID = 3
GO

PRINT CHAR(10) + 'Wait for 30 seconds' + CHAR(10)
GO

WAITFOR DELAY '00:00:30'

-- Make sure Guest has permissions to modify
-- and read the NewCategories table

GRANT ALL ON NewCategories TO Guest
GO

-- Impersonate the user Guest

SETUSER 'Guest'
GO

-- Modify Category 3 Name

UPDATE NewCategories
SET CategoryName = 'Confectionery'
WHERE CategoryID = 3

-- Show new values
-- Where the trigger modified automatically
-- the Modified and Modifier columns

SELECT *
FROM NewCategories
WHERE CategoryID = 3
GO

-- Impersonate the previous user (dbo)

SETUSER
GO
```

Listing 9.8: continued

```
-- Drop the demo table
-- it drops automatically the trigger

DROP TABLE NewCategories
```

OUTPUT

CategoryID	CategoryName	Modified	Modifier
3	Confections	2000-11-19 13:18:00	sa

```
Wait for 30 seconds
```

CategoryID	CategoryName	Modified	Modifier
3	Confectionery	2000-11-19 13:19:00	Guest

In INSERT and UPDATE operations, the Inserted table contains the same information as the base table for the affected rows.

In UPDATE operations, the Deleted table contains one row per every updated row in the table, but the information is not common to the base table because the Deleted table contains the previous values and the base table already contains the new values of the data.

In DELETE operations, the Deleted table does not contain any common rows with the base table, because the rows already have been removed from the base table.

Listing 9.9 shows an example of the contents of the Inserted and Deleted tables in different situations.

EXAMPLE

Listing 9.9: You Can Use the Inserted and Deleted Tables Inside Any Kind of Trigger

```
USE Northwind
GO

-- Create a new table

CREATE TABLE NewCategories (
CategoryID int NOT NULL
IDENTITY(1,1) PRIMARY KEY,
CategoryName nvarchar(15) NOT NULL ,
Modified smalldatetime
DEFAULT CURRENT_TIMESTAMP,
Modifier nchar(128)
DEFAULT SYSTEM_USER)
GO

-- Create an AFTER UPDATE trigger
```

Listing 9.9: continued

```
CREATE TRIGGER tr_NewCategories
ON NewCategories
AFTER UPDATE, INSERT, DELETE
AS

DECLARE @s varchar(80)
DECLARE @ni int, @nd int

SELECT @ni = COUNT(*)
FROM Inserted

SELECT @nd = COUNT(*)
FROM Deleted

SET @s = CASE
WHEN (@ni = @nd) AND @ni > 0
THEN 'AFTER UPDATE Trigger (compare Deleted and Inserted tables)'
WHEN @ni > @nd
THEN 'AFTER INSERT Trigger (look at the Inserted table)'
WHEN @ni < @nd
THEN 'AFTER DELETE Trigger (look at the Deleted table)'
ELSE 'TRIGGER fired by Null action (Inserted and Deleted are empty)' END

PRINT CHAR(10) + '##################################################'
PRINT @s
PRINT '##################################################' + CHAR(10)

PRINT CHAR(10) + 'Inserted Table' + CHAR(10)

SELECT *
FROM Inserted

PRINT CHAR(10) + 'Deleted Table' + CHAR(10)

SELECT *
FROM Deleted
GO

-- Insert Operation

INSERT NewCategories (CategoryName)
VALUES ('Food')

-- Multiple Insert Operation

INSERT NewCategories (CategoryName)
SELECT CategoryName
```

Listing 9.9: continued

```
FROM Categories

-- Delete one row

DELETE NewCategories
WHERE CategoryID = 7

-- Delete multiple rows

DELETE NewCategories
WHERE CategoryID BETWEEN 1 AND 4

-- Update one row

UPDATE NewCategories
SET CategoryName = 'Products'
WHERE CategoryID = 8

-- Update multiple rows

UPDATE NewCategories
SET CategoryName = UPPER(CategoryName)

-- Null operation because it does not affect any row

UPDATE NewCategories
SET CategoryName = UPPER(CategoryName)
WHERE CategoryID > 1000

-- Drop the demo table
-- it drops automatically the trigger

DROP TABLE NewCategories
###############################################################
AFTER INSERT Trigger (look at the Inserted table)
###############################################################
```

OUTPUT

```
Inserted Table

CategoryID  CategoryName    Modified                        Modifier
----------  -------------   ------------------------------  -------------
1           Food            2000-11-19 13:43:00             sa


Deleted Table
```

Listing 9.9: continued

```
CategoryID  CategoryName    Modified                      Modifier
----------  --------------  ----------------------------  -------------



############################################################
AFTER INSERT Trigger (look at the Inserted table)
############################################################

Inserted Table

CategoryID  CategoryName    Modified                      Modifier
----------  --------------  ----------------------------  -------------
2           Beverages       2000-11-19 13:43:00           sa
3           Condiments      2000-11-19 13:43:00           sa
4           Confections     2000-11-19 13:43:00           sa
5           Dairy Products  2000-11-19 13:43:00           sa
6           Grains/Cereals  2000-11-19 13:43:00           sa
7           Meat/Poultry    2000-11-19 13:43:00           sa
8           Produce         2000-11-19 13:43:00           sa
9           Seafood         2000-11-19 13:43:00           sa


Deleted Table

CategoryID  CategoryName    Modified                      Modifier
----------  --------------  ----------------------------  -------------



############################################################
AFTER DELETE Trigger (look at the Deleted table)
############################################################

Inserted Table

CategoryID  CategoryName    Modified                      Modifier
----------  --------------  ----------------------------  -------------


Deleted Table

CategoryID  CategoryName    Modified                      Modifier
----------  --------------  ----------------------------  -------------
7           Meat/Poultry    2000-11-19 13:43:00           sa
```

Listing 9.9: continued

```
################################################################
AFTER DELETE Trigger (look at the Deleted table)
################################################################

Inserted Table

CategoryID  CategoryName    Modified                      Modifier
----------- --------------- ----------------------------- --------------


Deleted Table

CategoryID  CategoryName    Modified                      Modifier
----------- --------------- ----------------------------- --------------
1           Food            2000-11-19 13:43:00           sa
2           Beverages       2000-11-19 13:43:00           sa
3           Condiments      2000-11-19 13:43:00           sa
4           Confections     2000-11-19 13:43:00           sa


################################################################
AFTER UPDATE Trigger (compare Deleted and Inserted tables)
################################################################

Inserted Table

CategoryID  CategoryName    Modified                      Modifier
----------- --------------- ----------------------------- --------------
8           Products        2000-11-19 13:43:00           sa


Deleted Table

CategoryID  CategoryName    Modified                      Modifier
----------- --------------- ----------------------------- --------------
8           Produce         2000-11-19 13:43:00           sa


################################################################
AFTER UPDATE Trigger (compare Deleted and Inserted tables)
################################################################

Inserted Table
```

Listing 9.9: continued

```
CategoryID  CategoryName    Modified                    Modifier
----------  --------------  --------------------------  -------------
5           DAIRY PRODUCTS  2000-11-19 13:43:00         sa
6           GRAINS/CEREALS  2000-11-19 13:43:00         sa
8           PRODUCTS        2000-11-19 13:43:00         sa
9           SEAFOOD         2000-11-19 13:43:00         sa


Deleted Table

CategoryID  CategoryName    Modified                    Modifier
----------  --------------  --------------------------  -------------
5           Dairy Products  2000-11-19 13:43:00         sa
6           Grains/Cereals  2000-11-19 13:43:00         sa
8           Products        2000-11-19 13:43:00         sa
9           Seafood         2000-11-19 13:43:00         sa



############################################################
TRIGGER fired by Null action (Inserted and Deleted are empty)
############################################################

Inserted Table

CategoryID  CategoryName    Modified                    Modifier
----------  --------------  --------------------------  -------------


Deleted Table

CategoryID  CategoryName    Modified                    Modifier
----------  --------------  --------------------------  -------------
```

Types of Triggers According to Their Order

SQL Server 2000 defines two different types of triggers:

- INSTEAD OF triggers that fire instead of the original action, before the base object is modified

- AFTER triggers that fire after the base table is modified

A table can have any number of AFTER triggers for every action, but only one INSTEAD OF trigger per action.

A view can have only INSTEAD OF triggers.

INSTEAD OF Triggers

INSTEAD OF triggers are fired automatically when you execute a statement by which the trigger is defined. In this case, the trigger fires before the action is executed. However, inside an INSTEAD OF trigger, you have access to the Inserted and Deleted virtual tables.

When the INSTEAD OF trigger starts its execution, the base table has not been modified yet. However, on INSERT actions the Inserted table contains the default values for columns with DEFAULT definitions, and it does not contain the values for the IDENTITY property.

Because the base table is not modified yet, constraints have not been checked yet. If inside the INSTEAD OF trigger you don't send any action to the base table, the base table is not modified at all.

You can use INSTEAD OF triggers to check the data before the actual modification, in a more complex way than with CHECK constraints. Depending on the results of your conditions, you can decide to apply the requested changes or decide not to apply them at all.

If you want to modify data in a table, you can use the INSERT, UPDATE, and DELETE statements. For each table or view, you can define only one INSTEAD OF trigger per each triggering action.

- An INSTEAD OF INSERT trigger allows you to cancel, partially or completely, an insert operation without rolling back any transaction.

- An INSTEAD OF UPDATE trigger offers you the possibility of checking changes before they are applied to the data. You can decide which changes to finally apply.

- An INSTEAD OF DELETE trigger allows you to cancel the deletion of specific rows, without rolling back transactions.

You cannot create an INSTEAD OF trigger in a table where you have defined a FOREIGN KEY with CASCADE operations.

Using SQL Server 2000, you can create INSTEAD OF triggers on views. In this way you can provide better updating functionality to your views, as in the following examples:

- In a view that shows a FullName field defined as LastName + ', ' + FirstName, you cannot execute an UPDATE statement to modify the FullName field directly, because it is a read-only computed column. You can create an INSTEAD OF UPDATE trigger to allow for modifications in the FullName field, resulting in changes in the FirstName and LastName fields. Listing 9.10 shows an example of this case.

Listing 9.10: Use INSTEAD OF Triggers to Update Computed Columns

```
USE Northwind
GO

-- Create a view based in the Employees table

CREATE VIEW EmployeesName
AS
SELECT ISNULL(EmployeeID, 0) AS EmployeeID,
LastName + ', ' + FirstName AS FullName
FROM Employees
GO

-- Show information related to the Employee 6

SELECT FullName
FROM EmployeesName
WHERE EmployeeID = 6

SELECT FirstName, LastName
FROM Employees
WHERE EmployeeID = 6
GO

-- Create INSTEAD OF INSERT trigger

CREATE TRIGGER isrEmployeesName
ON EmployeesName
INSTEAD OF INSERT
AS
INSERT Employees (LastName, FirstName)
SELECT LEFT(FullName, CHARINDEX(',', FullName) - 1),
LTRIM(RIGHT(FullName, LEN(FullName)
- CHARINDEX(',', FullName)))
FROM Inserted
GO

-- Create INSTEAD OF UPDATE trigger

CREATE TRIGGER udtEmployeesName
ON EmployeesName
INSTEAD OF UPDATE
AS
UPDATE Employees
SET LastName = LEFT(Inserted.FullName,
CHARINDEX(',', Inserted.FullName) - 1),
FirstName = LTRIM(RIGHT(Inserted.FullName,
```

Listing 9.10: continued

```
LEN(Inserted.FullName)
- CHARINDEX(',', Inserted.FullName) ))
FROM Employees
JOIN Inserted
ON Inserted.EmployeeID = Employees.EmployeeID
WHERE Employees.EmployeeID = Inserted.EmployeeID
GO


-- testing INSTEAD OF UPDATE Trigger

UPDATE EmployeesName
SET FullName = 'NewFamily, Michael'
WHERE EmployeeID = 6
GO


SELECT FullName
FROM EmployeesName
WHERE EmployeeID = 6

SELECT FirstName, LastName
FROM Employees
WHERE EmployeeID = 6
GO


-- testing INSTEAD OF INSERT Trigger

INSERT EmployeesName (EmployeeID, FullName)
VALUES (0, 'NewFamily, NewGuy')
GO


SELECT FullName
FROM EmployeesName
WHERE FullName LIKE 'New%'

SELECT FirstName, LastName
FROM Employees
WHERE LastName LIKE 'New%'
GO


-- deleting from this view
-- does not require an INSTEAD OF DELETE Trigger

DELETE EmployeesName
WHERE FullName = 'NewFamily, NewGuy'
GO
```

Listing 9.10: continued

```
SELECT FullName
FROM EmployeesName
WHERE FullName LIKE 'New%'

SELECT FirstName, LastName
FROM Employees
WHERE LastName LIKE 'New%'
GO

DROP VIEW EmployeesName
GO
```

OUTPUT

```
FullName
---------------------------------
Suyama, Michael

FirstName  LastName
---------- --------------------
Michael    Suyama

FullName
---------------------------------
NewFamily, Michael

FirstName  LastName
---------- --------------------
Michael    NewFamily

FullName
---------------------------------
NewFamily, Michael
NewFamily, NewGuy

FirstName  LastName
---------- --------------------
Michael    NewFamily
NewGuy     NewFamily

FullName
---------------------------------
NewFamily, Michael

FirstName  LastName
---------- --------------------
Michael    NewFamily
```

- You can create a view to obtain the total company budget, based on the individual budget per department. To increase the total budget, you can modify every department's individual budget. However, if you had a view to summarize the total budget, it could be useful to adjust individual budgets proportionally, by changing only the total budget field in the view.

Views based on aggregations are read-only, but you can create an INSTEAD OF UPDATE trigger on the summary view to accept changes in the total budget, and distribute these changes proportionally to every individual budget. Listing 9.11, applied to the Categories table, shows how to implement this solution.

EXAMPLE

Listing 9.11: Use INSTEAD OF Triggers to Distribute Changes in Summary Data

```
USE Northwind
GO

-- Modify the Categories table
-- To add a new field to store
-- Budget value

ALTER TABLE Categories
ADD Budget money NULL
GO
-- Add a random budget per category

UPDATE Categories
SET Budget = ROUND(SIN(CategoryID)* 10000 + 20000, -3)
GO

-- Create a view to see the total budget

CREATE VIEW TotalBudget
AS
SELECT SUM(Budget) AS TBudget
FROM Categories
GO

-- Create an INSTEAD OF trigger
-- to UPDATE budgets proportionally

CREATE TRIGGER udtTotalBudget
ON TotalBudget
INSTEAD OF UPDATE
AS

-- Share the new budget proportionally
```

Listing 9.11: continued

```
UPDATE Categories
SET Budget = ROUND(Budget *
(Inserted.TBudget /
Deleted.TBudget), -3)
FROM Inserted, Deleted

-- Adjust the difference to the biggest budget

UPDATE Categories
SET Budget = Budget +
    Inserted.TBudget -
        (SELECT SUM(Budget)
        FROM Categories)
FROM Inserted
WHERE CategoryID =
    (SELECT TOP 1 CategoryID
    FROM Categories
    ORDER BY Budget DESC)

GO

-- Test the view

PRINT CHAR(10) + 'Total Budget before the update' + CHAR(10)

SELECT *
FROM TotalBudget

PRINT CHAR(10) + 'Individual Budgets before the update' + CHAR(10)

SELECT CategoryID, Budget
FROM Categories

-- Increase the budget

UPDATE TotalBudget
SET TBudget = 200000

-- Test the update

PRINT CHAR(10) + 'Total Budget after the update' + CHAR(10)

SELECT *
FROM TotalBudget
```

Listing 9.11: continued

```
PRINT CHAR(10) + 'Individual Budgets after the update' + CHAR(10)

SELECT CategoryID, Budget
FROM Categories

-- Remove the view and the Budget column

DROP VIEW TotalBudget

ALTER TABLE Categories
DROP COLUMN Budget
```

OUTPUT

```
Total Budget before the update

TBudget
--------------------
174000.0000


Individual Budgets before the update

CategoryID  Budget
----------- --------------------
1              28000.0000
2              29000.0000
3              21000.0000
4              12000.0000
5              10000.0000
6              17000.0000
7              27000.0000
8              30000.0000


Total Budget after the update

TBudget
--------------------
200000.0000


Individual Budgets after the update

CategoryID  Budget
----------- --------------------
1              32000.0000
2              33000.0000
```

```
3              24000.0000
4              14000.0000
5              11000.0000
6              20000.0000
7              31000.0000
8              35000.0000
```

- If a view is defined as a query that joins several tables, you can only execute an UPDATE statement to modify through this view, if the statement affects only columns in a single table. In a view that joins two tables, you can create an INSTEAD OF UPDATE trigger to apply changes to columns on both tables simultaneously, as shown in Listing 9.12.

EXAMPLE

Listing 9.12: Use INSTEAD OF Triggers to Update Views Defined on Multiple Tables

```
USE Northwind
GO

-- Create a new table to store the Budget

CREATE TABLE CategoriesBudget(
CategoryID int NOT NULL
PRIMARY KEY
REFERENCES Categories (CategoryID)
,Budget money NOT NULL
DEFAULT 0)
GO
-- Add a random budget per category

INSERT CategoriesBudget
SELECT CategoryID, ROUND(SIN(CategoryID)* 10000 + 20000, -3)
FROM Categories


GO


-- Create a view to see the name and budget
-- for every Category

CREATE VIEW CategoriesNameBudget
AS
SELECT C.CategoryID,
C.CategoryName,
CB.Budget
FROM Categories C
JOIN CategoriesBudget CB
ON C.categoryID = CB.categoryID


GO
```

Listing 9.12: continued

```
-- Create an INSTEAD OF trigger
-- to UPDATE budgets proportionally

CREATE TRIGGER udtCategoriesNameBudget
ON CategoriesNameBudget
INSTEAD OF UPDATE
AS

-- Update the Category Name

UPDATE C
SET C.CategoryName = I.CategoryName
FROM Inserted I
JOIN Categories C
ON C.CategoryID = I.CategoryID

-- Update the Budget

UPDATE CB
SET CB.Budget = I.Budget
FROM Inserted I
JOIN CategoriesBudget CB
ON CB.CategoryID = I.CategoryID

GO

-- Test the view

PRINT CHAR(10) + 'Names and Budgets before the update' + CHAR(10)

SELECT *
FROM CategoriesNameBudget

-- Change name and budget of Category 7

UPDATE CategoriesNameBudget
SET Budget = 35000.0000,
CategoryName = 'Miscellaneous'
WHERE CategoryID = 7

-- Test the update

PRINT CHAR(10) + 'Names and Budgets after the update' + CHAR(10)

SELECT *
FROM CategoriesNameBudget
```

Listing 9.12: continued

OUTPUT

```
-- Back Categories to normal

UPDATE Categories
SET CategoryName = 'Produce'
WHERE CategoryID = 7

DROP VIEW CategoriesNameBudget

DROP TABLE CategoriesName
Names and Budgets before the update

CategoryID   CategoryName     Budget
..........   ...............  ....................
1            Beverages        28000.0000
2            Condiments       29000.0000
3            Confections      21000.0000
4            Dairy Products   12000.0000
5            Grains/Cereals   10000.0000
6            Meat/Poultry     17000.0000
7            Produce          27000.0000
8            Seafood          30000.0000


Names and Budgets after the update

CategoryID   CategoryName     Budget
..........   ...............  ....................
1            Beverages        28000.0000
2            Condiments       29000.0000
3            Confections      21000.0000
4            Dairy Products   12000.0000
5            Grains/Cereals   10000.0000
6            Meat/Poultry     17000.0000
7            Miscellaneous    35000.0000
8            Seafood          30000.0000
```

CAUTION

You cannot create an INSTEAD OF trigger in a view created using the WITH CHECK option.

AFTER Triggers

AFTER triggers execute after the data has been modified. However, because you are still inside the transaction, you can decide to cancel the action.

Unlike INSTEAD OF triggers, you do not have to do anything special to commit the transaction; it will be committed automatically unless you decide to roll it back.

You can create any number of AFTER triggers for every action on every table.

Creating and Dropping Triggers

To create a trigger, you can use the CREATE TRIGGER statement. In this statement, you must provide the name of the trigger, the object where the trigger is defined, and the action or actions that will fire the trigger.

The CREATE TRIGGER statement must be executed as the only statement in a batch. The same restriction applies to the CREATE PROCEDURE, CREATE VIEW, CREATE RULE, and CREATE FUNCTION statements.

You can use the WITH ENCRYPTION option to encrypt the trigger definition. In this way, you can prevent user access to the trigger's internal code. Be careful when using this option, because there is no way to decrypt an encrypted trigger. It is recommended that you save the CREATE TRIGGER script in a protected directory for further review and modification.

CAUTION

If you encrypt a trigger, it cannot be copied using replication.

You can prevent the execution of the trigger when receiving replicated data by using the NOT FOR REPLICATION option.

To define an AFTER trigger, you use either the FOR or the AFTER keywords. Use the INSTEAD OF keyword to define an INSTEAD OF trigger.

CAUTION

Because SQL Server 2000 accepts AFTER triggers and INSTEAD OF triggers, you should start using the AFTER keyword to create triggers that execute after the data is modified. The FOR keyword is still valid, as a synonym of the AFTER keyword, but it is provided only for backward compatibility.

Listing 9.13 shows some simplified examples of the CREATE TRIGGER statement.

EXAMPLE

Listing 9.13: Use the CREATE TRIGGER Statement to Create Triggers

```
-- Create a trigger on the customer table
-- to track INSERT, UPDATE and DELETE actions

CREATE TRIGGER tr_Customers
ON Customers
AFTER INSERT, UPDATE, DELETE
```

Listing 9.13: continued

```
AS
-- Your code here
GO


-- Create a trigger on the customer table
-- to track INSERT, UPDATE and DELETE actions
-- Using the FOR keyword

CREATE TRIGGER tr_Customers
ON Customers
FOR INSERT, UPDATE, DELETE
AS
-- Your code here
GO


-- Create a trigger on the customer table
-- to track INSERT actions

CREATE TRIGGER isr_Customers
ON Customers
AFTER INSERT
AS
-- Your code here
GO


-- Create a trigger on the customer table
-- to track INSERT, UPDATE and DELETE actions
-- With encryption

CREATE TRIGGER tr_Customers
ON Customers
WITH ENCRYPTION
AFTER INSERT, UPDATE, DELETE
AS
-- Your code here
GO


-- Create a trigger on the customer table
-- to track INSERT, UPDATE and DELETE actions
-- Preventing its execution when receiving
-- replicate data

CREATE TRIGGER tr_Customers
ON Customers
AFTER INSERT, UPDATE, DELETE
NOT FOR REPLICATION
```

Listing 9.13: continued

```
AS
-- Your code here
GO

-- Create an INSTEAD OF trigger
-- on the NewCustomers view
-- to execute on attempts to modify data through the view

CREATE TRIGGER iotr_NewCustomers
ON NewCustomers
INSTEAD OF INSERT, UPDATE, DELETE
AS
-- Your code here
GO

-- Create an INSTEAD OF INSERT trigger
-- on the NewCustomers view
-- to execute on attempts to insert data through the view

CREATE TRIGGER iotr_NewCustomers
ON NewCustomers
INSTEAD OF INSERT
AS
-- Your code here
GO
```

It is not recommended to execute SELECT statements inside a trigger because they should be executed in the background with minimum user interaction. This user interaction should be limited to error messages and warnings, which do not interfere with the results produced by the calling batch.

TIP

Execute the SET NOCOUNT ON statement at the beginning of the trigger code to avoid sending row counter information for every statement that affects data.

TIP

If you want to use specific environment settings during the execution of a trigger, execute the necessary SET statements at the beginning of the trigger code.

A trigger executes whenever the defined action is executed, regardless of the number of affected rows. To avoid the unnecessary execution of any statement inside the trigger when there are no affected rows, use the @@ROWCOUNT system function to test whether this value is bigger than 0.

When you create a trigger, SQL Server does not check for object names; it waits for execution time to check existence of the referenced objects. This is called *deferred name resolution*, and it can give some flexibility to the creation order of database objects.

Deciding the Order of Execution

You cannot decide on a specific order of execution for triggers defined against the same action, but you can select which trigger will be the first one to execute and which trigger will be the last one to execute. You can do this by using the sp_settriggerorder system-stored procedure, as in Listing 9.14.

EXAMPLE

Listing 9.14: You Can Change the Triggers' Order of Execution

```
-- Create multiple triggers on the customer table
-- to track UPDATE actions

CREATE TRIGGER tr1_Customers
ON Customers
AFTER UPDATE
AS
-- Your code here
PRINT 'This is the tr1 trigger'
GO

CREATE TRIGGER tr2_Customers
ON Customers
AFTER UPDATE
AS
-- Your code here
PRINT 'This is the tr2 trigger'
GO

CREATE TRIGGER tr3_Customers
ON Customers
AFTER UPDATE
AS
-- Your code here
PRINT 'This is the tr3 trigger'
GO

-- Test the order of execution
-- By using a MOCK operation

UPDATE Customers
SET ContactName = ContactName
GO
```

Listing 9.14: continued

```
-- Specify the tr3 trigger as first trigger to execute

EXEC sp_settriggerorder 'tr3_Customers', 'FIRST', 'UPDATE'

-- Specify the tr2 trigger as last trigger to execute

EXEC sp_settriggerorder 'tr2_Customers', 'LAST', 'UPDATE'

-- Specify the tr1 trigger as any order to execute

EXEC sp_settriggerorder 'tr1_Customers', 'NONE', 'UPDATE'

GO

-- Test the order of execution
-- By using a MOCK operation

PRINT CHAR(10) + 'After reordering' + CHAR(10)

UPDATE Customers
SET ContactName = ContactName
GO
```

OUTPUT

```
This is the tr1 trigger
This is the tr2 trigger
This is the tr3 trigger

After reordering

This is the tr3 trigger
This is the tr1 trigger
This is the tr2 trigger
```

CAUTION

Remember that INSTEAD OF triggers are always executed before the data is modified. Therefore, they execute before any of the AFTER triggers.

Checking for Updates on Specific Columns

To check inside a trigger if a column has been updated, you can use the IF UPDATE() clause. This clause evaluates to TRUE if the column has been updated.

To test for changes in multiple columns in a single statement, use the COLUMNS_UPDATED() function. This function returns a bitmap with the update status of every column in the base table. In other words, COLUMNS_UPDATED returns a sequence of bits, one bit for every column, and the bit is 1 if the column has been updated or otherwise it is 0.

Listing 9.15 shows an example of these two functions.

EXAMPLE

Listing 9.15: Inside a Trigger You Can Check Which Columns Have Been Updated

```
CREATE TRIGGER tr_OrderDetails
ON [Order Details]
AFTER UPDATE
AS
-- Testing for changes to the PRIMARY KEY
IF UPDATE(OrderID)
BEGIN
PRINT 'Changes to the PRIMARY KEY are not allowed'
ROLLBACK TRAN
END

-- Testing for changes on the 2nd, 3rd and 5th columns
IF ((COLUMNS_UPDATED() & (2 + 4 + 8)) > 0)
BEGIN
IF ((COLUMNS_UPDATED() & 2) = 2)
PRINT 'ProductID updated'
IF ((COLUMNS_UPDATED() & 4) = 4)
PRINT 'UnitPrice updated'
IF ((COLUMNS_UPDATED() & 8) = 8)
PRINT 'Quantity updated'
END
GO

PRINT CHAR(10) + 'Updating ProductID and UnitPrice'

UPDATE [Order Details]
SET ProductID = ProductID,
UnitPrice = UnitPrice

PRINT CHAR(10) + 'Updating Quantity only'

UPDATE [Order Details]
SET Quantity = Quantity

PRINT CHAR(10) + 'Updating OrderID'

UPDATE [Order Details]
SET OrderID = OrderID
```

OUTPUT

```
Updating ProductID and UnitPrice

ProductID updated
UnitPrice updated
```

```
Updating Quantity only

Quantity updated

Updating OrderID

Changes to the PRIMARY KEY are not allowed
```

Multiple-Row Considerations

Keep in mind that a trigger can be fired by an action that modifies a single row or multiple rows in a single statement.

If you define your trigger to work for single rows only, you should reject changes that affect multiple rows. In this case, you can check whether the system function @@ROWCOUNT returns a value greater than 1.

You can define your trigger to deal only with multiple-row operations. In this case, you could use aggregate functions or use cursors. None of these strategies is efficient for single-row operations.

The ideal situation would be to create a trigger with conditional logic to deal with either single-row or multiple-row operations depending on the value returned by @@ROWCOUNT. Listing 9.16 shows a new version of the example of Listing 9.6, optimized for both kinds of transactions.

EXAMPLE

Listing 9.16: You Can Use @@ROWCOUNT to Detect Multiple-Row Operations

```
- - - - - - - - - - - - - - - - - - - - - - - - - - - -
-- Create trigger for insert
- - - - - - - - - - - - - - - - - - - - - - - - - - - -

CREATE TRIGGER isrOrderDetails
ON [Order Details]
AFTER INSERT
AS
IF @@ROWCOUNT = 1
BEGIN

-- Single-row operation

UPDATE TC
SET TotalSales = TotalSales
+ I.UnitPrice * Quantity * (1 - Discount)
FROM TotalCategoriesSales TC
JOIN Products P
ON P.CategoryID = TC.CategoryID
JOIN Inserted I
ON I.ProductID = P.productID
```

Listing 9.16: continued

```
END
ELSE
BEGIN

-- Multi-row operation

UPDATE TC
SET TotalSales = TotalSales
+ (SELECT SUM(I.UnitPrice * Quantity * (1 - Discount))
FROM Inserted I
WHERE I.ProductID = P.productID)
FROM TotalCategoriesSales TC
JOIN Products P
ON P.CategoryID = TC.CategoryID

END
GO


-----------------------------
-- Create trigger for delete
-----------------------------

CREATE TRIGGER delOrderDetails
ON [Order Details]
AFTER DELETE
AS
IF @@ROWCOUNT = 1
BEGIN

-- Single-row operation

UPDATE TC
SET TotalSales = TotalSales
- D.UnitPrice * Quantity * (1 - Discount)
FROM TotalCategoriesSales TC
JOIN Products P
ON P.CategoryID = TC.CategoryID
JOIN Deleted D
ON D.ProductID = P.productID

END
ELSE
BEGIN

-- Multi-row operation
```

Listing 9.16: continued

```
UPDATE TC
SET TotalSales = TotalSales
- (SELECT SUM(D.UnitPrice * Quantity * (1 - Discount))
FROM Deleted D
WHERE D.ProductID = P.productID)
FROM TotalCategoriesSales TC
JOIN Products P
ON P.CategoryID = TC.CategoryID

END
GO


- - - - - - - - - - - - - - - - - - - - - - - - - -
-- Create trigger for Update
- - - - - - - - - - - - - - - - - - - - - - - - - -


CREATE TRIGGER udtOrderDetails
ON [Order Details]
AFTER UPDATE
AS
IF @@ROWCOUNT = 1
BEGIN

-- Single-row operation

UPDATE TC
SET TotalSales = TotalSales
+ I.UnitPrice * I.Quantity * (1 - I.Discount)
FROM TotalCategoriesSales TC
JOIN Products P
ON P.CategoryID = TC.CategoryID
JOIN Inserted I
ON I.ProductID = P.productID

UPDATE TC
SET TotalSales = TotalSales
- D.UnitPrice * D.Quantity * (1 - D.Discount)
FROM TotalCategoriesSales TC
JOIN Products P
ON P.CategoryID = TC.CategoryID
JOIN Deleted D
ON D.ProductID = P.productID

END
ELSE
BEGIN
```

Listing 9.16: continued

```
-- Multi-row operation

UPDATE TC
SET TotalSales = TotalSales
+ (SELECT SUM(I.UnitPrice * Quantity * (1 - Discount))
FROM Inserted I
WHERE I.ProductID = P.productID)
FROM TotalCategoriesSales TC
JOIN Products P
ON P.CategoryID = TC.CategoryID

UPDATE TC
SET TotalSales = TotalSales
- (SELECT SUM(D.UnitPrice * Quantity * (1 - Discount))
FROM Deleted D
WHERE D.ProductID = P.productID)
FROM TotalCategoriesSales TC
JOIN Products P
ON P.CategoryID = TC.CategoryID

END
GO
```

TIP

As shown previously in Listing 9.16, you can easily define a trigger for AFTER UPDATE as a sequence of the actions defined in the AFTER INSERT and AFTER DELETE triggers.

Altering Trigger Definitions

To modify the definition of a trigger, you can use the ALTER TRIGGER statement. In this case, the trigger will take the new definition directly. Listing 9.17 shows how to execute the ALTER TRIGGER statement to modify the tr_Employees trigger.

The syntax is identical to the CREATE TRIGGER statement. Moreover, because triggers are independent objects, no objects are depending on them. They can be dropped and re-created any time, if necessary.

CAUTION

You can change the name of a trigger using the sp_rename stored procedure, but this does not change the name of the trigger stored in the definition of the trigger in syscomments.

To rename a trigger, it is recommended to drop the trigger and re-create it with a different name.

Listing 9.17: You Can Use the ALTER TRIGGER Statement to Modify a Trigger

```
USE Northwind
GO

-- Create a trigger to restrict
-- modifications to the employees table
-- to the dbo

CREATE TRIGGER tr_Employees
ON Employees
AFTER UPDATE, INSERT, DELETE
AS
IF CURRENT_USER <> 'dbo'
BEGIN
RAISERROR ('Only Database Owners can modify Employees,
➥transaction rolled back', 10, 1)
ROLLBACK TRAN
END
GO

-- Modify the trigger to restrict
-- modifications to the employees table
-- to the members of the db_owner role

ALTER TRIGGER tr_Employees
ON Employees
AFTER UPDATE, INSERT, DELETE
AS
IF IS_MEMBER('db_owner') <> 1
BEGIN
RAISERROR ('Only Database Owners can modify Employees,
➥transaction rolled back', 10 ,1)
ROLLBACK TRAN
END
GO
```

Disabling Triggers

To prevent triggers from running when data arrives through replication, you can add the NOT FOR REPLICATION option to the CREATE TRIGGER or ALTER TRIGGER statements. In this case, the trigger will fire on direct modifications to the base table, but not from subscription actions.

Temporarily, you can disable a trigger to speed up some processes. To do so, you can use the ALTER TABLE statement with the DISABLE TRIGGER option, as in Listing 9.18.

Listing 9.18: You Can Disable a Trigger

```
USE Northwind
GO

-- To disable a single trigger

ALTER TABLE Employees
DISABLE TRIGGER tr_Employees --, isr_Employees, udt_Employees

-- To disable several triggers from the same table

ALTER TABLE Employees
DISABLE TRIGGER tr_Employees, isr_Employees, udt_Employees

-- To disable all the triggers from a table

ALTER TABLE Employees
DISABLE TRIGGER ALL
```

To reenable the trigger, use the ALTER TABLE statement with the ENABLE TRIGGER option. Listing 9.19 shows how to reenable the triggers that were disabled in Listing 9.18.

Listing 9.19: You Can Reenable a Trigger

```
USE Northwind
GO

-- To enable a single trigger

ALTER TABLE Employees
ENABLE TRIGGER tr_Employees --, isr_Employees, udt_Employees

-- To enable several triggers from the same table

ALTER TABLE Employees
ENABLE TRIGGER tr_Employees, isr_Employees, udt_Employees

-- To enable all the triggers from a table

ALTER TABLE Employees
ENABLE TRIGGER ALL
```

Nesting Triggers

A trigger can be defined to modify a table, which in turn can have a trigger defined to modify another table, and so on. In this case, triggers force the execution of other triggers, and the execution stops when the last action does not fire any more triggers.

Because triggers are a specialized form of stored procedures, you can nest trigger execution up to 32 levels. Triggers, stored procedures, scalar user-defined functions, and multistatement table-valued functions share this limit. If the execution of a sequence of nested triggers requires more than 32 levels, the execution is aborted, the transaction is rolled back, and the execution of the batch is cancelled.

Nested triggers are enabled by default. You can change this option at server level by setting the "nested triggers" option to 0, using the system stored procedure sp_configure.

You can read the system function @@NESTLEVEL to know how many levels of nesting you have during the execution of a trigger, stored procedure, or user-defined function.

NOTE

In a nested trigger situation, all the triggers are running inside the same transaction. Therefore, any errors inside any of the triggers could potentially roll back the entire transaction.

Listing 9.20 shows an example where you define triggers to maintain sales totals at different levels.

1. You insert, update, or delete data in the Order Details table. This data modification forces the execution of the AFTER UPDATE trigger.

2. The AFTER UPDATE trigger in the Order Details table updates the SaleTotal column in the Orders table.

3. Because the SaleTotal column in the Orders table has been updated, the existing AFTER UPDATE trigger in the Orders table runs automatically and updates the SaleTotal column in the Employees table and the Customers table.

EXAMPLE

Listing 9.20: You Can Create Triggers That Can Be Nested in Sequence

```
USE Northwind
GO

-- Add the column SaleTotal to the
-- Orders table

ALTER TABLE Orders
ADD SaleTotal money NULL

-- Add the column SaleTotal to the
-- Employees table

ALTER TABLE Employees
```

Listing 9.20: continued

```
ADD SaleTotal money NULL

-- Add the column SaleTotal to the
-- Customers table

ALTER TABLE Customers
ADD SaleTotal money NULL

GO

-- Initialize the data

UPDATE Orders
SET SaleTotal =
(SELECT SUM([Order Details].UnitPrice * Quantity * (1 - Discount))
FROM [Order Details]
WHERE [Order Details].OrderID = Orders.OrderID)

UPDATE Employees
SET SaleTotal =
(SELECT SUM(Orders.SaleTotal)
FROM Orders
WHERE Orders.EmployeeID = Employees.EmployeeID)

UPDATE Customers
SET SaleTotal =
(SELECT SUM(Orders.SaleTotal)
FROM Orders
WHERE Orders.CustomerID = Customers.CustomerID)

GO

-- Create nested triggers

CREATE TRIGGER isrTotalOrderDetails
ON [Order details]
AFTER INSERT, DELETE, UPDATE
AS

IF @@rowcount = 1

-- Single-row operation

UPDATE Orders
SET SaleTotal = SaleTotal
+ ISNULL(
(SELECT UnitPrice * Quantity * (1 - Discount)
```

Listing 9.20: continued

```
FROM Inserted
WHERE Inserted.OrderID = Orders.OrderID), 0)
- ISNULL(
(SELECT UnitPrice * Quantity * (1 - Discount)
FROM Deleted
WHERE Deleted.OrderID = Orders.OrderID), 0)

ELSE

-- Multi-row operation

UPDATE Orders
SET SaleTotal = SaleTotal
+ ISNULL(
(SELECT SUM(UnitPrice * Quantity * (1 - Discount))
FROM Inserted
WHERE Inserted.OrderID = Orders.OrderID), 0)
- ISNULL(
(SELECT SUM(UnitPrice * Quantity * (1 - Discount))
FROM Deleted
WHERE Deleted.OrderID = Orders.OrderID), 0)

GO


CREATE TRIGGER isrTotalOrders
ON Orders
AFTER INSERT, DELETE, UPDATE
AS

IF @@rowcount = 1
BEGIN
-- Single-row operation

UPDATE Employees
SET SaleTotal = SaleTotal
+ ISNULL(
(SELECT SaleTotal
FROM Inserted
WHERE Inserted.EmployeeID = Employees.EmployeeID), 0)
- ISNULL(
(SELECT SaleTotal
FROM Deleted
WHERE Deleted.EmployeeID = Employees.EmployeeID), 0)

UPDATE Customers
SET SaleTotal = SaleTotal
```

Listing 9.20: continued

```
+ ISNULL(
(SELECT SaleTotal
FROM Inserted
WHERE Inserted.CustomerID = Customers.CustomerID), 0)
- ISNULL(
(SELECT SaleTotal
FROM Deleted
WHERE Deleted.CustomerID = Customers.CustomerID), 0)

END
ELSE
BEGIN

-- Multi-row operation

UPDATE Employees
SET SaleTotal = SaleTotal
+ ISNULL(
(SELECT SUM(SaleTotal)
FROM Inserted
WHERE Inserted.EmployeeID = Employees.EmployeeID), 0)
- ISNULL(
(SELECT SUM(SaleTotal)
FROM Deleted
WHERE Deleted.EmployeeID = Employees.EmployeeID), 0)

UPDATE Customers
SET SaleTotal = SaleTotal
+ ISNULL(
(SELECT SUM(SaleTotal)
FROM Inserted
WHERE Inserted.CustomerID = Customers.CustomerID), 0)
- ISNULL(
(SELECT SUM(SaleTotal)
FROM Deleted
WHERE Deleted.CustomerID = Customers.CustomerID), 0)

END
GO

-- Updating Order Details
-- and forcing the nested triggers
-- execution

update [order details]
set quantity = 100
where orderid = 10248
```

Listing 9.20: continued

```
and productid = 11

-- Testing totals in Orders table

select CustomerID, EmployeeID, SaleTotal from orders
WHERE OrderID =  10248

SELECT SUM([Order Details].UnitPrice * Quantity * (1 - Discount))
FROM [Order Details]
WHERE OrderID =  10248

-- Testing totals in Employees

SELECT SaleTotal
FROM Employees
WHERE EmployeeID = 5

SELECT SUM(SaleTotal)
FROM Orders
WHERE EmployeeID =  5

-- Testing totals in Customers

SELECT SaleTotal
FROM Customers
WHERE CustomerID = 'VINET'

SELECT SUM(SaleTotal)
FROM Orders
WHERE CustomerID =  'VINET'
GO

-- Dropping triggers

DROP TRIGGER isrTotalOrderDetails

DROP TRIGGER isrTotalOrders
```

Analyzing the previous example, you can see that the data is updated only at the Order Details level, and two nested triggers maintain the summary information in the tables Orders, Employees, and Customers.

You can solve the same problem without using nested triggers. Create three triggers in the Order Details table: one trigger to update the SaleTotal column in the Orders table, a second trigger to update the Employees table, and a third one to update the Customers table. You can see in Listing 9.21 how to implement this solution (note, you must execute the code from Listing 9.20 before running the code from Listing 9.21).

TIP

Create one trigger per logical action, as in Listing 9.21, and avoid nested triggers. Your database application will be more modular and the maintenance will be easier.

EXAMPLE

Listing 9.21: Every Table Can Have Multiple Triggers for Each Action

```
USE Northwind
GO

CREATE TRIGGER tr_OrderDetails_TotalOrders
ON [Order details]
AFTER INSERT, DELETE, UPDATE
AS

IF @@rowcount = 1

-- Single-row operation

UPDATE Orders
SET SaleTotal = SaleTotal
+ ISNULL(
(SELECT UnitPrice * Quantity * (1 - Discount)
FROM Inserted
WHERE Inserted.OrderID = Orders.OrderID), 0)
- ISNULL(
(SELECT UnitPrice * Quantity * (1 - Discount)
FROM Deleted
WHERE Deleted.OrderID = Orders.OrderID), 0)

ELSE

-- Multi-row operation

UPDATE Orders
SET SaleTotal = SaleTotal
+ ISNULL(
(SELECT SUM(UnitPrice * Quantity * (1 - Discount))
FROM Inserted
WHERE Inserted.OrderID = Orders.OrderID), 0)
- ISNULL(
(SELECT SUM(UnitPrice * Quantity * (1 - Discount))
FROM Deleted
WHERE Deleted.OrderID = Orders.OrderID), 0)

GO


CREATE TRIGGER tr_OrderDetails_TotalEmployees
ON [Order details]
```

Listing 9.21: continued

```
AFTER INSERT, DELETE, UPDATE
AS

IF @@rowcount = 1

-- Single-row operation

UPDATE Employees
SET SaleTotal = SaleTotal
+ ISNULL(
(SELECT UnitPrice * Quantity * (1 - Discount)
FROM Inserted
JOIN Orders
ON Inserted.OrderID = Orders.OrderID
WHERE Orders.EmployeeID = Employees.EmployeeID), 0)
- ISNULL(
(SELECT UnitPrice * Quantity * (1 - Discount)
FROM Deleted
JOIN Orders
ON Deleted.OrderID = Orders.OrderID
WHERE Orders.EmployeeID = Employees.EmployeeID), 0)

ELSE

-- Multi-row operation

UPDATE Employees
SET SaleTotal = SaleTotal
+ ISNULL(
(SELECT SUM(UnitPrice * Quantity * (1 - Discount))
FROM Inserted
JOIN Orders
ON Inserted.OrderID = Orders.OrderID
WHERE Orders.EmployeeID = Employees.EmployeeID), 0)
- ISNULL(
(SELECT SUM(UnitPrice * Quantity * (1 - Discount))
FROM Deleted
JOIN Orders
ON Deleted.OrderID = Orders.OrderID
WHERE Orders.EmployeeID = Employees.EmployeeID), 0)

GO

CREATE TRIGGER tr_OrderDetails_TotalCustomers
ON [Order details]
AFTER INSERT, DELETE, UPDATE
AS
```

Listing 9.21: continued

```
IF @@rowcount = 1

-- Single-row operation

UPDATE Customers
SET SaleTotal = SaleTotal
+ ISNULL(
(SELECT UnitPrice * Quantity * (1 - Discount)
FROM Inserted
JOIN Orders
ON Inserted.OrderID = Orders.OrderID
WHERE Orders.CustomerID = Customers.CustomerID), 0)
- ISNULL(
(SELECT UnitPrice * Quantity * (1 - Discount)
FROM Deleted
JOIN Orders
ON Deleted.OrderID = Orders.OrderID
WHERE Orders.CustomerID = Customers.CustomerID), 0)

ELSE

-- Multi-row operation

UPDATE Customers
SET SaleTotal = SaleTotal
+ ISNULL(
(SELECT SUM(UnitPrice * Quantity * (1 - Discount))
FROM Inserted
JOIN Orders
ON Inserted.OrderID = Orders.OrderID
WHERE Orders.CustomerID = Customers.CustomerID), 0)
- ISNULL(
(SELECT SUM(UnitPrice * Quantity * (1 - Discount))
FROM Deleted
JOIN Orders
ON Deleted.OrderID = Orders.OrderID
WHERE Orders.CustomerID = Customers.CustomerID), 0)
GO

DROP TRIGGER tr_OrderDetails_TotalOrders

DROP TRIGGER tr_OrderDetails_TotalCustomers

DROP TRIGGER tr_OrderDetails_TotalEmployees

GO
```

NOTE

The examples in Listings 9.20 and 9.21 create a single trigger for the three actions: INSERT, DELETE, and UPDATE. Creating individual triggers per action is more efficient, as in Listing 9.16, from the execution point of view. I use this strategy here only to simplify the examples.

Recursive Triggers

If a trigger defined in the Products table modifies data in the Employees table, and the Employees table has a trigger that in turn modifies the Products table, the trigger defined in the Products table will fire again. This situation is called *indirect recursion*, because a single statement forces multiple executions of the same trigger, through the execution of other triggers. This is a special case of nested triggers, and everything said about it in the preceding section can be applied to this case.

In some scenarios, it is possible to have direct recursion, when a table has a trigger that modifies some data in the table again. In this case, by default, SQL Server will not fire the trigger again, avoiding this direct recursion.

To enable trigger recursion in a database you must set the 'recursive triggers' option to 'true' at database level using the sp_dboption system stored procedure, or set the option RECURSIVE_TRIGGERS ON in the ALTER DATABASE statement. Listing 9.22 shows both statements.

EXAMPLE

Listing 9.22: You Can Enable Recursive Triggers at Database Level Only

```
-- Enable Recursive triggers in Northwind

EXEC sp_dboption 'Northwind', 'recursive triggers', 'true'

-- Disable Recursive triggers in Northwind

ALTER DATABASE Northwind
SET RECURSIVE_TRIGGERS OFF
```

Consider the typical hierarchical table where you save cost and budget breakdown of a project cost control system. Every row in this table has a single ID as primary key, but it refers to another row as a parent row, excluding the root row: the project itself. Any change on Cost or Budget in a row has to be escalated to the highest level, and you introduce costs only in rows with no children.

This strategy is very flexible, adjusting changes easily on the distribution of activities in the project. Listing 9.23 shows the code to implement this example.

EXAMPLE

Listing 9.23: Use Triggers to Maintain Hierarchical Data

```
-- Create the base table

CREATE TABLE CostBudgetControl (
ID int NOT NULL
PRIMARY KEY,
Name nvarchar(100) NOT NULL,
ParentID int NULL
REFERENCES CostBudgetControl(ID),
Cost money NOT NULL DEFAULT 0,
Budget money NOT NULL DEFAULT 0,
HasChildren bit DEFAULT 0)

-- Insert Cost Structure
-- Create a text file (Gas.txt)
-- with the following contents:
/*
1, Gas Pipeline Project, 0, 85601000.0000, 117500000.0000, 1
2, Engineering, 1, 800000.0000, 950000.0000, 1
3, Materials, 1, 23400000.0000, 28000000.0000, 1
4, Construction, 1, 61000000.0000, 88000000.0000, 1
5, Supervision, 1, 401000.0000, 550000.0000, 1
6, Line, 2, 300000.0000, 400000.0000, 0
7, Stations, 2, 500000.0000, 550000.0000, 0
8, Pipes, 3, 14500000.0000, 16000000.0000, 0
9, Machinery, 3, 8900000.0000, 12000000.0000, 0
10, Section A, 4, 31000000.0000, 47000000.0000, 1
11, Section B, 4, 30000000.0000, 41000000.0000, 1
12, Welding, 5, 200000.0000, 250000.0000, 0
13, Civil, 5, 145000.0000, 200000.0000, 0
14, Buildings, 5, 56000.0000, 100000.0000, 0
15, Civil works, 10, 20000000.0000, 30000000.0000, 0
16, Civil works, 11, 18000000.0000, 25000000.0000, 0
17, Pipeline, 10, 11000000.0000, 17000000.0000, 0
18, Pipeline, 11, 12000000.0000, 16000000.0000, 0
*/

BULK INSERT Northwind.dbo.CostBudgetControl
   FROM 'C:\Gas.txt'
   WITH
      (
         FIELDTERMINATOR = ', ',
         ROWTERMINATOR = '\n'
      )
GO

UPDATE CostBudgetControl
SET ParentID = NULL
WHERE ID = 1
```

Listing 9.23: continued

```
GO

-- Create the recursive trigger

CREATE TRIGGER udtCostBudget
ON CostBudgetControl
AFTER UPDATE
AS
IF @@rowcount>0
UPDATE CostBudgetControl
SET Cost = Cost
+ ISNULL((SELECT SUM(Cost)
FROM Inserted
WHERE Inserted.ParentID = CostBudgetControl.ID), 0)
- ISNULL((SELECT SUM(Cost)
FROM Deleted
WHERE Deleted.ParentID = CostBudgetControl.ID), 0),
Budget = Budget
+ ISNULL((SELECT SUM(Budget)             .
FROM Inserted
WHERE Inserted.ParentID = CostBudgetControl.ID), 0)
- ISNULL((SELECT SUM(Budget)
FROM Deleted
WHERE Deleted.ParentID = CostBudgetControl.ID), 0)
WHERE ID IN
(SELECT ParentID
FROM Inserted
UNION
SELECT ParentID
FROM Deleted)
GO

-- Enable Recursive triggers

ALTER DATABASE Northwind
SET RECURSIVE_TRIGGERS ON
GO

-- Total Cost and Budget
-- Before the update

SELECT Cost, Budget
FROM CostBudgetControl
WHERE ID = 1

-- Update some cost
```

Listing 9.23: continued

```
UPDATE CostBudgetControl
SET Cost = 12500000.0000
WHERE ID = 17

-- Total Cost and Budget
-- After the update

SELECT Cost, Budget
FROM CostBudgetControl
WHERE ID = 1

GO

DROP TABLE CostBudgetControl
```

```
Cost                    Budget
--------------------    --------------------
85601000.0000           117500000.0000


Cost                    Budget
--------------------    --------------------
87101000.0000           117500000.0000
```

OUTPUT

Security Implications of Using Triggers

Only certain users can create triggers:

- The owner of the table on which the trigger has to be defined
- Members of the db_owner and db_ddladmin database roles
- Members of the sysadmin server role, because permissions don't affect them

The user who creates the trigger needs specific permissions to execute the statements defined in the code of the trigger.

CAUTION

If any of the objects referenced in the trigger don't belong to the same owner, you can have a broken ownership chain situation. To avoid this situation, it is recommended that dbo must be the owner of all the objects in a database.

Enforcing Business Rules: Choosing Among INSTEAD OF Triggers, Constraints, and AFTER Triggers

This is the final chapter that discusses techniques to enforce data integrity, and as a summary, you can propose which ways are recommended to enforce data integrity:

- To uniquely identify every row, define a PRIMARY KEY constraint. This is one of the first rules to apply to designing a normalized database. Searching for values contained in a PRIMARY KEY is fast because there is a UNIQUE INDEX supporting the PRIMARY KEY.

- To enforce uniqueness of required values in a column or group of columns, other than the PRIMARY KEY, define a UNIQUE constraint. This constraint does not produce much overhead because there is a UNIQUE INDEX supporting this constraint.

- To enforce uniqueness of optional values (columns that accept NULL), create a TRIGGER. You can test this uniqueness before the data modification with an INSTEAD OF trigger, or after the data modification with an AFTER trigger.

- To validate entries in a column, according to a specific pattern, range, or format, create a CHECK constraint.

- To validate values in a row, where values in different columns must satisfy specific conditions, create one or more CHECK constraints. If you create one CHECK constraint per condition, you can later disable specific conditions only, if required.

- To validate values in a column, among a list of possible values, create a *look-up table (LUT)* with the required values and create a FOREIGN KEY constraint to reference the look-up table. You could create a CHECK constraint instead, but using a LUT is more flexible.

- To restrict values in a column to the values contained in a column in a second table, create a FOREIGN KEY constraint in the first table.

- To make sure that every entry in a column is related to the primary key of another table, without exceptions, define the FOREIGN KEY column as NOT NULL.

- To restrict the values in a column to complex conditions involving other rows in the same table, create a TRIGGER to check these conditions. As an alternative, create a CHECK constraint with a user-defined function to check this complex condition.

- To restrict the values in a column to complex conditions involving other tables in the same or different database, create a TRIGGER to check these conditions.

- To declare a column as required, specify NOT NULL in the column definition.

- To specify a default value for columns where no value is supplied in INSERT operations, declare a DEFAULT property for the column.

- To declare a column as autonumeric, declare an IDENTITY property in the column and specify the seed value and the increment.

- To declare a default value, which depends on values in other rows or tables, declare a DEFAULT property for the column using a user-defined function as a default expression.

- To cascade changes on primary keys to related fields in other tables, declare a FOREIGN KEY with the ON UPDATE CASCADE clause. Do not create triggers to perform this operation.

- To delete in cascade related rows when the row in the primary table is deleted, declare a FOREIGN KEY with the ON DELETE CASCADE clause. Do not create triggers to perform this operation.

- To cascade complex operations to other tables to maintain denormalized data, create individual triggers to execute this operation.

- To validate INSERT, UPDATE, or DELETE operations applied through a view, define an INSTEAD OF trigger on the view.

- Do not use RULE objects unless you want to define self-contained user-defined data types. It is recommended to declare CHECK constraints instead.

- Do not use DEFAULT objects unless you want to define self-contained user-defined data types. It is recommended to declare DEFAULT definitions instead.

What's Next?

This chapter covered the creation and use of triggers as a way to enforce complex data integrity.

Chapter 10, "Enhancing Business Logic: User-Defined Functions (UDF)," covers user-defined functions, which can be used as part of the trigger definition and as an alternative to triggers, providing extra computing capabilities to CHECK constraints and DEFAULT definitions.

Chapter 12, "Row-Oriented Processing: Using Cursors," explains how to use cursors. This could be useful in some triggers to deal with multiple-row actions.

Triggers always work inside a transaction, and Chapter 13, "Maintaining Data Consistency: Transactions and Locks," covers specifically that: transaction and locks. There you can see the implications of modifying data through triggers and how to increase concurrency, preventing undesired blockings.

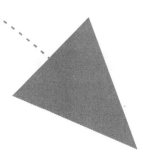

Enhancing Business Logic: User-Defined Functions (UDF)

Procedural languages are based mainly in the capability to create functions, encapsulate complex programming functionality, and return a value as a result of the operation. Using SQL Server 2000, you can define user-defined functions (UDF), which combine the functionality of stored procedures and views but provide extended flexibility.

This chapter teaches you the following:

- What the built-in user-defined functions are and how to use them

- How to define user-defined functions that return a scalar value

- How to define user-defined functions that return a result set

- How to convert stored procedures and views into user-defined functions

- How to extend the functionality of constraints with user-defined functions

Benefits of User-Defined Functions

You learned in Chapter 8, "Implementing Business Logic: Programming Stored Procedures," how to create stored procedures, which are similar to the way you create functions in other programming languages. However, using stored procedures from Transact-SQL is not very flexible, because you can use them only with the EXECUTE or INSERT...EXECUTE statements. If you have a stored procedure that returns a single value, you cannot use this procedure inside an expression. If your procedure returns a result set, you cannot use this procedure in the FROM clause of any Transact-SQL statement.

In Chapter 3, "Working with Tables and Views," you learned about views and how to use them anywhere as a replacement for tables. However, when you define a view, you are limited to a single SELECT statement. Unlike stored procedures, you cannot define parameters in a view.

Some user-defined functions are similar to views but they can be defined with more than one statement and they accept parameters. You can call user-defined functions in the same way you execute stored procedures, and you can use scalar user-defined functions as part of any expression anywhere in a Transact-SQL statement where an expression is valid. Furthermore, you can use a user-defined function that returns a table in the FROM clause of any Transact-SQL Data Manipulation Language (DML) statement.

User-defined functions have many benefits in common with stored procedures, as covered in Chapter 8. However, user-defined functions have more useful benefits. They enable you to

- Use the result set returned by a stored procedure in the FROM clause of a query

- Join the results of two stored procedures, without using temporary tables to store intermediate results

- Use the result of a stored procedure in the IN operator

- Use a stored procedure as a subquery in the WHERE clause

- Create a view that cannot be solved with a single SELECT statement

- Create a view with parameters similar to the way Microsoft Access creates queries with parameters

- Extend the list of built-in functions with any financial function

- Create new mathematical functions for any special scientific database applications that you might require

This chapter will help you discover how user-defined functions can help you solve these common programming problems.

Built-In User-Defined Functions

SQL Server 2000 implements some system functions as built-in user-defined functions. Many of them are not documented; Query Analyzer, Enterprise Manager, Profiler, Replication, and other client applications and system processes use some of these built-in user-defined functions internally. These functions can be used almost as any other user-defined function, but SQL Server itself implements them.

You cannot change the definition of these built-in user-defined functions. In some cases, you cannot see their definition using the sp_help or sp_helptext system stored procedures, and you cannot script them. However, their definition is stored in the syscomments system table as any other user-defined function.

CAUTION

Microsoft does not guarantee that undocumented built-in user-defined functions will remain unchanged in the future; however, we can use some of them as examples of what kind of operations a user-defined function can do.

In some cases, built-in user-defined functions return a single scalar value, and all of them are undocumented:

- fn_CharIsWhiteSpace(@nchar) returns 1 if the variable @nchar only contains a space, a tab character, a newline character, or carriage return character; it returns 0 otherwise.

- fn_MSSharedVersion(@len_minorversion) returns the major and minor version number of SQL Server. @len_minorversion specifies how many digits to show for the minor version.

- fn_MsGenSqeScStr(@pstrin) returns the string @pstring, converting single quotes into two single quotes so that you are able to concatenate this string with other strings to execute a dynamic statement.

- fn_IsReplMergeAgent() returns 1 if the present process is executed by the Replication Merge Agent.

- fn_GetPersistedServerNameCaseVariation(@servername) returns the server name of the server specified in @servername with exactly the same case it uses in the sysservers system table, regardless of the case used to call this function.

- fn_ReplGetBinary8LoDWord(@binary8_value) takes the lower four bytes from the @binary8_value binary variable and converts them into an integer value.

- `fn_ReplPrepadBinary8(@varbinary8_value)` converts the `varbinary(8)` value stored in `@varbinary8_value` into a fixed-length `binary(8)` value with leading zeros.

- `fn_ReplMakeStringLiteral(@string)` converts the value stored in the `@string` value into a `UNICODE` string, including quotes, such as `N'Hello'`, to be used in dynamically constructed statements.

- `fn_ReplQuoteName(@string)` returns the value stored in `@string` enclosed in square brackets. You can use this function in dynamic execution to select object names that contain spaces or keywords, such as `[Order Details]`.

- `fn_GenerateParameterPattern(@parameter)` returns a pattern string you can use with the `LIKE` operator to test for strings containing any case variation of the value stored in `@parameter`, such as converting `'Hello'` into `'%[hH][eE][lL][lL][oO]%'`. This is useful in case-sensitive servers, databases, or columns.

- `fn_UpdateParameterWithArgument`, `fn_SkipParameterArgument`, and `fn_RemoveParameterWithArgument` are internal functions, and their study is not the purpose of this book.

Listing 10.1 shows some examples of scalar built-in, user-defined functions and the partial result of some of them.

EXAMPLE

Listing 10.1: Using Undocumented Built-In User-Defined Functions

```
USE Northwind
GO

PRINT CHAR(10)
+ 'fn_chariswhitespace(CHAR(9))'
+ CHAR(10)

select fn_chariswhitespace(CHAR(9))
GO

PRINT CHAR(10)
+ 'fn_mssharedversion(1)'
+ CHAR(10)

select master.dbo.fn_mssharedversion(1)
GO

PRINT CHAR(10)
+ 'fn_replgetbinary8lodword(0x0304030401020102)'
+ CHAR(10)
```

Listing 10.1: continued

```
select fn_replgetbinary8lodword(0x0304030401020102)
GO

PRINT CHAR(10)
+ 'fn_replmakestringliteral(@a)'
+ CHAR(10)

declare @a varchar(100)

set @a = 'peter is right'

select fn_replmakestringliteral(@a)
GO

PRINT CHAR(10)
+ 'fn_replprepadbinary8(123456890123)'
+ CHAR(10)

select fn_replprepadbinary8(123456890123)
GO

PRINT CHAR(10)
+ 'fn_replquotename("hello")'
+ CHAR(10)

select fn_replquotename('hello')
fn_chariswhitespace(CHAR(9))
```

OUTPUT

```
....
1

fn_mssharedversion(1)


...........
80

fn_replgetbinary8lodword(0x0304030401020102)


...........
16908546

fn_replmakestringliteral(@a)
```

Listing 10.1: continued

```
- - - - - - - - - - - - - - - - - - - - - - - - - - - - - - -
N'peter is right'


fn_replprepadbinary8(123456890123)


- - - - - - - - - - - - - - - - - -
0x0C0000010BA59ABE


fn_replquotename("hello")


- - - - - - - - - - - - - - - - - - - - - - - - - - - - - - -
[hello]
```

In other cases, built-in, user-defined functions return a table. SQL Server documents some of them:

- fn_ListExtendedProperty produces a list of available extended properties for a given database or database objects, such as database users, user-defined data types, tables, views, stored procedures, user-defined functions, default objects, rule objects, columns of tables and views, parameters of stored procedures and user-defined functions, indexes, constraints, and triggers.

- fn_HelpCollations returns a list of the available collations.

- fn_ServerSharedDrives returns a list of the drives shared by a clustered server.

- fn_VirtualServerNodes returns the list of server nodes, defining a virtual server in a clustering server environment.

- fn_VirtualFileStats returns statistical I/O information about any file in a database, including transaction log files.

Listing 10.2 shows some examples of how to use these table-valued, built-in, user-defined functions.

NOTE

As you can see in Listing 10.2, you must call some of the built-in user-defined functions with double colons (::) to differentiate them from user-defined functions that are not built in and do not use the dbo as owner. Most of the built-in user-defined functions have a system owner called system_function_schema.

EXAMPLE

Listing 10.2: Table-Valued, Built-In, User-Defined Functions

```
USE Northwind
GO

PRINT CHAR(10)
+ 'fn_helpcollations'
+ CHAR(10)

select *
from ::fn_helpcollations()
WHERE name LIKE 'Cyrillic%'
GO

PRINT CHAR(10)
+ 'fn_listextendedproperty(NULL, NULL, NULL, NULL, NULL, NULL, NULL)'
+ CHAR(10)

select *
from ::fn_listextendedproperty(NULL, NULL, NULL, NULL, NULL, NULL, NULL)
GO

PRINT CHAR(10)
+ 'fn_MSFullText()'
+ CHAR(10)

select *
from master.dbo.fn_MSFullText()
GO

fn_helpcollations
```

OUTPUT

```
name                        description
--------------------------  ------------------------------------
Cyrillic_General_BIN        Cyrillic-General, binary sort
Cyrillic_General_CI_AI      Cyrillic-General, case-insensitive,
➥accent-insensitive, kanatype-insensitive, width-insensitive
Cyrillic_General_CI_AI_WS   Cyrillic-General, case-insensitive,
➥accent-insensitive, kanatype-insensitive, width-sensitive
Cyrillic_General_CI_AI_KS   Cyrillic-General, case-insensitive,
➥accent-insensitive, kanatype-sensitive, width-insensitive
Cyrillic_General_CI_AI_KS_WS Cyrillic-General, case-insensitive,
➥accent-insensitive, kanatype-sensitive, width-sensitive
Cyrillic_General_CI_AS      Cyrillic-General, case-insensitive,
➥accent-sensitive, kanatype-insensitive, width-insensitive
Cyrillic_General_CI_AS_WS   Cyrillic-General, case-insensitive,
➥accent-sensitive, kanatype-insensitive, width-sensitive
Cyrillic_General_CI_AS_KS   Cyrillic-General, case-insensitive,
➥accent-sensitive, kanatype-sensitive, width-insensitive
```

Listing 10.2: continued

```
Cyrillic_General_CI_AS_KS_WS  Cyrillic-General, case-insensitive,
➥accent-sensitive, kanatype-sensitive, width-sensitive
Cyrillic_General_CS_AI        Cyrillic-General, case-sensitive,
➥accent-insensitive, kanatype-insensitive, width-insensitive
Cyrillic_General_CS_AI_WS     Cyrillic-General, case-sensitive,
➥accent-insensitive, kanatype-insensitive, width-sensitive
Cyrillic_General_CS_AI_KS     Cyrillic-General, case-sensitive,
➥accent-insensitive, kanatype-sensitive, width-insensitive
Cyrillic_General_CS_AI_KS_WS  Cyrillic-General, case-sensitive,
➥accent-insensitive, kanatype-sensitive, width-sensitive
Cyrillic_General_CS_AS        Cyrillic-General, case-sensitive,
➥accent-sensitive, kanatype-insensitive, width-insensitive
Cyrillic_General_CS_AS_WS     Cyrillic-General, case-sensitive,
➥accent-sensitive, kanatype-insensitive, width-sensitive
Cyrillic_General_CS_AS_KS     Cyrillic-General, case-sensitive,
➥accent-sensitive, kanatype-sensitive, width-insensitive
Cyrillic_General_CS_AS_KS_WS  Cyrillic-General, case-sensitive,
➥accent-sensitive, kanatype-sensitive, width-sensitive


fn_listextendedproperty(NULL, NULL, NULL, NULL, NULL, NULL, NULL)

objtype  objname  name  value
-------- -------- ----- ------------------------


fn_MSFullText()

LCID
-----------
2052
1028
1043
2057
1033
1036
1031
1040
1041
1042
0
1053
```

Other built-in user-defined functions help you to manage user-defined
traces from Transact-SQL. You use system stored procedures to define
traces and built-in user-defined functions to get information about them.

- fn_trace_getinfo shows information about a specific trace or all the
  traces defined.

- fn_trace_gettable opens a trace file from disk and shows its information in a table format.

- fn_trace_geteventinfo shows information about the events defined for an active trace.

- fn_tracegetfilterinfo shows the filters applied to a specific trace.

There is a table-valued, built-in, user-defined function—fn_dblog—that is not documented, but it can be very useful in some cases. fn_dblog reads the information contained in the transaction log. This is an alternative to the DBCC LOG statement, undocumented as well, and less flexible than fn_dblog. Listing 10.3 shows an example of this function.

EXAMPLE

Listing 10.3: Use fn_dblog to Look at the Transaction Log

```
USE Northwind
GO

PRINT CHAR(10)
+ 'fn_log(NULL, NULL)'
+ CHAR(10)

select TOP 10
[Current LSN], Operation
from ::fn_dblog(NULL, NULL)
ORDER BY [Current LSN] DESC
GO

fn_log(NULL, NULL)
```

OUTPUT

```
Current LSN             Operation
--------------------    ---------------------------
0000002e:00000010:0006  LOP_COMMIT_XACT
0000002e:00000010:0005  LOP_DELTA_SYSIND
0000002e:00000010:0004  LOP_MODIFY_ROW
0000002e:00000010:0003  LOP_SET_FREE_SPACE
0000002e:00000010:0002  LOP_MODIFY_ROW
0000002e:00000010:0001  LOP_MODIFY_ROW
0000002d:000001e4:0001  LOP_BEGIN_XACT
0000002d:000001c3:0011  LOP_COMMIT_XACT
0000002d:000001c3:0010  LOP_DELTA_SYSIND
0000002d:000001c3:000f  LOP_MODIFY_ROW
```

NOTE

If you want to see the definitions of these built-in user-defined functions, you have them in the installation scripts. Using Query Analyzer, open the following files located in the INSTALL directory: procsyst.sql, replcom.sql, replsys.sql, repltran.sql, and sqldmo.sql.

Types of User-Defined Functions According to Their Return Value

You can define a user-defined function with a single statement or with multiple statements, as you will see later in this chapter in the "Creating and Dropping User-Defined Functions" section.

According to their return value, user-defined functions can be divided into three groups:

- Scalar functions that return a single scalar value.

- Table-valued functions that return a full result set, similar to a table.

- Inline user-defined functions are a special case of table-valued user-defined functions, but they are limited to a single SELECT statement.

Scalar Functions

Scalar user-defined functions return a single value, and they can be used wherever an expression is accepted, such as

- In the SELECT clause of a SELECT statement, as a part of an expression or as an individual column

- In the SET clause of an UPDATE statement, as a value to insert into a field of the table being updated

- In the FROM clause of any DML statement (SELECT, UPDATE, INSERT, DELETE), as a single-column, single-row result set–derived table

- In the FROM clause of any DML statement, as part of the joining conditions in the ON clause

- In the WHERE clause or HAVING clause of any DML statement

- In the GROUP BY clause, as part of any grouping condition

- In the ORDER BY clause of any statement, as sorting criteria

- As a DEFAULT value for a column

- Inside a CHECK CONSTRAINT definition

- Inside a CASE expression

- In a PRINT statement, if the user-defined function returns a string

- As part of the condition of IF or WHILE statements

- As part of the definition of a compute column

- As a parameter to call a stored procedure or another user-defined function

- As a return value of a stored procedure, if the user-defined function returns an integer value

- As a return value of another scalar user-defined function

Scalar user-defined functions can be combined with other functions in an expression, as long as the data types are compatible with the operation.

TIP

You can identify scalar user-defined functions because they return a scalar data type and their definition is enclosed in a BEGIN...END block.

CREATING SCALAR USER-DEFINED FUNCTIONS

To create a scalar user-defined function, you must use the CREATE FUNCTION statement, as shown in Listing 10.4.

The first example creates the MaxProductID function, which selects the maximum available ProductID from the Products table. This function returns a scalar integer value.

The second example creates the WhoWhere function, which returns a scalar string with information about which is the login of the connected user and from which machine the user is connected.

The third example returns the date of the latest executed process in SQL Server, which we can consider today's date in general.

The fourth example is a bit more complex; it generates a random number, between 0.0 and 1.0, based on the time of the latest statement executed in SQL Server. This function is similar to the system function Rand; however, Rand cannot be used inside a user-defined function, whereas this PRand function can be used.

EXAMPLE

Listing 10.4: Creating Scalar User-Defined Functions

```
USE Northwind
GO

-- Returns the maximum ProductID from Products

CREATE FUNCTION dbo.MaxProductID
()
RETURNS int
AS
BEGIN
RETURN (
SELECT MAX(ProductID)
FROM dbo.Products
)
```

Listing 10.4: continued

```
END
GO

-- Returns who and from where the query is executed

CREATE FUNCTION dbo.WhoWhere
()
RETURNS nvarchar(256)
AS
BEGIN
RETURN SYSTEM_USER
+ ' FROM '
+ APP_NAME()
END
GO

-- Returns the date of the latest executed statement
-- which is usually today

CREATE FUNCTION dbo.Today
()
RETURNS smalldatetime
AS
BEGIN
DECLARE @sdt smalldatetime

SELECT @SDT = CONVERT(varchar(10), MAX(last_batch), 112)
FROM master.dbo.sysprocesses

RETURN @SDT

END
GO

-- Function that produces a non-predictable
-- Pseudo-Random Number

CREATE FUNCTION dbo.PRand
()
RETURNS float
AS
BEGIN
DECLARE @dt datetime
DECLARE @dts varchar(3)
DECLARE @t1 float
DECLARE @t2 float
DECLARE @r float
```

Listing 10.4: continued

```
-- Obtain the time of latest executed statement

SET @dt = (
SELECT MAX(last_batch)
FROM master.dbo.sysprocesses
)

-- Select only the milliseconds

SET @dts = RIGHT(CONVERT(varchar(20), @dt, 114) , 3)

-- Scramble the digits

SET @t1 = CAST(SUBSTRING(@dts, 2, 1)
+ RIGHT(@dts, 1)
+ LEFT(@dts, 1) AS int)

-- Obtain the time of latest executed statement

SET @dt = (
SELECT MAX(last_batch)
FROM master.dbo.sysprocesses
)

-- Select only the milliseconds

SET @dts = RIGHT(CONVERT(varchar(20), @dt, 114) , 3)

-- Scramble the digits

SET @t2 = CAST(SUBSTRING(@dts, 2, 1)
+ RIGHT(@dts, 1)
+ LEFT(@dts, 1) AS int)

-- Select the random number

SET @r = '0' + LEFT(RIGHT(CONVERT(varchar(40), @t1 * @t2 / pi(), 2), 21), 16)

-- Return the random number

RETURN @r
END
GO
```

You can identify several parts in the CREATE FUNCTION syntax for a scalar user-defined function:

- CREATE FUNCTION ownername.functionname, where you can specify the owner of the function and the name of the function.

- () is an empty list of parameters. We will discuss parameters in the next section of this chapter.

- RETURNS datatype, where you define the data type for the returned value as the function's result.

- AS BEGIN...END to mark the function definition body.

- The function definition body.

You can define the body of the function in a way similar to a stored procedure, declaring and using variables, using control-of-flow statements, accessing data from other tables, and other databases and servers.

CAUTION

Remember that you cannot modify data in existing tables inside a user-defined function directly. This includes the creation of temporary tables.

Because writing long user-defined functions can be complex, you can break down long functions into smaller ones that can be reused more often. Listing 10.5 creates a new version of the PRand function, created in Listing 10.4. This version uses a base function, called Get3Rand, to generate the scrambled three-digit number. The NewPRand function uses the Get3Rand function to generate two values and combine them to provide the new random number.

EXAMPLE

Listing 10.5: New Definition for the Random Function Using Other Base Functions

```
USE Northwind
GO

-- Create a base function to extract a three-digits
-- number based on the scrambled version of the
-- milliseconds information of the latest executed
-- statement in SQL Server

CREATE FUNCTION dbo.Get3Rand
()
RETURNS int
AS
BEGIN
DECLARE @dt datetime
DECLARE @dts varchar(3)

SET @dt = (
SELECT MAX(last_batch)
FROM master.dbo.sysprocesses
)
```

Listing 10.5: continued

```
SET @dts = RIGHT(CONVERT(varchar(20), @dt, 114) , 3)

RETURN CAST(SUBSTRING(@dts, 2, 1)
+ RIGHT(@dts, 1)
+ LEFT(@dts, 1) AS int)

END
GO

-- Create the new NewPRand Random function
-- based on the Get3Rand function

CREATE FUNCTION dbo.NewPRand
()
RETURNS float
AS
BEGIN
DECLARE @r float

SET @r = '0' + LEFT(RIGHT(CONVERT(varchar(40),
dbo.Get3Rand() * dbo.Get3Rand() / pi(), 2), 21), 16)

RETURN (@r)
END
```

TIP

If your user-defined function requires using temporary tables, you can use table variables instead. Table variables are defined inside the user-defined function and can be modified inside it.

Listing 10.6 uses table variables defined internally inside a user-defined function to store intermediate results. This function calculates the medium UnitPrice for products stored in the Products table.

NOTE

The medium value is the central value of an ordered list of values. The medium does not have to be equal to the average value.

EXAMPLE

Listing 10.6: Using Table Variables Inside a Scalar User-Defined Function

```
USE Northwind
GO

CREATE FUNCTION dbo.MediumProductUnitPrice
()
RETURNS money
AS
```

Listing 10.6: continued

```
BEGIN

-- Create hosting table variable

DECLARE @t TABLE(
id int identity(1,1),
UnitPrice money)

-- Inserts the product prices in ascending order

INSERT INTO @t (UnitPrice)
SELECT UnitPrice
FROM Products
ORDER BY UnitPrice ASC

-- Selects the medium price

RETURN (
SELECT MAX(UnitPrice)
FROM @t
WHERE ID <=
(SELECT MAX(ID)
FROM @t) / 2
)

END
```

USING PARAMETERS IN USER-DEFINED FUNCTIONS

As you learned in Chapter 8, you can expand stored procedure capabilities by using parameters. You can create user-defined functions with parameters, too.

The examples from the preceding section do not use any parameter, which is why their execution does not depend on any value that the user might send. Most of the system-supplied mathematical functions accept one or more parameters and return a scalar result according to the mathematical operation to execute. Trigonometric functions use a number as a parameter and return a number as a result. String functions take one or more parameters and return a string.

You can create user-defined functions to expand the collection of system-supplied functions, using parameters. You must define a parameter list in the CREATE FUNCTION statement, after the function name. The parameters list is enclosed in parentheses. You must provide a data type for every parameter and, optionally, a default value.

CAUTION

The parameter list can be empty if the function does not use any input parameters. In this case, you must supply two parentheses ( ) to specify an empty parameters list.

If you do not specify a parentheses-enclosed parameter list, or at least an empty one, you will get a syntax error when trying to create the user-defined function.

Listing 10.7 shows some examples of user-defined functions using parameters.

The first function, `TotalPrice`, computes the total price of a specific sale. You must provide the quantity sold, the unit price to apply, the agreed discount, and then the function returns the total price of the sale.

The second function in Listing 10.7, `fn_FV`, computes the future value of an annuity, the `FV` financial formula, as described in Microsoft Excel and Microsoft Visual Basic.

The third and fourth functions provide an example of how to create a user-defined function to perform basic encryption.

CAUTION

The intention of the `SimpleEncrypt` and `SimpleDecrypt` user-defined functions is only to show how to define a function to modify a string. The encryption used in these functions is too simple to be used in a production environment.

EXAMPLE

Listing 10.7: Some Scalar User-Defined Functions Using Parameters

```
USE Northwind
GO

-----------------------------------------------------------
-- Generic function to compute the total price of a sale
-- from the quantity, unitprice and discount
-----------------------------------------------------------

CREATE FUNCTION dbo.TotalPrice
(@Quantity float, @UnitPrice money, @Discount float = 0.0)
RETURNS money
AS
BEGIN
RETURN (@Quantity * @UnitPrice * (1.0 - @Discount))
END
GO


-----------------------------------------------------------
-- Compute the future value of an annuity based on
-- periodic fixed payments with a fixed interest rate
-- Parameters:
-- @rate: interest rate between payments
```

Listing 10.7: continued

```
-- @nper: number of payments
-- @pmt: payment to be made on every period
-- @pv: present value. Default to 0.0
-- @type: 0 if the payment is made at the end of each period (default)
--        1 if the payment is made at the beginning of each period
-----------------------------------------------------------

CREATE FUNCTION dbo.fn_FV
(@rate float, @nper int, @pmt money, @pv money = 0.0, @type bit = 0)
RETURNS money
AS
BEGIN
DECLARE @fv money

IF @rate = 0
SET @fv = @pv + @pmt * @nper
ELSE
SET @fv = @pv * POWER(1 + @rate, @nper) +
@pmt * (((POWER(1 + @rate, @nper + @type) - 1) / @rate) - @type)

RETURN (-@fv)
END
GO


-----------------------------------------------------------
-- Encrypt the string increasing the Unicode value of every
-- character by the number of characters in the string
-----------------------------------------------------------

CREATE Function dbo.SimpleEncrypt
(@string nvarchar(4000))
RETURNS nvarchar(4000)
AS
BEGIN
DECLARE @output nvarchar(4000)
DECLARE @i int, @l int, @c int

SET @i = 1
SET @l = len(@string)
SET @output = ''

WHILE @i <= @l
BEGIN

SET @c = UNICODE(SUBSTRING(@string, @i, 1))
```

Listing 10.7: continued

```
SET @output = @output +
CASE
WHEN @c > 65535 - @l
THEN NCHAR(@c + @l - 65536)
ELSE NCHAR(@c + @l) END

SET @i = @i + 1

END

RETURN @output

END
GO



-------------------------------------------------------------
-- Decrypt the string decreasing the Unicode value of every
-- character by the number of characters in the string
-------------------------------------------------------------

CREATE Function dbo.SimpleDecrypt
(@string nvarchar(4000))
RETURNS nvarchar(4000)
AS
BEGIN
DECLARE @output nvarchar(4000)
DECLARE @i int, @l int, @c int

SET @i = 1
SET @l = len(@string)
SET @output = ''

WHILE @i <= @l
BEGIN

SET @c = UNICODE(SUBSTRING(@string, @i, 1))

SET @output = @output +
CASE
WHEN @c - @l >= 0
THEN NCHAR(@c - @l)
ELSE NCHAR(@c + 65535 - @l) END

SET @i = @i + 1
```

Listing 10.7: continued

```
END

RETURN @output

END
GO
```

Listing 10.8 shows a more complex example. In this case, we want to create functions to convert angles from and to HMS format (hours, minutes, and seconds, or degrees, minutes, and seconds). We want to be able to use angles either in sexagesimal (1 circle = 360°) or centesimal (1 circle = 400^g) units.

NOTE

Some mathematical books and scientific calculators refer to centesimal degrees as grades.

First, create the ANG_HMS user-defined function, which converts an angle into HMS format. To know the angle's units, define the @d_g parameter to specify the character that identifies the degrees unit. The @d_g parameter has only two possible values: 'g' (centesimal) or '°' (sexagesimal).

You can see in Listing 10.8 comments along the code of the ANG_HMS function, but in summary, it extracts from the angle in sequence: degrees, minutes, and seconds. The @precision parameter serves us to specify the number of digits to show for the fraction of the second.

Already having the generic ANG_HMS function, you can create the functions DEG_HMS and GRAD_HMS now to use directly in the ANG_HMS function.

Following a similar process, you can create the HMS_ANG, HMS_DEG, and HMS_GRAD functions.

EXAMPLE

Listing 10.8: Functions to Convert Angles to and from HMS Format

```
USE Northwind
GO

-----------------------------------------------------------
-- Generic function to convert an angle
-- into HMS format
-- @d_g indicates if the angle is measured in
-- sexagesimal degrees (CHAR(176) as the degrees symbol) or
-- centesimal degrees ('g', for grades)
-----------------------------------------------------------

CREATE FUNCTION dbo.ANG_HMS
(@angle float, @precision int = 0, @d_g CHAR(1))
RETURNS varchar(21)
```

Listing 10.8: continued

```
AS
BEGIN

-- Declare variables

DECLARE @sign float
DECLARE @ncircles int

DECLARE @degrees int
DECLARE @minutes int
DECLARE @seconds float
DECLARE @secInt int
DECLARE @secDec int

DECLARE @frac float

DECLARE @hms varchar(20)

-- Save the sign of the angle

SET @sign = SIGN(@angle)

-- Take out the sign of the angle
-- to avoid calculation problems

SET @angle = ABS(@angle)

-- Extract the integer part as degrees

SET @degrees = CAST(FLOOR(@angle) AS int)

-- Count how many complete circles the angle has

SET @ncircles = @degrees /
CASE @d_g WHEN 'g' THEN 400
ELSE 360 END

-- Convert the angle into an angle from the first circle

SET @degrees = @degrees %
CASE @d_g WHEN 'g' THEN 400
ELSE 360 END

-- Extract the decimal part from the angle

SET @frac = @angle - @degrees - (@ncircles *
```

Listing 10.8: continued

```
CASE @d_g WHEN 'g' THEN 400
ELSE 360 END
)

-- Extract minutes from the decimal part

SET @minutes = FLOOR(@frac *
CASE @d_g WHEN 'g' THEN 100
ELSE 60 END
)

-- Extract the number of seconds

SET @seconds = (@frac *
CASE @d_g WHEN 'g' THEN 100
ELSE 60 END
- @minutes) *
CASE @d_g WHEN 'g' THEN 100
ELSE 60 END

-- Calculate the number of complete seconds

SET @secInt = FLOOR(@seconds)

-- Set a limit for the fraction of a second to 9 digits

IF @precision > 9
SET @precision = 9

-- Extract the fraction of a second in the given precision

SET @secDec = (@seconds - @secInt) * POWER(10, @precision)

-- Start creating the resulting string with the sign
-- only for negative numbers

SET @hms = CASE @sign
WHEN -1 THEN '- '
ELSE '' END

-- Create the HMS format

SET @hms = @hms
+ CAST(@degrees AS varchar(3))
+ CHAR(176) + ' '
+ CAST(@minutes AS varchar(2))
+ 'm '
```

Listing 10.8: continued

```
+ CAST(@secInt AS varchar(2))
+ 's'
+ CAST(@secDec AS varchar(10))

RETURN @hms

END
GO


-- --------------------------------
-- Function to convert angles
-- measured in centesimal degrees
-- into HMS format
-- --------------------------------

CREATE FUNCTION dbo.GRAD_HMS
(@angle float, @precision int = 0)
RETURNS varchar(21)
AS
BEGIN

-- Call the ANG_HMS function with the 'g' format

RETURN dbo.ANG_HMS(@angle, @precision, 'g')

END
GO


-- --------------------------------
-- Function to convert angles
-- measured in sexagesimal degrees
-- into HMS format
-- --------------------------------

CREATE FUNCTION dbo.DEG_HMS
(@angle float, @precision int = 0)
RETURNS varchar(21)
AS
BEGIN

-- Call the ANG_HMS function with the CHAR(176) format

RETURN dbo.ANG_HMS(@angle, @precision, CHAR(176))

END
GO
```

Listing 10.8: continued

```
----------------------------------------------------------
-- Generic function to convert an angle
-- from HMS format
-- @d_g indicates if the angle is measured in
-- sexagesimal degrees (CHAR(176) as the degrees symbol) or
-- centesimal degrees ('g', for grades)
----------------------------------------------------------

CREATE FUNCTION dbo.HMS_ANG
(@hms varchar(22), @d_g char(1))
RETURNS float
AS
BEGIN

-- Declare variables

DECLARE @sign float

DECLARE @pos0 int
DECLARE @posg int
DECLARE @posm int
DECLARE @poss int

DECLARE @degrees float
DECLARE @angle float
DECLARE @minutes float
DECLARE @seconds float
DECLARE @secInt float
DECLARE @secDec float

-- Extract the sign

IF LEFT(@hms, 1) = '-'
SELECT @sign = -1, @pos0 = 2
ELSE
SELECT @sign = 1, @pos0 = 1

-- Search for the position in the string
-- of the character dividing degrees, minutes, and seconds

SET @posg = CHARINDEX(@d_g, @hms)
SET @posm = CHARINDEX('m', @hms)
SET @poss = CHARINDEX('s', @hms)

-- Extract the value of the degrees
```

Listing 10.8: continued

```
SET @degrees = SUBSTRING(@hms, @pos0, @posg - @pos0)

-- Extract the value of the minutes

SET @minutes = SUBSTRING(@hms, @posg + 1, @posm - @posg - 1)

-- Extract the value of the seconds
-- as integer and decimal part

SET @secInt = SUBSTRING(@hms, @posm + 1, @poss - @posm - 1)
SET @secDec = SUBSTRING(@hms, @poss + 1, len(@hms) - @poss)
/ POWER(10.0, len(@hms) - @poss)

-- Calculate the angle

SET @angle = @sign * (
@degrees +
@minutes /
CASE @d_g WHEN 'g' THEN 100.0
ELSE 60.0 END +
(@secInt + @secdec) /
CASE @d_g WHEN 'g' THEN 10000.0
ELSE 3600.0 END)

-- Return the value

RETURN @angle

END
GO


-- --------------------------------
-- Function to convert angles
-- measured in sexagesimal degrees
-- from HMS format
-- --------------------------------

CREATE FUNCTION dbo.HMS_DEG
(@hms varchar(22))
RETURNS float
AS
BEGIN

-- Call the HMS_ANG function with the CHAR(176) format

RETURN dbo.HMS_ANG(@hms, CHAR(176))
```

Listing 10.8: continued

```
END
GO


----------------------------------
-- Function to convert angles
-- measured in centesimal degrees
-- from HMS format
----------------------------------

CREATE FUNCTION dbo.HMS_GRAD
(@hms varchar(22))
RETURNS float
AS
BEGIN

-- Call the ANG_HMS function with the 'g' format

RETURN (dbo.HMS_ANG(@hms, 'g'))

END

GO
```

INVOKING SCALAR USER-DEFINED FUNCTIONS

You can use scalar user-defined functions anywhere in any Transact-SQL statement in which an expression is allowed.

If you want to invoke a user-defined function, you must qualify the function name with its owner, usually dbo. Listing 10.9 shows some statements using the MaxProductID in different valid ways.

EXAMPLE

Listing 10.9: How to Invoke a Scalar User-Defined Function

```
SELECT dbo.MaxProductID()
GO

SELECT ProductID, dbo.MaxProductID() AS 'MaxID'
FROM Products
GO

UPDATE [Order Details]
SET ProductID = dbo.MaxProductID()
WHERE ProductID = 25
GO

SELECT ProductID, MaxID
FROM Products
```

Listing 10.9: continued

```
CROSS JOIN (SELECT dbo.MaxProductID() AS 'MaxID') AS MI
GO

SELECT P.ProductID, Quantity
FROM Products AS P
JOIN [Order Details] AS OD
ON P.ProductID = OD.ProductID
AND P.ProductID = dbo.MaxProductID()
GO

SELECT P.ProductID, Quantity
FROM Products AS P
JOIN [Order Details] AS OD
ON P.ProductID = OD.ProductID
WHERE P.ProductID = dbo.MaxProductID()
GO

SELECT P.ProductID, SUM(Quantity)
FROM Products AS P
JOIN [Order Details] AS OD
ON P.ProductID = OD.ProductID
GROUP BY P.ProductID
HAVING P.ProductID = dbo.MaxProductID()
GO

SELECT ProductID, ProductName,
CASE ProductID
WHEN dbo.MaxProductID() THEN 'Last Product'
ELSE '' END AS Note
FROM Products
GO

DECLARE @ID int

SET @ID = dbo.MaxProductID()
```

CAUTION

User-defined functions are local to the database where they are created. Although it is possible to create global user-defined functions, Microsoft does not support this functionality.

If a user-defined function uses parameters, you must specify a value for each parameter on every call, even if they have default values. You can use the keyword DEFAULT to provide the default value for a parameter that has a default value. You cannot omit a parameter when calling a user-defined function—because it has a default value already—otherwise, you will receive a syntax error message, as in Listing 10.10, where you can use the `TotalPrice` function without providing a value for discount, hoping that the function will use the default value.

Listing 10.10: Failing to Provide a Parameter Produces a Syntax Error

```
USE Northwind
GO

-- This is an illegal call, because it does not provide
-- a value for the @discount parameter

SELECT dbo.TotalPrice (12, 25.4)
GO

-- This is a valid call, because it does provide
-- a value for every parameter

SELECT dbo.TotalPrice (12, 25.4, 0.0)
GO
```

```
Server: Msg 313, Level 16, State 2, Line 1
An insufficient number of arguments were supplied
➥for the procedure or function dbo.TotalPrice.

--------------------

304.8000
```

Listing 10.11 shows how to invoke some of the functions defined in Listings 10.4, 10.5, 10.6, 10.7, and 10.8. These examples show how to use these functions in different kinds of statements.

Listing 10.11: How to Invoke Scalar User-Defined Functions

```
USE Northwind
GO

-- dbo.MaxProductID

SELECT dbo.MaxProductID()
AS MaxProductID
GO

-- dbo.WhoWhere

SELECT dbo.WhoWhere() AS [Who from Where]
GO

-- Create a table using WHoWhere
-- As a DEFAULT constraint
```

Listing 10.11: continued

```
IF OBJECT_ID('TestWhoWhere') IS NOT NULL
DROP TABLE TestWhoWhere
GO

CREATE TABLE TestWhoWhere(
ID int IDENTITY (1,1)
PRIMARY KEY,
Name nvarchar(40),
WhoWhere nvarchar(256) DEFAULT dbo.WhoWhere())

INSERT TestWhoWhere (Name)
VALUES ('New record')

SELECT *
FROM TestWhoWhere
GO

-- Create a trigger to Update automatically
-- Who did it and from where the change was done

CREATE TRIGGER trWhoWhere
ON TestWhoWhere
AFTER INSERT, UPDATE
AS
    UPDATE TestWhoWhere
    SET WhoWhere = dbo.WhoWhere()
    FROM TestWhoWhere T
    JOIN Inserted I
    ON T.ID = I.ID
GO

INSERT TestWhoWhere
(Name, WhoWhere)
VALUES
('More records', 'nobody from nowhere')

SELECT *
FROM TestWhoWhere

-- dbo.Today

SELECT dbo.Today()
AS Today

-- Inserting an Order in the present month

INSERT Orders (CustomerID, OrderDate, ShippedDate)
```

Listing 10.11: continued

```
VALUES ('WELLI', '2000-11-23', '2000-12-12')

-- Searching for Orders in the last 30 days

SELECT OrderID, CustomerID, OrderDate, ShippedDate
FROM Orders
WHERE DATEDIFF(day, ShippedDate, dbo.Today()) < 30
GO

-- dbo.PRand

SELECT dbo.PRand() AS PRand
GO

-- dbo.Get3Rand

SELECT dbo.Get3Rand() as Get3Rand1
GO

SELECT dbo.Get3Rand() as Get3Rand2
GO

-- dbo.NewPRand

SELECT dbo.NewPRand() as NewPRand
GO

-- dbo.MediumProductUnitPrice

SELECT dbo.MediumProductUnitPrice()
GO

-- Get the Medium 10 products
-- by UnitPrice

PRINT CHAR(10) + 'Medium 10 Products' + CHAR(10)

SELECT *
FROM (SELECT TOP 6
UnitPrice, ProductID, ProductName
FROM Products
WHERE UnitPrice >= dbo.MediumProductUnitPrice()
ORDER BY UnitPrice ASC) AS A

UNION

SELECT *
```

Listing 10.11: continued

```
FROM (SELECT TOP 5
UnitPrice, ProductID, ProductName
FROM Products
WHERE UnitPrice <= dbo.MediumProductUnitPrice()
ORDER BY UnitPrice DESC) AS B

ORDER BY UnitPrice ASC

-- dbo.fn_FV

SELECT 0.07 AS Rate,
36 AS NPer,
1000 AS Pmt,
10000 AS Pv,
0 AS Type,
dbo.fn_FV(0.07, 36, 1000, 10000, 0) AS FV

-- dbo.SimpleEncrypt

SELECT dbo.SimpleEncrypt('Hello World')
AS [Encrypted Message]

-- dbo.SimpleDecrypt

SELECT dbo.SimpleDecrypt('Hello World')
AS [Decrypted version of a non-encrypted message]

SELECT dbo.SimpleDecrypt(dbo.SimpleEncrypt('Hello World'))
AS [Decrypted version of an encrypted message]

-- dbo.ANG_HMS

SELECT dbo.ANG_HMS(12.3456, 3, 'g') AS 'GRAD to HMS Using ANG_HMS'

SELECT dbo.ANG_HMS(12.3456, 3, CHAR(176)) AS 'DEG to HMS Using ANG_HMS'

-- dbo.GRAD_HMS

SELECT dbo.GRAD_HMS(12.3456, DEFAULT) AS 'GRAD to HMS Using GRAD_HMS'

-- dbo.DEG_HMS

SELECT dbo.DEG_HMS(12.3456, 2) AS 'DEG to HMS Using DEG_HMS'

-- dbo.HMS_ANG
```

Listing 10.11: continued

```
SELECT dbo.HMS_ANG('12g 34m 56s789', 'g') AS 'HMS to GRAD Using HMS_ANG'

SELECT dbo.HMS_ANG('12° 34m 56s789', '°') AS 'HMS to DEG Using HMS_ANG'

-- dbo.HMS_DEG

SELECT dbo.HMS_DEG('12° 34m 56s789') AS 'HMS to DEG Using HMS_DEG'

-- dbo.HMS_GRAD

SELECT dbo.HMS_GRAD('12g 34m 56s789') AS 'HMS to GRAD Using HMS_GRAD'

SELECT dbo.GRAD_HMS(dbo.HMS_GRAD('12g 34m 56s789'), 3)
AS 'HMS to GRAD and to HMS again using HMS_GRAD and GRAD_HMS'

GO
```

OUTPUT

```
MaxProductID
------------
77


Who from Where
------------------------------------------
SQLBYEXAMPLE\SQLAdmin FROM SQL Query Analyzer


ID        Name            WhoWhere
--------  --------------  -------------------------------------------
1         New record      SQLBYEXAMPLE\SQLAdmin FROM SQL Query Analyzer

ID        Name            WhoWhere
--------  --------------  -------------------------------------------
1         New record      SQLBYEXAMPLE\SQLAdmin FROM SQL Query Analyzer
2         More records    SQLBYEXAMPLE\SQLAdmin FROM SQL Query Analyzer


Today
------------------------------------------------------
2000-12-26 00:00:00


OrderID     CustomerID OrderDate                ShippedDate
----------  ---------- ------------------------ ------------------------
11109       WELLI      2000-11-23 00:00:00.000  2000-12-12 00:00:00.000
11110       WELLI      2000-11-23 00:00:00.000  2000-12-12 00:00:00.000
11111       WELLI      2000-11-23 00:00:00.000  2000-12-12 00:00:00.000


PRand
------------------------------------------------------
0.40721851426491701
```

Listing 10.11: continued

```
Get3Rand1
----------
475


Get3Rand2
----------
575


NewPRand
--------------------------------------------------------
5.2412061195157997E-2



--------------------
19.4500


Medium 10 Products

UnitPrice              ProductID   ProductName
--------------------  ----------  ----------------------------------------
18.0000                1           Chai
18.4000                40          Boston Crab Meat
19.0000                2           Chang
19.0000                36          Inlagd Sill
19.4500                44          Gula Malacca
19.5000                57          Ravioli Angelo
20.0000                49          Maxilaku
21.0000                11          Queso Cabrales
21.0000                22          Gustaf's Knäckebröd
21.0500                65          Louisiana Fiery Hot Pepper Sauce

Rate NPer     Pmt        Pv          Type         FV
---- ------   ----------  ----------  ----------  --------------------
.07  36       1000        10000       0           -263152.8817

Encrypted Message
--------------------------
Spwwz+bz}wo

Decrypted version of a non-encrypted message
--------------------------------------------
=Zaad_LdgaY

Decrypted version of an encrypted message
```

Listing 10.11: continued

```
------------------------------------------------
Hello World

GRAD to HMS Using ANG_HMS
-------------------------
12° 34m 55s999

DEG to HMS Using ANG_HMS
------------------------
12° 20m 44s159

GRAD to HMS Using GRAD_HMS
--------------------------
12° 34m 55s0

DEG to HMS Using DEG_HMS
------------------------
12° 20m 44s15

HMS to GRAD Using HMS_ANG
------------------------------------------------
12.345678899999999

HMS to DEG Using HMS_ANG
------------------------------------------------
12.582441388888888

HMS to DEG Using HMS_DEG
------------------------------------------------
12.582441388888888

HMS to GRAD Using HMS_GRAD
------------------------------------------------
12.345678899999999

HMS to GRAD and to HMS again using HMS_GRAD and GRAD_HMS
-------------------------------------------------------
12° 34m 56s788
```

You can use fields as parameters when calling a user-defined function in any statement, such as in Listing 10.12.

EXAMPLE

Listing 10.12: You Can Apply Scalar User-Defined Functions to Table Fields

```
USE Northwind
GO

-- Use the TotalPrice function to retrieve
```

Listing 10.12: continued

```
-- information from the Order Details table

SELECT OrderID, ProductID,
dbo.TotalPrice(Quantity, UnitPrice, Discount) AS TotalPrice
FROM [Order Details]
WHERE ProductID = 12


-- Use the SimpleEncrypt function to encrypt product names

SELECT ProductID,
dbo.SimpleEncrypt(ProductName) AS EncryptedName
FROM Products
WHERE CategoryID = 3


-- Use the SimpleDecrypt function to decrypt
-- a field encrypted with the SimpleEncrypt function

SELECT ProductID,
dbo.SimpleDecrypt(EncryptedName) AS ProductName
FROM (
SELECT ProductID, CategoryID,
dbo.SimpleEncrypt(ProductName) AS EncryptedName
FROM Products
) AS P
WHERE CategoryID = 3
```

OUTPUT

```
OrderID     ProductID   TotalPrice
----------- ----------- --------------------
10266       12          346.5600
10439       12          456.0000
10536       12          427.5000
10543       12          969.0000
10633       12          1162.8000
10678       12          3800.0000
10695       12          152.0000
10718       12          1368.0000
10968       12          1140.0000
10979       12          760.0000
11018       12          760.0000
11046       12          722.0000
11049       12          121.6000
11077       12          72.2000


ProductID   EncryptedName
----------- ---------------------------
16          Wh}sv}h
19          n {_ƒ‡ :],&}&†{_ :\ƒ_}_ƒ__
```

Listing 10.12: continued

```
20        i ^6h…z„{_=%6cw^ƒw,wz{
21        f|…3e,w_xŒ:†3fv,_x†
25        eŒeŒZx7eŒöDe†Œ~x‹DZ%|„|
26        Z^¤u÷…3Z^¤¤|u÷…v{x_
27        euz_yy{2euz_}_~svw
47        gnn{¤r-x|rxr{
48        Lqxlxujmn
49        Ui¤qtis}
50        fq|{ y~u~0ƒ…{|qq
62        bo¤,s.oƒ._ƒq¤s
68        fv,‡‡|†{3_,_zu…xtw†
```

```
ProductID    ProductName
..........   ...............................
11           Queso Cabrales
12           Queso Manchego La Pastora
31           Gorgonzola Telino
32           Mascarpone Fabioli
33           Geitost
59           Raclette Courdavault
60           Camembert Pierrot
69           Gudbrandsdalsost
71           Flotemysost
72           Mozzarella di Giovanni
```

A scalar user-defined function is a special form of stored procedure, and you can execute scalar user-defined functions in the same way you execute stored procedures. In this case, you can omit parameters that have a default value and alter the order of the parameters, providing the parameter name in the user-defined function call in the same way you do for stored procedures. Listing 10.13 shows some examples of how to call a scalar user-defined function using the EXECUTE statement.

EXAMPLE

Listing 10.13: You Can Use EXECUTE to Invoke Scalar User-Defined Functions

```
USE Northwind
GO

--Declare a variable to receive the result of the UDF

DECLARE @Total money

-- Use EXECUTE and provide values for every parameter

EXECUTE @Total = dbo.TotalPrice 12, 25.4, 0.0

SELECT @Total

-- Use EXECUTE and omit the @Discount parameter
```

Listing 10.13: continued

```
-- because it has a default value

EXECUTE @Total = dbo.TotalPrice 12, 25.4

SELECT @Total

-- Use EXECUTE and omit the UDF owner, because it defaults to dbo

EXECUTE @Total = TotalPrice 12, 25.4

SELECT @Total

-- Use EXECUTE and provide values for every parameter
-- specifying parameter names

EXECUTE @Total = TotalPrice
@Quantity = 12,
@UnitPrice = 25.4,
@Discount = 0.2

SELECT @Total

-- Use EXECUTE and provide values for every parameter
-- specifying parameter by order and by name on any order

EXECUTE @Total = TotalPrice 12,
@Discount = 0.2,
@UnitPrice = 25.4

SELECT @Total
```

```
--------------------
304.8000


--------------------
304.8000


--------------------
304.8000


--------------------
243.8400


--------------------
243.8400
```

TIP

If you invoke a user-defined function with the EXECUTE statement, you do not have to qualify the function with the owner name. However, it is always more efficient to qualify the objects you use, because in this way SQL Server does not have to search first for an object owned by you, before searching for the same object owned by dbo.

Inline Table-Valued User-Defined Functions

You can use views in any DML statement as if they were tables. You can use a WHERE clause inside the view definition to limit the view results to specific rows, but this restriction is fixed, because it is part of the view definition. In the query where you use the view, you can use another WHERE clause to limit the search. In this case, SQL Server combines both WHERE clauses in the final query plan, after the view definition is merged with the outer query.

SQL Server 2000 gives you a new feature to create something similar to parameterized views: inline user-defined functions.

An inline user-defined function contains a single SELECT statement but, unlike views, it can use several parameters to restrict the query, providing an easier call interface than views.

TIP

You can identify inline user-defined functions because they return a table and their definition has only a single SELECT statement, without a BEGIN...END block.

You can use an inline user-defined function wherever a table or view is accepted:

- In the SELECT clause of a SELECT statement, as part of a subquery that returns a single value (a single row and single column result set).

- In the SET clause of an UPDATE statement, as part of a subquery that provides a single value for a field in the table to be updated.

- In the FROM clause of any DML statement.

- In the WHERE or HAVING clauses of any DML statement, as part of a subquery that returns a single value to be compared to any field or variable.

- In the WHERE clause of any DML statement, as part of a subquery introduced by EXISTS or NOT EXISTS.

- In the WHERE or HAVING clause of any DML statement, as part of a subquery used with the IN or NOT IN operators, as long as the subquery returns a single column.

CREATING INLINE TABLE-VALUED USER-DEFINED FUNCTIONS

To create an inline user-defined function, you must use the CREATE
FUNCTION statement, as shown in Listing 10.14.

The first example creates the GetCustomersFromCountry function, which
selects customers based in a specific country. This function returns a result
set with the same structure as the original Customers table.

Based on the GetCustomersFromCountry function, you can create the
GetCustomersFromUSA function, which retrieves customers based in the
USA only.

The third example returns orders from a specific day using the
GetOrdersFromDay function.

The fourth example creates the GetOrdersFromToday function to retrieve
the list of today's orders. Note that you cannot base this function in
GetOrdersFromDay function, because you cannot invoke an inline user-
defined function using a scalar function as a parameter value.

NOTE

Inside the GetOrdersFromToday function you use the Today() scalar user-defined function, because Getdate() is not valid inside the definition of a user-defined function.

Later in this chapter, in the "Deterministic and Nondeterministic Functions" section, you
will see the lists of functions that are not valid inside a user-defined function.

The next function is the OrdersWithValue function, which uses the
TotalPrice scalar function to calculate the total value for every order. This
inline user-defined function retrieves a result set with the same structure
as the Orders table, plus the TotalValue field.

Based on the OrdersWithValue function, you can create the next two functions. OrdersByValue retrieves the orders where TotalValue is greater than
a specific target total value. TopTenOrders returns the top 10 orders by
TotalValue.

EXAMPLE

Listing 10.14: Inline User-Defined Functions Examples Using the CREATE FUNCTION Statement

```
USE Northwind
GO

-- Returns customers from a specific country

CREATE FUNCTION dbo.GetCustomersFromCountry
(@country nvarchar(15))
RETURNS TABLE
AS
RETURN (
SELECT *
```

Listing 10.14: continued

```
FROM Customers
WHERE Country = @country
)
GO


-- Returns USA-based customers

CREATE FUNCTION dbo.GetCustomersFromUSA
()
RETURNS TABLE
AS
RETURN (
SELECT *
FROM dbo.GetCustomersFromCountry(N'USA')
)
GO


-- Returns the orders from a specific day

CREATE FUNCTION dbo.GetOrdersFromDay
(@date as smalldatetime)
RETURNS TABLE
AS
RETURN (
SELECT *
FROM Orders
WHERE DATEDIFF(day, OrderDate, @date) = 0
)
GO


-- Returns orders from today

CREATE FUNCTION dbo.GetOrdersFromToday
()
RETURNS TABLE
AS
RETURN (
SELECT *
FROM Orders
WHERE DATEDIFF(day, OrderDate, dbo.Today()) = 0
)
GO


-- Returns Orders with the total order value

CREATE FUNCTION dbo.OrdersWithValue
```

Listing 10.14: continued

```
()
RETURNS TABLE
AS
RETURN (
SELECT O.*, TotalValue
FROM Orders O
JOIN (
SELECT OrderID, SUM(dbo.TotalPrice(Quantity, UnitPrice, Discount))
AS TotalValue
FROM [Order Details]
GROUP BY OrderID) AS OD
ON O.OrderID = OD.OrderID
)
GO


-- Returns orders with a value greater than
-- a specific target value

CREATE FUNCTION dbo.OrdersByValue
(@total money)
RETURNS TABLE
AS
RETURN (
SELECT *
FROM dbo.OrdersWithValue()
WHERE TotalValue > @total
)
GO


-- Returns the top 10 orders by total value

CREATE FUNCTION dbo.TopTenOrders
()
RETURNS TABLE
AS
RETURN (
SELECT TOP 10 WITH TIES *
FROM dbo.OrdersWithValue()
ORDER BY TotalValue DESC
)

GO
```

You can identify several parts of the CREATE FUNCTION syntax for inline user-defined function:

- `CREATE FUNCTION` *ownername.functionname*, where you can specify the owner of the function and the name of the function.

- `(parameter_lists)`, where every parameter is identified by its name and the data type. The parameter list can be empty.

- `RETURNS TABLE`, because inline user-defined functions always return a tablelike result set.

- `AS RETURN ()` marks the function definition body, which has to be enclosed inside the parenthesis block.

- The `SELECT` statement, which defines the result set to return.

In essence, the creation of an inline user-define function is not very different from the creation of a view, except for the parameters list, which gives inline user-defined functions extra functionality not available in views.

TIP

Inline user-defined functions have the same restrictions that apply to views; look at Chapter 3, "Working with Tables and Views," for more information about them. One of these restrictions is that you cannot use `ORDER BY`, but you can use `TOP 100 PERCENT...ORDER BY` to produce the same result. Listing 10.15 shows how to implement this trick.

EXAMPLE

Listing 10.15: Use `TOP 100 PERCENT` to Create an Inline User-Defined Function That Produces Sorted Data

```
USE Northwind
GO


-- Returns Products ordered by ProductName

CREATE FUNCTION dbo.OrderedProducts()
RETURNS TABLE
AS
RETURN (SELECT TOP 100 PERCENT *
FROM Products
ORDER BY ProductName ASC)
GO


-- Test the function

SELECT TOP 10 ProductID, ProductName
FROM dbo.OrderedProducts()
```

OUTPUT

```
ProductID   ProductName
----------- ------------------------------------------
17          Alice Mutton
3           Aniseed Syrup
40          Boston Crab Meat
60          Camembert Pierrot
```

Listing 10.15: continued

```
18        Carnarvon Tigers
1         Chai
2         Chang
39        Chartreuse verte
4         Chef Anton's Cajun Seasoning
5         Chef Anton's Gumbo Mix
```

INVOKING DATA FROM INLINE USER-DEFINED FUNCTIONS

You can invoke an inline user-defined function in the same way you invoke a table or a view in a DML statement, with the only exception that you must use parentheses after the function name, even if there are not any parameters to use.

SQL Server merges the definition of the Inline function with the definition of the query where the function is invoked, to create a unique query plan. This is the same way that SQL Server uses views to execute Transact-SQL statements.

Listing 10.16 shows how to invoke the inline user-defined functions defined in Listing 10.14 in different ways.

EXAMPLE

Listing 10.16: Invoking Inline User-Defined Functions

```
USE Northwind
GO

PRINT CHAR(10) + 'Use GetCustomersFromCountry(''Mexico'')' + CHAR(10)

SELECT CustomerID, CompanyName, City
FROM dbo.GetCustomersFromCountry('Mexico')

PRINT CHAR(10) + 'Use GetCustomersFromUSA()' + CHAR(10)

Select CustomerID, CompanyName, City
FROM dbo.GetCustomersFromUSA()

PRINT CHAR(10)
+ 'Use GetCustomersFromCountry(''Mexico'') with the IN operator'
+ CHAR(10)

SELECT OrderID,
CONVERT(varchar(10), OrderDate, 120) AS OrderDate
FROM Orders
WHERE CustomerID IN
(SELECT CustomerID
FROM dbo.GetCustomersFromCountry('Mexico'))
```

Listing 10.16: continued

```
PRINT CHAR(10)
+ 'Joins OrdersByValue to Customers'
+ CHAR(10)

SELECT CompanyName, OrderID, TotalValue,
CONVERT(varchar(10), OrderDate, 120) AS OrderDate
FROM dbo.OrdersByValue(10000) AS OBV
JOIN Customers C
ON OBV.CustomerID = C.CustomerID


PRINT CHAR(10)
+ 'Joins TopTenOrders to Customers'
+ CHAR(10)

SELECT CompanyName, OrderID, TotalValue,
CONVERT(varchar(10), OrderDate, 120) AS OrderDate
FROM dbo.TopTenOrders() AS OBV
JOIN Customers C
ON OBV.CustomerID = C.CustomerID

Use GetCustomersFromCountry('Mexico')
```

OUTPUT

```
CustomerID CompanyName                           City
---------- ------------------------------------- ---------------
ANATR      Ana Trujillo Emparedados y helados    México D.F.
ANTON      Antonio Moreno Taquería               México D.F.
CENTC      Centro comercial Moctezuma            México D.F.
PERIC      Pericles Comidas clásicas             México D.F.
TORTU      Tortuga Restaurante                   México D.F.


Use GetCustomersFromUSA()


CustomerID CompanyName                           City
---------- ------------------------------------- ---------------
GREAL      Great Lakes Food Market               Eugene
HUNGC      Hungry Coyote Import Store            Elgin
LAZYK      Lazy K Kountry Store                  Walla Walla
LETSS      Let's Stop N Shop                     San Francisco
LONEP      Lonesome Pine Restaurant              Portland
OLDWO      Old World Delicatessen                Anchorage
RATTC      Rattlesnake Canyon Grocery            Albuquerque
SAVEA      Save-a-lot Markets                    Boise
SPLIR      Split Rail Beer & Ale                 Lander
THEBI      The Big Cheese                        Portland
THECR      The Cracker Box                       Butte
```

Listing 10.16: continued

```
TRAIH      Trail's Head Gourmet Provisioners      Kirkland
WHITC      White Clover Markets                   Seattle


Use GetCustomersFromCountry('Mexico') with the IN operator

OrderID    OrderDate
..........  ..........
10259      1996-07-18
10276      1996-08-08
10293      1996-08-29
10304      1996-09-12
10308      1996-09-18
10319      1996-10-02
10322      1996-10-04
10354      1996-11-14
10365      1996-11-27
10474      1997-03-13
10502      1997-04-10
10507      1997-04-15
10518      1997-04-25
10535      1997-05-13
10573      1997-06-19
10576      1997-06-23
10625      1997-08-08
10676      1997-09-22
10677      1997-09-22
10682      1997-09-25
10759      1997-11-28
10842      1998-01-20
10856      1998-01-28
10915      1998-02-27
10926      1998-03-04
10995      1998-04-02
11069      1998-05-04
11073      1998-05-05


Joins OrdersByValue to Customers

CompanyName                          OrderID    TotalValue     OrderDate
...................................  ..........  .............  ..........
Simons bistro                        10417      11188.4000     1997-01-16
Rattlesnake Canyon Grocery           10479      10495.6000     1997-03-19
QUICK-Stop                           10540      10191.7000     1997-05-19
QUICK-Stop                           10691      10164.8000     1997-10-03
Königlich Essen                      10817      10952.8450     1998-01-06
```

Listing 10.16: continued

```
QUICK-Stop                       10865        16387.5000      1998-02-02
Rattlesnake Canyon Grocery       10889        11380.0000      1998-02-16
Hungry Owl All-Night Grocers     10897        10835.2400      1998-02-19
Hanari Carnes                    10981        15810.0000      1998-03-27
Save-a-lot Markets               11030        12615.0500      1998-04-17
```

```
Joins TopTenOrders to Customers

CompanyName                      OrderID      TotalValue      OrderDate
-------------------------------- ------------ --------------- ----------
QUICK-Stop                       10865        16387.5000      1998-02-02
Hanari Carnes                    10981        15810.0000      1998-03-27
Save-a-lot Markets               11030        12615.0500      1998-04-17
Rattlesnake Canyon Grocery       10889        11380.0000      1998-02-16
Simons bistro                    10417        11188.4000      1997-01-16
Königlich Essen                  10817        10952.8450      1998-01-06
Hungry Owl All-Night Grocers     10897        10835.2400      1998-02-19
Rattlesnake Canyon Grocery       10479        10495.6000      1997-03-19
QUICK-Stop                       10540        10191.7000      1997-05-19
QUICK-Stop                       10691        10164.8000      1997-10-03
```

You can update, insert, or delete rows in tables through inline user-defined functions with the same limits as updating, inserting, or deleting rows in tables through views. Listing 10.17 shows an example of how to insert, update, and delete rows in the Orders table through the GetOrdersWithValue inline user-defined function.

EXAMPLE

Listing 10.17: Modify Data Through Inline User-Defined Functions

```
USE Northwind
GO

PRINT CHAR(10) + 'Before the Insert' + CHAR(10)

SELECT CustomerID, CompanyName, Country
FROM dbo.GetCustomersFromUsa()
WHERE CustomerID > 'W'

INSERT dbo.GetCustomersFromUSA() (CustomerID, CompanyName, Country)
VALUES ('ZZZZZ', 'Dummy Customer', 'USA')

PRINT CHAR(10) + 'After the Insert' + CHAR(10)

SELECT CustomerID, CompanyName, Country
FROM dbo.GetCustomersFromUsa()
WHERE CustomerID > 'W'
```

Listing 10.17: continued

```
UPDATE dbo.GetCustomersFromUSA()
SET CompanyName = 'New Customer'
WHERE CustomerID = 'ZZZZZ'

PRINT CHAR(10) + 'After the Update' + CHAR(10)

SELECT CustomerID, CompanyName, Country
FROM dbo.GetCustomersFromUsa()
WHERE CustomerID > 'W'

DELETE dbo.GetCustomersFromUSA()
WHERE CustomerID = 'ZZZZZ'

PRINT CHAR(10) + 'After the Delete' + CHAR(10)

SELECT CustomerID, CompanyName, Country
FROM dbo.GetCustomersFromUsa()
WHERE CustomerID > 'W'
GO

DECLARE @ID int

PRINT CHAR(10) + 'Before the Insert' + CHAR(10)

SELECT CustomerID, OrderID, TotalValue, OrderDate
FROM dbo.OrdersWithValue()
WHERE CustomerID = 'VINET'

INSERT dbo.OrdersWithValue() (CustomerID, OrderDate)
SELECT 'VINET', dbo.Today()

-- Retrieve the latest Identity value in this session

SET @ID = SCOPE_IDENTITY()

INSERT [Order Details]
(OrderID, ProductID, Quantity, UnitPrice, Discount)
SELECT @ID, 28, 10, UnitPrice, 0.1
FROM Products
WHERE ProductID = 28

PRINT CHAR(10) + 'After the Insert' + CHAR(10)

SELECT CustomerID, OrderID, TotalValue, OrderDate
FROM dbo.OrdersWithValue()
WHERE CustomerID = 'VINET'
```

Listing 10.17: continued

```
DELETE [Order Details]
WHERE OrderID = @ID

DELETE Orders
WHERE OrderID = @ID

PRINT CHAR(10) + 'After the Delete' + CHAR(10)

SELECT CustomerID, OrderID, TotalValue, OrderDate
FROM dbo.OrdersWithValue()
WHERE CustomerID = 'VINET'
```

OUTPUT

```
Before the Insert

CustomerID CompanyName                               Country
---------- ----------------------------------------- ---------------
WHITC      White Clover Markets                      USA


After the Insert

CustomerID CompanyName                               Country
---------- ----------------------------------------- ---------------
WHITC      White Clover Markets                      USA
ZZZZZ      Dummy Customer                            USA


After the Update

CustomerID CompanyName                               Country
---------- ----------------------------------------- ---------------
WHITC      White Clover Markets                      USA
ZZZZZ      New Customer                              USA


After the Delete

CustomerID CompanyName                               Country
---------- ----------------------------------------- ---------------
WHITC      White Clover Markets                      USA


Before the Insert

CustomerID OrderID     TotalValue              OrderDate
---------- ----------- ----------------------- -----------------------
VINET      10248       440.0000                1996-07-04 00:00:00.000
```

Listing 10.17: continued

VINET	10274	538.6000	1996-08-06 00:00:00.000
VINET	10295	121.6000	1996-09-02 00:00:00.000
VINET	10737	139.8000	1997-11-11 00:00:00.000
VINET	10739	240.0000	1997-11-12 00:00:00.000

After the Insert

CustomerID	OrderID	TotalValue	OrderDate
VINET	10248	440.0000	1996-07-04 00:00:00.000
VINET	10274	538.6000	1996-08-06 00:00:00.000
VINET	10295	121.6000	1996-09-02 00:00:00.000
VINET	10737	139.8000	1997-11-11 00:00:00.000
VINET	10739	240.0000	1997-11-12 00:00:00.000
VINET	11118	410.4000	2000-12-26 00:00:00.000

After the Delete

CustomerID	OrderID	TotalValue	OrderDate
VINET	10248	440.0000	1996-07-04 00:00:00.000
VINET	10274	538.6000	1996-08-06 00:00:00.000
VINET	10295	121.6000	1996-09-02 00:00:00.000
VINET	10737	139.8000	1997-11-11 00:00:00.000
VINET	10739	240.0000	1997-11-12 00:00:00.000

NOTE

You cannot delete data from the OrdersWithValue function, because it joins multiple tables.

Table-Valued Functions

Multistatement table-valued user-defined functions (or table-valued functions) are similar to inline user-defined functions. Actually, you can use them in the same scenarios, but you are not restricted to defining them as a single SELECT statement.

A table-valued function returns a single result set—the contents of a table variable with a predefined format specified in the function declaration.

CAUTION

The result of a table-valued function is always read-only. The result of an inline user-defined function can be read-only or not, depending on the SELECT statement used to define the function.

As mentioned in the preceding section, inline user-defined functions are similar to views in both structure and use. Table-valued functions are similar to stored procedures, but they return a single result set.

You can define parameters in a table-valued function, as you did with scalar user-defined functions and stored procedures. However, you cannot create an OUTPUT parameter in a user-defined function.

CREATING TABLE-VALUED FUNCTIONS

To create a table-valued function, you must use the CREATE FUNCTION statement. Listing 10.18 shows functions similar to those in Listing 10.14, but in table-valued versions.

EXAMPLE

Listing 10.18: Table-Valued Version of the Inline User-Defined Functions Examples from Listing 10.14

```
USE Northwind
GO

CREATE FUNCTION dbo.tv_GetCustomersFromCountry
(@country nvarchar(15))
RETURNS @List TABLE
(CustomerID nchar(5),
CompanyName nvarchar(40),
Country nvarchar(15))
AS
BEGIN

INSERT @List
SELECT CustomerID, CompanyName, Country
FROM Customers
WHERE Country = @country

RETURN
END
GO

-- Returns USA-based customers

CREATE FUNCTION dbo.tv_GetCustomersFromUSA
()
RETURNS @List TABLE
(CustomerID nchar(5),
CompanyName nvarchar(40),
Country nvarchar(15))
AS
BEGIN
```

Listing 10.18: continued

```
INSERT @List
SELECT CustomerID, CompanyName, Country
FROM dbo.GetCustomersFromCountry(N'USA')

RETURN
END
GO


-- Returns the orders from a specific day

CREATE FUNCTION dbo.tv_GetOrdersFromDay
(@date as smalldatetime)
RETURNS @list TABLE
(OrderID int,
OrderDate datetime)
AS
BEGIN

INSERT @List
SELECT OrderID, OrderDate
FROM Orders
WHERE DATEDIFF(day, OrderDate, @date) = 0

RETURN
END
GO


-- Returns orders from today

CREATE FUNCTION dbo.tv_GetOrdersFromToday
()
RETURNS @list TABLE
(OrderID int,
OrderDate datetime)
AS
BEGIN

INSERT @List
SELECT OrderID, OrderDate
FROM Orders
WHERE DATEDIFF(day, OrderDate, dbo.Today()) = 0

RETURN
END
GO
```

Listing 10.18: continued

```
-- Returns Orders with the total order value

CREATE FUNCTION dbo.tv_OrdersWithValue
()
RETURNS @list TABLE
(OrderID int,
CustomerID nchar(5),
OrderDate datetime,
TotalValue money)
AS
BEGIN

INSERT @List
SELECT O.OrderID, CustomerID, OrderDate, TotalValue
FROM Orders O
JOIN (
SELECT OrderID, SUM(dbo.TotalPrice(Quantity, UnitPrice, Discount))
AS TotalValue
FROM [Order Details]
GROUP BY OrderID) AS OD
ON O.OrderID = OD.OrderID

RETURN
END
GO

-- Returns orders with a value greater than
-- a specific target value

CREATE FUNCTION dbo.tv_OrdersByValue
(@total money)
RETURNS @list TABLE
(OrderID int,
CustomerID nchar(5),
OrderDate datetime,
TotalValue money)
AS
BEGIN

INSERT @List
SELECT OrderID, CustomerID, OrderDate, TotalValue
FROM dbo.OrdersWithValue()
WHERE TotalValue > @total

RETURN
END
GO
```

Listing 10.18: continued

```
-- Returns the top 10 orders by total value

CREATE FUNCTION dbo.tv_TopTenOrders
()
RETURNS @list TABLE
(OrderID int,
CustomerID nchar(5),
OrderDate datetime,
TotalValue money)
AS
BEGIN

INSERT @List
SELECT TOP 10 WITH TIES
OrderID, CustomerID, OrderDate, TotalValue
FROM dbo.OrdersWithValue()
ORDER BY TotalValue DESC

RETURN
END
GO
```

You can identify several parts in the CREATE FUNCTION syntax for table-valued functions:

- CREATE FUNCTION *ownername.functionname*, where you can specify the owner of the function and the name of the function.

- (parameter_lists), where every parameter is identified by its name and the data type. The parameter list can be empty. Parameters can have default values.

- RETURNS @tablename TABLE, because table-valued functions always return a tablelike result set, which is the contents of the table variable defined in this line as @tablename.

- (Field definition, ...), definition of every field on the @tablename table variable, following the same rules as declaring fields in a standard table object.

- AS BEGIN...END marks the function definition body, which must be written inside the BEGIN END block.

- The RETURN statement, standalone, which sends the table variable back to the invoking process as a result set.

The contents of a table-valued function are similar to a stored procedure that uses a temporary table to store intermediate results and select from that temporary table at the end.

TIP

Inside scalar or table-valued user-defined functions you cannot create temporary tables; instead, you can use table variables. However, it is a good practice to replace temporary tables with table variables in stored procedures and scripts whenever this might be possible.

Looking at the examples in Listing 10.18, you could say that table-valued functions are similar to inline user-defined functions, except that you must declare the fields of the returning table explicitly. However, table-valued functions give you far more flexibility than inline user-defined functions, in a similar way as stored procedures give you more flexibility than views.

Listing 10.19 shows two more complex examples in which the creation of a table-valued function solves the problem.

The first function is called MakeList, and it converts a string with several items into a single column result set where every item is stored in a single row. You can specify any separator to divide values, or use the default '|'. This function can be useful in a WHERE clause introduced with the IN operator.

The second function is a bit more complex. It produces a subset of a fact table from the Order Details table, adding some extra information as the CategoryName, ProductName, CompanyName, and OrderDate from the Categories, Products, Customers, and Orders tables, and the TotalValue using the TotalPrice scalar user-defined function.

To call this function, you can specify whether you want a full list (@Key IS NULL), a list for a specific order (@Key = 'ORD' and @ID = OrderID), a specific Customer (@Key = 'CUS' and @ID = CustomerID), a product (@Key = 'PRO' and ID = ProductID), or a category (@Key = 'CAT' and @ID = CategoryID).

At the beginning of the function, you can find a sequence of IF structures to apply the most efficient method to every case to prepare the initial list of rows to return.

At the end of the OrderDetailsComplete function, fill the missing information with values coming from other tables.

EXAMPLE

Listing 10.19: Using Table-Valued Functions to Execute Complex Result Sets

```
USE Northwind
GO

-- Converts a string containing a list of items
-- into a single column table where every item
-- is in a separate row
```

Listing 10.19: continued

```
-- using any character as a separator

CREATE FUNCTION dbo.MakeList
(@ParamArray as nvarchar(4000), @Separator as char(1) = '|')
RETURNS @List TABLE
(Item sql_variant)
AS
BEGIN

DECLARE @pos int, @pos0 int

SET @pos0 = 0

WHILE 1=1
BEGIN

SET @pos = CHARINDEX(@Separator, @ParamArray, @pos0 + 1)

INSERT @List
SELECT CASE @pos
WHEN 0 THEN SUBSTRING(@ParamArray, @pos0+1,
LEN(@ParamArray) - @pos -1)
ELSE SUBSTRING(@ParamArray, @pos0+1, @pos - @pos0-1)
END

IF @pos = 0 BREAK

SET @pos0 = @pos

END

RETURN

END
GO

-- Produces a list of orders
-- with full descriptive information
-- ProductName, CategoryName, CompanyName
-- OrderDate and TotalValue
-- with every primary key to link to other tables
-- The list can be produced for every
-- Order (@Key = 'ORD'),
-- Product (@Key = 'PRO'),
-- Customer (@Key = 'CUS'),
-- Category (@Key = 'CAT')
-- Full List (@Key NOT IN ('ORD', 'PRO', 'CUS', 'CAT'))
```

Listing 10.19: continued

```
CREATE FUNCTION dbo.OrderDetailsComplete
(@ID sql_variant = NULL,
@Key char(3) = NULL)
RETURNS @Details TABLE
(OrderID int,
ProductID int,
CustomerID nchar(5) NULL,
CategoryID int NULL,
OrderDate smalldatetime NULL,
Value money NULL,
Category nvarchar(15) NULL,
Product nvarchar(40) NULL,
Company nvarchar(40) NULL)
AS
BEGIN

IF @Key = 'ORD'
BEGIN

INSERT @Details
(OrderID, ProductID, Value)
SELECT OrderID, ProductID,
dbo.TotalPrice(Quantity, UnitPrice, Discount)
FROM [Order Details]
WHERE OrderID = @ID

END
ELSE IF @Key = 'PRO'
BEGIN

INSERT @Details (OrderID, ProductID, Value)
SELECT OrderID, ProductID,
dbo.TotalPrice(Quantity, UnitPrice, Discount)
FROM [Order Details]
WHERE ProductID = @ID

END
ELSE IF @Key = 'CUS'
BEGIN

INSERT @Details (OrderID, ProductID, CustomerID, Value)
SELECT O.OrderID, ProductID, CustomerID,
dbo.TotalPrice(Quantity, UnitPrice, Discount)
FROM [Order Details] OD
JOIN Orders O
ON O.OrderID = OD.OrderID
WHERE CustomerID = @ID
```

Listing 10.19: continued

```
END
ELSE IF @Key = 'CAT'
BEGIN

INSERT @Details (OrderID, ProductID, CategoryID, Value)
SELECT OD.OrderID, P.ProductID, CategoryID,
dbo.TotalPrice(Quantity, OD.UnitPrice, Discount)
FROM [Order Details] OD
JOIN Products P
ON P.ProductID = OD.ProductID
WHERE CategoryID = @ID

END
ELSE
BEGIN

INSERT @Details
(OrderID, ProductID, Value)
SELECT OrderID, ProductID,
dbo.TotalPrice(Quantity, UnitPrice, Discount)
FROM [Order Details]

END

UPDATE D
SET D.CustomerID = O.CustomerID,
D.OrderDate = O.OrderDate
FROM @Details D
JOIN Orders O
ON O.OrderID = D.OrderID
WHERE D.CustomerID IS NULL

UPDATE D
SET D.CategoryID = P.CategoryID,
D.Product = P.ProductName
FROM @Details D
JOIN Products P
ON P.ProductID = D.ProductID
WHERE D.CategoryID IS NULL

UPDATE D
SET D.Category = C.CategoryName
FROM @Details D
JOIN Categories C
ON C.CategoryID = D.CategoryID

UPDATE D
```

Listing 10.19: continued

```
SET D.Company = C.CompanyName
FROM @Details D
JOIN Customers C
ON C.CustomerID = D.CustomerID

RETURN

END
GO
```

INVOKING TABLE-VALUED USER-DEFINED FUNCTIONS

You can invoke table-value functions the same way you do for inline user-defined functions. Listing 10.20 shows examples of how to call some functions defined in Listing 10.18.

NOTE

Listing 10.20 is a revised version of Listing 10.16, calling table-value functions instead of inline user-defined functions. The output is the same as in Listing 10.16; therefore, it is not necessary to show it again.

EXAMPLE

Listing 10.20: Calling Table-Value Functions

```
USE Northwind
GO

PRINT CHAR(10) + 'Use tv_GetCustomersFromCountry(''Mexico'')' + CHAR(10)

SELECT CustomerID, CompanyName, Country
FROM dbo.tv_GetCustomersFromCountry('Mexico')

PRINT CHAR(10) + 'Use tv_GetCustomersFromUSA()' + CHAR(10)

Select CustomerID, CompanyName, Country
FROM dbo.tv_GetCustomersFromUSA()

PRINT CHAR(10)
+ 'Use tv_GetCustomersFromCountry(''Mexico'') with the IN operator'
+ CHAR(10)

SELECT OrderID,
CONVERT(varchar(10), OrderDate, 120) AS OrderDate
FROM Orders
WHERE CustomerID IN
(SELECT CustomerID
FROM dbo.tv_GetCustomersFromCountry('Mexico'))
```

Listing 10.20: continued

```
PRINT CHAR(10)
+ 'Joins tv_OrdersByValue to Customers'
+ CHAR(10)

SELECT CompanyName, OrderID, TotalValue,
CONVERT(varchar(10), OrderDate, 120) AS OrderDate
FROM dbo.tv_OrdersByValue(10000) AS OBV
JOIN Customers C
ON OBV.CustomerID = C.CustomerID


PRINT CHAR(10)
+ 'Joins tv_TopTenOrders to Customers'
+ CHAR(10)

SELECT CompanyName, OrderID, TotalValue,
CONVERT(varchar(10), OrderDate, 120) AS OrderDate
FROM dbo.tv_TopTenOrders() AS OBV
JOIN Customers C
ON OBV.CustomerID = C.CustomerID
```

However, the way SQL Server executes table-valued functions and inline user-defined functions is completely different:

- The definition of inline user-defined functions is merged with the definition of the outer query, producing a single query plan, in which you cannot find any traces of the user-defined function. Figure 10.1 shows the query plan of this query, in which you can see an Index Scan on the Customers table's clustered index. Every time you use an inline user-defined function its definition must be merged again with the outer query, producing a new query plan.

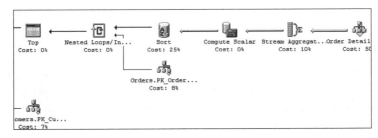

Figure 10.1: *Query plan of a query that uses an inline user-defined function.*

- The first time you call a table-valued function, it is compiled and a query plan is placed in memory. Every time you use this function, the calling query forces the execution of the saved query plan and the function returns the table variable, which will be used in the outer query. Figure 10.2 shows the query plan of this execution, simpler than the one from Figure 10.1, in which you can see a Table Scan on the table variable returned from the function. In this case, most of the work is done in a separate query plan, corresponding to the table-valued function.

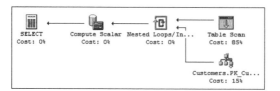

Figure 10.2: *Query plan of a query that uses a table-valued user-defined function.*

Dropping User-Defined Functions

To drop a user-defined function, ,you must use the DROP FUNCTION statement. Listing 10.21 shows a simple example of this statement.

EXAMPLE

Listing 10.21: Use DROP FUNCTION to Delete a User-Defined Function

```
USE Northwind
GO

DROP FUNCTION dbo.Today
```

CAUTION

Before dropping a user-defined function, as with any other database object, check its dependencies.

You cannot drop a user-defined function if it is used in a constraint definition. If you drop a user-defined function and it is used in other functions, views, triggers, or stored procedures, those functions will produce an error on next execution.

Preventing the Alteration of Dependent Objects: The SCHEMABINDING Option

You can prevent changes on the dependent objects of a user-defined function by using the SCHEMABINDING option. Using this option, you cannot modify the definition of the dependent objects using any of the ALTER statements, and you cannot drop dependent objects using any of the DROP statements. This link disappears when the function is dropped or when you alter the function definition without using the SCHEMABINDING option.

To use this option, you must ensure that the following conditions are met:

- Every function and view referenced in the function must be defined as SCHEMABINDING as well.

- Every object referenced in the function must be referenced using two-part names (owner.objectname).

- Every object referenced in the function belongs to the same database as the function.

- The user who creates the function (not necessarily the owner) has REFERENCES permissions on every object referenced inside the function. It is recommended that only members of the db_owner role execute the CREATE FUNCTION statement.

Listing 10.22 shows how to use the SCHEMABINDING option and the effect when you try to modify a dependent object. The process is as follows:

1. You create the NewCustomers table with data coming from the Customers table.

2. You create the GetCustomers table-valued function, reading the CustomerID and CompanyName fields from the NewCustomers table.

3. You try to alter the NewCustomers table, dropping the CompanyName column, and it is successful because the GetCustomers function was created without the SCHEMABINDING option.

4. Trying to use the GetCustomers function, you get error message 207 because the column CompanyName does not exist.

5. You start all over, with the creation of the NewCustomers table.

6. Create the GetCustomers function with the SCHEMABINDING option, and use the NewCustomers table without specifying the owner, and you get error 4512, because to use SCHEMABINDING you must use two part names.

7. Create the GetCustomers function with the SCHEMABINDING option and use two-part names this time. The operation succeeds.

8. Try to alter the NewCustomers table, dropping the CompanyName column. You get errors 5074 and 4922 because the function is created with the SCHEMABINDING option.

EXAMPLE

Listing 10.22: Effect of SCHEMABINDING on the Dependent Objects

```
USE Northwind
GO

IF OBJECT_ID('GetCustomers') IS NOT NULL
```

Listing 10.22: continued

```
DROP FUNCTION GetCustomers
GO

IF OBJECT_ID('NewCustomers') IS NOT NULL
DROP TABLE NewCustomers
GO

SELECT *
INTO NewCustomers
FROM Customers
GO

CREATE  FUNCTION dbo.GetCustomers()
RETURNS @List TABLE
(CustomerID nchar(5),
CompanyName nvarchar(40))
AS
BEGIN

INSERT @List
SELECT CustomerID, CompanyName
FROM NewCustomers

RETURN
END
GO

ALTER TABLE NewCustomers
DROP COLUMN CompanyName

PRINT CHAR(10)
+ 'ALTER TABLE statement successful without SCHEMABINDING'
+ CHAR(10)
GO

SELECT *
FROM GetCustomers()
GO

PRINT CHAR(10)
+ 'Execution of the GetCustomers table was unsuccessful'
+ CHAR(10)
+ 'because it references a non-existing field'
+ CHAR(10)
GO

IF OBJECT_ID('GetCustomers') IS NOT NULL
```

Listing 10.22: continued

```
DROP FUNCTION GetCustomers
GO

IF OBJECT_ID('NewCustomers') IS NOT NULL
DROP TABLE NewCustomers
GO

SELECT *
INTO NewCustomers
FROM Customers
GO


CREATE  FUNCTION dbo.GetCustomers()
RETURNS @List TABLE
(CustomerID nchar(5),
CompanyName nvarchar(40))
WITH SCHEMABINDING
AS
BEGIN

INSERT @List
SELECT CustomerID, CompanyName
FROM NewCustomers

RETURN
END
GO

PRINT CHAR(10)
+ 'CREATE FUNCTION failed with SCHEMABINDING'
+ CHAR(10)
+ 'because it did not use two part names'
+ CHAR(10)
GO

CREATE  FUNCTION dbo.GetCustomers()
RETURNS @List TABLE
(CustomerID nchar(5),
CompanyName nvarchar(40))
WITH SCHEMABINDING
AS
BEGIN

INSERT @List
SELECT CustomerID, CompanyName
FROM dbo.NewCustomers
```

Listing 10.22: continued

```
RETURN
END
GO


PRINT CHAR(10)
+ 'CREATE FUNCTION was successful with SCHEMABINDING'
+ CHAR(10)
+ 'because it did use two part names'
+ CHAR(10)
GO


ALTER TABLE NewCustomers
DROP COLUMN CompanyName
GO


PRINT CHAR(10)
+ 'ALTER TABLE statement failed with SCHEMABINDING'
+ CHAR(10)
GO
(91 row(s) affected)
```

OUTPUT

```
ALTER TABLE statement successful without SCHEMABINDING

Server: Msg 207, Level 16, State 3, Procedure GetCustomers, Line 12
Invalid column name 'CompanyName'.

Execution of the GetCustomers table was unsuccessful
because it references a non-existing field


(91 row(s) affected)

Server: Msg 4512, Level 16, State 3, Procedure GetCustomers, Line 14
Cannot schema bind function 'dbo.GetCustomers'
➥because name 'NewCustomers' is invalid for schema binding.
➥Names must be in two-part format and an object cannot reference itself.

CREATE FUNCTION failed with SCHEMABINDING
because it did not use two part names


CREATE FUNCTION was successful with SCHEMABINDING
because it did use two part names
```

Listing 10.22: continued

```
Server: Msg 5074, Level 16, State 3, Line 2
The object 'GetCustomers' is dependent on column 'CompanyName'.
Server: Msg 4922, Level 16, State 1, Line 2
ALTER TABLE DROP COLUMN CompanyName failed
➥because one or more objects access this column.

ALTER TABLE statement failed with SCHEMABINDING
```

Deterministic and Nondeterministic Functions

Some functions always return the same value when called with the same set of arguments. These functions are called *deterministic*. This is important if you want to create a clustered index on a view or any index on a computed column, because you can create these indexes only if they use deterministic functions.

Most of the built-in functions are deterministic, such as

ABS	DATEDIFF	PARSENAME
ACOS	DAY	POWER
ASIN	DEGREES	RADIANS
ATAN	EXP	ROUND
ATN2	FLOOR	SIGN
CEILING	ISNULL	SIN
COALESCE	ISNUMERIC	SQUARE
COS	LOG	SQRT
COT	LOG10	TAN
DATALENGTH	MONTH	YEAR
DATEADD	NULLIF	

Some built-in functions are deterministic or nondeterministic, depending on the way you use them:

- CAST is deterministic for every type of value except for conversion from datetime, smalldatetime, and sql_variant containing a date value, because the final results depend on regional settings.

- CONVERT is deterministic in the same cases as CAST and nondeterministic in the same cases as CAST, except if you specify a style when converting datetime and smalldatetime data, the result is always predictable and the function is deterministic in that case.

- CHECKSUM is deterministic if you specify the list of columns or an expression; it is nondeterministic if you specify CHECKSUM(*).

- ISDATE is nondeterministic unless it is used with CONVERT and with a predictable style different from 0, 100, 9, or 109.

- RAND is deterministic if a seed value is specified; it is nondeterministic without a seed value.

Most of the other built-in functions are nondeterministic. For a full list, you can search for the "Deterministic and Nondeterministic Functions" topic in Books Online.

A user-defined function is deterministic only if

- Every function—built-in or user-defined—referenced in the function is deterministic.

- The function is defined with the SCHEMABINDING option.

- The function does not references objects not defined inside the function itself, such as tables, views, extended stored procedures.

NOTE

Creating a nondeterministic user-defined function is fine, as long as you are aware of their limitations. Books Online incorrectly says that you cannot use built-in nondeterministic functions inside a user-defined function. The only functions you cannot use inside a user-defined function are contained in the list following this note.

Built-in functions that use the current time are not valid inside a user-defined function:

CURRENT_TIMESTAMP	GETDATE
GetUTCDate	IDENTITY
NEWID	TEXTPTR
@@DBTS	@@MAX_CONNECTIONS

Other functions that are not valid inside user-defined functions are the System Statistical functions:

@@CONNECTIONS	@@PACK_RECEIVED
@@CPU_BUSY	@@PACK_SENT
fn_virtualfilestats	@@TIMETICKS
@@IDLE	@@TOTAL_ERRORS
@@IO_BUSY	@@TOTAL_READ
@@PACKET_ERRORS	@@TOTAL_WRITE

Altering User-Defined Functions Definition

To modify the definition of a user-defined function, you can use the ALTER FUNCTION statement in exactly the same way you use the CREATE FUNCTION statement. In this case, the new definition replaces the old definition of the user-defined function with the same name.

Listing 10.23 shows an example of how to use the ALTER FUNCTION statement to modify a preexisting user-defined function and encrypt the definition with the WITH ENCRYPTION option.

EXAMPLE

Listing 10.23: Use ALTER FUNCTION to Modify a User-Defined Function

```
USE Northwind
GO

-- Returns the maximum ProductID from Products

ALTER FUNCTION dbo.MaxProductID
()
RETURNS int
WITH ENCRYPTION
AS
BEGIN

RETURN (
SELECT MAX(ProductID)
FROM dbo.Products
)

END
GO
```
a user-defined function, you can use the ALTER FUNCTION statement

---

CAUTION

Not using the SCHEMABINDING option when you execute the ALTER FUNCTION statement unbinds the dependent objects from the function.

CAUTION

Before encrypting a user-defined function definition, make sure you have a copy in a safe place, because it will be impossible to decrypt it.

Security Implications of Using User-Defined Functions

You can grant or deny the permissions to use user-defined functions depending on the type of function:

- For scalar user-defined functions, you can grant or deny permissions on EXECUTE and REFERENCES.

- For inline user-defined functions, you can grant or deny permissions on SELECT, UPDATE, INSERT, DELETE, or REFERENCES.

- For multistatement table-values user-defined functions, you can grant or deny permissions to SELECT and REFERENCES.

As in stored procedures and views, if every object referenced in a user-defined function belongs to the same owner as the user-defined function, and a user tries to use the function, permissions will be checked only on the function, not on every object referenced in the function.

Applying User-Defined Functions

You convert commonly used formulas into scalar user-defined functions. In this case, the function's compiled query plan remains in memory, as does any built-in function.

You can call user-defined functions from inside other user-defined functions, but only up to 32 levels, and this limit applies to the total of stored procedures, triggers, and scalar or table-valued user-defined functions you use.

NOTE

Use the @@NESTLEVEL system function to know how many nested levels you are using.

A good approach would be to create user-defined functions in a short number of layers, so the limit for nesting levels will never be surpassed. This contributes to the clarity of your database design as well.

Be aware that modifying underlying objects could affect the result of a user-defining function, unless you create the function with the SCHEMABINDING option.

This is still a new feature for Transact-SQL programmers, but client-application programmers will find user-defined functions very close to their normal programming methods.

Converting Stored Procedures into User-Defined Functions

If the only reason for a stored procedure is to supply an output parameter, you can create a scalar user-defined function instead. In this way, you can use this function in a more natural way than a stored procedure. Listing 10.24 shows an example of converting the fn_FV function into the sp_FV stored procedure and how to call them.

EXAMPLE

Listing 10.24: Comparing a Stored Procedure with a Scalar User-Defined Function

```
USE Northwind
GO

-- sp_fv with the same functionality
-- as the fn_fv function

CREATE PROCEDURE sp_fv
```

Listing 10.24: continued

```
@rate float, @nper int, @pmt money,
@pv money = 0.0, @type bit = 0,
@FV money output
AS

IF @rate = 0
SET @fv = @pv + @pmt * @nper
ELSE
SET @fv = @pv * POWER(1 + @rate, @nper) +
@pmt * (((POWER(1 + @rate, @nper + @type) - 1) / @rate) - @type)

SET @fv = -@fv
GO

-- Call the sp_fv stored procedure

DECLARE @fv money

EXECUTE sp_fv 0.10, 24, 1000, 10000, 0, @fv OUTPUT

SELECT @fv 'From sp_fv'
GO

-- Call the sp_fv stored procedure

SELECT dbo.fn_fv(0.10, 24, 1000, 10000, 0) as 'From fn_fv'
GO
```

OUTPUT

```
From sp_fv
--------------------
-186994.6535

From fn_fv
--------------------
-186994.6535
```

If a stored procedure returns a single read-only result set, you can convert it into a table-valued function with a similar code, and you can use the function in the FROM clause of any DML statement, providing a better programming flexibility. Listing 10.25 shows an example of a stored procedure with the same functionality as the tv_TopTenOrders and how to call them.

If you have a stored procedure that provides read/write access to a table through a client library, you can convert this procedure into an inline user-defined function.

EXAMPLE

Listing 10.25: Comparing Stored Procedures and Table-Valued User-Defined Functions

```
USE Northwind
GO

CREATE PROCEDURE sp_TopTenOrders
AS

DECLARE @list TABLE
(OrderID int,
CustomerID nchar(5),
OrderDate datetime,
TotalValue money)

INSERT @List
SELECT O.OrderID, CustomerID, OrderDate, TotalValue
FROM Orders O
JOIN (
SELECT OrderID, SUM(dbo.TotalPrice(Quantity, UnitPrice, Discount))
AS TotalValue
FROM [Order Details]
GROUP BY OrderID) AS OD
ON O.OrderID = OD.OrderID

SELECT TOP 10 WITH TIES
OrderID, CustomerID, OrderDate, TotalValue
FROM @List
ORDER BY TotalValue DESC
GO

EXECUTE sp_TopTenOrders
GO

SELECT *
FROM tv_TopTenOrders()
GO
```

OUTPUT

OrderID	CustomerID	OrderDate	TotalValue
10865	QUICK	1998-02-02 00:00:00.000	16387.5000
10981	HANAR	1998-03-27 00:00:00.000	15810.0000
11030	SAVEA	1998-04-17 00:00:00.000	12615.0500
10889	RATTC	1998-02-16 00:00:00.000	11380.0000
10417	SIMOB	1997-01-16 00:00:00.000	11188.4000
10817	KOENE	1998-01-06 00:00:00.000	10952.8450
10897	HUNGO	1998-02-19 00:00:00.000	10835.2400
10479	RATTC	1997-03-19 00:00:00.000	10495.6000
10540	QUICK	1997-05-19 00:00:00.000	10191.7000
10691	QUICK	1997-10-03 00:00:00.000	10164.8000

Listing 10.25: continued

OrderID	CustomerID	OrderDate	TotalValue
10865	QUICK	1998-02-02 00:00:00.000	16387.5000
10981	HANAR	1998-03-27 00:00:00.000	15810.0000
11030	SAVEA	1998-04-17 00:00:00.000	12615.0500
10889	RATTC	1998-02-16 00:00:00.000	11380.0000
10417	SIMOB	1997-01-16 00:00:00.000	11188.4000
10817	KOENE	1998-01-06 00:00:00.000	10952.8450
10897	HUNGO	1998-02-19 00:00:00.000	10835.2400
10479	RATTC	1997-03-19 00:00:00.000	10495.6000
10540	QUICK	1997-05-19 00:00:00.000	10191.7000
10691	QUICK	1997-10-03 00:00:00.000	10164.8000

Converting Views into User-Defined Functions

You can convert views into inline user-defined functions very easily, but in this case, the only benefit you will get is the possibility of having parameters. However, if you use a view to read data only, you will benefit from converting this view into a table-valued function because it will be optimized and compiled on the first execution, providing performance gains over a view.

Listing 10.26 shows the `fv_TopTenOrders` converted into a view, and how you call the view and the user-defined function. The output is the same as the one for Listing 10.25.

EXAMPLE

Listing 10.26: Comparing Views and Table-Valued User-Defined Functions

```
USE Northwind
GO

CREATE VIEW vw_TopTenOrders
AS

SELECT TOP 10 WITH TIES
O.OrderID, CustomerID, OrderDate, TotalValue
FROM Orders O
JOIN (
SELECT OrderID, SUM(dbo.TotalPrice(Quantity, UnitPrice, Discount))
AS TotalValue
FROM [Order Details]
GROUP BY OrderID) AS OD
ON O.OrderID = OD.OrderID
ORDER BY TotalValue DESC

GO

SELECT *
FROM tv_TopTenOrders()
```

Listing 10.26: continued

```
GO

SELECT *
FROM vw_TopTenOrders
GO
```

Using User-Defined Functions in Constraints

You can use a scalar user-defined function anywhere an expression is allowed, and that includes

- DEFAULT constraints

- CHECK constraints

- DEFAULT objects

- RULE objects

- A PRIMARY KEY constraint defined in a computed column using a user-defined function, as long as the returned values are unique

- A UNIQUE constraint defined in a computed column with a user-defined function, as long as the returned values are unique

Therefore, it is possible to access values from other tables from inside a constraint, as long as the constraint uses a user-defined function that searches for external data to produce its result.

The only place where you can use a table-valued user-defined function or an inline user-defined function is as a subquery in a CHECK constraint but, unfortunately, CHECK constraints do not support subqueries.

What's Next?

This chapter covered the creation and use of user-defined functions—an exciting new feature that provides extra programmability to the Transact-SQL language. The more you practice with user-defined functions, the more you will wonder how you could have survived without them before SQL Server 2000 offered this feature.

Chapter 11 teaches you how to write complex queries, and in some cases, using user-defined functions that could solve similar situations with less complexity.

In Chapter 12, you learn how to work with result sets row by row, using cursors. You can use cursors inside user-defined functions to achieve complex operations that are impossible using rowset-oriented programming.

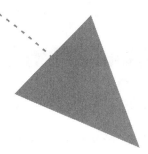

Using Complex Queries and Statements

In previous chapters, you learned how to execute queries to retrieve and modify data in SQL Server. You also learned how to create and use database objects, such as tables, views, stored procedures, user-defined functions, and triggers. Transact-SQL provides extended structures that can simplify the process of writing queries to solve complex requests.

This chapter teaches you the following:

- How to create subqueries, which are queries inside other queries, to solve complex problems

- How to use the EXISTS keyword to test for existence of rows in a subquery

- How to use the IN operator to check for values returned from a subquery

- How to use derived tables, which are subqueries that can be used as virtual tables in the FROM clause, to simplify complex queries

- How to use the CASE function to retrieve conditional values

- How to produce summary reports using the COMPUTE clause

- How to produce summary result sets using the CUBE and ROLLUP operators

- How to use optimizer hints to modify the way the query will be processed

Subqueries

A *subquery* is just a query contained inside another query. You can call the subquery an *inner* query contained within an *outer* query, which in turn can be a standard query or another subquery.

If you think about standard queries, you can define three kinds of queries, according to the type of result they provide:

- Scalar—Queries that produce a single value (one single row with only one column)

- List—Queries that produce a list of values (one or more rows with a single column only)

- Array—Queries that return a result set (one or more rows with one or more columns)

List queries can be considered single-column array queries. Scalar queries can be used as single-column, single-row array queries as well.

Listing 11.1 shows different scalar queries that return a single value. This value can be a single constant, the result of a system function, or the result of a standard query, as long as the query returns a single column and a single row.

EXAMPLE

Listing 11.1: Scalar Queries Return a Single Value

```
USE Northwind
GO

SET NOCOUNT ON
GO

-- Select a single constant

SELECT 1

-- Select a scalar system niladic function

SELECT SYSTEM_USER

-- Select a scalar system function

SELECT db_ID('Northwind')

-- Select the result of a User-Defined Function
-- Note this function does not exist

-- SELECT fn_getProductNameFromID(123)
```

Listing 11.1: continued

```
-- Select the result of an aggregate function applied to a number of rows

SELECT COUNT(*) as NRows
FROM Northwind.dbo.Products

-- Select a single column from a single row in a table

SELECT ProductName
FROM Northwind.dbo.Products
WHERE ProductID = 5
```

```
----------
1.00
```

OUTPUT

```
---------------------------------------------------------
SQLBYEXAMPLE\GuestUser


------
6.00

NRows
----------
77.00

ProductName
---------------------------------------
Chef Anton's Gumbo Mix
```

In Listing 11.2, you can see three examples of queries that provide a list of values. In the first example, you select values from a single column. In the second example, you aggregate data, grouping the results by another field. In the third example, you create a list query by combining several scalar queries using the UNION operator.

Listing 11.2: List Queries Return a List of Values

```
USE Northwind
GO
```

EXAMPLE

```
SET NOCOUNT ON
GO

-- Selecting a single column from a table

SELECT CategoryName
```

Listing 11.2: continued

```
FROM Northwind.dbo.Categories

-- Selecting aggregate values from a single column from a table using GROUP BY

SELECT COUNT(*) AS "Products per Supplier"
FROM Northwind.dbo.products
GROUP BY SupplierID

-- Selecting different constant values using the UNION operator

SELECT 1 AS "Numbers"
UNION
SELECT 2
UNION
SELECT 3
```

OUTPUT

```
CategoryName
---------------
Beverages
Condiments
Confections
Dairy Products
Grains/Cereals
Liquors
Liquors
Meat/Poultry
Produce
Seafood


Products per Supplier
---------------------
3.00
4.00
3.00
3.00
2.00
3.00
5.00
4.00
2.00
1.00
3.00
5.00
1.00
3.00
3.00
3.00
```

Listing 11.2: continued

```
3.00
2.00
2.00
3.00
2.00
2.00
3.00
3.00
2.00
2.00
1.00
2.00
2.00

Numbers
-----------
1.00
2.00
3.00
```

Listing 11.3 shows several array query examples that return result sets with multiple columns. The first example selects two columns from a table. The second example selects several constants. The third example selects the results of several scalar system functions. The last example combines the results of two array queries to produce a single array query, using the UNION operator.

EXAMPLE

Listing 11.3: Array Queries Return a Complete Result Set

```
USE Northwind
GO

SET NOCOUNT ON
GO

-- Selecting multiple columns from a table

SELECT ProductName, UnitPrice
FROM Northwind.dbo.Products
WHERE CategoryID = 1

-- Selecting multiple constants

SELECT 1 AS 'Lower',
2 AS 'Higher',
'Peter' AS 'Responsible'

-- Selecting values from system functions
```

Listing 11.3: continued

```
SELECT CURRENT_TIMESTAMP AS 'Now',
CURRENT_USER AS 'Database User',
SYSTEM_USER AS 'System Login'

-- Selecting data from multiple tables using the UNION operator

SELECT CompanyName, ContactName
FROM Northwind.dbo.Customers
WHERE Country = 'Brazil'
UNION
SELECT CompanyName, ContactName
FROM Northwind.dbo.Suppliers
WHERE Country = 'Brazil'
```

OUTPUT

```
ProductName                            UnitPrice
-------------------------------------- --------------------
Chai                                   $18.00
Chang                                  $19.00
Guaraná Fantástica                     $4.50
Sasquatch Ale                          $14.00
Steeleye Stout                         $18.00
Côte de Blaye                          $263.50
Chartreuse verte                       $18.00
Ipoh Coffee                            $46.00
Laughing Lumberjack Lager              $14.00
Outback Lager                          $15.00
Rhönbräu Klosterbier                   $7.75
Lakkalikööri                           $18.00


Lower       Higher      Responsible
----------- ----------- -----------
1.00        2.00        Peter


Now                      Database User   System Login
------------------------ --------------- ---------------------------
1/21/2001 4:38:42 PM     dbo             SQLBYEXAMPLE\AdminUser


CompanyName                            ContactName
-------------------------------------- ---------------------------
Comércio Mineiro                       Pedro Afonso
Familia Arquibaldo                     Aria Cruz
Gourmet Lanchonetes                    André Fonseca
Hanari Carnes                          Mario Pontes
Que Delícia                            Bernardo Batista
Queen Cozinha                          Lúcia Carvalho
Refrescos Americanas LTDA              Carlos Diaz
Ricardo Adocicados                     Janete Limeira
Tradição Hipermercados                 Anabela Domingues
Wellington Importadora                 Paula Parente
```

Most of the queries that use subqueries can be rewritten as simple queries without subqueries to produce the same results. Actually, the Query Optimizer can decide to apply the same query plan regardless of the way the query is written.

In the following sections, you will see the same solution with and without subqueries. In some cases, using a subquery makes the query easier to read.

Scalar Subqueries

A scalar query can be used as a subquery anywhere in a Transact-SQL statement where an expression is accepted:

- As part of any expression, because the result of the subquery is a scalar value.

- In the SELECT clause of a SELECT statement, as part of the output list.

- In the SET clause of an UPDATE statement, specifying the value to assign to a field.

- In the FROM clause of a SELECT statement, as a single row and single column derived table.

- In the WHERE clause, as a condition to test the value of a field, constant, variable, or the result of another scalar subquery.

- In the HAVING clause, in the same cases as in the WHERE clause.

Listing 11.4 shows several examples of how to use scalar subqueries in the SELECT, SET, FROM, WHERE, and HAVING clauses, inside other queries. The purpose of every query is documented throughout the code. You can see in Listing 11.5 how to solve the same queries from Listing 11.4, without using any subquery. Note that we do not show the output of Listing 11.5 because it is the same as for Listing 11.4.

NOTE

To use a query as a subquery inside another query, you must enclose the subquery in parentheses.

EXAMPLE

Listing 11.4: Use Scalar Subqueries Inside Other Queries

```
USE Northwind
GO

SET NOCOUNT ON
GO

-- In this case we combine the values returned by two subqueries
-- to get the medium unit price
```

Listing 11.4: continued

```
SELECT (
(SELECT MIN(Unitprice)
FROM Products) +
(SELECT MAX(Unitprice)
FROM Products))/2 as NewPrice

-- This query is not practically useful,
-- but it shows more choices on designing subqueries
SELECT 1, 2,
(SELECT 3)
GO

-- This query uses two subqueries to retrieve one single row
-- with the Maximum and Average UnitPrice

SELECT (
SELECT AVG(Unitprice)
FROM Products
) as AvgPrice
, (
SELECT MAX(Unitprice)
FROM Products
) as MaxPrice
GO

-- Compare the UnitPrice of every product
-- with the Average UnitPrice, produced by a subquery

SELECT ProductName, UnitPrice, (
SELECT AVG(Unitprice)
FROM Products
) as AvgPrice
FROM Products
WHERE CategoryID = 2
GO

-- Updates the UnitPrice of the product 11 to
-- 20% more than the maximum UnitPrice.


UPDATE Products
SET UnitPrice = (
SELECT MAX(Unitprice)
FROM Northwind..Products
) * 1.2
WHERE ProductID = 11
```

Listing 11.4: continued

```
-- Show the product with maximum UnitPrice

SELECT ProductName, UnitPrice
FROM Products P
WHERE Unitprice = (
SELECT Max(UnitPrice) MPrice
FROM Products
)

-- You want to retrieve the Categories with average Unitprice
-- greater than the overall products average price

SELECT CategoryID, AVG(UnitPrice) AS 'Average Price'
FROM Products P
GROUP BY CategoryID
HAVING AVG(UnitPrice) > (
SELECT AVG(UnitPrice) MPrice
FROM Products
)
```

NewPrice

$190.97

OUTPUT

```
---------- ---------- ----------
1.00        2.00        3.00

AvgPrice              MaxPrice
-------------------- --------------------
$33.88                $379.44
```

ProductName	UnitPrice	AvgPrice
Aniseed Syrup	$11.00	$33.88
Chef Anton's Cajun Seasoning	$24.20	$33.88
Chef Anton's Gumbo Mix	$23.49	$33.88
Grandma's Boysenberry Spread	$27.50	$33.88
Northwoods Cranberry Sauce	$44.00	$33.88
Genen Shouyu	$17.05	$33.88
Gula Malacca	$21.40	$33.88
Sirop d'érable	$31.35	$33.88
Vegie-spread	$48.29	$33.88
Louisiana Fiery Hot Pepper Sauce	$23.16	$33.88
Louisiana Hot Spiced Okra	$18.70	$33.88
Original Frankfurter grüne Soße	$14.30	$33.88

Listing 11.4: continued

```
ProductName                                UnitPrice
----------------------------------------   --------------------
Queso Cabrales                             $455.33
```

```
CategoryID  Average Price
----------  --------------------
1.00        $37.98
4.00        $72.16
6.00        $54.01
```

EXAMPLE

Listing 11.5: Solving the Scalar Subqueries Examples from Listing 11.4 Without Subqueries

```
USE Northwind
GO

SET NOCOUNT ON
GO

-- Get the medium unit price

SELECT (MIN(UnitPrice) +
MAX(UnitPrice))/2 AS NewPrice
FROM Products

-- Selects three constants

SELECT 1, 2, 3
GO

-- Retrieve one single row with the Maximum and Average UnitPrice

SELECT AVG(Unitprice) as AvgPrice,
MAX(Unitprice) as MaxPrice
FROM Products

GO

-- Compare the UnitPrice of every product
-- with the Average UnitPrice

DECLARE @UP money

SELECT @UP = AVG(Unitprice)
FROM Products

SELECT ProductName, UnitPrice, @UP AS AvgPrice
FROM Products
```

Listing 11.5: continued

```
WHERE CategoryID = 2
GO


-- Updates the UnitPrice of the product 11 to
-- 20% more than the maximum UnitPrice.

DECLARE @UP money

SELECT @UP = MAX(Unitprice)
FROM Products

UPDATE Products
SET UnitPrice = @UP * 1.2
WHERE ProductID = 11


-- You want to show the product with maximum UnitPrice

DECLARE @UP money

SELECT @UP = MAX(Unitprice)
FROM Products

SELECT ProductName, UnitPrice
FROM Products P
WHERE Unitprice = @UP


-- You want to retrieve the Categories with average Unitprice
-- greater than the overall products average price

DECLARE @UP money

SELECT @UP = AVG(Unitprice)
FROM Products

SELECT CategoryID, AVG(UnitPrice)
FROM Products P
GROUP BY CategoryID
HAVING AVG(UnitPrice) > @UP
```

List Subqueries

A List query can be used as a subquery inside a query in the following cases:

- In the WHERE clause of any query using the IN operator to specify the List query as a list of possible values.

- In the WHERE clause when using any comparison operator with the SOME, ANY, or ALL operators.

- In the FROM clause of a SELECT statement, as a multirow and single-column derived table.

- In the WHERE clause, using the EXISTS or NOT EXISTS keywords to test for existence of values in the List.

Listing 11.6 contains some examples of subqueries that produce lists of values. The first example uses a list subquery in the WHERE clause introduced with the IN operator. The second example uses a list subquery in the WHERE clause as well, with the ALL operator. The third example uses a list subquery as a derived table in the FROM clause. The last example shows a subquery in the WHERE clause using the EXISTS operator.

Listing 11.7 contains the same examples, but without using list subqueries. The output is the same as in Listing 11.6.

EXAMPLE

Listing 11.6: Using List Queries As Subqueries

```
USE Northwind
GO

SET NOCOUNT ON
GO

-- Orders placed by clients from London
-- and EmployeeID = 1

SELECT OrderID, CustomerID, EmployeeID, OrderDate
FROM Orders
WHERE CustomerID IN (
SELECT CustomerID
FROM Customers
WHERE City = 'London'
)
AND EmployeeID = 1

-- Select all the products with the UnitPrice
-- greater than all the products from Category 2

SELECT ProductID, ProductName, UnitPrice
FROM Products
WHERE UnitPrice > ALL (
SELECT UnitPrice
FROM Products
WHERE CategoryID = 2
)
```

Listing 11.6: continued

```
-- Select all the order details related to products from category 2
-- and OrderID between 10250 and 10300

SELECT OD.OrderID, OD.ProductID, OD.UnitPrice
FROM [Order Details] OD
JOIN (
SELECT ProductID
FROM Products
WHERE CategoryID = 2
) AS P
ON P.ProductID = OD.ProductID
WHERE OrderID BETWEEN 10250 AND 10300

-- List all the products only if there are any products never ordered

SELECT ProductID, ProductName
FROM Products
WHERE EXISTS (
SELECT Products.ProductID
FROM Products
LEFT OUTER JOIN [Order Details]
ON Products.ProductID = [Order Details].ProductID
WHERE [Order Details].ProductID IS NULL
)
```

OUTPUT

OrderID	CustomerID	EmployeeID	OrderDate
10,364.00	EASTC	1.00	11/26/1996 12:00:00 AM
10,377.00	SEVES	1.00	12/9/1996 12:00:00 AM
10,400.00	EASTC	1.00	1/1/1997 12:00:00 AM
10,453.00	AROUT	1.00	2/21/1997 12:00:00 AM
10,558.00	AROUT	1.00	6/4/1997 12:00:00 AM
10,743.00	AROUT	1.00	11/17/1997 12:00:00 AM
10,800.00	SEVES	1.00	12/26/1997 12:00:00 AM
11,023.00	BSBEV	1.00	4/14/1998 12:00:00 AM

ProductID	ProductName	UnitPrice
9.00	Mishi Kobe Niku	$97.00
11.00	Queso Cabrales	$455.33
18.00	Carnarvon Tigers	$62.50
20.00	Sir Rodney's Marmalade	$81.00
29.00	Thüringer Rostbratwurst	$123.79
38.00	Côte de Blaye	$263.50
51.00	Manjimup Dried Apples	$53.00
59.00	Raclette Courdavault	$55.00
62.00	Tarte au sucre	$49.30

Listing 11.6: continued

```
OrderID       ProductID    UnitPrice
-----------   -----------  -------------------

10,250.00     65.00        $16.80
10,251.00     65.00        $16.80
10,256.00     77.00        $10.40
10,257.00     77.00        $10.40
10,258.00     5.00         $17.00
10,262.00     5.00         $17.00
10,278.00     44.00        $15.50
10,278.00     63.00        $35.10
10,283.00     15.00        $12.40
10,284.00     44.00        $15.50
10,289.00     3.00         $8.00
10,290.00     5.00         $17.00
10,290.00     77.00        $10.40
10,291.00     44.00        $15.50
10,293.00     63.00        $35.10
10,300.00     66.00        $13.60


ProductID    ProductName
-----------  ----------------------------------------
```

Listing 11.7: Solving the List Subqueries Examples from Listing 11.6 Without Subqueries

```
USE Northwind
GO

SET NOCOUNT ON
GO


-- Orders placed by clients from London
-- and EmployeeID = 1

SELECT O.OrderID, O.CustomerID, O.EmployeeID, O.OrderDate
FROM Orders O
JOIN Customers C
ON O.CustomerID = C.CustomerID
WHERE City = 'London'
AND EmployeeID = 1


-- Select all the products with the UnitPrice
-- greater than all the products from Category 2

DECLARE @MP money

SELECT @MP = MAX(Unitprice)
FROM Products
WHERE CategoryID = 2
```

Listing 11.7: continued

```
SELECT ProductID, ProductName, UnitPrice
FROM Products
WHERE UnitPrice > @MP

-- Select all the order details related to products from category 2
-- and OrderID between 10250 and 10300

SELECT OD.OrderID, OD.ProductID, OD.UnitPrice
FROM [Order Details] OD
JOIN Products P
ON P.ProductID = OD.ProductID
WHERE CategoryID = 2
AND OrderID BETWEEN 10250 AND 10300

-- List all the products only if there are any products never ordered

DECLARE @n int

SELECT @n = COUNT(*)
FROM Products
LEFT OUTER JOIN [Order Details]
ON Products.ProductID = [Order Details].ProductID
WHERE [Order Details].ProductID IS NULL

SELECT ProductID, ProductName
FROM Products
WHERE ISNULL(@n, 0) > 0

-- OR

IF EXISTS(
SELECT Products.ProductID
FROM Products
LEFT OUTER JOIN [Order Details]
ON Products.ProductID = [Order Details].ProductID
WHERE [Order Details].ProductID IS NULL
)
SELECT ProductID, ProductName
FROM Products
```

Array Subqueries

An Array query, or standard query, can be used as a subquery inside a query in the following cases:

- In the FROM clause of a SELECT statement, as a multirow and multicolumn derived table.

- In the WHERE clause, using the EXISTS or NOT EXISTS keywords to test for existence of values in the List. The EXISTS function does not return any rows, it evaluates to TRUE if the subquery returns at least one row, and it evaluates to FALSE otherwise.

Listing 11.8 shows two examples of using array subqueries. The first example uses an array subquery in the FROM clause as a derived table. The second example combines two result sets with the UNION operator, introducing two array subqueries with the EXISTS operator.

Listing 11.9 solves the same problems from Listing 11.8 without using subqueries. Note that we do not show the output for Listing 11.9 because it is exactly the same as for Listing 11.8.

EXAMPLE

Listing 11.8: Using Array Queries As Subqueries

```
USE Northwind
GO

SET NOCOUNT ON
GO

-- Show name of product and category for products of categories 1 to 3

SELECT CategoryName, ProductName
FROM Products P
JOIN (
SELECT CategoryID, CategoryName
FROM Categories
WHERE CategoryID
BETWEEN 1 AND 3
) AS C
ON C.CategoryID = P.CategoryID
WHERE ProductName LIKE 'L%'

-- Show if we have beverage sales

SELECT 'We do have beverage Sales'
AS [Beverage Sales]
WHERE EXISTS(
SELECT *
FROM [Order details] O
JOIN Products P
ON O.ProductID = P.ProductID
WHERE P.CategoryID = 1
)

UNION
```

Listing 11.8: continued

```
SELECT 'We do not have any beverage Sales'
WHERE NOT EXISTS(
SELECT *
FROM [Order details] O
JOIN Products P
ON O.ProductID = P.ProductID
WHERE P.CategoryID = 1
)
```

OUTPUT

```
CategoryName     ProductName
--------------   ----------------------------------------
Beverages        Lakkalikööri
Beverages        Laughing Lumberjack Lager
Condiments       Louisiana Fiery Hot Pepper Sauce
Condiments       Louisiana Hot Spiced Okra


Beverage Sales
--------------------------------
We do have beverage Sales
```

EXAMPLE

Listing 11.9: Solving the Array Subquery Examples from Listing 11.8 Without Subqueries

```
-- Show name of product and category for products of categories 1 to 3

SELECT CategoryName, ProductName
FROM Products P
JOIN Categories AS C
ON C.CategoryID = P.CategoryID
WHERE P.CategoryID
BETWEEN 1 AND 3
AND ProductName LIKE 'L%'


-- Show if we have beverage sales
-- Note: CASE will be explained later in this chapter

DECLARE @N int

SELECT @N = COUNT(*)
FROM [Order details] O
JOIN Products P
ON O.ProductID = P.ProductID
WHERE P.CategoryID = 1

SELECT CASE
WHEN ISNULL(@n, 0) > 0
THEN  'We do have beverage Sales'
ELSE 'We do not have any beverage Sales'
END
AS [Beverage Sales]
```

CAUTION

In some cases, converting a query that uses a subquery into another query without a subquery can produce unexpected results, as in Listing 11.10. Make sure the query is defined properly to retrieve the desired results.

TIP

It is recommended to use IF EXISTS(SELECT * FROM ...) because Query Optimizer will select the best available index to investigate the existence of rows.

EXAMPLE

Listing 11.10: Rewriting a Query to Avoid the Use of a Subquery Can Produce Unexpected Results If Conditions Are Not Applied Properly

```
USE Northwind
GO

SET NOCOUNT ON
GO

-- Retrieve all the categories with products

-- This solution uses a subquery and retrieves 1 row

PRINT 'Using a Subquery' + CHAR(10)

SELECT CategoryName
FROM Categories
WHERE CategoryID IN
(SELECT CategoryID
FROM Products)
AND Description LIKE '%pasta%'

-- This solution does not use a subquery but it retrieves 7 rows

PRINT 'Without Using a Subquery' + CHAR(10)

SELECT CategoryName
FROM Categories
JOIN Products
ON Products.categoryID = Categories.CategoryID
WHERE Description LIKE '%pasta%'

-- This solution does not use a subquery but it retrieves 1 row again

PRINT 'Using DISTINCT Without a Subquery' + CHAR(10)

SELECT DISTINCT CategoryName
FROM Categories
```

Listing 11.10: continued

```
JOIN Products
ON Products.categoryID = Categories.CategoryID
WHERE Description LIKE '%pasta%'
```

Using a Subquery

```
CategoryName
--------------
Grains/Cereals
```

Without Using a Subquery

```
CategoryName
--------------
Grains/Cereals
Grains/Cereals
Grains/Cereals
Grains/Cereals
Grains/Cereals
Grains/Cereals
Grains/Cereals
```

Using DISTINCT Without a Subquery

```
CategoryName
--------------
Grains/Cereals
```

From the previous examples, you can get the impression that every query that uses subqueries can be defined as a standard query without any subquery. However, some problems can have an easier solution using subqueries than not using subqueries at all. What if you wanted to know the best-selling product by number of units and by total sale price? Listing 11.11 shows how to create subquery to solve this problem and how to do it without a subquery.

Listing 11.11: In Some Cases the Easiest Solution Is to Use Subqueries

```
USE Northwind
GO

SET NOCOUNT ON
GO

-- Retrieve the best selling product by number of units and by revenue

-- This solution uses subqueries
```

Listing 11.11: continued

```
SELECT 'By units' AS Criteria,
ProductName as 'Best Selling'
FROM Products
WHERE ProductID = (
SELECT ProductID
FROM [Order Details]
GROUP BY ProductID
HAVING SUM(Quantity) = (
SELECT MAX(SQ)
FROM (
SELECT SUM(Quantity) as SQ
FROM [Order Details]
GROUP BY ProductID
) AS OD))

UNION

SELECT 'By revenue' AS Criteria,
ProductName as 'Best Selling'
FROM Products
WHERE ProductID = (
SELECT ProductID
FROM [Order Details]
GROUP BY ProductID
HAVING SUM(UnitPrice * Quantity * (1-Discount)) = (
SELECT MAX(SQ)
FROM (
SELECT SUM(UnitPrice * Quantity * (1-Discount)) as SQ
FROM [Order Details]
GROUP BY ProductID
) AS OD))

-- This solution uses subqueries as well

SELECT 'By units' AS Criteria,
ProductName as 'Best Selling'
FROM Products P
JOIN (
SELECT TOP 1 ProductID,
SUM(Quantity) AS SQ
FROM [Order Details]
GROUP BY productID
ORDER BY SQ DESC
) AS OD
ON OD.ProductID = P.ProductID

UNION
```

Listing 11.11: continued

```
SELECT 'By revenue' AS Criteria,
ProductName as 'Best Selling'
FROM Products P
JOIN (
SELECT TOP 1 ProductID,
SUM(UnitPrice * Quantity * (1-Discount)) AS SR
FROM [Order Details]
GROUP BY ProductID
ORDER BY SR DESC
) AS OD
ON OD.ProductID = P.ProductID

-- This solution does not use subqueries.
-- However the execution is similar to the query that uses subqueries
SELECT ProductID,
SUM(Quantity) AS SQ,
CAST(SUM(UnitPrice * Quantity * (1.0-Discount))AS money) as SR
INTO #BestSelling
FROM [Order Details]
WHERE ProductID IS NOT NULL
GROUP BY productID

DECLARE @MQ int, @MR money
DECLARE @PQ int, @PR int

SELECT @MQ = MAX(SQ),
@MR = MAX(SR)
FROM #BestSelling

SELECT @PQ = ProductID
FROM #BestSelling
WHERE SQ = @MQ

SELECT @PR = ProductID
FROM #BestSelling
WHERE SR = @MR

SELECT 'By units' AS Criteria,
ProductName as 'Best Selling'
FROM Products
WHERE ProductID = @PQ

UNION

SELECT 'By revenue' AS Criteria,
ProductName as 'Best Selling'
FROM Products
```

Listing 11.11: continued

```
WHERE ProductID = @PR

-- drop temporary table

DROP TABLE #BestSelling
```

```
(Same output for every query)

Criteria    Best Selling
----------  ----------------------------------------
By revenue  Côte de Blaye
By units    Camembert Pierrot
```

Correlated Subqueries

In the previous examples, the subqueries were normal queries that you could run isolated from the outer query.

In some cases, you might need to write a subquery that depends on values from the outer query to retrieve its results. In these cases, you call the subquery a correlated subquery. This usually forces the execution of the subquery once per every row returned from the outer query.

TIP

You can easily identify a correlated subquery because it is enclosed in parentheses and it cannot be executed independently from the outer query.

Correlated subqueries can return a single scalar value, a list of values, or an array of values in the same way as standard subqueries.

Suppose you wanted to know the suggested UnitPrice for every product, together with the average and maximum selling price. You can solve this problem as in Listing 11.12.

Listing 11.12: Use Correlated Subqueries to Solve Complex Problems

```
-- Select the target UnitPrice, the minimum, average,
-- and maximum selling price for every product
-- show non-ordered products as well
```

```
-- With a Correlated Subquery

SELECT ProductID,
UnitPrice,
(SELECT AVG(UnitPrice)
FROM [Order Details]
WHERE [Order Details].ProductID =
Products.ProductID) AS AvgPrice,
```

Listing 11.12: continued

```
(SELECT MIN(UnitPrice)
FROM [Order Details]
WHERE [Order Details].ProductID =
Products.ProductID) AS MaxPrice,
ProductName
FROM Products
WHERE CategoryID = 1

-- With a standard (non-correlated) subquery

SELECT P.ProductID,
P.UnitPrice,
MMP.AvgPrice,
MMP.MinPrice,
P.ProductName
FROM Products P
LEFT OUTER JOIN (
SELECT ProductID,
MIN(UnitPrice) AS MinPrice,
AVG(UnitPrice) AS AvgPrice
FROM [Order Details]
GROUP BY ProductID
) AS MMP
ON MMP.ProductID =
P.ProductID
WHERE CategoryID = 1

-- Without subqueries

SELECT P.ProductID,
P.UnitPrice,
AVG(OD.UnitPrice) AS AvgPrice,
MIN(OD.UnitPrice) AS MinPrice,
P.ProductName
FROM Products P
LEFT OUTER JOIN [Order Details] OD
ON OD.ProductID =
P.ProductID
WHERE CategoryID = 1
GROUP BY P.productID, P.UnitPrice, P.ProductName
```

(Same output for every query)

OUTPUT

ProductID	UnitPrice	AvgPrice	MaxPrice	ProductName
1.00	$18.00	$17.15	$14.40	Chai
2.00	$19.00	$17.88	$15.20	Chang

Listing 11.12: continued

24.00	$4.50	$4.24	$3.60	Guaraná Fantástica
34.00	$14.00	$12.97	$11.20	Sasquatch Ale
35.00	$18.00	$17.00	$14.40	Steeleye Stout
38.00	$263.50	$245.93	$210.80	Côte de Blaye
39.00	$18.00	$16.68	$14.40	Chartreuse verte
43.00	$46.00	$43.04	$36.80	Ipoh Coffee
67.00	$14.00	$13.72	$11.20	Laughing Lumberjack Lager
70.00	$15.00	$14.15	$12.00	Outback Lager
75.00	$7.75	$7.38	$6.20	Rhönbräu Klosterbier
76.00	$18.00	$16.98	$14.40	Lakkalikööri

CAUTION

It is important to qualify the column names with the table name inside a subquery to avoid ambiguity. However, if you do not qualify column names, SQL Server will resolve them first from the subquery, and then from the outer query.

Using subqueries produces similar results to OUTER JOIN queries. To implement functionality similar to INNER JOIN queries, use EXISTS to test for existence in the inner table as in Listing 11.13.

EXAMPLE

Listing 11.13: Use EXISTS to Simulate Inner Queries When Using Subqueries

```
-- As in the first example from Listing 11-12
-- but in this case we select only products with orders
SELECT ProductID,
UnitPrice,
(SELECT AVG(UnitPrice)
FROM [Order Details]
WHERE [Order Details].ProductID =
Products.ProductID) AS AvgPrice,
(SELECT MIN(UnitPrice)
FROM [Order Details]
WHERE [Order Details].ProductID =
Products.ProductID) AS MaxPrice,
ProductName
FROM Products
WHERE EXISTS (
SELECT *
FROM [Order Details]
WHERE [Order Details].ProductID = Products.productID
)
AND CategoryID = 1
```

(Same output for every query)

OUTPUT

```
ProductID   UnitPrice   AvgPrice    MaxPrice    ProductName
..........  ..........  ..........  ..........  ........................
```

Listing 11.13: continued

1.00	$18.00	$17.15	$14.40	Chai
2.00	$19.00	$17.88	$15.20	Chang
24.00	$4.50	$4.24	$3.60	Guaraná Fantástica
34.00	$14.00	$12.97	$11.20	Sasquatch Ale
35.00	$18.00	$17.00	$14.40	Steeleye Stout
38.00	$263.50	$245.93	$210.80	Côte de Blaye
39.00	$18.00	$16.68	$14.40	Chartreuse verte
43.00	$46.00	$43.04	$36.80	Ipoh Coffee
67.00	$14.00	$13.72	$11.20	Laughing Lumberjack Lager
70.00	$15.00	$14.15	$12.00	Outback Lager
75.00	$7.75	$7.38	$6.20	Rhönbräu Klosterbier
76.00	$18.00	$16.98	$14.40	Lakkalikööri

It is common in correlated subqueries to use the same object inside and outside the subquery. In this case, you must provide an object alias to avoid ambiguity. In Listing 11.14, you want to know the list of customers who are based in the same city of at least one more customer.

EXAMPLE

Listing 11.14: Use Table Aliases to Avoid Ambiguity When Using Correlated Subqueries

```
USE Northwind
GO

SET NOCOUNT ON
GO

-- Retrieve the list of Cities where we have more than one customer,
-- ordered by City and CompanyName

-- With Correlated Subquery

SELECT City, CompanyName
FROM Customers C1
WHERE City IN (
SELECT City
FROM Customers C2
WHERE C2.CustomerID <> C1.CustomerID
)
AND Country = 'Argentina'
ORDER BY City, CompanyName

-- Without Subqueries

SELECT DISTINCT C1.City, C1.CompanyName
FROM Customers C1
JOIN Customers AS C2
ON C2.City = C1.City
WHERE C2.CustomerID <> C1.CustomerID
```

Listing 11.14: continued

```
AND C1.Country = 'Argentina'
ORDER BY C1.City, C1.CompanyName
```

OUTPUT

(Same output for every query)

```
City              CompanyName
--------------    -----------------------------------------
Buenos Aires      Cactus Comidas para llevar
Buenos Aires      Océano Atlántico Ltda.
Buenos Aires      Rancho grande
```

Derived Tables

Some of the examples from the previous section of this chapter can be solved using subqueries in the FROM clause. Subqueries work as tables in the query, and they are called *derived tables*. SQL Server considers these subqueries in the same way as ad hoc views, because the definition of the derived tables is merged with the outer query to produce a single query execution plan.

To use a derived table in a query, you must specify in the FROM clause a standard subquery with a table alias for the derived table (see Listing 11.15).

CAUTION

Correlated queries cannot be used as derived tables.

EXAMPLE

Listing 11.15: You Can Use Derived Tables to Solve Common Queries Without Defining Views or Temporary Tables

```
-- Using a Derived Table to compare UnitPrice
-- with the actual minimum and maximum prices
SELECT P.ProductID, P.UnitPrice
, (MinPrice + MaxPrice) / 2 AS MediumPrice
FROM Products P
JOIN (
SELECT ProductID,
MIN(UnitPrice) as MinPrice,
MAX(UnitPrice) as Maxprice
FROM [Order Details]
GROUP BY ProductID
) AS OD
ON OD.ProductID = P.ProductID

-- Using a Derived Table to produce a discounted price list

SELECT P.ProductID,
Discount * 100 AS Discount,
```

Listing 11.15: continued

```
P.UnitPrice * (1 - Discount) as Price
FROM Products P
CROSS JOIN (
SELECT 0.0 AS Discount
UNION ALL
SELECT 0.10
UNION ALL
SELECT 0.20
UNION ALL
SELECT 0.30
) AS OD
-- Partial result
```

OUTPUT

ProductID	UnitPrice	MediumPrice
23	9.0000	8.1000
46	12.0000	10.8000
69	36.0000	32.4000
77	13.0000	11.7000
31	12.5000	11.2500
15	15.5000	13.9500
62	49.3000	44.3500
38	263.5000	237.1500

```
-- Partial result
```

ProductID	Discount	Price
1	.00	18.000000
1	10.00	16.200000
1	20.00	14.400000
1	30.00	12.600000
2	.00	19.000000
2	10.00	17.100000
2	20.00	15.200000
2	30.00	13.300000

TIP

Derived tables are good candidates to be defined as views. After converted into views, some of them can be indexed, providing extra performance to your reporting queries. You can apply permissions to views but not to derived tables.

The CASE Function

You can use the CASE function to provide conditional values to an expression.

CAUTION

You cannot use the CASE function to provide conditional execution of statements as in other programming languages.

The result of a CASE function is always a scalar value. You can use CASE in two different ways:

- Select a result depending on the possible values that a variable, column, or expression can have. This is called Simple CASE. CASE returns the value correspondent to the first value that is equal to the searched expression. Listing 11.16 contains three examples using the CASE function to provide a verbose output.

- The CASE function evaluates in sequence several independent conditions. The CASE function returns the result correspondent to the first condition that evaluates to TRUE. This is called Searched CASE. Listing 11.17 shows three examples of Searched CASE.

EXAMPLE

Listing 11.16: Using Simple CASE Function to Provide an Easier-to-Understand Output

```
-- Use simple CASE to expand abbreviations

SELECT CASE Country
WHEN 'UK' THEN 'United Kingdom'
WHEN 'USA' THEN 'United States of America'
ELSE Country
END AS Country,
CompanyName
FROM Customers
ORDER BY 1, 2

-- Use simple CASE to define logical values

SELECT ProductName,
CASE Discontinued
WHEN 1 THEN 'Discontinued'
ELSE 'Available'
END AS Status
FROM Products

-- Use simple CASE to produce verbose results

SELECT CompanyName,
OrderID,
CASE YEAR(OrderDate)
WHEN YEAR(Getdate()) THEN 'This Year'
WHEN YEAR(GetDate()) - 1 THEN 'Last year'
ELSE CAST(DATEDIFF(year, OrderDate, Getdate()) AS varchar(5))
```

Listing 11.16: continued

```
+ ' years ago'
END AS 'When'
FROM Orders
JOIN Customers
ON Orders.CustomerID = Customers.CustomerID
```

(Partial output)

```
Country                 CompanyName
---------------------   ------------------------------------
United Kingdom          Around the Horn
United Kingdom          B's Beverages
United Kingdom          Seven Seas Imports
United States of America Great Lakes Food Market
United States of America Trail's Head Gourmet Provisioners
United States of America White Clover Markets
Venezuela               GROSELLA-Restaurante
Venezuela               LINO-Delicateses
```

OUTPUT

(Partial output)

```
ProductName                             Status
-------------------------------------   -----------
Gustaf's Knäckebröd                     Available
Singaporean Hokkien Fried Mee           Discontinued
Wimmers gute Semmelknödel               Available
```

(Partial output)

```
CompanyName                             OrderID     When
-------------------------------------   ----------  --------------
Furia Bacalhau e Frutos do Mar          10963       2 years ago
Furia Bacalhau e Frutos do Mar          10664       3 years ago
Furia Bacalhau e Frutos do Mar          10328       4 years ago
Princesa Isabel Vinhos                  11007       2 years ago
Princesa Isabel Vinhos                  10433       3 years ago
Princesa Isabel Vinhos                  10336       4 years ago
```

Listing 11.17: Using Searched CASE You Can Solve Complex Queries

```
-- Use searched CASE to define regions

SELECT CASE
WHEN Country IN ('Argentina', 'Brazil', 'Venezuela')
THEN 'South America'
WHEN Country IN ('Canada', 'USA')
THEN 'North America'
WHEN Country IN ('Mexico')
THEN 'Central America'
```

EXAMPLE

Listing 11.17: continued

```
WHEN Country IN ('Austria', 'Belgium', 'Denmark',
'Finland', 'France', 'Germany', 'Ireland', 'Italy',
'Norway', 'Poland','Portugal','Spain',
'Sweden', 'Switzerland', 'UK')
THEN 'Europe'
ELSE 'Undefined'
END AS Continent,
CompanyName
FROM Customers

-- Use searched CASE to define ranges of values

SELECT ProductName,
CASE
WHEN UnitPrice < 10 THEN 'Inexpensive'
WHEN UnitPrice < 50 THEN 'Fair'
WHEN UNitPrice < 100 THEN 'Expensive'
ELSE 'Very Expensive'
END AS Price
FROM products

-- Use searched CASE to get values that depend on data from other tables
-- in this example using a correlated subquery

SELECT CategoryName,
CASE
WHEN EXISTS (
SELECT *
FROM Products P
WHERE P.CategoryID = C.CategoryID)
THEN 'Yes' ELSE 'No' END AS 'Has products'
FROM Categories C
```

(Partial output)

OUTPUT

```
Continent       CompanyName
--------------  ----------------------------------------------
Europe          Around the Horn
Europe          Seven Seas Imports
North America   Great Lakes Food Market
North America   White Clover Markets
South America   GROSELLA-Restaurante
South America   LINO-Delicateses
```

(Partial output)

```
ProductName                                     Price
-----------------------------------------  -------------
```

Listing 11.17: continued

```
Gustaf's Knäckebröd                        Fair
Tunnbröd                                   Inexpensive
Singaporean Hokkien Fried Mee              Fair
Filo Mix                                   Inexpensive
Gnocchi di nonna Alice                     Fair

(Partial output)

CategoryName     Has products
..............   ...........
Beverages        Yes
Grains/Cereals   Yes
Meat/Poultry     No
Produce          Yes
Seafood          Yes
```

TIP

It is not necessary to create mutually exclusive conditions in a CASE function because the search will finish on the first condition that evaluates to true.

The COMPUTE Clause

In Chapter 4, you learned how to use aggregate functions to produce summary data. Queries using aggregate functions show only summary information by grouping data.

The Transact-SQL COMPUTE clause provides the capability to create reports that show detailed and summary information.

CAUTION

COMPUTE is not an ANSI standard feature.

To add summary information to any standard query, just add the COMPUTE clause at the end of the query, specifying which aggregate function to compute, as in Listing 11.18.

EXAMPLE

Listing 11.18: Use COMPUTE to Show Summary Information at the End of a Standard Query

```
-- This is a normal query to retrieve Price and Discount from Order details

SELECT OrderID,
ProductID,
(UnitPrice * Quantity * (1-Discount)) AS Price,
Discount
FROM [Order Details]
```

Listing 11.18: continued

```
-- This is the same query as before
-- but it shows the total of Price and the average discount

SELECT OrderID,
ProductID,
(UnitPrice * Quantity * (1-Discount)) AS Price,
Discount
FROM [Order Details]
COMPUTE SUM((UnitPrice * Quantity * (1-Discount))),
AVG(Discount)
```

With COMPUTE SUM and AVG (Partial results)

OUTPUT

OrderID	ProductID	Price	Discount
10250	41	77.0	0.0
10250	51	1261.4	0.15000001
10251	22	95.760002	5.0000001E-2
...			
11077	52	14.0	0.0
11077	60	63.919998	5.9999999E-2
11077	73	29.700001	9.9999998E-3
11077	77	26.0	0.0

```
                    sum
                    ============================
                    1265793.0396184921


                                             avg
                                             ============================
                                             5.6167054202260661E-2
```

As you saw previously in Listing 11.18, the output is not a result set. It is a report that can be sent to a printer, but it is difficult to use from a client application.

You can go one step further, because using the COMPUTE BY clause, you can show subtotals, as in Listing 11.19. In this case, you must use an ORDER BY clause in the query including, at least, the fields used in the COMPUTE BY clause, and in the same order.

EXAMPLE

Listing 11.19: Use COMPUTE BY to Show Subtotals at Different Levels

```
-- Retrieve Price and discount from Order details
-- plus Category, product and customer
-- and show the Price subtotal per Category

SELECT CategoryName AS Category,
ProductName AS Product,
```

Listing 11.19: continued

```
CompanyName AS Customer,
(OD.UnitPrice * Quantity * (1-Discount)) AS Price,
Discount
FROM [Order Details] OD
JOIN Orders O
ON O.OrderID = OD.OrderID
JOIN Products P
ON P.ProductID = OD.ProductID
JOIN Categories C
ON C.categoryID = P.CategoryID
JOIN Customers CS
ON CS.CustomerID = O.CustomerID
ORDER BY Category
COMPUTE SUM((OD.UnitPrice * Quantity * (1-Discount)))
BY Category

-- This is similar to the preceding query
-- but it shows the Average discount per Customer

SELECT CompanyName AS Customer,
(OD.UnitPrice * Quantity * (1-Discount)) AS Price,
Discount
FROM [Order Details] OD
JOIN Orders O
ON O.OrderID = OD.OrderID
JOIN Customers CS
ON CS.CustomerID = O.CustomerID
ORDER BY Customer
COMPUTE AVG(Discount)
BY Customer

-- This is a similar query as before
-- but it shows the Average discount per Category and Product
-- plus the overall average and grand total price

SELECT CategoryName AS Category,
ProductName AS Product,
(OD.UnitPrice * Quantity * (1-Discount)) AS Price,
Discount
FROM [Order Details] OD
JOIN Orders O
ON O.OrderID = OD.OrderID
JOIN Products P
ON P.ProductID = OD.ProductID
JOIN Categories C
ON C.categoryID = P.CategoryID
ORDER BY Category, Product
```

Listing 11.19: continued

```
COMPUTE AVG(Discount)
BY Category, Product
COMPUTE AVG(Discount)
BY Category
COMPUTE SUM((OD.UnitPrice * Quantity * (1-Discount)))
COMPUTE SUM(Price) BY Category (Partial results)
```

OUTPUT

Category	Product	Customer	Price	Discount
Beverages	Chartreuse verte	Alfreds Futterkiste	283.5	0.25
Beverages	Lakkalikööri	Alfreds Futterkiste	270.0	0.0
Beverages	Outback Lager	Ana Trujillo Emparedados	60.0	0.0
...				
Beverages	Steeleye Stout	Wolski Zajazd	54.0	0.0
Beverages	Guaraná Fantástica	Wolski Zajazd	54.0	0.0
Beverages	Rhönbräu Klosterbier	Wolski Zajazd	232.5	0.0

```
                                                 sum
                                                 ==================
                                                 267868.1805229187
```

Category	Product	Customer	Price	Discount
Condiments	Vegie-spread	Alfreds Futterkiste	878.0	0.0
Condiments	Aniseed Syrup	Alfreds Futterkiste	60.0	0.0
Condiments	Original Frankfurter	Alfreds Futterkiste	20.80	0.2
...				
Seafood	Inlagd Sill	White Clover Markets	665.0	0.0
Seafood	Boston Crab Meat	Wilman Kala	220.8	0.0
Seafood	Escargots de Bourgo	Wolski Zajazd	159.0	0.0

```
                                                 sum
                                                 ==================
                                                 131261.73742485046
```

Customer	Price	Discount
Alfreds Futterkiste	513.0	0.25
Alfreds Futterkiste	283.5	0.25
Alfreds Futterkiste	18.0	0.25
...		
Alfreds Futterkiste	503.5	5.0000001E-2
Alfreds Futterkiste	430.0	0.0

Listing 11.19: continued

```
                                             avg
                                             ====================
                                             0.08750000037252903


Customer                          Price    Discount
----------------------------      --------  --------
Ana Trujillo Emparedados y hel 28.799999  0.0
Ana Trujillo Emparedados y hel 60.0       0.0
...
Wolski  Zajazd                    232.5    0.0
Wolski  Zajazd                    591.59998 0.0

                                             avg
                                             ====================
                                             0.0
```

COMPUTE AVG(Discount) BY Category, product
and SUM(price) Grand Total   (Partial results)

```
Category     Product            Price    Discount
----------   ----------------   -------- -----------
Beverages    Chai               288.0    0.0
Beverages    Chai               144.0    0.0
Beverages    Chai               576.0    0.2
Beverages    Chai               72.0     0.2
...
Beverages    Chai               162.0    0.1
Beverages    Chai               337.5    0.25

                                             avg
                                             =====================
                                             7.7631580104169096E-2


Category     Product            Price    Discount
----------   ----------------   -------- -----------
Beverages    Chang              608.0    0.2
Beverages    Chang              304.0    0.2
...
Beverages    Steeleye Stout     360.0    0.0
Beverages    Steeleye Stout     54.0     0.0
Beverages    Steeleye Stout     720.0    0.0

                                             avg
                                             =====================
                                             4.7222223029368453E-2
```

Listing 11.19: continued

```
                                         avg
                                         ======================
                                         6.1881189077797501E-2


Category     Product            Price    Discount
..........   ................   ......   ..........
Condiments   Aniseed Syrup      400.0    0.0
Condiments   Aniseed Syrup      140.0    0.0
Condiments   Aniseed Syrup      60.0     0.0
...
Seafood      Spegesild          216.0    0.0
Seafood      Spegesild          252.0    0.0
Seafood      Spegesild          36.0     0.0


                                         avg
                                         ======================
                                         6.3703704625368118E-2


                                         avg
                                         ======================
                                         6.0242425080275899E-2


                              sum
                              ====================
                              1265793.0396184921

COMPUTE AVG(Discount) BY Customer (Partial results)
```

CAUTION

Avoid using COMPUTE and COMPUTE BY in client/server applications because they are difficult to manage from the client side. Every partial output in the report is a different recordset to the client application. COMPUTE is maintained only for backward compatibility.

TIP

To efficiently produce dynamic reports with summary information, take a look at SQL Server 2000 Analysis Services and Microsoft ActiveX Data Objects Multidimensional in Books Online.

The CUBE and ROLLUP Operators

To facilitate the use of summary information in client applications, SQL Server 2000 provides the ROLLUP and CUBE operators.

As you can see in Listing 11.20, using ROLLUP you can get aggregations at different levels in a single result set. Remember that using COMPUTE, you obtain a reportlike result set (see Listing 11.19).

Listing 11.20: Use ROLLUP to Produce a Result Set with Aggregations at Different Levels

```
SELECT CategoryName AS Category,
ProductName AS Product,
SUM((OD.UnitPrice * Quantity * (1-Discount))) AS Price,
AVG(Discount) AS AvgDiscount
FROM [Order Details] OD
JOIN Orders O
ON O.OrderID = OD.OrderID
JOIN Products P
ON P.ProductID = OD.ProductID
JOIN Categories C
ON C.categoryID = P.CategoryID
WHERE CategoryName LIKE 'C%'
GROUP BY CategoryName, ProductName
WITH ROLLUP
```

(Partial output)

Category	Product	Price	AvgDiscount
Condiments	Aniseed Syrup	3044.0	1.66666669150E-2
Condiments	Chef Anton's Cajun Seasoning	8567.89999389	7.50000009313E-2
...			
Condiments	Vegie-spread	16701.0950012	4.11764712018E-2
Condiments	NULL	106047.084989	5.26388897733E-2
Confections	Chocolade	1368.71252441	0.108333336810
Confections	Gumbär Gummibärchen	19849.1445426	0.051562501117
...			
Confections	Valkoinen suklaa	3437.6875	0.025000000372
Confections	Zaanse koeken	3958.07998657	7.38095243771E-2
Confections	NULL	167357.224831	5.69461086474E-2
NULL	NULL	273404.309821	5.52545463259E-2

Listing 11.20 shows a normal aggregate output, such as using GROUP BY, but you see three more rows than usual:

Category	Product	Price	AvgDiscount
Condiments	NULL	106047.084989	5.26388897733E-2
Confections	NULL	167357.224831	5.69461086474E-2
NULL	NULL	273404.309821	5.52545463259E-2

The first two rows have a NULL in Product, which means they have the aggregates for categories "Condiments" and "Confections". The last row has a NULL in both Category and Product because it shows the Total SUM and AVG for this result set.

Looking at the output from Listing 11.20, you don't see any subtotals per product because the subtotals are evaluated from left to right in the GROUP BY clause. If the GROUP BY clause has four fields, using ROLLUP you will have totals at four levels, including the grand total.

TIP

ROLLUP is usually more efficient than COMPUTE BY.

Use the CUBE operator to obtain every combination of totals (see Listing 11.21).

EXAMPLE

Listing 11.21: Use CUBE to Produce a Result Set with Aggregations at Every Combination of Levels

```
SELECT CategoryName AS Category,
ProductName AS Product,
SUM((OD.UnitPrice * Quantity * (1-Discount))) AS Price,
AVG(Discount) AS AvgDiscount
FROM [Order Details] OD
JOIN Orders O
ON O.OrderID = OD.OrderID
JOIN Products P
ON P.ProductID = OD.ProductID
JOIN Categories C
ON C.categoryID = P.CategoryID
WHERE CategoryName LIKE 'C%'
GROUP BY CategoryName, ProductName
WITH CUBE
```

OUTPUT

(Partial output)

Category	Product	Price	AvgDiscount
Condiments	Aniseed Syrup	3044.0	1.66666669150E-2
Condiments	Chef Anton's Gumbo Mix	5347.20000457	7.50000007450E-2
...			
Condiments	Sirop d'érable	14352.6001586	7.08333346992E-2
Condiments	Vegie-spread	16701.0950012	4.11764712018E-2
Condiments	NULL	106047.084989	5.26388897733E-2
Confections	Chocolade	1368.71252441	0.108333336810
Confections	Gumbär Gummibärchen	19849.1445426	0.051562501117
...			
Confections	Teatime Chocolate Biscuits	5862.61998462	5.54054060296E-2
Confections	Zaanse koeken	3958.07998657	7.38095243771E-2
Confections	NULL	167357.224831	5.69461086474E-2
NULL	NULL	273404.309821	5.52545463259E-2
NULL	Aniseed Syrup	3044.0	1.66666669150E-2
...			
NULL	Vegie-spread	16701.0950012	4.11764712018E-2
NULL	Zaanse koeken	3958.07998657	7.38095243771E-2

As you see in the preceding output, there are many rows where Category is NULL. Each one of these rows represents subtotals per Product. The rest of the output is identical to the Listing 11.20 output.

If the GROUP BY clause has 4 fields, using ROLLUP you will have totals at 15 levels: 4 single-field levels, 6 double-field levels, 4 triple-field levels, and one grand total level.

Checking for NULL values in a client application to detect summary data can be inaccurate if the field contained in the GROUP BY clause contain NULL values. SQL Server provides the function GROUPING to detect aggregate rows. GROUPING(Column1) returns 1 if the row shows aggregations for Column1. The example in Listing 11.22 adds two new columns, GrpCat and GrpProd, using the GROUPING function, to specify which values are subtotals produced by the CUBE operator.

EXAMPLE

Listing 11.22: Use the GROUPING Function to Detect Aggregate Rows

```
SELECT CategoryName AS Category,
GROUPING(CategoryName) AS GrpCat,
ProductName AS Product,
GROUPING(ProductName) AS GrpProd,
AVG(Discount) AS AvgDiscount
FROM [Order Details] OD
JOIN Orders O
ON O.OrderID = OD.OrderID
JOIN Products P
ON P.ProductID = OD.ProductID
JOIN Categories C
ON C.categoryID = P.CategoryID
WHERE CategoryName LIKE 'C%'
GROUP BY CategoryName, ProductName
WITH CUBE
```

OUTPUT

(Partial output)

Category	GrpCat	Product	GrpProd	AvgDiscount
Condiments	0	Aniseed Syrup	0	1.66666669150E-2
Condiments	0	Chef Anton's Cajun Seasoning	0	7.50000009313E-2
...				
Condiments	0	Sirop d'érable	0	7.08333346992E-2
Condiments	0	Vegie-spread	0	4.11764712018E-2
Condiments	0	NULL	1	5.26388897733E-2
Confections	0	Chocolade	0	0.108333336810
Confections	0	Gumbär Gummibärchen	0	0.051562501117
...				
Confections	0	Valkoinen suklaa	0	0.025000000372
Confections	0	Zaanse koeken	0	7.38095243771E-2
Confections	0	NULL	1	5.69461086474E-2

Listing 11.22: continued

NULL	1	NULL	1	5.52545463259E-2
NULL	1	Aniseed Syrup	0	1.66666669150E-2
NULL	1	Chef Anton's Cajun Seasoning	0	7.50000009313E-2
...				
NULL	1	Vegie-spread	0	4.11764712018E-2
NULL	1	Zaanse koeken	0	7.38095243771E-2

TIP

In a client application, you can hide the GROUPING columns because they make sense only to the programmer, not to the user.

Using Hints

In some cases, you might think that there is a better way to execute your queries than the query plan selected by the Query Optimizer. SQL Server 2000 provides several optimizer hints to tailor the execution to your needs.

You can specify the type of join to execute by using the LOOP, HASH, MERGE, or REMOTE hints of the JOIN clause. The query in Listing 11.23 forces a LOOP join to connect the Orders and Order Details tables, a MERGE join between the Products and Order Details table, and a HASH join to connect the Categories and Products tables. The purpose of this example is to show how to use the optimizer hints; the output is the same you can have without using these optimizer hints.

NOTE

Joins were covered in Chapter 5. The REMOTE hint allows you to select which server will execute the join when joining tables from different servers.

EXAMPLE

Listing 11.23: Use JOIN Optimizer Hints to Force One Specific Join Type

```
-- Force LOOP JOIN for the first JOIN,
-- MERGE JOIN for the second JOIN,
-- and HASH JOIN for the third JOIN

SELECT CategoryName,
ProductName,
OrderDate,
Quantity
FROM [Order Details] OD
INNER LOOP JOIN Orders O
ON O.OrderID = OD.OrderID
INNER MERGE JOIN Products P
ON P.ProductID = OD.ProductID
INNER HASH JOIN Categories C
ON C.CategoryID = P.CategoryID
```

Listing 11.23: continued

```
WHERE OrderDate
BETWEEN '1997-01-01'
AND '1997-03-31'
```

SQL Server selects automatically the order of joins, but you can specify a join order by using the FORCE ORDER optimizer hint.

You can control how to group data by using the HASH and ORDER hints of the GROUP BY or COMPUTE clause.

To select how to execute the UNION operator, you can select the MERGE, HASH, or CONCAT hints.

To create a query plan that will execute efficiently with a bigger number of rows that will allow for rapid growth, you can use the ROBUST PLAN optimizer hint.

The user usually perceives speed as how fast the server retrieves the first set of rows. SQL Server tries to optimize the query as a complete set, and this can produce slow perceived speed. You can use the FAST n to speed up the retrieval of the first n rows.

CAUTION

You should not use the FASTFIRSTROW optimizer hint because it is maintained only for backward compatibility. Use FAST 1 instead.

TIP

Use the FAST n optimizer hint, as in Listing 11.24, for gridlike client applications, and FAST 1 for single-record, form-based client applications.

EXAMPLE

Listing 11.24: Use the FAST Optimizer Hint to Improve the Response Time of Your Client Applications

```
-- Speed up the retrieval of the first 10 rows

SELECT ProductName,
OrderDate,
Quantity
FROM [Order Details] OD
INNER JOIN Orders O
ON O.OrderID = OD.OrderID
INNER JOIN Products P
ON P.ProductID = OD.ProductID
WHERE OrderDate
BETWEEN '1997-01-01'
AND '1997-03-31'
OPTION (FAST 10)
```

Query Optimizer selects the best indexes to use to execute the query efficiently, based on available statistics. In some cases, you can find a better query plan than Query Optimizer. In these cases, you can force the use of specific indexes by using the INDEX optimizer hint for every table (see Listing 11.25).

EXAMPLE

Listing 11.25: Use the INDEX Optimizer Hint to Force the Selection of Specific Indexes

```
-- This query uses a Clustered Index Scan (Table scan)

SELECT DISTINCT CustomerID,
OrderDate
FROM Orders
WHERE OrderDate
BETWEEN '1997-01-01'
AND '1997-03-31'

-- This query uses an Index Seek
-- On the OrderDate index

SELECT DISTINCT CustomerID,
OrderDate
FROM Orders (Index (OrderDate))
WHERE OrderDate
BETWEEN '1997-01-01'
AND '1997-03-31'
```

CAUTION

You can use the optimizer hint (INDEX (index1, index2, ...)) to force using a specific index. The (INDEX = index1) syntax is maintained for backward compatibility.

SQL Server selects automatically the correct locking strategy for every query. In some cases, you might have specific locking needs. For these cases, you can specify lock-optimizer hints, such as HOLDLOCK, SERIALIZABLE, PAGLOCK, UPDLOCK, and XLOCK. Locks will be covered in Chapter 13, "Maintaining Data Consistency: Transactions and Locks."

CAUTION

Always document the reasons for using an optimizer hint and test these reasons from time to time because, as volume of data increases, they might be invalid.

NOTE

We want to finish this chapter with a familiar note: Keep it simple.

Write your queries having performance and maintenance in your mind. Complex queries are difficult to optimize and difficult to maintain.

Query Optimizer usually does an excellent job. Use optimizer hints only when necessary, and document your reasons.

What's Next?

In this chapter, you learned the use of advanced query structures.

In Chapter 12, "Row-Oriented Processing: Using Cursors," you will learn how to use cursors to solve complex programming needs.

Chapter 13 covers transactions and locks. Understanding them provides the basis to improve concurrency in your database.

Working in a heterogeneous environment is a common scenario for a database programmer. Chapter 14, "Transferring Data to and from SQL Server," shows how to transfer data from different databases, and Chapter 15, "Working with Heterogeneous Environments: Setting Up Linked Servers," introduces the concept of distributed data by using linked servers.

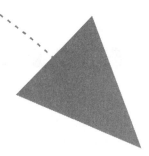

Row-Oriented Processing: Using Cursors

In previous chapters you learned how SQL Server processes complete result sets. SQL Server is optimized to work with operations that affect complete result sets, and Query Optimizer decides in which order to process the rows to get the job done in the most efficient way.

In some cases, you would be required to process individual rows from a result set in a specific order and, in these cases, you can use cursors. SQL Server supports Transact-SQL cursors and application cursors.

This chapter teaches you

- The differences between set- and row-oriented processing

- The type of cursors and when to use them

- How to implement Transact-SQL cursors

- The scope of cursors

- How to use cursor variables

- How to use cursors inside triggers to apply row-by-row processing in a multirow operation

- How to use application cursors

Row-by-Row Versus Set-Oriented Processing

You can apply a specific business process to a group of rows, in two completely different ways:

- Navigate the result set in the way you prefer, and apply the business process to every row individually, sending one or more Transact-SQL statements to SQL Server for every row.

- Send to SQL Server a single Transact-SQL statement that describes how to apply the business process to the entire result set, and let SQL Server decide how to apply it, in the optimal way.

I'll explain the difference between these two ways with a practical example.

Consider it is the end of the year and you want to increase product prices by 5%. The manual process will involve modifying each product's UnitPrice. The automatic process cannot be much different from this, because the final result must be new UnitPrice values 5% more expensive than before.

If you think about how to do this operation from a client application, such as Visual Basic, you could write a loop to retrieve one product at a time and modify its UnitPrice. Listing 12.1 shows how to use the ActiveX Data Object (ADO) library to access SQL Server and apply these changes row by row.

EXAMPLE

Listing 12.1: Access to SQL Server Row by Row from Visual Basic and ADO

```
Dim conNorthwind As ADODB.Connection
Dim rstProducts As ADODB.Recordset

Set conNorthwind = New ADODB.Connection

conNorthwind.Provider = "SQLOLEDB"

conNorthwind.Open "Server=MSSQLFGG\s2k;UID=sa;PWD=;Database=Northwind;"

Set rstProducts = New ADODB.Recordset

rstProducts.Open "select ProductID, UnitPrice FROM Products", _
conNorthwind, adOpenForwardOnly, adLockPessimistic

On Error GoTo CancelChanges

conNorthwind.BeginTrans

While Not rstProducts.EOF
rstProducts.Fields("UnitPrice").Value = _
rstProducts.Fields("UnitPrice").Value * 1.05
```

Listing 12.1: continued

```
rstProducts.Update

rstProducts.MoveNext
Wend

conNorthwind.CommitTrans

GoTo CloseObjects

CancelChanges:
conNorthwind.RollbackTrans

CloseObjects:

rstProducts.Close
conNorthwind.Close

Set rstProducts = Nothing
Set conNorthwind = Nothing
```

However, SQL Server can achieve this operation with a single UPDATE statement, as in Listing 12.2.

Listing 12.2: Convert a Cursor Operation into a Single Transact-SQL Statement

```
. . . . . . . . . . . . . . . . . . . . . .
-- From Query Analyzer
. . . . . . . . . . . . . . . . . . . . . .

UPDATE Products
SET UnitPrice = UnitPrice * 1.05


. . . . . . . . . . . . . . . . . . . . . .
-- From Visual Basic
. . . . . . . . . . . . . . . . . . . . . .

Dim conNorthwind As ADODB.Connection

Set conNorthwind = New ADODB.Connection

conNorthwind.Provider = "SQLOLEDB"

conNorthwind.Open "Server=MSSQLFGG\s2k;UID=sa;PWD=;Database=Northwind;"

conNorthwind.Execute "UPDATE Products SET UnitPrice = UnitPrice * 1.05"

conNorthwind.Close

Set conNorthwind = Nothing
```

Using Profiler, you can inspect which statements are sent to SQL Server by the Visual Basic client application. In Listing 12.1, you can see the output from Listing 12.3 (the output has been simplified to avoid repetitive lines).

OUTPUT

Listing 12.3: Execution Trace of the Visual Basic Example from Listing 12.1

```
TraceStart
SQL:StmtCompleted      select ProductID, UnitPrice FROM Products      61
RPC:Completed      declare @P1 int
set @P1=180150000
declare @P2 int
set @P2=2
declare @P3 int
set @P3=2
declare @P4 int
set @P4=-1
exec sp_cursoropen @P1 output, N'select ProductID, UnitPrice FROM Products',
➥@P2 output, @P3 output, @P4 output
select @P1, @P2, @P3, @P4      61
SQL:StmtCompleted      set implicit_transactions on      61
RPC:Completed      exec sp_cursorfetch 180150000, 32, 1, 1      61
SQL:StmtCompleted      UPDATE [Products] SET [UnitPrice]=@Param000004      61
RPC:Completed      exec sp_cursor 180150000, 33, 1, N'Products',
➥@UnitPrice = $19.8450      61
RPC:Completed      exec sp_cursorfetch 180150000, 32, 1, 1      61
SQL:StmtCompleted      UPDATE [Products] SET [UnitPrice]=@Param000004      61
RPC:Completed      exec sp_cursor 180150000, 33, 1, N'Products',
➥@UnitPrice = $20.9475      61
RPC:Completed      exec sp_cursorfetch 180150000, 32, 1, 1      61
SQL:StmtCompleted      UPDATE [Products] SET [UnitPrice]=@Param000004      61
... (output truncated here)
RPC:Completed      exec sp_cursor 180150000, 33, 1, N'Products',
➥@UnitPrice = $8.5444      61
RPC:Completed      exec sp_cursorfetch 180150000, 32, 1, 1      61
SQL:StmtCompleted      UPDATE [Products] SET [UnitPrice]=@Param000004      61
RPC:Completed      exec sp_cursor 180150000, 33, 1, N'Products',
➥@UnitPrice = $19.8450      61
RPC:Completed      exec sp_cursorfetch 180150000, 32, 1, 1      61
SQL:StmtCompleted      UPDATE [Products] SET [UnitPrice]=@Param000004      61
RPC:Completed      exec sp_cursor 180150000, 33, 1, N'Products',
➥@UnitPrice = $14.3325      61
RPC:Completed      exec sp_cursorfetch 180150000, 32, 1, 1      61
RPC:Completed      exec sp_cursorclose 180150000      61
SQL:StmtCompleted      IF @@TRANCOUNT > 0      61
SQL:StmtCompleted      COMMIT TRAN      61
SQL:StmtCompleted      61
TraceStop
```

However, as you can see in Listing 12.4, the trace produced by the example of Listing 12.2 is much simpler.

OUTPUT

Listing 12.4: Execution Trace of the Example from Listing 12.2

```
TraceStart
SQL:StmtCompleted    UPDATE Products SET UnitPrice = UnitPrice / 1.05    61
TraceStop
```

The difference between the outputs in Listing 12.3 and Listing 12.4 has a tremendous importance in terms of network traffic and server overhead. As you can imagine, sending one UPDATE statement plus two calls to stored procedures for every product cannot be as efficient as sending a single UPDATE statement for the complete list of products.

You can create a Transact-SQL script that works in a similar way as the Visual Basic application in Listing 12.1. Listing 12.5 shows an example of how to convert the Visual Basic program into a Transact-SQL script using cursors.

NOTE

Later in this chapter, you will learn the meaning of the statements used in Listing 12.5. The intention of this example is only to show the similarities between Transact-SQL cursors and Application cursors.

EXAMPLE

Listing 12.5: Using Transact-SQL Cursors to Apply Row-by-Row Changes

```
-- Declare host variables

DECLARE @ID int, @UnitPrice money

-- Declare the cursor

DECLARE MyProducts CURSOR LOCAL
FORWARD_ONLY
FOR
SELECT ProductID, UnitPrice
FROM Products

-- Open the cursor

OPEN MyProducts

-- Fetch the first row in the cursor

FETCH NEXT FROM MyProducts
INTO @ID, @UnitPrice
```

Listing 12.5: continued

```
WHILE @@FETCH_STATUS = 0

-- While the fetch is successful

BEGIN

-- Update the current product

UPDATE Products
SET UnitPrice = @UnitPrice * 1.05
WHERE CURRENT OF MyProducts

-- Fetch next product

FETCH NEXT FROM MyProducts
INTO @ID, @UnitPrice

END

-- Close the cursor

CLOSE MyProducts

-- Deallocate the cursor

DEALLOCATE MyProducts
```

Listing 12.6 shows the execution trace of the example in Listing 12.5. You can see that the trace in Listing 12.6 is structurally similar to the output from Listing 12.3. Note that the trace has been truncated to avoid too many repetitions.

OUTPUT

Listing 12.6: Execution Trace of Listing 12.5 (Simplified)

```
TraceStart
SQL:StmtCompleted    SELECT ProductID, UnitPrice FROM Products    52
SQL:StmtCompleted    OPEN MyProducts    52
SQL:StmtCompleted    FETCH NEXT FROM MyProducts INTO @ID, @UnitPrice    52
SQL:StmtCompleted    WHILE @@FETCH_STATUS = 0    52
SQL:StmtCompleted    UPDATE Products SET UnitPrice = @UnitPrice * 1.05
➥WHERE CURRENT OF MyProducts    52
SQL:StmtCompleted    FETCH NEXT FROM MyProducts INTO @ID, @UnitPrice    52
SQL:StmtCompleted            52
SQL:StmtCompleted    WHILE @@FETCH_STATUS = 0    52
SQL:StmtCompleted    UPDATE Products SET UnitPrice = @UnitPrice * 1.05
➥WHERE CURRENT OF MyProducts    52
SQL:StmtCompleted    FETCH NEXT FROM MyProducts INTO @ID, @UnitPrice    52
SQL:StmtCompleted            52
```

Listing 12.6: continued

```
... (Trace truncated)
SQL:StmtCompleted    WHILE @@FETCH_STATUS = 0    52
SQL:StmtCompleted    UPDATE Products SET UnitPrice = @UnitPrice * 1.05
➥WHERE CURRENT OF MyProducts    52
SQL:StmtCompleted    FETCH NEXT FROM MyProducts INTO @ID, @UnitPrice    52
SQL:StmtCompleted        52
SQL:StmtCompleted    WHILE @@FETCH_STATUS = 0    52
SQL:StmtCompleted    UPDATE Products SET UnitPrice = @UnitPrice * 1.05
➥WHERE CURRENT OF MyProducts    52
SQL:StmtCompleted    FETCH NEXT FROM MyProducts INTO @ID, @UnitPrice    52
SQL:StmtCompleted        52
SQL:StmtCompleted    WHILE @@FETCH_STATUS = 0    52
SQL:StmtCompleted    CLOSE MyProducts    52
SQL:StmtCompleted    DEALLOCATE MyProducts    52
TraceStop
```

It is obvious that SQL Server has to modify the UnitPrice column individually, regardless of the method used to send the UPDATE. However, if you do not use cursors, Query Optimizer can find the best strategy to modify this value without any constraints imposed by the way you navigate the cursor.

For example, if you want to retrieve information about orders placed by customers in the USA, and for every order you want to retrieve the order date and the name of the customer, you can do it in the following way:

1. Open a cursor in the Customers table.

2. Navigate the Customer cursor row by row, searching for customers in the USA.

3. For every customer in the USA, open a cursor in the Orders table for orders from this specific customer only.

4. Navigate the Orders cursor to show every order date.

5. After the last order of the current customer has been retrieved, you can go to the next customer and start with step 2.

Perhaps this strategy looks similar to a loop join—actually, SQL Server follows a similar process to execute loop joins. You can avoid using cursors to solve this problem by sending a simple query to SQL Server joining the Customers and Orders tables. If you send a standard join, Query Optimizer will have the final decision about which type of join is more appropriate to solve this particular query.

Listing 12.7 provides two examples on how to solve this problem using Transact-SQL language. The first example does not use cursors, and the second example does.

EXAMPLE

Listing 12.7: Solving a Business Problem With and Without Cursors

```
-----------------
-- Without cursors
-----------------

SELECT CompanyName, OrderDate
FROM Customers
JOIN Orders
ON Customers.CustomerID = Orders.CustomerID
WHERE Country = 'USA'
ORDER BY CompanyName, OrderDate


---------------
-- Using cursors
---------------


-- Declare host variables

DECLARE @ID nchar(5), @Name nvarchar(40),
@Country nvarchar(15), @OrderDate datetime

-- Declare products cursor

DECLARE MyCustomers CURSOR LOCAL
FOR
SELECT CustomerID, CompanyName, Country
FROM Customers

-- Open Customers Cursor

OPEN MyCustomers

-- Search for first customer

FETCH NEXT FROM MyCustomers
INTO @ID, @Name, @Country

WHILE @@FETCH_STATUS=0
BEGIN

IF @Country = 'USA'
BEGIN
```

Listing 12.7: continued

```
-- Declare Orders cursor

DECLARE MyOrders CURSOR LOCAL
FOR
SELECT OrderDate
FROM Orders
WHERE CustomerID = @ID

-- Open Orders cursor

OPEN MyOrders

-- Search for first Order

FETCH NEXT FROM MyOrders
INTO @OrderDate

WHILE @@FETCH_STATUS=0
BEGIN

SELECT @Name AS 'Company Name',
@OrderDate AS 'Order Date'

-- Search for next Order

FETCH NEXT FROM MyOrders
INTO @OrderDate

END

-- Close Orders cursor

CLOSE MyOrders

--Deallocate Orders cursor

DEALLOCATE MyOrders

END

-- Search for next Customer

FETCH NEXT FROM MyCustomers
INTO @ID, @Name, @Country

END
```

Listing 12.7: continued

```
-- Close Customers cursor

CLOSE MyCustomers

-- Deallocate Customers cursor

DEALLOCATE MyCustomers
```

TIP

Use cursors as a last resort. First, consider whether you can achieve the same results without using cursors.

To work with user-defined cursors, SQL Server must maintain specific memory structures and execute complex operations not required in standard, cursorless operations. In other words, using cursors is expensive for SQL Server. However, cursors are necessary to solve especially complex problems where result set operations cannot provide an easy solution. Later in this chapter, you will see an example of how to use cursors inside triggers to solve multirow operations, in which case, using cursors might be the only available choice.

Types of Cursors

SQL Server 2000 supports four types of cursors:

- *Forward-only* cursors can retrieve data from the first to the last row, without any other navigation capabilities.

- *Static* cursors provide a snapshot of the data to navigate without being affected by other connections.

- *Dynamic* cursors retrieve a dynamic result set that sees modifications to the data made from outside the cursor.

- *Keyset-driven* cursors create a fixed set of rows to navigate.

Static cursors use more storage space than dynamic or keyset-driven, but SQL Server uses fewer resources to navigate the data after their creation. Static cursors provide a fixed set of data that does not detect changes made by other connections.

Dynamic cursors use little storage space, but SQL Server uses more resources to navigate the data after their creation than static or keyset-driven cursors. Dynamic cursors provide a flexible set of data that reflects changes made to the data by other connections.

Keyset-driven cursors balance storage space requirements with navigation resources. Keyset-driven cursors provide a set of data with a fixed number of rows that reflects changes made by other connections.

Transact-SQL does not consider forward-only as a different kind of cursor, but as an optional property of the other types of cursors.

Forward-Only

A forward-only cursor does not provide the option to scroll through the data. Using this type of cursor, you can retrieve rows from the beginning of the result set to the end only.

Rows are not retrieved until they are requested by using the FETCH statement. For this reason, using this cursor type, you can see changes made to the data by any connection to data that is not yet retrieved. Changes to the data already retrieved cannot be seen because this cursor does not support scrolling backward.

By default, static, dynamic, and keyset-driven cursors are scrollable, unless you specify the FORWARD_ONLY keyword in the DECLARE CURSOR statement. Later in this chapter, you will learn about the syntax of the DECLARE CURSOR statement.

Microsoft provides an improvement to the forward-only cursors with the fast forward-only cursor. This option opens an optimized read-only forward-only cursor. To use this optimization, you must specify the FAST_FORWARD in the DECLARE CURSOR statement.

In some cases, it is not valid to create a fast forward-only cursor, and SQL Server must convert the cursor to the appropriate type. The following are some of these cases:

- The SELECT statement references BLOB columns, such as columns with text, ntext, or image data types.

- The cursor is not open as read-only.

- The query references remote tables from linked servers.

TIP

If you have to use a cursor, try to use a fast forward-only cursor, because it uses fewer resources in the server, providing a faster and more efficient operation.

Static

A static cursor provides a snapshot of the query. SQL Server builds the complete result set in TempDB when the cursor is open, and remains there untouched until the cursor is closed. Because the information is selected when the cursor is open, changes from other statements are not visible when you navigate the cursor. The creation of the worktable takes not only storage space, but some time as well, providing a slower start to the application that uses it.

NOTE

After the static cursor is populated, it contains a fixed number of rows with fixed column values until the cursor is closed.

When searching for rows, the cursor retrieves its information exclusively from the worktable created in `TempDB`. This is why static cursors provide fast data navigation.

The cursor does not detect the insertion of new rows, the deletion of existing ones, or changes to column values, unless you close the cursor and reopen it again.

If you create a static cursor on customers from London and retrieve 10 customers, you can navigate the rows returned from that cursor, and you will always retrieve the same values for the same 10 customers—regardless of any changes made to these customers from other statements in the same connection or different connections. Listing 12.8 shows the effect of changes in data used in a static cursor. Where the output does not show the change on `ProductName`, it still shows the row where `ProductID = 75`, after its deletion by a `DELETE` statement, and it does not show the new inserted row.

EXAMPLE

Listing 12.8: You Have an Isolated Result Set Using a Static Cursor

```
USE Northwind
GO

-- Start a new transaction
-- so we can rollback the changes

BEGIN TRAN

DECLARE @ID int, @name nvarchar(40)

-- Declare the cursor

DECLARE MyProducts CURSOR STATIC
FOR
SELECT ProductID, ProductName
FROM Products
WHERE ProductID > 70
ORDER BY ProductID
```

Listing 12.8: continued

```
-- Open the cursor

OPEN MyProducts

-- Search for a new row from the cursor

FETCH NEXT FROM MyProducts
INTO @ID, @name

-- Update directly the Products table

UPDATE Products
SET ProductName = 'NewName'
WHERE ProductID > 70

-- Delete one row from the Products table

DELETE [Order details]
WHERE ProductID = 75

DELETE Products
WHERE ProductID = 75

-- Add a new row to the Products table

INSERT Products (ProductName)
VALUES ('New Product')

-- While the fetch is successful

WHILE @@FETCH_STATUS <> -1
BEGIN

IF @@FETCH_STATUS = -2
-- Row has been deleted
PRINT CHAR(10) + 'Missing Row' + CHAR(10)
ELSE
-- Show the values from the cursor
SELECT @ID, @Name

-- Search for the new row

FETCH NEXT FROM MyProducts
INTO @ID, @Name
END
```

Listing 12.8: continued

```
-- Close the cursor

CLOSE MyProducts

-- Destroy the cursor

DEALLOCATE MyProducts

-- Undo changes

ROLLBACK TRAN
```

OUTPUT

```
---------- -----------------------------------------
71         Flotemysost


---------- -----------------------------------------
72         Mozzarella di Giovanni


---------- -----------------------------------------
73         Röd Kaviar


---------- -----------------------------------------
74         Longlife Tofu


---------- -----------------------------------------
75         Rhönbräu Klosterbier


---------- -----------------------------------------
76         Lakkalikööri


---------- -----------------------------------------
77         Original Frankfurter grüne Soße
```

NOTE

Later in this chapter, you will see, step by step, how to use cursors, covering the statements contained in Listing 12.8.

NOTE

Static cursors are read-only in SQL Server.

NOTE

In some documentation, you can find the term *snapshot* or *insensitive* applied to the same concept as static cursor.

CAUTION

Because the result of a static cursor must be stored in a worktable in TempDB, the total size of the columns selected in the cursor cannot exceed the maximum number of bytes in a standard row.

If your application makes extensive use of static cursors, make sure you have enough free space on TempDB.

Dynamic

A dynamic cursor reflects all the changes made by other connections. This type of cursor does not create a table in TempDB. Because this cursor does not require creating any temporary data in TempDB, it opens faster and uses less storage space than static cursors.

NOTE

After the dynamic cursor is opened, it contains an undefined number of rows with potentially changing column values until the cursor is closed.

Every time you need to fetch a new row, SQL Server must execute the required query plan to select the new row, and that operation takes some time, providing a slower navigation than static cursors.

Any changes to existing data, either by inserting new rows, deleting existing ones, or changing values in columns will be reflected in this type of cursor. Listing 12.9 shows how the dynamic cursor is affected by changes in the underlying data, where the output

- Shows the change on ProductName

- Hides the deleted row where ProductID = 75

- Shows the newly inserted row where ProductName = 'NewProduct'

EXAMPLE

Listing 12.9: Using Dynamic Cursors to See Changes from Other Connections—Same As Listing 12.8 Except

```
-- Declare the cursor

DECLARE MyProducts CURSOR DYNAMIC
FOR
SELECT ProductID, ProductName
FROM Products
WHERE ProductID > 70
ORDER BY ProductID
```

OUTPUT

```
71          Flotemysost
```

```
72          NewName
```

```
73          NewName
```

```
74          NewName
```

```
76          NewName
```

```
77          NewName
```

```
88          New Product
```

Changes to the data made in the same connection are always visible to the dynamic cursor. However, changes made by other connections are not visible until the transactions that modified the data are committed, unless you specify a Read Uncommitted isolation level for the transaction holding the cursor.

Keyset-Driven Cursors

To solve some of the problems of both static and dynamic cursors, you can create a keyset-driven cursor. This type of cursor creates in `TempDB` a list of unique values, called the keyset, from the original query, where every key uniquely identifies one single row in the result set. This keyset contains bookmarks to the actual data.

Because the keyset is completely built when the cursor is open, the number of rows is fixed until the cursor is closed. However, if some rows are deleted from the underlying tables, you will get a "row missing" message trying to fetch them, because the bookmarks of these cursor rows will point to an invalid location.

Rows inserted in the data that could be considered part of the cursor result set are not visible unless you close the cursor and reopen it again. Changes to column values made by any connections are visible inside the cursor, as long as the modified columns are not part of the keyset.

Listing 12.10 shows the same script as in Listing 12.8 and 12.9, but in this case the cursor is declared as KEYSET. As you can see in Listing 12.10, the output

- Shows the change on ProductName

- Produces an error message for the deleted row where ProductID = 75

- Does not show the newly inserted row where ProductName = 'NewProduct'

EXAMPLE

Listing 12.10: Using Keyset Cursors—Same As Listing 12.8 Except

```
-- Declare the cursor

DECLARE MyProducts CURSOR KEYSET
FOR
SELECT ProductID, ProductName
FROM Products
WHERE ProductID > 70
ORDER BY ProductID
```

OUTPUT

```
----------- ----------------------------------------
71          Flotemysost


----------- ----------------------------------------
72          NewName


----------- ----------------------------------------
73          NewName


----------- ----------------------------------------
74          NewName


Missing Row


----------- ----------------------------------------
76          NewName
```

Listing 12.10: continued

```
...........  ......................................
77          NewName
```

Steps to Use Cursors

As shown in Listing 12.8, to use a cursor you must follow this sequence:

1. Use the DECLARE statement to declare the cursor. This step specifies the type of cursor and the query that defines the data to retrieve. SQL Server creates the memory structures that support the cursor. No data is retrieved yet.

2. Execute the OPEN statement to open the cursor. In this step, SQL Server executes the query specified in the cursor definition and prepares the data for further navigation.

3. Execute the FETCH statement to search for rows. In this step, you move the cursor pointer to the required row and, optionally, retrieve column values into variables. Repeat this step as many times as necessary to complete the required task. Optionally, you can modify data through the cursor, unless the cursor is read-only.

4. Execute the CLOSE statement to close the cursor when the data contained is no longer necessary. The cursor is still created, but it does not contain any data. To retrieve the data again, you must execute the OPEN statement to open the cursor again.

5. Execute the DEALLOCATE statement to drop the cursor when you don't have intentions of reusing the cursor any longer.

The following sections look at these steps in more detail.

Declaring Cursors

To declare a cursor, you must use the DECLARE CURSOR statement. A simplified syntax of the DECLARE CURSOR statement could be

```
DECLARE CursorName CURSOR
[CursorScope]
[CursorBehavior]
[CursorType]
[CursorLock]
[TYPE_WARNING]
FOR SelectStatement
[UpdateOfColumns]
```

NOTE

SQL Server 2000 accepts the SQL-92 DECLARE CURSOR syntax as well.

Every cursor must have a name, and this name is a Transact-SQL identifier that must follow the same guidelines as for other object identifiers.

After the cursor name, you can specify whether the cursor is GLOBAL to the connection or LOCAL to the batch, stored procedure, trigger, or user-defined function where the cursor is created. Cursor scope is covered in more detail later in this chapter.

You can control cursor behavior by using two keywords: FORWARD_ONLY or SCROLL (see Listings 12.11 and 12.12). The default cursor behavior is FORWARD_ONLY, which means that the cursor can move only forward, using the FETCH NEXT statement, row by row to the end of the result set.

EXAMPLE

Listing 12.11: Using the FORWARD_ONLY Keyword

```
-- This is a LOCAL FORWARD_ONLY cursor

DECLARE MyProducts CURSOR
LOCAL FORWARD_ONLY
FOR
SELECT ProductID, ProductName
FROM Products
WHERE ProductID > 70
ORDER BY ProductID ASC
```

Declaring a cursor as SCROLL enables you to use any of the FETCH statements. Later in this chapter, you will learn the different FETCH options.

EXAMPLE

Listing 12.12: Using the SCROLL Keyword

```
-- This is a GLOBAL SCROLL cursor

DECLARE MyProducts CURSOR
GLOBAL SCROLL
FOR
SELECT ProductID, ProductName
FROM Products
WHERE ProductID > 70
ORDER BY ProductName DESC
```

CAUTION

FORWARD_ONLY and FAST_FORWARD are mutually exclusive. Declaring a cursor using both keywords produces a syntax error.

Cursor types have been explained earlier in this chapter. To define the cursor type, you can use the STATIC, KEYSET, DYNAMIC, or FAST_FORWARD keywords, as seen in Listings 12.1 to 12.3.

CAUTION

SCROLL and FAST_FORWARD are mutually exclusive. Declaring a cursor using both keywords produces a syntax error.

You can control how to lock the cursor data using the READ_ONLY, SCROLL_LOCKS, and OPTIMISTIC keywords in the DECLARE CURSOR statement.

Declaring a cursor as READ_ONLY prevents updates to the cursor using the UPDATE or DELETE statements with the WHERE CURRENT OF clause (see Listing 12.13). Using the SCROLL_LOCKS option forces the data to be locked when the cursor reads it, to guarantee potential updates. This locking behavior is often called pessimistic locking.

Using the OPTIMISTIC option frees the lock on the data after the data is loaded into the cursor, and will lock the data only to update or delete, if required. In this case, SQL Server must check whether the row has been modified by other connections between the reading and writing operations.

SQL Server can check for changes on the data by inspecting the actual value of a timestamp (rowversion) column and comparing this value to the value obtained during the read operation. If the data does not contain any timestamp column, SQL Server can use a checksum of the existing column values.

TIP

You can increase the concurrency of your application by selecting OPTIMISTIC concurrency.

STATIC and FAST_FORWARD cursors default to READ_ONLY locking. However, KEYSET and DYNAMIC cursors default to OPTIMISTIC locking.

CAUTION

SQL Server 2000 does not support OPTIMISTIC concurrency in a FAST_FORWARD cursor.

EXAMPLE

Listing 12.13: Use the READ_ONLY Option to Protect the Cursor from Updates

```
BEGIN TRAN

-- Declare the cursor

DECLARE MyProducts CURSOR
FORWARD_ONLY READ_ONLY
FOR
```

Listing 12.13: continued

```
SELECT ProductID, ProductName
FROM Products
WHERE ProductID > 70
ORDER BY ProductID

-- Open the cursor

OPEN MyProducts

-- Fetch the first row

FETCH NEXT FROM MyProducts

-- Try to update the data
-- in the current row
-- gives an error
-- on a READ_ONLY cursor

update Products
set productname = 'Modified name'
where current of MyProducts


-- Close the cursor

CLOSE MyProducts

-- Deallocate the cursor

DEALLOCATE MyProducts

ROLLBACK TRAN
```

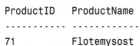

OUTPUT

```
ProductID    ProductName
----------   ------------------------------------
71           Flotemysost

(1 row(s) affected)

Server: Msg 16929, Level 16, State 1, Line 26
The cursor is READ ONLY.
The statement has been terminated.
```

In some cases, the cursor type must be changed because of restrictions in the definition of the cursor, as mentioned before in this chapter. In this case, you can get a notification of this change by using the TYPE_WARNING option (see Listing 12.14).

EXAMPLE

Listing 12.14: Using the TYPE_WARNING Option

```
-- Declare the cursor
-- as FAST_FORWARD
-- but it is converted into KEYSET
-- because it uses ntext fields
-- and ORDER BY

DECLARE MyCategories CURSOR
FAST_FORWARD READ_ONLY
TYPE_WARNING
FOR
SELECT CategoryID, CategoryName, Description
FROM Categories
ORDER BY CategoryName ASC

-- Open the cursor

OPEN MyCategories

-- Fetch the first row

FETCH NEXT FROM MyCategories

-- Close the cursor

CLOSE MyCategories

-- Deallocate the cursor

DEALLOCATE MyCategories
```

OUTPUT

```
Cursor created was not of the requested type.
CategoryID  CategoryName    Description
----------- --------------- -----------------------------------------------
1           Beverages       Soft drinks, coffees, teas, beers, and ales
```

The cursor must be defined for a SELECT statement. This is a normal SELECT statement with a few exceptions. You cannot use COMPUTE, COMPUTE BY, FOR BROWSE, or INTO in a SELECT statement that defines a cursor.

CAUTION

If the SELECT statement produces a result set that is not updatable, the cursor will be READ_ONLY. This can happen because of the use of aggregate functions, insufficient permissions, or retrieving read-only data.

You can restrict the columns to update inside the cursor using the FOR UPDATE clause, as shown in Listing 12.15. This clause can be used in two ways:

- FOR UPDATE OF Column1, ..., ColumnN—Use this option to define columns Column1 to ColumnN as updatable through the cursor.

- FOR UPDATE—This is the default option, and it declares all the cursor columns as updatable.

EXAMPLE

Listing 12.15: Using the FOR UPDATE Clause

```
DECLARE MyCategories CURSOR
KEYSET
FOR
SELECT CategoryID, CategoryName, Description
FROM Categories
ORDER BY CategoryName ASC
FOR UPDATE OF CategoryName, Description
```

NOTE

When you declare a cursor, SQL Server creates some memory structures to use the cursor, but the data is not retrieved until you open the cursor.

Opening Cursors

To use a cursor, you must open it. You can open a cursor using the OPEN statement. If the cursor was declared as STATIC or KEYSET, SQL Server must create a worktable in TempDB to store either the full result set, in a STATIC cursor, or the keyset only in a keyset-driven cursor. In these cases, if the worktable cannot be created for any reason, the OPEN statement will fail.

SQL Server can optimize the opening of big cursors by populating the cursor asynchronously. In this case, SQL Server creates a new thread to populate the worktable in parallel, returning the control to the application as soon as possible.

You can use the @@CURSOR_ROWS system function to control how many rows are contained in the cursor. If the cursor is using asynchronous population, the value returned by @@CURSOR_ROWS will be negative and represents the approximate number of rows returned since the opening of the cursor.

For dynamic cursors, @@CURSOR_ROWS returns -1, because it is not possible to know whether the full result set has been returned already, because of potential insertions by other operations affecting the same data.

CAUTION

The @@CURSOR_ROWS function returns the number of rows of the last cursor opened in the current connection. If you use cursors inside triggers, the result of this function from the main execution level could be misleading. Listing 12.16 shows an example of this problem.

To specify when SQL Server will decide to populate a cursor asynchronously, you can use the sp_configure system-stored procedure to change the server setting "cursor threshold", specifying the maximum number of rows that will be executed directly without asynchronous population.

CAUTION

Do not fix the "cursor threshold" value too low, because small result sets are more efficiently opened synchronously.

EXAMPLE

Listing 12.16: Using the @@CURSOR_ROWS System Function

```
-- Create a procedure to open
-- a cursor on Categories

CREATE PROCEDURE GetCategories
AS
DECLARE MyCategories CURSOR STATIC
FOR
SELECT CategoryID, CategoryName
FROM Categories

OPEN MyCategories

-- Shows the number of rows in the cursor

SELECT @@CURSOR_ROWS 'Categories cursor rows after open'

CLOSE MyCategories

DEALLOCATE MyCategories
GO

-- Create a cursor on Products

DECLARE MyProducts CURSOR STATIC
FOR
SELECT ProductID, ProductName
FROM Products

OPEN MyProducts

-- Shows the number of rows in the last opened cursor, which is MyProducts

SELECT @@CURSOR_ROWS 'Products cursor rows'

EXEC GetCategories
```

Listing 12.16: continued

```
-- Shows the number of rows in the last opened cursor
-- in the current connection, which is MyCategories

SELECT @@CURSOR_ROWS 'Categories cursor rows after close and deallocated'

CLOSE MyProducts

DEALLOCATE MyProducts
```

OUTPUT

```
Products cursor rows
-------------------
77


Categories cursor rows after open
---------------------------------
8


Categories cursor rows after close and deallocated
--------------------------------------------------
0
```

Fetching Rows

You can use the FETCH statement to navigate an open cursor, as shown in Listing 12.17. Every time you execute the FETCH statement, the cursor moves to a different row.

FETCH FROM CursorName retrieves the next row in the cursor. This is a synonym of FETCH NEXT FROM CursorName. If the FETCH statement is executed right after the OPEN statement, the cursor is positioned in the first row. If the current row is the last one in the result set, executing FETCH NEXT again will send the cursor beyond the end of the result set and will return an empty row, but no error message will be produced.

CAUTION

After opening a cursor with the OPEN statement, the cursor does not point to any specific row, so you must execute a FETCH statement to position the cursor in a valid row.

FETCH PRIOR moves the cursor to the preceding row. If the cursor was positioned already at the beginning of the result set, using FETCH PRIOR will move the pointer before the starting of the result set, retrieving an empty row, but no error message will be produced.

FETCH FIRST moves the cursor pointer to the beginning of the result set, returning the first row.

FETCH LAST moves the cursor pointer to the end of the result set, returning the last row.

FETCH ABSOLUTE n moves the cursor pointer to the n row in the result set. If n is negative, the cursor pointer is moved n rows before the end of the result set. If the new row position does not exist, an empty row will be returned and no error will be produced. If n is 0, no rows are returned and the cursor pointer goes out of scope.

FETCH RELATIVE n moves the cursor pointer n rows forward from the current position of the cursor. If n is negative, the cursor pointer is moved backward n rows from the current position. If the new row position does not exist, an empty row will be returned and no error will be produced. If n is 0, the current row is returned.

You can use the @@FETCH_STATUS system function to test whether the cursor points to a valid row after the last FETCH statement. @@FETCH_SATUS can have the following values:

- 0 if the FETCH statement was successful and the cursor points to a valid row.

- -1 if the FETCH statement was not successful or the cursor points beyond the limits of the result set. This can be produced using FETCH NEXT from the last row or FETCH PRIOR from the first row.

- -2 the cursor is pointing to a nonexistent row. This can be produced by a keyset-driven cursor when one of the rows has been deleted from outside the control of the cursor.

CAUTION

@@FETCH_STATUS is global to the connection, so it reflects the status of the latest FETCH statement executed in the connection. That is why it is important to test it right after the FETCH statement.

EXAMPLE

Listing 12.17: Use FETCH to Navigate the Cursor

```
DECLARE MyProducts CURSOR STATIC
FOR
SELECT ProductID, ProductName
FROM Products
ORDER BY ProductID ASC

OPEN MyProducts

SELECT @@CURSOR_ROWS 'Products cursor rows'

SELECT @@FETCH_STATUS 'Fetch Status After OPEN'
```

Listing 12.17: continued

```
FETCH FROM Myproducts

SELECT @@FETCH_STATUS 'Fetch Status After first FETCH'

FETCH NEXT FROM MyProducts

SELECT @@FETCH_STATUS 'Fetch Status After FETCH NEXT'

FETCH PRIOR FROM Myproducts

SELECT @@FETCH_STATUS 'Fetch Status After FETCH PRIOR'

FETCH PRIOR FROM Myproducts

SELECT @@FETCH_STATUS 'Fetch Status After FETCH PRIOR the first row'

FETCH LAST FROM Myproducts

SELECT @@FETCH_STATUS 'Fetch Status After FETCH LAST'

FETCH NEXT FROM Myproducts

SELECT @@FETCH_STATUS 'Fetch Status After FETCH NEXT the last row'

FETCH ABSOLUTE 10 FROM Myproducts

SELECT @@FETCH_STATUS 'Fetch Status After FETCH ABSOLUTE 10'

FETCH ABSOLUTE -5 FROM Myproducts

SELECT @@FETCH_STATUS 'Fetch Status After FETCH ABSOLUTE -5'

FETCH RELATIVE -20 FROM Myproducts

SELECT @@FETCH_STATUS 'Fetch Status After FETCH RELATIVE -20'

FETCH RELATIVE 10 FROM Myproducts

SELECT @@FETCH_STATUS 'Fetch Status After FETCH RELATIVE 10'

CLOSE MyProducts

SELECT @@FETCH_STATUS 'Fetch Status After CLOSE'

DEALLOCATE MyProducts
```

Listing 12.17: continued

```
Products cursor rows
--------------------
77


Fetch Status After OPEN
-----------------------
0


ProductID   ProductName
----------- ----------------------------------------
1           Chai


Fetch Status After first FETCH
------------------------------
0


ProductID   ProductName
----------- ----------------------------------------
2           Chang


Fetch Status After FETCH NEXT
-----------------------------
0


ProductID   ProductName
----------- ----------------------------------------
1           Chai


Fetch Status After FETCH PRIOR
------------------------------
0


ProductID   ProductName
----------- ----------------------------------------


Fetch Status After FETCH PRIOR the first row
--------------------------------------------
-1


ProductID   ProductName
----------- ----------------------------------------
77          Original Frankfurter grüne Soße


Fetch Status After FETCH LAST
-----------------------------
```

Listing 12.17: continued

```
0

ProductID    ProductName
----------   -----------------------------------------

Fetch Status After FETCH NEXT the last row
----------------------------------------
-1

ProductID    ProductName
----------   -----------------------------------------
10           Ikura

Fetch Status After FETCH ABSOLUTE 10
-----------------------------------
0

ProductID    ProductName
----------   -----------------------------------------
73           Röd Kaviar

Fetch Status After FETCH ABSOLUTE -5
-----------------------------------
0

ProductID    ProductName
----------   -----------------------------------------
53           Perth Pasties

Fetch Status After FETCH RELATIVE -20
-----------------------------------
0

ProductID    ProductName
----------   -----------------------------------------
63           Vegie-spread

Fetch Status After FETCH RELATIVE 10
-----------------------------------
0

Fetch Status After CLOSE
-----------------------
0
```

At the same time you are moving the cursor with the FETCH statement, you can use the INTO clause to retrieve the cursor fields directly into user-defined variables (see Listing 12.18). In this way, you later can use the values stored in these variables in further Transact-SQL statements.

EXAMPLE

Listing 12.18: Use FETCH INTO to Get the Values of the Cursor Columns into Variables

```
SET NOCOUNT ON
GO

DECLARE @ProductID int,
@ProductName nvarchar(40),
@CategoryID int

DECLARE MyProducts CURSOR STATIC
FOR
SELECT ProductID, ProductName, CategoryID
FROM Products
WHERE CategoryID BETWEEN 6 AND 8
ORDER BY ProductID ASC

OPEN MyProducts

FETCH FROM Myproducts
INTO @ProductID, @ProductName, @CategoryID

WHILE @@FETCH_STATUS = 0
BEGIN

SELECT @ProductName as 'Product',
CategoryName AS 'Category'
FROM Categories
WHERE CategoryID = @CategoryID

FETCH FROM Myproducts
INTO @ProductID, @ProductName, @CategoryID

END

CLOSE MyProducts

DEALLOCATE MyProducts
```

OUTPUT

```
Product                                   Category
----------------------------------------- ---------------
Uncle Bob's Organic Dried Pears           Produce
```

Listing 12.18: continued

```
Product                                     Category
------------------------------------------- ---------------
Mishi Kobe Niku                             Meat/Poultry

Product                                     Category
------------------------------------------- ---------------
Ikura                                       Seafood

Product                                     Category
------------------------------------------- ---------------
Konbu                                       Seafood

Product                                     Category
------------------------------------------- ---------------
Tofu                                        Produce

Product                                     Category
------------------------------------------- ---------------
Alice Mutton                                Meat/Poultry

Product                                     Category
------------------------------------------- ---------------
Carnarvon Tigers                            Seafood

Product                                     Category
------------------------------------------- ---------------
Rössle Sauerkraut                           Produce

Product                                     Category
------------------------------------------- ---------------
Thüringer Rostbratwurst                     Meat/Poultry

Product                                     Category
------------------------------------------- ---------------
Nord-Ost Matjeshering                       Seafood

Product                                     Category
------------------------------------------- ---------------
Inlagd Sill                                 Seafood

Product                                     Category
------------------------------------------- ---------------
Gravad lax                                  Seafood
```

Listing 12.18: continued

Product	Category
Boston Crab Meat	Seafood

Product	Category
Jack's New England Clam Chowder	Seafood

Product	Category
Rogede sild	Seafood

Product	Category
Spegesild	Seafood

Product	Category
Manjimup Dried Apples	Produce

Product	Category
Perth Pasties	Meat/Poultry

Product	Category
Tourtière	Meat/Poultry

Product	Category
Pâté chinois	Meat/Poultry

Product	Category
Escargots de Bourgogne	Seafood

Product	Category
Röd Kaviar	Seafood

Product	Category
Longlife Tofu	Produce

If the cursor is updatable, you can modify values in the underlying tables sending standard UPDATE or DELETE statements and specifying WHERE CURRENT OF CursorName as a restricting condition (see Listing 12.19).

EXAMPLE

Listing 12.19: Using WHERE CURRENT OF to Apply Modifications to the Current Cursor Row

```
BEGIN TRAN

-- Declare the cursor

DECLARE MyProducts CURSOR
FORWARD_ONLY
FOR
SELECT ProductID, ProductName
FROM Products
WHERE ProductID > 70
ORDER BY ProductID

-- Open the cursor

OPEN MyProducts

-- Fetch the first row

FETCH NEXT FROM MyProducts

-- UPdate the name of the product
-- and the UnitPrice in the current cursor position

update Products
set ProductName = ProductName + ' (to be dicontinued)',
UnitPrice = UnitPrice * (1.0 + CategoryID / 100.0)
where current of MyProducts

SELECT *
from Products

-- Close the cursor

CLOSE MyProducts

-- Deallocate the cursor

DEALLOCATE MyProducts

ROLLBACK TRAN
```

NOTE

You can update through cursor columns that are not part of the cursor definition, as long as the columns are updatable.

Closing Cursors

Use the CLOSE statement to close a cursor, freeing any locks used by it. The cursor structure is not destroyed, but it is not possible to retrieve any data from the cursor after the cursor is closed.

TIP

It is a good practice to close cursors as soon as they are not necessary. This simple practice can provide better concurrency to your application.

Most of the listings in this chapter use the CLOSE statement.

Deallocating Cursors

To destroy the cursor completely, you can use the DEALLOCATE statement. After this statement is executed, it is not possible to reopen the cursor without redefining it again.

After DEALLOCATE you can reuse the cursor name to declare any other cursor, with identical or different definition.

TIP

To reuse the same cursor in different occasions in a long batch or a complex stored procedure, you should declare the cursor as soon as you need it and deallocate it when it is no longer necessary. Between the DECLARE and DEALLOCATE statements, use OPEN and CLOSE to access data as many times as necessary to avoid long-standing locks. However, consider that each time you open the cursor the query has to be executed. This could produce some overhead.

Scope of Cursors

In the DECLARE CURSOR statement, you can specify the scope of the cursor after its name. The default scope is GLOBAL, but you can change the default scope, changing the database option default to local cursor.

CAUTION

You should not rely on the default cursor scope of SQL Server. It is recommended that you declare the cursor explicitly as either LOCAL or GLOBAL, because the default cursor scope might change in future versions of SQL Server.

You can use a global cursor anywhere in the same connection in which the cursor was created, whereas local cursors are valid only within the scope of the batch, procedure, user-defined function, or trigger where the cursor is created. The cursor is automatically deallocated when it goes out of scope (see Listing 12.20).

EXAMPLE

Listing 12.20: Using Global Cursors

```
-- Declare the cursor as GLOBAL

DECLARE MyProducts CURSOR GLOBAL
FOR
SELECT ProductID, ProductName
FROM Products
WHERE ProductID > 70
ORDER BY ProductID
```

However, you can assign the cursor to an OUTPUT parameter in a stored procedure. In this case, the cursor will be deallocated when the last cursor variable that references the cursor goes out of scope.

> **NOTE**
>
> Cursor variables are covered later in this chapter.

Global and local cursors have two different name spaces, so it is possible to have a global cursor with the same name as a local cursor, and they can have completely different definitions. To avoid potential problems, SQL Server use local cursors.

Local Cursors

Local cursors are a safety feature that provides the creation of local cursors inside independent objects, such as stored procedures, triggers, and user-defined functions. Local cursors are easier to manage than global cursors because you do not have to consider potential changes to the cursor in other procedures or triggers used by your application.

Global Cursors

Global cursors are useful in scenarios where different procedures must manage a common result set, and they must dynamically interact with it. It is recommended you use local cursors whenever possible. If you require sharing a cursor between two procedures, consider using a cursor variable instead, as is covered in the next section.

Using Cursor Variables

It is possible to declare variables using the cursor data type, which is very useful if you need to send a reference of your cursor to another procedure or user-defined function. Using cursor variables is similar to using standard cursors (see Listing 12.21).

EXAMPLE

Listing 12.21: Using Cursor Variables

```
-- Declare the cursor variable

DECLARE @Products AS CURSOR

-- Assign the cursor variable a cursor definition

SET @Products = CURSOR STATIC
FOR
SELECT ProductID, ProductName
FROM Products

-- Open the cursor

OPEN @Products

-- Fetch the first cursor row

FETCH NEXT FROM @Products

-- Close the cursor

CLOSE @Products

-- Deallocate the cursor

DEALLOCATE @Products
```

SQL Server provides system stored procedures to retrieve information about cursors. These procedures use cursor variables to communicate its data:

- sp_cursor_list produces a list of available cursors in the current connection.

- sp_describe_cursor retrieves the attributes of an open cursor. The output is the same as the output produced with sp_cursor_list, but sp_describe_cursor refers to a single cursor.

- `sp_describe_cursor_columns` describes the columns retrieved by the cursor.

- `sp_describe_cursor_tables` gets information about the tables used in the cursor.

These stored procedures use cursor variables to retrieve results. In this way, calling procedures and batches can use the result one row at a time.

Listing 12.22 shows how to execute these system stored procedures to get information about cursors and cursors variables.

EXAMPLE

Listing 12.22: Retrieving Information About Cursors with System Stored Procedures

```
USE Northwind
GO

-- Declare some cursors

DECLARE CCategories CURSOR LOCAL
DYNAMIC
FOR
SELECT CategoryName
FROM Categories

DECLARE CCustomers CURSOR LOCAL
FAST_FORWARD
FOR
SELECT CompanyName
FROM Customers

DECLARE COrdersComplete CURSOR GLOBAL
KEYSET
FOR
SELECT O.OrderID, OrderDate,
C.CustomerID, CompanyName,
P.ProductID, ProductName,
Quantity, OD.UnitPrice, Discount
FROM Orders O
JOIN [Order Details] OD
ON OD.OrderID = O.OrderID
JOIN Customers C
ON C.CustomerID = O.CustomerID
JOIN Products P
ON P.ProductID = OD.ProductID

-- Declare a cursor variable to hold
-- results from the stored procedures
```

Listing 12.22: continued

```
DECLARE @OutputCursor AS CURSOR

-- Get information about declared local cursors

EXEC sp_cursor_list @OutputCursor OUTPUT, 1

-- deallocate the cursor, so we can reuse the cursor variable

DEALLOCATE @OutputCursor

-- Or get information about declared global cursors

EXEC sp_cursor_list @OutputCursor OUTPUT, 2

-- deallocate the cursor, so we can reuse the cursor variable

DEALLOCATE @OutputCursor

-- Or get information about declared global and local cursors
-- note that status = -1 means cursor closed

PRINT CHAR(10) + 'sp_cursor_list cursor OUTPUT' + CHAR(10)

EXEC sp_cursor_list @OutputCursor OUTPUT, 3

FETCH NEXT FROM @OutputCursor

WHILE @@FETCH_STATUS = 0
FETCH NEXT FROM @OutputCursor

-- deallocate the cursor, so we can reuse the cursor variable

DEALLOCATE @OutputCursor

-- Open the CCategories cursor

OPEN CCategories

-- Get information about a cursor
-- note that status = 1 means cursor open

EXEC sp_describe_cursor @OutputCursor OUTPUT,
N'local', N'CCategories'

PRINT CHAR(10) + 'sp_describe_cursor cursor OUTPUT' + CHAR(10)
```

Listing 12.22: continued

```
FETCH NEXT FROM @OutputCursor

WHILE @@FETCH_STATUS = 0
FETCH NEXT FROM @OutputCursor

-- deallocate the cursor, so we can reuse the cursor variable

DEALLOCATE @OutputCursor

CLOSE CCategories

-- Open the CCustomers cursor

OPEN CCustomers

-- Get information about a cursor
-- note that status = 1 means cursor open

EXEC sp_describe_cursor_columns @OutputCursor OUTPUT,
N'local', N'CCustomers'

PRINT CHAR(10) + 'sp_describe_cursor_columns cursor OUTPUT' + CHAR(10)

FETCH NEXT FROM @OutputCursor

WHILE @@FETCH_STATUS = 0
FETCH NEXT FROM @OutputCursor

-- deallocate the cursor, so we can reuse the cursor variable

DEALLOCATE @OutputCursor

CLOSE CCustomers

-- Open the CCategories cursor

OPEN COrdersComplete

-- Get information about a cursor
-- note that status = 1 means cursor open

EXEC sp_describe_cursor_tables @OutputCursor OUTPUT,
N'global', N'COrdersComplete'

PRINT CHAR(10) + 'sp_describe_cursor_tables cursor OUTPUT' + CHAR(10)
```

Listing 12.22: continued

```
FETCH NEXT FROM @OutputCursor

WHILE @@FETCH_STATUS = 0
FETCH NEXT FROM @OutputCursor

DEALLOCATE @OutputCursor

CLOSE COrdersComplete

DEALLOCATE CCategories

DEALLOCATE CCustomers

DEALLOCATE COrdersComplete
```

NOTE

Books Online contains a full description of the sp_cursor_list, sp_describe_cursor, sp_describe_cursor_columns, and sp_describe_cursor_tables system stored procedures.

Use this information to interpret the output from Listing 12.22.

Using Cursors to Solve Multirow Actions in Triggers

In many cases, dealing with multirow operations inside triggers is not an easy task. If the single-row solution is solved, you can use cursors to convert multirow operations into single-row operations inside the trigger, to apply to them the same proved logic of the single-row cases.

Consider the following example: You want to assign a credit limit to every customer following an automated process applied by the AssignCreditLimit stored procedure. To automate the process, you can create a trigger AFTER INSERT to calculate the credit limit for every new customer.

The AssignCreditLimit stored procedure can work with only one customer at a time. However, an INSERT operation can insert multiple rows at the same time, using INSERT SELECT.

You can create the trigger with two parts; one will deal with single row and the other with multiple rows, and you will check which part to apply using the result of the @@ROWCOUNT function as described in Listing 12.23.

EXAMPLE

Listing 12.23: Using Cursors to Convert Multirow Operations into Single-Row Operations Inside Triggers

```
USE Northwind
GO

ALTER TABLE Customers
ADD CreditLimit money
GO

CREATE PROCEDURE AssignCreditLimit
@ID nvarchar(5)
AS

-- Write here your own CreditLimit function

   UPDATE Customers
   SET CreditLimit = 1000
   WHERE CustomerID = @ID
GO

CREATE TRIGGER isr_Customers
ON Customers
FOR INSERT AS

SET NOCOUNT ON

DECLARE @ID nvarchar(5)

IF @@ROWCOUNT > 1
-- Multirow operation
BEGIN

-- Open a cursor on the Inserted table

DECLARE NewCustomers CURSOR
FOR SELECT CustomerID
FROM Inserted
ORDER BY CustomerID

OPEN NewCustomers

FETCH NEXT FROM NewCustomers
INTO @ID

WHILE @@FETCH_STATUS = 0
BEGIN
```

Listing 12.23: continued

```
-- Assign new Credit Limit to every new customer

EXEC AssignCreditLimit @ID

FETCH NEXT FROM NewCustomers
INTO @ID
END

-- close the cursor

CLOSE NewCustomers
DEALLOCATE NewCustomers
END

ELSE
-- Single row operation
BEGIN
SELECT @ID = CustomerID
FROM Inserted

IF @ID IS NOT NULL

-- Assign new Credit Limit to the new customer

EXEC AssignCreditLimit @ID
END

GO

-- Test it

INSERT customers (CustomerID, CompanyName)
VALUES ('ZZZZZ', 'New Company')

SELECT CreditLimit
FROM Customers
WHERE CustomerID = 'ZZZZZ'
```

Application Cursors

When a client application requests information from SQL Server using the
default settings in ADO, OLE DB, ODBC, or DB-Library, SQL Server must
follow this process:

1. The client application sends a request to SQL Server in a network package. This request can be any Transact-SQL statement or a batch containing multiple statements.

2. SQL Server interprets the request and creates a query plan to solve the request. The query plan is compiled and executed.

3. SQL Server packages the results in the minimum number of network packets and sends them to the user.

4. The clients start receiving network packets, and these packets are waiting in the network buffer for the application to request them.

5. The client application receives the information contained in the network packages row by row.

The client application cannot send any other statement through this connection until the complete result set is retrieved or cancelled.

This is the most efficient way to retrieve information from SQL Server, and it is called a *default result set*. It is equivalent to a FORWARD_ONLY READ_ONLY cursor with a row set size set to one row.

NOTE

Some articles and books refer to the default result set as a "Firehose" cursor, which is considered an obsolete term.

SQL Server supports three types of cursors:

- Transact-SQL cursors—These are the cursors you studied in the previous sections of this chapter.

- Application Programming Interface (API) server cursors—These are cursors created in SQL Server, following requests from the database library, such as ADO, OLE DB, ODBC, or DB-Library. Listings 12.1 and 12.3 contain examples of this type of cursor.

- Client cursors—These cursors are implemented in the client side by the database library. The client cache contains the complete set of rows returned by the cursor, and it is unnecessary to have any communication to the server to navigate the cursor.

CAUTION

Do not mix API cursors with Transact-SQL cursors from a client application, or SQL Server will try to map an API cursor over Transact-SQL cursors, with unexpected results.

TIP

Use Transact-SQL cursors in stored procedures and triggers and as local cursors in Transact-SQL batches, to implement cursors that do not require user interaction.

Use API cursors from client applications where the cursor navigation requires user interaction.

Using a default result set is more efficient than using a server cursor, as commented in previous sections in this chapter.

CAUTION

You cannot open a server cursor in a stored procedure or batch if it contains anything other than a single SELECT statement with some specific Transact-SQL statements. In these cases, use a client cursor instead.

Using server cursors is more efficient than using client cursors because client cursors must cache the complete result set in the client side, whereas server cursors send to the client the fetched rows only. To open a client cursor using ADO, you can set the CursorLocation property to adUseClient in the Connection or Recordset objects. The default value is adUseServer for server API cursor.

What's Next?

In this chapter, you learned how to use Transact-SQL cursors.

In Chapter 13, you will learn about transactions and locks, which are both important aspects of using cursors.

The concurrency of a database application depends directly on how the application manages transactions and locks.

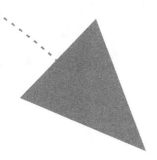

Maintaining Data Consistency: Transactions and Locks

SQL Server 2000 is designed to serve multiuser environments. If multiple users try to access the same data, SQL Server must protect the data to avoid conflicting requests from different processes. SQL Server uses transactions and locks to prevent concurrency problems, such as avoiding simultaneous modifications to the same data from different users.

This chapter teaches you the following:

- Basic concepts about transactions
- How to use Transact-SQL statements to manage transactions
- How to understand the common concurrency problems and avoid them when they arise
- How to apply the right transaction isolation level
- Lock types available in SQL Server
- How to detect and avoid deadlocks

Characteristics of Transactions (ACID)

A *transaction* is a sequence of operations executed as a single logical operation, which must expose the ACID (Atomicity, Consistency, Isolation, and Durability) properties. These are as follows:

- Atomicity—The transaction must be executed as an atomic unit of work, which means that it either completes all of its data modifications or none at all.

- Consistency—The data is consistent before the transaction begins, and the data is consistent after the transaction finishes. To maintain consistency, all integrity checks, constraints, rules, and triggers must be applied to the data during the transaction. A transaction can affect some internal SQL Server data structures, such as allocation maps and indexes, and SQL Server must guarantee that these internal modifications are applied consistently. If the transaction is cancelled, the data should go back to the same consistent state it was in at the beginning of the transaction.

- Isolation—The transaction must be isolated from changes made to the data by other transactions, to prevent using provisional data that is not committed. This implies that the transaction must either see the data in its previous state or the transaction must wait until the changes from other transactions are committed.

- Durability—After the transaction completes, its changes to the data are permanent, regardless of the event of a system failure. In other words, when a client application receives notification that a transaction has completed its work successfully, it is guaranteed that the data is changed permanently.

Every RDBMS uses different ways to enforce these properties. SQL Server 2000 uses Transact-SQL statements to control the boundaries of transactions to guarantee which operations must be considered as an atomic unit of work.

Constraints and other integrity mechanisms are used to enforce logical consistency of every transaction. SQL Server internal engines are designed to provide physical internal consistency to every operation that modifies data, maintaining allocation structures, indexes, and metadata.

The programmer must enforce correct transaction and error management to enforce an appropriate atomicity and consistency. Later in this chapter, in the "Transactions and Runtime Errors" section, you will learn about transaction and error management.

Programmers can select the right level of isolation by specifying Transaction Isolation Level or using locking hints. Later in this chapter, in the "Isolation Levels" section, you will learn how to apply transaction isolation levels. The section "Types of Locks" gives you details on how to use locking hints.

SQL Server guarantees durability by using the Transaction log to track all the changes to the database and uses the recovery process when necessary to enforce data consistency in case of system failure or unexpected shutdown.

Using Transactions

To consider several operations as members of the same transaction, it is necessary to establish the transaction boundaries by selecting the transaction starting and ending points.

You can consider three different types of transactions:

- Auto commit transactions—SQL Server always starts a transaction whenever any statement needs to modify data. SQL Server automatically commits the transaction if the statement finishes its work successfully. However, if the statement produces any error, SQL Server will automatically roll back all changes produced by this incomplete statement. In this way, SQL Server automatically maintains data consistency for every statement that modifies data.

- Explicit transactions—The programmer specifically declares the transaction starting point and decides either to commit or rollback changes depending on programming conditions.

- Implicit transactions—SQL Server starts a transaction automatically whenever any statement needs to modify data, but it is the programmer's responsibility to specify the transaction ending point and confirm or reject applied changes.

NOTE

It is impossible to instruct SQL Server to disable the creation of Auto commit transactions. This is why inside a trigger you are always inside a transaction.

A Transact-SQL batch is not a transaction unless stated specifically. In Listing 13.1, Operations 1 through 3 are independent; there is no link between them, so they don't form a single transaction. If there is an error in one of the operations, the others can still be committed automatically. However, operations 4 through 6 are part of the same transaction, and either all of them or none of them will be applied permanently.

Using the @@IDENTITY function can be wrong in this case, because this system function returns the latest Identity value generated in this connection. If a trigger inserts data in a table where you have an Identity field, the @@IDENTITY function will return the value generated inside the trigger, not the one generated by the original action that fired the trigger.

TIP

Use the SCOPE_IDENTITY() function to retrieve the latest Identity value inserted in the current scope.

EXAMPLE

Listing 13.1: Setting the Transaction Boundaries

```
USE Northwind
GO


-----------------------
-- Without Transactions
-----------------------


DECLARE @CatID int,
@ProdID int

-- Operation 1
-- Create a new Category

INSERT Categories
(CategoryName)
VALUES ('Cars')

-- Retrieves the latest IDENTITY value inserted

SET @CatID = SCOPE_IDENTITY()

-- Operation 2
-- Create a new product
-- in the new Category

INSERT Products
(ProductName, CategoryID)
VALUES ('BigCars', @CatID)

-- Retrieves the latest IDENTITY value inserted

SET @ProdID = SCOPE_IDENTITY()

-- Operation 3
```

Listing 13.1: continued

```
-- Change UnitsInStock
-- for the new product

UPDATE Products
SET UnitsInStock = 20
WHERE ProductID = @ProdID


-----------------------
-- With Transactions
-----------------------


-- Start a new transaction

BEGIN TRAN

-- Operation 4
-- Create a new Category

INSERT Categories
(CategoryName)
VALUES ('HiFi')

IF @@ERROR <> 0 GOTO AbortTransaction

SELECT @CatID = CategoryID
FROM Categories
WHERE CategoryName = 'HiFi'

-- Operation 2
-- Create a new product
-- in the new Category

INSERT Products
(ProductName, CategoryID)
VALUES ('GreatSound', @CatID)

IF @@ERROR <> 0 GOTO AbortTransaction

SELECT @ProdID = ProductID
FROM Products
WHERE ProductName = 'GreatSound'

-- Operation 3
-- Change UnitsInStock
-- for the new product
```

Listing 13.1: continued

```
UPDATE Products
SET UnitsInStock = 50
WHERE ProductID = @ProdID

IF @@ERROR <> 0 GOTO AbortTransaction

COMMIT TRAN
PRINT 'Transaction committed'

GOTO EndTransaction

AbortTransaction:

ROLLBACK TRAN
PRINT 'Transaction rolled back'

EndTransaction:

PRINT 'Transaction finished'
```

BEGIN TRAN

To start a new local transaction, you can use the BEGIN TRANSACTION (or BEGIN TRAN) statement. This statement starts a new transaction, if there aren't any transactions already started, or creates a new level of nested transactions if the execution was already inside another transaction.

As mentioned before, any time you execute a statement that modifies data, SQL Server automatically starts a new transaction. If you were already inside a transaction when the statement started to run and this operation fired a trigger inside the trigger, you will be in the second level of a nested transaction.

The same situation happens if you define a stored procedure to apply some data changes, and you need to apply these data changes as a single transaction. In this case, you start a new transaction inside the stored procedure and decide at the end of it whether you want to commit or roll back. This stored procedure will execute its statements in a transaction state regardless of the existence of a transaction in the calling procedure or batch.

It is possible to have any number of nested transactions in SQL Server 2000. The @@TRANCOUNT system function gives you the number of levels of nested transactions you have open at any given time. Any time you execute BEGIN TRAN, the result of the function @@TRANCOUNT is increased by one. Listing 13.2 shows an example of how the @@TRANCOUNT function works.

EXAMPLE

Listing 13.2: Values of the @@TRANCOUNT Function After Using BEGIN TRAN

```
BEGIN TRAN

SELECT @@TRANCOUNT 'First Transaction'

BEGIN TRAN

SELECT @@TRANCOUNT 'Second Transaction'

BEGIN TRAN

SELECT @@TRANCOUNT 'Third Transaction'

BEGIN TRAN

SELECT @@TRANCOUNT 'Fourth Transaction'

ROLLBACK TRAN
```

OUTPUT

```
First Transaction
-----------------
1

Second Transaction
-----------------
2

Third Transaction
-----------------
3

Fourth Transaction
-----------------
4
```

> **NOTE**
>
> Using nested transactions is not considered a good practice. SQL Server considers nested transactions as one single transaction, starting on the first BEGIN TRAN and finishing on the last COMMIT TRAN or the first ROLLBACK TRAN. Having multiple transaction levels in the same batch or stored procedure makes the code harder to understand and maintain.
>
> The reason for having nested transactions is to be able to start a new transaction inside a stored procedure, or trigger, regardless of the existence of a previous transaction in the process.

You can assign a name to a transaction to easily identify it in code. In this case, this name only helps you to identify possible errors in code, but you cannot commit or roll back an individual transaction by providing its name, unless you save the transaction. You learn how to do this later in this chapter in the "ROLLBACK TRAN" section. Listing 13.3 uses transactions with names and shows how they are written to the transaction log.

Listing 13.3: Transactions with Names Can Be Identified in the Transaction Log

```
USE Northwind
GO

BEGIN TRAN ChangeNameAllCustomers

UPDATE Customers
SET CompanyName = CompanyName
WHERE COUNTRY = 'USA'

SELECT [Current LSN], Operation, [Transaction Name]
FROM ::fn_dblog(NULL, NULL)

COMMIT TRAN
```

EXAMPLE

(Partial output)

OUTPUT

Current LSN	Operation	Transaction Name
00000046:000000ca:0002	LOP_BEGIN_CKPT	NULL
00000046:000000cb:0001	LOP_END_CKPT	NULL
00000046:000000cc:0001	LOP_BEGIN_XACT	ChangeNameAllCustome
00000046:000000cc:0002	LOP_DELETE_ROWS	NULL
00000046:000000cc:0003	LOP_MODIFY_HEADER	NULL
00000046:000000cc:0004	LOP_SET_BITS	NULL
00000046:000000cc:0005	LOP_DELETE_ROWS	NULL
00000046:000000cc:0006	LOP_INSERT_ROWS	NULL
00000046:000000cc:0007	LOP_INSERT_ROWS	NULL
00000046:000000cc:0008	LOP_DELETE_ROWS	NULL
00000046:000000cc:0009	LOP_DELETE_ROWS	NULL
00000046:000000cc:000a	LOP_INSERT_ROWS	NULL
00000046:000000cc:000b	LOP_INSERT_ROWS	NULL
00000046:000000cc:000c	LOP_DELETE_ROWS	NULL
00000046:000000cc:000d	LOP_DELETE_ROWS	NULL
00000046:000000cc:000e	LOP_INSERT_ROWS	NULL
00000046:000000cc:000f	LOP_INSERT_ROWS	NULL

```
. . . [deleted rows from output]
```

CAUTION

Microsoft does not support the fn_dblog function. It is used here only to show how transactions are written to the Transaction log.

NOTE

Before using the fn_dblog function, you should change the Northwind database to Full Logging mode and perform a full database backup.

Whenever you start a new transaction, it is marked in the transaction log, as you saw in Listing 13.3. You can restore a transaction log, specifying to stop the restore process either before or after a specific marked transaction. To achieve this, you must use the WITH MARK option in the BEGIN TRAN statement, as you can see in Listing 13.4.

EXAMPLE

Listing 13.4: Starting Transactions Using the WITH MARK Option

```
USE Northwind
GO

BEGIN TRAN ChangeUnitsInStock_1_10_20
WITH MARK

UPDATE Products
SET UnitsInStock = UnitsInStock * 1.1
WHERE ProductID in (1, 10, 20)

COMMIT TRAN
```

CAUTION

Mark your long complex administrative transactions with a name and use WITH MARK, so you can restore the database in the same state it was before the execution of this complex, and potentially dangerous, operation.

NOTE

Using named nested transactions, only the name of the outermost transaction is recorded in the transaction log.

COMMIT TRAN

To confirm the changes made inside a transaction, you must execute the COMMIT TRANSACTION (or COMMIT TRAN) statement.

CAUTION

Explicit transactions must be committed using COMMIT TRAN; otherwise, they will be rolled back when the connection is closed, or during the recovery process in case of a system shutdown or failure.

If the transaction was at the first level of transactions, executing COMMIT TRAN forces SQL Server to consider the changes made to the database as permanent. If the transaction was inside another transaction or transactions, changes to the database must wait until the outermost transaction is committed. In this case, the value of @@TRANCOUNT decreases by 1, but no changes to the data are confirmed yet. Only when the value of @@TRANCOUNT changes from 1 to 0 because of a COMMIT TRAN statement are changes on the data considered permanent.

While the transaction is not finally committed, the modified data is locked to other transactions. SQL Server will free these locks as soon as the transaction finally terminates, and this happens only when the outermost transaction terminates.

Listing 13.5 shows the effect of COMMIT TRAN in the value of @@TRANCOUNT.

EXAMPLE

Listing 13.5: Every Time You Execute COMMIT TRAN, @@TRANCOUNT Is Decreased by One

```
USE Northwind
GO

BEGIN TRAN Customers

UPDATE Customers
SET ContactTitle = 'President'
WHERE CustomerID = 'AROUT'

SELECT @@TRANCOUNT 'Start Customers Transaction'

BEGIN TRAN Products

UPDATE Products
SET UnitPrice = UnitPrice * 1.1
WHERE CategoryID = 3

SELECT @@TRANCOUNT 'Start Products Transaction'

BEGIN TRAN Regions

INSERT Region
VALUES (5, 'Europe')
```

Listing 13.5: continued

```
SELECT @@TRANCOUNT 'Start Regions Transaction'

COMMIT TRAN Regions

SELECT @@TRANCOUNT 'Commit Regions Transaction'

BEGIN TRAN Orders

UPDATE Orders
SET ShippedDate = CONVERT(VARCHAR(10), Getdate(), 120)
WHERE OrderID = 10500

SELECT @@TRANCOUNT 'Start Orders Transaction'

COMMIT TRAN Orders

SELECT @@TRANCOUNT 'Commit Orders Transaction'

COMMIT TRAN Products

SELECT @@TRANCOUNT 'Commit Products Transaction'

COMMIT TRAN Customers

SELECT @@TRANCOUNT 'Commit Customers Transaction'
```

OUTPUT

```
Start Customers Transaction
--------------------------
1

Start Products Transaction
--------------------------
2

Start Regions Transaction
--------------------------
3

Commit Regions Transaction
--------------------------
2

Start Orders Transaction
--------------------------
3
```

Listing 13.5: continued

```
Commit Orders Transaction
------------------------
2


Commit Products Transaction
------------------------
1


Commit Customers Transaction
------------------------
0
```

CAUTION

Although you can provide a transaction name to the COMMIT TRAN statement, this name is ignored and the latest open transaction is committed instead. However, it is a good practice to provide names to transactions in long scripts and stored procedures to provide extra help to detect code errors.

ROLLBACK TRAN

To cancel the changes applied during a transaction, you can use the ROLLBACK TRANSACTION (or ROLLBACK TRAN) statement. Calling ROLLBACK TRAN inside a nested transaction undoes all the changes applied from the starting point of the outermost transaction. Because ROLLBACK TRAN cancels the active transaction, all the resources locked by the transaction are freed after the transaction terminates. After the execution of the ROLLBACK TRAN statement, the TRANCOUNT function returns 0.

SQL Server 2000 supports the ANSI standard statement ROLLBACK WORK, which is equivalent to ROLLBACK TRAN, but in this case you cannot specify a transaction name.

Listing 13.6 shows the effect of ROLLBACK TRAN in the value of @@TRANCOUNT.

EXAMPLE

Listing 13.6: When You Execute ROLLBACK TRAN, @@TRANCOUNT Is Decremented to Zero

```
BEGIN TRAN Customers

UPDATE Customers
SET ContactTitle = 'President'
WHERE CustomerID = 'AROUT'

SELECT @@TRANCOUNT 'Start Customers Transaction'

BEGIN TRAN Products
```

Listing 13.6: continued

```
UPDATE Products
SET UnitPrice = UnitPrice * 1.1
WHERE CategoryID = 3

SELECT @@TRANCOUNT 'Start Products Transaction'

BEGIN TRAN Orders

UPDATE Orders
SET ShippedDate = CONVERT(VARCHAR(10), Getdate(), 120)
WHERE OrderID = 10500

SELECT @@TRANCOUNT 'Start Orders Transaction'

COMMIT TRAN Orders

SELECT @@TRANCOUNT 'Commit Orders Transaction'

-- Note: the following statement produces an error,
-- because the specified transaction name is invalid

ROLLBACK TRAN Products

SELECT @@TRANCOUNT 'Rollback Products Transaction'

ROLLBACK TRAN Customers

SELECT @@TRANCOUNT 'Rollback Customers Transaction'
```

OUTPUT

```
Start Customers Transaction
---------------------------
1

Start Products Transaction
---------------------------
2

Start Orders Transaction
------------------------
3

Commit Orders Transaction
-------------------------
2

Server: Msg 6401, Level 16, State 1, Line 29
```

Listing 13.6: continued

```
Cannot roll back Products.
➥No transaction or savepoint of that name was found.

Rollback Products Transaction
----------------------------
2

Rollback Customers Transaction
----------------------------
0
```

The way that ROLLBACK TRAN works depends on the point from which you execute it:

- When executed inside a batch, it cancels the active transaction, but the execution continues with the remaining statements of the batch. To prevent this situation, check the value of the @@TRANCOUNT function.

- Using ROLLBACK TRAN inside a stored procedure cancels the active transaction, even if the outermost transaction was declared outside the stored procedure. However, the execution continues with the remaining statements of the stored procedure. In this case, the process that called this procedure receives a warning because @@TRANCOUNT changed its value inside the procedure.

- If you execute ROLLBACK TRAN inside a trigger, the transaction is completely cancelled but the execution of the trigger continues. Any changes made inside the trigger after ROLLBACK TRAN are made permanent, because these modifications are not inside a transaction anymore. However, when the execution of the trigger terminates, the batch is cancelled and no more instructions will be executed.

TIP

You can cancel the operation that fires the trigger, without using ROLLBACK TRAN, using the information contained in the Inserted and Deleted tables to execute an action that compensates the action just made. For example, you can cancel a DELETE operation reinserting in the target table the content of the Deleted table.

In some cases, it could be interesting to consider part of a transaction as provisional, being able to roll back this portion without affecting the outer transaction status. In this case, you can create a savepoint and roll back only to the savepoint.

As an example, consider a transaction has been created to insert a new order and to insert some rows in Order Details. As a part of the same transaction, you want to try a 10% discount to products ordered in more than 5 units in this transaction, but only if the order costs more than $500 after the discount. To solve this problem, you can declare a savepoint before applying the extra discount. After the extra discount is applied, you can test whether the total price of this order is lower than $500, in which case this extra discount, and only this extra discount, must be rolled back. Listing 13.7 shows this example.

EXAMPLE

Listing 13.7: Use Savepoints to Roll Back a Portion of a Transaction

```
USE Northwind
GO

BEGIN TRAN NewOrder

-- Insert a new Order

DECLARE @ID int

INSERT Orders (CustomerID, OrderDate)
VALUES ('BOTTM', '2000-11-23')

-- Obtain the newly inserted OrderID

SET @ID = @@IDENTITY

-- Insert [Order details] data

INSERT [Order Details]
(OrderID, ProductID, UnitPrice, Quantity, Discount)
SELECT @ID, 23, 9, 12, 0.10

INSERT [Order Details]
(OrderID, ProductID, UnitPrice, Quantity, Discount)
SELECT @ID, 18, 62.5, 5, 0.05

INSERT [Order Details]
(OrderID, ProductID, UnitPrice, Quantity, Discount)
SELECT @ID, 32, 32, 5, 0.05

INSERT [Order Details]
(OrderID, ProductID, UnitPrice, Quantity, Discount)
SELECT @ID, 9, 97, 4, 0.10
```

Listing 13.7: continued

```
-- try the discount

-- Create a Savepoint

SAVE TRAN Discount

-- Increase the discount to
-- products where Quantity >= 5

UPDATE [Order Details]
SET Discount = Discount + 0.1
WHERE OrderID = @ID
AND QUANTITY >= 5

-- Check the total price, after the extra discount, to see if
-- this order qualifies for this discount.

IF (SELECT SUM(Quantity * UnitPrice * (1-Discount))
FROM [Order Details]
WHERE OrderID = @ID) < 500

-- Does not qualify, roll back the discount

ROLLBACK TRAN Discount

-- Commit the transaction, inserting the order permanently

COMMIT TRAN NewOrder
```

CAUTION

Transaction names are case sensitive in SQL Server 2000.

CAUTION

In a ROLLBACK TRAN statement, the only names allowed are the name of a saved transaction or the name of the outermost transaction.

Using Implicit Transactions

As commented earlier in this chapter, SQL Server starts a transaction automatically every time you modify data. However, these transactions are automatically committed when the operation terminates. In this way, each statement by itself is a transaction in SQL Server.

You can set a connection in Implicit Transactions mode. In this mode, the first time you modify data, SQL Server starts a transaction and keeps the transaction open until you decide explicitly to commit or roll back the transaction.

To set the Implicit Transactions mode in a connection, you must execute the SET IMPLICIT_TRANSACTIONS ON statement. Listing 13.8 shows an example of implicit transactions.

CAUTION

SQL Server 2000 connections start with Implicit Transactions mode off, so any change you make to a database is permanent, unless it is executed inside a user-defined transaction.

EXAMPLE

Listing 13.8: Using the Implicit Transactions Mode

```
USE Northwind
GO

SET NOCOUNT ON
SET IMPLICIT_TRANSACTIONS ON
GO

SELECT @@TRANCOUNT
AS 'Transactions levels before UPDATE'

UPDATE Customers
SET ContactName = 'Peter Rodriguez'
WHERE CustomerID = 'ANATR'

SELECT @@TRANCOUNT
AS 'Transactions levels after UPDATE'

ROLLBACK TRAN

SELECT @@TRANCOUNT
AS 'Transactions levels after ROLLBACK TRAN'
```

OUTPUT

```
Transactions levels before UPDATE
------------------------------
0

Transactions levels after UPDATE
------------------------------
1

Transactions levels after ROLLBACK TRAN
--------------------------------------
0
```

TIP

Use Implicit Transactions mode in testing environments. In this mode, you can always roll back your actions.

Transactions and Runtime Errors

It is a common misconception that errors inside a transaction force the transaction to roll back. However, this is not always true, and you should provide the appropriate error control to decide when to roll back the changes after an error.

You can use the @@ERROR system function to detect the error caused by the latest statement sent to SQL Server in your connection. If the statement was successful, @@ERROR will return 0.

In some cases, you can consider an error as something that is perfectly valid for SQL Server. For example, you can execute an INSERT statement, and because of the restricting conditions, the statement does not insert any row. For SQL Server, the statement was completed successfully and @@ERROR returned 0. However, if you called the @@ROWCOUNT function, you can see that it returns 0 as well, because 0 rows were affected by the latest statement.

Another potential problem might be trying to commit a nonexistent transaction, because of a previous rollback in the same connection. A rollback does not cancel the batch, and the execution continues, potentially arriving at a COMMIT TRAN or ROLLBACK TRAN again, producing a runtime error.

Listing 13.9 shows the following sequence:

1. You start a transaction.

2. You try to create a new product in category 10 and get an error message because category 10 does not exist.

3. You create a new order.

4. Unaware of the previous product error, the execution continues and you try to insert the new product in an existing order, thinking that this product exists. You do not get an error message, but nothing is actually inserted.

5. You commit the transaction thinking that the order contains a product, but actually it doesn't.

6. You start a new transaction.

7. You try to create a new product in category 10 and you get an error message because category 10 does not exist.

8. The batch detects the error and decides to roll back the transaction.

Listing 13.9: The Same Transaction With and Without Error Control

```
USE Northwind
GO

----------------------
-- Without Error Control
----------------------

DECLARE @PID int, @OID int

PRINT CHAR(10) + 'Start a transaction without error control' + CHAR(10)

BEGIN TRAN

INSERT Products (ProductName, CategoryID, UnitPrice)
VALUES ('New Cars Magazine Year Subscription', 10, 35.0)

SET @PID = SCOPE_IDENTITY()

INSERT Orders (CustomerID, OrderDate)
VALUES ('COMMI', '2000-11-23')

SET @OID = SCOPE_IDENTITY()

INSERT [Order Details]
(OrderID, ProductID, UnitPrice, Quantity, Discount)
SELECT @OID, ProductID, UnitPrice, 1, 0.3
FROM Products
WHERE ProductID = @PID

COMMIT TRAN

PRINT CHAR(10)
+ 'The transaction has been partially applied'
+ CHAR(10)

SELECT ProductName
FROM Products
WHERE ProductID = @PID

SELECT CustomerID, OrderDate
FROM Orders
WHERE OrderID = @OID

SELECT UnitPrice, Quantity
FROM [Order Details]
```

Listing 13.9: continued

```
WHERE ProductID = @PID
GO


--------------------
-- With Error Control
--------------------

DECLARE @PID int, @OID int

PRINT CHAR(10)
+ 'Start a transaction with error control'
+ CHAR(10)

BEGIN TRAN

INSERT Products (ProductName, CategoryID, UnitPrice)
VALUES ('New Cars Magazine Year Subscription', 10, 35.0)

IF @@ERROR <> 0
GOTO CancelOrder

SET @PID = SCOPE_IDENTITY()

INSERT Orders (CustomerID, OrderDate)
VALUES ('COMMI', '2000-11-23')

IF @@ERROR <> 0
GOTO CancelOrder

SET @OID = SCOPE_IDENTITY()

INSERT [Order Details]
(OrderID, ProductID, UnitPrice, Quantity, Discount)
SELECT @OID, ProductID, UnitPrice, 1, 0.3
FROM Products
WHERE ProductID = @PID

IF @@ERROR <> 0 OR @@ROWCOUNT=0
GOTO CancelOrder

COMMIT TRAN
GOTO CheckOrder

CancelOrder:

ROLLBACK TRAN
```

Listing 13.9: continued

```
CheckOrder:

PRINT CHAR(10)
+ 'The transaction has been completely rolled back'
+ CHAR(10)

SELECT ProductName
FROM Products
WHERE ProductID = @PID

SELECT CustomerID, OrderDate
FROM Orders
WHERE OrderID = @OID

SELECT UnitPrice, Quantity
FROM [Order Details]
WHERE ProductID = @PID
```

Start a transaction without error control

```
Server: Msg 547, Level 16, State 1, Line 1
INSERT statement conflicted with COLUMN
➡FOREIGN KEY constraint 'FK_Products_Categories'.
➡The conflict occurred in database 'Northwind',
➡table 'Categories', column 'CategoryID'.
The statement has been terminated.

(1 row(s) affected)


(0 row(s) affected)


The transaction has been partially applied

ProductName
----------------------------------------

(0 row(s) affected)

CustomerID OrderDate
---------- ---------------------------------------------------------
COMMI      2000-11-23 00:00:00.000

(1 row(s) affected)

UnitPrice             Quantity
```

Listing 13.9: continued

```
.................... ........

(0 row(s) affected)


Start a transaction with error control

Server: Msg 547, Level 16, State 1, Line 1
INSERT statement conflicted with COLUMN
➥FOREIGN KEY constraint 'FK_Products_Categories'.
➥The conflict occurred in database 'Northwind',
➥table 'Categories', column 'CategoryID'.
The statement has been terminated.


The transaction has been completely rolled back


ProductName
--------------------------------------

(0 row(s) affected)

CustomerID OrderDate
---------- --------------------------------------------------------

(0 row(s) affected)

UnitPrice            Quantity
-------------------- --------

(0 row(s) affected)
```

Concurrency Problems

In a multiuser environment, as several users try to access the same data at the same time, trying to perform different actions, you can encounter various concurrency problems.

In the following sections you learn every potential problem and, later in this chapter, you will see how to use the right isolation level to solve the concurrency problem and how SQL Server uses locks to support these isolation levels.

Every concurrency problem is illustrated with a figure. Every figure shows two connections, called Connection A and Connection B. These two connections can be made from the same computer or from different computers, and by the same user or by different users. SQL Server has to solve concurrency problems between connections, regardless of which user or client computer is used to establish these connections.

Lost Updates

You can experience a lost update situation whenever two connections modify the same data in sequence, because SQL Server will maintain only the last successful update. Consider the example of Figure 13.1:

1. Connection A retrieves the UnitPrice of Product 25 in the variable @UP for later use.

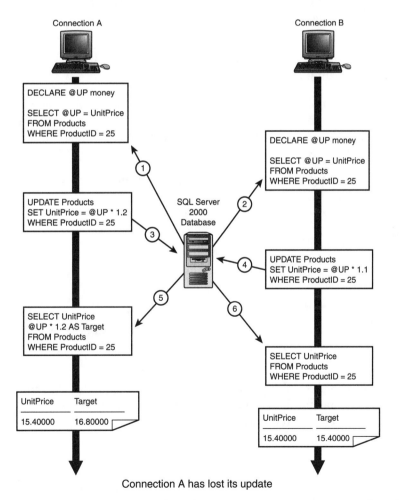

Figure 13.1: *Updating data from two connections can produce lost updates.*

2. Connection B retrieves the UnitPrice of Product 25 in the variable @UP for later use.

3. Connection A updates the price of Product 25, increasing the price 20% over the price saved in the variable @UP. The change is permanent.

4. Connection B updates the price of Product 25, increasing the price 10% over the price saved in the variable @UP. Connection B is unaware that Connection A changed the product after step 2. The new price is changed permanently—overwriting the price modified by Connection A in step 3.

5. Connection A checks the new price and compares it with the calculated price and finds that they are different. The update from Connection A is lost.

6. Connection B checks the new price and it is the same as the intended computed value.

This problem can be prevented by writing atomic UPDATE statements in both Connection A and Connection B. An atomic UPDATE contains the reading operation and the writing operation in a single statement, as in Listing 13.10.

EXAMPLE

Listing 13.10: Write Atomic UPDATE Statements to Prevent Lost Updates

```
USE Northwind
GO

UPDATE Products
SET UnitPrice = UnitPrice * 1.2
WHERE ProductID = 25
```

Uncommitted Dependency (Dirty Read)

Reading data without using locks can produce unexpected results. Other connections can modify data temporarily, and you can use that new data in your calculations, driving you to incorrect results.

In this case, you could say that you are reading dirty data, because the data has not been committed yet. In other words, your calculations depend on uncommitted data.

Figure 13.2 shows an example of this situation:

1. Connection A starts a new transaction to update product prices. Inside the transaction, Connection A increases product prices by 20%. The transaction is not committed yet, so these changes are provisional.

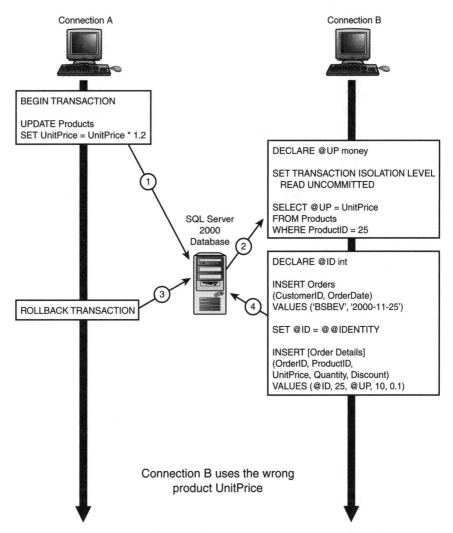

Connection A

```
BEGIN TRANSACTION

UPDATE Products
SET UnitPrice = UnitPrice * 1.2
```

```
ROLLBACK TRANSACTION
```

SQL Server
2000
Database

Connection B

```
DECLARE @UP money

SET TRANSACTION ISOLATION LEVEL
    READ UNCOMMITTED

SELECT @UP = UnitPrice
FROM Products
WHERE ProductID = 25
```

```
DECLARE @ID int

INSERT Orders
(CustomerID, OrderDate)
VALUES ('BSBEV', '2000-11-25')

SET @ID = @@IDENTITY

INSERT [Order Details]
(OrderID, ProductID,
UnitPrice, Quantity, Discount)
VALUES (@ID, 25, @UP, 10, 0.1)
```

Connection B uses the wrong
product UnitPrice

Figure 13.2: Reading data without using locks can produce dirty reads.

2. Connection B decides to work reading uncommitted data. Connection B retrieves the price for product 25. This price is dirty, because Connection A has changed this value temporarily to be 20% higher than before.

3. Connection A changes its mind and decides to roll back the changes on product prices. In this case, product 25 recovers its original price.

4. Connection B, unaware of the changes made by Connection A in step 3, creates a new Order and a new Order Detail for product 25, using the price incorrectly retrieved in step 2. These insertions in the database are permanent.

SQL Server 2000 prevents this problem automatically by using READ COMMITTED as the default isolation level. In this way, other connections cannot see the changes before they are considered permanent. Listing 13.11 shows how to declare the same operation in Connection B as READ COMMITTED, using an atomic INSERT instead of a SELECT followed by INSERT. In this case, Connection B must wait for Connection A to liberate its locks before proceeding with the UPDATE operation.

EXAMPLE

Listing 13.11: Do Not Use the READ UNCOMMITTED Isolation Level If You Want to Prevent Dirty Reads

```
USE Northwind
GO

SET TRANSACTION ISOLATION LEVEL READ COMMITTED

DECLARE @ID int

INSERT Orders
(CustomerID, OrderDate)
VALUES ('BSBEV', '2000-11-25')

SET @ID = @@IDENTITY

INSERT [Order Details]
(OrderID, ProductID, UnitPrice, Quantity, Discount)
SELECT @ID, ProductID, UnitPrice, 10, 0.1
FROM Products
WHERE ProductID = 25
```

NOTE

Later in this chapter, you will learn the READ UNCOMMITTED and READ COMMITTED isolation levels.

Inconsistent Analysis (Nonrepeatable Read)

In a multiuser environment, other users dynamically modify the data stored in a database.

Trying to execute a long-running process, such as a monthly report, can produce some inconsistencies because of changes produced in the database from the beginning of the report to the end. This can be considered an inconsistent analysis, because every time you read data, the data is different. This situation is called *nonrepeatable reads*.

To produce a long-running report, you must retrieve the number of orders from the Order Details table because you are interested only in orders with Order Details. Later in the report, you might want to calculate the average of total price per order, using the value retrieved previously.

Figure 13.3 shows an example of this situation:

1. Connection A retrieves the total number of orders with at least one row in the Order Details table, and stores this value in the @Count variable.

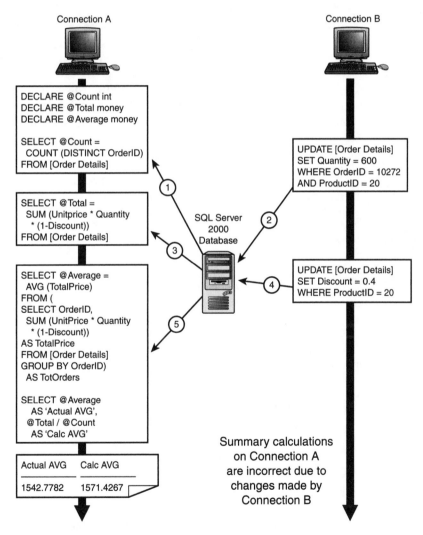

Figure 13.3: This is an example of inconsistent analysis.

2. Connection B updates the Order Details table changing the quantity of the Product 20 in the Order 10272.

3. The total number of rows has not been changed from Connection B, and now you can calculate the total price of the complete Order Details table and store this value in the @Total variable. This total includes the change made by Connection B in step 2.

4. Connection B updates the Order Details table again, changing the discount to Product 20.

5. Connection A is not aware of the changes on discount that Connection B applied to Product 20. So, it does not know that the content of the variable @Total is invalid. Connection A calculates the average price per order in two ways and every way provides a different result.

This problem can be prevented by minimizing the repeated reads and trying to convert them into atomic operations, or using the REPEATABLE READ isolation level. When using the REPEATABLE READ isolation level, the retrieved data is locked until the transaction terminates, preventing changes to the data from other connections.

Listing 13.12 shows that the average price calculated directly or indirectly produces the same results in an atomic SELECT statement.

EXAMPLE

Listing 13.12: Use Atomic SELECT Statements to Prevent Repeatable Reads

```
USE Northwind
GO

SELECT AVG(TotalPrice) AS 'Actual AVG',
SUM(TotalPrice) / COUNT(OrderID) AS 'Calc AVG'
FROM (
SELECT OrderID, SUM(UnitPrice * Quantity * (1 - Discount))
AS TotalPrice
FROM [Order Details]
GROUP BY OrderID) AS TotOrders
```

NOTE

Later in this chapter, you will learn the REPEATABLE READ isolation levels.

Phantom Reads

In the preceding section, you covered the concurrency problem due to updates in data previously read. If other connections are inserting data in the range of data you are analyzing, you can find that those new rows appear in your result sets with no apparent reason, from your connection point of view. These new rows are called *phantoms*.

This problem produces inconsistent analysis as well, because your previous totals are no longer valid after the insertion of new rows.

Figure 13.4 shows a very simple example of this problem:

1. Connection A retrieves the list of orders that includes the Product 25, and it produces a result set with 6 rows, including orders 10259, 10337, 10408, 10523, 10847, and 10966.

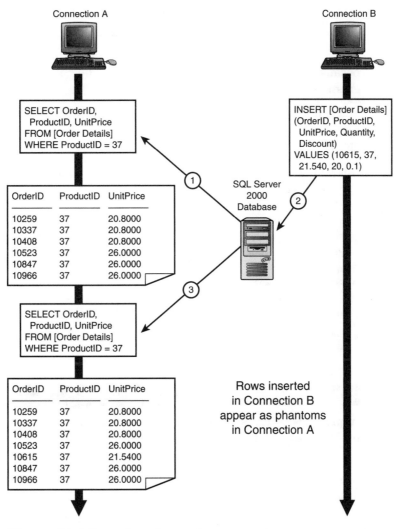

Figure 13.4: *Insertions from other connections can appear in your results as phantom rows.*

2. Connection B inserts a new order detail in the Order 10615 with the product 25.

3. Connection A resends the same statement as in step 1, but it retrieves a new row, correspondent to the Order 10615. Connection A was unaware of this insertion, so it considers this row to be a phantom.

CAUTION

Having phantoms is nothing to avoid per se, unless they produce inconsistent analysis as well, which is the usual case.

Preventing this problem is more difficult than in the previous cases, because SQL Server needs to lock rows that do not exist yet, locking non-existing data.

You can use the SERIALIZABLE isolation level, or the SERIALIZABLE optimizer hint, to prevent phantom reads. Listing 13.13 shows how to use the SERIALIZABLE optimizer hint.

EXAMPLE

Listing 13.13: Using SERIALIZABLE Optimizer Hint Inside a Transaction to Prevent Phantom Reads

```
USE Northwind
GO

SELECT OrderID,
ProductID, UnitPrice
FROM [Order Details] (SERIALIZABLE)
WHERE ProductID = 37
```

NOTE

Later in this chapter, you will learn how SQL Server implements the SERIALIZABLE isolation level.

Isolation Levels

In previous sections of this chapter, you learned about the concurrency problems experienced in a multiuser environment.

It is important to decide how changes from other connections can affect your results, or when to allow other connections to apply changes to the data you use in your connection.

You can select the isolation level of your transactions in SQL Server 2000 either per transaction or per table. You can use the SET ISOLATION LEVEL statement to specify the isolation level at the transaction level. To select the isolation level per table, you can use locking hints.

SQL Server 2000 supports four isolation levels:

- READ COMMITTED
- READ UNCOMMITTED
- REPEATABLE READ
- SERIALIZABLE

Isolation levels are defined to solve specific concurrency problems as shown in Figure 13.5.

		Isolation Level			
P Problem S Solution X Solved by standard exclusive locks inside transactions		READ UNCOMMITTED	READ COMMITTED	REPEATABLE READ	SERIALIZABLE
Concurrency Problem	Lost Update	X	X	X	X
	Dirty Reads	P	S	S	S
	Inconsistent Analysis	P	P	S	S
	Phantom Reads	P	P	P	S

Figure 13.5: *Every isolation level solves specific concurrency problems.*

NOTE

Note that SQL Server avoids lost updates automatically by using exclusive locks inside transactions. However, after the transaction terminates, other connections can modify the same data again, and SQL Server will always keep the latest modified value.

READ COMMITTED

SQL Server 2000 uses by default the READ COMMITTED isolation level. Using this setting, transactions cannot see changes from other connections while they are not committed or rolled back. SQL Server implements this isolation level, locking the modified data exclusively; therefore, other transactions cannot read the modified data.

NOTE

ANSI-92 specifies that if a connection tries to read data that is being modified by another connection, it can either wait for data to be unlocked or it must see the previous state of the data.

SQL Server implements exclusive locks to solve this situation, so other connections must wait. Other RDBMS products implement the other way, so users can see the previous state of the data until changes are made permanent.

Every implementation has advantages and disadvantages.

Using this isolation level you can prevent dirty reads, because you cannot see data modifications from other connections that have not been committed; however, other connections can change some of the data you have read already during your transaction, producing nonrepeatable reads, or add new rows to the data set you are reading, producing phantoms.

TIP

Try to use the READ COMMITTED isolation table as a standard isolation level because it is less intrusive than REPEATABLE READ and SERIALIZABLE, and it provides a better concurrency to your database application.

Setting the READ COMMITTED locking hint for a table, in the FROM clause of a query, overrides the transaction isolation level. Listing 13.14 shows how to use the READ COMMITTED isolation level and READCOMMITTED locking hint.

EXAMPLE

Listing 13.14: Use READ COMMITTED to Prevent Dirty Reads

```
USE Northwind
GO


-- Use the READCOMMITTED optimizer hint for a table

SELECT *
FROM Products (READCOMMITTED)
GO


-- Use the READ COMMITTED ISOLATION LEVEL for a transaction

SET ISOLATION LEVEL READ COMMITTED
GO


SELECT *
FROM Products
```

READ UNCOMMITTED

In some cases, it might be interesting to read data without being affected by any potential lock held by other connections. A typical example is to search for some general information about the data contained in a table—such as the total number of rows—while the table is being modified by other connections. In these cases, you don't care about dirty reads, and reading provisional data is acceptable.

Using the READ UNCOMMITTED isolation level, SQL Server does not check for exclusive locks affecting the data, and does not lock the data being read with shared locks. You can use this isolation level by using the SET TRANSACTION ISOLATION LEVEL READ UNCOMMITTED statement.

You can use the READUNCOMMITTED locking hint to specify the READ UNCOMMITTED isolation level for a specific table in a query, regardless of the current transaction isolation level. Listing 13.15 shows an example of this locking hint.

NOTE

The READUNCOMMITTED and NOLOCK locking hints are equivalent.

EXAMPLE

Listing 13.15: Using the READ UNCOMMITTED Isolation Level

```
USE Northwind
GO

-- Use the READUNCOMMITTED or the NOLOCK locking hint
-- to avoid lockings on specific tables

SELECT COUNT(*)
FROM [Order Details] (READUNCOMMITTED) -- or (NOLOCK)
GO

-- Use the READ UNCOMMITTED Isolation level
-- to specify this setting for the current connection

SET TRANSACTION ISOLATION LEVEL READ UNCOMMITTED
GO

SELECT COUNT(*)
FROM [Order Details]

SELECT MAX(OrderID)
FROM Orders
```

CAUTION

Using the READ UNCOMMITTED isolation level makes sense only when you are reading for data. Applying this isolation level to a table that is being modified by the same transaction does not prevent the production of exclusive locks on this table.

REPEATABLE READ

Use the REPEATABLE READ isolation level to guarantee that the retrieved data will not change during the transaction. To achieve this isolation level, SQL Server must lock the data retrieved, preventing updates from other connections. This is important on long-running processes where the results must be consistent all during the process, such as during long-running reports.

This isolation level provides consistent analysis, but it does not prevent the appearance of phantom reads.

You can override the default transaction isolation level for one specific table in a query using the REPEATABLEREAD locking hint in the FROM clause of the query, as in Listing 13.16.

EXAMPLE

Listing 13.16: Use the REPEATABLE READ Isolation Level to Prevent Inconsistent Analysis

```
USE Northwind
GO

-- Use the REPEATABLEREAD to prevent inconsistent analysis
-- when reading from a table
-- that is being modified by other connections

SELECT COUNT(*)
FROM [Order Details] (REPEATABLEREAD)
GO

-- Set REPEATABLE READ isolation level at connection setting
-- to affect every table used in the connection

SET TRANSACTION ISOLATION LEVEL REPEATABLE READ
GO

SELECT COUNT(*) AS NRows
FROM [Order Details]

SELECT SUM(Quantity * UnitPrice * (1-Discount)) AS Total
FROM [Order Details]
```

CAUTION

Use the REPEATABLE READ isolation level with caution, because it locks connections that try to modify the data affected by this transaction.

SERIALIZABLE

Use the SERIALIZABLE isolation level to prevent all the concurrency problems, including the appearance of phantom reads.

SQL Server must lock enough resources to prevent the possibility that other connections could insert or modify data covered by the range specified in your query. The way SQL Server enforces this isolation level depends on the existence of a suitable index, adequate to the WHERE clause of the query or queries to protect:

- If the table does not have a suitable index, SQL Server must lock the entire table.

- If there is an appropriate index, SQL Server locks the keys in the index corresponding to the range of rows in your query, plus the next key to the range.

TIP

Create an index according to the fields used in the WHERE clause of a query that references a table with a SERIALIZABLE locking hint, to prevent locks at table level.

CAUTION

Applying a SERIALIZABLE isolation level to a table used in a query without a WHERE clause will lock the entire table.

You can use the SERIALIZABLE locking hint to apply this isolation level to a specific table in a query, overriding the actual transaction isolation level.

NOTE

The SERIALIZABLE locking hint is equivalent to the HOLDLOCK locking hint.

This isolation level is important to prevent insertion that could invalidate your analysis. Listing 13.17 shows an example of this isolation level.

Listing 13.17: Use the SERIALIZABLE Locking Hint to Prevent an Inconsistent Analysis Because of Phantom Reads

```
USE Northwind
GO

-- Use the SERIALIZABLE or HOLDLOCK locking hints to prevent
-- inconsistent analysis due to Phantom Reads

DECLARE @ID int

BEGIN TRANSACTION

SELECT @ID = MAX(RegionID)
FROM Region (SERIALIZABLE)

INSERT Region
(RegionID, RegionDescription)
SELECT @ID + 1, 'Europe Union'

COMMIT TRANSACTION
GO

-- Use the SERIALIZABLE Isolation level to prevent
-- inconsistent analysis due to Phantom Reads in a long running process

SET TRANSACTION ISOLATION LEVEL SERIALIZABLE
GO

BEGIN TRANSACTION

-- Your queries

COMMIT TRANSACTION
```

CAUTION

SERIALIZABLE is the isolation level that allows the lowest concurrency. Use it only when necessary and with the shortest possible transactions.

Types of Locks

SQL Server uses locks to provide concurrency while maintaining data consistency and integrity. Whenever you read data, SQL Server locks the data while reading, to prevent other connections from modifying provide the data at the same time.

If you modify data, SQL Server locks that data as long as the transaction lasts to avoid dirty reads in other connections. These locks are called exclusive locks, and they are incompatible with any other locks.

SQL Server uses other types of locks to prevent specific concurrency problems and to guarantee the consistency of internal operations.

Locks are maintained as long as they are necessary, depending on the isolation level selected. It is the programmer's responsibility to design short transactions that execute quickly and do not lock the data for a long time.

If a connection is trying to get a lock in a resource that is locked by another connection, the connection has to wait until the resource is free or is locked in a compatible mode to continue the execution. SQL Server does not produce any error message when a connection is being blocked by another transaction. Usually, this blocking disappears shortly and the transaction continues.

If a connection is blocked for a longer time than the query timeout specified in the client database access library, the application can determine whether the transaction should continue or should be aborted, perhaps with the user's consent. In this case, it is the responsibility of the client application to search for the reasons for this timeout, because SQL Server does not report specifically the existence of any blocking situation.

If necessary, SQL Server can lock any of the following resources:

- A row in a table, or RID.
- A key in an index page.
- A page in a table.
- A page in an index.
- An extent in a database. SQL Server locks extents during the process of allocation and deallocation of new extents and pages.
- An entire table.
- An index.
- A database. SQL Server always grants a shared lock on a database to the process that connects to a database. This is helpful to detect whether users are connected to a database before trying intrusive actions, such as dropping or restoring the database.

In some cases, SQL Server decides to escalate locks to an upper level to keep locking costs at an appropriate level. By using locking hints (PAGLOCK, ROWLOCK, TABLOCK, TABLOCKX), you can suggest that Query Optimizer use locks at a certain level.

You can use the sp_lock system stored procedure to list the locks currently existing in the server. Specifying the SPID (system process ID) of an existing process when calling sp_lock, you will retrieve the list of locks that belong to a specific process. Listing 13.18 shows how to use sp_lock to get information about locks.

Listing 13.18: Use sp_lock to Get Information About Lockings

```
USE Northwind
GO

BEGIN TRAN

DECLARE @UP money

-- Read and lock the data to prevent updates

SELECT @UP = AVG(UnitPrice)
FROM [Order Details] (REPEATABLEREAD)
WHERE ProductID = 37

-- Update the Product 37

UPDATE Products
SET UnitPrice = @UP
WHERE ProductID = 37

-- List locks server wide

EXECUTE sp_lock

-- List locks for this connection only

EXECUTE sp_lock @@SPID

-- Cancel changes

ROLLBACK TRAN
```

spid	dbid	ObjId	IndId	Type	Resource	Mode	Status
52	8	0	0	DB		S	GRANT
53	6	0	0	DB		S	GRANT
54	6	0	0	DB		S	GRANT
56	6	0	0	DB		S	GRANT
56	6	325576198	4	KEY	(84006690ff8d)	S	GRANT
56	6	117575457	0	TAB		IX	GRANT
56	6	325576198	1	KEY	(cd0058f4cb88)	S	GRANT

Listing 13.18: continued

```
56   6   325576198   1   KEY  (fb00d3668ea6)   S    GRANT
56   6   117575457   1   KEY  (2500ef7f5749)   X    GRANT
56   6   325576198   1   PAG  1:148            IS   GRANT
56   6   325576198   1   KEY  (4000a82ec576)   S    GRANT
56   6   325576198   1   PAG  1:182            IS   GRANT
56   6   325576198   1   PAG  1:181            IS   GRANT
56   6   325576198   4   PAG  1:198            IS   GRANT
56   6   325576198   1   PAG  1:200            IS   GRANT
56   6   325576198   1   PAG  1:208            IS   GRANT
56   6   325576198   4   KEY  (38008da3b95f)   S    GRANT
56   6   117575457   1   PAG  1:276            IX   GRANT
56   6   325576198   4   KEY  (86009acb8f9e)   S    GRANT
56   6   325576198   1   KEY  (840022f8faea)   S    GRANT
56   6   325576198   0   TAB                   IS   GRANT
56   6   325576198   4   KEY  (cd00166aca95)   S    GRANT
56   1   85575343    0   TAB                   IS   GRANT
56   6   325576198   4   KEY  (fb00d769ae1d)   S    GRANT
56   6   325576198   1   KEY  (860044a822ed)   S    GRANT
56   6   325576198   1   KEY  (3800a93e5703)   S    GRANT
56   6   325576198   4   KEY  (400055e1cf9b)   S    GRANT
57   6   0           0   DB                    S    GRANT
58   8   0           0   DB                    S    GRANT

spid dbid  ObjId      IndId Type Resource      Mode Status
---- ----  ---------- ----- ---- -------------- ---- ------
56   6   0           0   DB                    S    GRANT
56   6   325576198   4   KEY  (84006690ff8d)   S    GRANT
56   6   117575457   0   TAB                   IX   GRANT
56   6   325576198   1   KEY  (cd0058f4cb88)   S    GRANT
56   6   325576198   1   KEY  (fb00d3668ea6)   S    GRANT
56   6   117575457   1   KEY  (2500ef7f5749)   X    GRANT
56   6   325576198   1   PAG  1:148            IS   GRANT
56   6   325576198   1   KEY  (4000a82ec576)   S    GRANT
56   6   325576198   1   PAG  1:182            IS   GRANT
56   6   325576198   1   PAG  1:181            IS   GRANT
56   6   325576198   4   PAG  1:198            IS   GRANT
56   6   325576198   1   PAG  1:200            IS   GRANT
56   6   325576198   1   PAG  1:208            IS   GRANT
56   6   325576198   4   KEY  (38008da3b95f)   S    GRANT
56   6   117575457   1   PAG  1:276            IX   GRANT
56   6   325576198   4   KEY  (86009acb8f9e)   S    GRANT
56   6   325576198   1   KEY  (840022f8faea)   S    GRANT
56   6   325576198   0   TAB                   IS   GRANT
56   6   325576198   4   KEY  (cd00166aca95)   S    GRANT
56   1   85575343    0   TAB                   IS   GRANT
56   6   325576198   4   KEY  (fb00d769ae1d)   S    GRANT
```

Listing 13.18: continued

```
56    6    325576198   1    KEY   (860044a822ed)   S    GRANT
56    6    325576198   1    KEY   (3800a93e5703)   S    GRANT
56    6    325576198   4    KEY   (400055e1cf9b)   S    GRANT
```

Using the SET LOCK_TIMEOUT statement, you can specify the number of milliseconds that a session will wait for any lock to be released before reporting a timeout error in the current session, independently of the query timeout defined in the client application. Use the @@LOCK_TIMEOUT system function to get the current lock timeout value, which can be

- @@LOCK_TIMEOUT = 0—SQL Server cancels the query as soon as it detects a blocking situation, sending the error 1222 "Lock request time out period exceeded."

- @@LOCK_TIMEOUT = -1—SQL Server waits until the block disappears.

- @@LOCK_TIMEOUT > 0—Indicates the number of milliseconds that SQL Server will wait before sending the error 1222.

When the lock timeout occurs, the batch is cancelled and the execution goes to the next batch. Listing 13.19 shows an example of LOCK_TIMEOUT for two connections.

EXAMPLE

Listing 13.19: Use LOCK_TIMEOUT to Control How Much Time a Connection Will Wait for Locks to Be Released

```
-- Connection A

USE Northwind
GO

BEGIN TRANSACTION

SELECT *
FROM Products (HOLDLOCK)

-- Note that we do not terminate the transaction.


---------------
-- Connection B
---------------


USE Northwind
GO

-- Specify 2000 milliseconds (2 seconds) as lock timeout

SET LOCK_TIMEOUT 2000
```

Listing 13.19: continued

```
GO

UPDATE Products
SET UnitPrice = UnitPrice * 0.9
GO

IF @@ERROR = 1222
PRINT CHAR(10) + 'Lock Timeout produced' + CHAR(10)

SELECT GetDate() as Now
```

OUTPUT

```
Server: Msg 1222, Level 16, State 1, Line 1
Lock request time out period exceeded.

Lock Timeout produced

Now
```
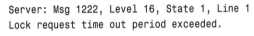
```
2000-12-11 00:55:48.210
```

SQL Server uses the following lock types:

- Shared locks
- Exclusive locks
- Update locks
- Intent locks
- Schema locks
- Bulk Update locks

NOTE

Bulk Update locks are used to prevent other connections from using a table while importing data in the table using the TABLOCK hint or setting the Table lock on Bulk Load option for the target table with the sp_tableoption system stored procedure.

SQL Server can grant a lock in a resource depending on other existing locks. Figure 13.6 shows the compatibility between locks.

CAUTION

The locks produced in a process do not affect any statement in the same process, so it is impossible to get blocked by any action performed in the same process.

A transaction is not affected by its own locks.

Existing granted mode	Requested mode	Intent shared (IS)	Shared (S)	Update (U)	Intent exclusive (IX)	Shared with intent exclusive (SIX)	Exclusive (X)
Intent shared (IS)		Yes	Yes	Yes	Yes	Yes	No
Shared (S)		Yes	Yes	Yes	No	No	No
Update (U)		Yes	Yes	No	No	No	No
Intent exclusive (IX)		Yes	No	No	Yes	No	No
Shared with intent exclusive (SIX)		Yes	No	No	No	No	No
Exclusive (X)		No	No	No	No	No	No

Figure 13.6: This table shows the compatibility between locks.

Shared Locks

During the process of reading data, SQL Server uses shared locks (S) to prevent changes to the data from other processes. However, shared locks do not prevent reading operations from other connections. SQL Server releases shared locks as soon as possible, unless the reading operation is inside a user-defined transaction with an isolation level of REPEATABLE READ or SERIALIZABLE.

If a query reads many rows from a table, in a transaction with the default isolation level, only portions of that table are locked at any given time. In this case, as soon as the statement terminates, the shared locks are released without waiting to finish the transaction. Use the HOLDLOCK lock hint to maintain these shared locks until the end of the transaction.

NOTE

Any DML statement (SELECT, UPDATE, INSERT, or DELETE) can produce shared locks, as long as these statements are reading data from one or more tables.

Listing 13.20 shows how, after executing a SELECT statement, locks are released; however, after the INSERT statement, you can see shared locks in the Products and Orders tables, because you use them for the HOLDLOCK and REPEATABLEREAD lock hints.

Listing 13.20: Examples of Shared Locks

```
USE Northwind
GO

-- Start a transaction

BEGIN TRAN

-- Get OBJECT_IDs to interpret the sp_lock output

SELECT OBJECT_ID('Order details') as 'Order details'
SELECT OBJECT_ID('Orders') as 'Orders'
SELECT OBJECT_ID('Products') as 'Products'

-- Get current locks to use as a baseline to further executions of sp_lock

PRINT 'Initial lock status' + CHAR(10)

EXEC sp_lock

-- Execute a standard SELECT statement

SELECT MAX(OrderID)
FROM Orders
WHERE CustomerID = 'ALFKI'

-- Get locks status after the SELECT statement

PRINT CHAR(10) + 'Lock status after SELECT' + CHAR(10)

EXEC sp_lock

-- Perform an INSERT statement in Order details,
-- reading from Orders and Products

INSERT [Order Details]
(OrderID, ProductID, Unitprice, Quantity, Discount)
SELECT
(SELECT MAX(OrderID)
FROM Orders (HOLDLOCK)
WHERE CustomerID = 'ALFKI'),
ProductID, UnitPrice, 10, 0.1
FROM Products (REPEATABLEREAD)
WHERE ProductName = 'Tofu'
```

Listing 13.20: continued

```
-- Get locks status after the INSERT statement

PRINT CHAR(10) + 'Lock status after INSERT' + CHAR(10)

EXEC sp_lock

ROLLBACK TRAN

-- Get locks status after the ROLLBACK statement

PRINT CHAR(10) + 'Lock status after ROLLBACK' + CHAR(10)

EXEC sp_lock
```

OUTPUT

```
Order details
-------------
325576198

(1 row(s) affected)

Orders
----------
21575115

(1 row(s) affected)

Products
----------
117575457

(1 row(s) affected)

Initial lock status
```

spid	dbid	ObjId	IndId	Type	Resource	Mode	Status
51	4	0	0	DB		S	GRANT
52	4	0	0	DB		S	GRANT
53	10	0	0	DB		S	GRANT
54	7	0	0	DB		S	GRANT
55	1	85575343	0	TAB		IS	GRANT
55	6	0	0	DB		S	GRANT
56	10	0	0	DB		S	GRANT
57	6	0	0	DB		S	GRANT

Listing 13.20: continued

```
-----------
11011

(1 row(s) affected)
```

Lock status after SELECT

spid	dbid	ObjId	IndId	Type	Resource	Mode	Status
51	4	0	0	DB		S	GRANT
52	4	0	0	DB		S	GRANT
53	10	0	0	DB		S	GRANT
54	7	0	0	DB		S	GRANT
55	1	85575343	0	TAB		IS	GRANT
55	6	0	0	DB		S	GRANT
56	10	0	0	DB		S	GRANT
57	6	0	0	DB		S	GRANT

```
(1 row(s) affected)
```

Lock status after INSERT

spid	dbid	ObjId	IndId	Type	Resource	Mode	Status
51	4	0	0	DB		S	GRANT
52	4	0	0	DB		S	GRANT
53	10	0	0	DB		S	GRANT
54	7	0	0	DB		S	GRANT
55	6	117575457	0	TAB		IS	GRANT
55	6	0	0	DB		S	GRANT
55	6	325576198	5	PAG	1:189	IX	GRANT
55	6	325576198	4	PAG	1:187	IX	GRANT
55	6	325576198	3	PAG	1:202	IX	GRANT
55	6	325576198	2	PAG	1:201	IX	GRANT
55	6	325576198	1	PAG	1:211	IX	GRANT
55	6	21575115	3	PAG	1:248	IS	GRANT
55	6	21575115	3	KEY	(d300d99e322e)	RangeS-S	GRANT
55	6	117575457	1	PAG	1:276	IS	GRANT
55	6	117575457	4	PAG	1:281	IS	GRANT
55	6	21575115	0	TAB		IS	GRANT
55	6	325576198	1	KEY	(1100203d3739)	X	GRANT
55	6	325576198	2	KEY	(1100203d3739)	X	GRANT
55	6	325576198	3	KEY	(1100203d3739)	X	GRANT

Listing 13.20: continued

55	6	325576198	0	TAB		IX	GRANT
55	6	21575115	3	KEY	(18013d14dae8)	RangeS-S	GRANT
55	6	117575457	4	KEY	(c80063450f36)	S	GRANT
55	1	85575343	0	TAB		IS	GRANT
55	6	325576198	5	KEY	(11004b34faa9)	X	GRANT
55	6	325576198	4	KEY	(11004b34faa9)	X	GRANT
55	6	117575457	1	KEY	(0e00d057643e)	S	GRANT
56	10	0	0	DB		S	GRANT
57	6	0	0	DB		S	GRANT

Lock status after ROLLBACK

spid	dbid	ObjId	IndId	Type	Resource	Mode	Status
51	4	0	0	DB		S	GRANT
52	4	0	0	DB		S	GRANT
53	10	0	0	DB		S	GRANT
54	7	0	0	DB		S	GRANT
55	1	85575343	0	TAB		IS	GRANT
55	6	0	0	DB		S	GRANT
56	10	0	0	DB		S	GRANT
57	6	0	0	DB		S	GRANT

Exclusive Locks

SQL Server uses exclusive locks (X) to protect the modified data from other processes until the transaction terminates. This lock mode is incompatible with any other lock. In the preceding section, you can see in Listing 13.20 how an INSERT statement produces exclusive locks.

SQL Server creates exclusive locks when necessary, regardless of the selected isolation level. Inserted, deleted, or updated resources are always locked exclusively until the transaction terminates.

You can still see these resources from other processes using the READ UNCOMMITTED isolation level or the NOLOCK locking hint.

TIP

You can use mock updates to produce an exclusive lock in a row without modifying it. To SQL Server, you have modified the data, even if the new values are the same as the old ones, as in Listing 13.21.

EXAMPLE

Listing 13.21: Modifying Data Produces Exclusive Locks

```
-- Start a transaction

BEGIN TRAN

-- Get OBJECT_ID to interpret the sp_lock output

SELECT OBJECT_ID('Products') as 'Products'

-- Get current locks to use as a baseline to further executions of sp_lock

PRINT 'Initial lock status' + CHAR(10)

EXEC sp_lock

-- Execute a mock UPDATE statement

UPDATE Products
SET UnitPrice = UnitPrice
WHERE ProductID = 28

-- Get locks status after the mock UPDATE statement

PRINT CHAR(10) + 'Lock status after the mock UPDATE' + CHAR(10)

EXEC sp_lock

-- Execute a real UPDATE statement

UPDATE Products
SET UnitPrice = UnitPrice * 1.5
WHERE ProductID = 35

-- Get locks status after the real UPDATE statement

PRINT CHAR(10) + 'Lock status after the real UPDATE' + CHAR(10)

EXEC sp_lock

ROLLBACK TRAN
```

OUTPUT

```
Products
-----------
117575457

(1 row(s) affected)
```

Listing 13.21: continued

Initial lock status

spid	dbid	ObjId	IndId	Type	Resource	Mode	Status
51	4	0	0	DB		S	GRANT
52	4	0	0	DB		S	GRANT
53	10	0	0	DB		S	GRANT
54	7	0	0	DB		S	GRANT
55	1	85575343	0	TAB		IS	GRANT
55	6	0	0	DB		S	GRANT
56	10	0	0	DB		S	GRANT
57	6	0	0	DB		S	GRANT

(1 row(s) affected)

Lock status after the mock UPDATE

spid	dbid	ObjId	IndId	Type	Resource	Mode	Status
51	4	0	0	DB		S	GRANT
52	4	0	0	DB		S	GRANT
53	10	0	0	DB		S	GRANT
54	7	0	0	DB		S	GRANT
55	6	117575457	0	TAB		IX	GRANT
55	6	0	0	DB		S	GRANT
55	6	117575457	1	PAG	1:276	IX	GRANT
55	1	85575343	0	TAB		IS	GRANT
55	6	117575457	1	KEY	(1c00c4c874c4)	X	GRANT
56	10	0	0	DB		S	GRANT
57	6	0	0	DB		S	GRANT

(1 row(s) affected)

Lock status after the real UPDATE

spid	dbid	ObjId	IndId	Type	Resource	Mode	Status
51	4	0	0	DB		S	GRANT
52	4	0	0	DB		S	GRANT
53	10	0	0	DB		S	GRANT
54	7	0	0	DB		S	GRANT
55	6	117575457	0	TAB		IX	GRANT

Listing 13.21: continued

55	6	0	0	DB		S	GRANT
55	6	117575457	1	KEY	(230033203c6c)	X	GRANT
55	6	117575457	1	PAG	1:276	IX	GRANT
55	1	85575343	0	TAB		IS	GRANT
55	6	117575457	1	KEY	(1c00c4c874c4)	X	GRANT
56	10	0	0	DB		S	GRANT
57	6	0	0	DB		S	GRANT

> **NOTE**
>
> Modifying a row in a table with no clustered index produces a RID (Row ID) lock. If the table has a clustered index, the index leaf level is the collection of data pages; this is why the row lock is considered a key lock in the sp_lock output.

Update Locks

Update locks are an intermediate state between a shared lock and an exclusive lock. You use an update lock when you are reading some data with intentions of modifying the same data. To prevent modifications from other connections, you could lock the data exclusively, but in that case, you are preventing readings from other connections. Using update locks prevents undesired modifications, while allowing read access to the data from other connections.

If you used only a shared lock in the resource lock, and other connection gets another shared lock in the same resource, you can get a deadlock situation if both connections tried to convert their shared lock into exclusive locks.

In Listing 13.22, you can see an example of update locks. To execute this example, you must establish two connections to SQL Server:

1. Execute the first part of the script in Connection A, which reads a row from the Products table, using the UPDLOCK locking hint.

2. Attempt to execute an UPDATE statement of the same row from Connection B. The statement waits for locks to be released, because the existing update lock is incompatible with the exclusive lock required to modify data.

3. Execute an UPDATE statement from Connection A. Because this is the connection that holds the update lock, it is possible to update the data directly. In this case, the update lock is converted into an exclusive lock.

4. Connection B is still waiting because the existing exclusive lock is incompatible with the requested exclusive lock.

EXAMPLE

Listing 13.22: An Example of How to Use UPDLOCK

```
USE Northwind
GO

-- Start a transaction

BEGIN TRAN

-- Get OBJECT_ID to interpret the sp_lock output

SELECT OBJECT_ID('Products') as 'Products'

-- Get current locks to use as a baseline to further executions of sp_lock

PRINT 'Initial lock status' + CHAR(10)

EXEC sp_lock

SELECT ProductID, ProductName, UnitPrice
FROM Products (UPDLOCK)
WHERE ProductID = 28

PRINT CHAR(10) + 'lock status after SELECT' + CHAR(10)

EXEC sp_lock

-- Change to connection B and execute:
/*

UPDATE Products
SET UnitPrice = UnitPrice
WHERE ProductID = 28

*/

-- Change to connection A and execute:

PRINT CHAR(10) + 'lock status after UPDATE from Connection B' + CHAR(10)

EXEC sp_lock

-- Execute a mock UPDATE statement

UPDATE Products
SET UnitPrice = UnitPrice
WHERE ProductID = 28

-- Get locks status after the mock UPDATE statement
```

Listing 13.22: continued

```
PRINT CHAR(10) + 'Lock status after the mock UPDATE' + CHAR(10)

EXEC sp_lock

ROLLBACK TRAN
```

OUTPUT

```
Products
-----------
117575457

(1 row(s) affected)

Initial lock status

spid   dbid   ObjId        IndId   Type Resource              Mode       Status
------ ------ ------------ ------- ---- ---------------------- --------   ------
51     4      0            0       DB                          S          GRANT
52     4      0            0       DB                          S          GRANT
53     10     0            0       DB                          S          GRANT
54     7      0            0       DB                          S          GRANT
55     6      0            0       DB                          S          GRANT
55     1      85575343     0       TAB                         IS         GRANT
56     10     0            0       DB                          S          GRANT
57     6      0            0       DB                          S          GRANT
58     6      0            0       DB                          S          GRANT


ProductID    ProductName                               UnitPrice
-----------  ----------------------------------------- ---------------------
28           Rössle Sauerkraut                         45.6000

lock status after SELECT

spid   dbid   ObjId        IndId   Type Resource              Mode       Status
------ ------ ------------ ------- ---- ---------------------- --------   ------
51     4      0            0       DB                          S          GRANT
52     4      0            0       DB                          S          GRANT
53     10     0            0       DB                          S          GRANT
54     7      0            0       DB                          S          GRANT
55     6      0            0       DB                          S          GRANT
55     6      117575457    0       TAB                         IX         GRANT
55     6      117575457    1       PAG  1:276                  IU         GRANT
55     1      85575343     0       TAB                         IS         GRANT
55     6      117575457    1       KEY  (1c00c4c874c4)         U          GRANT
56     10     0            0       DB                          S          GRANT
57     6      0            0       DB                          S          GRANT
58     6      0            0       DB                          S          GRANT
```

Listing 13.22: continued

lock status after UPDATE from Connection B

spid	dbid	ObjId	IndId	Type	Resource	Mode	Status
51	4	0	0	DB		S	GRANT
52	4	0	0	DB		S	GRANT
53	10	0	0	DB		S	GRANT
54	7	0	0	DB		S	GRANT
55	6	0	0	DB		S	GRANT
55	6	117575457	0	TAB		IX	GRANT
55	6	117575457	1	PAG	1:276	IU	GRANT
55	1	85575343	0	TAB		IS	GRANT
55	6	117575457	1	KEY	(1c00c4c874c4)	U	GRANT
56	10	0	0	DB		S	GRANT
57	6	0	0	DB		S	GRANT
58	6	0	0	DB		S	GRANT
58	6	117575457	1	KEY	(1c00c4c874c4)	X	WAIT
58	6	117575457	1	PAG	1:276	IX	GRANT
58	6	117575457	0	TAB		IX	GRANT

Lock status after the mock UPDATE

spid	dbid	ObjId	IndId	Type	Resource	Mode	Status
51	4	0	0	DB		S	GRANT
52	4	0	0	DB		S	GRANT
53	10	0	0	DB		S	GRANT
54	7	0	0	DB		S	GRANT
55	6	0	0	DB		S	GRANT
55	6	117575457	0	TAB		IX	GRANT
55	6	117575457	1	PAG	1:276	IX	GRANT
55	1	85575343	0	TAB		IS	GRANT
55	6	117575457	1	KEY	(1c00c4c874c4)	X	GRANT
56	10	0	0	DB		S	GRANT
57	6	0	0	DB		S	GRANT
58	6	0	0	DB		S	GRANT
58	6	117575457	1	KEY	(1c00c4c874c4)	X	WAIT
58	6	117575457	1	PAG	1:276	IX	GRANT
58	6	117575457	0	TAB		IX	GRANT

Intent Locks

SQL Server can lock resources at different hierarchical levels: rows, pages, extents, tables, and databases. If one process holds a lock in a row, a different process could get a lock on the page where this row is stored, compromising the lock in the other connection. Another process could get a lock on the table, adding more complexity to this locking situation.

To prevent this situation, SQL Server uses intent locks at a higher level in the hierarchy, preventing incompatible levels from other connections.

If SQL Server grants shared locks at row level to a process, it grants an intent share (IS) lock at page and table level also, protecting the requested shared row lock. Figure 13.7 shows this case.

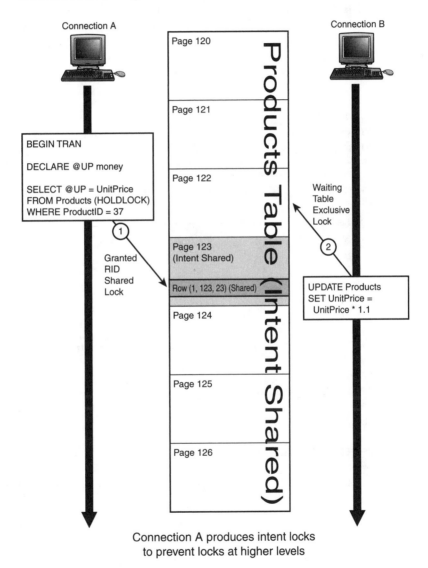

Connection A produces intent locks
to prevent locks at higher levels

Figure 13.7: *SQL Server uses intent locks to protect granted locks at lower hierarchical levels.*

To protect an exclusive (X) row lock, SQL Server grants an intent exclusive (IX) lock at page and table level.

In some cases, a SQL Server transaction requests shared locks on some rows and exclusive locks on other rows. In these cases, SQL Server will produce intent shared (IS) locks to protect the data pages that have only rows with shared locks. However, if a data page has at least one row with an exclusive lock, SQL Server will protect this page with an intent exclusive (IX) lock. Because some pages have intent shared locks and other pages have exclusive shared locks, at the table level SQL Server will use the shared with intent exclusive (SIX) lock.

Schema Locks

When SQL Server receives Data Definition Language (DDL) statements, it locks the object being created or modified with a schema modification lock (Sch-M), as in the example of Listing 13.23.

EXAMPLE

Listing 13.23: SQL Server Uses Schema Modification Locks to Protect Objects During Creation or Modification

```
USE Northwind
GO

BEGIN TRAN

CREATE TABLE TestSchema
(ID int)

-- Show names of the objects 1, 2 and 3 of Northwind,
-- because they are used in sp_lock

SELECT object_name(1) AS ID1

SELECT object_name(2) AS ID2

SELECT object_name(3) AS ID3

-- Show the ID of TestSchema table to identify locks on this table

SELECT Object_ID('TestSchema') AS TestSchemaID

EXEC sp_lock

ROLLBACK TRAN
```

Listing 13.23: continued

OUTPUT

```
ID1
- - - - - - - - - - - - -
sysobjects

ID2
- - - - - - - - - - - - -
sysindexes

ID3
- - - - - - - - - - - - -
syscolumns

TestSchemaID
- - - - - - - - - - - - -
1813581499


(1 row(s) affected)
```

spid	dbid	ObjId	IndId	Type	Resource	Mode	Status
51	4	0	0	DB		S	GRANT
52	4	0	0	DB		S	GRANT
53	10	0	0	DB		S	GRANT
54	7	0	0	DB		S	GRANT
55	6	0	0	DB		S	GRANT
56	10	0	0	DB		S	GRANT
57	6	0	0	DB		S	GRANT
57	6	1	0	TAB		IX	GRANT
57	6	3	0	TAB		IX	GRANT
57	6	2	0	TAB		IX	GRANT
57	6	1	3	KEY	(bb006c403485)	X	GRANT
57	6	2	1	KEY	(bb00da29dced)	X	GRANT
57	6	1813581499	0	TAB		Sch-M	GRANT
57	6	1	2	KEY	(f00169258f34)	X	GRANT
57	6	3	2	KEY	(04018aa462b1)	X	GRANT
57	1	85575343	0	TAB		IS	GRANT
57	6	1	1	KEY	(bb00194052c1)	X	GRANT
57	6	3	1	KEY	(bc00403fd981)	X	GRANT
58	6	0	0	DB		S	GRANT

As you saw in the output of Listing 13.23, there is a schema modification (Sch-M) lock on the table TestSchema and exclusive locks on some rows of the system tables sysobjects, syscolumns, and sysindexes.

During the process of compiling a query plan, SQL Server uses a schema stability (Sch-S) lock on the objects used in the query plan to prevent modifications on their definition that could potentially invalidate the query plan being compiled.

Changes to objects referenced in an existing compiled query plan force the query plan to be invalid, and SQL Server marks the query plan to be recompiled next time it is executed.

Key-Range Locks

SQL Server uses key-range locks to avoid phantom reads. As commented in the "Concurrency Problems" section earlier in this chapter, this is a special case of inconsistent analysis because of the insertion of rows from other processes in the range of rows affected by the process.

Key-range locks help serialize the following operations:

- Queries restricted by a range of values, to prevent other rows from being inserted in this range by other processes.

- Fetching a nonexistent row, with intentions of inserting the row at a later point in the transaction.

- Insert operations.

SQL Server implements range locks by locking keys in an index when you select the SERIALIZABLE isolation level, as you can see in Listing 13.24.

EXAMPLE

Listing 13.24: Use the SERIALIZABLE Locking Hint to Force Range Locks

```
USE Northwind
GO

-- Start a transaction

BEGIN TRAN

-- Get OBJECT_ID to interpret the sp_lock output

SELECT OBJECT_ID('Products') as 'Products'

-- Get current locks to use as a baseline to further executions of sp_lock

PRINT 'Initial lock status' + CHAR(10)

EXEC sp_lock

SELECT ProductID, ProductName, UnitPrice
FROM Products (SERIALIZABLE)
WHERE CategoryID = 3
```

Listing 13.24: continued

```
PRINT CHAR(10) + 'lock status after SELECT' + CHAR(10)

EXEC sp_lock

ROLLBACK TRAN
```

OUTPUT

```
Products
-----------
117575457


(1 row(s) affected)

Initial lock status

spid   dbid   ObjId         IndId   Type Resource          Mode      Status
------ ------ ------------  ------  ---- ----------------   --------  ------
51     4      0             0       DB                      S         GRANT
52     4      0             0       DB                      S         GRANT
53     10     0             0       DB                      S         GRANT
54     7      0             0       DB                      S         GRANT
55     6      0             0       DB                      S         GRANT
56     10     0             0       DB                      S         GRANT
57     6      0             0       DB                      S         GRANT
58     6      0             0       DB                      S         GRANT
61     6      0             0       DB                      S         GRANT
61     1      85575343      0       TAB                     IS        GRANT
62     6      0             0       DB                      S         GRANT
63     6      0             0       DB                      S         GRANT
68     6      0             0       DB                      S         GRANT
69     6      0             0       DB                      S         GRANT


ProductID     ProductName                                 UnitPrice
-----------   --------------------------------------      --------------------
16            Pavlova                                     17.4500
19            Teatime Chocolate Biscuits                  9.2000
20            Sir Rodney's Marmalade                      81.0000
21            Sir Rodney's Scones                         10.0000
25            NuNuCa Nuß-Nougat-Creme                     14.0000
26            Gumbär Gummibärchen                         31.2300
27            Schoggi Schokolade                          43.9000
47            Zaanse koeken                               9.5000
48            Chocolade                                   12.7500
49            Maxilaku                                    20.0000
50            Valkoinen suklaa                            16.2500
```

Listing 13.24: continued

```
62          Tarte au sucre                      49.3000
68          Scottish Longbreads                 12.5000

(13 row(s) affected)


lock status after SELECT

spid   dbid   ObjId         IndId   Type   Resource           Mode       Status
------ ------ ------------- ------- ----   ----------------   ---------  ------
51     4      0             0       DB                        S          GRANT
52     4      0             0       DB                        S          GRANT
53     10     0             0       DB                        S          GRANT
54     7      0             0       DB                        S          GRANT
55     6      0             0       DB                        S          GRANT
56     10     0             0       DB                        S          GRANT
57     6      0             0       DB                        S          GRANT
58     6      0             0       DB                        S          GRANT
61     6      0             0       DB                        S          GRANT
61     6      117575457     0       TAB                       IS         GRANT
61     6      117575457     1       KEY    (310027bf2c96)     S          GRANT
61     6      117575457     1       KEY    (3200c9109984)     S          GRANT
61     6      117575457     1       KEY    (3e0071af4fce)     S          GRANT
61     6      117575457     1       KEY    (2f008b9fea26)     S          GRANT
61     6      117575457     2       KEY    (1700bde729cb)     RangeS-S   GRANT
61     6      117575457     2       KEY    (1e00ebf74a93)     RangeS-S   GRANT
61     6      117575457     1       KEY    (1b007df0a359)     S          GRANT
61     6      117575457     1       KEY    (14002be0c001)     S          GRANT
61     6      117575457     1       PAG    1:276              IS         GRANT
61     6      117575457     2       PAG    1:277              IS         GRANT
61     6      117575457     2       KEY    (32001d9803ec)     RangeS-S   GRANT
61     6      117575457     2       KEY    (4100e7a8a604)     RangeS-S   GRANT
61     6      117575457     2       KEY    (3400b1b8c55c)     RangeS-S   GRANT
61     6      117575457     2       KEY    (35005f17704e)     RangeS-S   GRANT
61     6      117575457     1       PAG    1:360              IS         GRANT
61     1      85575343      0       TAB                       IS         GRANT
61     6      117575457     1       KEY    (440089efcdca)     S          GRANT
61     6      117575457     1       KEY    (300042d8902e)     S          GRANT
61     6      117575457     2       KEY    (1c00603f4339)     RangeS-S   GRANT
61     6      117575457     2       KEY    (1d008e90f62b)     RangeS-S   GRANT
61     6      117575457     2       KEY    (160004dffe56)     RangeS-S   GRANT
61     6      117575457     2       KEY    (1300ea704b44)     RangeS-S   GRANT
61     6      117575457     2       KEY    (1800d8809573)     RangeS-S   GRANT
61     6      117575457     1       KEY    (15004e877cb9)     S          GRANT
61     6      117575457     1       KEY    (130092d8179c)     S          GRANT
```

Listing 13.24: continued

61	6	117575457	1	KEY	(10007c77a28e)	S	GRANT
61	6	117575457	1	KEY	(1900f638aaf3)	S	GRANT
61	6	117575457	1	KEY	(1a0018971fe1)	S	GRANT
61	6	117575457	2	KEY	(3300d4df79e4)	RangeS-S	GRANT
61	6	117575457	2	KEY	(0f006da996c9)	RangeS-S	GRANT
61	6	117575457	2	KEY	(47001fe82400)	RangeS-S	GRANT
62	6	0	0	DB		S	GRANT
63	6	0	0	DB		S	GRANT
68	6	0	0	DB		S	GRANT
69	6	0	0	DB		S	GRANT

A Serious Problem to Avoid: Deadlocks

Imagine that your database application has two users: Paul and Mary.

Paul starts a transaction and modifies some attributes of the Acme Ltd. customer. Later, inside the same transaction, Paul tries to modify this customer's payments. However, Paul cannot modify these payments because Mary holds an exclusive lock on these payment records. Paul must wait for these records to be unlocked before completing the transaction.

Mary is modifying customers' payments, and that's why this information is locked. Inside the same transaction, Mary tries to modify some data about the Acme Ltd. customer. At this moment, Paul, who modified this record just a few minutes ago, locks this information.

Mary cannot update this information because Paul is holding an exclusive lock on it, so Mary must wait for this resource to be unlocked before proceeding with her transaction. However, Paul cannot continue with his transaction because he's waiting for Mary to unlock the information he needs to update.

This situation of mutual blockings is called *deadlock*. If SQL Server detects this situation, it decides which process has a bigger execution cost, and selects this process as a winner. After the winner is selected, SQL Server notifies the other processes waiting in this deadlock situation with error 1205, telling them that they have been selected as victims in a deadlock situation.

If two processes involved in a deadlock situation are blocking one another in a circular reference, SQL Server selects which process can be selected to break the deadlock with the least overall cost, and notifies this process with error 1205.

NOTE

You can propose your specific session as a potential deadlock victim by using the statement SET DEADLOCK_PRIORITY LOW.

Two processes can create a deadlock situation when they access resources in opposite orders and try to convert a shared lock into an exclusive lock at the same time. Figure 13.8 illustrates this scenario:

1. Connection A starts a transaction and reads the UnitPrice column from the Product 37. This connection uses the HOLDLOCK locking hint to maintain the shared lock on the row corresponding to Product 37.

2. Connection B starts a transaction and reads the average UnitPrice from the Order Details table for Product 37. This connection uses the HOLDLOCK locking hint to maintain the shared lock on the Order Details rows from Product 37.

3. Connection A tries to update the Order Details table to reset the unit price of Product 37 to the value stored in the Products table. To execute this statement, Connection A needs an exclusive lock on the affected rows, but this exclusive lock must wait because Connection B holds a shared lock on the same rows.

4. Connection B tries to update Product 37 in the Products table with the average unit price retrieved from the Order Details table. Connection B requests an exclusive lock on Product 37, but this lock must wait because Connection A holds a shared lock on it.

5. SQL Server detects this deadlock situation, selects Connection B as victim of this situation, and sends message 1205 to Connection B. Resources locked by Connection B are unlocked.

6. After Connection B has been selected as a victim and its locks have been released, Connection A can continue its operation.

Another typical case is when two transactions want to convert an existing shared lock on a common locked resource into an exclusive lock. To prevent this situation, you should use the UPDLOCK locking hint in transactions in which you read data with intentions of updating it later in the same transaction.

CAUTION

When a transaction is selected as a victim in a deadlock situation, the process is cancelled and changes applied are rolled back. However, the calling application could usually resend the transaction and, hopefully, the previous locks have disappeared.

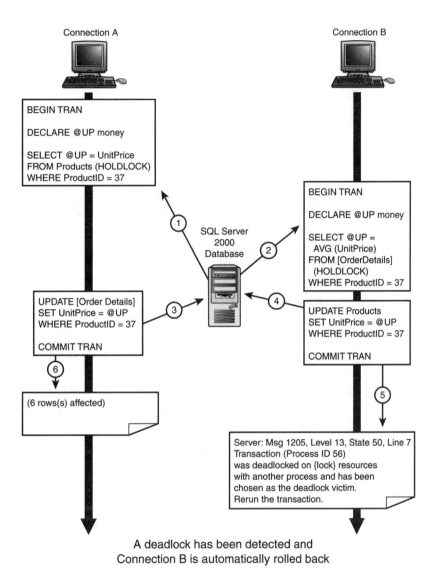

Figure 13.8: A typical deadlock situation.

Avoiding deadlock is not always possible; however, you can help to reduce deadlocks by following these guidelines:

- Keep transactions as short as possible.

- Avoid user interaction inside transactions. In other words, start a transaction only when required and release it as soon as possible.

- Always access resources in the same order and check for potential circular references.

- Use the READ COMMITTED isolation level if possible, because it produces fewer locks than higher isolation levels. Try to avoid SERIALIZABLE as much as possible.

- If an application uses several connections, bind them to share the same locking space. You can execute the stored procedure sp_bindsession to keep more than one session in the same transaction.

What's Next?

Transactions and locks are key aspects to provide the adequate concurrency to your database application in a multiuser environment. However, they are restricted, as covered in this chapter, to a single-server operation. The following two chapters focus on the multiserver environment from two different perspectives:

- Chapter 14 shows how to transfer data to and from SQL Server databases stored in the same or different servers. Data Transformation Services (DTS) is a feature-rich application which, integrated in SQL Server or as a standalone subsystem, transfers data between heterogeneous systems, including all the required transformations.

- Chapter 15 discusses the multiserver environment and the implications of the distributed transactions. In Chapter 15, you learn how to use linked servers to maintain data in multiple servers, as an alternative to DTS and Replication.

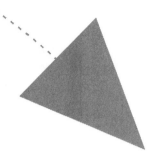

Transferring Data to and from SQL Server

In a standard business environment, it is quite common to have different system platforms, different operating systems, heterogeneous networks, and different database systems. Linking existing data from different sources is a convenient way to work with heterogeneous data to gain data consistency through the company without creating any data redundancy. However, in some cases, you might need to transfer data from one system to another.

Importing and exporting data is a common task for a database administrator, and it is not our intention to cover this subject in detail. However, as a database programmer, you should know the basics of importing and exporting data, and this chapter will teach you how to solve this problem.

This chapter teaches you the following:

- Why you need to transfer and transform data
- SQL Server 2000 tools for transferring data
- How to use the BULK INSERT statement
- How to use the bcp command-line utility
- How to use the Copy Database Wizard

The Need for Transferring Data

If your company has a single database, in a single server, and you never need to receive data from other systems or send data to other servers, you could skip this chapter.

Many systems receive their data through direct user input. However, there are some cases where transferring data is important:

- You want to migrate to a new system and you want to populate the new database with data coming from your old system.

- Your accounting system works in a mainframe and you do not want to change this system. However, it would be useful to have some accounting information in the SQL Server Sales database. In this case, you must periodically refresh this information from the mainframe.

- The post office changes the national postal code information and they distribute this new information as a CSV file. You need to import this file into your system to update the Customer Management application.

- The Inland Revenue changes their requirements and now the annual accounts must be sent in a different format. You must create the process of exporting data in exactly the way they require.

- You create a testing server in your network and you want to have the same databases as in your production server to test a new indexing strategy.

- Your sales managers visit customers, and they want to have a copy of the Sales System database in their laptops so they can look at sales figures when they are at the customer site.

- Your corporation has many different companies in different countries, and you want to receive periodic financial information from them. Every one of these companies uses a different system, and the only way to receive data is by text files, so you can import them easily.

- You have a Documents database and you receive many documents from different sources. You want to import them into the Documents database efficiently.

- You are running a Geographical Information System and your field teams send you files every week with their field measurements. You need to integrate this new data with your existing GIS database.

- You just finished a new Agricultural Census in your county and you want to compare this new data with the latest census's data. The old data is in a different system and you want to import the old data to consolidate both databases.

- Your remote offices need to produce reports about their local sales figures. They complain because they need to access your central mainframe to produce these reports, but the mainframe connection is not always available. You decide that a good solution is to have a local database with local data to produce reports locally. You need to refresh these local databases periodically to have their data synchronized with the central database.

- Your network administrators are concerned about a potential bottleneck on your central database system. A feasible solution is to install departmental servers with replicated data. In this way, users can receive data from a local server, in the same network segment, without traversing the entire network to arrive to the data center.

SQL Server 2000 provides different tools to transfer data from any source to any destination. Depending on your specific requirements, one tool can be more appropriate than another. You will learn about the SQL Server 2000 tools used to transfer data in the next section of this chapter.

In other cases, the problem is not only transferring data, but also modifying data from the source database to meet the requirements of the destination database system. Some examples are as follows:

- You have a relational database and you need to create a data warehouse database with a different database schema; in this case, it could be a star schema.

- Your legacy system in the USA stores dates in a different format (mmddyyyy) from the legacy system you have in France (ddmmyyyy). You want to make sure you can import dates correctly to your central server in Indonesia, which uses the ISO/ODBC standard format (yyyy-mm-dd).

- After a company merge, you need to consolidate data from two different systems. In one system, the codes used in lookup tables are different from the codes used in the other system. In the Spanish system, end users can be S (solteros), C (casados), D (divorciados o separados), V (viudos). In the British system, end users can be S (single), M (married), D (divorced), W (widow or widower). You need to agree about new codes and transform the old ones.

- You just bought a bank in Morocco, and you see that their database system identifies customer accounts by their full name, including title. You want to provide a new account identification number and store title, family name, and first name in separate fields.

- You work in an international project and you need to integrate data in different currencies. Your system selects Euro as the standard internal currency and you must transform all quantities into Euros and store the exchange rate applied to every amount in a different field.

- You created a weather database to help on global weather forecasts. This system receives continuous information from weather systems around the world, each one using different units for temperature, rainfall, pressure, and so on. You must convert the data to uniform units to be able to produce consistent results.

Data Transformation Services 2000 can help you create complex packages that transfer and transform the data to meet the requirements of the destination database.

Tools for Transferring Data Using SQL Server 2000

SQL Server 2000 offers many different choices to transfer data. Every tool has advantages and disadvantages. You can use the following examples as guidelines to select the data distribution tool to use:

- Using distributed queries, you can directly access data from different servers. Chapter 15, "Working with Heterogeneous Environments: Setting Up Linked Servers," covers distributed queries in detail.

- You can use replication to copy data from one server to another, on demand or at regular intervals. If you need to distribute data to mobile users, and they need to modify data locally, merge replication is an excellent solution. Transactional replication is a very efficient mechanism to distribute data changes to remote servers, if the latency inherent to replication is acceptable in your case. Replication is not covered in this book. Books Online contains a full section about replication, with comprehensive information about how replication works.

- You can back up a database in a SQL Server 7.0 or 2000 server and restore it in another SQL Server 2000 server. If you restore a SQL Server 7.0 database into SQL Server 2000, the restore process modifies the database internal physical structure to adapt it to the new SQL Server 2000 physical structure. Restoring SQL Server 2000 databases into SQL Server 7.0 is not supported. Backup is not covered in this book because it is an administrative task. Books Online contains the "Backing Up and Restoring Databases" section, where you can find more information about this topic.

NOTE

Contrary to what happened with SQL Server 7.0, in SQL Server 2000 you can restore databases from servers with different collations, because every database has its own collation, independent from the server default collation.

- You can detach a database from a server running SQL Server 7.0 or
  2000, copy the database files to another server, and attach them to the
  destination server. This procedure is more efficient than using backup
  and restore. After you attach a SQL Server 7.0 database into SQL
  Server 2000, it is converted to the new database structure. Attaching
  SQL Server 2000 databases into SQL Server 7.0 is not supported.
  Look in Books Online for information on how to use the stored procedures sp_detach_db and sp_attach_db.

NOTE

In SQL Server 2000, you can attach databases that have been detached from servers
with different collations, because every database has its own collation, independent
from the server default collation.

- You can convert SQL Server 6.5 databases into SQL Server 2000 running
  the SQL Server Upgrade Wizard. Look in Books Online for information
  on "Upgrading Databases from SQL Server 6.5 (Upgrade Wizard)."

- Data Transformation Services (DTS) is a flexible and powerful tool
  that you can use to import and export data, and transform the data as
  well. You will learn how to import and export data using DTS later in
  this chapter, in the "Using Data Transformation Services" section.

- Use the bcp command-line utility to import and export data to and
  from SQL Server 2000. You learn how to use bcp in the next section of
  this chapter.

- Use the new BULK INSERT statement in a batch or stored procedure to
  import data from a file into a SQL Server 2000 table. The next section
  of this chapter covers this tool in detail.

- You can use the ODBC bulk copy application programming interface
  (API), as the bcp utility does, using any programming language to create your own transferring application. To get more information about
  this interesting programming solution, search in Books Online for the
  section "How to Bulk Copy with the SQL Server ODBC Driver (ODBC)."

- You can write an application using the SQL-DMO library, and use the
  Transfer and Transfer2 objects' properties and methods to transfer
  data and schema between SQL Server 2000 or SQL Server 7.0 servers.
  Search in Books Online for the "Transfer Object" topic.

The BULK INSERT Statement and bcp

You can use the bcp command-line utility to export a table or the result of a
query to an external data file. You can copy this file over the network or the

Internet, or use any media to send it to its destination. It also can be used to import the data file into a single table.

You can use the bcp native mode to export data to and from SQL Server databases. If you export data from SQL Server in native mode, you cannot import that data into any other database system than SQL Server. However, using character-based files provides better flexibility, because the data can be exported to any database system that supports importing from text files.

TIP

Using bcp in native mode, between SQL Server databases, is more efficient than using character mode.

To use bcp, you must open a command prompt window and execute this utility from there.

If you want to import data from a data file into SQL Server, using Transact-SQL language, you can use the new BULK INSERT statement. This method of importing data is highly efficient, and you should use it to perform simple import operations of big data files.

Using bcp and BULK INSERT is faster than inserting the same information, row by row, either manually or from a client application.

By default, constraints and triggers are ignored when importing data using bcp or BULK INSERT, providing a faster inserting operation. However, you should check the data to guarantee that it complies with the existing constraints.

TIP

If you define triggers in your tables to maintain denormalized data in other tables, you should create a stored procedure with similar functionality to apply to the imported data after the bulk operation terminates. In this case, it is better if the stored procedure executes both operations in sequence: the import process and the post-import maintenance operations.

In the next section, you will see how to enable or disable constraint checking and trigger execution during the bulk copy operations.

If your destination database uses a full recovery model, the import operation must be fully logged, and you will be potentially running out of space in the transaction log.

The fastest way to import data into SQL Server is by executing a minimally logged bulk-copy operation, which can be performed if all these conditions are met:

- The database recovery model is set to simple or bulk-logged.
- The destination table is not replicated.
- The destination table does not have any triggers.
- The destination table is empty or does not have any indexes.
- You run the bulk copy operation, specifying the TABLOCK hint.

If the destination of the bulk copy operation does not meet any of these conditions, the operation will be logged.

TIP

If the destination table has indexes, it is recommended to drop the indexes before importing the data and re-creating them after the data is imported. In this case, the sequence should be as follows:

1. Drop nonclustered indexes.

2. Drop the clustered index, if it exists.

3. Import the data.

4. Create the clustered index.

5. Create the nonclustered indexes.

However, for extremely big tables, when the data to import does not represent an appreciable percentage of the existing volume of data, this technique is not recommended, because the internal index maintenance during the importing process will be more efficient than the full rebuild of existing indexes.

TIP

The first time you import a new type of file using a bulk-copy operation, you should import the data to a provisional table first, check the data you just imported to see whether the importing process is done correctly, and when you are certain that the operation works as expected, you can consider the process as valid, and perform the bulk-copy operation on the destination table.

Using the bcp Command-Line Utility

The bcp command-line utility copies data from SQL Server to an external data file and imports data from an external data file into SQL Server.

NOTE

The bcp utility uses the ODBC Bulk Copy Application Programming Interface (API). It is compatible with any version of SQL Server.

To test the bcp utility, open a command prompt window and execute bcp /?, as in Listing 14.1.

EXAMPLE

Listing 14.1: Get Syntax Help About How to Execute bcp

```
C:\TEMP>bcp /?

usage: D:\Program Files\Microsoft SQL Server\80\Tools\BINN\bcp.exe {dbtable |
query} {in | out | queryout | format} datafile
    [-m maxerrors]           [-f formatfile]           [-e errfile]
    [-F firstrow]            [-L lastrow]              [-b batchsize]
    [-n native type]         [-c character type]       [-w wide character type]
    [-N keep non-text native] [-V file format version] [-q quoted identifier]
    [-C code page specifier] [-t field terminator]     [-r row terminator]
    [-i inputfile]           [-o outfile]              [-a packetsize]
    [-S server name]         [-U username]             [-P password]
    [-T trusted connection]  [-v version]              [-R regional enable]
    [-k keep null values]    [-E keep identity values]
    [-h "load hints"]
```

In this section, we will take a look at some of these options, step by step.

Now, in the same command prompt window, you can write the instruction from Listing 14.2 to export the `Northwind.dbo.Region` table to the external file `region.txt` in character format, and use your NT or Windows 2000 credentials to connect to SQL Server.

EXAMPLE

Listing 14.2: Export the Region Table to the `region.txt` External File Using bcp

```
C:\TEMP>bcp northwind.dbo.region out region.txt
➥-S YourServer\YourInstance -T -c
Starting copy...
```

OUTPUT

```
4 rows copied.
Network packet size (bytes): 4096
Clock Time (ms.): total       20
```

Looking at the instruction you just typed, see the following options:

- bcp is the program to execute.

- northwind.dbo.region is the fully qualified name of the table to export. You can specify the name of a view, an inline user-defined function, or a table-valued function, as shown in Listing 14.3.

- out specifies that you want to export data.

- region.txt is the name of the file to fill with the exported data.

- -S YourServer\YourInstance specifies the server and instance to connect to. If you want to export from the default instance, use -S YourServer instead.

- -T instructs bcp to use your NT or Windows 2000 credentials to connect to SQL Server, using integrated authentication.

- -c means the data is exported using text mode.

EXAMPLE

Listing 14.3: Export the Result of the dbo.TopTenOrders Inline User-Defined Function to the topten.txt External File Using bcp

```
C:\TEMP>bcp northwind.dbo.toptenorders() out topten.txt
➥-S YourServer\YourInstance -T -c

Starting copy...

10 rows copied.
Network packet size (bytes): 4096
Clock Time (ms.): total      541
```

NOTE

You created the TopTenOrders inline user-defined function in Listing 10.14 from Chapter 10, "Enhancing Business Logic: User-Defined Functions (UDF)."

To look at the file region.txt, you can use the type command, as seen in Listing 14.4.

EXAMPLE

Listing 14.4: Inspect the Contents of the Exported File region.txt

```
C:\TEMP>type region.txt
1       Eastern
2       Western
3       Northern
4       Southern
```

Now, you can try to import the file into a new table, using bcp again. In the same command-prompt window, write the instruction contained in Listing 14.5.

EXAMPLE

Listing 14.5: Import the region.txt File into a New Table Called NewRegions Using bcp

```
C:\TEMP>bcp northwind.dbo.NewRegions in region.txt
➥-S YourServer\YourInstance -T -c
SQLState = S0002, NativeError = 208
Error = [Microsoft][ODBC SQL Server Driver][SQL Server]Invalid object name
'northwind.dbo.NewRegions'.
```

You got an error message because bcp can import data only into existing tables, either directly, through appropriate views, or inline user-defined functions.

To solve this problem, you must create the destination table first. You can do it easily from Query Analyzer with the CREATE TABLE statement, or graphically in Enterprise Manager. However, you can do it as well from the command prompt, using the osql utility to connect to SQL Server and execute the CREATE TABLE statement. Listing 14.6 shows the execution of both osql and bcp.

EXAMPLE

Listing 14.6: Create the NewRegions Table and Import the region.txt File

```
C:\TEMP>osql -S YourServer\YourInstance -E -d Northwind -Q "CREATE TABLE
➥NewRegions (ID int, Name nchar(50))"

C:\TEMP>bcp northwind.dbo.NewRegions in region.txt -S
➥YourServer\YourInstance -T -c
Starting copy...

4 rows copied.
Network packet size (bytes): 4096
Clock Time (ms.): total       311
```

Now, you can use osql again, as in Listing 14.7, to look at the new table NewRegions and test whether the import operation succeeded.

EXAMPLE

Listing 14.7: Use osql to Read Data from the NewRegions Table

```
C:\TEMP>osql -S YourServer\YourInstance -E -d Northwind
➥-Q "SELECT * FROM NewRegions"
ID          Name
----------- --------------------------------------------------
          1 Eastern
          2 Western
          3 Northern
          4 Southern

(4 rows affected)
```

You can use bcp to export the result from any query into a file, using the queryout option, as in Listing 14.8.

EXAMPLE

Listing 14.8: Export the Result of a Query to the query.txt External File Using bcp and the queryout Option

```
C:\TEMP>bcp "SELECT CategoryID, CategoryName FROM Northwind.dbo.Categories"
➥queryout query.txt -S YourServer\YourInstance -T -c
Starting copy...

10 rows copied.
Network packet size (bytes): 4096
Clock Time (ms.): total       1
```

You can limit the number of errors to accept during the bulk copy operation by using the -m option. The default value is 10. Every row that produces an error is disregarded by bcp, and the execution continues until the number of errors is greater than 10 or the number specified within the -m option, in which case the operation is cancelled.

Using the -e err_file option, bcp sends rows with transfer errors to the err_file file. You can later review this file, correct any error, and retry the import operation only with these rows.

If you want to import specific rows only from the data file, use -F first_row and -L last_row to specify the first and last rows to import. If you do not use the -F option, the transfer process starts from the first row. If you do not use the -L option, the transfer continues to the end of the file.

The default field terminator is the tab character (\t or CHAR(9)), but you can specify your own field terminator with the -t option. The default row terminator is the newline character (\n or CHAR(10)), but you can specify your own row terminator with the -r option.

In the examples from Listings 14.1 through 14.8, we always used character format. However, bcp accepts more formats:

- -n uses native SQL Server mode; therefore, every field is exported using its native storage format. This mode is very efficient if you need to transfer data between SQL Server databases. Use the -N option to send character data as UNICODE, and any other data type in its native format.

- -c uses the character data type. This option uses the tab character (\t) as field separator and the newline character (\n) as row terminator. Use this format to transfer data to non-SQL Server databases. Use the -w option if you want to output data in UNICODE (double byte) format.

- -V60, -V65, -V70 uses data types from old versions of SQL Server.

If the query to execute is too long to be written inline with the bcp command, you can create a text file and use it as an input file with the -i input_file option. For similar reasons, if you expect too many messages to fit in the command-prompt window, you can specify an output file with the -o output_file option.

In the preceding examples, we used integrated authentication (with the -T option) to connect bcp to SQL Server, but you can use SQL Server authentication using the -U login_id and -P password options.

By default, bcp does not fire any AFTER INSERT or INSTEAD OF INSERT triggers on the destination table, but you can force the execution of triggers using the -h "FIRE_TRIGGERS" hint. This option is valid only if the in option is specified. The triggers are fired only once per batch during the bulk copy operation, and the inserted and deleted tables contain the complete set of imported rows on that batch.

As with triggers, constraints are not checked during data import operations using bcp. If you want to enforce constraints for every imported row, you can use the -h "CHECK_CONSTRAINTS" hint.

If you want to perform a minimum logged bulk copy operation, you must use the -h "TABLOCK" hint as well, as mentioned earlier in this chapter.

If you want to use more than one hint, you can specify them using a single -h option with every hint separated by commas, such as -h "FIRE_TRIGGERS, CHECK_CONSTRAINTS, TABLOCK".

You can use the format option, instead of the in, out, or queryout options, to produce a format file. By editing the format file, you can perform complex import operations, such as selecting which columns to import from the file, change the order of the columns to import, or specify different delimiters for every column. Later in this chapter, you will see how to use the format file to import WAV files into SQL Server. You can search in Books Online for the "Using Format Files" topic to get information about the different options you have when using the format file.

Using the BULK INSERT Statement

The BULK INSERT statement imports a data file into a table either directly or through a view. This way is similar to the bcp utility, but you use BULK INSERT from Transact-SQL, not from the command prompt. Listing 14.9 shows a simple example to import data from the region.txt file created in Listing 14.2. To execute this example, you can open a session in SQL Server using Query Analyzer.

EXAMPLE

Listing 14.9: Use the BULK INSERT Statement to Import a Data File into a Table

```
USE Northwind
GO

TRUNCATE TABLE NewRegions
GO

SELECT *
FROM NewRegions
GO

BULK INSERT NewRegions FROM 'C:\Temp\region.txt'
GO

SELECT *
FROM NewRegions
```

Listing 14.9: continued

```
ID          Name
----------- ------------------------------------------------

(0 row(s) affected)


(4 row(s) affected)

ID          Name
----------- ------------------------------------------------
1           Eastern
2           Western
3           Northern
4           Southern

(4 row(s) affected)
```

You can use the FIRSTROW and LASTROW options in the same way you used
the -F and -L options in bcp. Listing 14.10 show an example of importing
rows 5 to 8 from the topten.txt file produced in Listing 14.3.

Listing 14.10: Use the FIRSTROW and LASTROW Options to Specify Which Rows to Import

```
USE Northwind
GO

-- Create the destination table
-- with no rows and the same structure as
-- the result set from TopTenOrders function

SELECT *
INTO TopTen
FROM dbo.TopTenOrders()
where OrderID < 1000
GO

-- Import rows 5 to 8 from the file

BULK INSERT TopTen FROM 'C:\Temp\topten.txt'
WITH
(
FIRSTROW = 5,
LASTROW = 8
)
GO

-- Test the rows imported
```

Listing 14.10: continued

```
SELECT OrderID, CustomerID
FROM TopTen
```

```
ID          Name
----------- ---------------------------------------------

(0 row(s) affected)


(4 row(s) affected)

ID          Name
----------- ---------------------------------------------
1           Eastern
2           Western
3           Northern
4           Southern

(4 row(s) affected)
```

BULK INSERT has a similar functionality as bcp for importing operations. Table 14.1 maps every option in the bcp utility to the corresponding option in the BULK INSERT statement.

Table 14.1: Options Equivalence Between BULK INSERT and bcp

BULK INSERT	bcp
FROM 'data_file'	in data_file
BATCHSIZE = batch_size	-b batch_size
CHECK_CONSTRAINTS	-h "CHECK_CONSTRAINTS"
CODEPAGE = 'ACP'	-C ACP
CODEPAGE = 'OEM'	-C OEM
CODEPAGE = 'RAW'	-C RAW
CODEPAGE = 'code_page'	-C code_page
DATAFILETYPE = 'char'	-c
DATAFILETYPE = 'native'	-n
DATAFILETYPE = 'widechar'	-w
DATAFILETYPE = 'widenative'	-N
FIELDTERMINATOR = 'field_terminator'	-t field_term
FIRSTROW = first_row	-F first_row
FIRE_TRIGGERS	-h "FIRE_TRIGGERS"
FORMATFILE = 'format_file'	-f format_file
KEEPIDENTITY	-E
KEEPNULLS	-k
KILOBYTES_PER_BATCH = kb_per_batch	(Not available)
(Not available)	-a packet_size

Table 14.1: continued

BULK INSERT	bcp
LASTROW = last_row	-L last_row
MAXERRORS = max_errors	-m max_errors
ORDER (column [ASC|DESC],... n)	-h "ORDER (column [ASC|DESC],... n)"
ROWS_PER_BATCH = rows_per_batch	-h "ROWS_PER_BATCH = bb"
ROWTERMINATOR = 'row_terminator'	-r row_term
(Not available)	out
(Not available)	queryout
(Not available)	format
(Not available)	-e err_file
(Not available)	format
(Not available)	-V 60
(Not available)	-V 65
(Not available)	-V 70
(Not available)	-6
(Not available)	-q
(Not available)	-o output file
(Not available)	-i input file
(Not available)	-S server_name\instance
(Not available)	-U login_id
(Not available)	-P password
(Not available)	-T
(Not available)	-v
(Not available)	-R

NOTE

For descriptions of individual options not described in this chapter, look at the "BULK INSERT" topic in Books Online.

CAUTION

Only members of the sysadmin role can execute the BULK INSERT statement. SQL Server uses the SQL Server service account to read the file. Therefore, you should make sure that the service account has permissions to read the file.

It is not required to be a member of the sysadmin role to execute the bcp command-line utility, but the user needs to have appropriate permissions on the source and destination tables, as well as the files and directories used by bcp.

BULK INSERT imports data into a table, but you do not have a BULK EXPORT statement to export data from a table to an external file. You can execute bcp from the command prompt to export data from SQL Server to a file. Can you execute bcp from Transact-SQL?

You can use the xp_cmdshell system stored procedure to execute any OS command, and that includes bcp. Listing 14.11 shows an example of how to export a table to an external file, using bcp with xp_cmdshell, create a new destination table, and import the file into the new table using BULK INSERT.

EXAMPLE

Listing 14.11: Use bcp with xp_cmdshell to Export Data from Transact-SQL

```
USE Northwind
GO

PRINT CHAR(10)
+ 'Exporting the Products Table in widenative mode'
+ CHAR(10)

EXECUTE master.dbo.xp_cmdshell 'bcp northwind.dbo.products
➥out c:\temp\products.txt -S MSSQLFGG\S2K -T -N'
GO

PRINT CHAR(10)
+ 'Creating the NewProducts table '
+ 'with the same structure as '
+ CHAR(10)
+ 'the Products table but empty'
+ CHAR(10)

SELECT *
INTO NewProducts
FROM Products
WHERE ProductID = -1
GO

PRINT CHAR(10)
+ 'Checking the NewProducts table'
+ CHAR(10)

SELECT COUNT(*)
FROM NewProducts
GO

PRINT CHAR(10)
+ 'Importing the Products.txt file into the NewProducts Table'
+ CHAR(10)

BULK INSERT NewProducts FROM 'c:\temp\Products.txt'
WITH
(
DATAFILETYPE = 'widenative'
)
GO
```

Listing 14.11: continued

```
PRINT CHAR(10)
+ 'Checking the NewProducts table'
+ CHAR(10)

SELECT COUNT(*) AS NRows
FROM NewProducts
GO
```

Exporting the Products Table in widenative mode

output

```
NULL
Starting copy...
NULL
77 rows copied.
Network packet size (bytes): 4096
Clock Time (ms.): total      411
NULL


(7 row(s) affected)

Creating the NewProducts table with the same structure as
the Products table but empty

(0 row(s) affected)

Checking the NewProducts table


-----------
0

(1 row(s) affected)

Importing the Products.txt file into the NewProducts Table

(77 row(s) affected)

Checking the NewProducts table

NRows
-----------
77

(1 row(s) affected)
```

Another common problem is inserting images, or any document, from individual files into a table. This case is more difficult than reading data from a single file because in this case, the individual files are not part of any data file exported from a database application.

To solve this problem, you must create a format file to import every file, one by one. As an example, you can create the WAVFiles table, as in Listing 14.12, to store WAV files, and you want to save the WAV files included in the WINNT\MEDIA directory in this table. Using one of these files (START.WAV), you must first know how big it is, to write a format file for it. When you look at the directory, you will find that the START.WAV file is exactly 1,192 bytes in size. The format file to create it is included in Listing 14.12. Create a file called wav.fmt in the WINNT\MEDIA directory with the contents of Listing 14.13.

EXAMPLE

Listing 14.12: Create the WAVFiles Table

```
USE Northwind
GO

CREATE TABLE WAVFiles (
ID int NOT NULL
IDENTITY(1,1)
PRIMARY KEY,
FullFileName varchar(1024) NULL,
WAV image NULL)
GO
```

EXAMPLE

Listing 14.13: WAV.FMT File to Import the START.WAV File Using BULK INSERT

```
8.0
1
1 SQLIMAGE 0 1192 "" 3 wav ""
```

The WAV.FMT file created on Listing 14.13 contains the following sections:

- First line (8.0)—This is the version number of the bcp.exe application, corresponding to SQL Server 2000.

- Second line (1)—This is the number of fields the source file contains. In this case, the file contains a single field: the wav field.

- Third line (1)—Field number in the file. There is only one field in this case:

SQLIMAGE	Data file in the destination database. Because this is nontext BLOB information, the data type should be SQLIMAGE.
0	Prefix length. In this case, you want to read from the beginning of the file.

1192	Length of the field. In this case, it is the length of the file: 1192 bytes.
" "	Field terminator. In this case, it must be empty, because there is only one field in the file.
3	Import this information in the third field of the table.
wav	Target field name.
" "	Target field collation. It must be empty for an image field.

Now, you execute the BULK INSERT statement to import this file into the table, as in Listing 14.14. After importing the file, the script updates the record with the original filename and tests the length of the information just imported.

EXAMPLE

Listing 14.14: Import the WAV File into the WAVFile Table

```
USE Northwind
GO

DECLARE @ID int

BULK INSERT WAVFiles FROM 'd:\winnt\media\start.wav'
WITH (
FORMATFILE = 'd:\winnt\media\wav.fmt'
)

SET @ID = IDENT_CURRENT('WAVFiles')

UPDATE WAVFiles
SET FullFileName = 'D:\WINNT\MEDIA\start.wav'
WHERE ID = @ID

SELECT ID,
DATALENGTH(wav) AS WAVELength,
FullFileName
FROM WAVFiles
WHERE ID = @ID
```

```
ID          WAVELength  FullFileName
----------- ----------- ------------------------------------
1           1192        D:\WINNT\MEDIA\start.wav
```

OUTPUT

To automate the process, you can create the stored procedure ImportWavFiles, as defined in Listing 14.15. The ImportWavFiles stored procedure uses the CreaWavFmt stored procedure, defined in Listing 14.15 as well, to automatically create the WAV.FMT file for every WAV file in the required directory.

TIP

The CreaWavFmt stored procedure uses the DOS ECHO command to write text to a file. You can use xp_cmdshell to execute ECHO commands and write information to a short file from Transact-SQL, as in this example.

EXAMPLE

Listing 14.15: Stored Procedures to Import WAV Files from Any Directory into the WAVFile Table

```
USE Northwind
GO


.........................
-- CreaWavFmt
.........................
CREATE PROCEDURE CreaWavFmt
@dir varchar(255), -- directory ended with '\'
@length int -- file length
AS
/*
** This is the required step to import
** image files with BULK INSERT
**
** We should do it manually, but we
** have xp_cmdshell for?
*/

DECLARE @cmd varchar(8000)

-- Remove wav.fmt file if exists

SET @cmd = 'del '
+ @dir + 'wav.fmt'

EXEC master.dbo.xp_cmdshell @cmd, no_output

-- Create the first line of the format file

SET @cmd = 'echo 8.0 >>'
+ @dir + 'wav.fmt'

EXEC master.dbo.xp_cmdshell @cmd, no_output

-- Write the second line to the file

SET @cmd = 'echo 1 >>'
+ @dir + 'wav.fmt'

EXEC master.dbo.xp_cmdshell @cmd, no_output
```

Listing 14.15: continued

```
/*
** Add the third line to the file, specifying:
** 1 (the first field = entire file)
** SQLIMAGE as datatype
** 0 as field prefix length
** length of the field (file in this case)
** no field separator
** third field on the table
** Wav field
** Empty collation
*/

SET @cmd = 'echo 1 SQLIMAGE 0 '
+ CONVERT(varchar(10), @length)
+ ' "" 3 wav "" >>'
+ @dir + 'wav.fmt'

EXEC master.dbo.xp_cmdshell @cmd, no_output

-- wav.fmt is created already for this file

GO

---------------------------
-- InsertWavFiles
---------------------------

CREATE PROCEDURE InsertWavFiles
@dir varchar(255)
AS

DECLARE @sdir varchar(256)

/*
** Create temporary table to hold
** directory contents
*/

CREATE TABLE #tdir(
FileDir varchar(200) NULL,
length int NULL)

SET @sdir = 'dir '
+ @dir + '*.WAV'

INSERT #tdir (FileDir)
```

Listing 14.15: continued

```
EXEC master.dbo.xp_cmdshell @sdir

-- Filter undesired rows
-- you can add your own conditions

DELETE #tdir
WHERE FileDir NOT LIKE '%.WAV'
OR FileDir IS NULL

-- Obtain file length and
-- filename cleansing
--
-- You could check with
-- EXEC master.dbo.xp_cmdshell 'dir c:\*.*'
-- that lengths are correct

UPDATE #tdir
SET length = CONVERT(int,
CONVERT(money,
LTRIM(RTRIM(SUBSTRING(FileDir, 20, 20)))), 1)),
FileDir = LTRIM(RTRIM(SUBSTRING(FileDir, 40, 40)))

DECLARE @file varchar(256)
DECLARE @length int
DECLARE @sql varchar(8000)

DECLARE c_files CURSOR
FOR SELECT FileDir, length
FROM #tdir

OPEN c_files

FETCH NEXT FROM c_files INTO @file, @length

WHILE @@FETCH_STATUS = 0
BEGIN

-- Create bcp.fmt file to import the file

EXEC CreaWavFmt @dir, @length

-- Import the file

SET @sql ='BULK INSERT WAVFiles FROM '''
+ @dir
+ @file
```

Listing 14.15: continued

```
+ ''' WITH (FORMATFILE = '''
+ @dir
+ 'wav.fmt'')'

EXECUTE (@sql)

-- Update the imported record

UPDATE WAVFiles
SET FUllFileName = @dir + @file
WHERE ID = IDENT_CURRENT('WAVFiles')

FETCH NEXT FROM c_files INTO @file, @length
END

CLOSE c_files

DEALLOCATE c_files

DROP TABLE #tdir

GO


------------------------------------
-- Test the InsertWavFiles procedure
------------------------------------


EXEC InsertWavFiles 'd:\winnt\media\'

SELECT ID,
DATALENGTH(wav) AS WAVELength,
FullFileName
FROM WAVFiles
```

```
ID          WAVELength  FullFileName
----------- ----------- ------------------------------------
1           55776       d:\winnt\media\chimes.wav
2           97016       d:\winnt\media\chord.wav
3           80856       d:\winnt\media\ding.wav
4           15906       d:\winnt\media\ir_begin.wav
5           42728       d:\winnt\media\ir_end.wav
6           75508       d:\winnt\media\ir_inter.wav
7           119384      d:\winnt\media\notify.wav
8           25434       d:\winnt\media\recycle.wav
9           10026       d:\winnt\media\ringin.wav
10          5212        d:\winnt\media\ringout.wav
11          1192        d:\winnt\media\start.wav
```

OUTPUT

Listing 14.15: continued

12	171100	d:\winnt\media\tada.wav
13	135876	d:\winnt\media\The Microsoft Sound.wav
14	95708	d:\winnt\media\Utopia Asterisk.WAV
15	4616	d:\winnt\media\Utopia Close.WAV
16	5824	d:\winnt\media\Utopia Critical Stop.WAV
17	9946	d:\winnt\media\Utopia Default.WAV
18	24596	d:\winnt\media\Utopia Error.WAV
19	13026	d:\winnt\media\Utopia Exclamation.WAV
20	14922	d:\winnt\media\Utopia Maximize.WAV
21	3462	d:\winnt\media\Utopia Menu Command.WAV
22	2692	d:\winnt\media\Utopia Menu Popup.WAV
23	14990	d:\winnt\media\Utopia Minimize.WAV
24	10760	d:\winnt\media\Utopia Open.WAV
25	13084	d:\winnt\media\Utopia Question.WAV
26	98330	d:\winnt\media\Utopia Recycle.WAV
27	5120	d:\winnt\media\Utopia Restore Down.WAV
28	15372	d:\winnt\media\Utopia Restore Up.WAV
29	86798	d:\winnt\media\Utopia Windows Exit.WAV
30	156760	d:\winnt\media\Utopia Windows Start.WAV
31	344108	d:\winnt\media\Windows Logoff Sound.wav
32	486188	d:\winnt\media\Windows Logon Sound.wav

TIP

You can use a similar strategy to import any kind of files or documents into SQL Server.

Using Data Transformation Services

Data Transformation Services is a powerful tool introduced with SQL Server 7.0. It is a versatile tool that enables developers to design packages that transfer and transform the data efficiently between two data sources.

Using Data Transformation Services, you can

- Select any data source, not necessarily SQL Server, if you have an ODBC driver or OLE DB provider to access its data.

- Select any data destination (it doesn't have to be SQL Server) if you have the ODBC driver or OLE DB provider to connect to it.

- Define the transformation process to convert the source data into the structure and format required on destination.

- Define complex tasks using Transact-SQL or any scripting language.

- Transfer database objects between two SQL Server databases in the same or different servers.

- Define a package with a complete sequence of DTS tasks with rich flow control, to specify the order of execution.

- Save the DTS package in SQL Server 2000's msdb database, SQL Server 2000 Meta Data Services, a COM structured file, or as a Visual Basic file.

It is not the purpose of this book to cover in detail this important tool. However, we want to show you how to perform two common tasks, step by step:

- How to transfer database objects between two Microsoft SQL Server 2000 databases.

- How to export tables and views from Microsoft SQL Server 2000 to Microsoft Access 2000.

NOTE

To execute the examples from the next three sections, you must have two instances of SQL Server 2000 installed, or access to two different severs in your network with SQL Server 2000 installed.

Transfer Objects Between Two SQL Server 2000 Databases

In this section, you learn how to transfer database objects from the Northwind database in a SQL Server 2000 instance to a new database in a different SQL Server 2000 instance in the same server. Note that this example works as well between two different servers.

To perform this task, you will use the DTS Import/Export Wizard.

To start the wizard, you can run Enterprise Manager, open the Tools menu, select Wizards, Data Transformation Services, and DTS Export Wizard.

A different way to start the wizard is by choosing All Tasks, Export Data from the context menu of the Databases folder, as shown in Figure 14.1.

You see the DTS Import/Export Wizard Welcome screen. Here you can click Next.

Figure 14.2 shows the next step, which is to choose a data source. If you started the wizard from a specific database context menu, you will find the selected server and database here. If you started the wizard from the Databases folder, you will see the selected server and the default database for your connection.

In this step, you can select any data source and specify any required settings to connect to the data source. In this case, we accept the following default settings:

- Microsoft SQL OLE DB provider for SQL Server.

- Server SQLBE\Inst3, which is the named instance Inst3 in the SQLBE server.

- DTS uses Windows Authentication Mode to connect to the SQLBE\Inst3 server. You could select SQL Server authentication instead, and, in that case, you must supply a valid username and password.

- Use the Northwind database as data source.

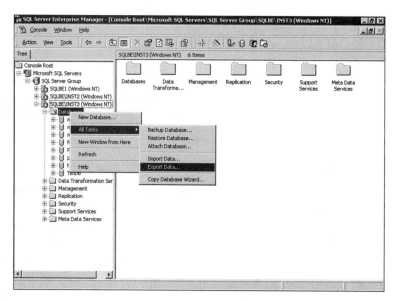

Figure 14.1: *Start the DTS Export Wizard using the context menu of the Databases folder.*

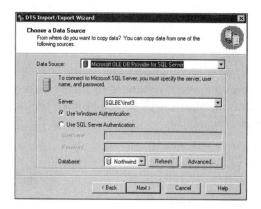

Figure 14.2: *You can select the data source from where to read the data.*

Click Next to arrive at the next step, which is to choose a destination, as you can see in Figure 14.3. In this step, you can select the following settings:

- Microsoft SQL OLE DB Provider for SQL Server.

- Server SQLBE\Inst2, which is the named instance Inst2 in the SQLBE server.

- DTS will use Windows Authentication mode to connect to the SQLBE\ Inst3 server. You could select SQL Server Authentication instead and, in that case, you must supply a valid username and password.

- Use a new database as destination.

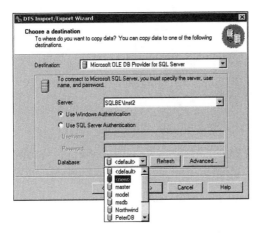

Figure 14.3: *You can select the destination where the data will be sent.*

When you select New database, the DTS Import/Export Wizard will show you the Create Database form, as shown in Figure 14.4. In this form, you can specify the name of the new database, NewNorthwind, and the initial size of the data and log files—in this case, 2MB for each file.

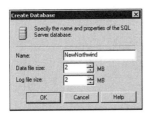

Figure 14.4: *You can create a new destination database, if required.*

TIP

We recommend that you create the destination database using the Transact-SQL CREATE DATABASE statement before starting the wizard, because the CREATE DATABASE statement gives you greater flexibility in how and where to create the new database.

When you accept the creation of the new database, you return to the wizard and you can see the new database selected, as in Figure 14.5.

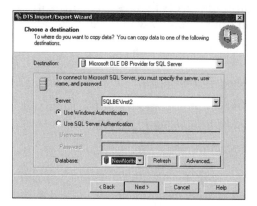

Figure 14.5: *You can select the newly created database as the destination database.*

Click Next and you arrive at the Specify Table Copy or Query step, as shown in Figure 14.6. This step is different, depending on which data source and destination you selected in the previous steps. In this case, from SQL Server to SQL Server, you have three choices:

- Copy Table(s) and View(s) from the Source Database—Selecting this option, you will be presented with a list of available tables and views to select, as in Figure 14.16, in the next section of this chapter.

- Use a Query to Specify the Data to Transfer—This is a very flexible way of defining the data source, because you can write your own SELECT statement to retrieve the required data.

- Copy Objects and Data Between SQL Server Databases—This option is available only when you select SQL Server as a source and destination. Using this option, you can transfer objects with or without data.

In this case, select Copy Objects and Data Between SQL Server Databases, and click Next.

The next step is to Select Objects to Copy, as shown in Figure 14.7. In this step, you can select

- Whether or not to create destination objects—In this case, you can specify to drop the object first, include all dependent objects, and include extended properties.

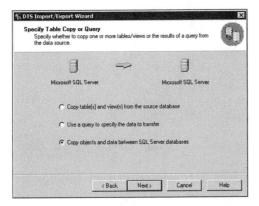

Figure 14.6: *You can select different ways to select which data to copy.*

CAUTION

If you do not select Include All Dependent Objects, you can find errors when scripting objects that depend on objects that will be created later in the same package. If you try to export a view, and its base tables are not transferred, SQL Server throws an error during the transfer process.

- Transfer the data—You can uncheck this option to transfer only the schema: the definition of the database objects. If you selected to transfer the data, you can select to overwrite the existing data or to append the new data to the existing data.

- Specify to translate collations—When transferring data between SQL Server 2000 databases, this setting affects only data added to an existing table. If your DTS package creates the destination object, the columns will have the same collation as in the source database.

TIP

Using UNICODE data when working with servers or databases with different code pages saves translation problems. If you work only with SQL Server 2000, specify the collation at database or column level, if necessary, and the columns will be transferred with their collation definition.

- Select to copy all objects or only some of them.

- Use default security and table options—Uncheck this option and you can select to transfer logins, permissions, indexes, triggers, and constraints.

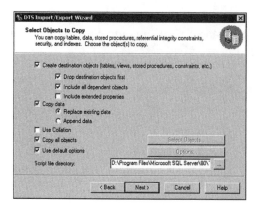

Figure 14.7: *You can select which database objects to copy.*

Accept the default options in the Select Objects to Copy step and click Next.

You are now in the Save, Schedule, and Replicate Package step, as you can see in Figure 14.8. In this step, you can set several options that affect how and when the package will be executed:

- Run Immediately—To execute the package right after the wizard completes.

- Use Replication to Publish Destination Data—This option starts the Create Publication Wizard after the DTS Import/Export Wizard completes.

- Schedule DTS Package for Later Execution—This option causes a SQL Server Agent job to be executed automatically, according to the required schedule.

- Save DTS Package—Use this option to store the package so you can modify it later. You can store the package in the MSDB database in SQL Server, in the SQL Server Meta Data Services, in a COM structured storage file, or as a Visual Basic File.

Select SQL Server as the storage location for the package, and click Next. You arrive at the Save DTS Package step, and you will see something similar to Figure 14.9. In this step, you can specify several options:

- Name and description of the package.

- Owner Password—This password will be required for users trying to modify the package.

- User Password—Users must specify this password to run the package.

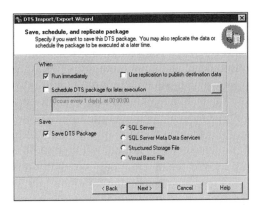

Figure 14.8: *You can select where to save the DTS package and when to execute it.*

NOTE

DTS packages can be stored outside SQL Server. Therefore, the authentication mode selected in SQL Server will not necessarily protect the DTS packages from being modified or executed.

- Server—You can select in which server to store the package and specify the authentication mode to connect to the server.

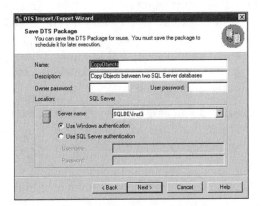

Figure 14.9: *To save the DTS package, you must specify a name and provide a description, as well as owner and user passwords.*

After setting the required options, click Next and you will arrive at the last step in the DTS Import/Export Wizard, the Completing the DTS Import/Export Wizard. In this stage, you can still cancel the execution of the package by clicking Cancel.

Click Finish, and the wizard creates the package according to the settings you selected. Because you selected to run the package immediately, the package will run right after the wizard completes, as you see in Figure 14.10.

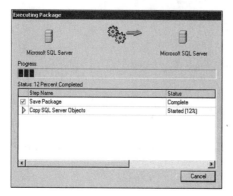

Figure 14.10: *You can see the execution progress of the package.*

When the package finishes its execution, you will receive a confirmation message.

You saved this package in SQL Server, so you can open it again and modify its definition if you need to.

You can open the Data Transformation Services folder in Enterprise Manager and inside Local Packages you could find the CopyObjects package you just created. Open the package and you will see, as in Figure 14.11, a single Copy SQL Server Objects task. You are now in the DTS Designer environment, where you can modify the package adding more tasks, modifying the sequence of execution, and so on.

Double-click on the task and you can see its properties. Figure 14.12 shows the Data Source properties, and it shows the same settings you selected previously in the Wizard in the Choose a Data Source step, as shown in Figure 14.12.

Click the Copy tab, and what you will see, as shown in Figure 14.13, is very similar to the Select Objects to Copy step shown in Figure 14.7.

Now that the package has been created and saved, you can execute it any time you need it. To run the package at any time, just right-click it and select Execute Package.

Export a SQL Server Table to an Access Database

In this case, you are going to copy the tables and views from the Northwind database in SQL Server to a database in Access 2000.

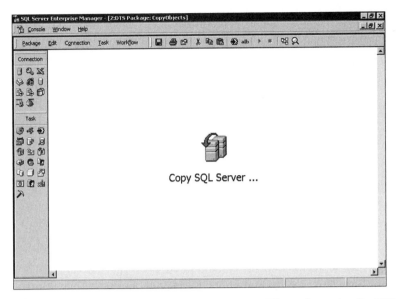

Figure 14.11: *You can open an existing DTS package in the DTS package designer.*

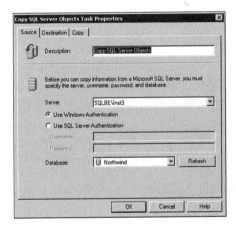

Figure 14.12: *You can see the data source properties in the Source tab of the Object Transfer Task Properties form.*

The first task you must do is to create an empty Access database, named DTS.MDB, in a well-known location in your hard disk. For this example, we selected the location D:\SQL.

You must select the DTS Import/Export Wizard, as in the previous section, and you will arrive at the welcome screen.

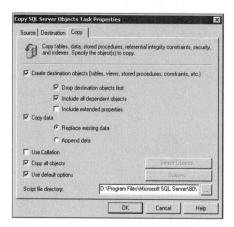

Figure 14.13: *Use the Copy tab in the Object Transfer Task Properties form to see which database objects are selected to be copied.*

Click Next and you will arrive at the Choose a Data Source step as described earlier in this chapter. Refer to Figure 14.3, which shows the default options for this example.

Click Next to arrive at the Choose a Destination step. In this case, you must select the Microsoft Access destination, and the form, as shown in Figure 14.14, will be different from the form displayed in Figure 14.3.

As you select the Access destination, you must provide

- File Name—In this case, D:\SQL\DTS.MDB, or the full path of the file you created at the beginning of this section, if it is different.

- Username and Password—If you have a secured Access environment, you must provide a valid username and password. Otherwise, you can provide Admin as username and a blank password.

Click the Advanced button if you want to specify different extra settings for the Jet OLE DB Provider.

Click Next to go to the Specify Table Copy or Query step, as shown in Figure 14.15. This figure is similar to the one in Figure 14.6, but you cannot copy objects from SQL Server to Access; that is why this option is not available.

Select Copy Table(s) and View(s) from the Source Database, and click Next to arrive at the Select Source Tables and Views step, as shown in Figure 14.16. In this step, you can

- Select which tables and views to copy. For this example, click Select All to select all tables and views.

- Select the name for every destination table.

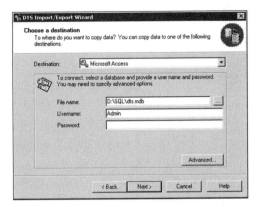

Figure 14.14: *Specify the Access file to export to, as well as a valid user-name and password for Access.*

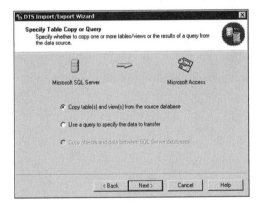

Figure 14.15: *You can select whether to read data from tables or views, or create your own queries.*

NOTE

Both tables and views are transferred as tables to the Access database.

- Specify how to transform the data between source and destination, clicking the "..." button under the Transform column.

Now you have to follow the same steps as those in Figures 14.8 and 14.9 to save and schedule the DTS package.

After this process, the package will be saved and executed, as shown in Figure 14.17. Note that this figure is different from Figure 14.10. In this case, there are several tasks running in parallel. You will see later in this section that this DTS package is made out of individual subpackages for every table or view to copy.

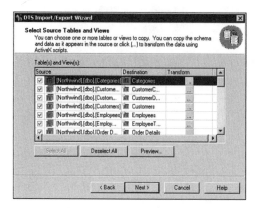

Figure 14.16: *Select which tables and views to select as data source.*

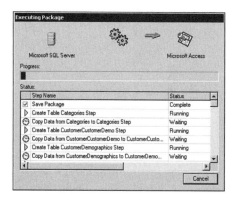

Figure 14.17: *You can see how SQL Server executes different DTS tasks in parallel.*

When the package finishes its execution, you will see a confirmation message with information about how many objects have been transferred from Microsoft SQL Server to Microsoft Access.

Now you can edit the package, using the DTS Designer. You can use Enterprise Manager to open the Local Packages folder in the Data Transformation Services section, and you will see the ExportAccess package (see Figure 14.18).

Right-click the package and select Design Package, and the DTS Designer environment will show a similar screen as shown in Figure 14.19.

Figure 14.19 shows the package in design mode and you can see many little tasks there. Use the Zoom icon in the toolbar to show the package design at 100%, and your screen will show something similar to Figure 14.20.

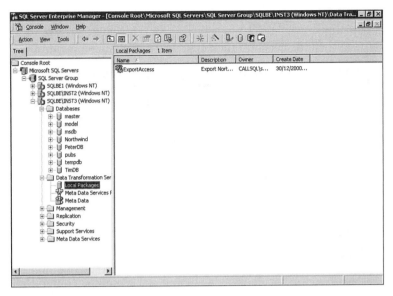

Figure 14.18: You can see the list of local DTS packages from Enterprise Manager.

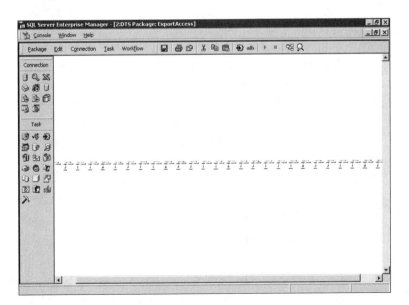

Figure 14.19: The DTS Designer Environment shows the ExportAccess package.

You can see in Figure 14.20 that for every table or view, the DTS package contains three elements:

- An Execute SQL Task to create the table in Access

- A connection to SQL Server
- A connection to Access

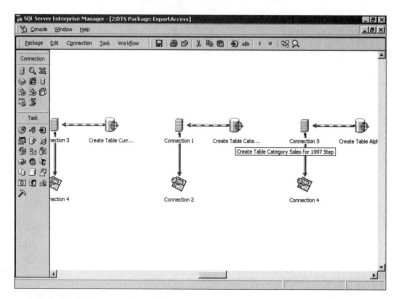

Figure 14.20: *Zoom 100% to see every task in the DTS Designer window.*

Note that DTS opens two connections to SQL Server—Connection 1 and Connection 3—and two connections to Access—Connection 2 and Connection 4. In this way, the package can run tasks in parallel.

There is an arrow between the Execute SQL Task and the SQL Server Connection. If you right-click on this arrow, you will be prompted with a context menu.

Selecting Properties in the context menu will bring you to the Workflow Properties form (see Figure 14.21). There you can specify the source and destination steps, as well as the precedence criteria:

- Select None for independent tasks, with no precedence declared between them.

- Select Completion for unconditional precedence, where the destination task will be executed after the source task completes, regardless of the execution success or failure.

- Select Failure to execute the destination task only in the event of a source task execution failure.

- Select Success to execute the destination task only if the execution of the source tasks is successful.

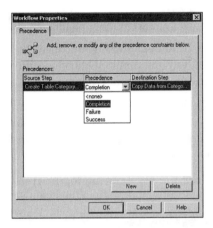

Figure 14.21: *You can select precedence properties based on completion, failure, or success of the preceding task.*

If you open the destination Access database, you will see the table list, where every table and view in the source database has been converted into an Access table (see Figure 14.22).

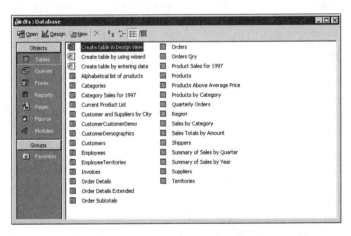

Figure 14.22: *You can see the tables list in the Destination Access database.*

You can create a similar package to import data from Access into SQL Server or export from an Access database into another Access database, if this is what you need to do.

NOTE

Remember that you can create a DTS package to transfer data from ANY data source to ANY destination, as long as you have an ODBC driver or an OLEDB provider for the data source and the destination.

The Copy Database Wizard

SQL Server includes a new tool to copy databases between two servers: the Copy Database Wizard. The Copy Database Wizard is implemented as a custom DTS package with the following custom tasks:

- Database Move/Copy Task—Using this task, you can select source and destination servers, as well as a database or databases to move or copy. Using this custom task, you specify the location for the database files in the destination server.

- Logins Copy Tasks—Used to copy existing logins from the source to the destination server.

- Master Stored Procedures Copy Task—Used to copy user-defined stored procedures from the master database in the source server to the master database in the destination server.

- Jobs Copy Task—Used to copy jobs from the msdb database, in the source server, to the msdb database, in the destination server.

- Error Messages Copy Task—Used to copy the messages contained in the master.dbo.sysmessages system table between the source and destination servers.

TIP

The Copy Database Wizard Custom tasks can be very useful in your own DTS packages.

To illustrate how the Copy Database Wizard works, copy a database from one instance of SQL Server to another instance in the same server. If you have two servers in your network with SQL Server 2000 installed, you can follow this example to copy a database from one server to another.

Before starting with the wizard, you must create a new database. In this example, we created a new database called TimDB.

To start the Copy Database Wizard from Enterprise Manager, you can display the context menu for the Databases folder, as in Figure 14.23.

When you start the Copy Database Wizard, you get the Welcome to the Copy Database Wizard form, where you can find a summary of the actions that this wizard will execute.

Click Next, and you will see the Select a Source Server step (see Figure 14.24). In this form, you must select the SQL Server source server and specify which authentication mode the package will use to connect to the source server.

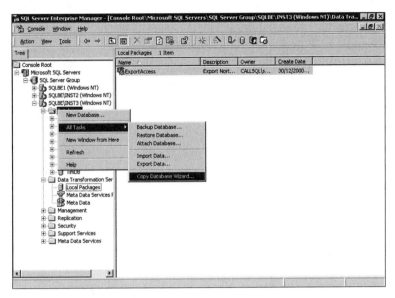

Figure 14.23: *Start the Copy Database Wizard from the Databases context menu.*

NOTE

It is not necessary to register a server in Enterprise Manager to be able to select the server as source or destination server.

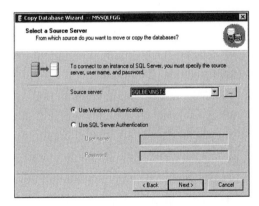

Figure 14.24: *Select a source server for the Copy Database Wizard.*

Click Next and the wizard will take you to the Select a Destination Server step (see Figure 14.25). Here you will select another instance of SQL Server 2000 in the same or a different server from the source server.

NOTE

You cannot select the same server as both source and destination.

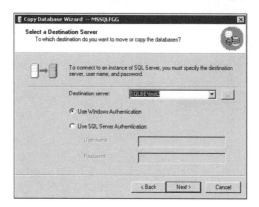

Figure 14.25: *Select a destination server for the Copy Database Wizard.*

The next step is Select the Databases to Move or Copy (see Figure 14.26). In this form, you will see that only databases that do not exist in the destination server are available for moving or copying. This excludes system databases, because they exist in both servers. In this example, you must select to copy the database you just created at the beginning of this section.

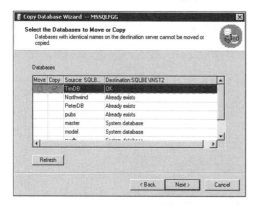

Figure 14.26: *Select valid databases to move or copy.*

Click Next and you will arrive at the Database File Location step (see Figure 14.27). In this form, you will see every file used by every database selected in the previous step.

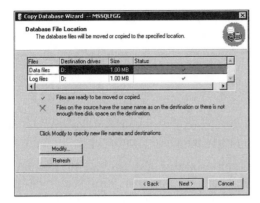

Figure 14.27: *Select the location of the database files.*

The wizard selects as the destination the default data directory of the destination server, which is the directory where the master database primary data file is stored. You can change the directory of these files to any valid folder in the destination server.

Click Modify to go to the Database Files form, where you can change the name and location of every file individually (see Figure 14.28). If the file already exists on the destination directory, you will see a conflict mark. Note that you cannot change the file size in this wizard. Database files retain their size after the transfer to the destination server.

NOTE

Filenames are unique per database, not serverwide. You can have conflicts only if the destination's physical file already exists.

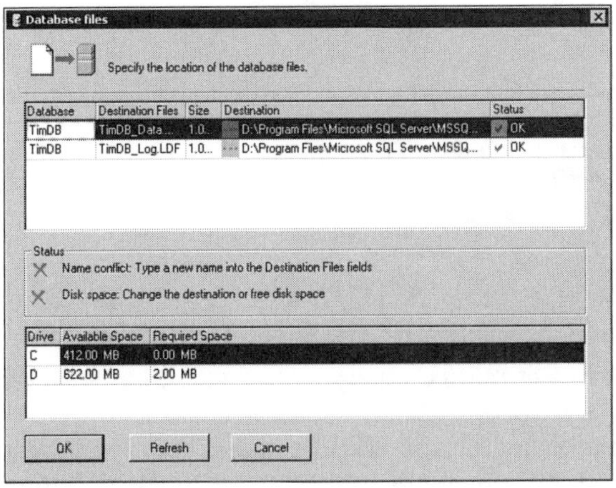

Figure 14.28: *The Database Files form enables you to change database filenames and locations.*

In SQL Server 2000, every database is as self-contained as possible. However, your database might need some objects that are defined in other databases. This is why the Copy Database Wizard contains the Select Related Objects step (see Figure 14.29). In this step, you can

- Select to copy logins from the source server to the destination. This is a recommended practice to avoid orphan database users in the destination database, because of nonexisting logins in the destination server. You can specify which logins to copy.

- If you created stored procedures in the master database to be shared by every database, you can transfer them, too. Perhaps the source database contains stored procedures and triggers that access the shared stored procedures from a master.

- You can have jobs defined in msdb that are referenced from your source database. You can copy them to the destination server, also.

- Perhaps you defined custom error messages in the source server and your stored procedures, triggers, and user-defined functions use these custom messages; then, you will need to transfer them to the destination server.

CAUTION

Have clear numbering criteria for your custom messages, so you can avoid overlapped messages from one database system to another. Before copying messages to the destination server, check that these messages do not exist in the destination server.

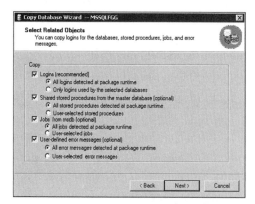

Figure 14.29: *Select related objects, such as logins, jobs, and messages.*

The next step is Schedule the DTS Package, because the Copy Database Wizard creates a DTS package and stores it in the destination server. Figure 14.30 shows this form, where you can provide a name to the DTS package and specify a schedule in the usual way.

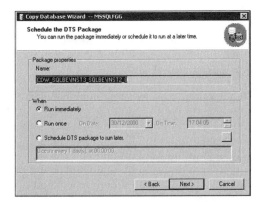

Figure 14.30: *You can schedule when to execute the Copy Database Wizard DTS package.*

The Completing the Copy Database Wizard form will show a summary of the tasks to execute, and you can click Finish to complete the wizard's work.

The package execution starts, as you see in Figure 14.31, and you can click More Info to get a full description of the tasks to execute (see Figure 14.32).

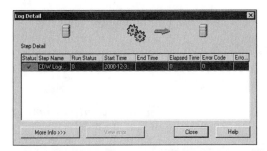

Figure 14.31: *Copy Database Wizard. Log details, without extra details.*

As you can see in Figure 14.33, the Copy Database Wizard executed the following tasks successfully:

1. Copied selected logins to the destination server.

2. Copied selected stored procedures to the destination server.

3. Copied selected jobs from the source to the destination server.

4. Copied selected messages from the source to the destination server.

5. Checked that the source database does not have active connections.

6. Put the source database in single-user mode.

7. Detached the source database.

8. Copied the database files to the destination server.

9. Attached the database to the destination server.

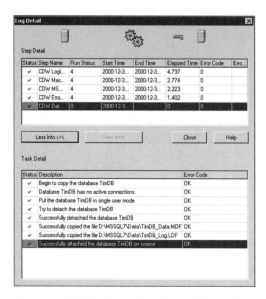

Figure 14.32: *Copy Database Wizard. Log details, with extra details.*

Figure 14.33: *The Copy Database Wizard execution completed successfully.*

What's Next?

Transferring and transforming data is a common administrative task in multiserver environments.

Chapter 15, "Working with Heterogeneous Environments: Setting Up Linked Servers," discusses the multiserver environment and the implications of distributed transactions. In Chapter 15, you learn how to use linked servers to maintain data in multiple servers, as an alternative to DTS and replication.

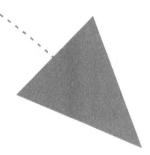

Working with Heterogeneous Environments: Setting Up Linked Servers

Chapter 14, "Transferring Data to and from SQL Server," introduced the idea of transferring data between different databases, servers, or platforms. In this chapter, you will practice with SQL Server 2000 features that enable you to execute queries that span multiple servers.

In some cases, you might want to access data that is not stored in SQL Server, that perhaps is not even relational. As long as you have an ODBC driver or an OLE DB provider to connect to this particular data, you can use linked servers, or rowset functions, to access this data from any Transact-SQL batch, stored procedure, trigger, or user-defined function.

This chapter teaches you the following:

- What distributed queries are and why you might need them
- How to use Transact-SQL rowset functions to execute queries in remote servers
- How to define linked servers
- How to execute queries using linked servers
- How to run queries that are executed remotely in a remote server
- How to design and use partitioned views

Distributed Queries

Using any programming language, you can use ADO and OLE DB to connect to any data source. SQL Server 2000 uses OLE DB to give you access to any available data source.

You can write ad hoc queries in SQL Server to access external data using a rowset function in the FROM clause, as if it were a result set from a local table. All you need to use this functionality is an OLE DB provider and the properties required to establish a connection to the data.

For common queries, it is more efficient to define a linked server, declaring the connection properties permanently, so any user connected to the local server will have access to the remote server without specifying any connection property manually.

NOTE

For this chapter, you should install SQL Server 2000 three times:

- Default instance: SQLBE

- First named instance: SQLBE\Inst2

- Second named instance: SQLBE\Inst3

Read Appendix A, "Using SQL Server Instances," to learn about how to install and work with SQL Server 2000 instances.

TIP

If your server has a different name than SQLBE, you can use the SQL Server 2000 Client Network Utility to create an alias to your first available SQL Server 2000 server or instance and call it SQLBE. Select two more SQL Server 2000 servers and create aliases for them called SQLBE\Inst2 and SQLBE\Inst3.

In this way, you can execute the examples of this chapter with minimal or no changes.

Ad Hoc Queries

SQL Server 2000 provides, two rowset functions to access heterogeneous data from any query:

- OPENDATASOURCE—To open any relational data source that exposes the data organized in catalogs, schemas, and data objects. SQL Server is a typical example, because it exposes data as DatabaseName.ObjectOwner.ObjectName, where the object can be a table, view, stored procedure, or user-defined function.

- OPENROWSET—To open any data source, relational or nonrelational, as long as you can connect to the data source through OLE DB.

Both rowset functions provide a similar functionality. The main difference is the way you invoke them, although the result is the same in both cases: a result set.

USING OPENDATASOURCE

Any database object in SQL Server can be identified by its fully qualified name: ServerName.CatalogName.SchemaName.ObjectName. In SQL Server, the CatalogName is the name of the database in which the object is stored. The SchemaName is usually the name of the owner of the object.

NOTE

In SQL Server 2000, although not very common, you can create schemas using the CREATE SCHEMA statement. If you are interested in this topic, you can take a look at the topic "CREATE SCHEMA" in Books Online.

Working with ADO, from any programming language, you need to establish a connection to a server before trying to access its data. In Transact-SQL, use the OPENDATASOURCE function to connect to a server and retrieve data from there (see Listing 15.1).

Listing 15.1: Use OPENDATASOURCE to Connect to a Server and Retrieve Data

```
SELECT ProductID, ProductName
FROM OPENDATASOURCE(
'SQLOLEDB',
'Data Source=SQLBE\Inst3;User ID=sa;Password=;').Northwind.dbo.Products
WHERE UnitPrice > 50.0
```

EXAMPLE

OUTPUT

```
ProductID    ProductName
----------   ------------------------------------------
9            Mishi Kobe Niku
18           Carnarvon Tigers
20           Sir Rodney's Marmalade
29           Thüringer Rostbratwurst
38           Côte de Blaye
51           Manjimup Dried Apples
59           Raclette Courdavault
```

As you saw in Listing 15.1, you use OPENDATASOURCE as a server name to fully qualify a table in a remote server. The OPENDATASOURCE function has two parameters:

- The OLE DB provider to use. In this example, you use the SQLOLEDB OLE DB provider to access a SQL Server 2000 server. You can use this provider to access any version of SQL Server.

- The connection string, required by the OLE DB provider, to connect to the data source.

Every OLE DB provider requires a different connection string. In this case, the connection string contains the following data:

- `Data Source=SQLBE\Inst3;`—In this case, it is the name of the SQL Server 2000 server you want to connect to, `SQLBE`, and the instance name `Inst3`. You can use the `Server` keyword instead of `Data Source`.

- `User ID=sa;`—This is the SQL Server login used to connect to the remote SQL Server. In this example, you connect to SQL Server using the sa account. You can use the `UID` keyword instead of `User ID`.

- `Password=;`—In this case, you provide a blank password. You can substitute the `Password` keyword with `PWD`.

CAUTION

Try to avoid using the sa account to connect to SQL Server; use integrated security instead. However, if you must use the sa account, provide a hard-to-guess password to the sa account as soon as possible, and restrict the number of users who know this password.

To run the examples in this chapter, you should connect to SQL Server using integrated security, as in Listing 15.2.

The example in Listing 15.2 uses integrated security to connect to SQL Server through `OPENDATASOURCE`. As you can see in that example, the only difference is the inclusion of the `Integrated Security=SSPI;` string, or `Trusted_Connection=yes;`, instead of `User ID=sa;Password=;`.

EXAMPLE

Listing 15.2: You Can Use Integrated Security When Using OPENDATASOURCE to Connect to SQL Server

```
SELECT CustomerID, CompanyName
FROM OPENDATASOURCE(
'SQLOLEDB',
'Server=SQLBE;Integrated Security=SSPI;').Northwind.dbo.Customers
WHERE City = 'London'
```

OUTPUT

```
CustomerID CompanyName
---------- ----------------------------------------
AROUT      Around the Horn
BSBEV      B's Beverages
CONSH      Consolidated Holdings
EASTC      Eastern Connection
NORTS      North/South
SEVES      Seven Seas Imports
```

In the examples from Listings 15.1 and 15.2, you might think that SQL Server connects to the remote servers, retrieves the data from the specified table, and locally applies the filter declared in the WHERE clause. However, the Query Processor is intelligent enough to detect that the WHERE clause applies exclusively to remote data and send the query to the remote server to be filtered remotely. In this way, the overall performance is improved, because the data is filtered where it belongs. Figure 15.1 shows the query plan of the query in Listing 15.2. In this query plan, you can see only one step, a remote query, defined as

```
SELECT Tbl1001."CustomerID" Col1003
,Tbl1001."CompanyName" Col1004
FROM "Northwind"."dbo"."Customers" Tbl1001
WHERE Tbl1001."City"=N'London'
```

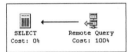

Figure 15.1: *The Query Processor sends the* WHERE *clause to the remote server to be processed remotely.*

You can use the OPENDATASOURCE function to join it to a local table (see Listing 15.3). In this case, the query plan is shown in Figure 15.2, where you can still see the remote query, with a merge join to connect the remote result set with the local result set.

EXAMPLE

Listing 15.3: You Can Join the Result of OPENDATASOURCE to a Local Table

```
SELECT OrderID, OrderDate, O.CustomerID, CompanyName
FROM OPENDATASOURCE(
'SQLOLEDB',
'Server=SQLBE;Integrated Security=SSPI;').Northwind.dbo.Customers
AS C
JOIN Northwind.dbo.Orders
AS O
ON O.CustomerID = C.CustomerID
WHERE City = 'London'
AND OrderDate BETWEEN '1996-12-01'
AND '1996-12-15'
```

OUTPUT

```
OrderID  OrderDate                  CustomerID CompanyName
-------- -------------------------- ---------- -------------------
10377    1996-12-09 00:00:00.000    SEVES      Seven Seas Imports
```

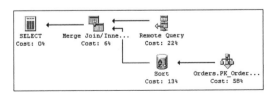

Figure 15.2: *You can join a Remote Query to a local table.*

If you modify the example from Listing 15.3 to retrieve the Customer information from the SQLBE server and the Orders information from the SQLBE\Inst2 server, the query should be as in Listing 15.4, and the query plan is shown in Figure 15.3.

EXAMPLE

Listing 15.4: Use OPENDATASOURCE to Connect to a Server and Retrieve Data

```
SELECT OrderID, OrderDate, O.CustomerID, CompanyName
FROM OPENDATASOURCE(
'SQLOLEDB',
'Server=SQLBE;Integrated Security=SSPI;').Northwind.dbo.Customers
AS C
JOIN OPENDATASOURCE(
'SQLOLEDB',
'Server=SQLBE\Inst2;Integrated Security=SSPI;').Northwind.dbo.Orders
AS O
ON O.CustomerID = C.CustomerID
WHERE City = 'London'
AND OrderDate BETWEEN '1996-12-01'
AND '1996-12-15'
```

OUTPUT

```
OrderID  OrderDate                   CustomerID CompanyName
-------- --------------------------- ---------- --------------------
10377    1996-12-09 00:00:00.000     SEVES      Seven Seas Imports
```

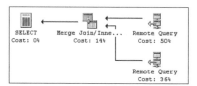

Figure 15.3: *You can join a remote query to another remote query.*

CAUTION

You can use OPENDATASOURCE only to retrieve data from tables and views. Stored procedures and user-defined functions are not allowed in OPENDATASOURCE.

You can use OPENDATASOURCE to retrieve data from an Access database, as the DTS.MDB database defined in Chapter 14, in the "Export a SQL Server Table to an Access Database" section. Listing 15.5 shows how to use the Microsoft Jet OLE DB provider to connect to an Access database, and Figure 15.4 shows its query plan.

EXAMPLE

Listing 15.5: Use OPENDATASOURCE to Connect to a Remote SQL Server and an Access Database

```
SELECT OrderID, OrderDate--, O.CustomerID, CompanyName
FROM OPENDATASOURCE(
'SQLOLEDB',
'Server=SQLBE;Integrated Security=SSPI;').Northwind.dbo.Customers
```

Listing 15.5: continued

```
AS C
JOIN OPENDATASOURCE(
'Microsoft.Jet.OLEDB.4.0',
'Data Source="D:\SQL\DTS.MDB";User ID=Admin;Password=;')...Orders
AS O
ON O.CustomerID = C.CustomerID
WHERE City = 'London'
AND OrderDate BETWEEN '1996-12-01'
AND '1996-12-15'
```

```
OrderID  OrderDate                CustomerID CompanyName
-------- ------------------------ ---------- --------------------
10377    1996-12-09 00:00:00.000  SEVES      Seven Seas Imports
```

OUTPUT

Figure 15.4: You can join a remote query to SQL Server to a remote query to Access.

If you compare the query plan from Figure 15.4 to the one from Figure 15.3, you can see two extra steps after retrieving the Orders data from Access:

- A filter to select the data range.

- A sort operation to be able to execute the merge join.

These extra steps are required because SQL Server cannot ask the Jet OLE DB provider to execute these tasks remotely.

You can use OPENDATASOURCE to modify a table in an UPDATE, DELETE, or INSERT statement, as in Listing 15.6.

Listing 15.6: Use OPENDATASOURCE to Specify a Source for UPDATE, INSERT, or DELETE Statements

```
PRINT 'Before moving BSBEV from London' + CHAR(10)

SELECT CustomerID, CompanyName, City
FROM OPENDATASOURCE(
'SQLOLEDB',
'Server=SQLBE\Inst3;Integrated Security=SSPI;').Northwind.dbo.Customers
WHERE CustomerID = 'BSBEV'

PRINT CHAR(10) + 'Moving BSBEV from London to Southampton' + CHAR(10)

UPDATE OPENDATASOURCE(
```

EXAMPLE

Listing 15.6: continued

```
'SQLOLEDB',
'Server=SQLBE\Inst3;Integrated Security=SSPI;').Northwind.dbo.Customers
SET City = 'Southampton'
WHERE CustomerID = 'BSBEV'

PRINT CHAR(10) + 'After BSBEV moved from London to Southampton' + CHAR(10)

SELECT CustomerID, CompanyName, City
FROM OPENDATASOURCE(
'SQLOLEDB',
'Server=SQLBE\Inst3;Integrated Security=SSPI;').Northwind.dbo.Customers
WHERE CustomerID = 'BSBEV'

PRINT CHAR(10) + 'Moving BSBEV back to London' + CHAR(10)

UPDATE OPENDATASOURCE(
'SQLOLEDB',
'Server=SQLBE\Inst3;Integrated Security=SSPI;').Northwind.dbo.Customers
SET City = 'London'
WHERE CustomerID = 'BSBEV'
```

OUTPUT

```
Before moving BSBEV from London

CustomerID CompanyName                              City
---------- ---------------------------------------- ---------------
BSBEV      B's Beverages                            London

(1 row(s) affected)

Moving BSBEV from London to Southampton

(1 row(s) affected)

After BSBEV moved from London to Southampton

CustomerID CompanyName                              City
---------- ---------------------------------------- ---------------
BSBEV      B's Beverages                            Southampton

(1 row(s) affected)

Moving BSBEV back to London

(1 row(s) affected)
```

USING OPENROWSET

You can use OPENROWSET to retrieve result sets from any data source, in a way similar to OPENDATASOURCE. The main difference is that you can send the query to the data source, using the syntax that the OLE DB provider accepts, and the OLE DB provider will return the requested result set.

Listing 15.7 shows how to use OPENROWSET to retrieve data from an instance of SQL Server, in a way similar to that seen earlier in Listing 15.1. However, you can send the entire query, including the WHERE clause, directly to the OPENROWSET function, as shown in the second example of Listing 15.7.

EXAMPLE

Listing 15.7: Use OPENROWSET to Connect to a Server and Retrieve Data

```
SELECT ProductID, ProductName
FROM OPENROWSET(
'SQLOLEDB',
'Server=SQLBE\Inst3;UID=sa;PWD=;', Northwind.dbo.Products)
WHERE UnitPrice > 50.0

SELECT *
FROM OPENROWSET(
'SQLOLEDB',
'Server=SQLBE\Inst3;UID=sa;PWD=;',
'SELECT ProductID, ProductName
FROM Northwind.dbo.Products
WHERE UnitPrice > 50.0')
```

OUTPUT

```
ProductID    ProductName
-----------  ----------------------------------------
9            Mishi Kobe Niku
18           Carnarvon Tigers
20           Sir Rodney's Marmalade
29           Thüringer Rostbratwurst
38           Côte de Blaye
51           Manjimup Dried Apples
59           Raclette Courdavault
```

The query plans of the two queries shown in Listing 15.7 are not the same. In Figure 15.5, you can see a remote query step for the first query and a remote scan for the second query; however, the results are the same, and in both cases the query is sent to the remote server to be executed there.

You can join the result set returned by OPENROWSET to other result sets. Listing 15.8 shows an example similar to Listing 15.4, but in this case you retrieve the same result in three different ways:

- The first query joins two OPENROWSET functions against two servers (SQLBE\Inst2 and SQLBE\Inst3).

- The second query joins two OPENROWSET functions against the same server (SQLBE\Inst2).

- The third query uses OPENROWSET just once to retrieve the entire result set from a single server (SQLBE\Inst2).

Figure 15.5: *OPENROWSET produces either a remote query or a remote scan when reading remote data.*

EXAMPLE

Listing 15.8: Use OPENROWSET to Retrieve a Result Set to JOIN to Other Result Sets

```
PRINT 'Using OPENROWSET twice againt two servers' + CHAR(10)

SELECT OrderID, OrderDate, O.CustomerID, CompanyName
FROM OPENROWSET(
'SQLOLEDB',
'Server=SQLBE\Inst2;Trusted_Connection=yes;',
Northwind.dbo.Customers)
AS C
JOIN OPENROWSET(
'SQLOLEDB',
'Server=SQLBE\Inst3;Trusted_Connection=yes;',
Northwind.dbo.Orders)
AS O
ON O.CustomerID = C.CustomerID
WHERE City = 'London'
AND OrderDate BETWEEN '1996-12-01'
AND '1996-12-15'


PRINT 'Using OPENROWSET twice againt one server' + CHAR(10)

SELECT OrderID, OrderDate, O.CustomerID, CompanyName
FROM OPENROWSET(
'SQLOLEDB',
'Server=SQLBE\Inst2;Trusted_Connection=yes;',
Northwind.dbo.Customers)
AS C
JOIN OPENROWSET(
'SQLOLEDB',
'Server=SQLBE\Inst2;Trusted_Connection=yes;',
Northwind.dbo.Orders)
AS O
ON O.CustomerID = C.CustomerID
WHERE City = 'London'
AND OrderDate BETWEEN '1996-12-01'
```

Listing 15.8: continued

```
AND '1996-12-15'

PRINT 'Using OPENROWSET once' + CHAR(10)

SELECT *
FROM OPENROWSET(
'SQLOLEDB',
'Server=SQLBE\Inst2;Trusted_Connection=yes;',
'SELECT OrderID, OrderDate, O.CustomerID, CompanyName
FROM Northwind.dbo.Customers AS C
JOIN
Northwind.dbo.Orders AS O
ON O.CustomerID = C.CustomerID
WHERE City = ''London''
AND OrderDate BETWEEN ''1996-12-01''
AND ''1996-12-15''')
```

OUTPUT

```
Using OPENROWSET twice againt two servers


OrderID  OrderDate                  CustomerID CompanyName
-------- -------------------------- ---------- ------------------
10377    1996-12-09 00:00:00.000    SEVES      Seven Seas Imports


Using OPENROWSET twice againt one server

OrderID  OrderDate                  CustomerID CompanyName
-------- -------------------------- ---------- ------------------
10377    1996-12-09 00:00:00.000    SEVES      Seven Seas Imports


Using OPENROWSET once

OrderID  OrderDate                  CustomerID CompanyName
-------- -------------------------- ---------- ------------------
10377    1996-12-09 00:00:00.000    SEVES      Seven Seas Imports
```

Figure 15.6 shows the query plan produced to execute the first query from Listing 15.8. You can see that this query plan is similar to the query plan shown in Figure 15.3.

Figure 15.7 shows the query plan produced when the second query from Listing 15.8 is executed. Because both OPENROWSET functions connect to the same server, only one remote query step is required to retrieve the final result set. This is more efficient than returning two complete result sets and joining them locally. The Query Processor makes this decision automatically, and through this way you can save network bandwidth because only the requested data is transferred from the remote server.

Figure 15.6: *You can join a remote query to another remote query using OPENROWSET.*

Figure 15.7: *The Query Processor optimizes access to remote servers when you connect twice, using OPENROWSET.*

Finally, you can use OPENROWSET to send a complex query to a remote SQL Server, as seen in the third example in Listing 15.8. Figure 15.8 shows the query plan produced to execute this query. This query contains only one OPENROWSET function, whereas the query plan shows a single remote scan step.

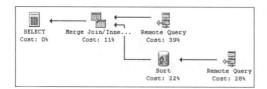

Figure 15.8: *You can use OPENROWSET to send complex queries to a remote server.*

In the examples in this section, you used the same kind of connection string as in the OPENDATASOURCE function. You can use a different syntax in OPENROWSET to specify the server name, the user ID, and the password, as illustrated in Listing 15.9.

EXAMPLE

Listing 15.9: You Can Use a Simplified Syntax in OPENROWSET to Connect to a Data Source

```
PRINT 'From SQL Server' + CHAR(10)

SELECT CategoryID, CategoryName
FROM OPENROWSET(
'SQLOLEDB',
'SQLBE\Inst3';'sa';'', Northwind.dbo.Categories)

PRINT 'From Access' + CHAR(10)

SELECT CategoryID, CategoryName
FROM OPENROWSET(
'Microsoft.Jet.OLEDB.4.0',
```

Listing 15.9: continued

```
'D:\SQL\DTS.MDB';'Admin';'',
'SELECT * FROM Categories
ORDER BY CategoryName DESC')
```

From SQL Server

OUTPUT

```
CategoryID  CategoryName
..........  ...............
1           Beverages
2           Condiments
3           Confections
4           Dairy Products
5           Grains/Cereals
6           Meat/Poultry
7           Produce
8           Seafood
```

From Access

```
CategoryID  CategoryName
..........  ...............
8           Seafood
7           Produce
6           Meat/Poultry
5           Grains/Cereals
4           Dairy Products
3           Confections
2           Condiments
1           Beverages
```

TIP

Avoid the syntax from Listing 15.9, because with the syntax of Listings 15.7 and 15.8 you can reuse the same connection string used in any application that uses OLE DB to connect to the data source.

You can use OPENROWSET, with the OLE DB provider for ODBC, to connect to any Data Source Name (DSN) defined in the ODBC Manager. Listing 15.10 uses the LocalServer system DSN, which points to the default SQL Server instance. You can use this provider to establish DSN-less connections to any data source also, specifying the ODBC driver to use as seen in the second example in Listing 15.10.

CAUTION

Test the LocalServer DSN with the ODBC Manager before trying the example from Listing 15.10.

EXAMPLE

Listing 15.10: You Can Use the OLE DB Provider for ODBC with OPENROWSET to Access Any ODBC Data Source Name

```
SELECT *
FROM OPENROWSET('MSDASQL',
'DSN=LocalServer',
'SELECT * FROM Northwind.dbo.Region')
```

OUTPUT

```
RegionID    RegionDescription
----------  ------------------------------------------------------
1           Eastern
2           Western
3           Northern
4           Southern
```

TIP

You can use OPENROWSET to invoke system functions or administrative stored procedures from the local server as result sets to be filtered in a SELECT statement, as in Listing 15.11, where you use OPENROWSET to execute sp_who remotely.

EXAMPLE

Listing 15.11: Use OPENROWSET to Work with Transact-SQL Administrative Statements As Result Sets

```
SELECT spid, cmd, dbname
FROM OPENROWSET('SQLOLEDB',
'Server=SQLBE;Trusted_Connection=yes;',
'EXEC sp_who')
WHERE dbname = 'Northwind'
```

OUTPUT

```
spid    cmd               dbname
------  ----------------  ----------------
62      SELECT            Northwind
63      AWAITING COMMAND  Northwind
65      AWAITING COMMAND  Northwind
```

You can retrieve results from remote stored procedures or user-defined functions by using OPENROWSET, as illustrated in Listing 15.12.

EXAMPLE

Listing 15.12: Use OPENROWSET to Open Remote User-Defined Functions

```
SELECT OrderID, CustomerID, TotalValue, ShipCountry, OrderDate
FROM OPENROWSET('SQLOLEDB',
'Server=SQLBE;Trusted_Connection=yes;',
'Select * FROM Northwind.dbo.TopTenOrders()')
```

OUTPUT

```
OrderID   CustomerID TotalValue      ShipCountry     OrderDate
--------- ---------- --------------  --------------- ------------------------
10865     QUICK      16387.5000      Germany         1998-02-02 00:00:00.000
10981     HANAR      15810.0000      Brazil          1998-03-27 00:00:00.000
11030     SAVEA      12615.0500      USA             1998-04-17 00:00:00.000
10889     RATTC      11380.0000      USA             1998-02-16 00:00:00.000
10417     SIMOB      11188.4000      Denmark         1997-01-16 00:00:00.000
10817     KOENE      10952.8450      Germany         1998-01-06 00:00:00.000
10897     HUNGO      10835.2400      Ireland         1998-02-19 00:00:00.000
```

Listing 15.12: continued

```
10479    RATTC    10495.6000    USA        1997-03-19 00:00:00.000
10540    QUICK    10191.7000    Germany    1997-05-19 00:00:00.000
10691    QUICK    10164.8000    Germany    1997-10-03 00:00:00.000
```

If you want to update data through the OPENROWSET function, you must use the OPENROWSET function in the UPDATE clause as if it were a table. Listing 15.13 shows an example of UPDATE, INSERT, and DELETE statements using OPENROWSET.

EXAMPLE

Listing 15.13: You Can UPDATE, INSERT, and DELETE a Result Set Returned by OPENROWSET

```
DECLARE @ID int

PRINT 'Insert a new Category' + CHAR(10)

INSERT OPENROWSET('SQLOLEDB',
'Server=SQLBE;Trusted_Connection=yes;',
Northwind.dbo.Categories)
(CategoryName)
VALUES ('New Category')

PRINT 'Retrieve the CategoryID' + CHAR(10)

SELECT @ID = CategoryID
FROM OPENROWSET('SQLOLEDB',
'Server=SQLBE;Trusted_Connection=yes;',
'SELECT CategoryID
FROM Northwind.dbo.Categories
WHERE CategoryName = ''New Category''')

PRINT 'Update the name of the new Category' + CHAR(10)

UPDATE OPENROWSET('SQLOLEDB',
'Server=SQLBE;Trusted_Connection=yes;',
Northwind.dbo.Categories)
SET CategoryName = 'Other'
WHERE CategoryID = @ID

PRINT 'Delete the new Category' + CHAR(10)

DELETE OPENROWSET('SQLOLEDB',
'Server=SQLBE;Trusted_Connection=yes;',
Northwind.dbo.Categories)
WHERE CategoryID = @ID
```

Listing 15.13: continued

```
Insert a new Category

(1 row(s) affected)

Retrieve the CategoryID

Update the name of the new Category

(1 row(s) affected)

Delete the new Category

(1 row(s) affected)
```

NOTE

You cannot use the SCOPE_IDENTITY function in the example from Listing 15.13 because the insertion takes place in a remote server.

You can use OPENROWSET to create a more accurate version of the scalar user-defined function dbo.Today(), created in Listing 10.4, because using OPENROWSET you can actually reconnect to SQL Server. Almost any instruction is available in OPENROWSET, including not valid built-in functions in user-defined functions, such as GetDate. Listing 15.14 shows how to implement the Today() function using OPENROWSET.

EXAMPLE

Listing 15.14: You Can Use OPENROWSET Inside User-Defined Functions

```
USE Northwind
GO

IF OBJECT_ID('Today', 'FN') IS NOT NULL
DROP FUNCTION dbo.Today
GO
-- Returns the actual system date
-- obtained by using OPENROWSET as a callback function

CREATE FUNCTION dbo.Today
()
RETURNS smalldatetime
AS
BEGIN
DECLARE @sdt smalldatetime

SELECT @SDT = CONVERT(varchar(10), TodaysDate, 120)
FROM OPENROWSET('SQLOLEDB',
'Server=SQLBE;Trusted_Connection=yes;',
'SELECT Getdate() AS TodaysDate')
```

Listing 15.14: continued

```
RETURN @SDT

END
GO

SELECT dbo.Today()
AS Today
```

Today

- -

2001-01-02 00:00:00

OUTPUT

Linked Servers

Any client application can establish connections to more than one server at a time, but it is not possible to join directly result sets from different connections.

Using the rowset functions from the last section, you can execute queries that relate information coming from different data sources. However, SQL Server must establish a connection on every call to OPENDATASOURCE or OPENROWSET, using the connection string or connection parameters sent along with the function call.

If you are a Microsoft Access user, you will be familiar with the concept of a linked table. This is a permanent definition of a logical connection to an external data source.

SQL Server 2000 implements links to any OLE DB data source, as linked servers, to any SQL Server instance. Any user connected to an instance of SQL Server can access any linked server defined in that instance without knowing the parameters to connect to this particular data source. In this way, you have the flexibility of the OPENROWSET and OPENDATASOURCE functions without exposing to the users the complexity inherent to any OLE DB connection.

CAUTION

Having a SQL Server registered in Enterprise Manager does not mean that you have declared that server as a linked server. This is only a setting in a client application, Enterprise Manager, stored in a specific client computer, perhaps the server itself, and it does not have to be visible to any other client connecting to the server.

Users can access objects on linked servers, using fully qualified four-part names and using any data access statement. In this way, you can use any kind of information exposed by the OLE DB provider as if it were a table on a database, and join that information to other tables in the local server.

In the following sections, you will learn how to set up and use linked servers.

SETTING UP AND QUERYING LINKED SERVERS

The first thing you need to set up a linked server, which connects to an external data source, is an appropriate OLE DB provider. Microsoft has tested the following OLE DB providers to use in a linked server:

- Microsoft OLE DB Provider for SQL Server (SQLOLEDB)—Use this provider to connect to SQL Server 6.5, 7.0, and 2000.

- Microsoft OLE DB Provider for ODBC (MSDASQL)—Use this provider to connect to any data source, as long as you have a valid ODBC driver for this particular data source.

- Microsoft OLE DB Provider for Jet (Microsoft.Jet.OLEDB.4.0)—This provider connects you to Microsoft Access databases, Microsoft Excel spreadsheets, and text files.

- Microsoft OLE DB Provider for DTS Packages (DTSPackageDSO)—This provider gives you access to the result set of a transformation step from a DTS package.

- Microsoft OLE DB Provider for Oracle (MSDAORA).

- Microsoft OLE DB Provider for Microsoft Directory Services (ADSDSOObject)—Use this provider to get information from the Active Directory information on Microsoft Windows 2000 or Microsoft Exchange 2000.

- Microsoft OLE DB Provider for Microsoft Indexing Service (MSIDXS)—This provider gives you access to local files indexed by the Microsoft Indexing Service.

- Microsoft OLE DB Provider for DB2 (DB2OLEDB)—This provider is part of the Microsoft Host Integration Server, and gives you connectivity to IBM DB2 databases.

To set up a linked server, you can use the sp_addlinkedserver system stored procedure. Listing 15.15 shows how to create a linked server in the SQLBE server to connect to the SQLBE\Inst2 instance of SQL Server.

EXAMPLE

Listing 15.15: Setting Up a Linked Server Using the sp_addlinkedserver System Stored Procedure

```
-- Use sp_addlinkedserver with
-- SQL Server as a product name

EXEC sp_addlinkedserver
@server = N'SQLBE\Inst3',
@srvproduct = N'SQL Server'
```

Listing 15.15: continued

```
GO


-- Use sp_addlinkedserver with
-- SQLOLEDB as a provider name

EXEC sp_addlinkedserver
@server = N'SQLBEInst2',
@srvproduct = N'',
@provider = N'SQLOLEDB',
@datasrc = N'SQLBE\Inst2'
GO


-- Use sp_addlinkedserver with
-- SQLOLEDB as a provider name
-- and with an initial catalog

EXEC sp_addlinkedserver
@server = N'NewSQLBEInst2',
@srvproduct = N'',
@provider = N'SQLOLEDB',
@datasrc = N'SQLBE\Inst2',
@catalog = N'Northwind'
GO
```

To execute the sp_addlinkedserver system stored procedure to create a linked server to a SQL Server instance, you must supply

- The actual name of the SQL Server default instance or named instance (@server)

- N'SQL Server' as product name (@srvproduct)

or

- The logical name you want to provide to the linked server (@server).

- N'' as product name (@srvproduct).

- The name of the OLE DB provider used to connect to the data source—in this case, N'SQLOLEDB' (@provider).

- The actual name of the SQL Server default instance or named instance to connect (@datasrc).

- Optionally, you can specify the catalog or database to which to connect (@catalog). However, this parameter is used only to specify an initial database to connect. After the connection is made, you can access any database on that server, providing you have permissions to use it and the @catalog parameter is disregarded.

To query a linked server, you must use a fully qualified name, using four-part names, as seen in Listing 15.16. In this way, tables from linked servers can be used as any local table on any DML operation, such as SELECT, INSERT, UPDATE, or DELETE. The last example on Listing 15.16 shows how to link remote tables to other remote and local tables, as if all these tables were local tables.

EXAMPLE

Listing 15.16: You Can Use Linked Servers to Access Remote Tables Using Fully Qualified Names

```
PRINT 'Selecting data from a linked server'
+ CHAR(10)

SELECT CategoryID, CategoryName
FROM [SQLBE\Inst3].northwind.dbo.categories
WHERE CategoryID BETWEEN 1 AND 3

PRINT 'Inserting a row into a linked server'
+ CHAR(10)

INSERT SQLBEInst2.Northwind.dbo.Categories
(CategoryName)
VALUES('More products')

PRINT 'Updating a row from a linked server'
+ CHAR(10)

UPDATE SQLBEInst2.Northwind.dbo.Categories
SET CategoryName = 'Extra Products'
WHERE CategoryName = 'More products'

PRINT 'Deleting a row from a linked server'
+ CHAR(10)

DELETE NewSQLBEInst2.Northwind.dbo.Categories
WHERE CategoryName = 'Extra Products'

PRINT 'Join data coming from linked servers'
+ CHAR(10)

SELECT OrderDate, Quantity, OD.UnitPrice,
CategoryName, ProductName
FROM [SQLBE\Inst3].northwind.dbo.categories C
JOIN SQLBEInst2.Northwind.dbo.Products P
ON P.CategoryID = C.CategoryID
JOIN NewSQLBEInst2.Northwind.dbo.[Order Details] OD
ON OD.ProductID = P.ProductID
JOIN Northwind.dbo.Orders O
```

Listing 15.16: continued

```
ON O.OrderID = OD.OrderID
WHERE P.CategoryID = 1
AND Year(OrderDate ) = 1998
AND CustomerID = 'BSBEV'
```

Selecting data from a linked server

OUTPUT

```
CategoryID  CategoryName
----------- ---------------
1           Beverages
2           Condiments
3           Confections

(3 row(s) affected)

Inserting a row into a linked server

(1 row(s) affected)

Updating a row from a linked server

(1 row(s) affected)

Deleting a row from a linked server

(1 row(s) affected)

Join data coming from linked servers

OrderDate               Quantity UnitPrice  CategoryName     ProductName
----------------------- -------- ---------- ---------------- -----------
1998-04-14 00:00:00.000 30        46.0000   Beverages        Ipoh Coffee

(1 row(s) affected)
```

CAUTION

You cannot omit any of the four parts of the fully qualified name when referencing a remote table from a linked server.

If you want to execute a stored procedure from a linked server, you must first enable RPC (Remote Procedure Calls) on the linked server. Listing 15.17 shows an example of how to enable RPC in a linked server by using the sp_serveroption system stored procedure, and how to call a stored procedure remotely.

EXAMPLE

Listing 15.17: You Can Execute Remote Stored Procedures in a Linked Server

```
-- Set RPC OUT true
-- to accept remote procedure calls

EXECUTE sp_serveroption N'SQLBEinst2', 'RPC OUT', 'true'

-- Execute a remote procedure
```

OUTPUT

```
EXECUTE sqlbeinst2.northwind.dbo.CustOrderHist 'BSBEV'
ProductName                              Total
---------------------------------------- -----------
Aniseed Syrup                            30
Boston Crab Meat                         10
Geitost                                  15
Gnocchi di nonna Alice                   20
Gustaf's Knäckebröd                      21
Ipoh Coffee                              30
Konbu                                    23
Manjimup Dried Apples                    3
Maxilaku                                 6
Mozzarella di Giovanni                   1
Outback Lager                            7
Raclette Courdavault                     4
Ravioli Angelo                           6
Sir Rodney's Scones                      29
Spegesild                                15
Steeleye Stout                           20
Tarte au sucre                           10
Uncle Bob's Organic Dried Pears          34
Wimmers gute Semmelknödel                9

(19 row(s) affected)
```

You can define a linked server to connect to an Access database. Listing 15.18 shows how to create a linked server to connect to the DTS.MDB Access database created in Chapter 14. In this example, you must write in @datasrc the location of the MDB file.

NOTE

Linking an Access database, the value of @srvproduct is only informative. And the location of the database must be sent using the @datasrc parameter, not the @location parameter.

EXAMPLE

Listing 15.18: Setting Up a Linked Server to an Access Database

```
EXEC sp_addlinkedserver
@server = N'DTSMDB',
@srvproduct = N'Access 2000',
```

Listing 15.18: continued

```
@provider = N'Microsoft.Jet.OLEDB.4.0',
@datasrc = N'd:\sql\dts.mdb'
GO

-- Map every login in SQL Server
-- to the Admin login in Access

EXEC sp_addlinkedsrvlogin
@rmtsrvname = 'DTSMDB',
@useself= false,
@locallogin = NULL,
@rmtuser = 'Admin',
@rmtpassword = NULL
GO

-- Read data from Access
-- through the linked server

SELECT ProductName, UnitPrice
FROM DTSMDB...Products
WHERE UnitPrice > 100
GO
```

OUTPUT

```
ProductName                                    UnitPrice
------------------------------------------     --------------------
Thüringer Rostbratwurst                        123.7900
Côte de Blaye                                  263.5000
```

As you saw in Listing 15.18, it is not enough to create the linked server to access its data. In some cases, it is necessary to map the local logins to remote logins to be able to connect to the linked server. To map logins, use the `sp_addlinkedsrvlogin` system stored procedure. This procedure accepts the following parameters:

- `@rmtsrvname`—The name of the linked server. In this case, it is `'DTSMDB'`.

- `@useself`—True to map every local account to the same account in the linked server, so the `@locallogin`, `@rmtuser`, and `@rmtpassword` parameters will be ignored. In this case, you don't want to automatically map every local user to a remote user, because your Access database is not secured in this case, so you give a value of `@rmtuser = false`.

- `@locallogin`—Name of the local login to map, only if `@useself = false`. You specify NULL in this case because you want to map all local logins to the same remote login.

- @rmtuser—Name of the remote login to map the @locallogin. If you use an unsecured Access database, @rmtuser = 'Admin'.

- @rmtpassword—Password to use in the remote server for the remote user specified in @rmtuser. In this case, it must be a blank password, @rmtpassword = NULL.

You can create a linked server to read text files from a directory. To test it, you can create a little text file, like the one in Listing 15.19, in the D:\SQL directory.

Listing 15.19: Ages.txt File

```
ID    Age    Name
1     55     Joseph
2     32     John
3     34     Frederick
4     70     Antony
5     65     Francis
6     75     Jon
7     43     Manfred
8     21     Dick
9     18     Louis
```

EXAMPLE

Now, you can create a linked server to read files in any directory, as in the example in Listing 15.20, using the OLE DB provider for Jet.

Listing 15.20: Setting Up a Linked Server to a Disk Directory

```
-- Create a Linked Server
-- To read text files from
-- the D:\SQL directory

EXEC sp_addlinkedserver
@server = N'TextFiles',
@srvproduct = N'Text files',
@provider = N'Microsoft.Jet.OLEDB.4.0',
@datasrc = N'D:\SQL',
@provstr='Text'

GO

-- Map every login in SQL Server
-- to the Admin login in Jet

EXEC sp_addlinkedsrvlogin
@rmtsrvname = 'TextFiles',
@useself= false,
@locallogin = NULL,
@rmtuser = 'Admin',
```

EXAMPLE

Listing 15.20: continued

```
@rmtpassword = NULL
GO


-- Read data from the Ages.txt file

SELECT *
FROM TextFiles...ages#txt
GO
```

OUTPUT

```
ID_Age_Name
-----------------------------------
1    55    Joseph
2    32    John
3    34    Frederick
4    70    Antony
5    65    Francis
6    75    Jon
7    43    Manfred
8    21    Dick
9    18    Louis
```

NOTE

Note that, as in Listing 15.20, you must convert the character "." ("ages.txt") from the filename into the character '#' ("ages#txt"), because the character "." is not valid inside a table name in SQL Server.

PASS-THROUGH QUERIES

When working with linked servers, SQL Server 2000 always tries to send the queries to the linked servers to be processed remotely. This decreases the network traffic. In particular, the query execution is more efficient because it is performed in the same server in which the affected data is stored. In this case, the query is "passed through" the linked server for remote execution.

You can force the execution of pass-through queries remotely by using the OPENQUERY function. OPENQUERY is similar to the OPENDATASOURCE and OPENROWSET functions, because it connects to a remote data source and returns a result set. However, OPENQUERY uses a linked server definition to connect to the remote server. In this way, you have a persistent definition of the connection properties, providing easier maintenance of your database application.

As you can see in the examples from Listing 15.21, the syntax of OPENQUERY is very simple: You provide the linked server name to send the query and the query to be executed.

Listing 15.21: Using OPENQUERY to Send Pass-Through Queries to a Linked Server

```
-- Gets the date and time in the linked server

SELECT *
FROM OPENQUERY(SQLBEinst2,
'SELECT Getdate() AS Now')

-- Reads some data from the linked server

SELECT DISTINCT ProductName, UnitPrice
FROM OPENQUERY(SQLBEinst2,
'SELECT DISTINCT P.ProductID, ProductName,
OD.UnitPrice
FROM Northwind.dbo.Products P
JOIN Northwind.dbo.[Order details] OD
ON OD.ProductID = P.ProductID
WHERE OD.UnitPrice > 100')

-- Updating data through OPENQUERY

UPDATE OPENQUERY(SQLBEinst2,
'SELECT *
FROM Northwind.dbo.Categories')
SET CategoryName = 'Obsolete'
WHERE CategoryID = 3

-- Testing changes

SELECT categoryname
FROM SQLBEInst2.Northwind.dbo.categories
WHERE CategoryID = 3
GO
```

```
Now
-----------------------------------------------------
2001-02-20 17:33:16.370

ProductID    ProductName                                  UnitPrice
-----------  -------------------------------------------  --------------------
29           Thüringer Rostbratwurst                      123.7900
38           Côte de Blaye                                210.8000
38           Côte de Blaye                                263.5000

categoryname
--------------
Obsolete
```

The first query in Listing 15.21 retrieves the system data and time from the linked server.

The second query remotely executes a query that joins two tables. When the combined result set is returned, the local server performs the DISTINCT operation.

The third query updates data remotely using the OPENQUERY function.

CAUTION

OPENROWSET, OPENDATASOURCE, and OPENQUERY accept only string constants as values for their parameters. String variables are not accepted.

PARTITIONED VIEWS

Consider you have a very big table, SalesInfo, with your worldwide sales information. You have different regions and you want to be able to execute queries to any subset of the complete sales table, regardless of the region.

This table is too big and the maintenance is starting to be difficult. You decide to divide the table among four servers, North, West, South, and East, each one storing data from only one region.

To ensure that you store on every server only data related to that specific server, create a check constraint that enforces the value for the particular regions this server manages.

Now you want to access any data from anywhere, so, on every server you create a view that combines the data from every server with the data from the other servers by a UNION ALL. Use UNION ALL because you do not want to remove duplicates in the final result set. This view is called a *partitioned* view.

You can test a simple version of this technique using the example from Listing 15.22. This script can be run in a single server and single instance, and still it uses the partitioned view technique. This is the only simplification used in this example. You can change this script to create every table in a different instance or server and modify the view to retrieve every table from the appropriate server, as shown in Listing 15.22.

EXAMPLE

Listing 15.22: Create a Partitioned View Based on Four Tables

```
USE Northwind
GO

-- Create the partitioned table
-- RegionID is the partitioning column
-- it is part of the PRIMARY KEY
-- and it has a check constraint
```

Listing 15.22: continued

```
-- to delimit ranges per table

-- RegionID = 3 North

CREATE TABLE SalesInfoNorth (
OrderID int NOT NULL,
RegionID int NOT NULL
CHECK (RegionID = 3),
SaleDate datetime,
Amount money,
EmployeeID int,
CONSTRAINT PK_SI_North
PRIMARY KEY (OrderID, RegionID))


-- RegionID = 4 South

CREATE TABLE SalesInfoSouth (
OrderID int NOT NULL,
RegionID int NOT NULL
CHECK (RegionID = 4),
SaleDate datetime,
Amount money,
EmployeeID int,
CONSTRAINT PK_SI_South
PRIMARY KEY (OrderID, RegionID))

-- RegionID = 1 East

CREATE TABLE SalesInfoEast (
OrderID int NOT NULL,
RegionID int NOT NULL
CHECK (RegionID = 1),
SaleDate datetime,
Amount money,
EmployeeID int,
CONSTRAINT PK_SI_East
PRIMARY KEY (OrderID, RegionID))

-- RegionID = 2 West

CREATE TABLE SalesInfoWest (
OrderID int NOT NULL,
RegionID int NOT NULL
CHECK (RegionID = 2),
SaleDate datetime,
Amount money,
```

Listing 15.22: continued

```
EmployeeID int,
CONSTRAINT PK_SI_West
PRIMARY KEY (OrderID, RegionID))
GO


-- Create a View that gets the entire
-- SalesInfo informations
-- Note the use of UNION ALL
-- This is the Partitioned View

CREATE VIEW SalesInfo
AS
SELECT *
FROM SalesInfoNorth
UNION ALL
SELECT *
FROM SalesInfoSouth
UNION ALL
SELECT *
FROM SalesInfoEast
UNION ALL
SELECT *
FROM SalesInfoWest
GO


-- Populate the partitioned tables
-- using the SalesInfo view directly
-- The partitioned view mechanism
-- will send every row to the appropriate
-- destination table automatically.

INSERT SalesInfo
SELECT o.OrderID,
T.RegionID,
O.OrderDate,
sum(UnitPrice * Quantity * (1-Discount)),
O.EmployeeID
FROM Orders O
JOIN [Order Details] OD
ON O.OrderID = OD.OrderID
JOIN EmployeeTerritories ET
ON ET.EmployeeID = O.EmployeeID
JOIN Territories T
ON T.TerritoryID = ET.TerritoryID
GROUP BY O.OrderID, T.RegionID, O.OrderDate, O.EmployeeID
GO
```

Listing 15.22: continued

```
-- Checking number of rows in every table and total

SELECT COUNT(*) AS CountNorth
FROM SalesInfoNorth

SELECT COUNT(*) AS CountSouth
FROM SalesInfoSouth

SELECT COUNT(*) AS CountEast
FROM SalesInfoEast

SELECT COUNT(*) AS CountWest
FROM SalesInfoWest

SELECT COUNT(*) AS CountTotal
FROM SalesInfo
GO
```

OUTPUT

```
CountNorth
-----------
147


CountSouth
-----------
127


CountEast
-----------
417


CountWest
-----------
139


CountTotal
-----------
830
```

As you have seen in Listing 15.22, it is not necessary to insert data in the individual tables, because SQL Server detects that you are using a partitioned view and sends every row to the appropriate table (even if the table is stored in a different server).

CAUTION

The term *partitioned view*, although it is the official term that Microsoft gives to this technique, can be misleading: The view is not partitioned; actually, it is the data that is

continued

> divided, or partitioned, across different tables. Using this technique, the view integrates the entire data set from the partitioned table.

If every individual table is stored in a different server, or instance, the view is called a distributed partitioned view. This technique provides great improvements on performance. Microsoft used this technique to execute the SQL Server 2000 performance tests sent to the Transaction Processing Council (www.tpc.org).

NOTE

You can use partitioned views to speed up data retrieval in SQL Server 7.0. However, only SQL Server 2000 supports updatable partitioned views. If you update a field that is part of the partitioned key, SQL Server 2000 moves the affected rows to the appropriate table, according to the defined partition schema.

When selecting data from the partitioned view, SQL Server decides automatically which table and server must serve the request, and then divides the execution across the relevant servers.

Distributed Transactions

As you learned on Chapter 13, "Maintaining Data Consistency: Transactions and Locks," you can consider a group of Transact-SQL statements as part of the same transaction. If the data affected by a transaction is spread across different servers, you need to create a distributed transaction.

To create a distributed transaction, you must start the Microsoft Distributed Transaction Coordinator service (MS-DTC), and the connection must use the SET XACT_ABORT ON setting.

MS-DTC implements a two-phase commit mechanism to guarantee transaction consistency across different servers. This process can be described as follows:

1. You connect to a SQL Server instance and start a distributed transaction, using the SET XACT_ABORT ON and BEGIN DISTRIBUTED TRANSACTION statements.

2. You send a DML statement to another instance or server. MS-DTC running on your server must contact the MS-DTC running on the other server to start a distributed transaction and to send the DML statement to be executed remotely.

3. You can send other commands to other instances or servers, including the server you are connected to. In every case, MS-DTC will check

whether this connection already has a distributed transaction with the target server.

4. When your operations have terminated and you want to commit all changes, send the COMMIT TRAN statement.

5. MS-DTC takes control of the commit process and asks every participant server whether they are ready to commit.

6. Every server answers the commit request, sending an affirmative or negative vote.

7. MS-DTC counts the votes received. If there is one negative vote, it informs every participant server that they must roll back the operation. If all votes are affirmative, MS-DTC informs them that they can finally commit.

Listing 15.23 shows an example of a distributed transaction, where you can update from two different instances as part of the same transaction.

EXAMPLE

Listing 15.23: Use Distributed Transactions to Maintain Transaction Consistency Across Multiple Servers

```
-- This setting is required
-- to start Distributed Transactions

SET XACT_ABORT ON
GO


-- Start a Distributed Transaction

BEGIN DISTRIBUTED TRANSACTION

-- Modify data locally

UPDATE Northwind.dbo.Products
SET UnitPrice = UnitPrice * 1.1
WHERE CategoryID = 2


-- Modify the same data remotely

UPDATE SQLBEInst2.Northwind.dbo.Products
SET UnitPrice = UnitPrice * 1.1
WHERE CategoryID = 2


-- Confirm changes

COMMIT TRANSACTION
GO
```

Listing 15.23: continued

```
(12 row(s) affected)


(12 row(s) affected)
```

You can create the `DistSalesInfo` distributed partitioned view, as shown in Listing 15.24. This view is created based on the tables `SalesInfoNorth` and `SalesInfoSouth` that you created in the local server with Listing 15.22. Now you must create the `SalesInfoEast` and `SalesInfoWest` tables in the SQLBE\Inst2 instance, using the same script from Listing 15.22.

You can modify a record from the distributed partitioned view, as in Listing 15.24, to change the `RegionID` field from North (3) to East (1). You can see how the record has been moved automatically from the `SalesInfoNorth` table in the local server to the `SalesInfoEast` table in the linked server. The output shows one row less in the local `SalesInfoNorth` table, and one more row in the remote `SalesInfoEast` table.

In this case, it is not necessary to start a distributed transaction, because SQL Server does it automatically for you, executing this statement in auto-committed mode.

EXAMPLE

Listing 15.24: Use Distributed Transactions to Maintain Transaction Consistency Across Multiple Servers

```
--------------------------------------------------
-- NOTE NOTE NOTE NOTE NOTE NOTE NOTE NOTE NOTE NOTE
--
-- Execute this script in the SQLBE\Inst2 instance
--
-- NOTE NOTE NOTE NOTE NOTE NOTE NOTE NOTE NOTE NOTE
--------------------------------------------------


USE Northwind
GO

-- RegionID = 1 East

CREATE TABLE SalesInfoEast (
OrderID int NOT NULL,
RegionID int NOT NULL
CHECK (RegionID = 1),
SaleDate datetime,
Amount money,
EmployeeID int,
CONSTRAINT PK_SI_East
PRIMARY KEY (OrderID, RegionID))
GO
```

Listing 15.24: continued

```
-- RegionID = 2 West

CREATE TABLE SalesInfoWest (
OrderID int NOT NULL,
RegionID int NOT NULL
CHECK (RegionID = 2),
SaleDate datetime,
Amount money,
EmployeeID int,
CONSTRAINT PK_SI_West
PRIMARY KEY (OrderID, RegionID))
GO


-------------------------------------------
-- NOTE NOTE NOTE NOTE NOTE NOTE NOTE NOTE
--
-- Execute from here in the SQLBE instance
-- and make sure that MS-DTC is running
--
-- NOTE NOTE NOTE NOTE NOTE NOTE NOTE NOTE
-------------------------------------------

USE Northwind
GO

SET XACT_ABORT ON
GO

-- Populate the new table with information
-- from the same table in the SQLBE instance

INSERT SQLBEInst2.Northwind.dbo.SalesInfoEast
SELECT *
FROM SalesInfoEast

INSERT SQLBEInst2.Northwind.dbo.SalesInfoWest
SELECT *
FROM SalesInfoWest
GO

-- Create a View that gets the entire
-- SalesInfo informations
-- Note the use of UNION ALL

CREATE VIEW DistSalesInfo
AS
SELECT *
```

Listing 15.24: continued

```
FROM Northwind.dbo.SalesInfoNorth
UNION ALL
SELECT *
FROM Northwind.dbo.SalesInfoSouth
UNION ALL
SELECT *
FROM SQLBEInst2.Northwind.dbo.SalesInfoEast
UNION ALL
SELECT *
FROM SQLBEInst2.Northwind.dbo.SalesInfoWest
GO

SELECT COUNT(*) AS NorthBefore
FROM SalesInfoNorth

SELECT COUNT(*) AS EastBefore
FROM SQLBEInst2.Northwind.dbo.SalesInfoEast

UPDATE DistSalesInfo
SET RegionID = 1
WHERE OrderID = 10602

SELECT COUNT(*) AS NorthAfter
FROM SalesInfoNorth

SELECT COUNT(*) AS EastAfter
FROM SQLBEInst2.Northwind.dbo.SalesInfoEast
GO
```

OUTPUT

```
NorthBefore
-----------
147


EastBefore
-----------
417


NorthAfter
-----------
146


EastAfter
-----------
418
```

What's Next?

In this chapter, you learned how to work with data from different instances, different servers, or even different environments.

To execute the exercises in this chapter, review Appendix A, "Using SQL Server Instances," where you can learn how to set up multiple SQL Server 2000 instances in the same server.

In this book, we tried to show you how to use SQL Server 2000 from a database developer's point of view. Now you can try to apply these techniques to your own database environment.

You can obtain support and updated code from this book on

```
http://www.sqlserverbyexample.com
```

You can find extra SQL Server support in the Microsoft SQL Server public newsgroups, where Microsoft SQL Server engineers, SQL Server Most Valuable Professionals (MVP), and many SQL Server professionals try every day to learn a bit more about SQL Server and share their knowledge with their colleagues:

```
news://msnews.microsoft.com/microsoft.public.sqlserver.ce
news://msnews.microsoft.com/microsoft.public.sqlserver.clients
news://msnews.microsoft.com/microsoft.public.sqlserver.clustering
news://msnews.microsoft.com/microsoft.public.sqlserver.connect
news://msnews.microsoft.com/microsoft.public.sqlserver.datamining
news://msnews.microsoft.com/microsoft.public.sqlserver.datawarehouse
news://msnews.microsoft.com/microsoft.public.sqlserver.dts
news://msnews.microsoft.com/microsoft.public.sqlserver.fulltext
news://msnews.microsoft.com/microsoft.public.sqlserver.mseq
news://msnews.microsoft.com/microsoft.public.sqlserver.odbc
news://msnews.microsoft.com/microsoft.public.sqlserver.olap
news://msnews.microsoft.com/microsoft.public.sqlserver.programming
news://msnews.microsoft.com/microsoft.public.sqlserver.replication
news://msnews.microsoft.com/microsoft.public.sqlserver.security
news://msnews.microsoft.com/microsoft.public.sqlserver.server
news://msnews.microsoft.com/microsoft.public.sqlserver.setup
news://msnews.microsoft.com/microsoft.public.sqlserver.tools
news://msnews.microsoft.com/microsoft.public.sqlserver.xml
news://msnews.microsoft.com/microsoft.public.ae.arabic.sqlserver
news://msnews.microsoft.com/microsoft.public.de.sqlserver
news://msnews.microsoft.com/microsoft.public.es.sqlserver
news://msnews.microsoft.com/microsoft.public.espanol.sqlserver.administracion
news://msnews.microsoft.com/microsoft.public.espanol.sqlserver.olap
news://msnews.microsoft.com/microsoft.public.fr.sqlserver
news://msnews.microsoft.com/microsoft.public.il.hebrew.sqlserver
news://msnews.microsoft.com/microsoft.public.jp.sqlserver.server
```

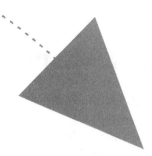

Using SQL Server Instances

In previous versions of SQL Server, it was possible to install more than one instance of the SQL Server engine in the same machine using some Registry tricks. Although this method did the trick, it was very tedious and, more importantly, it was not supported by Microsoft. One of the new features Microsoft introduced in SQL Server 2000 is the capability to run more than one copy or instance of SQL Server in the same computer. This new feature is called *multi-instance support* and basically allows you to maintain multiple installations of SQL Server running independently in just one server.

In some cases, it might be beneficial to maintain separate installations of SQL Server in one computer for various reasons. For example, suppose two different customers of an application-hosting company need administrative access to SQL Server, and the hosting company doesn't want each SQL administrator to interfere with the activities of the other customer's administrator. To deal with this issue, the hosting company can manage two different installations of SQL Server, one for each customer, keeping each one of them from interfering with the other's installation. Previously, the way to overcome this limitation was to use one server for each installation. However, using multi-instance support in SQL Server 2000, all installations can run simultaneously and independently in just one server. In general, multi-instance is a cost-effective solution, because you need to buy and manage just one server, instead of maintaining as many servers as installations you have to support.

This appendix teaches you the following:

- How to install a new SQL Server instance
- How to connect to different instances of SQL Server in the same machine
- System functions used in multi-instance installations
- Current limitations of SQL Server instances

Installing SQL Server Instances

A SQL Server instance is a completely independent installation of the SQL Server engine and its related services, such as SQL Agent. There are two types of SQL Server instances: default and named. A default instance is identified by the name of the server where it runs, whereas named instances are identified by the server name and the instance name (*servername\ instancename*). There can be just one default instance running in a server, and it works exactly as previous versions of SQL Server. Regarding named instances, you can install as many named instances as you want in a specific server, even if there isn't a default instance installed. However, Microsoft supports only a maximum of 16 named instances per machine.

A named instance can only be SQL Server 2000, whereas the default instance can be either SQL Server 6.5, 7.0, or 2000. Furthermore, the default instance can use version switching between SQL Server 6.5 and 7.0, or between SQL Server 6.5 and 2000. Version switching enables you to keep two versions installed as default, but only one of them is active at a time. Therefore, you can maintain three versions of SQL Server (6.5, 7.0, and 2000) in the same machine, using the following configuration:

- Version switching between 6.5 and 7.0 as a default instance

- One or more named instances of SQL Server 2000

This type of environment is great for developers who must develop and test applications in multiple versions of SQL Server.

Using named instances, different versions of SQL Server 2000 can be installed on the same machine. In particular, you might have an instance running the standard edition of SQL Server, and another one running the Enterprise Edition in the same machine. Regarding licensing, an additional license must be purchased for each new instance installed in a server. As you can see, multi-instance can be useful for testing purposes, because you can test the features of the Standard Edition and the Enterprise Edition using just one server, instead of two. Moreover, because every instance runs independently, you can have the same version of SQL Server 2000 in different instances with different service packs.

CAUTION

Be aware that all instances in one server share the system memory of the server. This is the reason it is usually not recommended to install multiple instances in production systems.

In regard to related services, each SQL Server instance has its own instance of SQL Server Agent. Nevertheless, the Microsoft Distributed Transaction Coordinator (MSDTC) service and the Full text search service have only one instance, which is shared among all SQL Server instances. Similarly, client tools, such as Enterprise Manager, Query Analyzer, Profiler, Server Network Utility, Client Network Utility, isql, and osq, are shared among instances.

In this appendix, you will install a new named instance of SQL Server 2000 Enterprise Edition in a server called SQLBYEXAMPLE. Be aware that Internet Explorer 5.0 is a prerequisite of the installation of SQL Server 2000, because the MMC (SQL Server snap-in) and the Books online are HTML based. Maybe you already have this prerequisite if there's already a default instance or another named instance of SQL Server 2000 in the machine where the new named instance will be installed.

Also, make sure that any service related to SQL Server is stopped before proceeding with the installation process of the new SQL Server named instance. For example, if you have a Web server or a transaction server connecting to SQL Server, stop these services first, and proceed to install the new instance.

To begin the installation process, insert the SQL Server Enterprise Edition CD and this will automatically begin the installation process.

The first step is to choose whether it will be a local or a remote install. If you choose the remote install option, SQL Server creates an unattended installation file called setup.iss, copies the installation files to the remote server, and then performs the actual installation. In our case, you have to choose Local Computer because you will be performing a local installation, as shown in Figure A.1.

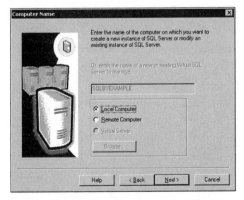

Figure A.1: *Performing a local or remote installation.*

In the next window, you must choose the type of task to perform in the installation. By choosing the first choice (the one you will choose), a new instance of SQL Server is installed. The second choice allows you to modify an existing installation of SQL Server, and the last option is used to manage cluster installations, rebuild the Registry, or create an unattended installation file (an `.iss` file). Figure A.2 shows this window.

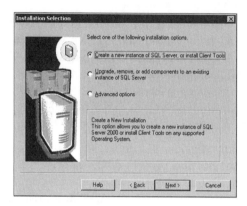

Figure A.2: *Choosing the action to take in the installation process.*

Next, you are required to enter your name and company name, and then you have to accept the license agreement. In the next window, you must choose the components that you want to install. In this case, Server and Client Tools is selected because you want to install the SQL Server engine and also the client tools. Using the third option, you can install just the Microsoft Data Access Components (MDAC 2.6).

This window is shown in Figure A.3. Be aware that if you select the first or the second option, the installation process overwrites any client tools that you have previously installed on the server, because there can be only one copy of the client tools in a server, regardless of the number of instances running.

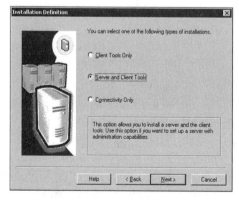

Figure A.3: *Choosing the components to be installed.*

In the next window, you must specify the type of instance to install, either default or named. If there's already a default instance installed on the server, the first choice (install a default instance) is grayed out because there can be only one default instance, and you will only be allowed to enter an instance name, as Figure A.4 shows. The name of the instance you'll be installing is APPENDIXA.

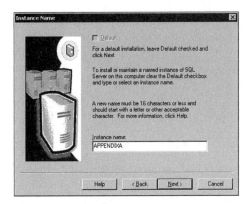

Figure A.4: *Choosing the type of instance to install.*

Then, choose the type of installation of SQL Server you are performing (Typical, Minimum, or Custom), and also the path where files will be installed. Specifically, the elements of the SQL Server installation are the SQL Server engine, replication tools, full-text search, client tools, client connectivity, Books Online, upgrade tools, development tools, and code samples. The typical installation includes all elements except the code samples, and the minimum installation includes only the engine, replication, full-text search, and client connectivity. These options appear in Figure A.5.

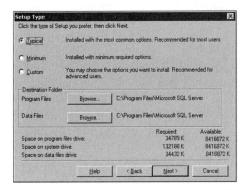

Figure A.5: *Type of installation and path of files.*

If you chose Custom installation, you will see the screen shown in Figure A.6, in which you must choose the elements to install. Otherwise, if you choose either Typical or Minimum, the installation process takes you directly to the screen shown in Figure A.7.

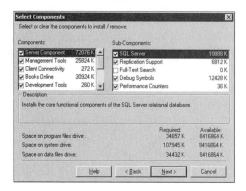

Figure A.6: *Choosing each individual component to install.*

In the next window, you configure the accounts that will be used by the SQL Server service and the SQL Agent service of the new instance, as shown in Figure A.7. Also, these services can be set to start automatically when Windows starts up. You can configure both services to use the same account or to use different ones.

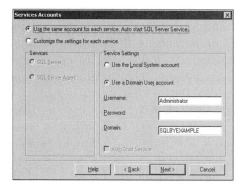

Figure A.7: *Configuring the service accounts.*

The account(s) used by SQL Server and SQL Agent can be either localsystem, which is an account with administrative privileges on the local server (similar to a local administrator), or a domain account. If SQL Server won't be performing any activity that involves any other server in the domain, localsystem may be the solution. However, if SQL Server performs activities that involve other servers—for example, taking backups and storing them in another server—SQL Server must use a domain account that has appropriate permissions on the server where the backup files will be stored.

In the next window, Figure A.8, the authentication mode used by SQL Server is set up. Windows authentication mode is the recommended one and the default one in the installation process (the installation is secure out of the box). Using this type of authentication, SQL Server doesn't store passwords; it just stores the SID, which is an identifier of Windows login, and users don't have to specify a password when connecting to SQL Server (because they were already validated by Windows). Therefore, any user who has a Windows NT 4.0 or Windows 2000 account can benefit from using the Windows authentication mode or trusted connections.

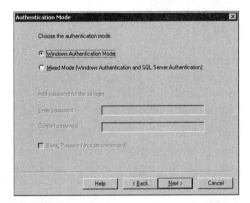

Figure A.8: *Configuring the Authentication mode.*

Mixed mode allows users to connect to SQL Server using a SQL Server login and password. This mode is useful when you have non-Windows clients connecting to SQL Server. If you choose SQL Server and Windows authentication (mixed mode), you have the choice to leave the sa password blank, which is not recommended because this leaves the system unprotected (any user can log in as sa with a blank password). In this case, it's highly recommended that you change the sa password immediately after the installation process.

You must choose the default collation (sort order plus character set) used by this installation of SQL Server. The collation defines the way data is stored and compared in SQL Server. In some cases, it might be beneficial to change the default collation if you want to store data in a different language.

In SQL Server 2000, you can have different collations in the same instance, even at column level; thus, a single table can have different collations. This window is shown in Figure A.9.

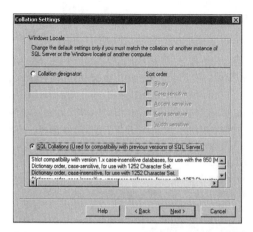

Figure A.9: *Choosing the default collation.*

In the next window, the network libraries used by this instance of SQL Server are configured. The only ones you can choose when installing a named instance are named pipes, TCP/IP, and NWLink because you cannot connect to a SQL Server named instance using any of the other network libraries.

Basically, a network library enables different clients to communicate with SQL Server. To be able to communicate with SQL Server, clients must connect to the server using a network library used by the server. Also, SQL Server might be using more than one network library simultaneously. For example, if the enabled network libraries in SQL Server are named pipes and TCP/IP, some clients can connect using named pipes, and others can connect using TCP/IP.

If you leave the port number as the default (0) in the TCP/IP network library, the TCP port used by the SQL Server instance is automatically chosen by SQL Server every time it is started, unless you specify a port different from zero at installation time. To check the current TCP port used by a SQL Server instance, use the Server Network utility, and check the properties of the TCP/IP network library.

After the installation process, network libraries can be reconfigured using the Server Network Utility. Figure A.10 shows the window used to configure network libraries.

Afterward, a window states that to complete the setup process it only needs the licensing information, which is configured in the next window of the installation process.

Two licensing modes are available: *per seat* and *per processor*. Use per seat mode when you know beforehand how many clients will be connecting to

SQL Server. In this mode, you need a server license for each server or instance, and a client access license (CAL) for each device that will be connecting to SQL Server.

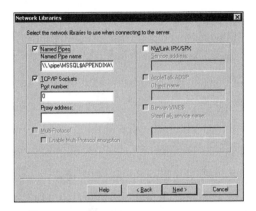

Figure A.10: *Configuring the server network libraries.*

Use per processor mode if you want to allow unlimited connections to SQL Server, directly or indirectly. For example, if you run a Web site, you can use per processor licensing to allow unlimited connections to SQL Server from the Web server (indirect connections). In this mode, a license for each processor of the server is required. For example, if SQL Server has two processors, you need two per processor licenses (even if SQL Server is configured to use just one processor).

The licensing window is shown in Figure A.11.

CAUTION
The Internet connector license was used in previous versions of SQL Server to allow unlimited connections to SQL Server. This type of license was discontinued in SQL Server 2000. Now, use the per processor license instead.

After the installation process gathers all necessary information, it begins the actual installation of the components in the following order:

1. Microsoft Data Access Components (MDAC)

2. Distributed Transaction Coordinator (MSDTC)

3. SQL Server engine

4. Run configuration scripts

5. Register ActiveX components

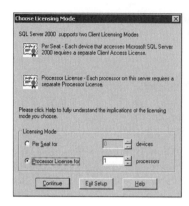

Figure A.11: *Choosing the licensing mode.*

Each SQL Server instance has its own directory with its data files. However, the common tools (client tools) for all instances are stored in a directory called 80 that is located inside the Microsoft SQL Server folder.

Every SQL Server named instance has its own SQL Server and SQL Agent services. The names of these services are mssql$instancename (SQL Server service) and sqlagent$instancename (SQL Agent). These services are listed in the Services window (located in the Control Panel in Windows NT 4.0, or in the Administrative tools folder in Windows 2000), which is shown in Figure A.12.

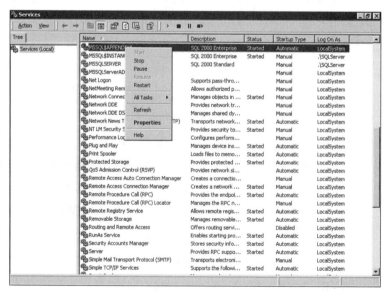

Figure A.12: *The Services window.*

These services can be started, stopped, and paused from the Services window, the command prompt, Enterprise Manager, or the SQL Server Service Manager. In particular, to start, stop, or pause the SQL Server service of an instance from the command prompt, use the following commands, respectively:

```
net start mssql$instancename
net stop mssql$instancename
net pause mssql$instancename
```

To uninstall a SQL Server named instance, use one of these two approaches:

- Use the Add/Remove Programs window located in the Control Panel. In this window, shown in Figure A.13, you can see a list of all instances installed in the local server and the option to change or completely remove the instance from the server.

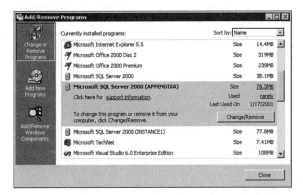

Figure A.13: *Uninstalling a SQL Server instance.*

- Rerun the SQL Server installation program and choose the Remove Components option.

Connecting to Instances

After an instance is completely installed, you can verify that the installation was successful connecting to this new instance. In particular, to connect to a named instance, use the following syntax: *servername\instancename*. Notice that when there are many instances in one server, from the client's point of view, each instance works as a completely different server.

There are many ways to test the connection to SQL Server. For example, you can use osql, which is a command-line utility that connects to SQL Server using ODBC. Figure A.14 shows how this command is used from the DOS prompt.

```
C:\WINNT\System32\cmd.exe - osql -S SQLBYEXAMPLE\APPENDIXA -E        _ □ ×

C:\>osql -S SQLBYEXAMPLE\APPENDIXA -E
1> SELECT @@SERVERNAME
2> GO



SQLBYEXAMPLE\APPENDIXA


(1 row affected)
1> _
```

Figure A.14: *Using* osql *to test connectivity to SQL Server.*

Clients that connect to a named instance of SQL Server 2000 must have installed at least the Microsoft Data Access Components (MDAC) 2.6, which are the ones installed by SQL Server 2000. Therefore, if you install SQL Server 2000's client utilities in a client machine, you will be able to connect to named instances. However, you can install MDAC 2.6 separately in a client machine without installing the client tools of SQL Server 2000. MDAC 2.6 can be downloaded directly from Microsoft's Web site (http://www.microsoft.com/data).

Another way to connect to a named instance of SQL Server 2000 is by creating an alias in the client machine using the Client Network utility, which is one of the SQL Server client tools. When creating the alias, you must specify the name of the alias (this is the one you will use to connect to the named instance), the network library, and the name of the instance—for example, SQLBYEXAMPLE\APPENDIXA. Figure A.15 shows the creation of an alias called TESTINSTANCE using the Client Network utility.

Figure A.15: *Using the Client Network utility to create aliases.*

After the alias is created, you can connect to the named instance using the alias name (TESTINSTANCE), instead of *servername\instancename*. Figure A.16 shows how to connect to a named instance using an alias in the Query Analyzer.

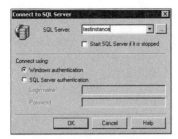

Figure A.16: *Connecting to a SQL Server instance using an alias.*

If you create an alias using the TCP/IP network library, it is recommended you set the Dynamically Determine Port option, because a SQL Server named instance, by default, chooses an available TCP port every time it is started. Therefore, you don't know the TCP port used by the named instance to accept incoming connections beforehand, unless you specify a port for the named instance in the Server Network utility. Figure A.17 shows how to configure a SQL Server 2000 named instance to use a specific TCP port (8888 in this case).

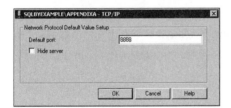

Figure A.17: *Specifying the TCP port used by an instance to accept incoming connections.*

CAUTION

If you change the TCP port used by a named instance, the SQL Server service of this instance must be restarted for this change to take effect.

Then, you can create an alias to connect to the named instance using the port specified in the Server Network utility. This is shown in Figure A.18.

Usually, applications connect to SQL Server using either ODBC or OLE DB. Specifically, in OLE DB connection strings, the name of the server is specified using the following syntax: Data Source=*computername**instancename*. The network library can also be specified in the connection string. For example, Listing A.1 shows a connection string that connects to the Northwind database located in SQLBYEXAMPLE\APPENDIXA, using integrated security (Integrated Security=SSPI) and the TCP/IP network library (Network Library=dbmssocn).

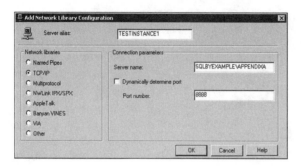

Figure A.18: *Specifying the TCP port when creating an alias.*

Listing A.1: An OLE DB Connection String Used to Connect to a Named Instance

```
"Provider=SQLOLEDB.1;Data Source=dev08\instance2;Integrated Security=SSPI;
Initial Catalog=Northwind;Network Library=dbmssocn"
```

EXAMPLE

You can issue distributed queries to a named instance through a linked server. Specifically, when querying tables in the linked server use the following syntax:

[*servername\instancename*].database.username.objectname

Listing A.2 shows how a linked server is configured when connecting to a named instance, and then it issues a query against the linked server.

Listing A.2: Creating a Linked Server Using Instances

```
sp_addlinkedserver @server = 'dev08\instance1'
GO

SET ANSI_NULLS ON
SET ANSI_WARNINGS ON
GO

SELECT * FROM [dev08\instance1].Northwind.dbo.Shippers
GO
```

```
(1 row(s) affected)
```

OUTPUT

```
(1 row(s) affected)

ShipperID   CompanyName                               Phone
----------  ----------------------------------------  -----------------------
1           Speedy Express                            (503) 555-9831
2           United Package                            (503) 555-3199
3           Federal Shipping                          (503) 555-9931

(3 row(s) affected)
```

System Functions Used in Multi-Instance Installations

Two system functions return information related to instances:

- SERVERPROPERTY—This function takes one parameter and returns information about the server where the instance is installed. If the parameter is *machinename*, this function returns the name of the server. If the parameter used is *servername*, it returns the name of the server, along with the name of the instance. If *instancename* is used as the parameter, the function returns the name of the current instance, and if it's the default instance, it returns NULL. Listing A.3 shows how to use this function with the parameters described.

Listing A.3: Using the SERVERPROPERTY Function

EXAMPLE

```
USE Master

SELECT SERVERPROPERTY('machinename')
SELECT SERVERPROPERTY('servername')
SELECT SERVERPROPERTY('instancename')
GO
```

OUTPUT

```
- - - - - - - - - - - - - - - - - - - - - -
SQLBYEXAMPLE

(1 row(s) affected)


- - - - - - - - - - - - - - - - - - - - - -
SQLBYEXAMPLE\APPENDIXA

(1 row(s) affected)


- - - - - - - - - - - - - - - - - - - - - -
APPENDIXA

(1 row(s) affected)
```

- @@SERVERNAME—This function returns the name of the server and current instance of SQL Server. This is equivalent to SERVERPROPERTY using the servername parameter. @@SERVERNAME is shown in Listing A.4.

Listing A.4: Using the @@SERVERNAME Function

EXAMPLE

```
USE Master

SELECT @@SERVERNAME
GO
```

Listing A.4: continued

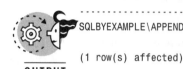

```
SQLBYEXAMPLE\APPENDIXA

(1 row(s) affected)
```

OUTPUT

Current Limitations

As any other new feature, SQL Server's multi-instances has a lot of great and useful characteristics, but also has some limitations.

- First of all, not all network libraries work with instances. Specifically, only named pipes, TCP/IP, and NWLink can be configured in a server with multiple instance installations. The remaining ones that don't work with SQL Server instances are Multiprotocol, AppleTalk, and Banyan VINES, which Microsoft didn't enhance in SQL Server 2000. This is the reason they cannot be used to communicate with named instances.

- In a server with multiple instances, there's only one version of the client tools. For example, if there's a default instance running SQL Server 7.0, and then a SQL Server 2000 named instance is installed, the client tools of SQL Server 2000 overwrite SQL Server 7.0's tools. Therefore, you cannot have different versions of the client utilities installed in one machine. The only exception is Books Online, which is kept in the system even if a newer version of the client tools is installed. For example, you can browse the Books Online of SQL Server 7.0 and 2000 in the same computer.

- A limitation of the installation process is that the client tools are always installed in the system drive (usually C). Sometimes, this can be a serious problem if no space is available in the system drive.

Finally, any suggestion that you might have regarding instances or any other aspect of SQL Server can be sent by email to sqlwish@microsoft.com. The SQL Server development team constantly monitors this email address; therefore, there's a good chance that your comment will reach the right person, and eventually, it might become a feature of an upcoming version of SQL Server.

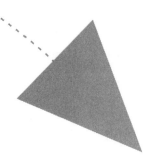

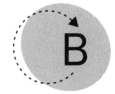

Using SQL Query Analyzer

As a relational database management system, SQL Server stores data, enforces security, maintains data integrity, and executes user queries to retrieve any requested data.

In a client/server environment, the client application sends queries to SQL Server to be executed at the server side and is the client application that manages the query results and presents them to the user. SQL Server provides a client application to execute queries and retrieve results; this application is SQL Query Analyzer.

Although SQL Query Analyzer does not pretend to substitute the role of a standard application, you cannot expect users to work with SQL Query Analyzer as their standard front end for database applications. However, SQL Query Analyzer is very useful for specific activities such as the following:

- Creating and testing the database objects during the development process
- Tuning and optimizing the database while in production
- Executing common administrative tasks

In this book, you use SQL Query Analyzer version 8.00.194, as included in the original release (RTM) of Microsoft SQL Server 2000.

This appendix teaches you how to

- Connect to SQL Server
- Set user options
- Write and execute queries
- Search for database objects
- Use the Object Browser to navigate your database structure
- Analyze queries
- Use the Transact-SQL Debugger

Installing SQL Query Analyzer

You install SQL Query Analyzer as part of the SQL Server 2000 installation process. The Typical and Minimum setups both install SQL Query Analyzer by default, but the Custom setup gives you the option of installing this tool, as you can see in Figure B.1.

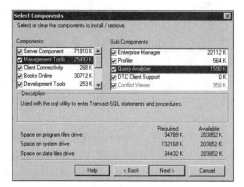

Figure B.1: *Using the Custom setup, you can select which SQL Server components to install.*

It is possible to install SQL Query Analyzer on a client computer even if the server components are not installed on the same computer. This allows for remote access to SQL Server.

A special case is the remote access to a computer through the Internet. In this case, the simplest way is to create a server alias using the Client Network utility, specifying the IP address as server name and a server alias name to be used when connecting by SQL Query Analyzer and other client tools. Figure B.2 shows a typical example of this alias creation form.

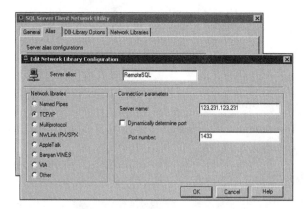

Figure B.2: *Using the Client Network utility to define a server alias simplifies the access to remote servers.*

The Query Analyzer Workplace

When you run SQL Query Analyzer, you will get a connection form, as you can see in Figure B.3, where you can select which server or server instance to connect to, and which authentication mode to use. If you selected SQL Server Authentication mode, you must provide a valid login and password to connect.

Figure B.3: *In the Logon screen, you can select the server you want to connect to and which authentication mode to use.*

CAUTION

If you try to connect to SQL Server using the SQL Server authentication mode and you fail to supply a valid login name, SQL Query Analyzer will not try to connect using your Windows NT 4.0 or Windows 2000 credentials, as it did in previous versions, so the connection will be rejected. It is recommended to use integrated security if possible.

Initially, the Server drop-down list will not contain any entries. The server name will be added to the list only after successful connection to a server.

TIP

SQL Query Analyzer will try to connect to the local default instance if you leave the server name blank or write a dot '.' or '(local)' as the server name.

CAUTION

If you installed SQL Server 2000 with SQL Server 7.0 or 6.5 on the same computer, the default instance will be either SQL Server 7.0 or SQL Server 6.5, which means that many of the examples in this book will not work because of the different functionality between SQL Server 2000 and earlier versions. So, make sure you connect to the right instance of SQL Server 2000 before trying any of the examples.

When connected, SQL Query Analyzer will show a workplace as shown in Figure B.4.

As in other Windows applications, you can see some common elements such as the menu bar, the toolbar, and the status bar.

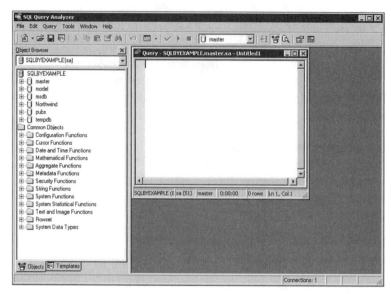

Figure B.4: *The SQL Query Analyzer workplace is similar to all Windows applications in look and feel.*

SQL Query Analyzer is a *Multi Document Interface (MDI)* application where every connection to SQL Server uses its own child window, inside the parent window. You can select the connection window by using the application window menu as usual, and you can arrange the windows in the common ways: Cascade, Tile Horizontally, and Tile Vertically.

TIP

If you have established more than one connection to SQL Server from SQL Query Analyzer, it is usually better to maximize the connection window to have extra visible space to work with the Editor and Results panes. As soon as you maximize one of the connection windows, all the other connection windows will be maximized as well.

The Editor Pane

The Editor pane of a connection window is a text editor you can use to edit your queries and SQL statements. These statements can come from different sources as follows:

- Scripts written directly in the Editor pane
- Saved SQL script files you can retrieve in the Editor pane for further editing
- Scripts produced from the Object Browser and Object Search, as you will see later

- Predesigned templates you can reuse to speed up and facilitate the process of writing code

This is a code-oriented text editor with many features to help you write SQL language code. You can find information about these features in Books Online, but it is interesting to pay attention to the following points:

- The text is color coded to differentiate between keywords, system objects and system stored procedures, operators, comments, and so on.

- You can use shortcuts to speed the editing process. You can find the full shortcut list in the topic "SQL Query Analyzer Keyboard Shortcuts" in Books Online, but the more frequently used are in Table B.1.

- It is possible to select the font, tab length, and other options, as you can see in Figures B.13 and B.15 later in this appendix.

- You can select which part of the code to execute by selecting the block either with the mouse or with the keyboard combining the Shift key with the navigation keys.

Table B.1: SQL Query Analyzer's More Useful Shortcuts

Shortcut	Action
F5, Ctrl+E, or Alt+X	Executes the selected query
Ctrl+F5	Checks the syntax of the selected query
Alt+Break	Cancels the execution of the query that is being executed
Shift+F1	Searches in Books Online for the selected word, SQL statement, keyword, or SQL Server object in Books Online
Ctrl+Shift+Del	Clears the current Editor pane window to provide an empty window to start editing again (see the tip following this table)
Ctrl+C or Ctrl+Insert	Copies the marked block to the Clipboard
Ctrl+X or Shift+Del	Cuts the marked block and send it to the Clipboard
Ctrl+V or Shift+Insert	Pastes the contents of the Clipboard
Ctrl+Shift+C	Marks the current block of text as comments (adds -- at the beginning of every line)
Ctrl+Shift+R	Uncomment the current block of text (removes the -- from the beginning of every line)
Ctrl+Shift+L	Converts the selected text to lowercase
Ctrl+Shift+U	Converts the selected text to uppercase; this is useful to highlight keywords in the code
Ctrl+Z	Undoes the latest editing action

The Object Browser

Writing queries requires precise knowledge of database objects definition and complete syntax of statements, functions, and stored procedures. Developers can use the SQL Query Analyzer Object Browser to get information about database objects. Moreover, Object Browser is a dynamic tool with embedded scripting capabilities that can greatly improve your coding productivity.

As you can see in Figure B.5, Object Browser has two main sections: the server structure, with information about databases and database object of the server that the user is connected to, and the common objects, with information about system functions and data types.

Figure B.5: *In the Object Browser structure, you can see two main sections: server and common objects.*

As you can see in Figure B.6, you can right-click any object to see a context menu from where you can create a script of that object either to the

Clipboard, a new window, or a file. Depending on the object type, it is possible to script different statements. In the example shown in Figure B.6, a user table, the available statements are CREATE, DROP, SELECT, INSERT, UPDATE, and DELETE. For stored procedures, you can choose to script the CREATE, ALTER, DROP, and EXECUTE statements.

TIP

During the coding process, scripting to the Clipboard is usually more flexible than scripting to a new window because after it is in the Clipboard, you can paste the script anywhere in your code, even several times.

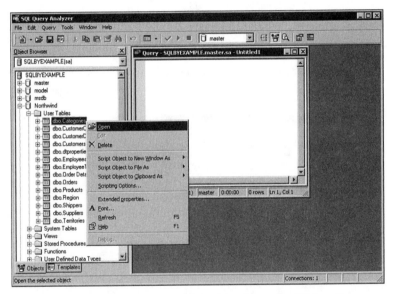

Figure B.6: *Right-click any object to show the Object Browser context menu.*

In Figure B.7, you can see how the Object Browser shows object dependencies, as well as definitions of columns and parameters. The Object Browser enables the user to drag and drop any object's name to the Editor Pane, reducing the likelihood of misspelling an object name.

CAUTION

Always check dependencies before altering or dropping any object. Failing to do so could produce errors when other objects must reference the modified or missing object.

An interesting feature in SQL Server 2000 is the possibility of defining extended properties for databases and database objects. From the Object Browser it is possible to edit them using the context menu, as you can see in Figure B.8.

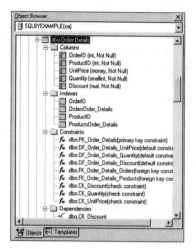

Figure B.7: *Object Browser shows complete information about tables such as Columns, Indexes, Constraints, Dependencies, and Triggers.*

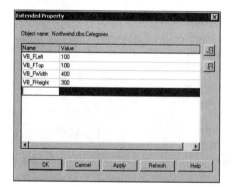

Figure B.8: *Extended properties for a table, identifying the default form position and size for a fictitious Visual Basic client application.*

The Object Search

Working with several databases, and hundreds or thousands of objects, makes it difficult to find specific objects in Object Browser. Using the Object Search you can efficiently search for any object on any database.

Figure B.9 shows the Object Search window. You can use wildcards in the Object name field, as seen in Figure B.9. Searching for ___help* means any three characters followed by the word help followed by any string. Other combinations, such as *sys* sys* or authors, are valid as well.

You can search for objects with specific extended properties values.

TIP

Object Search is especially useful when you want to know which table contains the information you need to select in your query. In this case, provide an approximate column name, using wildcards, and specify Column as object type.

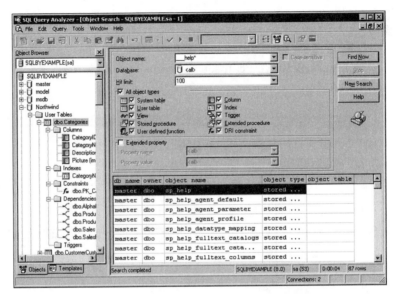

Figure B.9: *Searching for an object is very efficient using the Object Search window.*

The Results Pane

The lower section of every connection's window, below the Editor pane, is the Results pane, in which SQL Query Analyzer shows the results of the queries and any output message from SQL Server.

SQL Query Analyzer can show results in Text or Grid, in a spreadsheetlike format. It is possible to send results directly to a file, in which case the Results pane shows only SQL Server messages and confirmation of the file write operation as shown in Listing B.1.

To send results to a file, select the menu Query—Results to File. With this setting, whenever you execute a query, SQL Query Analyzer will prompt you to provide a filename, and the results will be sent to the selected file. To test how SQL Query Analyzer sends results to a file, make sure the menu Query—Results to File is checked and execute the example of Listing B.1.

EXAMPLE

Listing B.1: The Results of a Query Can Be Sent to a File

```
USE Northwind
GO

SELECT *
FROM Products
```

OUTPUT

```
(77 row(s) affected)
The following file has been saved successfully:
C:\WINNT\Profiles\Administrator\My Documents\fn.rpt 14242 bytes
```

In Figure B.10, you can see the same results in text, and in Figure B.11 in grid.

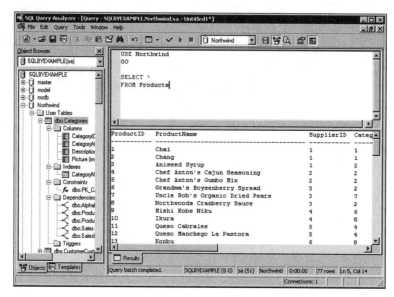

Figure B.10: *You can show query results in text mode.*

NOTE

Results in grid are read-only. If you want to edit table values directly in a grid from SQL Query Analyzer, go to Object Browser, right-click in the object, and select Open. This way, SQL Query Analyzer will open a new window with a fully editable grid.

CAUTION

Executing more than a single query in the same batch when Grid mode is selected produces several grids in the Result pane. This can be a bit confusing because of the number of different slide bars in the Result pane. The main slider belongs to the Result pane, and every individual grid has its own slider, too.

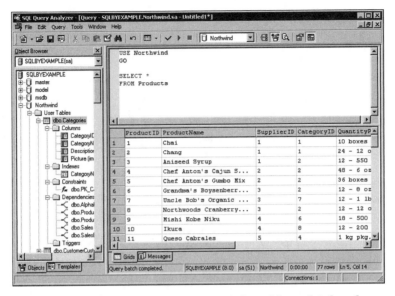

Figure B.11: *Dealing with query results with multiple columns is easier in grid mode.*

Managing User and Connection Options

SQL Query Analyzer is a flexible environment that can be customized to specific user needs, as you can do in Microsoft Office applications. Some of these settings affect the way SQL Query Analyzer looks, the way it shows information. and how it interacts with the user, whereas other settings affect the way it connects to SQL Server.

Customizing SQL Query Analyzer

You can change SQL Query Analyzer settings using two different menus under the Tools menu title: Options and Customize. In Figure B.12, you can see how to change some general settings about SQL Query Analyzer.

TIP

Check the Select SQL Query Analyzer as the Default Editor for Query File Extensions option, because it can help you open files using Windows Explorer or any standard folder window.

CAUTION

You are not forced to use the recommended extensions. However, if every computer uses different extensions for scripts, results, or templates, sharing files will be more complex, and association of filename extensions to Query Analyzer can be a more complex task.

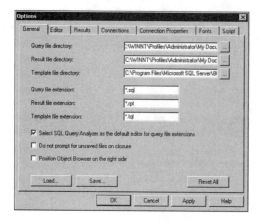

Figure B.12: You can select SQL Query Analyzer as the default editor for scripts file with the general options.

In Figure B.13, SQL Query Analyzer enables you to change some settings that influence how it displays the Editor pane.

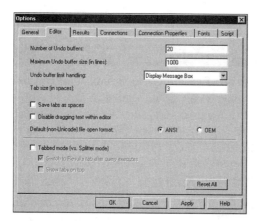

Figure B.13: You can change tab size and tabbed mode using the Editor Options.

Adjust the tab size to a value big enough to facilitate the programming logic readability, but not too high or you will be forced to use the horizontal sliders to read the code, and it will not print properly. Normal values for tab size are 3, 4, or 5, but feel free to select your own value if it suits you better.

The lower part of the form offers you the choice of showing the connection window as a tabbed window, with the Edit and Results panes under different tabs.

In Figure B.14, you can see how to change the way SQL Query Analyzer produces results. You can change the default results target in a way similar to the toolbar.

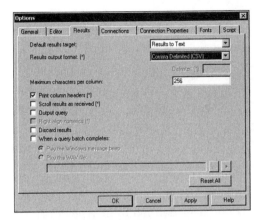

Figure B.14: *It is possible to control the results output.*

TIP

If you intend to export the results to a spreadsheet application, you should consider setting the Results Output Format option to Comma Delimited (CSV).

CAUTION

The Maximum Characters per Column setting is useful to limit the output in the Results pane, but if you selected results in a file, be aware that columns results will be truncated to the maximum characters per column value you selected.

SQL Query Analyzer uses different font settings to help the developers identify statements, operators, system objects, and other specific system-supplied keywords during the code-writing process. You can change these settings as shown in Figure B.15. For every category, you can select which font SQL Query Analyzer will use for text, but for the Editor category, you can specifically select which font to use to highlight every keyword type.

It is possible to set how SQL Query Analyzer produces scripts using the Script tab in the Options form.

It is useful to select the Prefix the Script with a Check for Existence option because this will avoid unnecessary error messages when running the script, if the objects to be created already exist in the destination database.

Select Script Object-Level Permissions to guarantee the destination objects will have the same access level as the original ones.

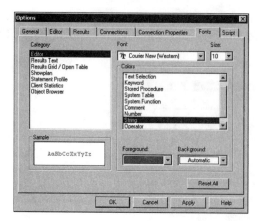

Figure B.15: *Selecting the right fonts for every part of the code makes it more readable.*

Unless you have the same user-defined data types in the destination database, you should select the Convert Specification of User-Defined Data Types to the Appropriate SQL Server Base Data Type option so that only native data types will be scripted. If the destination server is SQL Server 7.0 or 6.5, check that the data types are supported in the target version.

In Figure B.16, you can see some of the scripting options that SQL Query Analyzer offers you.

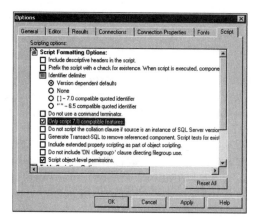

Figure B.16: *SQL Query Analyzer offers many options to create scripts according to the programmer's needs.*

CAUTION

If you had to use the script to re-create objects on any previous version, including SQL Server 7.0, make sure you check the script completely to test that it includes only available features in the target version. Selecting the Only Script 7.0 Compatible Features option does not always produce the expected results.

It is possible to create user-defined shortcuts to speed up writing some repetitive sentences. SQL Query Analyzer provides the following predefined shortcuts:

Shortcut	Action
Alt+F1	sp_help
Ctrl+1	sp_who
Ctrl+2	sp_lock

The previous shortcuts are fixed and cannot be changed, but programmers can define actions for shortcuts Ctrl+F1, Ctrl+0, and Ctrl+3 to Ctrl+9.

When you use these shortcuts, nothing is written to the Editor pane, the sentence is sent to SQL Server, and the Results pane shows the results of the statement.

Figure B.17 shows the Customize form, where you can define new shortcuts or modify or remove existing ones.

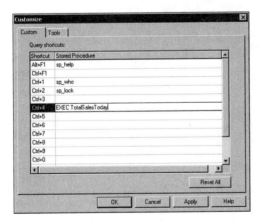

Figure B.17: *It is possible to create shortcuts using the Customize menu.*

Connection Settings

Every connection to SQL Server uses different settings, which affect the way SQL Server produces results and, in some cases, the way SQL Server performs some operations.

SQL Query Analyzer offers three ways to change connection settings:

- Use the Tools, Options menu to change the default connection settings for new connections.

- Use the Query, Current Connection Properties menu, or the correspondent icon in the toolbar, to modify specific settings for the current connection.

- Write the required SET commands, in the Editor Pane, to change specific settings for the current connection.

The settings of the current connection are changed any time the default connection settings change, but not vice versa.

TIP

If you want to start a new connection with the same settings as the current connection, you can click the New Query icon in the toolbar, press Ctrl+N, or choose File, New, Blank Query Window. Otherwise, a new connection with the default settings will be created.

Figure B.18 shows some connection options. You can access this configuration form from the Tools, Options menu.

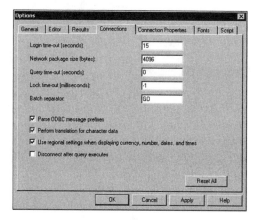

Figure B.18: *SQL Query Analyzer provides full connection settings control using the Options menu.*

The value for Query Time-Out and Lock Time-Out are related to each other. By default, SQL Query Analyzer assumes unlimited Lock Time-Out and Query Time-Out, but it is possible to change this setting to abort queries that have waited for longer than a specified time for locks to be released by adjusting the Lock Time-Out to a shorter time than the Query Time-Out.

CAUTION

Take care to remember that Query Time-Out is specified in seconds and Lock Time-Out in milliseconds.

The default value for Query Time-Out is 0 seconds, which means indefinite waiting time. It is impossible to set Query Time-Out to no waiting time because SQL Server would be unable to execute any query.

You can select 0 milliseconds to specify "no waiting time" for Lock Time-Out, so as soon as the query detects any locks on required resources, the execution of the query will be cancelled.

If your client and your server use different collation settings, you should check the Perform Translation for Character Data option. This instructs the driver to translate the character data between collations. This option is useful when, for example, the client has a Western European collation and the server uses an Eastern European collation.

The last setting, Use regional settings when displaying currency, number, dates, and times, formats the query results according to the regional settings specified in Control Panel.

CAUTION

Setting Use regional settings when displaying currency, number, dates, and times affects only the way results are formatted, but not the format of input values. To change the format for input date values, you should execute the SET DATEFORMAT statement first.

The connection properties manage the way SQL Server executes the query. Figure B.19 shows the connection properties for the default connection.

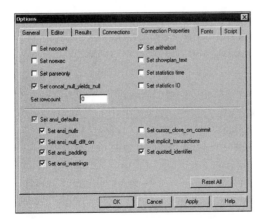

Figure B.19: *It is possible to manage specific connection properties for the current connection or default properties for new connections.*

Selecting Set parseonly instructs SQL Server to check the syntax correctness of the query, without executing it. Object names are not resolved with this option set, so it is possible to have some nonexistent objects referenced in your queries.

Selecting Set noexec instructs SQL Server to check syntax, resolve names, and compile the query, saving the compiled query plan in the procedure cache but without executing the query.

To avoid unnecessary network traffic it is best to select the Set nocount option.

Later in this appendix, you'll learn how to use the execution options that provide execution statistic information. To select the default options, you can click the Reset All button.

Defining and Using Templates for Query Analyzer

To help in the writing of repetitive queries, SQL Query Analyzer provides templates. These are scripts, saved in the directory Templates/SQL Query Analyzer, with special directives to SQL Query Analyzer to accept template parameters.

To define a new template, write your script as usual and save it with the .tql extension in the SQL Query Analyzer templates directory (it is `C:\ Program Files\Microsoft SQL Server\80\Tools\Templates\SQL Query Analyzer` by default).

To use a template, you can use the templates pane of the Object Browser or the Edit, Insert template menu. Whichever one you use, the template will be inserted in the Editor pane. Figure B.20 shows the Templates pane of the Object Browser.

If the template uses parameters, you can either edit the template to change values manually, use the Edit, Replace Template Parameters menu, or Ctrl+Shift+M to edit in the Replace Template Parameters form as shown in Figure B.21.

TIP

It is more efficient to save frequent scripts as templates, instead as normal scripts, because they provide parameters functionality, and they are listed in the Templates pane, which makes it easy to reuse these scripts.

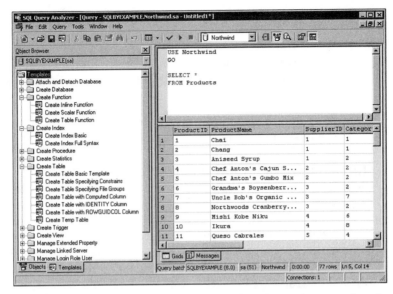

Figure B.20: *By using templates, you can save time reusing frequent scripts.*

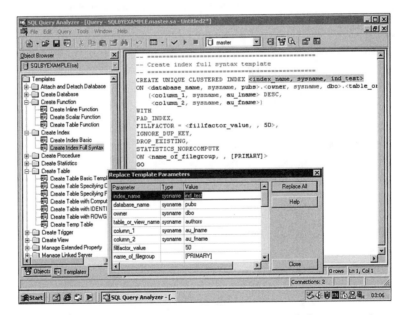

Figure B.21: *Specifying parameter values and data types is easy using the Replace Template Parameters form.*

Analyzing Queries

SQL Query Analyzer is not only a client tool to edit SQL queries and to show the correspondent results. SQL Query Analyzer provides analyzing capabilities that can help tune our databases and the queries they have to answer.

Analyzing queries is an advanced task, but it is important to at least show the very basic analyzing tasks every programmer should know.

Obtaining Information About Query Execution

The first question about query execution is usually: How long will it take to execute?

To answer this question, you can execute the SET STATISTICS TIME ON statement, or you can use the connection properties page and check the Set Statistics Time check box. Programmers can use these results to compare different strategies to retrieve the same results. Listing B.2 shows a typical output of Statistics time.

EXAMPLE

Listing B.2: Execution of a Query with Information About Time Statistics

```
USE Northwind
GO

SET STATISTICS TIME ON

SELECT Products.ProductID,
    Products.ProductName,
    [Order Details].OrderID,
    [Order Details].Quantity,
    [Order Details].UnitPrice,
    [Order Details].Discount
FROM Products
    JOIN [Order Details]
    ON Products.ProductID = [Order Details].ProductID
WHERE Products.ProductID = 50

SET STATISTICS TIME OFF
```

OUTPUT

```
SQL Server Execution Times:
   CPU time = 0 ms,  elapsed time = 0 ms.
SQL Server parse and compile time:
   CPU time = 0 ms, elapsed time = 0 ms.

SQL Server Execution Times:
   CPU time = 0 ms,  elapsed time = 0 ms.
ProductID  ProductName          OrderID    Quantity  UnitPrice  Discount
---------- -------------------- ---------- --------- ---------- ------------
```

Listing B.2: continued

```
50.00        Valkoinen suklaa    10,350.00   15.00    £13.00    0.10
50.00        Valkoinen suklaa    10,383.00   15.00    £13.00    0.00
50.00        Valkoinen suklaa    10,429.00   40.00    £13.00    0.00
50.00        Valkoinen suklaa    10,465.00   25.00    £13.00    0.00
50.00        Valkoinen suklaa    10,637.00   25.00    £16.25    5.0000001E-2
50.00        Valkoinen suklaa    10,729.00   40.00    £16.25    0.00
50.00        Valkoinen suklaa    10,751.00   20.00    £16.25    0.10
50.00        Valkoinen suklaa    10,920.00   24.00    £16.25    0.00
50.00        Valkoinen suklaa    10,948.00   9.00     £16.25    0.00
50.00        Valkoinen suklaa    11,072.00   22.00    £16.25    0.00


(10 row(s) affected)


SQL Server Execution Times:
   CPU time = 10 ms,  elapsed time = 151 ms.
```

Execution time depends mainly on the amount of data to access. It is possible to obtain this information by executing the SET STATISTICS IO ON statement, or selecting the Set Statistics IO check box in the Connection Properties form. Listing B.3 shows an example using the same query from Listing B.2 as a basis.

EXAMPLE

Listing B.3: Execution of a Query with Information About Data Access Statistics

```
USE Northwind
GO

SET STATISTICS IO ON

SELECT Products.ProductID,
    Products.ProductName,
    [Order Details].OrderID,
    [Order Details].Quantity,
    [Order Details].UnitPrice,
    [Order Details].Discount
FROM Products
    JOIN [Order Details]
    ON Products.ProductID = [Order Details].ProductID
WHERE Products.ProductID = 50

SET STATISTICS IO OFF
```

OUTPUT

```
ProductID   ProductName          OrderID     Quantity  UnitPrice  Discount
----------  -------------------  ----------  --------  ---------  -----------
50.00       Valkoinen suklaa     10,350.00   15.00     £13.00     0.10
50.00       Valkoinen suklaa     10,383.00   15.00     £13.00     0.00
```

Listing B.3: continued

50.00	Valkoinen suklaa	10,429.00	40.00	£13.00	0.00
50.00	Valkoinen suklaa	10,465.00	25.00	£13.00	0.00
50.00	Valkoinen suklaa	10,637.00	25.00	£16.25	5.0000001E-2
50.00	Valkoinen suklaa	10,729.00	40.00	£16.25	0.00
50.00	Valkoinen suklaa	10,751.00	20.00	£16.25	0.10
50.00	Valkoinen suklaa	10,920.00	24.00	£16.25	0.00
50.00	Valkoinen suklaa	10,948.00	9.00	£16.25	0.00
50.00	Valkoinen suklaa	11,072.00	22.00	£16.25	0.00

```
(10 row(s) affected)

Table 'Order Details'. Scan count 1, logical reads 22, physical reads 10,
    read-ahead reads 0.
Table 'Products'. Scan count 1, logical reads 2, physical reads 2,
    read-ahead reads 0.
```

As you can see in the results of Listing B.3, to execute the query, SQL Server had to

- Scan the table [Order Details] once, reading 10 pages from disk and reading data pages 22 times in total, so it had to read some of the pages several times.

- Scan the Products table once, reading 2 pages from disk and reading data from data pages 2 times in total.

Analyzing Query Execution Plan

According to the comments of the previous section, there is information on how long it takes to execute a query and how much data SQL Server must access to achieve the expected result. However, how does SQL Server actually execute this query?

SQL Query Analyzer provides a graphical tool to show the query plan selected by SQL Server to execute the query. To see this query plan on query execution, you can select the Show Execution Time menu, or press Ctrl+K. To show the estimated query plan without actually executing the query, click the Display Estimated Execution Plan icon in the toolbar, or press Ctrl+L.

Figure B.22 shows the graphical execution plan for the query from Listing B.2.

NOTE

Query optimization is both an art and a science. Showing in detail how to master the analytical capabilities of Query Analyzer to optimize queries is not the purpose of this book.

Extra information is available in Books Online in the topic "Graphically Displaying the Execution Plan Using SQL Query Analyzer."

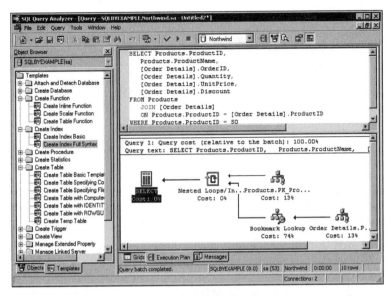

Figure B.22: *SQL Server uses the graphical execution plan to show how the query is executed.*

Managing Indexes from Query Analyzer

Indexes have an important role to play in the execution of queries. SQL Query Analyzer provides index management from the same environment. The menu Tools, Manage Indexes gives you access to the Manage Indexes form. Figure B.23 shows this form.

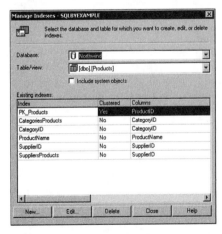

Figure B.23: *Managing indexes from SQL Query Analyzer facilitates query tuning and optimization.*

From the graphical query plan it is possible to manage indexes for a given table by right-clicking the table object and selecting Manage Indexes from the table's context menu. This is just another way to arrive at the Manage Indexes form.

Indexes are discussed in detail in Chapter 6, "Optimizing Access to Data: Indexes."

Working with the Transact-SQL Debugger

Transact-SQL is a rich and powerful programming language designed to be used on databases. Visual Basic programmers appreciate the debugging features of this popular language, and for SQL Server–stored procedures they benefit from a Transact-SQL debugger add-in. However, some SQL Server programmers don't use Visual Studio and they would appreciate having a full-featured Transact-SQL debugger to test the execution of stored procedures, triggers, and user-defined functions. This new version of SQL Query Analyzer integrates a Transact-SQL debugger.

To test how Transact-SQL Debugger works, create a user-defined function and a stored procedure as in Listing B.4.

CAUTION

If the MSSQLSERVER service uses the system account as login account, the Transact-SQL debugger will have very limited functionality. Select an appropriate Windows account as service account for SQL Server, and you will benefit from many advantages, such as being able to use the Transact-SQL debugger with all its features.

EXAMPLE

Listing B.4: The User-Defined Function and the Stored Procedure You Can Debug Using the Transact-SQL Debugger

```
CREATE FUNCTION testdebug(@a int, @b int)
RETURNS int
AS
BEGIN
    SET @a = @a * 2
    SET @b = @b * 4

    DECLARE @c int

    SET @c = @a * @b

    SET @c = @c + @a

    SET @c = @c + @b

    RETURN @c
END
GO
```

Listing B.4: continued

```
CREATE PROCEDURE spTestdebug
AS
    DECLARE @a0 int, @b0 int
    DECLARE @c0 int

    SET @a0 = 1
    SET @b0 = 10

    SET @c0 = dbo.testdebug(@a0, @b0)

    SELECT @c0
GO
```

You will now use Object Search to search for the procedure you just created. Figure B.24 shows the Object Search form and the results, as well as the context menu for the selected stored procedure.

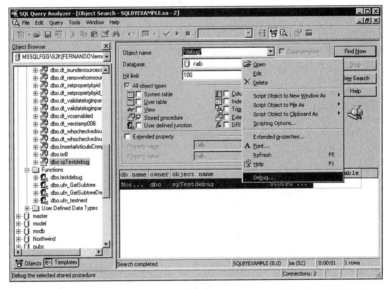

Figure B.24: *Searching for objects is easy using the SQL Query Analyzer Object Search.*

Select Debug from the context menu to open the Transact-SQL Debugger window, where you can trace the execution of this stored procedure step by step by pressing F11. When the stored procedure execution arrives at the step where the user-defined function must be evaluated, the debugger goes to the user-defined function code and opens the code to start the debug process there as well. Figure B.25 shows the Debugger window while debugging the user-defined function TestDebug. The following are the components of the window:

- The Debugger toolbar controls the procedure's execution.

- The Source Code window uses a yellow arrow to indicate the next step to execute and a red bullet to indicate the breakpoints.

- The Local Variables window shows local variables, including parameters, available in the current scope. In this window, you can change the values of the variables.

- The Globals window shows the value of several system functions. By default in this window, you can see the system functions `@@connections` and `@@trancount`, but it would be useful to add `@@error` as well as any other useful system function.

- The Callstack window shows the logical sequence of procedure calls up to this execution point. As you see in Figure B.25, this case shows two procedures: the `Northwind.dbo.TestDebug` user-defined function and the `Northwind.dbo.spTestDebug` stored procedure. Double-click any of these procedures and the debugger shows the selected procedure's code and a yellow arrow points to the local execution point.

- The Results Text window shows any results your procedure might produce.

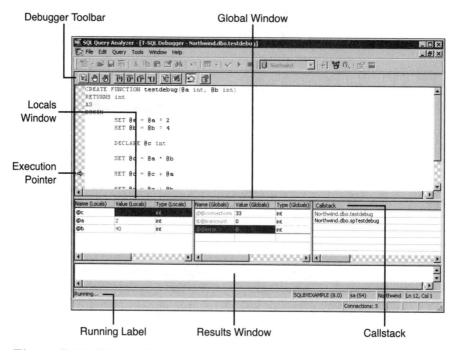

Figure B.25: Use the Transact-SQL Debugger to trace the execution of stored procedures, triggers, and user-defined functions.

TIP

To debug the execution of triggers, create a stored procedure to modify the table, forcing the trigger to be executed. When the debugger arrives at the DML statement, which fires the trigger, it will jump to the trigger code to continue debugging.

Summary

In this chapter, you learned how to use SQL Query Analyzer. This is an important tool that helps you to design, test, and tune a database in SQL Server.

The Object Browser helps you identify the definition of any object, without using metadata stored procedures or external tools. Using drag-and-drop helps you avoid misspellings.

You learned how to use the scripting facilities of Object Browser and Object Search. Now, you know how to produce results in text, grid, or to a file, according to your needs.

As any client tool, you can manage connection settings that help you adjust the connection to the user requirements.

Query Analyzer is a powerful analysis tool that helps you understand how SQL Server executes queries. Graphical Query Plan and the Transact-SQL debugger are great tools that will help you during the development and maintenance of a database system.

SQL Query Analyzer is the main tool that you use to test the examples provided in this book, and the main client tool you use in the development environment as a database developer.

We tried to cover in this appendix the main uses of SQL Query Analyzer. However, if you still need more information, Books Online contains a comprehensive description of the functionality of this powerful and useful tool.

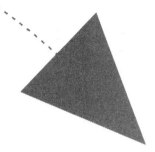

Index

Companion CD-ROM Installation Information

SQL Server 2000 120-Day Enterprise Evaluation Edition

SYSTEM REQUIREMENTS:

- A PC with an Intel or compatible Pentium 166MHz or higher processor

- Microsoft Windows NT Server 4.0 with Service Pack 5 or later, Windows NT Server 4.0 Enterprise Edition with Service Pack 5 or later, Windows 2000 Server, Windows 2000 Advanced Server, or Windows 2000 Datacenter Server operating system

- Minimum of 64MB of RAM (128MB or more recommended)

- Hard-disk space required:

  - 95MB–270MB for database server; approximately 250MB for typical installation

  - 50MB minimum for Analysis Services; 130MB for typical installation

  - 80MB for Microsoft English Query (supported on Windows 2000 operating system but not logo certified)

- Microsoft Internet Explorer 5.0 or later

- CD-ROM drive

- VGA or higher resolution monitor

- Microsoft Mouse or compatible pointing device